LANGUAGE
LEARNING
DISABILITIES
IN
SCHOOL-AGE
CHILDREN

LANGUAGE
LEARNING
DISABILITIES
IN
SCHOOL-AGE
CHILDREN

Edited by

GERALDINE P. WALLACH, PH.D.

Associate Professor, Division of Communication Disorders
Emerson College
Boston, Massachusetts

KATHARINE G. BUTLER, PH.D.

Director, Division of Special Education and Rehabilitation
Professor, Communicative Disorders
Syracuse University
Syracuse, New York

WILLIAMS & WILKINS
Baltimore • London • Los Angeles • Sydney

Copyright ©, 1984
Williams & Wilkins
428 East Preston Street
Baltimore, MD 21202, U.S.A.

Printed in the United States of America

Library of Congress Cataloging in Publication Data

Main entry under title:

Language learning disabilities in school-age children.

  Includes index.
  1. Learning disabilities—Addresses, essays, lectures. 2. Language disorders in children—Addresses, essays, lectures. 3. Reading disability—Addresses, essays, lectures. 4. Remedial teachng—Addresses, essays, lectures. I. Wallach, Geraldine P. II. Butler, Katharine G. [DNLM: 1. Learning disorders. 2. Language disorders—In infancy and childhood. WL 340 L2877]   LC4704.L37   1983   371.91'4
83-1377   ISBN 0-683-08707-X

Composed and printed at the   86 87 88 89 90
Waverly Press, Inc.   10 9 8 7 6 5 4 3 2

Preface

Language, learning, and reading problems. We have learned much about them over the past two or three decades. But it is only recently, and as a result of exciting and innovative research, that we have begun to appreciate the impact of early language disorders upon other aspects of children's growth and development. While the first three-quarters of the 20th century have seen the advent of compulsory education and the public's increasing insistence that literacy is an attainable goal for every individual, not until the mid-1970's was there national recognition and support for the education of all handicapped children and youth. Access to education not only implies but, in essence, virtually requires that the children acquire sufficient language skills to benefit from instruction.

It is at the intersection of language and instruction that we find ourselves in the 1980's. Evidence from research and clinical history indicates that language-disordered preschoolers are at high risk for academic failure, thus leading us to a much closer scrutiny of both the similarities and differences extant among various clinical and educational populations. Professionals from a variety of disciplines are engaged in identification of those factors which may link or separate children and adolescents amorphously labeled "language disordered," "learning disabled," or "reading disabled."

As professionals in the midst of a new decade of research and practice, we continue our quest by asking new and provocative questions about old and continuing problems. What cognitive and linguistic strategies underpin speaking and reading? What is literacy, and what level of inferencing does it require? What instructional variables may facilitate or deter classroom learning? What do we really mean by "developmental delay"? Does "dyslexia" really exist as an entity unto itself? Do language-disordered preschoolers ever catch up? Can early language programs make a difference? Who are these children we call "learning disabled"?

Language Learning Disabilities in School-Age Children is the result of the editors' self-questioning, research, and successes and failures with special children. Realizing that there are no easy answers to complex questions, nonetheless, we believe that the questions need to be asked. Can we derive some sense of order from the results of current investigations conducted among such heterogeneously labeled clinical

groups? As we reflected upon the current and controversial state of the art in language learning disabilities, it became apparent that it would be necessary to call upon a group of authors who could collectively articulate the complexity of the issues involved and provide that sense of a continuum from theory to practice which illuminates the best clinical efforts. Thus, we have worked together to construct a text with three major goals in mind: first, to provide readers with an in-depth and integrated view of some of the research that links language acquisition, development, and disorders to learning and reading disabilities; second, to present readers with some organizational principles that would help them integrate language and academic programming for students with language learning disabilities in school settings; and third, to offer realistic and practical suggestions for the development of contemporary language assessment and intervention strategies for older children and adolescents with language learning disabilities.

The book is divided into four major sections: (I) Basic Issues in Language Learning Disabilities; (II) Normal Processes: Implications for the Source of Language and Learning Problems; (III) Assessment and Intervention Strategies for Language Learning-disabled Students; (IV) Organization and Delivery of Services for Language Learning-disabled Students.

Section I outlines a number of basic questions and issues in language learning disabilities. The four chapters in this section, while differing in foci and emphases, address various aspects of the interactions among what the child knows (cognitive abilities), the environment, and the demands of task or the situation. Some of the controversies regarding a neurological base for language learning disabilities are introduced. Wallach and Liebergott open with a discussion of the problems attached to labeling and categorizing heterogeneous populations of children. Definitions are presented, and a conceptual framework is offered that sets the stage for the remainder of the text. The next two chapters deal with a number of the complex issues surrounding the natural progression of early language disorders. Maxwell and Wallach ask, "What *does* happen to preschoolers with language disorders as they become older?" Maxwell hypothesizes a neurological schema which may underlie various aspects of language growth and development. Butler's chapter completes the section by reviewing current models of language processing, bringing the reader back to some of the behavioral symptoms and cognitive strategies so often seen among language-disabled students. Interactions observed between "memory," "comprehension," and "selective attention" are discussed. Butler raises a number of significant questions regarding assessment and intervention procedures and rationale for those procedures, which are followed up in greater detail throughout the remainder of the text.

Section II provides a fascinating look at newly developed areas of research and practice. The four chapters in this section cover a broad scope of interrelated aspects of language development that readers will find important in clinical research and practice. The authors each offer implications from their research to apply with language learning-disabled students. Wallach outlines some basic hypotheses about later language learning, discussing some of the syntactic-semantic strategies that develop as children embark upon their school careers. Westby provides insight into the development of children's narrative abilities, moving from the primitive narrative schemata used by young children to more expert productions, requiring the use of maturing inferencing skills in the process. Van Kleeck provi :es a thoughtful discussion of the development of metalinguistic skills. Her analysis of language awareness, its development, and relationship with Piagetian constructs provides a frame of reference in which language intervention may be placed in context. Nelson complements the section by bringing us into elementary school classrooms. She outlines the changes in teachers' language through the grades and reminds us of the interactions between a child's inherent language abilities, the environment, and the changing demands of the school curriculum.

Section III outlines a number of contemporary and forward-looking assessment and intervention strategies. Van Kleeck opens the section with an important review of some of the current and not so current models that underpin assessment and intervention planning for children with language learning disabilities. She raises questions about the appropriateness and efficacy of standardized tests and programs. Looking toward the future, she offers alternative strategies. Miller continues with an innovative look at problem solving as it relates to language

and learning disabilities. She notes how important it is for the clinician or teacher to make a careful study of the child's language and communication functioning so that the appropriate problems may be presented, i.e., those that are within the child's linguistic and communicative functioning. To do less obviates the purposes of instruction. Israel covers word knowledge and word retrieval strategies, and Klein-Konigsberg follows with a chapter that blends research and practice. The chapters complement one another by looking at some of the qualitative changes in the language-processing abilities of older children. Both authors relate traditional notions of vocabulary, word association, and memory abilities to newer and more dynamic constructs. The nature of memory strategies and information retrieval are described and provide insights into the area of semantic integration. Blachman shifts to the study of phonological abilities and their relationship to reading acquisition. Her discussion covers some of the most interesting research in children's early reading. The chapter sheds new light on our interpretation of decoding, "phonics," and auditory skills such as "blending" and "auditory discrimination." She stresses the importance of rate of presentation of various task components, noting that "the basic connections between speech and print seem to elude many children with learning disabilities." Indeed, it may be supposed that the presumed basic connections between spoken language and written language have eluded, at least to some extent, practicing professionals, a matter this chapter may rectify to some degree. Silliman ends Section III with an in-depth summary of the cognitive and social components of language learning disabilities. Complementing Nelson's chapter from Section II, Silliman brings us back into the classroom and provides us with some specific ideas for the assessment and intervention of language within the instructional context. She highlights the role of teaching discourse within the educational process and stresses the importance of interactional competencies for successful academic achievement.

Section IV presents some hard-line questions about the development and organization of school programs for language learning-disabled students. Schery forces us to reconsider the earlier question raised about whether preschoolers with language disorders ever "catch up" to their peers. She evaluates the effectiveness of early language therapy programs. She notes the pervasive lack of a data base and the difficulties inherent in clinical research studies. However, she also notes that there is accumulating evidence that language intervention may help children gain communication skills above that which would be expected if no treatment had been provided. The Lee and Fine chapter takes us into the high school and provides us with previously unavailable information about high school language-disordered students. They also provide practical suggestions for organization, assessment, and intervention. In conclusion, the "final word" by Butler and Wallach deals with our inability to achieve the final word on language learning disabilities. It reflects upon our incomplete search for the origin of such disabilities and the eventual outcome of currently proposed language assessment and intervention strategies. A play on words, it is anything but final.

In order to achieve the goals outlined earlier in the Preface, we have brought together a group of research-oriented practitioners. The authors have a broad range of "child-related" experiences and interests. Although many of the contributors hold university affiliations, the text is not the effort of a group of "armchair" theorists esconced in ivory towers of various hues. The editors, as well as all other contributors to this text, continue to provide clinical services to the population reported upon herein.

Language Learning Disabilities in School-Age Children is intended to serve as a substantial text for students in speech-language pathology and professionals in related areas. The theme and content of the book, with emphasis upon the connections between language proficiency, language learning, and school success, should also be useful to learning disabilities specialists, reading specialists, special educators, and psychologists. We leave it to our readers to take from this text a conceptual framework within which they may place their emerging clinical and research questions. We hope the text has also provided some answers to those same questions and will lead to the further development of inquiry into this puzzling professional arena.

Geraldine P. Wallach, Ph.D.
Katharine G. Butler, Ph.D.

Acknowledgments

As editors, it is difficult for us to put into words our appreciation of, and respect for, the contributors to this text. We are sincerely indebted to them for their efforts. Multi-authored texts are frequently fraught with difficulties. Our experience has been to the contrary. We have found the authors not only to be responsive to the overall conceptualization of the book as a whole, but, in addition, they provided superb individual contributions of significant scope and diversity.

At this time we would like to acknowledge specific colleagues. The editors wish to thank a number of individuals, including Dr. Joel Stark, Dr. Paula Menyuk, and Dr. Robin Chapman, for their suggestions relating to the initial stages of this work. A number of the authors wish to note others as well: S. Maxwell and G. Wallach thank Dr. Anthony Bashir for his support. His ongoing research in the area of language learning disabilities continues to provide information about the way symptoms of language disability change over time and across learning tasks. G. Wallach also wishes to thank Dr. Audrey Holland for her suggestions regarding the neurological correlates of language development and disorders. A van Kleeck is indebted to Dr. Joel Stark who suggested that she ask herself two tough questions—i.e., was she merely pouring old wine into a new bottle? And, regardless of the vintage, when application is to be considered, does "meta" really matter? In addition, van Kleeck would like to thank Cheryl Gunter for several ideas regarding metalinguistic procedures in language development, and Susan Scoggins for her assistance in developing the word-referent differentiation task appearing in this text. L. Miller gives special thanks to Doris Downey, friend and colleague, who provided invaluable assistance in the chapter related to problem solving. D. Lee and J. Shapero-Fine wish to acknowledge the administrators, teachers, and students of the Scarborough Board of Education, without whom their efforts could not have been realized. They also thank Corinne Brown for technical assistance.

We jointly thank our respective friends, colleagues, superiors, and spouses, as well as the secretaries, children, and students who have supported us as we labored to find the right word, the right phrase, and, most assuredly, the right reference. We offer this text, a summary of our joint endeavors, to our readers for their critical review and use. We trust that it will assist them in their continuing search for further understanding of the fascinating area of language learning disabilities.

G.P.W.
K.G.B.

Contributors

Benita Blachman, Ph.D. (13)
Division of Special Education and
Rehabilitation
Syracuse University
Syracuse, NY

**Katharine G. Butler,
Ph.D. (4, 17)**
Division of Special Education and
Rehabilitation
Syracuse University
Syracuse, NY

Leonard Israel, Ph.D. (11)
Speech-Language Pathologist in Private
Practice
West Palm Beach, FL

**Estelle Klein-Konigsberg,
Ph.D. (12)**
Speech-Language Pathologist in Private
Practice
Aurora, CO

A. Donna Lee, M.S. (16)
Language and Speech Services
The Board of Education for the Borough
of Scarborough
Scarborough, Ontario, Canada

**Jacqueline Weis Liebergott,
Ph.D. (1)**
Division of Communication Disorders
Emerson College
Boston, MA

David L. Maxwell, Ph.D. (3)
Division of Communication Disorders
Emerson College
Boston, MA

**Sara E. Maxwell, M.S.,
M.Ed. (2)**
Preschool Language and Learning Program
Westwood Public Schools
Westwood, MA

Lynda Miller, Ph.D. (10)
Speech-Language Pathologist in Private
Practice
Chicago, IL

Nickola Wolf Nelson, Ph.D. (8)
Department of Speech Pathology and
Audiology
Western Michigan University
Kalamazoo, MI

Janice Shapero-Fine, M.A. (16)
Language and Speech Services
The Board of Education for the Borough of
Scarborough
Scarborough, Ontario, Canada

Elaine R. Silliman, Ph.D. (14)
Communication Sciences Program
Hunter College of the City University of
New York
New York, NY

Teris K. Schery, Ph.D. (15)
Department of Speech Communication
California State University at Los Angeles
Los Angeles, CA

Anne van Kleeck, Ph.D. (7, 9)
Department of Speech Communication
The University of Texas at Austin
Austin, TX

**Geraldine P. Wallach, Ph.D.
(1, 2, 5, 17)**
Division of Communication Disorders
Emerson College
Boston, MA

Carol E. Westby, Ph.D. (6)
Programs for Children; Divisions of
Communication Disorders and Child
Psychiatry
University of New Mexico
Albuquerque, NM

Contents

SECTION I

Basic Issues in Language Learning Disabilities

CHAPTER ONE

Who Shall Be Called "Learning Disabled": Some New Directions

GERALDINE P. WALLACH, Ph.D., and JACQUELINE WEIS LIEBERGOTT, Ph.D.

Marketing experts tell us that labels and catch-all phrases are powerful devices that convince consumers, either consciously or subconsciously, to buy a product. Consider, for example, the use of such popular labels as Ultra-Brite Toothpaste, Rapid Shave, Fresh Start, and My Sin. While a great deal of marketing research underlies the choice of a product's label, there is no guarantee that a label will conjure up a desirable image for everyone. We are reminded of a group of irate consumers who informed a large soap company that "Irish Spring" was an inappropriate name for a new product in view of the political situation in Northern Ireland. In this case, as in others we might think of, the company's referent and the consumer's referent were quite different. Past experience, background, sociopolitical orientation, and level of sensitivity, among other factors, contribute to the use and interpretation of labels.

Labels such as "learning disabilities," "dyslexia," "specific reading disabilities," "minimal brain dysfunction," and "childhood dysphasia" have their own marketing histories. As summaries of complex problems and heterogeneous populations, they continue to provoke controversy. In spite of tremendous research and clinical advances over the past decade alone, we are still asking, "Who are these children?" (Stark, 1980) and "Why are they in trouble?"

As stated by Eisenberg (1978, p. 40),

these labels appear to "reflect differences in terminology rather than differences in children." Lately, rather than new labels we see new label combinations to describe school-age children and adolescents with problems. Terms include: language learning disabilities (LLD), language-reading disorders, learning/reading disabilities, and language disorders and learning disabilities. Subtleties in punctuation often reflect differences in professionals' orientations toward the disorders. Some individuals prefer using "and" to ensure that the problems remain separate. Others, more apt to accept interactions, yet not ready to accept the total integration of areas, prefer the hyphen or the slash.

The label combinations described above are attempts to make some of the connections between language, learning, and reading more explicit. However, in some cases, new terminology only adds to the confusion. For example, one could say that "Bill has a language disorder and a learning disability." This could be interpreted as (1) Bill has two separate problems; or (2) Bill is part of a subgroup of children within the learning-disabled (LD) population whose language problems are causing his learning disability; or (3) Bill's problems with language and learning overlap and manifest themselves differently at various points in his development.

As we shall see, children with language disorders, reading disabilities, and learning disabilities are not necessarily members of distinct populations. Thus, interpretation 1—Bill has two completely separate problems—appears to be the least satisfactory. Interpretation 2 says more about cause-effect relationships than it does about Bill. Interpretation 3 views learning disabilities as a *continuation* of early language disorders. This point of view is one taken by many of the authors of chapters in this book, and it seems to have the potential for clarifying differences found among learning-disabled children. Other aspects of these three possibilities will be explored throughout this text.

DEFINITIONS OF LEARNING DISABILITIES AND DYSLEXIA: PROBLEMS OF CIRCULAR REASONING

Historically, learning disabilities and reading disabilities have been associated with one another. However, the definitions that professionals and professional organizations write tend to focus more on issues of causality and frequently bypass the developmental nature of the disability.

Consider this dialogue (Lahey, 1980, p. 79):

Question: Why are these children with normal intelligence having difficulty learning to read?
Answer: Because they are "learning disabled."
Question: How do you know that?
Answer: Because they have normal intelligence and are having difficulty learning to read.

This example provided by Lahey brings to mind a number of issues that have surrounded learning disabilities controversies. First, it demonstrates the circular reasoning attached to the use of such labels. Second, it points out that labels sometimes lead us to assume that we are dealing with a real entity rather than an abstraction based on some common behaviors. Third, it suggests that homogeneity exists within a population when, in fact, it does not. Given all the problems involved in labeling, it is difficult to avoid since federal and state mandates require labeling to enter children into programs (Gaskins, 1982).

Gaskins (1982), in a recent article entitled, "Let's End the Reading Disabilities/ Learning Disabilities Debate," vents her frustration over the use of labels by educational personnel. She states that the question of who should teach a poor reader is often determined by a label. For example, poor readers who have been labeled LD tend to be placed with a LD specialist certified in special education. Children with reading problems, without a special education label, usually receive remedial instruction from a reading specialist. Gaskins (1982) goes on to make a number of perceptive comments: (1) the separation of the two fields, reading and LD, is artificial and "fraught with territorial dispute"; (2) recent research suggests that there is no uniquely identifiable collection of symptoms associated with a reading disability or with a learning disability; and (3) labels are often used to determine programming (as in the above example) "yet the experts . . . do not agree on a clearly definitive way to decide whether a poor reader should be labeled 'reading disabled' or 'learning disabled'" (Gaskins, 1982, p. 81). Let us look at a number of definitions to see what, if any, guidance they offer professionals.

The National Joint Committee on Learning Disabilities (NJCLD) at its January 1981 meeting provided the following definition of Learning Disabilities (Legislative Council Report, ASHA, 1982, p. 200):

"Learning disabilities is a generic term that refers to a heterogeneous group of disorders manifested by significant difficulties in the acquisition and use of listening, speaking, reading, writing, reasoning, or mathematical abilities. These disorders are intrinsic to the individual and presumed to be due to central nervous system dysfunction.

Even though a learning disability may occur concomitantly with other handicapping conditions, (e.g. sensory impairment, mental retardation, social and emotional disturbance) or environmental influences (e.g. cultural differences, insufficient/inappropriate instruction, psychogenic factors), it is not the direct result of those conditions or influences."

The federal definition of LD is similar, although it does not indicate as explicitly the notion of heterogeneity, the intrinsic nature of LD, or the occurrence of concomitant conditions. Children with specific learning disabilities are defined as (U. S. Office of Education, 1976):

". . . those children who have a disorder in one or more of the basic psychological processes involved in understanding or in using language, spoken or written, which disorder may manifest itself in imperfect ability to listen, think, speak, read, write, spell, or do mathematical calculations. The term includes such conditions as perceptual handicaps, brain injury, minimal brain dysfunction, dyslexia, and developmental aphasia. The term does not include children who have learning problems which are primarily the result of visual, hearing, or motor handicaps, of mental retardation, of emotional disturbance, or environmental, cultural, or economic disadvantage."

By comparison, the World Federation of

Neurology offers a definition (taken from Rutter, 1978, p. 12) of "specific developmental dyslexia" by stating that it is:

". . . a disorder manifested by difficulty in learning to read despite conventional instruction, adequate intelligence and sociocultural opportunity. It is dependent upon fundamental cognitive disabilities which are frequently of constitutional origin."

Rutter (1978) reflects on the above definition of dyslexia by saying that "as a piece of logic this definition is a nonstarter" (p. 12). Certainly, the definition begs a whole series of other questions. He reminds us that issues related to "constitutional origin," "neurological base," and IQ warrant clarification. He also points out that dyslexia (as a learning disability) is a diagnosis of exclusion. Professionals have taken issue with this in that individuals from low socioeconomic backgrounds, the largest group of retarded readers in the United States, are excluded by definition (Blank, 1978; Eisenberg, 1978). Rutter (1978) goes on to say that reading problems have many causes and encompass a variety of symptoms. Even if, as suggested, some reading disorders are due to an inherent/intrinsic factor, i.e., factors within children, such as central nervous system involvement, these factors do not necessarily lead to a unitary problem (see also, Taylor et al., 1979).

There are many similarities between these definitions. All of them attempt to define LD and dyslexia by exclusion. All of them deal with causality and imply a unitary cause. All of them avoid the issue of the changing nature of language, learning, and reading problems over time (see Chapter 2). Although the definition of the National Joint Committee on Learning Disabilities recognizes the heterogeneous nature of the population, it too does not attempt to capture descriptively differences between groups of children.

THE LANGUAGE COMPONENT OF LEARNING AND READING DISABILITIES

Bryan et al. (1980) point out that the classification of children into programs for learning disabilities is weighted heavily on various language-dependent skills. Mastery of oral expression, reading comprehension, mathematical calculation, mathematical reasoning, and spelling (U. S. Office of Education, 1976, 52407) requires some prior mastery of language during the preschool period. The only generally accepted manifestation of specific learning disabilities is a significant disparity between potential or expected academic performance and actual performance (Eisenberg, 1978; Stark and Wallach, 1980). However, the disparity between potential or expected academic performance and actual performance may result more from the difference between children's linguistic skills and, for example, their reading ability, than the disparity between children's IQ scores and level of reading.

The prevalence of language problems within the learning disabilities population has been well documented (Johnson and Myklebust, 1967; Berry, 1969, Kirk et al., 1968; Wiig and Semel, 1976; Benton and Pearl, 1978; Gerber and Bryen, 1981). "Language-conceptual" orientations in the 1970's and 1980's have helped us re-evaluate "perceptual deficit" orientations in learning disabilities that were more predominant in the 1960's than they are now.

A Bit of History

The presence of reading disabilities within the learning disabilities population led to the notion that visual perceptual problems underpinned children's learning disabilities. By visual perceptual problems educators often meant that "the child did not recognize, sequence, and/or discriminate written stimuli in the correct way—the way an intact neurological system enables normally achieving children to deal with these written characters on the page" (Wallach, 1982, p. 82). It was felt that the diagnosis and remediation of deficits in these areas, e.g., training a child to sequence visual stimuli, would improve reading (Frostig and Horne, 1964). As will be discussed in Chapter 2 and elsewhere in this text, this notion has been challenged.

Disenchanted with the visual perceptual model, some professionals shifted to an auditory processing hypothesis. This hypothesis suggests that "auditory perceptual" problems underpin learning and reading problems. As put by Stark (1980), we hear of auditory processing disorders, auditory sequencing disorders, auditory recognition disorders, auditory figure/ground disorders, and so on, to describe a variety of difficulties. Considerable controversy surrounds this view, as many have questioned whether the dysfunction is specifically auditory (Rees, 1973; Bloom and Lahey, 1978; Tallal, 1975) and have also questioned the viability of the concept for explaining the problems of the learning disabled. The reader is further directed to Benton and Pearl (1978), Stark and Wallach (1980), Gerber and Bryen (1981), and Wallach (1982) for additional information about historical perspectives.

A New Decade in Language Learning Disabilities

A recent article by Wallach and Lee (1981), entitled "Too Late, Too Early, Didn't Test the Right Things Anyway," discussed the dilemmas faced by practicing professionals. The authors were faced with the task of designing a program to provide language and speech services for a population of children from junior kindergarten (3- and 4-year-olds) through high school. The students in question manifested a variety of communication problems, some more subtle than others. Recognizing the need for ongoing language and speech assessments throughout grade levels, they questioned the use of standardized tests as a primary means for measuring children's growth and development. Some of the standardized language tests available "missed" children at various points in their school careers and raised questions concerning *which* language factors were predictive of later learning disabilities. While Wallach and Lee preferred to use descriptive-informal methods of language assessment, they found themselves under constant pressure from administrators to provide standardized scores (Well, what *did* Susie score on the Peabody Picture Vocabulary Test?), to make test-retest comparisons (You gave Susie the Illinois Test of Psycholinguistic Abilities (ITPA) in September; how did she do in June?), and to make statements about factors that seemed to have little to do with the child's academic performance (Has Susie's digit span improved?). Their analysis of the standardized test data available to them on the children revealed that many of the children who had been listed on caseloads as "delayed language" reappeared in learning disability classes as they became older.

The examples provided by Wallach and Lee (1981) represent their personal experiences in a particular school system. In order to avoid the problems of "Too Late, Too Early, Didn't Test the Right Things Anyway," the following organizing principles are suggested:

1. Early language disorders (preschool) are related to later learning disabilities (school age). Knowledge of the way that symptoms of language disability change over time provides a basis for evaluating available tests, assessment, and educational placement procedures.

2. The relation between spoken and written language represents a complex interplay between implicit and explicit language knowledge.

3. The interactive relations among form, content, and use suggest that language is acquired (and needs to be facilitated) in an integrated manner.

4. Qualitative and quantitative analyses of children's language behavior are necessary for formulating appropriate goals. These goals must relate to the child's language needs as well as to the demands of the learning environment.

Early and Later Disabilities

Bloom and Lahey (1978) describe language "as a code whereby ideas about the world are represented through a conventional system of arbitrary signals for communication" (p. 4). They provide us with the FORM-CONTENT-USE paradigm for language assessment and intervention.

FORM includes phonology, morphology, and syntax. *Phonology* is viewed as knowledge about sounds and sound sequences permissible in one's native language. *Morphology* is that part of the grammar that provides rules for combining morphemes into words. Sounds combine together to form morphemes. A morpheme is the smallest meaning unit of language, so that the phrase "unhappy cat" represents three morphological units—"un" (meaning not), "happy," and "cat." *Syntax* is that part of a grammar that describes the structures of language. Syntax includes rules for combining words into sentences. CONTENT includes various aspects of semantics or the meaning component of language. It involves word knowledge (vocabulary), knowledge of word relationships, and understanding of time and event relationships. More specifically, *semantics* is a translation of what one knows about the world into one's language. Finally, to complete the Bloom and Lahey (1978) model, USE includes the pragmatic aspects of language. *Pragmatics* is the study of the functions of language in varying contexts—or the ways in which differing social situations affect the linguistic forms one uses to communicate. Functions include a speaker's intention, the various purposes of a communication (e.g., to get information, to comment on a situation, etc.), and the like. Contexts include both linguistic (e.g., a previous sentence) and nonlinguistic (e.g., a picture, a gesture) dimensions in which language is embedded. A number of authors in this text will provide assistance in looking at the components of language in integrative and innovative ways (see Chapter 10).

Language problems in preschool and school-age children take a number of forms. Problems reflecting the interactions between form, content, and use occur in varying degrees and manifest themselves in comprehension and/or production. The question of how overt symptoms of a language disability, e.g., expressive syntax problems, change over time and across learning tasks is a provocative one. It may be that more obvious language problems become covert as children get older. It is interesting to speculate about what type(s) of early language problems "turn into" more subtle problems. Perhaps certain symptoms of language disability "wash away" over time, while others change their form.

A beautiful example of this phenomenon is suggested by Bryan et al. (1980). Their studies of the conversational abilities of learning-disabled children and their normally achieving peers reveal that, although neither group of children showed overt syntactic problems, the learning-disabled children made more competitive utterances and had more difficulty seeking clarification than their peers. Given these findings, the authors then raise the issue of whether the deficits that they observed in these communicative interactions were remnants of a developmental language disorder. Discussion of the principle that the form of a behavior may change over time has not been restricted to the area of language. Others have described this same type of change in academic and social performance (see Chapter 2).

We still know relatively little about the continuum of language failure. However, researchers who have initiated follow-up studies of children with language disorders early in life suggest that, even after intervention, language disorders persist through the school years and even through adulthood (Hall and Tomblin, 1978; Weiss et al., 1979; Synder, 1980). Language-disabled children are at the highest risk for academic failures, particularly in reading (Snyder, 1980). The notion of such children "catching up" is now seriously questioned. Certainly, the need to evaluate various types of ongoing assessment and intervention procedures is warranted (see Chapters 2 and 15).

In summary, there are a number of ways that symptoms of early language disability change over time: (1) overt symptoms frequently seen in younger children with language disorders (e.g., reduced mean length of utterance, limited vocabulary, etc.) may become more subtle (e.g., they show up as inferential processing problems, word retrieval problems, pragmatic difficulties, etc.); (2) language problems may show up in reading and spelling, i.e., spoken language problems "turn into" written language problems; and (3) verbal language problems (listening-speaking) may persist and, in addition, are evidenced in reading and writing.

The Relation between Spoken and Written Language

This brings us to principle 2. It concerns the relation between spoken and written language, i.e., the translation of language "in the air" to language "on the paper" (Menyuk, 1980). Reading and writing requires both an implicit and explicit understanding of the language system.

Implicit language knowledge means the less conscious abstraction of phonological-syntactic-semantic-pragmatic rules during the various stages of language acquisition. *Explicit* language knowledge refers to conscious judgments and analyses of various aspects of language structure and various uses of language (e.g., language for problem solving, language of instruction). Linguists have referred to this as a distinction between competence and performance. For example, a child follows the phonological rules of his language in order to combine sounds into recognizable words. Thus, phonological rules require that it be /g/, /r/,/i/,/n/ and not /r/,/g/,/i/,/n/. This represents an example of implicit language knowledge. When the teacher asks the child to draw a circle around all of the green ones and the child performs correctly, he is demonstrating his knowledge explicitly (see Chapter 10).

When faced with the task of decoding a word for reading, the child must manipulate phonemes on a more conscious level. He must talk about sounds and their relation to the letters on the page. This ability has been called metalinguistic ability, i.e., the use of language to describe language. Other examples of metalinguistic skills are judgments of grammaticality, ambiguity, and synonymy. Figurative language, humor, and the like, are also expressions of metalinguistic awareness. As discussed in Chapters 7 and 9 and elsewhere in this text, the study of metalinguistics has had a tremendous effect on our understanding of later language learning. For example, an understanding of metalinguistic ability has helped us to realize that many tests and subtests are more difficult than they appear. The *Lindamood Auditory Conceptualization Test,* the *Rosner Test,* and the *Goldman-Fristoe Sound Analysis Subtest* require a child to make sophisticated judgments about the phonemic structure of the language. Identifying the first sound in a word requires that a child understand, at an abstract level, the concept of a sound, reflect on the auditory pattern, and segment an *individual* sound from the unsegmented speech stream. The term "phonemic segmentation" is often applied to this ability (Liberman, 1980; Chapter 13).

The relationship between spoken and written language systems reflects an interplay between implicit and explicit language rather than a simple auditory-to-visual transfer. Notions like "Johnny is a visual learner" and "Anne is an auditory learner" are limited concepts. Many aspects of syntactic-semantic-phonological and pragmatic components of spoken language are brought to the surface so to speak during the act of reading and/or writing. Current diagnostic and intervention efforts appear to be increasingly directed toward the interplay of components rather than increasing discrete skills (see Chapter 6).

From Discrete Skills to Integrative Views of Language

The discrete skills approach to assessment and programming, as seen in the ITPA model, frequently ignores the dynamic and overlapping nature of the various language components. It is this dynamic relation that principle 3 addresses. Models such as these often lead to the separating and segmenting of memory, per-

ceptual, and linguistic factors beyond recognition (Wallach, 1980; see Chapter 9). One's ability to discriminate words auditorially is certainly related to one's knowledge of vocabulary, the context, and prior experience. One's ability to visually process and recall written words is influenced by verbal strategies or verbal mnemonics (Gupta et al., 1978; Swanson, 1978; see Chapter 2). One's memory will be affected by many things, including interest in a topic, linguistic competence, supporting contextual and other cues (see Chapter 12). Statements such as "Johnny has an auditory memory problem," "Mary has a visual sequential memory problem," and the like, sometimes make it sound as though "memory," like "language," appears as a box or a "unified thing" that can easily be simplified or isolated as a problem or a skill.

The discrete skills approach has been theoretically challenged (e.g., Rees, 1973; Bloom and Lahey, 1978), as has the application of this approach to the teaching of language (Mann and Goodman, 1973; Stark and Wallach, 1980). For example, Bloom and Lahey (1978, p. 533) question the usefulness of digit span and related exercises by stating:

"It is not clear how many unrelated words one must be able to repeat in order to learn language—perhaps only one or two, or perhaps more. The correlation between memory span for sequential auditory information and language development ... may be related to some third factor influencing both, and improvement in one skill may not influence the other."

Certainly, many alternatives to the discrete skills approach are currently available. The Bloom and Lahey model (1978) is one alternative. Blank et al. (1978) offer practitioners another alternative with their schema for analyzing children's discourse (see also Chapter 14). Roth and Perfetti (1980) and Westby (Chapter 6) offer other approaches and show how the structures of children's narratives can be analyzed and translated into therapy.

GOAL SETTING: THE TEACHER, THE CLASSROOM, THE CURRICULUM

Principle 4 suggests that our analysis of the language learning-disabled child's behavior must include more than an analysis of the child in a clinical setting. It should include analyses of (1) teacher-child interactions and how the teacher interprets and deals with the child's language learning problem; (2) the language of the classroom; and (3) the language of the curriculum.

The following scenario involving a first-grade child is offered as an illustration of the need for multiple types of analyses. The language clinician reported to the teacher that a child she had seen in November was having problems answering inferential questions, such as "Why" and "How." The child was also having difficulty with more complex syntactic forms (both receptively and expressively) involving subordination, relativization, and the like. Skills requiring syllable-sound analyses, such as those tapped by the *Rosner Screening Test* (1975) and the *Wepman Test of Auditory Discrimination* were also weak. In brief, the clinician was generally concerned about this child's comprehension processing and ability to deal with certain metalinguistic judgments involving sounds. The clinician discussed these findings with the teacher. The teacher reported that the child was doing fine in the classroom. "He is reading his sight words, and he certainly talks a blue streak in class." Unfortunately, they both then went their separate ways. Toward the end of grade 1, when the teacher became concerned about the child's reading comprehension, she did not know where to turn.

Too late? Too early? Not looking for the right factors? Self-fulfilling prophecy? Where do we go from here? Perhaps we should consider in-service programs for both teachers and clinicians, as well as preassessment checklists and the like, to get the education-communication process to work more efficiently. Many checklists, for example, are available for review (e.g., Lynch, 1979; Wallach and Lee, 1981). Silliman (Chapter 14) discusses a checklist by Damico and Oller (1980). This checklist is structured so that teachers can be guided in their observations of pragmatic behaviors in children. In addition, Lee and Fine (Chapter 16) have developed a checklist for secondary referrals.

Classroom Language

Nelson (Chapter 8) discusses the complexity of language through the grades, while Silliman (Chapter 14) provides numerous schemas for the coding of components of classroom language. She discusses the dimensions of *function* (communicative intent), *structure* (participant, turn-taking features), and *content* (construction and maintenance of conversational sequences). In addition to providing a useful framework, Silliman discusses some fascinating differences between special education and regular grade classes. The assessment of classroom language is a complex issue in need of further investigation. As we shall see, "objective awareness of the components of teaching discourse should lead to a better coordination of classroom objectives with therapeutic goals" (Silliman and Leslie, 1980, p. 10).

The Curriculum

A child's linguistic and communicative abilities interact with the content and structure of the curriculum. While spoken language is more obviously linked with the reading process, researchers and practitioners have begun to study the dynamic interactions between cognitive and linguistic variables that may interfere with the acquisition of types of content. For example, Carlson et al. (1980) reflect upon how language ability interacts with math. As put by Carlson et al.: "A child having difficulty with a particular math task will benefit most from an initial assessment by the teacher of the language interaction involved in that task" (p. 61). (For further information see Chapters 8 and 10).

COMPONENTS OF LANGUAGE, LEVELS OF PROCESSING, AND LANGUAGE LEARNING DISABILITIES

As practitioners dealing with language learning-disabled students, we need to keep in mind three issues: (1) How are the language components related to children's school problems? (2) In what ways do content, structure, and context interact to facilitate or interfere with learning? (3) What strategies are needed to complete a given task successfully? The checklist for analyzing testing and teaching presented in Table 1.1 allows for the integration of information about a child's language learning disabilities. It is by no means complete. Rather, the checklist serves as an example of the kinds of questions we might ask ourselves in our attempts to understand children and adolescents with language learning disabilities. This discussion may also provide a foundation for issues that will be pursued by other authors in this text. Any separation of components and levels of processing is recognized as being artificial in that communication is both cyclical and interactional (see Chapter 8).

Language Components Revisited

A number of questions should come to mind as we embark on testing or teaching language learning-disabled students. Why have we chosen to test a particular language component? Will standardized tests or language sampling provide the depth of information needed to assess the older child? What do we need to know about semantic strategies? Are the language symptoms of learning-disabled students more likely to surface along pragmatic domains (Bryan et al., 1980)? Will some of the problems of school-age children occur at the metalinguistic level of language?

As we learn to ask the right questions, we may also develop a better perspective about the usefulness, or appropriateness, of various tests and programs. For example, the *Lindamood Auditory Conceptualization Test* or subtests of the *Goldman-Fristoe-Woodcock Auditory Perceptual Test* have traditionally been given to obtain information about the child's ability to discriminate and sequence phonemes. We have looked at the child's score on this test and made statements about causality and/or the child's discrimination ability in relation to his peers. What we ignored was the usefulness of these tasks for revealing the child's strategies for dealing with phonological elements, the child's ability or inability to make metalinguistic judgments about phonemes, the child's knowledge of vocabulary, the child's skillfulness at making distinctions among classes of sounds, etc. (Atkinson and Canter, 1979).

Other questions we might ask ourselves about the language components and their relationship to learning disabilities include: How does semantic-syntactic-pragmatic-phonological knowledge relate to problem-solving ability (see Chapter 10)? How does an individual's knowledge and use of the components for spoken language relate to his or her use of the same components for reading? How do deficits or differences in one or more of these areas differentially affect academic performances? By asking the right questions, we may generate more educationally useful answers.

The Information Load

Every situation a child encounters places differing amounts of emphasis on the linguistic and nonlinguistic environment. Asking children to report on their summer vacations is different than asking them to discuss a recent news event. In the first case they have experienced the event and know a great deal about it; in the second case, they have not been a part of the event and must relate it to information that is understood only vaguely. Underpinning tasks such as these are considerations like (1) the *type* of information given to child, (2) the *amount* of information given, and (3) the *context* in which the information is presented.

Our ability to understand these dimensions is important. Let us look at some of these interactions as they relate to reading. For example, providing a child with *less*

Table 1.1.
A Checklist For Analyzing Testing and Teaching[a]

The Area	Description	Sample Questions
I. The components of language	Syntax-semantics-pragmatics-phonology	Why have we chosen to assess and/or teach one or more of the components?
		Will standardized tests measure up? Is the level appropriate for a LD child?
		How do oral language deficits in one or more of the components relate to written language deficits? to math? to problem solving?
		Are we testing and teaching implicit or metalinguistic aspects of language?
		In what context have breakdowns occurred?
II. The information load	Type of information STRUCTURE (word-phrase-sentence-story) CONTENT (concrete-abstract, etc.)	Is the material and its presentation appropriate or inappropriate for the child's level? Is it "our" problem and/or the child's?
	Amount of information	Has the child been given enough information?
	Contextual support	What is it about the content (or ideas presented) that is difficult?
		What types of contextual support (e.g., visual or linguistic) accompany the material presented?
		Can stories be analyzed in the same way as individual sentences (see Chapter 6)?
III. Strategies facilitated	Verbatim response (rote repetition)	What was the child asked to do?
	Literal meaning (who-what-whom)	Were the instructions explicit?
	Inferential-integrative (fill in missing parts, read between the lines, etc.) (Perfetti, 1977)	Did the task "encourage" one kind of response and not another?
		Do standardized tests provide the information needed?
		What strategies are needed in the older grades?

[a] See Wallach, 1982; see also Chapters 9, 14, and 16 for additional checklists.

information (e.g., one sentence as opposed to two in a reading comprehension task) does not necessarily mean the task is "easier to do" (Pearson and Spiro, 1980). Blachowicz (1978) discusses how oversimplifying syntax in children's early readers can actually "go against comprehension." She found that a series of simple declarative sentences—The man is big, The man is fat, The man is my daddy—are more difficult for second graders to comprehend than the supposedly more complex sentence, The big fat man is my daddy (see also Chapter 12). Blank (1980) shows how children's early readers may require "inferential jumps" across sentences even though the text itself is relatively simple. Consider the two sentences, "Jill was at Stan's house. Stan and Jill sat on the grass." Blank notes that one could not easily predict the second sentence after reading the first. Thus, even though the individual sentences might be easy to process, *when put together* they change the demands of the task.

Strategies Facilitated or Levels of Processing Required

This area is an important one for clinician or teacher observation. It requires an analysis of the child's behavior to determine the strategies he is using to perform a task. This is most often done by an analysis of error responses. When a child "gets it wrong," rather than totaling scores, the clinician needs to ask how the child achieved that answer. The clinician who can ascertain the child's strategy has an understanding of what the child is doing and how to intervene. An example of this can be seen in the work of Prizant and Duchan (1981) with autistic children. From an analysis of these children's echolalic behavior, they determined the functional uses of echolalia. They then suggested intervention strategies that built on the echolalia rather than suggesting its elimination. This type of approach, i.e., the analysis of strategies, is critical to understanding a child's reading and language behavior.

Both listeners and readers have numerous strategies available to them. Whereas one listener may take a speaker's remarks literally, the next one easily draws the inference behind the message. One student may get stuck on an isolated point in a lecture, whereas another may integrate the information in a lecture with past lectures—or courses (Wallach, 1982). Perfetti (1977) provided the strategy hierarchy used in section III of our checklist (Table 1.1). It includes verbatim, literal meaning, and inferential-integrative meaning levels. Perfetti's 1977 model provides us with some guidelines; it does not represent a rigid, or simplistic, step-by-step hierarchy (see Chapter 4).

The first aspect of comprehension described by Perfetti is the verbatim level. At this level, a child repeats and/or reads utterances, but does not understand them. Perfetti gives an example of how a child can get stuck at this level of processing, noting that children who read sentences aloud correctly without being able to answer questions about what they have read are manifesting level 1, or verbatim processing. He calls them "sentence surfers" because they seem to glide across the surface of sentences without getting to the "deeper" meanings. The implications of "sentence surfing" can be applied to oral and written language. Do some children approach information without the degree of analysis required for true comprehension? Was the child directed by the teacher to read aloud without being told that he/she would have to answer questions? Perhaps language learning-disabled children need instructions that are more explicit.

The aspect of comprehension described by Perfetti as the "basic-literal" level of comprehension (level 2) involves the semantic-syntactic analysis of a sentence. For example, one could answer a question like "Who kissed Tom?" after hearing the sentence "Jane kissed Tom." Figuring out WHO DID WHAT TO WHOM requires a literal translation. On the other hand, questions like: "How did Tom feel about it?" are not answerable from the given information alone and require more complex processing.

Constructive comprehension (level 3) requires that the child go on to obtain more information, integrating details, themes, character descriptions, motivations, etc., to answer questions appropriately. Numerous examples of sentence comprehension strategies of levels 2 and 3 types appear in the literature (see Chapter 5).

At level 3 listeners and readers are active

participants in the process of comprehension. They actively construct meaning by using their knowledge of the world and past experience for interpreting what they hear, see, and need to learn (Blachowicz, 1978; Bransford and Nitsch, 1978). The critical unit of comprehension, then, is larger than the sentence. As put by Blachowicz (1978, p. 198):

"Comprehension is not a passive process of storing and retrieving linguistic entities . . . but involves accounts of . . . the changes within the (mind) of the comprehender as well as the situational and contextual variables surrounding the comprehension act."

Bransford and Johnson (1973) provide a number of examples to show how individual sentences can be incomprehensible without appropriate context or prior knowledge. Consider two classic examples taken from their work:

The notes were sour because the seam was split.

The haystack was important because the cloth had ripped.

While these sentences are syntactically simple for adults, comprehension of them eludes us unless we can construct a context, or we have heard the sentences before, or we have read Bransford and Johnson's article. We could certainly apply a literal translation to the sentences and answer such questions as "What was sour?" or "Why was the haystack important?" However, the full meaning of the sentences remains vague.

Consider the two sentences again, this time with linguistic contexts provided:

John's bagpipe concert was a terrible failure. He attempted to play a number of tunes. However, the notes were sour because the seam was split.

Bill insists on going to that skydiving club. His parachute failed in mid-air. Luckily, he landed in a field. The haystack was important because the cloth had ripped.

Research and Its Influence in Language Learning Disabilities

The trend toward integrative analyses of syntactic, semantic, and pragmatic competencies has made it clear that our assessments need to be broad (Siegel, 1975; Miller, L., 1978; Miller, J., 1978, Chapter 9; Swisher and Aten, 1981). Current information about language acquisition above the age of 5 contributes to our ability to perform comprehensive assessments and plan and provide creative intervention procedures (see Chapter 5). Increased understanding of the notion that language cannot be tested or taught in the isolation of a therapy room has allowed language specialists and classroom teachers to be more involved in joint ventures for the educational programming of students with language learning disabilities.

CLOSING REMARKS

The problems of school-age children with language learning disabilities are varied and complex. There are no easy answers to the questions, "Who are these children?" (Stark, 1980) and "Why are they in trouble?" What we do know, however, is that we are talking about children and adolescents with problems along certain dimensions of language input and/or output—in spoken and/or written form. Normal and learning-disabled individuals have knowledge of spoken language that interacts with their ability to learn new things. Reading and speaking are creative, active processes. Indeed, "to learn to read is to learn a system of rules and strategies for extracting information from text" (Gibson and Levin, 1975, p. 332; see also Myers and Paris, 1978).

A number of questions will be explored in the chapters that follow. It is our hope that the answers to these questions will result in all of us providing better service. Some of these questions are:

1. What does one need to know about a child's verbal language system in order to understand that child's written language abilities?

2. What perceptual, conceptual, linguistic, and metalinguistic factors are most significant for learning and school success?

3. When do language delays turn into deviance?

4. Can language learning strategies be

taught, or can we only lead children to develop strategies on their own?

5. Do currently available standardized tests and programs meet the needs of older students with language learning problems?

6. What are some of the differences between everyday discourse, classroom language, text language, and the language of reasoning and problem solving?

As we learn more about "who these children are" and "how they develop," we may learn more about "how to get them out of trouble."

References

American Speech-Language and Hearing Association Committee on Language Learning Disabilities: The role of the speech-language pathologist in language learning disabilities. *ASHA* 24:937–944, 1982.

Atkinson M, Canter GJ: Variables influencing phonemic discrimination performance in normal and learning disabled children. *J Speech Hear Disord* 44:543–556, 1979.

Benton AL, Pearl D: *Dyslexia: An Appraisal of Current Knowledge.* New York, Oxford University Press, 1978.

Berlin L, Blank M, Rose S: "The language of instruction: the hidden complexities." *Top Language Disord* 1 (1):47–58, 1980.

Berry MF: *Language Disorders of Children: The Bases and Diagnoses.* New York, Appleton-Century-Crofts, 1969.

Blachowicz CLZ: "Semantic constructivity in children's comprehension." *Read Res Q* 13:187–199, 1978.

Blank M: Review of "Toward an understanding of dyslexia: psychological factors in specific reading disability." In Benton AL, Pearl D: *Dyslexia: An Appraisal of Current Research.* New York, Oxford University Press, 1978, pp 113–122.

Blank M: Reading ability and early oral language. Presented at the symposium on Language, Learning and Reading Disabilities: A New Decade, City University of New York, May, 1980.

Blank M, Rose S, Berlin L: *The Language of Learning: The Preschool Years.* New York, Grune and Stratton, 1978.

Bloom L, Lahey M: *Language Development and Language Disorders.* New York, John Wiley & Sons, 1978.

Bransford JD, Johnson M: "Considerations of some problems in comprehension." In Chase W: *Visual Information Processing.* New York, Academic Press, 1973, pp 383–438.

Bransford JD, Nitsch KE: Coming to understand things we could not previously understand. In Kavanagh J, Strange W: *Speech and Language in the Laboratory, School, and Clinic.* Cambridge, MA, MIT Press, 1978, pp 267–307.

Bryan T, Donahue M, Pearl R: Learning disabled children's communicative competence and social relationships. Presented at the symposium on Language, Learning and Reading Disabilities: A New Decade, City University of New York, May, 1980.

Carlson J, Gruenewald L, Nyberg B: "Everyday math is a story problem: the language of the curriculum." *Top Language Disord* 1 (1):59–70, 1980.

Damico J, Oller JW: Pragmatic versus morphological/syntactic criteria for language referrals. *Language, Speech, Hear Serv Schools* 11:85–94, 1980.

Dunn L: *Peabody Picture Vocabulary Test.* Circle Pines, MN, American Guidance Service, 1969.

Eisenberg L: "Definitions of dyslexia: Their consequences for research and policy." In Benton AL, Pearl D: *Dyslexia: An Appraisal of Current Knowledge.* New York, Oxford University Press, 1978, pp 31–42.

Frostig M, Horne D: *The Frostig Program for the Development of Visual Perception.* Chicago, Follett Publishing Company, 1964.

Gaskins I: "Let's end the reading disabilities/learning disabilities debate." *J Learn Disabil* 15:81–83, 1982.

Gerber A, Bryen D: *Language and Learning Disabilities.* Baltimore, University Park Press, 1981.

Gibson E, Levin H: *The Psychology of Reading.* Cambridge, MA, MIT Press, 1975.

Goldman R, Fristoe M, Woodcock R: *Auditory Skills Test Battery.* Circle Pines, MN, American Guidance Service, 1974.

Gupta R, Ceci SJ, Slater AM: "Visual discrimination in good and poor readers." *J Spec Educ,* 12:409–416, 1978.

Hall P, Tomblin B: "A follow-up study of children with articulation and language disorders." *J Speech Hear Disord* 43:227–241, 1978.

Johnson D, Myklebust H: *Learning Disabilities: Educational Principles and Practices.* New York, Grune and Stratton, 1967.

Kirk S, McCarthy J, Kirk WD: *The Illinois Test of Psychological Ability.* Chicago, University of Illinois Press, 1968.

Lahey M: "Learning disabilities: a puzzle without a cover picture?" Presented at the symposium on Language, Learning and Reading Disabilities: A New Decade, City University of New York, May, 1980.

Legislative Council Report: American Speech-Language and Hearing Association, Los Angeles, California, November 20–24, 1981. *ASHA* 24:195–208, 1982.

Liberman I: Phonological disorders and reading. Presented at the symposium on Language, Learning and Reading Disabilities: A New Decade, City University of New York, May, 1980.

Lindamood CH and Lindamood PC: *Auditory Conceptualization Test.* Austin, TX, Teaching Resources Company, 1971.

Lynch J: "Use of a prescreening checklist to supplement speech, language, and hearing screening." *Language Speech Hear Serv Schools* 10:249–258, 1979.

Mann L, Goodman L: Perceptual motor training: a critical retrospect. Presented at First International Leo Kanner Colloquium on Child Development, Deviations, and Treatment, University of North Carolina, Chapel Hill, 1973.

Menyuk P: Syntactic competence and reading. Presented at the symposium on Language, Learning and Reading Disorders: A New Decade, City University of New York, May, 1980.

Miller J: "Assessing children's language behavior: developmental process approach." In Schiefelbusch RL: *Bases of Language Intervention.* Baltimore, University Park Press, 1978, pp 269–318.

Miller L: "Language pragmatics and early child language disorders." *J Speech Hear Disord* 43:419–436, 1978.

Myers M, Paris S: "Children's metacognitive knowledge about reading." *J Educ Psychol* 70:680–690, 1978.

Pearson PD, Spiro RJ: "Toward a theory of reading comprehension instruction." *Top Language Disord* 1 (1):71–88, 1980.

Perfetti C: "Language comprehension and fast decoding." In Guthrie J: *Cognition, Curriculum, and Comprehension.* Newark, DE, International Reading Association, 1977, pp 20–41.

Prizant B, Duchan J: "The functions of immediate echolalia in autistic children." *J Speech Hear Disord* 46:241–249, 1981.

Rees N: "Auditory processing factors in language disorders: the view from Procurstes' bed." *J Speech Hear Disord* 38:304–315, 1973.

Rees N: The speech pathologist and the reading process. *ASHA* 16:225–258, 1974.

Rees N: "Art and science of diagnosis in hearing, language and speech." In Singh S, Lynch J: *Diagnostic Procedures in Hearing, Language, and Speech.* Baltimore, University Park Press, 1978, pp 3–24.

Rees N, Shulman M: "I don't understand what you mean by comprehension." *J Speech Hear Disord* 43:208–219, 1978.

Rosner J: *Helping Children Overcome Learning Disabilities.* New York, Walker and Company, 1975.

Roth S, Perfetti CA: "A framework for reading, language comprehension, and language disability." *Top Language Disord* 1 (1):15–28, 1980.

Rutter M: "Prevalence and types of dyslexia." In Benton AL, Pearl D: *Dyslexia: An Appraisal of Current Knowledge.* New York, Oxford University Press, 1978, pp 3–28.

Siegel G: "The use of language tests." *Language Speech Hear Serv Schools* 6:211–217, 1975.

Silliman E, Leslie S: Instructional language: a comparison of a regular and special education classroom. Presented at ASHA, Detroit, November, 1980.

Snyder L: "Have we prepared the language-disordered child for school?" *Top Language Disord* 1 (1):29–49, 1980.

Stark J: "Some views from the back row." Keynote speech presented at the symposium on Language, Learning, and Reading Disabilities: A New Decade, City University of New York, May, 1980.

Stark J, Wallach GP: "The path to a concept of language learning disabilities." *Top Language Disord* 1 (1):1–14, 1980.

Swanson L: "Verbal encoding effects on the visual short-term memory of learning disabled and normal readers." *J Educ Psychol* 70:539–544, 1978.

Swisher L, Aten J: "Assessing comprehension of spoken language: a multifaceted task." *Top Language Disord* 1 (1):75–86, 1981.

Tallal P: "A different view of auditory processing factors in language disorders." *J Speech Hear Disord* 40:313–314, 1975.

Taylor HG, Satz P, Friel J: Developmental dyslexia in relation to other childhood reading disorders; significance and clinical utility. *Read Res Q* 25:84–100, 1979.

US Office of Education: *Federal Register,* 1976, p 52407.

Vellutino F: "Toward an understanding of dyslexia: psychological factors in specific reading disability." In Benton AL, Pearl D: *Dyslexia: An Appraisal of Current Knowledge.* New York, Oxford University Press, 1978, pp 61–111.

Vellutino F: "The validity of perceptual deficit explanations of reading disability: a reply to Fletcher and Satz." *J Learn Disabil* 12:160–167, 1979.

Wallach GP: "I don't care who said it or what it means, just tell me what to do." Reaction to Liberman, Menyuk, and Bryan. Presented at Language, Learning and Reading Disabilities: A New Decade, City University of New York, May, 1980.

Wallach GP: "Language processing and reading deficiencies: assessment and intervention of children with special learning problems." In Lass N, McReynolds L, Northern J, et al: *Speech, Language, and Hearing.* Philadelphia, WB Saunders, 1982, vol 2, pp 819–838.

Wallach GP, Lee AD: "So you want to know what to do with language-disabled children above the age of six." *Top Language Disord* 1 (1):99–113, 1980.

Wallach GP, Lee AD: "Language screening in the schools." *Semin Speech Language Hear* 2:53–73, 1981.

Weiss R, Hansen K, Heubelein T: Pragmatic psycholinguistic therapy for language disorders in early childhood. Short course presented at ASHA, Atlanta, 1979.

Wepman JM: *Auditory Discrimination Test.* Beverly Hills, CA, Learning Research Associates, 1958.

Wiig E, Semel E: *Language Disabilities in Children and Adolescents.* Columbus, OH, Charles E Merrill, 1976.

CHAPTER TWO

The Language-Learning Disabilities Connection: Symptoms of Early Language Disability Change over Time

SARA E. MAXWELL, M.S., C.C.C., M.Ed., and GERALDINE P. WALLACH, Ph.D.

"Language deficits which begin early in life ... may persist into young adulthood and emerge again and again in later life. They tend to come out when new circumstances—perhaps a new line of study, a new job, or a promotion—place different and unexpected demands upon language processing and use in speaking or writing" (Wiig and Semel, 1980, p. 20).

A psychologist is presenting a diagnostic report to a school placement and review committee. Mark is an 8-year-old boy. He repeated grade 1 and is currently experiencing difficulty with reading and spelling in grade 2. Special class placement is being considered. Test scores and numerous hypotheses about Mark's problems are discussed by the group.

Mark's verbal IQ score was 92. His performance score was 130. In addition, the psychologist noted that test scores suggest that Mark is "*auditorially*—perceptually impaired." She points out that Mark had difficulty with the *Wepman Test of Auditory Discrimina-*

tion, the Auditory Attention Span for Related Syllables subtest of the *Detroit Test*, and "auditory" subtests of the *Illinois Test of Psycholinguistic Abilities* (ITPA). Of specific concern is Mark's poor "auditory memory." It is reported that he cannot remember a series of commands (or the Detroit sentences).

The case is complicated further because Mark also has "language problems." He scored at the 5-year level on the Detroit "free association" subtest that required his saying as many words as he could within a 3-minute period. The psychologist goes on to say that "Mark has difficulty organizing his thoughts and expressing his feelings." He is easily frustrated and somewhat withdrawn in school. His parents report that he frequently "acts out" at home.

The team considers whether further testing (neurological, perceptual, psychological) would pinpoint the factors "blocking" Mark's learning. The question also arises as to whether Mark needs a "language class," a "perceptual class" (an *auditory* "perceptual class," of course), or a "behavioral class" (Wallach, 1981, p. 84).

The foregoing examples illustrate various aspects of the relationship between language disorders and learning disabilities. Wiig and Semel (1980) remind us that children do not necessarily outgrow their early language disabilities. However, the symptoms or observable manifestations of early language disabilities do not remain static. Clinical anecdotes describing older children with language disorders frequently include the following: They cannot appreciate humor. They are too literal. The idioms of language elude them. They fail to learn to read or they read with great difficulty. Their social language skills are deficient (see Chapter 7). As we have learned from research in semantics and pragmatics, language proficiency involves much more than learning correct language forms. Language learning after 5 includes many higher level skills, some of which are quite subtle (see Chapter 5). Research during the past decade has contributed to our knowledge, but there is still much to be learned about how higher level language abilities differentially affect academic success. More information is also needed about how and why higher level language problems begin (see Chapter 16).

What does happen to preschoolers with language disorders? It is suggested that they do not catch up in spite of early intervention (Snyder, 1980). Are some of these children relabeled "learning disabled" after encountering various degrees of school failure? In what ways do their symptoms of early language disability change over time and across tasks (ASHA Committee on Language Learning Disabilities, 1982)? How are language failures revealed in new situations?

Mark's case brings some of these questions into a practical setting. While we recognize that children like Mark do not experience sudden onset of "specific learning disabilities" in grade 2 or grade 4, we also recognize that descriptions of their early language behavior are not always available. The possibility that learning disabilities are a continuation of early language disabilities is a provocative and complicated notion. It has encouraged reevaluation of the ways we view language and learning problems that surface during the school years.

We might ask a number of questions about Mark and children like him. How does his poor performance on tests of auditory perception relate to later language learning? Is Mark having problems with auditory perception, per se, or is he having problems making metalinguistic judgments about the phonemic structure of language (see Chapters 9 and 13)? How are Mark's "auditory memory problems" related to comprehension and processing problems? Are his word-naming difficulties characteristic of older children with learning and reading problems (see Chapter 11)?

Mark's case represents a practical dilemma. The attempt to separate perceptual, memory, linguistic, and social problems ignores the dynamic interaction among them. Unfortunately, many class placements and intervention recommendations are based on standardized tests that encourage inappropriate and/or rigid categorizations of language abilities. Language abilities are too often compartmentalized into simplistic receptive-expressive, auditory-visual, and perceptual-linguistic groupings. Equally unfortunate is the realization that most standardized tests do not tap language functions at integrative levels appropriate for Mark's age (see Chapter 1).

The changes brought about by maturation are magnified when one studies children with problems. This chapter will address a number of related issues. The effect of a child's preschool language disorder upon subsequent academic performance (Aram and Nation, 1980) will be examined. A comparison of follow-up studies will reveal the interaction betwen language disabilities and reading disabilities. As we shall see, many of the questions being raised in dyslexia research are similar to those being raised in language research. Specific examples of ways in which symptoms of language disability change over time will be presented. A final section will concern issues relating to neurocognitive development and reorganization. A discussion of the infant-preschooler-older child continuum will provide topics for future research in language learning disabilities.

LANGUAGE DISABILITIES BECOME LEARNING AND READING DISABILITIES
Follow-up Studies of Language-delayed Children

The connection between language proficiency and school success appears obvious. Yet, a strange separation exists in theory and practice between "language disabilities" and "learning disabilities." One develops an appreciation for the effect that the development and use of language have upon learning and later academic success by considering the experiences of children who were found to have language disabilities during the preschool years. In a 9-year follow-up study, Strominger and Bashir (1977) asked whether children who are recognized early as having a language disability experience reading, spelling, and writing problems as they get older. They wondered whether a continuum of failure would become apparent. Strominger and Bashir (1977) examined their clinical records. Forty children, who had been seen in their clinic before the age of 5, were seen again between the ages of 9 and 11. "Delayed language," including vocabulary and syntactic problems, had been the original complaint. "Unintelligible speech" was also noted as a problem for some of these children. However, none of the children had been diagnosed as mentally retarded, severely emotionally disturbed, or motorically impaired. A number of tests were administered during the follow-up period including the *WISC-R*, the *Token Test for Children*, and the *Boston Naming Test* (Kaplan and Goodglass, 1975). Reading and writing skills were also assessed.

Of the forty children studied, 33 were boys. Thirty children showed a 10- to 15-point discrepancy between verbal and performance subtests of the *WISC-R*, with the majority of children (26) scoring higher on the performance subtest. Of the four children who demonstrated the reversed pattern, i.e., higher verbal scores, three were girls. These data are important to consider as we explore differences between language-disordered boys and girls. They are also important because we need to learn more about the significance of IQ verbal-performance discrepancies.

Strominger and Bashir (1977) report that "no child was found without residual deficits" (p. 3). Only two children in the entire sample were reported to be on or above grade level on tests of oral reading, reading comprehension, and written language. Interestingly, these two subjects continued to experience problems with sound sequencing and spelling. They also manifested "mild naming problems" (see Chapters 11 and 13). Symptoms of language disabilities that had been identified in the preschool years had not disappeared completely. However, these two children did perform significantly better than the 38 remaining children in the follow-up group. Both obtained full-scale IQ scores of 120, with less than a 5-point discrepancy between verbal and performance scores. This is interesting in view of the point made earlier about IQ subtest discrepancies. Clearly, we need to know more about language-disabled children who achieve academic success. Are the achievers in full-time regular classrooms? Are their social language skills appropriate? What might be different about their family life? their early school experiences? their early language symptomatology? the strategies they have developed for learning new tasks? their preferred learning style?

Most of the remaining 38 children from the Strominger and Bashir (1977) sample continued to manifest problems in both spoken and written language. Only 17 were reading above third-grade level. Written language problems were the most obvious deficits noted. Persistent deficits in mean length and complexity of written sentences were noted. It was also found that available expressive vocabulary and the degree of naming problems had "a high degree of concomitant association with reading deficit" (Strominger and Bashir, 1977, p. 4). This study lends support to the concept of a continuum of language failure. Other recent studies support the finding that word knowledge and word retrieval problems frequently coexist with reading problems (see Chapter 11). Future research must examine the individual differences among children more closely. Study of individual strategy preferences among subjects warrants careful consideration. As Strominger and Bashir (1977) have indicated, "the child who evidences early disruption of language acquisition is at the highest risk for future educational failure or difficulty in reading and written language (p. 4)." They go on to explain that early problems with oral language should not be viewed as the *cause* of reading and writing problems. Rather, such problems are part of an underlying problem that continues and shows itself differently as a child gets older.

Aram and Nation (1980) studied 63 children whose language disorders had been identified during their preschool years. The children were followed up 4 to 5 years after initial diagnosis. Aram and Nation asked questions similar to those raised by Stromnger and Bashir. They also wanted to know if subsequent academic performance could be predicted on the basis of the nature and severity of a child's preschool language disorder. Aram and Nation (1980) believed that descriptions of a child's initial language disorder might begin to clarify some of the interrelationships among speech, language, and academic abilities.

Aram and Nation used parent and teacher questionnaires and school records to gather their data. Their subjects were between 4:7 and 10:4 years old, with a mean age of 7:11, at the time of the follow-up. They were all under age 5, with a mean age of 32 months, when they were first seen for speech and language evaluations.

Although problems persisted in 80% of the original group, the outcome of early language disabilities was not the same for all children. Half of the group with persistent problems continued to manifest obvious speech and language difficulties well into the school years. The other half, though apparently not manifesting overt language problems, were reported as having "other" learning problems. Children in the latter group were not in regular classrooms and were showing below-normal achievement in reading and in math. Some immediate questions come to mind: What factors (such as age and nature of communication problem) differentiated these two groups originally? Does the second group have more subtle language-processing problems characteristic of later language learning? What similarities are there between groups? What is different about the 20% who do "make it"?

Aram and Nation addressed the above questions. However, they indicated that we need to proceed with caution when attempting to predict subsequent classroom placement in the elementary grades from preschool levels of language comprehension, formulation, phonological abilities, etc. They present interesting findings for further consideration. Additional analyses of the follow-up data revealed the following: severity ratings, which were completed by a team of clinicians during the initial preschool intake period, correlated significantly with subsequent classroom placement. As Strominger and Bashir (1977) had reported previously, early problems with language comprehension were shown to place children at high risk for academic failure. Interestingly, preschoolers' auditory reception measures, such as responses to nonlinguistic auditory stimuli, did not correlate with later classroom placements. This was the case even if children were rated as having severe problems with auditory reception originally (Aram and Nation, 1980, p. 165). Preschoolers rated in the mild or moderate speech and language impairment category "had a high probability of being in normal classes with either same-age or younger peers, or in L.D. placements" (Aram and Nation, 1980, p. 166).

Another important finding was reported in the Aram and Nation study. Therapy during the preschool years did not significantly circumvent later speech, language, and academic disabilities. This finding reiterates the provocative question that Snyder (1980) has asked about preschool language therapy, i.e., "Have we prepared the language-disordered child for school?" It also reminds us of the pervasive nature of language disorders and the need for long-term intervention programs.

These and other studies appear to indicate that we do not yet have sufficient knowledge about how etiological, maturational, and environmental factors "play off" one another. There is evidence to suggest that these factors interact differently at different points in time (Bashir et al.,

1983). As Aram and Nation (1980) point out, future studies must examine the language-disordered child in a broader language-learning context. More comprehensive preschool interventions can then be designed (see Chapter 15).

In addition, Aram and Nation point out that the only preschool dimension that correlated significantly with the duration of later school therapy was the severity of phonology ratings. They ask why phonology stands out as the preschool language dimension related to the duration of school therapy. Do severe phonological problems persist into the school years? It appears as if school speech-language pathologists, who are well versed in the nature and treatment of articulation problems, are more likely to provide treatment for this group of children after they enter school. Whether the articulation problems of Aram and Nation's group remained severe enough to warrant therapy deserves scrutiny. Perhaps this finding reflects the state of the art in language learning disabilities to some extent. It is unclear why some of the language-impaired preschool children are dismissed from therapy and are not included on school caseloads. It may be that currently available tests are not sufficiently sensitive to delineate language problems of the school-age child (see Chapters 12 and 15). It may also be the case that some preschool language problems, as suggested earlier, emerge as "other" problems (reading, difficulty with the classroom curricula, etc.). Thus, professionals' involvement changes, e.g., the reading specialist takes over for the speech-language pathologist (Bashir, et al., 1983; see Chapter 1).

King et al. (1982) conducted a 15-year follow-up study of speech- and language-disordered children. Their subjects were older than those studied by Strominger and Bashir (1977) and Aram and Nation (1980). Fifty subjects ranged in age from 13 years 10 months to 20 years 5 months at the time of follow-up. As in the other studies, all members of the group had been under 5 years of age at initial intake. Question-

naires were sent to their families to obtain information about communicative, social, academic, and occupational outcomes. Forty-two per cent of the subjects were perceived by their families as still having communication problems. King et al. (1982, p. 30) provide some examples from the reports that provide a description of the symptomatology:

... "trouble finding words and expressing himself ... he can't understand complicated directions ..."
... "he's not good at expressing his feelings ..."
... "infantile ... skips small words ... difficulty in pronouncing some combination of sounds ..."
... "says answers, but can't write them ..."

School problems of varying degrees and types were also reported. Many of the subjects had delayed admissions, repeated grades, or tutors and special placements. Both language and articulation problems appeared concomitantly with reading problems. However, subjects initially diagnosed as having a "language" problem were at the highest risk for a continuation of problems into adolescence and young adulthood. Subjects initially diagnosed as having "articulation" problems appeared to have a better prognosis (King et al., 1982, p. 30). This finding is substantiated elsewhere. In a 13- to 20-year follow-up study, Hall and Tomblin (1978) observed differences between preschoolers designated as "language impaired" and those considered to be "articulation impaired." They indicate that "the language-impaired group consistently achieved at a lower level than the articulation-impaired group, particularly in reading" (p. 235). They go on to report that, although all subjects from both language-impaired and articulation-impaired groups were completing or had completed high school, fewer language subjects than articulation subjects were obtaining higher education.

The issue of what happens to the different groups within the general category of "early preschool communication problems" is raised throughout the research. Although there is some suggestion that language-impaired and articulation-impaired children take "different paths," this notion should be entertained with caution. Indeed, the nature of particular interactions among early syntactic-semantic-pragmatic and phonological abilities (and disabilities) continues to be investigated (Schwartz et al., 1980). The nature of changes in children's abilities as they go through the grades, as well as the type of remediation they receive, may contribute to our understanding of this complex problem. Hall and Tomblin (1978) indicate that the differences between their language and articulation subjects increased from the third through the fifth grade. Differences, while still evidenced, declined somewhat from sixth through eighth grade. In all their analyses, the language-impaired children continued to manifest a wider range of difficulties and showed greater within-group variance than the articulation group. Problems with mathematics were also reported for the language group, suggesting that language disorders cut across subject areas (see Chapters 8 and 10).

The evidence presented thus far appears discouraging. Nevertheless, it may provide us with a resolve to reevaluate current models, methods, and myths in language disabilities. One myth, that the majority of children "outgrow" their early language disabilities, is dispelled by the research. However, we are also reminded that low levels of academic achievement cannot be predicted for *all* language-disabled children (King et al., 1982). As children with language disabilities are carefully followed up, we may learn about the variables and the intervention techniques that are effective in facilitating school, social, and communication success (Griffiths, 1969; Weiner, 1974; DeAjuriaguerra, et al., 1976). We may also find that children who lack overt verbal language symptoms are later labeled "learning disabled." Let us continue with our discussion of the language-learning disabilities continuum by considering questions being raised by researchers in reading disabilities.

Follow-up Studies of Children with Reading Problems

The study of children with school problems may be approached from a number of different perspectives. One might ask what happens to preschoolers with language problems. It is also possible to ask what children with specific reading disabilities were like before they came to school. The two streams of research frequently come together in the sense that the same questions are being addressed from various viewpoints. What are the early predictors of school failure? of reading failure? While some have chosen to study the long-term effects of early verbal language deficits, others have chosen to study the long-term effects of visual perceptual and visual-motor difficulties in young children.

An interesting dilemma arises when children with reading and learning problems are not referred for clinical and educational evaluations until 9 or 11 years old (Satz et al., 1978). Mark's case, presented earlier, is an example of this phenomenon. Can symptoms of verbal language disabilities remain covert, only to surface when the demands of the school curricula increase? Are there times when certain aspects of learning and reading problems predominate over others?

VISUAL PERCEPTUAL DIFFICULTIES

As part of a longitudinal research project, Robinson and Schwartz (1973) administered a battery of psychological tests to 142 children between 5 and 6 years of age who were about to enter grade 1. Forty-one children were identified as having difficulties with visual perception, visual-motor coordination, or both. They were designated as being "at risk" for academic problems. Skills such as the visual organization of wholes from parts, visual discrimination, and copying were found to be weak. When retested 3 years later, the high-risk group continued to manifest visual perceptual and visual-motor difficulties. However, they had no more difficulty reading than a control group randomly selected from the original 142 children. Since the reading scores of the high-risk group were not significantly lower than those of the control group by grade 3, it appears that reading difficulties could not be predicted from early differences in those visual perceptual and visual-motor abilities they examined. While the persistence of visual deficits does not, according to Robinson and Schwartz (1973), appear to signal later reading failures, this area warrants further investigation.

The question of which symptoms are the most reliable predictors of. reading problems appears unanswered at this point in time. Much more needs to be learned about developmental changes which occur between the ages of 5 and 7 years (see Chapter 5). Satz et al. (1978) point out that many high-risk children, such as those in the Robinson and Schwartz (1973) study, "catch up" on certain developmental skills but not on others. They found that, during kindergarten, some of the best predictors of later reading disability included difficulties with finger localization, alphabet recitation, and visual recognition-discrimination. When their "high-risk" children were retested on the same prediction tasks at the end of grade 2, they performed as well as the children who were not "at risk." However, the high-risk children were still behind in reading and writing (Satz et al., 1978, p. 342). Satz et al. reflect upon developmental neurology (see Chapter 3). They hypothesize that "high risk children will eventually 'catch up' on these earlier developing skills but will then lag on those more cognitive-linguistic skills ... because they have a slower and later ontogenetic development" (p. 341). Satz et al. conclude that, if the same subjects had been tested initially on the predictive tasks at 8 years old, no group differences would have been found. For clinicians and educators, this represents a most important point. It may be inappropriate to use the same tests and procedures with 9-year-olds that are used with 5-year-olds. We need to know more

about how and why symptoms "wash away" or become obscured over time. We must consider the test/retest paradigm with caution (see Chapter 15).

Visual perceptual difficulties which have been associated with reading difficulties in younger children are not necessarily important correlates of severe and persistent reading difficulties (Rutter and Yule, 1973; Rutter, 1978). In an ongoing dialogue, Fletcher and Satz (1979) and Vellutino (1979b) debate the relative importance of visual perceptual versus verbal linguistic skills in reading. Fletcher and Satz indicate that visual perceptual skills may be more important at the earlier stages of reading. The period between the ages of 5 and 7 years represents a time when visual perceptual abilities appear to play a predominant role in reading acquisition. Children come to rely less on visual-processing strategies as their verbal linguistic strategies become stronger. "Reading", between 5 and 7 years, is largely a single-word recognition task (Rourke, 1978). Thus, perceptual errors are more likely to show up during this period. Between the ages of 9 and 11 years, reading requires higher order language comprehension and conceptual abilities. This shift in reading process demands, along with other curricula demands, may explain why some children are not referred for some learning and reading disabilities until the age of 9 or 11 years (see Chapter 8).

There is support for the contention that naming errors in children with reading problems also change as a function of age. Younger children with reading problems (6- to 9-year-olds) reportedly make errors that reflect "visually based" mistakes. Thus, children say "carrot" for "dart." On the other hand, older children (10- and 11-year olds) make "semantically based" errors involving circumlocutions (Wolf, 1979; in Wiig et al., 1982, p. 12). According to Israel (Chapter 11), many shifts occur in children's word-processing abilities between the ages of 5 and 7 years. These also reflect perceptual-conceptual progressions. Israel points out, for example, that when children are asked why two words go together, e.g., boy and girl, younger children tend to give perceptually based answers. That is, 5-year-olds tend to say "a boy and a girl go together because a girl has long hair and a boy has short hair." Older children (above 7 years) make conceptual judgments. The 7-year-old might say: "a boy and a girl go together because they are human beings" (see Chapter 11). Muma (1978), among others, also discusses how children move from iconic processing (they try to remember the shape, the way something looks) to symbolic processing (they use verbal labels when possible) as they get older. Both visual and verbal strategies are important, but we need to recognize how they develop and interact with each other over time. This knowledge base influences the way we use assessment and intervention tools.

THE VERBAL DEFICIT HYPOTHESIS AND READING FAILURE

Vellutino (1978, 1979a) has taken one of the strongest positions against the proposal that visual perceptual delays or deficits underlie reading difficulties. He indicates that, by the time most children are diagnosed as "reading disabled," their apparent "perceptual problems" are secondary manifestations of "verbal mediation deficiencies, possibly associated with basic language problems" (Vellutino, 1978, p. 107). Vellutino points out that we must look at the interaction among visual errors, materials, and tasks more closely. In a series of experiments, Vellutino asked good and poor readers between grades 2 and 6 to copy three, four, and five-item words, scrambled letters, numbers, and geometric designs. He also asked children to read the words and "spell out" the letters. The items were flashed in front of the subjects, who then wrote them from memory. Real words included items such as "fly," "loin," and "chair." Scrambled letters and numbers included items like: dnv, jpyc, ztbrc, 382, 4328, and 96842. Geometric designs included circles, squares, triangles, and other visual forms (Vellutino et al., 1975a). Overall, the poor readers performed as well as

the good readers in copying the sequences. For example, both groups copied words such as "lion" and "loin" with equal accuracy. However, differences between groups surfaced when they were asked to read the same words aloud. The disabled readers could not read accurately many of the same words that they had copied correctly. According to Vellutino (1978), it is not surprising that poor readers do not read as well as good readers. What the study demonstrates is that "visual perception of a given word is not necessarily reflected in the pronunciation or verbal labeling of that word" (p. 83). Vellutino goes on to say that reading substitutions for both groups ("lion" for "loin" and "clam" for "calm") are due to "linguistic intrusion errors" and not to visual perceptual errors. By linguistic intrusion errors, he meant that children substitute a more familiar vocabulary word for a stimulus word, particularly when contextual cues are unavailable. The "carrot-dart" substitution mentioned earlier may serve as another example of a linguistic intrusion error even though it was characterized as a "visual" error. Vellutino (1978) also reports that differences between the reading-disabled and normally achieving children widened as they got older. That is, although there was steady improvement on the copying task, there was not as much improvement on the reading tasks for the poor readers. By grade 6, the copying differences between the two groups had disappeared. The linguistic differences had not.

Vellutino and his colleagues (1973, 1975b) completed numerous studies to support the hypothesis that verbal strategy deficits are the most plausible explanation for the majority of reading failures. In one study, they used Hebrew word stimuli to control for previous experiences with letters and words. Consistent with what one might expect, poor readers performed as well as good readers on copying tasks, but both groups had difficulty when language demands (e.g., say the word, recall its name) were increased. Vellutino also reports that both good and poor readers, unfamiliar with the Hebrew right-left orientation, revert to left-right scanning strategies. This finding is at variance with the suggestion that "poor readers cannot establish a left-right directional set in reading because of visuospatial confusion" (Vellutino, 1978, p. 85). Vellutino (1978) goes on to say that, "whatever else reading may be, it is a decidedly linguistic function" (p. 110). Vellutino's work is currently being scrutinized by neurolinguists and neuropsychologists who believe the "verbal deficit" model does not sufficiently explain all aspects of reading disabilities. However, many of his data provide provocative questions for future research on the nature of the linguistic aspects of reading performance.

The suggestion that age-related changes must be considered when discussing both visual and verbal learning strategies is reflected throughout the research. Research also suggests that, even if visual perceptual problems persist, they are not the solitary cause of reading problems. Rutter (1978, p. 8) reiterates a number of important points when he writes:

"While reading disabled children may be 'perceptually impaired' compared with their peers, they still have sufficient skills in discrimination to learn to read. Besides this, it is apparent that good listeners do not listen to every phoneme, and good readers do not discriminate each individual word when reading."

Blank (1978) reminds us that symptoms of learning and reading failure often coexist. Some visual perceptual tasks, and other tasks such as reciting the alphabet, may be *predictive* of reading and school problems at certain points in time, but they should not be thought of as causes of such problems. Blank (1978) provides a classic example. She finds that many young children with reading problems also have problems with color naming. She points out that their difficulty with this task may correlate with some factor, or factors, that cause reading failures; however, color naming itself may not be relevant to reading performance. Blank's example and similar issues raised in Chapter 1 deal with cause and effect relationships in language learning disabilities. We must look beyond specific errors children make to better understand how skills involved in reading are interrelated. Nevertheless, gaps between theory, research, and practice sometimes impede progress. Stark (1981) emphasizes this reality. He states that, although linguistic rather than visual difficulties may be the more important source of a majority of reading problems by the school years. ". . . well-meaning teachers spend endless time in training visual-motor processes" (p. 90).

Delay versus Difference

It is important to "be aware of the potential pitfalls which can be encountered when phenomena such as 'spurts' and 'plateaus' in development are overlooked" (Rourke, 1978, p. 171). Rourke (1975) reports that certain tests may be powerful discriminators of learning- and reading-disabled children at different points in time. He indicates that tasks used to measure dichotic listening, reaction time, and similar behavioral responses are more sensitive to detecting differences between groups at ages between 6 and 8. Tests of attention, measured by auditory and visual reaction times, also appear to reflect differences between normal and reading-disabled children only at younger age ranges. Rourke and Czudner (1972) found that the performances of older reading-disabled children (i.e., 9 to 14 years old) were not different from those of normal 9- to 14-year-olds on various reaction time tasks. On the other hand, Rourke (1978) found that verbal-performance IQ score discrepancies were more closely correlated with academic achievement in children above 10 years. This is also reported by Robinson and Schwartz (1973). These findings suggest, as with the visual perceptual data, that some abilities develop relatively early in normal children. Thus, there may be adequate time for "catch up" for *some* children, in *some* instances, on *some* skills. The larger body of data from both the reading and language research suggests that reading problems identified in childhood persist during adolescence (Satz et al., 1978). If symptoms change over time, early reading problems may manifest themselves in the form of spelling difficulties in adults (Rutter, 1978). In general, poor readers make progress as they mature. However, there is little evidence to suggest that they "outgrow" their reading disabilities completely or that they approximate the performance of proficient readers (Rourke, 1976, 1978).

A CLOSER LOOK AT LANGUAGE SYMPTOMATOLOGY

It has been suggested that language abilities and disabilities cannot be separated from reading acquisition and reading failure. The need for longitudinal research is apparent. Research in language learning and reading should result in refined descriptions of the developmental unfolding of normal and disordered sequences (see Chapter 7). The heterogeneous nature of language disabilities requires that descriptions of "language symptomatology" receive careful scrutiny.

Dyslexia Subgroups

Mattis et al. (1975) and Denckla and Rudel (1976), among others, have observed different subgroups (or syndromes) within populations identified as dyslexic. Such terms as "anomia," "verbal memorization disorders," and "dysphonemic sequencing difficulty" have been used to describe some of the language symptoms one might see in dyslexic children. Mattis et al. (1975) isolated three major dyslexia syndromes. One group of children were predominantly "language disordered." The second group manifested "articulatory and graphomotor dyscoordination." The third group demonstrated "visuospatial perceptual disorders." Mattis and his colleagues remind us that some overlap exists between "cluster groups." A number of interesting symptoms are described by Mattis (1978).

Disorders of speech sound discrimination were indicated as one of the problems of the language-disordered group. This group

also manifested "disorders of comprehension," as defined by the *Token Test.* Weak performance on the *ITPA* Sound Blending subtest was observed in the articulatory and graphomotor group. This group, unlike the language group, demonstrated "receptive language processes within normal limits." Some questions should be raised. Are both groups manifesting problems with metalinguistic skills that relate to the phonological component of language? Are sound blending and speech sound discrimination more closely related than they might appear (see Chapters 9 and 13)? Do both groups have difficulty with the integrative and inferential aspects of comprehension? Mattis's language group was reported as having difficulty with the *Token Test,* i.e., subjects scored at least 1 SD below the mean. What kinds of errors did they make? What strategies did they employ? Are the language and articulation groups a similar group at different points in time or do they represent different neurological subgroups (see Chapter 3)? Further examination is warranted.

The smallest percentage of subjects in the Mattis et al. (1975) study fell into the category labeled "visuospatial group." They had performance-verbal IQ score discrepancies in excess of 10 points, with the higher scores obtained on the verbal subtests (as in Strominger and Bashir, 1977). Other tasks were used to determine that this group had problems in the visual areas. What is interesting to note is whether visual-*motor* skills, such as copying and writing, and visual *perceptual* skills, such as looking-discriminating-sequencing, differentiated subjects. Indeed, children may have difficulty *copying* something even though they "see" (perceive, discriminate) it correctly. Thus, the umbrella term—"visual problems"—can be misleading. The Mattis et al. (1975) data remind us to consider the effects of coexisting symptomatology and to exercise caution when using labels (see Chapter 1). Closer scrutiny of reading subgroups is certainly warranted, and this research represents an important contribution toward that end.

The study of homogeneous subgroups within a heterogeneous population is extremely complex. Nevertheless, research and clinical data from a variety of sources and orientations continue to suggest that the largest percentage of learning- and reading-disabled children have language problems (Denckla, in Mattis et al., 1975). Changes in early language symptoms that occur over time are demonstrated when they manifest themselves in reading and writing performance. Difficulties in verbal language (listening and speaking) frequently accompany more overt written language difficulties.

Communicative Competence and Learning Disabilities: From Overt to Subtle

In a series of studies, Bryan and her colleagues (1981) addressed the issues of "symptoms changing" and "subtle" language problems. Children diagnosed as learning disabled between grade 1 and grade 8 were evaluated on numerous communicative skills. Bryan et al. were concerned with the competence of learning-disabled children as conversational partners. They assessed such skills as asking questions appropriately, leading group discussions, and altering communication to fit various situations. Learning-disabled children were observed in both listener and speaker roles.

PICKING UP ON LISTENER FEEDBACK: THE SPEAKER ROLE

In one experiment, children were asked to describe a series of abstract figures to an adult experimenter. The adult was to find the picture being described from a large array of similar pictures. Children were told that they could give additional verbal clues if they thought their partner (the experimenter) needed them. Experimenters modified feedback to the child so as to determine how astute the child was in knowing when the listener was confused. Four possible experimenter responses were used: (1) The correct picture was chosen. (2) The

child was asked directly for another clue, e.g., "Tell me something else about it." (3) A less direct comment was made, i.e., the experimenter looked at the array of pictures and said, "I don't understand." (4) The experimenter used puzzled facial expressions, making sure that eye contact was established.

Developmental changes in responses to the different types of listener feedback were noted. Differences were also found between the normally achieving and learning-disabled subjects. Even the youngest subjects (first graders) responded to requests for more information. They responded to direct questions and "I don't understand" requests from experimenters. However, children in grades 1 to 4 were less likely to respond to facial feedback alone. It was not until grades 7 and 8 that children were equally likely to respond to all three types of feedback. Learning-disabled and normal children differed only in their responses to facial feedback, and only in the first and second grades. Learning-disabled boys responded to facial feedback *more often* than the normal-achieving boys. Learning-disabled girls were less likely to respond to facial feedback than the normal-achieving girls. The reasons for these differences are not clear; however, the results indicate a number of patterns. The comprehension of subtle, nonverbal feedback appears to develop relatively late. The prediction that learning-disabled children are less responsive to facial feedback than normals was not upheld, since learning-disabled boys actually responded to facial feedback at an earlier age than the other children. The findings remain tentative because factors such as personality dimensions and other levels of academic status and performance and their relationship to these differences need to be studied more closely (see Chapters 8 and 14). However, the research demonstrates a method for studying conversational interactions. It also demonstrates that differences exist within the learning-disabled population. These data appear to support the observation that "deficits" do not necessarily occur across the board (Pearl et al., 1979).

ASKING FOR CLARIFICATION: THE LISTENER ROLE

In another experiment, Donahue et al. (1980) examined learning-disabled children's understanding of conversational rules for repairing communication breakdowns. That is, when a message is not understood, clarification must be requested. The children were instructed to select one of four pictures after hearing a clue from the experimenter. The pictures were constructed in such a way that explicit clues from the experimenter were needed in order for children to select the correct one. For example, one set of pictures showed a seal. Only certain features differentiated the pictures: (1) a seal with a hoop around his neck *sitting on a stand* balancing a ball; (2) a seal with a hoop around his neck *standing on the floor* balancing a ball; (3) a seal *without a hoop around his neck* standing on the floor balancing a ball; and (4) a seal without a hoop around his neck *sitting on a stand* balancing a ball. Thus, a statement such as, "Pick up the picture of the seal balancing the ball," would not provide sufficient information for the listener. The children would need to ask the experimenter for more information. This would be an appropriate conversational strategy.

The results showed several similarities and differences between normal and learning-disabled children. Learning-disabled children did not differ from normal children in their ability to choose the correct picture when the experimenter gave enough information; however, they were less likely than the normal children to request additional information when they needed it. Thus, they were less able to select the correct picture overall. Even more interesting is the finding that, ". . . the linguistic skills required to produce appropriate requests for more information were well within these children's productive language abilities" (Donahue et al., 1980, p. 16). On this task

then, failure to request more information could not be attributed to deficits in comprehension or production of syntactic-semantic structures. Any syntactic-semantic differences that may exist between the two groups warrant further investigation. The Donahue et al. (1980) study reflects one way in which symptoms change across learning tasks—syntactic problems go underground and pragmatic ones surface—and this is a topic for future research (Bryan and Pflaum, 1978). Donahue et al. (1982) point out that we must continue to explore the ways in which syntactic proficiency interacts with communicative competence. They remind us that some learning-disabled children's productive language deficits, obscured in some situations, may be less subtle than was previously thought.

Language Strategies: From Delays to Differences

Wallach (1977) investigated a different aspect of the language-learning disability connection. She asked about older learning-disabled children's comprehension processing difficulties. Are their patterns of comprehension the same as, or different from, those of normally achieving children of the same age? Can performance on an individual sentence comprehension task be generalized to performance on other tasks, such as story processing or free recall of word lists? Fifty learning-disabled children between the ages of 8 years, 6 months and 13 years, 3 months were compared with a group of normally achieving children on a number of comprehension tasks.

In the first experiment, the children were asked to manipulate objects in order to demonstrate comprehension for a series of complex relative clause sentences such as: (1) The giraffe that bites the hippo kicks the wolf, (subject relative); and (2) The giraffe bites the hippo that kicks the wolf (object relative). Errors were analyzed in order to determine the comprehension strategies employed. Both quantitative and qualitative results differentiated the normal and learning-disabled groups. The normally achieving children above 9½ years achieved perfect or near-perfect (one error) scores. Thus, while the sentences were quite difficult, they were comprehended by the 9½-year-olds. On the other hand, only eight learning-disabled children obtained perfect or near-perfect scores. These were spread across the different age ranges. Perhaps the most interesting finding relates to the nature of errors. The learning-disabled children did not perform uniformly like younger normals. A different pattern of errors was noted. It was found that the normal and learning-disabled subjects employed different comprehension strategies. The younger normals preferred temporal order strategies. They followed the sequence of noun-verb-noun and manipulated objects accordingly. The learning-disabled children used "first noun/actor" and "parallel function strategies." A first noun/actor strategy occurred when children assumed that the first noun mentioned was the actor/doer of all the actions in the sentence. Thus, if a child picked "the giraffe" for the object relative in sentence 2, it became the doer/actor of all the actions, which led to an incorrect interpretation of part of the sentence. The strategy can work, however, for the subject relative. A parallel function strategy occurred when a child tried to fit an animal into a coherent semantic role. For example, they decided that "the hippo" in sentence 2 has the role of recipient/object of *all* the actions.

Another interesting finding was reported from the Wallach data. "Comprehension subgroups" were isolated within the learning-disabled group. There were children, regardless of their strategy preferences, who were clearly "strategy users." That is, they were consistent in their approach to the task. There were others within the learning-disabled group who could not be defined as strategy users. They approached each sentence differently, sometimes following word order, sometimes using first noun/actor strategies, sometimes performing randomly. Wallach (1977) found evidence for differential performances between the two learning-disabled groups on other tasks. The performance of the learning-disabled strategy users was superior to that of the inconsistent children in certain story tasks and on free recall word tasks. Neither group, however, approximated the performance of the normal group (see Chapter 5 for additional information on these various strategies).

Further investigation of comprehension differences within the learning-disabled population is clearly warranted. Indeed, there are problems inherent in the research. What differentiates the learning-disabled children who perform well on these kinds of tasks from those who do not? As indicated throughout this text, one needs to be cautious about making generalizations across learning-disabled populations. Nevertheless, studies of this kind may help us put traditional developmental delay models into perspective. Learning-disabled children may not always follow the same path as normally acquiring children. In some instances, they perform as well as normally acquiring children but manifest different approaches or strategies when completing tasks (Goldsmith et al., 1974; Wallach and Brown, in preparation). In addition, understanding of the complex reorganizations and subsequent changes that occur in the performance of normally acquiring children, as well as children with problems, may provide us with a greater understanding of the language-learning disability connection. Further study of the nature of individual developmental differences among children is necessary.

DEVELOPMENTAL ISSUES AND THE CONCEPT OF "CHANGING SYMPTOMS"

Growing attention to the work of Piaget (1952), Flavell (1977), Luria (1976), Travers (1982), and others in the area of cognition has encouraged researchers and practitioners to ask provocative questions relating to the role of conceptual development in language acquisition (Whitehurst and Zimmerman, 1979). It has also encouraged us to consider the reciprocal effects of language performance upon cognitive development. Karmiloff-Smith (1981) reminds us that, regardless of disagreements we may have about the language-cognition/cognition-language sequence, Piaget has shown us how to view the child as a developing whole—an increasingly integrated network of interacting systems rather than as a series of fragmented pieces (p. 151). She goes on to say that "modifications in children's behavior, linguistic or nonlinguistic, cannot be explained by external influences alone" (p. 154). This does not discount environmental influences, but it suggests that changes within the child also program growth and development. Emerging data about the effects of various functions of the nervous system upon maturation are helping us understand some of the intrinsic mechanisms that underpin cognitive and linguistic development (see Chapter 3).

Gleitman (1981) has asked a number of important questions relating to language and cognitive development. She asks whether certain subcomponents of language are more environmentally influenced than others? In studies of young children, Gleitman and her colleagues found that morphological changes, such as use of can, have, and "ed" word endings, appeared to be a function of maternal speech style. Conversely, children's increasing use of predicates (verbs) and their obligatory noun agreements was more predictable from maturation. These findings emphasize the importance of considering the effects of experience upon the developing child's neural maturation. The dynamic nature of these two aspects of development explains difficulties encountered when we attempt to determine changes in behavior that occur over time.

Gleitman (1981) also asked whether cognitively delayed or impaired children, such as those with Down's syndrome, took longer to learn language because they "formed inductions over different, and shallower, units of language" (p. 110). Gleitman and her colleagues looked at a group of 12-year-old Down's syndrome children. Through a careful series of analyses, they matched this group to a group of normal controls for language skills. It was found that the Down's syndrome children's language approximated that of the normal controls who were 2½ years of age. Both groups had MLU's (mean length of utterances) between 3.0 and 3.5. An interesting discrepancy surfaced. The mental age of the Down's syndrome group was approximately 6 years. Yet, their language was at the 2½-year range. Thus, the Down's syndrome group did not show a mental age-language age match-up. They appeared to be taking longer to learn language. However, Gleitman and her colleagues were not convinced that this was the case. They compared the performance of older Down's syndrome children to a group of Down's syndrome 7-year-olds, who appeared to be a younger version of the 12-year-olds. They found that the language of these two groups was very similar. That is, the younger Down's syndrome group already "knew" as much language as the 12-year-olds. Based upon their observations, Gleitman and her colleagues concluded that Down's syndrome children between 4 and 6 years learn as much as normal children learn from 1 to 3 years. They conjecture, although tentatively, that these children are not necessarily slower to form generalizations. Rather, "they arrive late at the stage that allows learning to begin, and the learning stops early, owing to the failure to reach the mental state in which normal learners rework the data, achieving mature grammar" (Gleitman, 1981, p. 111). In a sense, Gleitman seems to be addressing the question of "delay versus deviance" raised by Wallach and Liebergott (Chapter 1). She and her colleagues suggest the need for longitudinal studies with disordered populations so that we might better understand the spurts and plateaus in their development.

Miller et al. (1981) also challenge the slow motion view of language performance in certain populations. Miller et al. (1981) studied a group of mentally retarded children. They found that language performances could not be predicted from cognitive levels of functioning. Interestingly, 50% of their subjects were at, or beyond, language levels one would expect based upon their cognitive performances. These researchers reiterate the complexities attached to studying children with problems. They remind us of the heterogeneity within populations, including those labeled "developmentally disabled." The attempt to improve our understanding of development, disorders, and changes that occur in children over time continues.

Where Do We Begin?

Study of the earliest stages of child development may provide us with new directions for the future. Cognitive development can be observed in its earliest forms during infancy (Weiner and Elkind, 1972; Bower, 1974, 1977; Lewis, 1976; Kagan, et al., 1978, Travers, 1982). Recognition of the importance of affective and sensory motor experience emphasizes the need for a holistic approach if the cognitive matrix for language learning is to be accurately understood. The quality of operation of the entire neurocognitive system depends upon the extent to which sensory, affective, and motor components are intact at the central integrative or cortical level and upon the speed and efficiency with which they interact. Gleitman has shown that the time elapsed since conception, when neurological development begins, is a better predictor of language onset in premature children than time elapsed since birth (exposure time). One could go on to ask whether normal learners first exposed to language data at later ages learn in qualitatively different ways? (Gleitman, 1981, p. 111). Some children "catch up" and others do not.

The integrative capacity of the nervous system, or the ability to coordinate neurocognitive functions that occur between a stimulus and response, determines the intellectual aspect of human individual experience and behavior. This capacity is re-

flected in processes long referred to as attending, discrimination, memory, sequencing, classification, integration, and analysis. These activities are closely tied to, and facilitate, language learning. However, their definitions undergo modification when applied to infants, to preschoolers, and to school-age children. When the very young child engages in what appears to be a simple act, such as waving "bye-bye," attending, discriminating, planning of a motor sequence, and memory all occur simultaneously. The child is also reacting affectively in a spatially and temporally complex environment. When school-age children read a passage, they apply language knowledge to attend, scan, and predict outcomes (see Chapter 8).

It can be seen that, as the neurocognitive system matures, overt responses to identical learning tasks might differ. This notion is supported by the observation that identical stimuli appear to interest a young child at one point in his development but cause distress or fail to interest him at another. It appears that the child's differing reactions are a function of his changing levels of ability to cognitively analyze and predict possible response outcomes or logical consequences. The effects of his actions or the possible effect of the stimulus situation upon him would be analyzed differently at various levels of maturity.

Disruptions or delays that occur in the orderly acquisition of specific skills, as the result of certain interruptions or deviations in neurocognitive activity, further complicate the attempt to understand learning. They may or may not occur during a period when their effect is minimized by compensatory development in other areas of the nervous system. When an interruption is minimal, development in other areas may provide strategies for compensating. The child may only experience difficulty in situations where unfamiliar situational stimuli, for which a compensatory strategy has not yet developed, render old modes of responding ineffective. Furthermore, weaknesses occur on a continuum from severe to negligible. An interruption may be subtle. Its effect may not be measurable by currently available assessment procedures which can only evaluate overt responding or observable behavior.

The concept of interacting developmental processes is complicated. The notion that symptoms change over time complicates this concept even further. The woven threads of a piece of fabric still on a loom provide us with a visual analogy. The warp threads represent the various cognitive-linguistic schemas or raw materials within the child. The shuttle represents experience. It moves back and forth, weaving an increasingly intricate pattern that grows in complexity over time. The warp threads represent internal processes and continue to provide the basic foundation through which strands of experience are woven. They become absorbed into the increasingly integrated spatial and textural pattern. We might conceive of the color and shading as being determined by personality variables. The completed piece will represent a subtle blending of basic processes with externally determined and changing variables which contribute to a unique "whole." Such a blending process can explain the individual differences found in every child.

The Development of Strategies: From Infancy to School Age

ATTENDING

It appears that many of the symptoms associated with language learning disabilities represent a "tip of the iceberg" phenomenon. Problems with the observable behavioral aspects of attention, discrimination, memory, sequencing, and other intellectual processes do not comprise the disability itself. They appear to be manifestations of a more all-encompassing problem. They appear to play off one another in particular ways that are difficult to pinpoint or measure. As practitioners, we need to ask ourselves numerous questions about the symptomatology we observe. For example, we accept the notion that during

learning attention must be selectively focused on the important aspect of a stimulus or task. Irrelevant information must be filtered. Do learning-disabled children know which stimuli are relevant and appropriate? Klein-Konigsberg (Chapter 12) suggests that learning-disabled children often pay attention to the wrong thing. Some learning-disabled children need to be directed explicitly to important aspects of a stimulus (Perfetti, 1977). Studies of the synthetic (constructive) or analytic aspects of comprehension have also shown how individuals "selectively ignore" information—shifting and focusing their attention to various aspects of a stimulus or situation as required (Ross, 1976). Teachers often describe learning-disabled children as having a short attention span. We might ask, "Short for what?" As we all know, many learning-disabled children, as well as normally acquiring children, attend for very long periods of time—to the things that interest them.

Clearly, the ability of children to redirect attention is part of expanding competence related to maturation of the nervous system. Developmental studies of attending behavior may provide us with important information about perceptual, cognitive, and linguistic influences. Studies have shown that infants generally prefer a human voice to other types of auditory stimuli (Sherrod et al., 1978). It is interesting to speculate whether the prosodic features of speech constitute novel stimuli which retard habituation and thus prolong attending. If this were true, it might be said that human infants are biologically programmed to focus upon a speech sound model made by a caregiver. Soon after birth, infants appear to react differently to different types of human speech and it becomes apparent that they have begun to associate speech sounds to the important events in their own life. As children's ability to attend to selected stimuli and to inhibit irrelevant stimulation matures, they become increasingly able to shift and to redirect attentional sets. Children learn to attend to several apparently simultaneous stimuli. Research along these lines may help us to understand the beginnings of problems seen later in children of school age (Ross, 1976).

DISCRIMINATION

Studies have also shown that infants can discriminate environmental sounds from speech sounds quite early. Indeed, infants have been shown to perceive distinctions between similar speech sounds as early as 2 weeks (Wingfield, 1979). Some infants show discriminative behavior for auditory stimuli as young as 48 hours (Sherrod et al., 1978). Perhaps this occurs in utero. It should be remembered that discriminative behavior in infants can be measured by changes in heart rate and sucking responses. This suggests a neurological preprogramming for the reception of auditory information and the subsequent development of language. The structure of mental organization appears to predipose children to language behavior. The connection between these early infant patterns and later associative learning warrants further investigation.

"Auditory discrimination deficits" in language learning-disabled children are now understood within the broader context of metalinguistic development. Van Kleeck (Chapters 7 and 9), Nelson (Chapter 8), and Blachman (Chapter 13) will explore this phenomenon in greater detail. Higher levels of discrimination are different from those behaviors observed in infancy. Higher level functions include discriminations of multiple attributes, distinctions between fantasy and reality, discriminations that result in matching language with certain social situations, and the like.

MEMORY AND SEQUENCING

Numerous examples presented throughout this text contribute to a better understanding of language learning disabilities symptomatology. As we shall see later, many memory and sequencing or temporal ordering problems, such as those with two-clause sentences (see Chapters 5 and 12)

are related to the acquisition and use of comprehension strategies. Inductive and deductive reasoning, as well as simultaneous and successive processing (Das et al., 1979), are among methods employed by children during learning and problem solving. They involve development of sensory and symbolic integration at higher levels (see Chapter 10). Different learning strategies, such as self-verbalization, appear to be more effective at different stages of a child's growth and development (Maxwell, 1981). Developmental achievements are recycled at successively higher levels so that the child is equipped to deal with increasingly complex physical and social stimuli. The child's growing awareness of the predictability of the environment, as well as of ways in which he can reduce the punishing consequences of ambiguity and uncertainty, appears to be an important aspect of learning and social development.

CLOSING REMARKS

Developmental patterns are not represented in the form of neatly organized sequences through which an individual progresses. The normally acquiring population certainly manifests regularity. However, it is not plausible to propose that children move from an early stage to a more mature stage "in a way that preserves the categories and functions of the stage before" (Gleitman, 1981, p. 112). The developmental patterns of language-disordered children are still being investigated. Comparative studies have shown both similarities and differences between language-disabled children and children learning language normally (Snyder, 1980). For example, Gallagher and Darnton (1978) found that the revision strategies of young language-disordered children were different from those employed by normal children. By contrast, Skarakis and Greenfield (1979) found that many conversational strategies at later stages of language development were similar for language-disordered children and their normal agemates. Thus, differences found at the one-word stage of development do not always remain differences in the later stages of acquisition. Language difficulties, although subtle, may be significant (see Chapter 8).

The follow-up studies of children with language and reading problems may not reveal as positive an outcome as desired. However, Gleitman (1981) indicates that we do not yet know the potential of children learning—or relearning—language at later stages. According to Gleitman (1981, p. 111), "... older relearners may be capable of mature conceptual representations of linguistic data, at certain points in time." As more is learned about brain-related "spurts" of development, more successful intervention programs for older language learning-disabled students may be devised. Schery (Chapter 15) observes that we can and do make changes. However, careful evaluation of methods and procedures is greatly needed. Lee and Fine (Chapter 16) provide suggestions for the modifications of high school programs for the language learning disabled.

Relatively little is known about how symptoms of language disability change over time. It is hoped that this chapter has stimulated ideas about some ways to look at children across time. It is possible that systematic studies of various subgroups within the language learning-disabled populations may provide us with direction. As we embark on longitudinal research, we may learn more about the specific visual, auditory, cognitive, and linguistic functions which operate in the reading process. We may also learn more about those factors which are causative, contributory, or merely coincidental to language learning and reading failures (Valtin, 1982). The questions continue: Which language and learning changes are significant predictors of school success? When does metalinguistic awareness really begin? It may be that we should begin to study aspects of children's behavior that are already in their repertoire with the hope of understanding their changing function (Karmiloff-Smith, 1981). Perhaps we need to look more closely

at the tasks in which language learning-disabled children are successful (Goldsmith et al., 1974).

Recent advances in the study of language acquisition suggest that the theoretical and clinical model for the 1980's must be a dynamic, interactive one (Maxwell, 1980; Maxwell and Hale, 1981). The relationship between form, content, and use warrants continued study. Furthermore, a system of symbols, such as verbal language, cannot be understood independent of development in other behavioral domains which coincide with it (Woodruff and Maxwell, 1981). A child's behavioral repertoire must be understood as only the observable aspects of the neurocognitive circuitry and chemistry which interact with it. Increasing sophistication of methodological approaches to the study of brain maturation and its correlation with learning may result in more efficacious approaches to diagnosis and remediation of language learning disabilities (see Chapter 3).

We have a long way to go. This chapter has outlined a hypothesis. That hypothesis reflects a connection between language, learning, and reading disabilities. The data are presented for further reflection. We have explored some important relationships. Indeed, we are reminded of the power of such relationships in the quote, "Before I spoke to people, I did not think these things, for there was no one to think them for" (spoken by John Merrick from the play, *The Elephant Man*).

References

American Speech-Language-Hearing Association Committee on Language Learning Disabilities: The role of the speech-language pathologist in learning disabilities. *ASHA* 24:937–944, 1982.
Aram DM, Nation JE: Preschool language disorders and subsequent language and academic difficulties. *J Commun Disord* 13:159–170, 1980.
Baker H, Leland B: *Detroit Test of Learning Aptitude.* Indianapolis Bobbs Merrill, 1967.
Bashir A, Kuban K, Kleinman S, et al: *Issues in Language Disorders: Considerations of Cause, Maintenance, and Change.* In Miller J, Yoder D, Schieflebush R: *ASHA Report No 12,* 1983, 92–106.
Blank M: Review of "Toward an understanding of dyslexia: psychological factors in specific reading

disability." In Benton AL, Pearl D: *Dyslexia: An Appraisal of Current Knowledge.* New York, Oxford University Press, 1978, pp 115–122.

Bower TGR: *Development in Infancy.* San Francisco, Freeman, 1974.

Bower TGR: *The Perceptual World of the Child.* Cambridge, MA, Harvard University Press, 1977.

Bryan T, Donahue M, Pearl R: Learning disabled children's communicative competence and social relationships. In *Language, Learning, and Reading Disabilities: A New Decade.* Preliminary Proceedings of an Interdisciplinary Conference. Department of Communication Arts and Sciences, Queens College of the City University of New York, 1981, 67–77.

Bryan T, Pflaum S: Linguistic, cognitive and social analyses of learning disabled children's interactions. *Learn Disabil Q* 1:70–79, 1978.

Das JP, Kirby JR, Jarman RF: *Simultaneous and Successive Processing.* New York, Academic Press, 1979.

DeAjuriaguerra J, Jaeggi A, Guignard F, et al: The development and prognosis of dysphasia in children. In Morehead D, Morehead A: *Normal and Deficient Child Language.* Baltimore, University Park Press, 1976.

Denchkla MB, Rudel R: Naming of object-drawings by dyslexia and other learning disabled children. *Brain Language* 3:1–15, 1976.

DiSimoni F: *The Token Test for Children.* Hingham, MA, Teaching Resources, 1978.

Donahue M, Pearl R, Bryan T: Conversational competence in LD children: responses to uninformative messages. Presented at the Conference of the Association for Children with Learning Disabilities, Milwaukee, February, 1980.

Donahue M, Pearl R, Bryan T: Learning disabled children's syntactic proficiency on a communicative task. *J Speech Hear Disord* 47:397–403, 1982.

Flavell JH: *Cognitive Development.* Englewood Cliffs, NJ, Prentice-Hall, 1977.

Fletcher JM, Satz P: Unitary Deficit Hypotheses of Reading Disabilities: Has Vellutino Led us Astray? *J Learn Disabil* 12:155–171, 1979.

Gallagher T, Darnton B: Conversational aspects of the speech of language disordered children: revision behaviors. *J Speech Hear Res* 21:118–125, 1978.

Gleitman L: Maturational determinants of language growth. *Cognition* 10:103–114, 1981.

Goldsmith S, Wallach GP, Beilin H: Variables in Processing Time Sentences: Linguistic and cognitive considerations. Presented at the Northeastern Modern Language Association Convention, Pennsylvania State University, April, 1974.

Griffiths CPS: A follow-up study of children with disorders of speech. *J Disord Commun* 4:46–56, 1969.

Hall PK, Tomblin JB: A follow-up study of children with articulation and language disorders. *J Speech Hear Disord* 43:227–241, 1978.

Kagan J, Kearsley R, Zelaza P: *Infancy.* Cambridge, MA, Harvard University Press, 1978.

Kaplan E, Goodglass H: *Boston Naming Test: Experimental Edition,* 1975.

Karmiloff-Smith A: Getting developmental differences or studying child development? *Cognition* 10:151–158, 1981.

King RR, Jones C, Lasky E: In retrospect: a fifteen-year follow-up report of speech-language-disorders children. *Language Speech Hear Serv Schools* 13:24–32, 1982.

Kirk S, McCarthy J, Kirk W: *The Illinois test of Psycholinguistic Abilities.* Urbana, University of Illinois, 1968.

Lewis M: *Origins of Intelligence, Infancy and Early Childhood.* New York, Plenum Press, 1976.

Ludlow CL, Doran-Quine ME: *The Neurological Bases of Language Disorders in Children: Methods and Directions for Research.* Washington DC, United States Department of Health, Education and Welfare, National Institute of Neurological Communicative Disorders and Stroke Monograph no. 22, 1978.

Luria AR: *Cognitive Development.* Cambridge, MA, Harvard University Press, 1976.

Mattis S: Dyslexia syndromes: a working hypothesis that works. In Benton AL, Pearl D: *Dyslexia: An Appraisal of Current Knowledge.* New York, Oxford University Press, 1978, pp 43–58.

Mattis S, French JH, Rapin I: Dyslexia in children and young adults: three independent neuropsychological syndromes. *Dev Med Child Neurol* 17:150–163, 1975.

Maxwell SE: Transdisciplinary model for diagnosis and remediation in early childhood. In *Proceedings of the 18th Congress.* Washington DC, International Association of Lozopedics and Phoniatrics, vol 1, 1980, pp 191–196.

Maxwell SE: The Effect of Self-Verbalization on Cognitive Performance in Four-Year Old Children. Unpublished study, Boston College, 1981.

Maxwell SE, Hale A: Transdisciplinary Diagnosis and Clinical Management: A Model Program. Workshop presented at 59th Annual International Convention, Council for Exceptional Children, New York, April, 1981.

Miller JF, Chapman R, MacKenzie H: Individual differences in language acquisition of mentally retarded children. Presented at the Second International Congress for the Study of Child Language, University of British Columbia, Vancouver, August, 1981.

Muma J: *Language Handbook: Concepts, Assessment, Intervention.* Englewood Cliffs, NJ, Prentice-Hall, 1978.

Pearl R, Donahue M, Bryan T: Learning disabled children's responses to requests for clarification which may vary in explicitness. Presented at the 4th Annual Boston University Conference on Language Development, Boston, September, 1979.

Perfetti C: Language comprehension and fast decoding: some psycholinguistic prerequisites for skilled reading comprehension. In Guthrie J: *Cognition, Curriculum, and Comprehension.* Newark, DE, International Reading Association, 1977, pp 20–41.

Piaget J: *The Origins of Intelligence in Children.* New York, International Universities Press, 1952.

Robinson ME, Schwartz LB: Visuo-motor skills and reading ability: a longitudinal study. *Dev Med Child Neurol* 15:281–286, 1973.

Ross AO: *Psychological Aspects of Learning Disabilities and Reading Disorders.* New York, McGraw-Hill, 1976.

Rourke BP: Brain-behavior relations in children with learning disabilities. *Am Psychol* 30:911–920, 1975.

Rourke BP: Reading retardation in children: developmental lag or deficit?" In Knights RM, Bakker DJ: *The Neurospychology of Learning Disorders.* Baltimore, University Park Press, 1976, pp 125–137.

Rourke BP: Neuropsychological research in reading retardation: a review. In Benton AL, Pearl D: *Dyslexia: An Appraisal of Current Knowledge.* New York, Oxford University Press, 1978, pp 139–172.

Rourke BP, Czudner G: Age differences in auditory reaction time of 'brain damaged' and normal children under regular and irregular preparatory interval conditions. *J Exp Child Psychol* 14:372–378, 1972.

Rutter M: Prevalence and Types of Dyslexia. In Benton AL, Pearl D: *Dyslexia: An Appraisal of Current Knowledge.* New York, Oxford University Press, 1978, pp 3–28.

Rutter M, Yule W: Specific reading retardation. In Mann L, Sabatino D: *The First Review of Special Education.* Philadelphia, Buttonwood Farms, 1973.

Satz P, Taylor HG, Friel J, et al: Some developmental and predictive precursors of reading disabilities: a six-year follow-up. In Benton AL, Pearl D: *Dyslexia: An Appraisal of Current Knowledge.* New York, Oxford University Press, 1978, pp 313–347.

Schwartz RG, Leonard LB, Folger MK, et al: Early phonological behavior in normal-speaking and language disordered children: evidence for a synergistic view of linguistic disorders. *J Speech Hear Disord* 45:357–377, 1980.

Sherrod K, Vietze P, Friedman S: *Infancy.* Monterey, CA, Brooks/Cole, 1978.

Skarakis E, Greenfield P: The role of old and new information in the linguistic expression of language disabled children. Presented at the Boston University Conference on Language Development, Boston, September, 1979.

Snyder L: Have we prepared the language disordered child for school? *Top Language Disord* 1:29–46, Dec 1980.

Stark J: Reading: what needs to be assessed? *Top Language Disord* 1:87–94, June 1981.

Strominger AZ, Bashir AS: A nine-year follow-up of language-delayed children. Presented at the Annual Convention of the American Speech-Language and Hearing Association, Chicago, 1977.

Travers JF: *The Growing Child.* Glenview, IL, Scott Foresman, 1982.

Valtin R: Deficiencies in research on reading deficiencies. In Kavanaugh JF, Venezky RL: *Orthography, Reading, and Dyslexia.* Baltimore, University Park Press, 1980, pp 271–286.

Vellutino FR: *Dyslexia: Theory and Research.* Cambridge, MA, MIT Press, 1979a.

Vellutino FR: The validity of perceptual deficit explanations of reading disability: a reply to Fletcher and Satz. *J Learn Disabil* 12:160–167, 1979b.

Vellutino FR: Toward an understanding of dyslexia: psychological factors in specific reading disability.

In Benton AL, Pearl D: *Dyslexia: An Appraisal of Current Knowledge.* New York, Oxford University Press, 1978, pp 61–112.

Vellutino FR, Pruzek KR, Steger JA, et al: Immediate visual recall in poor and normal readers as a function of orthographic-linguistic familarity. *Cortex* 9:368–384, 1973.

Vellutino FR, Smith H, Steger JA, et al: Reading disability: age differences and the preceptual-deficit hypothesis. *Child Dev* 46:487–493, 1975a.

Vellutino FR, Steger JA, Karman M, et al: Visual form perception in deficient and normal readers as a function of age and orthographic linguistic familarity. *Cortex* 11:22–30, 1975b.

Wallach GP: The implications of different language comprehension strategies in learning disabled children: effects of thematization. Unpublished doctoral dissertation, The Graduate School and University Center of the City University of New York, 1977.

Wallach GP: I don't care who said it or what it means, just tell me what to do. In *Language, Learning and Reading Disabilities: A New Decade.* Preliminary Proceedings of an Interdisciplinary Conference. Department of Communication Arts and Sciences. Queens College of the City University of New York, 1981, 84–90.

Wallach GP, Brown S: Older children's ability to perform metalinguistic judgments of synonymy: a normal and learning disabled population. *J Speech Hear Disord,* in preparation.

Wechsler D: *Wechsler Intelligence Scale for Children.* New York, Psychological Corporation, 1974.

Weiner IB, Elkind D: *Readings in Child Development.* New York, John Wiley & Sons, 1972.

Weiner P: A language-delayed child at adolescence. *J Speech Hear Disord* 39:202–212, 1974.

Wepman JM: *Auditory Discrimination Test.* Beverly Hills, CA, Learning Research Associates, 1958.

Whitehurst GJ, Zimmerman BJ: *The Functions of Language and Cognition.* New York, Academic Press, 1979.

Wiig E, Semel E: *Language Assessment and Intervention for the Learning Disabled.* Columbus, OH, Charles E. Merrill, 1980.

Wiig E, Semel E, Nystrom L: Comparison of rapid naming abilities in language-learning-disabled and academically achieving eight-year-olds. *Language Speech Hear Serv Schools* 13:11–22, 1982.

Wingfield A: *Human Learning and Memory: An Introduction.* New York, Harper and Row, 1979.

Wolf M: The relationship of disorders of word-finding and reading in children and apasics. Doctoral dissertation, Harvard School of Education, 1979.

Woodruff G, Maxwell SE: The Transdisciplinary Approach to Service Delivery. Short course presented at 33rd Annual Meeting, American Association of Psychiatric Services for Children, San Francisco, November, 1981.

CHAPTER THREE

The Neurology of Learning and Language Disabilities: Developmental Considerations

DAVID L. MAXWELL, Ph.D.

"Modern psychology takes completely for granted that behavior and neural function are perfectly correlated, that one is completely caused by the other" (Hebb, 1949).

The term "learning disability" is a relatively gross generic label that is commonly used in reference to a poorly understood heterogeneous group of performance deficits. To invoke this term solely on the basis of certain performance criteria is frequently circuitous (See Wallach and Liebergott's discussion of problems surrounding tautological definitions in Chapter 1.) Statistical approaches to definition, although adding a degree of operational precision, are nonetheless quite arbitrary. Thus, in a recent study by Taylor et al., (1979), learning-disabled readers were defined as those children who were reading at a level at least 1 SD below the mean of the entire sample.

Following the long tradition of behaviorism, specialists in many fields of human management have adhered to one or more versions of the stimulus-response model of learning while ignoring or denying the mediating influences of neural processes. Nevertheless, several authorities have recently pointed to the limitations of theories and teaching methods that fail to consider the importance of such processes to the development and regulation of many higher order activities: information processing, problem solving, reading, writing, and the use of oral language (Gaddes, 1969; Geschwind, 1979; Cruickshank, 1979; Rourke, 1981). The ontogeny of such complex skills, while no doubt influenced by the psychosocial milieu, is inextricably bound to corresponding developments in the neural substrata.

Remarkable methodological advances in approaches to the study of brain maturation and neurobehavioral correlates are beginning to illuminate the contents and processes of the previously inscrutable "black-box." The effectiveness of educators and clinical scientists will be enhanced by a better understanding of the central neural mechanisms—their manner of transforming and storing information, extracting meaning, generating responses, and predicting and evaluating the consequences for behavior. Ultimately, learning disabilities involve problems in one or more of these areas. Within the brief confines of this chapter, an effort is made to catalyze the reader's interest in the morphological, chemical, and electrical regulators of neural activity and the relation of these factors to certain cognitive-linguistic deficits. The implications of such data for the development of effective teaching programs and learning strategies are discussed as warranted.

MORPHOLOGICAL ASPECTS OF BRAIN MATURATION

In the study of learning disabilities, it is important to bear in mind the significance of the emerging neuroanatomical components and the relation of their own biological timetables to the ontogeny of particular functions. At the same time, as many neuropsychologists have noted (Vygotsky, 1956; Luria, 1966; Lenneberg, 1967), caution ought to be exercised in deducing direct causal relationships between specific aspects of brain maturation and certain cognitive and linguistic milestones. According to these and other writers, more important to the understanding of higher brain function is the manner of the differentiation and ultimate integration of various sensory and motor regions in the formation of functional cerebral systems. Although such "holistic" approaches to the study of complex human mental activity have merit, educators, psychologists, and neural scientists should also remember what the Apostle Paul said in the 1st century A.D.: "If one member suffers, all other members suffer with it" (I Corinthians 12:26).

The Neuron

The elementary structural and functional units of the nervous system are the neurons (nerve cells), which are specialized for receiving and transmitting electrochemical information. Although the morphology of the neurons differs in different parts of the nervous system, they typically possess three features: a long axon, several dendrites, and a cell body (Fig. 3.1).

The axon projects from the cell body to terminate in presynaptic end feet called teledendria bouton. These microscopic filaments secrete into the synaptic spaces various chemical transmitters which excite or suppress neural activity on the postsynaptic surfaces of adjacent cells. At a cellular level, perhaps one of the more significant aspects of neural maturation entails the progressive elaboration of the postsynaptic surfaces of neurons. These major receptor zones—called dendrites—constitute more than 95% of the cerebral cortex available for synaptic inputs. The tree-like arborizations of dendrites receive, compute, and integrate a vast number of neural messages transmitted from other cells across hundreds of thousands of synaptic junctions. Thus, the information-processing capability of a particular neuron is determined, in part, by the configuration or "reach" of its dendritic branches.

The surface areas of cortical dendrites contain excrescences called gemmules, thorns, or, more commonly, spines. Spines are believed to be the recipient zones for most dendritic synapses. Some neurons in the cerebral cortex have about 4,000 spines per cell, which greatly enlarges the total area of synaptic contact. It has been speculated that variations in the size and shapes of spines might influence the amount of current allowed to pass into the core of the dendrite (Pellionisz and Llinas, 1977). Repetitive stimulation does appear to be associated with an increase in the size of the necks of dendritic spines (Fifková and van Harrelel, 1977). This might lessen the resistance between the synapse and dendritic core of the neuron. By allowing more current to reach the cell body, neural conduction is augmented. Mechanisms underlying the shrinking and swelling behavior of spines might play significant roles in learning, memory, and other cognitive and linguistic processes.

Environmental and Nutritional Influences

The possible significance of the number of synaptic connections between neurons has yet to be determined. However, studies of animal models during early development sugggest that the extent of dendritic branching and the number of dendritic spines varies in proportion to the richness

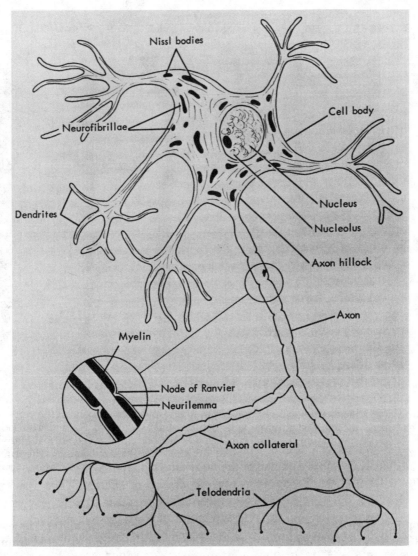

Figure 3.1. Illustration of a neuron showing cell body and processes. (Reprinted from Zemlin WR: *Speech and Hearing Science: Anatomy and Physiology*, ed 2. Englewood Cliffs, NJ, Prentice-Hall, 1981, with permission.)

of the sensory environment (Móllgaard et al., 1971; Volkmar and Greenough, 1972; Greenough, 1976; Rosenzweig and Bennett, 1977). Furthermore, there is some evidence that sensory deprivation may result in atrophy of dendritic spines (Gyllensten et al., 1965, 1966; Fifková and Hassler, 1969; Ryugo et al., 1975). Purpura (1974) has suggested that a deficiency in spine formation could be a cause of mental retardation and other learning deficits (Fig. 3.2).

The effects of nutritional deprivation on brain growth are similar to those which result from environmental impoverishment. Studies of animal models suggest that deficits in brain weight which result from severe malnutrition during the growing period of the brain are irreversible. Some of the deleterious consequences include a reduction in the thickness of the cerebral cortex, a decrement in the total DNA and overall number of cells, and a

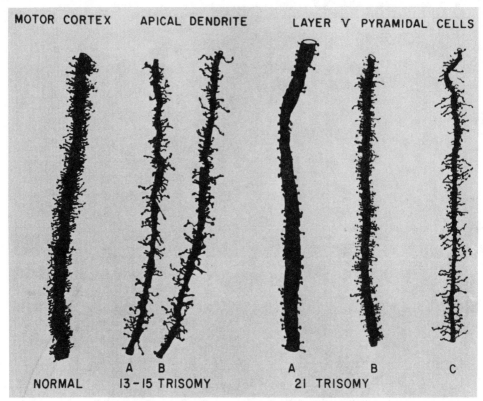

MOTOR CORTEX   APICAL DENDRITE   LAYER V PYRAMIDAL CELLS

A   B   A   B   C
NORMAL   13–15 TRISOMY   21 TRISOMY

Figure 3.2. Camera lucida drawings obtained from rapid Golgi preparations of the cerebral cortex of normal and mentally retarded children with chromosomal trisomies. These drawings illustrate more clearly than the photographs the morphological characteristics of the normal and abnormal dendritic spines. The labels under the different drawings are self-explanatory. (Reprinted from Marin-Padilla M: Neuron differentiation in mental retardation. In Bergsma D: *Morphogenesis and Malformation of the Face and Brain.* New York, Allan R. Liss, 1975, with permission.)

retardation in the growth of newly formed neurons (Lewis et al., 1975; Krigman and Hogan, 1976; Griffin et al., 1977). The number of connections in the malnourished brain is also reduced (Cragg, 1972), as is the thickness of dendrites (West and Kemper, 1976) and the number of spines (Salas et al., 1974). These pathological structural changes would likely have an impact on learning and problem-solving abilities.

Care should be taken in extrapolating the consequences of malnutrition in experimental animals to humans. Nevertheless, a substantial portion of the human population of children is at nutritional risk during the preschool years—a time span in which 90% of the total brain growth occurs. Behar (1968) reported that close to 60% of the

world's preschool population, an estimated 400 million children, suffered from undernutrition in 1967. More recent data, compiled by the UNICEF organization, indicate that 17 million children died of malnutrition in 1980 to 1981 and 100 million go to bed hungry each night (Grant, 1982). While most of these children are in the underdeveloped nations, there is evidence that a significant number in such affluent countries as the United States are also undernourished and in jeopardy for poor brain growth and development (Livingston et al., 1975).

In the industrialized countries, 15 to 20% of the school-age children have learning disabilities in the presence or absence of behavioral problems, and perhaps 25 to

40% exhibit specific skill-related deficits, as in reading (Coursin, 1975). In addition to environmental deprivation, chronic nutritional deficiencies can retard the development of the cognitive abilities of affected individuals (Ashem and Janes, 1978). As Franková (1974, p. 202) noted, "... for optimum development of the brain and of subsequent behavior, an adequate supply of both nutrients and external stimuli during the decisive developmental periods is essential. A typical picture of malnutrition involves reduction both of the available nutrients and of the environmental stimulation."

Importance of Brain Growth

Brain growth stages are no doubt related to increments in the complexity of the neural network with increased elongation and branching of axons and dendrites. Epstein (1974, 1978) has concluded that increments in the brain size of mammals are closely associated with the appearance of new behavioral competencies. In humans, sensory discrimination abilities as well as mental age values correlate well with specific age-related stages of brain growth. Of particular interest is Epstein's observation that the first four stages of brain growth (3 to 10 months; 2 to 4, 6 to 8, and 10 to 12 years) coincide with the four main stages of cognitive development found by Piaget (1969) and his associates. However, Epstein identified a fifth postnatal stage of brain growth (14 to 16+ years) with no heretofore identifiable Piagetian counterpart. He posited that, if brain and mind growth stages are developmentally correlated a fifth Piagetian stage should be discovered. This prediction was supported in a study by Arlin (1975), who reported the first evidence for such a cognitive stage having its onset in the 14- to 16-year period.

Are these data pertaining to brain growth stages and their functional manifestations merely esoteric given the "practical concerns" of educators and clinicians? Epstein (1979) does not think so. He suggests that the concordant analysis of the maturation of the brain and behavior may help to explain the failure of such programs as Head Start to improve the cognitive abilities of children from deprived environments. (See Chapter 15 for an alternative analysis of the Head Start data.) Typically, children are enrolled and participate in such programs during a period of minimal brain growth. The failure of some preschool language-disabled children to "catch up," as described by Maxwell and Wallach in the previous chapter, may be related to this phenomenon. The data of Hunt (1975) indicate that earlier intervention programs beginning at the age of 2 years, a period of active brain growth, resulted in greater and more stable increments in IQ and school performance. Still another quite interesting speculation by Epstein (1979) pertains to the adjustment problems often experienced by junior high school students. He suggested that their social and educational difficulties may be more closely tied to a brain-related growth plateau than to sexual maturation. These findings, while interesting, must also be assessed with caution.

Development of Neural Circuitry

There is no one explanation for neural development; the morphology of neurons, their connective patterns, and their manner of functioning with one another all result from complex interactions between genetic make-up, environmental conditioning, and behavior.

The timetables for mitotic cell division, migration, and differentiation have characteristic patterns for each region of the brain. Neuromorphologists employ these characteristics in the study of brain maturation. Such approaches have resulted in the classification of neurons on the basis of size, functional connectivities, malleability to environmental influences, and other factors (Rámon y Cajal, 1899; Jacobson, 1969, 1970; Llinas and Hillman, 1975). Most large neurons are the projection type, having long axons, dendrities, and a cell body. They arise early in the embryo and have relatively fixed, genetically predetermined connections which evolve into the primary afferent and efferent pathways of the brain. Smaller neurons called local circuit neurons form later than projection neurons, continue to develop throughout the first 2 years of postnatal life, have positions and arrangements less subject to genetic control, and depend more for their development and maintenance on sensory stimulation than do projection neurons.

Local circuit neurons, which have no axons or relatively short axons, are so designated because they mediate neural activity within nearby functional cell groups rather than between distant cell groups. In the cerebral cortex, local circuit neurons outnumber projection neurons three to one, and 95% of the neurons in some forebrain nuclei are of the former type. From their structure and pattern of functional organization, local circuit neurons no doubt play an important role in the processing of information. It is thought that many serve to inhibit or grade the level of activity of adjacent cells so that signals can be interpreted and processed appropriately (Coltman and McGaugh, 1980).

To function efficiently, the circuits of the brain must develop correctly, i.e., must follow the right "wiring diagrams." The neurons of the six-layered cerebral cortex are so thickly packed that they can only be recognized as individual units through the use of special staining procedures applied to histological sections (Fig. 3.3). They are arranged both in terms of horizontal laminations and vertical columns throughout the depth of the cortex. According to the well known cytoarchitectural map of Brodmann, the cerebral hemispheres can be divided into more than 40 discrete areas (Fig. 3.4).

Sensorimotor Cortex

The vertical strips or columns of cells might be regarded as the elementary functional units of the cortex. Specific afferent pathways project from the nuclei of the thalamus to converge on specific cells in the columnar units. Data from specific sensory modalities are processed at these sites and relayed by intercortical connections to other cells in the vertical column. Excitation may also extend horizontally through cell layers, progressively recruiting greater numbers of vertical units.

Some of the functional cellular counterparts of the vertical columns which have been verified according to specific afferent inputs include the primary somesthetic cortex (areas 3, 1, 2) of the parietal lobe and the primary visual cortex (area 17) of the occipital lobe (Hubel and Wiesel, 1972; Powell and Mountcastle, 1972). A similar cellular arrangement is believed to exist in the primary auditory cortex (areas 41, 42) of the temporal lobe (Merzenich and Brugge, 1973). The cells in these sensory zones are the basic localized cortical areas concerned with the discrimination of specific forms of sensory stimuli. They are most highly developed in horizontal layer IV, representing the terminal projections of afferent fibers. On the other hand, layer IV is practically nonexistent in the primary motor cortex (area 4) of the frontal lobe, but layers III and V contain large numbers of pyramidal cells, the origins of descending motor fibers. Damage to any of the primary cortical zones, although resulting in specific forms of sensory and motor deficits, has little effect on the higher cognitive-linguistic functions.

Association Cortex

A large portion of the human cerebral cortex consists of areas without designated specific sensory or motor functions. These secondary or association areas overlap or lie close to the primary cortical sensorimotor zones. The association cortex is thought to be involved in the integrative and interpretative aspects of information processing. Hence, damage to the association areas of the somesthetic (areas 5, 7, 40) or visual (areas 18, 19) cortex results in various forms of recognition or discrimination deficits (agnosias). Even more complex are the verbal deficits resulting from damage to the angular gyrus (area 39) and Wernicke's area (area 22). These areas mediate the comprehension of the written and spoken syllables of language. Associated impairments frequently include disabilities in reading, writing, and in the syntactic-

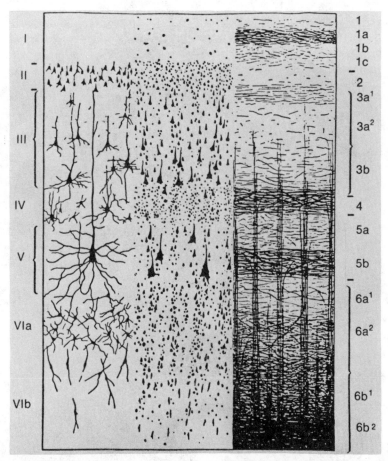

Figure 3.3.   Diagram of the structure of the cerebral cortex. *Left*, from a Golgi preparation; *center*, from a Nissl preparation; *right*, from a myelin sheath preparation. *I*, lamina zonalis; *II*, lamina granularis externa; *III*, lamina pyramidalis; *IV*, lamina granularis interna; *V*, lamina ganglionaris; *VI*, lamina multiformis. (After K. Brodmann and O. Vogt. Reprinted from Brodal A: *Neurological Anatomy in Relation to Clinical Medicine.* New York, Oxford University Press, 1969, with permission.)

semantic aspects of oral speech. Concomitant and interrelated memory problems may also occur (see Chapters 10 and 12).

In the posterior part of the inferior frontal lobe is Broca's area (areas 44, 45) which is involved in formulating the phonological and graphic aspects of oral and written language. Broca's area is connected with Wernicke's area and the angular gyrus through an arched bundle of nerve fibers called the arcuate fasciculus. Verbal symbols comprehended by these latter zones are transmitted via the pathway of the arcuate fasciculus to Broca's area for encoding into the appropriate oral and written

forms. Disturbances in Broca's area and its connecting pathways to the posterior cortical association areas are reflected in misarticulation of speech sounds, effortful telegraphic utterances, agrammatical syntax and various forms of dysgraphia.

Still other regions of association cortex, located even more anteriorly in the prefrontal lobe, are believed to mediate selective attention. Luria (1973) noted that damage to these areas in humans impairs those attentional skills important for planning, problem solving, and the initiation of action. Studies of infrahuman primates indicate that rich connections exist between

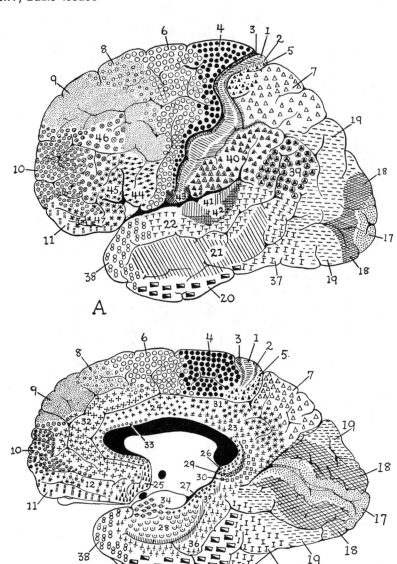

Figure 3.4. Cytoarchitectual map of the human cortex. *A*, convex surface; *B*, medial surface. (After K. Brodmann. Reprinted from Carpenter M: *Human Neuroanatomy*. Baltimore, Williams & Wilkins, 1976, with permission.)

the adjacent prefrontal cortical loci, and there are interhemispheric pathways to the temporal, parietal, and occipital cortex (Pandya and Kuypers, 1969; Pandya and Vignola, 1971; Tobias, 1975; Goldman and Nauta, 1977; Jacobson and Trajanowski, 1977). Connections linking the prefrontal hemispheres through the corpus collosum

and to certain subcortical nuclei have also been found (Akert, 1964; Nauta, 1964; Kemp and Powell, 1970; Pandya and Vignola, 1971; Goldman and Nauta, 1977). After an extensive review of these and other behavioral and electrophysiological studies, Goldman (1979) concluded that the dorsolateral prefrontal cortex is highly specialized for processing and retaining temporal-spatial information. Experimental lesions in animal models result in severe performance deficits on a variety of spatial-delayed response tasks. The extent to which these data can be generalized to the functioning of the frontal association areas in humans must be determined through further research. Nevertheless, there is already some evidence of correlations between neural tissue in specific parts of the brain and certain forms or types of intelligence.

Intelligence and Related Brain Structures

In recent years, psychologists and educators have expanded their concepts of intelligence as more has been learned about the complex cognitive processes that structure and guide the modes for expressing mental activity. According to Luria (1973), the prefrontal lobes form a superstructure above all other parts of the cerebral cortex. This concept is similar to Halstead's (1947) premise that the frontal lobes possess a type of "biological" intelligence essential for most forms of adaptive behavior, making possible the highest reaches of human intellect. Similar notions are embedded in the constructs of Hebb's "type A" intelligence (1949) and Cattell's "fluid" intelligence (1963). All of these constitute a form of global or general intelligence that is used to solve problems and deal with new and unfamiliar material. Perhaps such a form can best be seen as a basic irreducible intelligence network through which more specific forms of intelligence are processed. In this respect, it is interesting that lesions in the prefrontal lobes do not result in specific sensory or motor disturbances. Rather, what are disturbed are the more universal functions related to rational goal-directed behavior. Perseveration, distraction, concrete attitudes, and lability in anticipating and assessing response contingencies are characteristic of prefrontal lobe disturbances. The emergence of the inhibitory, activating, and modulating influences appear related to the growth of the frontal lobe and the maturation of constituent neurons.

The ontogeny of the prefrontal regions follows a relatively protracted course of development, showing a major growth spurt between 1 and 4 years and another toward the age of 7 to 8 years (Fig. 3.5). The possibility that the mental development of children is governed by such underlying cortical changes should hold considerable interest for educators and developmental specialists concerned with the role of "metacognition," "metalinguistics," and other executive processes in regulating behavior (see Chapter 7). Luria (1970, 1973) has found that frontal disturbances may impair a variety of intellectual functions, including the ability to self-direct and regulate one's actions and to perform complex memory activities related to motivation, recall, persistence of effort, and shifting attention according to task requirements. As one example of such deficits, Luria (1973) cites problems in performing arithmetical exercises which necessitate holding in memory a series of calculations and switching from one operation to another. Frontal disturbances lead to fragmentation in performing the necessary operations and to stereotypic errors resulting from the inability to search for and implement new strategies. It seems reasonable to assume that similar traits underpin the concrete attitudes, maladaptive emotional reactions, and socially inappropriate behaviors that frequently accompany prefrontal lobe impairments.

Many tests of intelligence do tap brain-related behaviors and abilities associated with storing, processing, and retrieving learned information. Such a form of intelligence can be seen as a second class of mental activity described as "type B" (Hebb, 1949), "psychometric" (Halstead, 1947), or "crystallized" (Cattell, 1963). A close neurological substratum for this form of activity is found in the lateral-posterior regions of the cortex whose primary function is the reception, analysis, and storage of information (Luria, 1973). Specific anatomical structures include the occipital (visual), temporal (auditory), and parietal

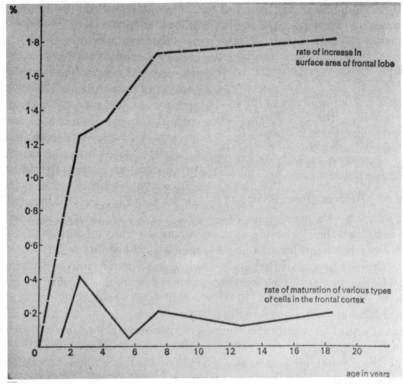

Figure 3.5.   Rate of increase in area of the frontal lobes and rate of increase in size of nerve cells in ontogeny. (After Moscow Brain Institute. Reprinted from Luria AR: *The Working Brain*. New York, Basic Books, 1973, with permission.)

(somesthetic) regions. Projection fibers convey sensory data first to the primary cortical areas of these lobes, where they are sorted and analyzed in terms of their elementary components. These data are then conveyed to the association regions, where they are synthesized and compared with other data arriving from multiple sensory sources. This hierarchical arrangement forms the basis for most of the cognitive information-processing activities of the brain.

Simultaneous and Successive Processing

The so-called specific learning disabilities may stem from relatively focalized disturbances in the posterior-lateral regions of the association cortex, reflecting difficulties in simultaneous or successive processing. Borrowing from the earlier work of Luria, Das and his associates (1975) derived a cognitive model of neural integration based on these constructs.

Simultaneous processing is said to involve the integration or synthesis of the separate elements of a stimulus cluster into groups. Such skill is important for the recognition of the spatial relations among stimuli forming meaningful patterns and for grasping information as a whole. Deficits in simultaneous processing would be reflected in the inability to solve such problems as those involved in copying figures or in correctly identifying analogous visual patterns. Luria (1973) noted that deficits in simultaneous synthesis may also be evident in the failure to carry out complex intellectual operations. Although children may grasp the meaning of a school exercise, "... they are hopelessly perplexed by the grammatical wording of the conditions which it incorporates. They cannot understand the meaning of expressions 'so much larger' and 'so many times more' . . . and as a result, they are completely unable to solve the problem" (p. 155).

The other type of neural integration, successive processing, entails the serial ordering of sensory data into meaningful units. Unlike simultaneous processing, wherein information is surveyable at any point in time, successive processing depends ". . . upon a system of cues which consecutively activates the components" (Das et al., 1979, p. 52). Such syntactic language disturbances as phoneme reversals, word order confusions, errors in phrasing, etc., represent difficulties in the successive processing of grammatical information. Although the processing of verbal material has successive characteristics (Das et al., 1975), proficient listeners and readers do a great deal of simultaneous processing as well. Simultaneous processing would seem a necessary ingredient for converting the consecutive individual elements of linguistic information into unitary logical-grammatical constructions.

Such constructs as simultaneous and successive processing hold promise for gaining a better view of cognition and language functioning from the perspective of antecedent neurological mechanisms. Neurodevelopmental impairments in poor readers, including deficits in spatial and temporal organization, appear to be the correlative expression of some more basic underlying variable. Problems in these areas may be reflective of a generalized neurological immaturity or vulnerability. These issues were raised by Maxwell and Wallach in the previous chapter.

Myelination of the Brain

Much can be learned about neurobehavioral development by studying the sequence in which the pathways of the central nervous system mature. The axon projections of many neurons undergo numerous anatomical and chemical changes as they are wrapped progressively in several alternating spiral layers of lipids and proteins—the myelin sheath. Myelination (the produc-

tion of myelin) occurs at different rates and sequences in different parts of the nervous system. Yakovlev and Lecours (1967) reported that myelination of certain fibers begins early in the fetus during the period of rapid brain growth and, depending on the anatomical area, may take weeks to years for completion.

First and foremost, the chronicity of myelination appears related to the importance of certain pathways involved in the mediation of basic physiological needs while those that regulate complex mental activity are myelinated later. For example, the sensorimotor pathways concerned with the sucking reflex myelinate quite early as do the acoustic nerve and the auditory tracts important for environmental awareness. On the other hand, the pyramidal pathways, important to the development of skilled motor behavior, are not myelinated until the second or third postnatal year, whereas many intracortical association fibers only complete the process during the third or fourth decade (Fig. 3.6).

The functional relevance of myelin to the development of behavior is still poorly understood. Because of its insulating properties, myelin is thought to bear some relationship to the speed of neural conduction. In myelinated fibers, neural impulses are propagated due to sequential depolarizations occurring at regularly dispersed unmyelinated points along the axon (Fig. 3.1). This form of neural transmission—known as salatory conduction—is associated with an increased rate of conduction because impulses "skip" along the neuron from one unsheathed node to the next. In certain demyelinating diseases, such as multiple sclerosis, there is a gradual decrement in the velocity of neural conduction as the insulating sheaths of axons are progressively destroyed.

Schulte et al. (1969) suggested that the significance of myelin to central nervous system development may not stem entirely from changes in the velocity of neural conduction but to corresponding developments in other electrical and physiological param-

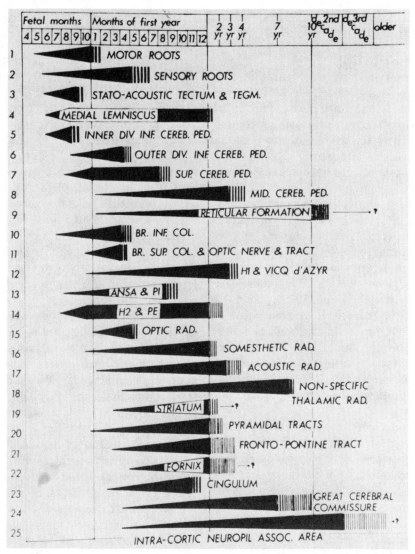

Figure 3.6. Comparative chronology of myelination. The width and length of lines represent the progression in the intensity of staining and density of myelinated fibers; the attached vertical stripes indicate the approximate age range of myelinations. *ANSA*, ansa lenticularis of pallidum; *H1*, fasciculus lenticulothalamicus; *H2* fasciculus lenticularis; *PE*, outer segment of pallidum; *PI*, inner segment of pallidum. (Redrawn from Yakovlev PI, Lecours AR: In Minkowski AM: *Regional Development of the Brain in Early Life.* Blackwell Scientific Publications, 1967, with permission.

eters. For example, the maximum spike frequencies and amplitudes of action potentials increase with increments in the thickness of the myelin sheath. The size of the action potential is thought to influence the amount of neurotransmitter released at interneuronal synapses, with larger action potentials being associated with greater amounts of neurotransmitter release. In turn, it is the amount of transmitter that determines activities which culminate in organized behavior.

Is it reasonable to assume that neural fibers do not function at optimal levels until myelination is completed, i.e., that various types of neurological immaturity will be manifest in children whose myelination is particularly slow? Taking an affirmative position, Gardner (1979, p. 120) noted that those: ". . . children with such lags may only represent the lower end of the bell-shaped curve for myelination rate. In others, disease processes may have caused the retarded myelin development. And in others, there may be a combination of factors: myelination lag and exposure to detrimental influences may bring about developmental lag."

With respect to linguistic development, the long projection axons of the cortex are important for establishing communicative channels between the language centers and other centers as those involved in neuromotor control. Some investigators have believed that only at a young age, while the cell systems of such pathways are still developing, can new language centers be formed (Penfield and Roberts, 1959; Lenneberg, 1967). Assuming that the completion of myelination reflects the functional maturation of the brain and may be taken to mean, as Lecours (1975) has suggested, that impulse conduction in such fibers is "space committed in an invariable path," certain types of clinical and educational programs designed to intervene in language lags or disturbances ought to begin as early as possible. The plasticity of such cell systems, as indicated by their ability to change neuronal organizations for information processing, especially in relation to the expressive aspects of language output, falls off sharply after the age of 6 to 8 years (Diller, 1981). As noted previously, the fiber systems of the local circuit neurons, important for some of the higher aspects of cognition and language learning, mature later and ought to be malleable to the influences of intervention over a longer period of time. The fact that underlying changes in the neurology give rise to increasing differentiation and hierarchization of mental activities suggests the need for tailoring the form and direction of childhood education accordingly. This latter issue is addressed in greater depth by many of the authors of this textbook.

Cerebral Asymmetries

There has been long-standing interest in the functional organization of the cerebral hemispheres in the mediation of learning and verbal behavior. Beginning with the early reports of Dax (1865), Broca (1865), and other 19th-century investigators, a vast literature pertaining to the asymmetrical distribution of certain hemispheric functions has steadily accumulated (Oppenheimer, 1977).

There is general agreement that the left hemisphere, in the large majority of individuals and irrespective of handedness, provides the anatomical substratum for most verbal, analytic, and complex motor functions (Penfield and Roberts, 1959; Wada and Rasmussen, 1960; Geschwind, 1972; Dimond and Beaumont, 1974). On the other hand, the right hemisphere is thought to be predominantly involved with nonverbal, visual perceptual and some tactile perceptual processes (Milner and Taylor, 1972; Boll, 1974; Dimond and Beaumont, 1974; Segalowitz and Gruber, 1977; Kinsbourne, 1978).

Despite the speculations of many theorists, the issue of whether various features of cerebral lateralization are related to particular cognitive and language disabilities has yet to be resolved. Progress in this area has been hampered by ambiguity surrounding the nature of basic hemispheric mechanisms for localizing certain functions in normal individuals. For several years, it was believed that functional hemispheric asymmetries emerge and become increasingly lateralized with advancing age (Penfield and Roberts, 1959; Basser, 1962; Lenneberg, 1967). However, more recent evidence suggests that the two hemispheres may be functionally asymmetrical for the processing of certain auditory and visual stimuli from the time of birth or shortly thereafter (Entus, 1977; Wada and Davis, 1977). Moreover, the left hemisphere may be already specialized for the processing of speech material in infants less than 12 months of age (Molfese et al., 1975; Molfese, 1977). Cross-sectional studies of age-related behavioral asymmetries suggest that the lateralization of language may be complete by the age of 3 years at the latest (Kinsbourne and Hiscock, 1977).

Anatomical asymmetries of some language centers in the cerebral hemispheres, especially in the area of the planum temporale (a portion of Wernicke's area) have also been reported by several investigators (Pfeifer, 1936; Geschwind and Levitsky, 1968; Galaburda et al., 1978). On the average, the planum is about one-third larger on the left side than on the right (Fig. 3.7). Asymmetries in this region are likewise apparent in the brains of fetuses and newborn infants (Wada, 1969; Chi, et al., 1972; Tezner, et al., 1972; Witelson and Pallie,

1973). The fact that the degree of asymmetry is greater in adults than in infants has led to the suggestion that the anatomical disparity between the two hemispheres increases with age (Wada et al., 1975). Commenting on these and other data, Geschwind (1979, p. 148) said: "I am confident there will exist not only asymmetries of structures on the two sides, but there will also be asymmetries of the process of development." A counterview of this position is offered by Kinsbourne (1981, p. 405), which, because of its challenging character, is worth presenting at length:

"The case of the asymmetrical hemisphere is a good illustration of hasty interpretation. In fact, at the present state of knowlege, nothing can be concluded from these asymmetries beyond the fact that they exist.

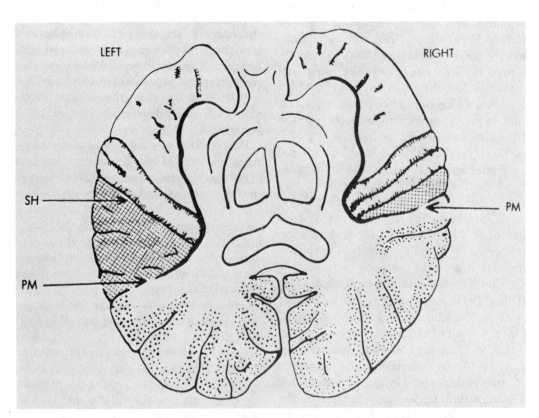

Figure 3.7. Asymmetry of the human superior temporal lobes. Typical left-right differences are shown. The posterior margin (*PM*) of the planum temporale slopes back more sharply on the left than on the right, and the anterior margin of the sulcus of Heschl (*SH*) slopes forward more sharply on the left. (Reprinted from Geschwind N, Levitsky W: Human brain: Left-right asymmetries in temporal speech region. *Science* 161:186–187, 1968, with permission.)

There is no evidence of an invariant relationship between surface landmarks and volume of the underlying brain. The more extensive planum could represent more cortex or cortex stretched thin. Further, one cannot unequivocally relate brain volume to excellence of functioning of the neuronal systems concerned. Does the increased volume represent more neurons, more neural connections or more connective tissue cells or extracellular fluid?. ... In short, not only can asymmetries of limited areas of the brain not be interpreted, but the time is probably far off when they will become interpretable. ... To pin an argument about language in general post hoc on some subsection of language territory is arbitrary."

As noted previously, efforts to relate cognitive and linguistic deficits or a learning disabilities such as dyslexia to delays in lateralizing certain perceptual or motor functions have produced inconclusive results. One type of experimental approach that may prove useful in defining the neural morphology of developmental learning disorders is illustrated in a radiological study by Hier and his associates (1978). Computerized tomography brain scans were collected on a group of 24 children diagnosed as dyslexic. The parieto-occipital region on the right side was found to be wider than that on the left in 42% of these subjects—a number significantly larger than would have been predicted for a population of normal subjects. This was an intriguing result since these areas in the left hemisphere are believed to be critical for reading, writing, and other language functions. Nevertheless, the authors cautioned against deriving excessive etiological significance from such isolated occurrences of reversed asymmetry. Such caution is justified in view of the fact that reversals in asymmetry are considerably more frequent in the population than is the prevalence of dyslexia. While this fact contraindicates the presence of a direct cause and effect relationship, it does appear that the risk of dyslexia may be greater for children with reversals in asymmetry than for those who do not illustrate such reversals.

Gradually, the older concept of brain dominance—a belief in the strict duality of cerebral functioning—is being replaced as more is learned about the special yet complementary activities of the two hemispheres. Lateralization of brain function ought not to be viewed as an all or none phenomenon but as a matter of the degree to which each hemisphere exhibits a given function (Harnod and Doty, 1977). Studies which support this concept are of the kind reported by Zaidel (1978a, 1978b), whose findings suggest that the right hemisphere may play a more important role in linguistic functions than was previously suspected. Although the language performance of the right hemisphere was found inferior to that of the left, it could still comprehend an array of verbal material, including abstract words and a variety of complex syntactic structures.

More research is needed to better understand basic mechanisms underlying the origin of lateralized cognitive and linguistic functions, their anatomical counterparts and maturational timetables. Meanwhile, in the absence of sufficient data, educational programs designed to reverse, facilitate or otherwise alter processes of brain lateralization are presumptuously founded and prematurely conceived.

NEUROELECTRICAL ASPECTS OF DEVELOPMENT

Electroencephalography

Thus far, several structural features of brain maturation and their functional correlates have been reviewed. Another topic having relevance to learning and language acquisition pertains to the concomitant development of cortical and subcortical electrical activity. In Figure 3.8, it can be seen that such activity progresses steadily from the relatively disorganized, slow electrical rhythms of the perinatal period to the more regular and rapid alpha rhythms that appear as the nervous system matures. Such electroencephalographic (EEG) recordings reflect spontaneous electrical potentials generated by neurons. The alpha rhythm is detectable in the motor cortex shortly after birth but is not seen in the occipital cortex until approximately the fourth postnatal month. In the frontal cortex, a character-

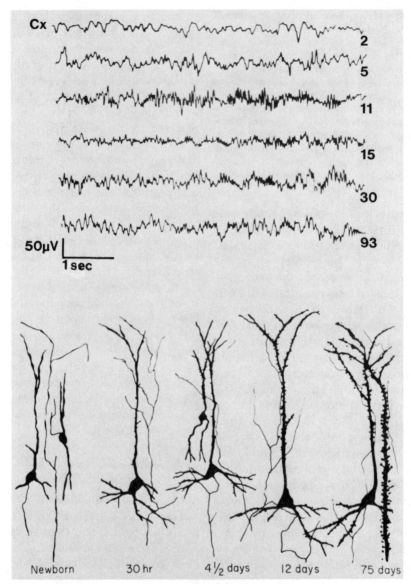

Figure 3.8. Some structural and functional correlates of cortical maturation. Upper series of EEG traces follows development from 2 to 93 days with the appearance of spindle bursts (day 11) and the appearance of increasingly mature alpha-rich records by day 30. The lower series of drawings from Golgi material summarizes the maturation of somata, dendrites, and axons. (Reprinted from Scheibel M, Scheibel A: *Electroencephalogr Clin Neurophysiol* (Suppl 24), 1963, with permission of Elsevier-North Holland, Inc.)

istically mature alpha pattern is not obtained until the nineteenth or twentieth year and in some individuals not before the age of 30. The ontogeny of EEG patterns roughly parallels the progressive morphological changes in cortical neurons, perhaps reflecting the relative closure of the extra-cellular spaces with advancing maturation (Deza and Eidelberg, 1967).

The diagnostic-prognostic utility of the EEG pattern as an indicator of mental development is limited. Efforts to correlate aspects of "intelligence" or language development with EEG recordings, such as alpha modal frequency, have produced equivocal results. Although more success has been obtained when subjects are recorded during active tasks as opposed to passive test conditions, there is still no agreement that alpha activity discriminates among particular neuropsychological factors or between children with such learning disabilities as dyslexia and normal readers. Galin (1979), who provided an extensive review of this literature, has been developing methods for the study of alpha hemispheric asymmetry in an effort to correlate it with cognitive processes. At the time of his 1979 publication, he had yet to apply such methods to the study of dyslexia and other learning disabilities.

Averaged Evoked Potentials

Another index of the functional maturation of the central nervous system is the evoked potential (EP)—an electrical characteristic of the EEG that is time locked to a particular stimulus. The computer averaging of such potentials (AEP's) to repetitive auditory, visual, or somatosensory stimulation can be used to reflect information processing in the pathways of specific sensory systems and their terminal cortical projections. The study of the sequential activation of the neural generators has provided valuable information about the different stages of serial information processing. Human AEP data have been amassed for such processing from the events of sensory reception to the longer latency components of conscious awareness (Table 3.1).

Such brain electrical activity related to sensory and cognitive styles of processing can provide normative models against which the processing functions of the learning disabled might usefully be compared. According to Thatcher (1980, p. 566), "The diagnostic capacities of such functional analyses will likely be of fundamental importance in the development of remediation and therapeutic intervention." Although studies in this area are sparse, there is some evidence that the late components of visually evoked potentials (100 to 250 msec)

Table 3.1.
Human Averaged Evoked Potentials (AEP's) Reflecting Different Stages of Serial Information Processing, from Sensory Reception to Conscious Awareness

Parameter	Latency of Component	Data Source
	msec	
Stimulus intensity	70–110	Armington, 1964
		Diamond, 1964
		Vaughn, 1966
Pattern appearance and disappearance	100–130	Spekreijse et al., 1977
		Harter, 1968
		Jeffreys, 1971
Selective attention	280	Hillyard et al., 1973
		Picton and Hillyard, 1974
Expectancy, prediction, information delivery	280–390	Sutton et al., 1967
		Tueting, 1979
Semantic matching	400–500	Friedman et al., 1974
		Thatcher, 1977
Logical information processing	600	Thatcher, 1976

after stimulus onset) are smaller for the mentally retarded than for the normally intelligent child (Rhodes et al., 1969). Also, a flattening in the amplitude of visually evoked responses over the left parietal area in a family of dyslexics has been reported (Connors, 1970). More recently, computer procedures for brain electrical activity mapping (BEAM) have shown dyslexic patients to illustrate EP differences overlying the entire cortical system believed to be active in speech and reading (Duffy et al., 1980).

Behavioral studies pertaining to temporal order perception in school-age children suggest that poor readers may perform more poorly on verbal and nonverbal sequential tests than normal readers (Bakker, 1972; Gaddes, 1981). In his study, Gaddes found that the between-group differences were most apparent at very fast speeds of stimulus presentation (exposure time: 100 msec). It is noteworthy that such a stimulus duration approximates the lower limit of the neural processing time for the appearance and disappearance of pattern information (Table 3.1). Thus, it appears that deficits in temporal order perception, especially when subtle, are more likely to surface when stress is placed on the central processing systems. This principle should be borne in mind in designing diagnostic tests and related evaluation instruments.

NEUROCHEMISTRY OF LEARNING DISABILITIES

Complex learning and language development are dependent upon the emergence of communication networks among neighboring neurons and their long distance connections to specialized sensing and motor devices. Electrically induced chemical changes at the synaptic junctions of neurons provide the means for transmitting information from the fibers of one cell to the next, comprising the pathways of nerves.

Transmitter Substances

A number of chemicals or "transmitter substances" are released by the end feet of axons into the synaptic spaces, and these, in turn, induce electrical changes in the dendrites of the adjacent cells. These electrical changes involve either an *excitation* or *inhibition* of neural activity depending on the character of the chemical transmitter and its interaction with the postsynaptic receptor surfaces of dendrites. The acquisition, refinement, and skilled expression of learned behavior ultimately depend upon how the forces of excitation and inhibition modulate one another so as to sculpt patterns of neural activity into appropriate responses and integrated response systems.

The development and use of selective staining procedures have led to the discovery of perhaps 30 or more transmitter substances which are localized in relatively specific neuronal circuits within the brain. Some of the best mapped transmitters, in terms of the anatomical pathways in which they operate, are the monoamines norepi-

nephrine, dopamine, serotonin, and acetylcholine. The anatomy of their chemical circuitry is beyond the scope of this review, but it should be noted that some transmitters are excitatory in one part of the brain and inhibitory in another; yet, they usually exert a characteristic effect at any one interneuronal site of secretion.

Coltman and McGaugh (1980, p. 191) have noted that, "Synaptic transmission displays plasticity: it is a function of previous stimulus history, strengthening and weakening under different conditions." The effect of transmitters on neurons is to generate graded electrical responses which are translated and spatiotemporally encoded into messages (firing patterns) in accord with previous experience. Several studies suggest that the integration of higher neural activity involving the consolidation, storage, and retrieval of information may be influenced by transmitter substances. For example, there is evidence that learning and memory deficits in animals may be induced by the administration of drugs which interfere with the synthesis of norepinephrine and that the degree of impairment varies in proportion to drug dosage (Randt et al., 1971; Haycock et al., 1977; Spanis, et al., 1977). Similar impairments have been noted for drugs which block the action of acetylcholine at the nerve terminals of synapses (Deutsch, 1971). Although the precise location of acetylcholine synapses in the central nervous system are still unknown, this transmitter appears to be rich in the cells of the hippocampus (Lewis et al., 1964; Steiner, 1968), a structure lying deep within the temporal lobe which, together with its cortical connections, is thought to play an important role in memory functions.

The relevance of the neurotransmitter substances to learning and memory may lie in their activating influences on such forebrain mechanisms as those involved in selective attention and perception. Mere receptor activation does not guarantee either attention to or perception of a stimulus. Yet, the organism must be sufficiently aroused for either to occur. According to the so-called Yerkes-Dodson law (1908), for any task there is an optimal level of arousal such that performance is related to arousal in a curvilinear or U-shaped fashion. There is a considerable body of data on both animal and human learning which supports this claim. In general, it has been found that performance suffers under conditions in which the experimentally defined arousal level is either too weak or excessive given the demands of the task. In an early review of relevant literature, Easterbrook (1959) concluded that the number of cues utilized in any situation becomes smaller with increments in emotion (arousal). Such narrowing of attention improves efficiency when a task requires attention to only a small number of cues as involved in a simple task but may have a deleterious effect when the task is more complex, requiring attention to a wide range of cues (Hockey, 1979).

Pharmacotherapy

The biochemical importance of arousal mechanisms in the causation and/or exacerbation of certain learning disabilities has yet to be resolved. The terms "hyperkinetic syndrome" or "minimal brain damage" (MBD) are commonly used in reference to a cluster of behavioral, cognitive, and social disorders found in many disabled children including: short attention span, distractibility, perseveration, impulsivity, problems in auditory and visual perception, decreased sensitivity to reinforcement, emotional maladjustment, and other impairments (Strauss and Lehtinen, 1947; Laufer and Denhoff, 1957; Wender, 1972).

Although the terms are often used synonymously, some investigators have argued that a distinction ought to be made between hyperactivity and MBD since not all hyperactive children have learning disabilities, an important feature of MBD. Furthermore, not all MBD children are hyperactive (Safer and Allen, 1976). The American Psychiatric Association's *Diagnostic and Statistical Manual of Mental Disorders* (DSM-III, 1981) uses the term "attention deficit disorder" to describe signs of inappropriate inattention and impulsivity. However, two subtypes of children are noted—those with and those without hyperactivity.

Studies which have sought to examine the etiological and physiological bases of hyperactivity in children have resulted in equivocal findings. Contradictions in data have no doubt arisen from such experimental errors as the failure to use uniform study populations and methods for neurological and behavioral assessment. This is particularly true in the area of drug research where the data have also been clouded by misconceptions and unwarranted conclusions. An example of the latter problem was the tendency, especially among early investigators, to ascribe hyperactivity to overarousal. However, there is evidence that at least some portion of the learning disabled may suffer from underarousal rather than overarousal (Wender, 1971, 1973; Satterfield and Dawson, 1971; Cohen and Douglas, 1972; Sroufe and Stewart, 1973; Spring et al., 1974). Wender (1974), a strong proponent of this view, suggested that there may be different forms of biochemical lesions affecting monoamine metabolism in learning-disabled children. If valid, such an interpretation might help to account for the "paradoxical effect" of the psychostimulants in reducing hyperactivity.

Psychotropic drugs are administered more often for hyperactivity than for any other disorder in children (Gadow, 1979). It appears that some children respond better to stimulant medication and others seem to be more sensitive to the tricyclic antidepressants. The major difference in these drugs is that the stimulants appear to facilitate the action of dopamine-containing neurons whereas tricyclic antidepressants interfere with the uptake of norepinephrine and serotonin. On the basis of these considerations and other findings relevant to the differential responsiveness of children to drugs with known mechanisms of action, Wender (1974) concluded that there may be subgroups of learning-disabled children—some with lesions of the noradrenergic systems and others wherein the predominant disturbance is in the dopaminergic system. The varied manifestations of hyperactivity may lead to its subdivision into different clinical categories as more is learned about the condition (Loney et al., 1978).

As van Duyne (1976) noted, statements pertaining to remediation aspects of drugs are most often too general and unrelated to the effect of specific educational procedures on various learning tasks. It is important to recognize that complex and often curvilinear relations exist among certain arousal, task, and performance variables, as was discussed previously in relation to the Yerkes-Dodson law. The manner of the interaction of these variables with various drug therapies for hyperkinesis is an area deserving further research.

An interesting approach to this problem is reflected in the work of Sprague and Sleator (1976), who have devised models for the study of different drug dosages on the performance of certain tasks. The theoretical curves shown in Figure 3.9 were used to summarize three important points. First, increasing drug dosages appear to have an inverted U-shape effect on both cognitive and social aspects of performance. To the extent that increments in drug dosage may lead to increased arousal, such findings are consonant with the predictions of the Yerkes-Dodson law. Second, it was noted that the zone of "peak enhancement" differed for the cognitive and social factors. Thus, the "right" drug dosage varies according to the type of behavior treated. Third, what is "right" in one case may be "wrong" in another. Increasing drug dosages to attain desirable modifications in behavior may exert an unfavorable influence on cognitive learning (Swanson et al., 1978). The reverse is also true. Reducing drug dosages to obtain gains in cognitive performance may have an undesirable impact on a child's social adjustment.

All of these factors, in addition to the physiological side effects associated with drug usage, ought to be carefully weighed in designing appropriate drug therapies for hyperactive children. In addition, the nature of the learning impairment must also be considered. Drug therapy may only be appropriate for learning disabilities stemming from attentional deficits rather than from more primary or basic deficits in learning and memory. In the words of Douglas (1972, p. 259), drugs may merely increase an ability to "stop, look, and listen." Clearly, the relative responsiveness of learning disabilities, having different origins and characteristics, to various forms of pharmaceutical management poses complex problems for future research.

CLOSING REMARKS

The brain is the executor of behavior in all its myriad forms. The evolution of the neurons, their developmental history and changing patterns through time, their internal communications, and systems for communicating with other brains are frontiers for study transcending the scope of any one speciality.

Clinicians, educators, and developmental specialists in many fields are beginning to broaden their horizons, beyond mere parochial concern with materials and methods of management, to include a consideration of brain-behavior relationships. The explosion of interest in cognitive psychology is indicative of the failure of strict behavioristic approaches to deal adequately with the "higher order" mental activities. This is not to refute the programmatic value of many operant technologies for teaching. Yet, teachers and clinicians are increasingly acknowledging the need to better understand the role of covert processes in regulating overt responses.

Many problems remain to be solved. How is the nervous system organized for learning? Is the brain merely a biological computer that *passively* accumulates and organizes chains of individual reflex elements into complex behavioral patterns? On the other hand, is the brain capable of *actively*

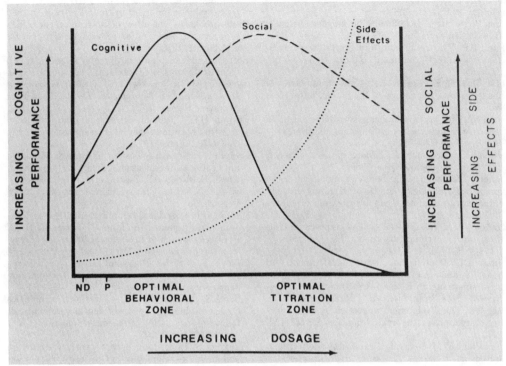

I igure 3.9. Theoretical dose-response curves. (Reprinted from Sprague R, Sleator E: Drugs and dosages: implications for learning disabilities. In Knight R, Bakker D: *The Neuropsychology of Learning Disorders.* Baltimore, University Park Press, 1976, with permission.)

(consciously) participating in the mediation of stimulus inputs and response outputs?

To the extent that different tasks might be associated with different styles and strategies of learning, what neurological mechanisms might account for such variance? From another viewpoint, how might the acquisition and development of linguistic, visual-spatial, and other problem-solving abilities affect neurological reorganization? Problems surrounding the auditory and visual transfer of linguistic and nonlinguistic information are complex and require additional investigation (see Chapters 1 and 4). Furthermore, the morphological, chemical, and electrical correlates of intersensory competence are still unknown. Knowledge of this kind may one day lead to a better definition of learning and language disabilities and, hopefully, to improvements in instructional materials and teaching programs.

References

Akert K: Comparative anatomy of the frontal cortex and thalamocortical connections. In Warren JM, Akert K: *The Frontal Granular Cortex and Behavior.* New York, McGraw-Hill, 1964.

American Psychiatric Association. *Diagnostic and Statistical Manual of Mental Disorders,* ed 3. Washington DC, American Psychiatric Association, 1980.

Arlin PK: Cognitive development in adulthood: a fifth stage? *Dev Psychol* 11:602–606, 1975.

Armington JC: Adaptational changes in the human electroretinogram and occipital response. *Vision Res* 4:179–192, 1964.

Ashem B, Janes MD: Deleterious effects of chronic undernutrition on cognitive abilities. *J Child Psychol Psychiatry* 19:23–31, 1978.

Bakker DJ: *Temporal Order in Disturbed Reading.* Rotterdam, Rotterdam University Press, 1972.

Basser LS: Hemiplegia of early onset and the faculty of speech with special reference to the effects of hemispherectomy. *Brain* 85:427–460, 1962.

Behar M: Prevalence of malnutrition among preschool children. In Scrimshaw NS, Gordon JE: *Malnutrition, Learning and Behavior.* Cambridge, MA, MIT Press, 1968.

Bogen J: The other side of the brain. (1) Dysgraphia and dyscopia following cerebral commissurotomy. *Bull LA Neurol Soc* 34:73–105, 1969.

Boll TJ: Right and left cerebral hemisphere damage and tactile perception: performance of the ipsilateral and contralateral sides of the body. *Neuropsychologia* 12:235–238, 1974.

Broca P: Du Siege de la faculte du language articule. *Bull Soc Anthropol* 6:377–393, 1865.

Cattell RP: Theory of fluid and crystallized intelligence: a critical experiment. *J Educ Psychol* 54:1–22, 1963.

Chi J, Dooling E, Giles F: Left-right asymmetries of the temporal speech areas of the human fetus. *Arch Neurol* 34:346–348, 1972.

Cohen NJ, Douglas VI: Characteristics of the orienting response in hyperactive and normal children. *Psychophysiology* 9:238–245, 1972.

Coltman C, McGaugh J: *Behavioral Neuroscience.* New York, Academic Press, 1980.

Conners CK: Symposium: behavior modification by drugs. II. Psychological effects of stimulant drugs in children with minimal brain dysfunction. *Pediatrics* 49:702–708, 1972.

Connors CA: Cortical visual evoked response in children with learning disorders. *Psychophysiology* 7:418–428, 1970.

Coursin DB: Malnutrition, brain development and behavior: anatomic, biochemical and electrophysiologic constructs. In Brazier MA: *Growth and Development of the Brain.* New York, Raven Press, 1975.

Cragg BG: The development of cortical synapses during starvation in the rat. *Brain Res* 95:143–150, 1972.

Cruickshank WM: Learning disabilities: a definitional statement. In Polak E: *Issues and Initiatives in Learning Disabilities. Selected Papers from the First National Conference on Learning Disabilities.* Ottawa, Canadian Association for Children with Learning Disabilities, 1979.

Curry F: A comparison of left-handed and right-handed subjects on verbal and nonverbal dichotic listening tasks. *Cortex* 3:342–352, 1967.

Das JP, Kirby J, Jarman RF: Simultaneous and successive synthesis, an alternative model for cognitive abilities. *Psychol Bull* 82:87–103, 1975.

Das JP, Kirby JR, Jarman RF: *Simultaneous and Successive Cognitive Processing.* New York, Academic Press, 1979.

Dax G: Lesions de la moitie gauche de l'encephale coincident avec l'oubli des signes de la pensee. *Gaz Hebdom Med Chir* 2:259–262, 1865.

Deutsch JA: The cholinergic synapse and the site of memory. *Science* 174:788–794, 1971.

Deza L, Eidelberg F: Development of cortical electrical activity in the rat. *Exp Neurol* 17:425–438, 1967.

Diamond SP: Input-output relations. *Ann NY Acad Sci* 112:160–171, 1964.

Diller K: Natural methods of foreign language teaching. In Winitz H: *Native Language and Foreign Language Acquisition.* New York, New York Academy of Sciences, 1981, vol 379.

Dimond SJ, Beaumont JG: Experimental studies of hemispheric functions in the human brain. In Dimond SJ, Beaumont JG: *Hemisphere Functions in the Human Brain.* New York, John Wiley & Sons, 1974.

Douglas VI: Stop, look, and listen: The problem of sustained attention and impulse control in hyperactive and normal children. *Can J Behav Sci* 4:259–282, 1972.

Duffy FH, Denckla MB, Bartels PH, et al: Dyslexia: regional differences in brain electrical activity by topographic mapping. *Ann Neurol* 7:412–420, 1980.

Easterbrook JA: The effect of emotion on cue utilization and the organization of behavior. *Psychol Rev* 66:183–201, 1959.

Entus AK: Hemispheric asymmetry in processing of dichotically presented speech and nonspeech stimuli by infants. In Segalowitz SJ, Gruber F: *Language Development and Neurological Theory.* New York, Academic Press, 1977.

Epstein HT: Phrenoblysis: special brain and mind growth. II. Human mental development. *Dev Psychobiol* 7:217–224, 1974.

Epstein HT: Growth spurts during brain development: implications for educational policy and practice. In Chall JS, Mirsky AF: *Education and Brain Yearbook of the N.S.S.E.* Chicago, University of Chicago Press, 1978.

Epstein HT: Correlated brain and intelligence development in humans. In Hahn M, Jensen C, Dudek B: *Development and Evolution of Brain Size: Behavioral Implications.* New York, Academic Press, 1979.

Fifková E, Hassler R: Quantitative morphological changes in visual centers of rats after unilateral deprivation. *J Comp Neurol* 135:167–178, 1969.

Fifková E, van Harrelel A: Long lasting morphological change in dendrite spines of dentate granular cells following stimulation of the entorhinal area. *J Neurocytol* 6:211–230, 1977.

Franková S: Interaction between early malnutrition and mental development. In Cravioto J, Hambraeus L, Vahlquist B: *Swedish Nutrition Foundation Symposium XII.* Uppsala, Almquist and Wiksell, 1974.

Friedman D, Simpson R, Ritter W, et al: The late positive component (P-300) and information processing in sentences. *Electroencephalogr Clin Neurophysiol* 37:1–9, 1974.

Gaddes WH: Can educational psychology be neurologized? *Can J Behav Sci* 1:38–49, 1969.

Gaddes WH: A review of some research in the area of serial order behavior. In Cruickshank WM, Lerner J: *The Best of ACLD 1981.* Syracuse, Syracuse University Press, 1981, vol 3.

Gadow KD: *Children on Medication: A Primer for School Personnel,* Reston, VA. Council for Exceptional Children, 1979.

Galaburda A, Lemay M, Kemper T, et al: Right-left asymmetries in the brain. *Science* 199:852–856, 1978.

Galin D: EEG studies of lateralization of verbal process. In Ludlow CL, Doran-Quine ME: *The Neurological Bases of Language Disorders in Children: Methods and Questions for Research.* NINCDS monograph no. 22, Bethesda, MD, United States Department of Health, Education and Welfare, 1979.

Gardner RA: *The Objective Diagnosis of Minimal Brain Dysfunction.* Cresskill, NJ, Creative Therapeutics, 1979.

Geschwind N: Language and the brain. *Sci Am* 226:76–83, 1972.

Geschwind N: Anatomical foundations of language and dominance. In Ludlow CL, Doran-Quine ME: *The Neurological Bases of Language Disorders in Children: Methods and Directions for Research.* NINCDS monograph no. 22, Bethesda, MD, United States Department of Health, Education and Welfare, 1979.

Geschwind N, Levitsky W: Human brain: Left-right asymmetries in temporal speech region. *Science* 161:186–187, 1968.

Goldman PS: Development and plasticity of frontal association cortex in the infrahuman primate. In Ludlow CL, Doran-Quine ME: *The Neurological Bases of Language Disorders in Children: Methods and Directions for Research.* NINCDS monograph no. 22, Bethesda, MD, United States Department of Health, Education and Welfare, 1979.

Goldman PS, Nauta WH: Columnar distribution of cortico-cortical fibers in the frontal association, limbic and motor cortex of the developing rhesus monkey. *Brain Res* 122:293–413, 1977.

Grant JP: The state of the world's children, 1981–1982. New York, UNICEF, 1982.

Greenough WT: Enduring brain effects of differential experience and training. In Rosenzweig MR, Bennett EL: *Neurological Mechanisms of Learning and Memory.* Cambridge, MA, MIT Press, 1976.

Greulich WW: Growth of children of the same race under different environmental conditions. *Science* 127:515–516, 1958.

Griffin WS, Woodward DJ, Chanda R: Cerebellar weight, DNA, RNA, protein and histological correlations. *J Neurochem* 28:1269–1279, 1977.

Gyllensten L, Malmfors T, Norrlin M: Effects of visual deprivation on the optic centers of growing and adult mice. *J Comp Neurol* 124:149–160, 1965.

Gyllensten L, Malmfors T, Norrlin M: Growth alterations in the auditory cortex of visually deprived mice. *J Comp Neurol* 126:463–470, 1966.

Halstead WC: *Brain and Intelligence: A Quantitative Study of the Frontal Lobes.* Chicago, University of Chicago Press, 1947.

Harnod S, Doty R: Introductory overview. In Harnod S, Doty R, Goldstein L, et al: *Lateralization in the Nervous System.* New York, Academic Press, 1977.

Harter MR: Effects of contour sharpness and checksize on visually evoked cortical potentials. *Vision Res* 8:701–711, 1968.

Haycock JW, van Buskirk R, McGaugh JL: Effects of catecholaminergic drugs upon memory storage process in mice. *Behav Biol* 29:281–310, 1977.

Hebb DO: *The Organization of Behavior.* New York, John Wiley & Sons, 1949.

Hier D, LeMay M, Rosenberger P, et al: Developmental dyslexia. *Arch Neurol* 35:90–92, 1978.

Hillyard SA, Hink RF, Schwent VL, et al: Electrical signs of selective attention in the human brain. *Science* 182:171–173, 1973.

Hockey R: Stress and the cognitive components of skilled performance. In Hamilton V, Warburton D: *Human Stress and Cognition.* New York, John Wiley & Sons, 1979.

Hubel DH, Wiesel TN: Laminar and columnar distribution of geniculocortical fibers in the macaque monkey. *J Comp Neurol* 146:421–450, 1972.

Hunt JM: Reflections on a decade of early education. *J Abnorm Child Psychol* 3:275–336, 1975.

Jacobson M: Development of specific neuronal connections. *Science* 163:543–547, 1969.

Jacobson M: *Developmental Neurobiology.* New York, Holt, 1970.

Jacobson S, Trojanowski JQ: Prefrontal granular cortex of the rhesus monkey, II. Interhemispheric cortical afferents. *Brain Res* 132:235–346, 1977.

Jeffreys DA: Cortical source locations of pattern-related VEPs (visual evoked potentials) recorded from the human scalp. *Nature* 229:501–502, 1971.

Kemp JM, Powell TS: The cortico-striate projection in the monkey. *Brain Rev* 93:793–820, 1970.

Kinsbourne M: Cerebral control and mental evolution. In Kinsbourne M, Smith W: *Hemispheric Disconnection and Cerebral Function.* Springfield, IL, Charles C Thomas, 1974.

Kinsbourne M: Biological determinants of functional bisymmetry and asymmetry. In Kinsbourne M: *Asymmetrical Function of the Brain.* Cambridge, Cambridge University Press, 1978.

Kinsbourne M: The development of cerebral dominance. In Filskov SD, Boll TJ: *Handbook of Clinical Neuropsychology.* New York, John Wiley & Sons, 1981.

Kinsbourne M, Hiscock M: Does cerebral dominance develope. In Segalowitz SJ, Gruber FA: *Language Development and Neurological Theory.* New York, Academic Press, 1977.

Krigman MR, Hogan EL: Undernutrition in the developing rat: effect upon myelination. *Brain Res* 107:239–256, 1976.

Laufner MW, Denhoff E: Hyperkinetic behavior syndrome in children. *J Pediatr* 50:463–473, 1957.

Lecours AR: Myelogenetic correlates of the development of speech and language. In Lenneberg EH, Lenneberg E: *Foundations of Language Development I.* New York, Academic Press, 1975.

Lenneberg EH: *Biological Foundations of Language.* New York, John Wiley & Sons, 1967.

Lewis PD, Balazs R, Patel AJ, et al: The effect of undernutrition in early life on cell generation in the rat brain. *Brain Res* 83:235–247, 1975.

Lewis PR, Shute C, Silver A: Confirmation from choline acetylase analysis of a massive cholinergic innervation to the hippocampus. *J Physiol (Lond)* 172:9–10, 1964.

Livingston RB, Calloway DH, MacGregor JS, et al: U. S. poverty impact on brain development. In Brazier MA: *Growth and Development of the Brain.* New York, Raven Press, 1975, pp. 377–394.

Llinas R, Hillman DE: A multipurpose tridimensional reconstructive computer system for neuroanatomy. In Santini M: *Golgi Centennial Symposium: Perspective in Neurobiology.* New York, Raven Press, 1975.

Loney J, Langhorne JE, Paternite CE: An empirical basis for subgrouping the hyperkinetic/MBD syndrome. *J Abnorm Psychol* 87:431–441, 1978.

Luria AR: *Human Brain and Psychological Processes.* New York, Harper and Row, 1966.

Luria AR: *Traumatic Aphasia.* The Hague, Mouton Press, 1970.

Luria AR: *The Working Brain.* New York, Basic Books, 1973.

Merzenich MM, Brugge JF: Representation of the cochlear partition on the superior temporal plane of the macaque monkey. *Brain Res* 50:275–296, 1973.

Milner B, Taylor L: Right hemispheric superiority in tactile pattern-recognition after cerebral commissurotomy. Evidence for nonverbal memory. *Neuropsychologia* 10:1–10, 1972.

Molfese DL: Infant cerebral asymmetry. In Segalowitz SJ, Gruber FA: *Language Development and Neurological Theory.* New York, Academic Press, 1977.

Molfese D, Freeman R, Palermo D: The ontogeny of brain lateralization for speech and nonspeech stimuli. *Brain Language* 2:356–368, 1975.

Møllgaard K, Diamond MC, Bennett LL, et al: Quantitative synaptic changes with differential experience in rat brain. *Int J Neurosci* 2:113–128, 1971.

Nauta WM: Some efferent connections of the prefrontal cortex in the monkey. In Warren JM, Kert KE: *The Frontal Granular Cortex and Behavior.* New York, McGraw-Hill, 1964.

Nebes R: Superiority of the minor hemisphere in commissurotomized man for the perception of part-whole relations. *Cortex* 7:333–349, 1971.

Nebes R: Perception of spatial relationships by the right and left hemisphere in commissurotomized man. *Neuropsychologia* 11:285–289, 1973.

Oppenheimer JM: Studies of brain asymmetry: historical perspective. In Dimond S, Blizard D: Evolution and lateralization of the brain. *Ann NY Acad Sci* 299:4–17, 1977.

Pandya DN, Kuypers HG: Cortico-cortical connections in the rhesus monkey. *Brain Res* 13:13–36, 1969.

Pandya DN, Vignola LA: Intra- and interhemispheric projections of the precentral, premotor and arcuate areas of the rhesus monkey. *Brain Res* 26:217–233, 1971.

Pellionisz A, Llinas R: A computer model of cerebellar Purkinge cells. *Neuroscience* 2:37–48, 1977.

Penfield W, Roberts L: *Speech and Brain Mechanisms.* Princeton, NJ, Princeton University Press, 1959.

Pfeifer AA: Pathologie der Horstrahlung und der corticalen Horsphare. In Bumke O, Foerster E: *Handbuch der Neurologie.* Berlin, Springer, 1936, vol 6.

Piaget J: *Psychology of Intelligence.* Totowa, NJ, Littlefield, Adams, 1969.

Picton TW, Hillyard SA: Human auditory evoked potentials. II. Effects of attention. *Electroencephalogr Clin Neurophysiol* 36:191–200, 1974.

Powell TP, Mountcastle VB: The cytoarchitecture of the postcentral gyrus of the monkey macaca mulatta. *Bull Johns Hopkins Hosp* 146:421–450, 1972.

Purpura DP: Approaches, advantages and limitations. In Purpura DP, Perkins GP: *Methodological Approaches to the Study of Brain Maturation.* Baltimore, University Park Press, 1974.

Rámon y Cajal S: *Comparative Study of the Sensory Areas of the Human Cortex.* Worcester, MA, Clark University Press, 1899.

Rámon y Cajal S: *Recollections of my life. Mem Am Philosoph Soc* 7: 1937.

Randt CT, Quartermain D, Goldstein M, et al: Norepinephrine biosynthesis inhibition: effects on memory in mice. *Science* 172:498–499, 1971.

Rhodes LE, Dustman RE, Beck EG: The visual evoked response: a comparison of bright and dull children. *Electroencephalogr Clin Neurophysiol* 27:364–372, 1969.

Rosenzweig MR, Bennett EL: Effects of environmental enrichment or impoverishment on learning and on brain values in rodents. In Oliverio A: *Genetics, Environment and Intelligence.* Amsterdam, Elsevier-North Holland, 1977.

Rourke BP: Reading and spelling disabilities: a developmental neuropsychological perspective. In Kirk U: *Neuropsychology of Language, Reading and Spelling.* New York, Academic Press, 1981.

Ryugo DK, Ryugo R, Globus A, et al: Increased spine density in auditory cortex following visual or somatic deafferentiation. *Brain Res* 90:143–146, 1975.

Safer DJ, Allen RP: *Hyperactive Children: Diagnosis and Management.* Baltimore, University Park Press, 1976.

Salas M, Diaz S, Nieto A: Effects of neonatal food deprivation on cortical spines and dendritic development of rats. *Brain Res* 73:139–144, 1974.

Satterfield JH, Dawson ME: Electrodermal correlates of hyperactivity in children. *Psychophysiology* 8:191–197, 1971.

Scheibel ME, Scheibel AB: Selected structural-functional correlations in postnatal brain. In Sterman MB, McGinty DJ, Adinolfi AM: *Brain Development and Behavior.* New York, Academic Press, 1971.

Schulte FJ, Linke I, Michaelis R, et al: Excitation, inhibition, and impulse conduction in spinal motoneurons of preterm, term and small-for-dates newborn infants. In Robinson RJ: *Brain and Early Behavior.* New York, Academic Press, 1969.

Segalowitz SJ, Gruber FA: *Language Development and Neurological Theory.* New York, Academic Press, 1977.

Silver AA, Hagin R: Specific reading disability: Delineation of the syndrome and relationship to cerebral dominance. *Compr Psychiatry* 1:126–134, 1960.

Silver AA, Hagin R: Specific reading disability: follow-up studies. *Am J Orthopsychiatry* 34:95–102, 1964.

Spanis CW, Haycock JW, Handwerker MJ, et al: Impairment of retention of avoidance response in rats by post-training diethyldithiocarbamate. *Psychopharmacology* 53:213–215, 1977.

Spekrijse H, Estevez O, Reits D: Visual evoked potentials and the physiological analysis of visual processes in man. In Desmedt JE: *Visual Evoked Potential in Man: New Developments.* Oxford, Clarendon Press, 1977.

Sprague RL, Sleator EK: Drugs and dosages: implications for learning disabilities. In Knights RM, Bakker DJ: *The Neurology of Learning Disorders.* Baltimore, University Park Press, 1976.

Spring C, Greenberg L, Scott J, et al: Electrodermal activity in hyperactive boys who are methylphenidate responders. *Psychophysiology* 11:436–442, 1974.

Sroufe LA, Stewart MA: Treating problem children with stimulant drugs. *N Engl J Med* 289:407–413, 1973.

Steiner FA: Influences of microelectrophoretically applied acetylcholine on the responsiveness of hippocampal and lateral geniculate neurons. *Pflugers Arch* 303:173–180, 1968.

Strauss AA, Lehtinen LE: *Psychopathology and Education in the Brain-injured Child.* New York, Grune and Stratton, 1947.

Sutton S, Tueting P, Zubin J, et al: Information delivery and sensory evoked potential. *Science* 155:1436–1439, 1967.

Swanson J, Kinsbourne M, Roberts W, et al: Time-response analysis of the effect of stimulant medication on the learning ability of children referred for hyperactivity. *Pediatrics* 61:21–29, 1978.

Taylor HG, Satz P, Friel J: Developmental dyslexia in relation to other childhood reading disorders: significance and clinical utility. *Res Q* 15:84–101, 1979.

Tezner D, Tzavaros A, Gruner J, et al: Etude e anatomique de l'asymetrie droite-gauche du planum temporale. *Rev Neurol* 126:444, 1972.

Thatcher RW: Electrophysiological correlates of animal and human memory. In Terry RD, Gershon S: *The Neurobiology of Aging.* New York, Raven Press, 1976.

Thatcher RW: Electrophysiological correlates of hemispheric lateralization during semantic information processing. In Harnod S, Doty R, Goldstein L, et al: *Lateralization in the Nervous System.* New York, Academic Press, 1977.

Thatcher RW: Spatial synchronization of brain electrical activity related to cognitive information processing. In Thompson RF, Hicks LA, Shvyrkov VB: *Neural Mechanism of Goal Directed Behavior and Learning.* New York, Academic Press, 1980.

Tobias TJ: Afferents to prefrontal cortex from the thalamic mediodorsal nucleus in the rhesus monkey. *Brain Res* 83:191–212, 1975.

Tueting P: Event related potentials, cognitive events, and information processing. In Otto D: *Perspectives in Event Related Brain Potential Research.* Washington DC, United States Government Printing Office, 1979.

van Duyne HJ: Effects of stimulant drug therapy on learning behaviors in hyperactive/MBD children. In Knights RM, Bakker DJ: *The Neuropsychology of Learning Disorders.* Baltimore, University Park Press, 1976.

Vaughn HG: The perceptual and physiologic significance of visual evoked responses from the scalp of man. *Vision Res (Suppl.)* 203–223, 1966.

Volkmar FR, Greenough WT: Rearing complexity affects branching of dendrites in the visual cortex of the rat. *Science* 76:1445–1447, 1972.

Vygotsky LS: Thinking and speech. In Leontiev AN, Luria AR: *Selected Psychological Investigations.* Moscow, Agentstvo Pechati Novosti, 1956.

Wada JA: Interhemispheric sharing and shift of cerebral speech function. *Excerpta Med Int Congr Ser* 193:296–297, 1969.

Wada JA, Clark R, Hamm A: Cerebral hemispheric asymmetry in humans. *Arch Neurol* 32:239–246, 1975.

Wada JA, Davis A: Fundamental nature of human infants' brain asymmetry. *Can J Neurol Sci* 4:203–207, 1977.

Wada JA, Rasmussen T: Intra-carotid injections of sodium amytal for the lateralization of cerebral speech dominance. *J Neurosurg* 17:266–282, 1960.

Wender PH: *Minimal Brain Dysfunction in Children.* New York, Wiley-Interscience, 1971.

Wender PH: The minimal brain dysfunction syndrome in children. *J Nerv Ment Dis* 155:55–71, 1972.

Wender PH: Minimal brain dysfunction in children: diagnosis and management. *Pediatr Clin North Am* 20:187–202, 1973.

Wender PH: Some speculations concerning a possible biochemical basis of minimal brain dysfunction. *Life Sci* 14:1605–1621, 1974.

West CD, Kemper TL: The effect of a low protein diet on the anatomical development of the rat brain. *Brain Res* 107:221–237, 1976.

Witelson SF, Pallie W: Left hemisphere specialization of language in the newborn: neuroanatomical evidence of asymmetry. *Brain* 96:641–646, 1973.

Yakovlev PL, Lecours AR: The myelogenetic cycles of regional maturation of the brain. In Minkowski A: *Regional Development of the Brain in Early Life.* Oxford, Blackwell, 1967.

Yerkes RM, Dodson JD: The relation of strength of stimulus to rapidity of habit formation. *J Comp Neurol Psychol* 18:459–482, 1908.

Zaidel E: Lexical organization in the right hemisphere. In Busser PA, Rougeul-Busser T: *Cerebral Correlates of Conscious Experience* (INSERM Symposium no. 6). Amsterdam, Elsevier-North Holland, Biomedical Press, 1978a.

Zaidel E: Concepts of cerebral dominance in the split brain. In Busser PA, Rougeul-Busser T: *Cerebral Correlates of Conscious Experience* INSERM Symposium no. 6). Amsterdam, Elsevier-North Holland, Biomedical Press, 1978b.

CHAPTER FOUR

Language Processing: Halfway Up the Down Staircase

KATHARINE G. BUTLER, Ph.D.

Pause a moment before you begin this chapter. You will need a stopwatch, pencil, and paper. Have them nearby as you begin to read the second paragraph. As the title of this chapter suggests, we will be discussing how information is processed, stored, and retrieved. In order to gain some notion of how complex a seemingly simple task may be, let us conduct a small experiment.

Task one: Say the alphabet aloud *as rapidly as you can.* Time yourself.
Write down the number of seconds which elapsed from a to z.
Write down "how" you think you recalled the alphabet from long-term memory. What mnemonic strategy did you use?

Task two: Close your eyes and "see" the alphabet in your mind's eye. Look at each letter. Time yourself. Take as long as you need.
Write down the number of seconds which elapsed between "seeing" a and z.
Write down your perception of how you performed this task. Did you use a different strategy?

Are there significant differences in the temporal duration of each task? There should be. It frequently takes almost twice as long to perform task two.

How would you judge the difficulty of the tasks you have just completed with, for example, a request to "say as rapidly as you can the names of 15 state capitols." Can you predict whether you could complete this request in, say, 30 seconds?

As you may recall from Chapter 1, "information load" and processing strategies are important concepts in the evaluation of language disorders. There is much we can learn from normal processing to assist us in our assessment and intervention of disordered language and learning. Let us briefly examine some of the characteristics of the tasks you have completed. Your level of performance resulted from your ability to retrieve from long-term memory, under both speeded and nonspeeded conditions, information which is well esconced in your memory. In our literate culture, we can anticipate that most children will have been "taught" the alphabet during their early years. We can also anticipate that some specific mnemonic strategy was utilized; very probably you learned the alphabet through a song which assisted you in chunking this originally unrelated and meaningless information. Certainly, you were required to overlearn the material, to go beyond 100% learning. You were required to practice it, i.e., to rehearse it, code it, and store it in long-term memory. Later you were required to form sound-symbol associations, again assigning meaning to originally unknown visual stimuli. Even here, the importance of the "context" of language should be noted. As Reid (1981) notes, nearly all children recognize some words by sight prior to reading instruction. You will find references to the connections between context, memory, and oral and printed language throughout this volume.

As you review your performance on tasks one and two, you will note that your memory search for the required information tended to be both rapid and automatic. The processing load was light and may have required some attention to task but relatively little effort. Compare the outcome of those tasks with the untried task of naming state capitols under speeded conditions. Unless you happen to be a geographer or, perchance, a social studies teacher, you may predict that you will have much greater difficulty. The information may be difficult to access from long-term memory, partially at least because it is likely that it was stored through differing strategies, is embedded in a number of disparate contexts, is less well known, requires controlled search of paired associates (state *and* city names), and may be subject to associative interference. However, given a few moments to organize, you may be able to identify a system by which your recall would be aided (perhaps, visualizing a map of the United States, or by selecting your own state and moving "outward" in some kind of pattern). As Glaser (1981, p. 932) points out, competent individuals utilize learning and experience to organize their knowledge "into a fast-access pattern recognition or encoding system that greatly reduces the mental processing load." In addition, mature learners (such as yourself) have developed self-regulatory and metacognitive skills (see also Chapter 7). If you answered the questions "what mnemonic strategies did you use?" and "write down your perception of how you performed this task," you were involved in a metacognitive task. Metacognitive skills do not represent specific performance but rather enable one to reflect upon and monitor one's own performance. Knowing the extent of your knowledge, predicting the correctness of a response, apportioning cog-

nitive resources, and checking the outcome of attempted solutions are all metacognitive in nature (Glaser, 1981). These regulatory skills are known to develop with maturity and may be less developed in children with language learning disabilities. As Glaser points out: "The especially interesting characteristic of these skills is that they may be the particular aspect of performance that facilitates transfer from learning and training situations to new situations" (p. 934). He notes that metacognitive tasks may be important candidates for assessment, and adds that tests of self-regulatory skills may be important predictors for successful problem solving and learning.

We started out by saying that in this chapter will be discussed how language is processed, stored, and retrieved. To this we must add information about problem solving and metacognition, if we are to arrive at effective assessment and intervention. (See Chapters 7, 9, 10, and 11 for such information in greater detail.)

In order to understand how information is processed, or at least how cognitive psychologists currently view such processing, it is helpful to recognize that there are a number of viewpoints or perspectives. Much has been written over the past several years regarding "bottom-up" processing (data driven) versus "top-down" (cognitive) processing. It is important that one understand the assumptions behind the various viewpoints, since the assumptions may directly affect theory and practice. As the title of this chapter suggests, it is probable that the higher order cognitive processes hold sway. There is a need, however, to consider data-driven incoming (upgoing?) sensory and perceptual stimuli as well. From a theoretical position halfway up the down staircase, then, let us look at how information is processed.

INFORMATION PROCESSING

To more fully appreciate what is meant by language processing, it is well to look briefly at the outlines of the broader field of information processing. As Anderson

(1980) describes, information processing grew out of both information theory and research on human skills and performance (human-factor theory) and achieved prominence during and after World War II. He reports (p. 9):

"Information theory is a branch of communication sciences that provides an abstract way of analyzing the processing of knowledge. The work of the British psychologist Donald Broadbent . . . was probably most influential in integrating . . . and developing the information processing approach."

A second influence on information processing reflects the developments in computer science and artificial intelligence. A third influence is linguistics and Noam Chomsky's work in analyzing the structure of language (Anderson, 1980). These three influences—human factor theory, information theory, and linguistics—have resulted in increasing emphasis on higher order mental processes, thought, and language in the years since 1940. Throughout this text, the reader will be able to trace the impact of those influences on the way in which speech-language pathologists view language acquisition, development, and disorders. We have turned our attention to *how* individuals acquire information, in addition to our earlier interest in *what* information was acquired and how it was comprehended and expressed.

Implicit within the information-processing approach is that there is a reciprocal and integrative relationship between and among perceptual, attentional, and memorial functions, and that such functions are under the control of higher order mental processes. Although we know a great deal about language, problem solving, memory, and perception, the form of the theory which specifies how all these subdomains interconnect is still very unclear (Anderson, 1980). For the practitioner who faces the challenge of what to do on Monday morning, it also means that there is not complete certitude about the clinical process. Indeed, the tasks which confront practicing professionals are highly inferential. As we shall see, the ability to make infer-

ences calls for considerable world knowledge and word knowledge.

The Multi-Store Model of Processing

The multi-store model of memory and processing began almost 100 years ago when William James (1890) noted the difference between primary and secondary memory. Since the 1960's, a number of models have been proposed (Baddely, 1966; Craik, 1968, 1970; Wickelgren, 1965; Atkinson and Shiffrin, 1968, 1971; Waugh and Norman, 1965). Such models have focused upon the movement of information from the sensory stores (or registers) through short-term store and into long-term or permanent store (Naus et al., 1978).

Short-term memory is thought to be limited in its capacity and bound by time, whereas long-term memory is thought to be essentially unlimited in capacity but is affected by interference factors and temporary irretrievability. The Atkinson and Shiffrin model is neatly summarized as follows (Naus et al., 1978, p. 221):

" . . . modality-specific stimulus information is assumed first to enter the appropriate sensory register. Information in this initial store is thought to be a relatively complete copy of the physical stimulus, which is only available for further processing for a maximum of 3–5 seconds. From the sensory register, information may be transferred into limited-capacity short term store."

The practicing professonal who attempts to utilize the multi-store model in assessment must heed the implications of viewing incoming auditory and visual stimuli as being available in the sensory registers for only very brief periods of time before transfer to short-term memory store. Indeed, short-term memory, known also as working memory or primary memory, although easily defined as that which holds knowledge currently in use (Anderson, 1980), is not as easily measured. The capacity of short-term memory varies according to the meaningfulness of the material, an important point. Anderson illustrates this point by noting that adults can successfully repeat back four nonsense syllables, but not six. They can repeat back six one-syllable words, but not nine one-syllable words. They can usually repeat three four-syllable words (i.e., 12 syllables) but not six four-syllable words. In addition, they can repeat back a 19-word sentence: Richard Milhous Nixon, former President of the United States, wrote a book about his career in the White House (pp. 167–168). Why the variability? As you will recall from our alphabet task, the information is chunked and the units of memory are less related to physical units, such as letters, syllables, or words, and more related to how the information is assigned meaning, i.e., chunked.

Thus, for an examiner to state in a report that short-term memory has been assessed, when in reality only a digit span test, an unrelated word test, or a sentence imitation task has been administered, does not do justice to short-term memory, no matter what model may be used. In addition, it is not yet clear that changes in short-term memory tasks (such as recall of a list of items) is age related. Ornstein (1978, p. 5) reports that the research data imply that "recall from short-term store is similar in children over a wide age range, but that there are developmental changes in the recall of information from long-term store." Information-processing strategies such as rehearsal are of particular interest since maintenance rehearsal is thought to keep information active in short-term memory and coding rehearsal is thought to assist in the transfer of information from short-term store to long-term store.

In the multi-store model, rehearsal is viewed as just one of a number of strategies under an individual's conscious control. Rehearsal can expedite the movement of information throughout the structural components of the memory system. As has been noted elsewhere in this volume, information-processing strategies can only be effective with those items which have been selectively attended to. Unattended information is subject to rapid loss from short-term store. However, the loss can be delayed by means of verbal rehearsal, which also may assist in placing the information in long-term memory (Naus et al., 1978, p. 221)

As information moves through the sensory system to the short-term store and (if all is well) into long-term memory, a number of important factors come into play. Although short- and long-term memory can be thought of as "separate" entities within the multi-store system, they are not opposite or even distinct from each other in real life. There is probably considerable overlap between short-term memory (STM) and long-term memory (LTM). Attempts to measure the contents of memory must take this into account.

Typically, short-term memory is thought to hold a small amount of information that is actively being worked on, while long-term memory is a large body of information which is relatively permanently encoded (Anderson, 1980). This "permanent" information is not directly accessible to us, however. It must be moved from LTM to STM if it is to be used. (Just think of your grandmother's telephone number, or the color of the clothes you wore to your senior high graduation prom.) In the multi-store model, it is hypothesized that one reason it takes longer to recall information from long-term memory than from short-term memory is that the information in long-term store must be "reactivated" and moved into short-term store. Returning to our example of the names of state capitols, we now see that such information may be recalled with difficulty. It is unlikely, for example, that the names of state capitols represent well known and easily retrievable information. These to-be-remembered facts may, indeed, be associationally weak, and the memory network may not provide the information needed. This is particularly true if the information was only partially learned or attended to at the moment of learning. If, however, you were provided with a list of city names and state names and asked to match the city to the state, your success rate would probably be much higher. As you know, having taken hundreds of quizzes over your academic life, a recognition task is considered to be easier than a recall task from long-term memory. The memory search process is enhanced by the addition of this information, and the strategies required for completion are less sophisticated. The implications for testing language- and learning-disordered children may include, therefore, reviewing test items to see whether they call for recognition or recall. Analysis of test items from standardized or nonstandardized instruments will reflect the type of memorial task presented and will give some notion as to the level of sophistication of the required cognitive strategy.

There has been considerable criticism of the multi-store model (Duchan, 1981; Craik and Lockhart, 1972). This bottom-up processing model has served a number of useful purposes, however. It has assisted language specialists in directing their attention to memory processing and information retrieval as important components of language comprehension and production. It has given us new ways of thinking about attention, perception, memory, cognitive and mnemonic strategies, as well as recall, recognition, and retrieval.

In the multi-store model, memorial strategies are of particular interest because such strategies are assumed to be under the subject's conscious control. There is accumulating evidence that those strategies under a child's conscious control are both "knowable" and "teachable." At least certain strategies are thought to be relatively susceptible to change by development or environmental manipulation (Tarver et al, 1976; Finch and Spirito, 1980; Hall, 1980). A word of caution is necessary, however, since certain variables (such as attention, memorial "slots," speed of retrieval, and some academic behaviors) may not be as amenable to teaching and training (Tarver et al, 1976: Keogh and Glover, 1980; Torgeson, 1981).

We have said that the multi-store models have been criticized for presenting a perhaps simplified version of what must go on in the movement of information from the sensory registers through short-term memory and into long-term memory. As Norman (1979, p. 121) succinctly states:

"I cannot believe that the human mind is divided up into little compartments—this one doing perception, that one memory, this one emotional, that one rational. We are integrated, wholistic organisms, functioning in a complex diverse environment."

However, at the level of the clinic and the school, it is almost impossible to think about all things at once and to assess an "integrated organism" who may well be displaying some lack of integration in communication and learning. Thus, while it is important to recognize that the mind is not made up of compartments and that problems are not clean cut nor solutions definitive, it is also helpful to have some way of viewing the organism and the environment. Beginning clinicians are often overwhelmed by the challenges presented in assessment and intervention and in applying theory to practice. (See Chapter 17 for a summary of such difficulties.)

The Levels-of-Processing Models

In 1972, Craik and Lockhart proposed that the multi-store models needed to be revised in view of research conducted in the late 1960's and early 1970's. Essentially, it was hypothesized that remembering information rested upon the depth (or level) to which incoming perceptual information was processed. Here again we note a "series" approach, but this time it begins with the analysis of incoming sensory information (i.e., shallow processing) and progresses to the semantic and abstract level (i.e., deeper levels of processing). These models focus upon the specific information which is to be processed and require that one envision the processing stages as a series or a hierarchy "where greater 'depth' implies a greater degree of semantic or cognitive analysis. . . .analysis proceeds through a series of sensory stages to levels associated with matching or pattern recognition and finally to semantic-associative stages of stimulus enrichment" (Norman,

1979, pp. 122–123.) The emphasis in the Craik and Lockhart model (1972) is on (1) the importance of the *amount* of processing an item receives, rather than its placement in long-term or short-term memory; (2) the characteristics of the memory for an item which depends on how much processing it has received; (3) two different rehearsal processes existing—one type to maintain a memory image and the other to actively organize the information and, thus, to increase retrieval strength. In this model, the function of short-term memory is to hold information temporarily. That information is examined in the light of what is already in the long-term memory system and undergoes active organization (i.e., elaborative rehearsal) if it is to be processed at the deeper "levels" of semantic analysis. On the other hand, if information is to be held only temporarily in working memory, then maintenance rehearsal will suffice and the information will be forgotten.

Research with learning-disabled children has consistently demonstrated that they tend to use a less active and organized approach to memory tasks than do children who learn normally (Torgesen, 1980). Language learning-disabled children appear to be less successful in elaborative encoding processes, failing to rehearse either as much or as successfully (Torgesen and Goldman, 1977.)

It is obvious that there are components of top-down processing inherent in the levels-of-processing models. Information in long-term memory interacts with incoming data as it is being processed, permitting "new associations and new structures to be formed between the newly presented material and information currently stored in long-term memory" (Norman, 1979, p. 126). As noted earlier, sensory processing is thought to be highly transient, whereas semantic processing is thought to be more resistant to forgetting, i.e., is processed at a deeper level (Ornstein, 1978). In essence, "the levels of processing reflect the level of organization applied to information" (Norman, 1979, p. 128.) An example of this

might be the use of mnemonic strategies, those cues that we use to assist us in encoding difficult or lengthy material. You will read further about mnemonic strategies in this text under such terms as grouping, clustering, categorization, rhyming, and attention to critical elements. Imagery, spatial position, and organization are also powerful.

Of equal importance to students of all ages is the effect of context on encoding. The context at the moment of learning is thought to be linked with the newly formed memory units. That context can be either physical or emotional and, when replicated at the time of recall, will facilitate the recall of to-be-remembered items. A fascinating example is the study by Godden and Baddeley (1975). They requested that divers memorize a list of 40 unrelated words either 20 feet under the sea or on the shoreline. The subjects were asked to recall the unrelated words either in the same context in which the words were studied or in a different environment, i.e., "wet recall environment" or "dry recall environment." Recall was clearly superior under the same conditions of learning and retrieval. As you might suspect, neither "wet" nor "dry" conditions permitted the subjects to recall 40 unrelated words, a task of considerable difficulty. In fact, recall was limited to less than 12 unrelated words (still a goodly number for those of us who are landlubbers at heart and in mind). The experiment illustrates in a most dramatic fashion that context *is* important and that the context in which learning takes place facilitates recall if replicated at the time of testing. In this case, being "all wet" not once, but twice, appears to have its advantages.

Similar results are found when the emotional context is held constant (Bower et al., 1978). Interestingly enough, this is true whether the emotional state is positive or negative. Better recall appears to be the case when the emotional state at the time of testing is matched to the emotional state at the time of study (Anderson, 1980). As other research indicates, this may also be true of learning under certain drug-induced conditions (Eich et al., 1975; Parker et al., 1976). Such research findings raise interesting questions for practitioners concerned with the effects of medication on children (whether prescribed or nonprescribed), the emotional status of their clients, or even such a mundane but important issue as "carryover," that essential transfer of speech and language skills from the clinic to the real world of interactive communication.

We have said that the level to which information is processed is affected by the various encoding conditions present at the time of learning. In the level-of-processing memory models, recall is considered to be a by-product of the type of processing carried out on the material. In fact, as Craik and Tulving (1975, p. 269) state, it is "the operations carried out on the material, not the intention to learn, as such, (which determines) retention." Thus in more recent level-of-processing models of memory, there is a shift from viewing processing as proceeding sequentially from "shallow" to "deep" processing to a "spread" of processing (Mandler, 1979). Basic to the notion of the "spread" of processing is the interpretation of incoming information in terms of the individual's semantic knowledge. In fact, it may be that it is a "child's existing semantic knowledge (which) determines in a real sense what is remembered" (Naus et al., 1978, p. 228.) What is encoded in long-term memory reflects how many associations, both contextual and semantic, a child can make, not *necessarily* the child's intention to learn. That is an important distinction. Simply saying to a child, "Here is something I want you to remember" (i.e., directing his attentional resources) is clearly not enough.

Attempting to apply some of the things we have learned about levels of processing to children's memorial strategies requires us to deal with the difference between deliberate and nondeliberate (automatic) associative processing. Meyers and Perlmutter (1978) note that automatic associative processing in younger as well as older children may simply reflect the repeated use of certain activities, skills, and meanings, permitting recall from activation of an associational network (Collins and Loftus, 1975). How a child responds to questions reflects the activation of meaning in long-term memory with which the incoming information (in this case a question) interacts.

The following is a real-life example of automatic associative processing adapted from Butler, 1982, p. 25):

(1) Robert, age 2:11, is standing in a waiting room, with several pennies clenched securely in his fist. His father (attempting to teach the value of money) asks: What do you want to buy?

Robert: Meat.
Father: What else?
Robert: Ketchup.
Father: What do you *need* to get meat and ketchup?
Robert: French fries.
Father: French fries. What do you *have* to pay for the food?
Robert: (Nonintelligible response)
Father: *How* do you pay for the food?
Robert: (Nonintelligible response)
Mother: (Intervening) He doesn't understand the question, can't you see that?

Another example, this time provided by a boy, age 7:3, who was being examined by a speech-language pathologist for a language disorder, reveals a somewhat different processing strategy:

Examiner: Where does your father work?
Steven: Sicgo.
Examiner: What's that?
Steven: You know . . . when you're sick, you got to go.
(Examiner later determined that the father works at a Citgo service station.)

Yet a third example will permit us to look at *nonautomatic* (controlled) processing. Note how the child's search strategies utilize prior knowledge. Note also how other children respond when Tom's memory search does not immediately provide the required information. The scene is a later elementary classroom. The teacher is providing group instruction. It is a day like any other day in that such instruction requires extensive cognitive processing skills (adapted from Mosenthal, 1982):

Teacher: OK, Tom. What's a "contraction"?
Tom: It's like when ... a contraction ... you contract stuff.
Teacher: Yes, but what does "contraction" mean?
Tom: (No immediate response)
Students: I know! I know! (Susan among them)
Teacher: OK, Susan.
Susan: It's when you make something smaller.
Tom: Yea. When the road contracts, it gets broken up. Our driveway got contracts and broken up.
Lisa: You mean "cracks up."
Teacher: But what about the kind of contraction we learned about yesterday?
Robert: Oh, a "word contraction."
Teacher: Yes, What is a "word contraction"?
Susan: It's when you make a word smaller.
Tom: The word ... it gets broken up.
Teacher: Right. Excellent!

These three examples reflect the differences in memory performance across a number of dimensions. Developmental psychologists tend to support the level-of-processing model because they feel that it is the knowledge available in semantic memory which has implications both for what and how currently presented information can be remembered (Chi, 1977). It is easy to see that Robert, age 2:11, has less knowledge available to him in semantic memory then the older children in the other two examples. It is also easy to see that Steven's response to the question concerning where his father works reflects how the information was originally stored in memory and how he goes about attempting to retrieve it from long-term store. The third example provides yet another view of encoding and retrieval and focuses upon the differences among children. Susan's semantic and associational strengths are apparent throughout the example; Tom's responses are slower and reflect less adequate search strategies. Overall, however, one can see how the increasing semantic and conceptual knowledge of older children increases the extent to which they successfully encode information and are able to recall it from long-term memory. (Note the teacher's comment: "But what about the kind of

contraction we learned about yesterday?").

It is important to remember that both the multi-store model and the levels-of-processing model were designed to explain what goes on in adult memory. It has only been relatively recently that attempts have been made to apply the models to children. We shall discuss children's memory processing following a brief summary of the two models.

A Comparison between Multi-Store and Levels-of-Processing Models

DIFFERENCES

These models differ in theoretical orientation and in some basic assumptions about the memory system. Such differences lead to asking research questions differently, performing experiments differently, and interpreting the outcomes differently. For the clinician who attempts to derive applications to assessment and intervention, it also leads to thinking about test instruments and remediation approaches differently. In fact, it is possible to use the same test for entirely different reasons and interpret the results in distinctly different ways, all based upon the selection of a certain framework for verbal learning and memory.

Multi-store models permit one to think about at least three types of memory storage: sensory register, short-term, and long-term. Information comes in through the sensory system (e.g., visual or auditory) and flows through the system in a well regulated way, entering first short-term store and then, if attended to, rehearsed, and encoded, into long-term store. Under the individual's conscious control are certain processes or strategies for maintaining and processing information. Such control processes may change according to the task and the type of incoming stimuli. As we know from our own experience, not all information is retained. It may be lost from short-term store due to decay of the memory trace (Remember when you could not remember a telephone number you had just looked up in the telephone book?) or by displacement of information by other incoming information (Remember how you could not remember the names of all the people you met at last night's party?) Information may also be lost from long-term store due to interference or temporary irretrievability (Naus et al., 1978). Not everything that goes into long-term store can be retrieved easily on a "demand basis," a factor well known to clinicians attempting to teach vocabulary, for example. In fact, how and why one forgets may be as important as how and why one remembers (Spear, 1976) (Parenthetically, forgetting can be attributed to one of two general causes: (1) the failure to retrieve formerly stored information due to ineffective or inefficient recall of the attributes of that memory unit or (2) the failure to have stored the information appropriately during encoding of the attributes. As Estes notes, it is not currently possible to assess forgetting and to identify whether it is due to a retrieval failure or to a storage failure, since the two factors cannot be measured independently.)

Important to the multi-store model is the concept that short-term memory is limited in capacity, whereas long-term memory is seen as essentially unlimited. It is thought that information is "held in short-term store in an auditory-verbal-linguistic code, whereas storage (is) primarily semantic in long-term store" (Naus et al., 1978, p. 220). Within the multi-store model, the storage and retrieval of information is under the subject's direct control and involves rehearsal strategies, coding, and search plans. The structural features of the model of the memory system are considered similar to a computer system's hardware. The various memory stores (sensory, short- and long-term) are relatively fixed and remain the same across memory tasks. On the other hand, control processes might be considered as software, with the individual processing the information as the programmer who is capable of varying his storage and retrieval operations according to the task at hand (Naus et al., 1978).

The multi-store model also permits the viewing of memory in another manner, as *episodic* and *semantic*. Episodic memories are those recalled as specific, temporally dated events. They are autobiographical, in the sense that your recollection of your twenty-first birthday is unlike another individual's recall of the same point in his life history. Episodic memories can be lost or transformed. (Try to recall your third birthday or your first day in a new school; try, even, to recall what your supervisor told you about how you might better conduct your most recent diagnostic session.) It is highly likely that each of those three events has either been lost or has been transformed, and no longer represents the actual events. Semantic memories are language based and, as such, have lost their relationship to specific autobiographical references. Rather, semantic memories represent recall of generalized knowledge. (If you were asked to describe an apple, you might say "It's a fruit; it's red, you eat it; it tends to be more round then oblong; it's crunchy," despite the fact that at lunch today you ate a yellow apple which was mealy and in which you discovered an unappetizing worm.) In the next section, we will look at semantic-episodic distinctions as currently proposed by researchers interested in children's memory processing.

Let us now look at the levels-of-processing models. They essentially provide for interpretation of incoming information in terms of the contents of the long-term memory system. The initial level of processing involves sensory features, and analysis starts with the "shallow" sensory processing and progresses through deeper and deeper levels of abstract and semantic processing. Presumably, the retention of information has to do with the *depth* of processing; information processed at the shallower levels will not be retained as easily as information which has been processed to greater depths. The conditions at the time of encoding also have an effect on what is stored in memory. Central to the levels-of-processing model is the notion that the *manner* of studying the to-be-remembered material is critical for ultimate retrievability. In this model, structural features (i.e., the memory "stores") are much less important, whereas the control processes (i.e., how one consciously processes incoming information) are seen as central. It is the nature of the activity at the moment of learning which is seen as primary to how one retains and retrieves information. Recall is thought to be a by-product of the type of processing carried out on the material as that information interacts with the individual's semantic knowledge. It is hypothesized that material that is deeply processed will be remembered more effectively.

SIMILARITIES

Both multi-store and levels-of-processing models have undergone significant revisions over the past few years (Craik and Jacoby, 1975; Lockhart et al., 1976; Jacoby and Craik, 1978). "Memory processes" are now important in both models (Shiffrin and Schneider, 1977; Naus and Halasz, 1978). Although the terminology and the emphasis may differ between the models, many of the same processes are observed, albeit from varying points of view (Ornstein, 1978). Developmental psychologists have found the levels-of-processing model to be somewhat more appealing since it lends itself to looking at children's processing of information more easily. However, as Naus et al. (1978) point out, both memory frameworks are quite general and it may be that both can account equally well (or poorly) for the information we now have about memory.

Application of Multi-Store and Levels-of-Processing Models to Children's Memory Development

Naus et al. (1978) reviewed both models and attempted to determine the extent to which each might be applicable to the understanding of memory in children. They concluded that, despite the problems inherent in both models, it is "possible that the models can serve as alternate metaphors

which are differentially useful for assessment of memory development" (p. 225).

MULTI-STORE MODEL

In this model, there may be no major age-related changes in memory structures. Rather, the age changes that are seen (what others might call "the development of memory") are, in reality, substantial changes in the control processes (rehearsal, search plans, etc.). Thus, increased recall of information is presumed to reflect increased use of mnemonic strategies or control processes. Children of different ages, according to Naus et al., differ in the techniques used to control the movement of information through the multi-storage system. They point out that, by the age of 12 or so, children's use of organizational and rehearsal techniques has developed into a series of task-appropriate strategies. A difficulty with the multi-store model is that it does not explain how memory can occur when it is unintended (i.e., nondeliberate). Incidental learning and recall seem to be important aspects of how children learn (Corsale and Ornstein, 1977) and are more difficult to explain in this model.

LEVELS-OF-PROCESSING MODEL

In this model, children become more skilled in the processing of information, encoding material to deeper levels. Memory improves because processing reaches greater semantic depths. Naus et al. (1978) note that the major developmental trends in memory performance appear to be related to how children become more efficient in their use of strategies and that the levels-of-processing model accomodates to this domain somewhat more easily. In addition, because it is concerned with the semantic knowledge base, the model provides a way of looking at memory as a by-product of other activities (increases in nondeliberate memory). It also provides a way of looking at children's everyday use of memory which may be helpful in determining how semantic integration occurs (see Chapters 11 and 12). The reader is referred to Paris (1978) for a review of how children's comprehension of sentences influences recall and of the importance of the ability to establish inferential relationships within sentences to memory retention. The levels-of-processing model emphasizes semantic and conceptual knowledge and its influence on successful encoding; the multi-store models emphasize the importance of short-term store and its control over incoming stimuli and entrance into long-term store. Just how newly acquired information is integrated into the child's changing "storehouse of knowledge" is not clearly identified in either model, however (Naus et al., 1978).

Developmental psychologists have been puzzled by the evidence that young children are capable of various mnemonic activities long before they spontaneously use such strategies (Flavell, 1970). Paris (1978) concludes that it is the child's perception of the task demands and his motivation for remembering which may account for this evidence. It is the child's goals which are important; not the goals of the examiner or teacher, at least for a young child. As Paris (1978, p. 154) notes:

"... constructive skills of comprehension are relative to the child's standards and goals within a given task or context. That is why the young child's memory may not be inefficient, incorrect, or deficient by the child's standards. The child's means of remembering are often consistent with his goals and commensurate with his perceptions of remembering as a skill."

In addition, the failure to use processing strategies, and the errors in performance which reflect that failure, may not truly reflect the capacities of children (Roberts, 1981, p. 71). It is important to look at both successes and failures in the assessment process, or, for that matter, in the intervention process. Roberts believes that there has been an overemphasis on children's limitations and that normal children's failure of a task does not necessarily reflect their skill in the components of the domain being tested. He points out that there are multiple sources of error, including what he considers to be unnecessary task complexities among some Piagetian tasks. He notes that most 3- or 4-year-olds are able to sort a set of blocks by their colors *or* their shapes, if done separately (Fischer and Roberts, 1980). However, when they are required to sort blocks simultaneously by both shape and color, the sorting becomes random and their ability to sort by color *or* shapes is not apparent. Thus, although children may have certain skills, these skills are not always used or combined in a higher order task (Fischer, 1980; Siegler, 1976). Given such a conclusion, it behooves examiners to analyze any assessment task or battery to determine the matrix of skills necessary for a correct response.

As noted earlier, episodic and semantic memories are considered to be different *types* of memory. Tulving (1972, p. 386) first attempted to describe semantic memory as "a mental thesaurus, organized knowledge a person possesses about words and other verbal symbols, their meaning and referents, about relations among them, and about rules, formulas, and algorithms for the manipulation of these symbols, concepts and relations." The two systems (episodic and semantic) are thought to differ from one another "in terms of: (1) the nature of the stored information; (2) autobiographical versus cognitive reference; and (3) the conditions and consequences of retrieval" (Nelson and Brown, 1978, p. 234). However, there appears to be some general confusion about the application of those terms to laboratory and real-life tasks, particularly when one attempts to measure the memory performance of younger children. Nelson and Brown claim that simply because young children are poor at memorizing isolated lists of words or materials under laboratory conditions does not mean that they have poor episodic memories, in the autobiographical and short-term sense. They point out that if the term episodic is used to refer to all autobiographical real-world occurrences, then young children's memory is "all episodic and only later develops a semantic component" (p. 239). They also point out that, while episodic memories are multimodal (verbal, imagic), what eventually emerges in the semantic system is a language-based organization which no longer reflects the episodic origins. However, in some manner not yet clearly understood, from the basic episodic event comes semantic memories which permit us to speak about cognitive maps, scripts, story structures, categorical relationships, and the like.

SUMMARY

We have seen that multi-store and levels-of-processing models both address the matter of how information is registered, coded, stored, and retrieved. We have also seen that because the levels-of-processing model appears to be somewhat more appropriate for dealing with children's memorial strategies, it has been used recently as a framework for the investigation of children's memorial processing, since it tends to focus upon semantic knowledge and the changing base of that knowledge. A number of the chapters in this text deal with the child's semantic knowledge (see Chapters 11 and 12) and suggest how one might approach measurement and intervention. Prior to suggesting some principles for such assessment and remediation, it is necessary to consider a third model, one which draws upon both the multi-store and levels-of-processing models and provides a way of utilizing information about bottom-up and top-down processing. Norman (1979) has attempted to combine recent research in perception, memory, and mental processes within a framework of cognitive processing which incorporates "schema-driven" analysis.

Cognitive Processing

Norman (1979) points out that bottom-up (data-driven) analysis of incoming sensory information and top-down (conceptually guided) analysis are not necessarily conflicting models. Both are necessary, he states, but neither is sufficient (p. 125). The importance of attention, perception, and memory requires that they be considered together. As Norman emphasizes, thought,

language, and problem solving all "result from processes that operate on knowledge structures; and because only the outcome of the processing is observable, psychological studies cannot distinguish between structure and process" (p. 123). Despite our inability to sort out how information is represented in memory from the processing of that information, there *are* a number of phenomena which appear to be well established. Norman points out that:

1. Given a perceptual task, expectations can improve performance. While "one cannot perceive the whole without perceiving the parts, . . . the perception of the parts is guided by the perception of the whole" (p. 122).

2. The ability to retrieve information depends on the activity undertaken at the time of encoding. But, as Norman indicates, the activity at the time of learning is dependent upon, and guided by, memories of similar or related events, and there is a matching process between the current task and past events.

3. Processing becomes more difficult when novel tasks or complex stimuli must be learned. Conscious attention to processing calls for attentional resources which are then withdrawn from other activities. However, when information or skills are well practiced, the processing load is lightened, and little attention or conscious processing may be required.

Norman essentially proposed that the perceptual analysis of incoming stimuli is "guided by the overall goal of establishing an integrated interpretation of the events of the world" (p. 126). Such an integrated interpretation requires that perceptual events be interpreted though existing memory schemas. In his view, schemas control the analysis and interpretation of both perceptual and memorial information. Such schema-driven analysis goes well beyond the sequential, serial processing mechanisms observed in the multi-store models. Norman believes there is evidence for multiple processing structures which interact in some controlled fashion with each other but also are able to perform independently (p. 134). He also believes that the conceptually driven (top-down) model is insufficient for all situations. Memory schema analysis, on the other hand, provides for the flow of processing that is simultaneously data driven and cognitively driven:

"Data-driven analysis starts from the bottom . . . and flows upward, attempting to identify the sensory information on the basis of the features present. Conceptually driven analysis uses the preliminary results of the data-driven analyses to make suggestions about possible patterns, guiding the efforts of the data-driven process" (p. 137).

As these two analyses continue, a "memory schema" is selected, which further assists in guiding the search for interpretation. If there is sufficient perceptual data to support that interpretation, the memory schema is confirmed. If not, the search proceeds through other memory schemas, until a schema is found which efficiently organizes the incoming information in an appropriate manner. Basic to this concept of "analysis by a pool of memory schemas" is that the flow of information is *not* characterized by "down" or "up." Stages of processing disappear in this particular model of cognitive processing.

Schemas represent our previous experience which is embedded in both an internal and external context, and thus memory schema analysis has also been identified as "inside-out" processing (Pearson, 1982). When we hear the word "bear" without a surrounding context, we do not know whether to relate it to "bear" or "bare," or even (if we have faulty perceptual knowledge or a great thirst!) to "beer" (Butler, 1982). The words in such sentences as "I saw a bear in the woods," "I saw that the baby's bare feet were dirty," and "He wanted to bare his soul" certainly call forth differing memory schemas if they are to be interpreted within the context of the sentence.

Experience tends to create vast numbers of memory units or schemas, and it is well for us that they do. Learning and problem solving require that we engage in schema-based processing, in all likelihood. How new information is integrated into memory schemas (i.e., old information) is not yet fully understood. Norman (1979) indicates that there may be no single, uniform representation of knowledge. There are probably important differences between procedural knowledge (i.e., knowledge for doing things) and declarative knowledge (i.e., knowledge about things.) While there may not be fundamentally different representations for procedural and declarative knowledge, Norman hypothesizes that declarative knowledge may not always be as easily accessible since it may be embedded within procedures that apply the knowledge. Note how often examiners ask children to "define," "describe," "itemize," or "identify" objects or concepts but how rarely they ask children to reveal, perhaps in nonverbal terms, "how" to apply a concept or use an object. Again, we see that children may "know" but not know that they know. Worse, those who test children's knowledge and language skills may not know that they know, since the information is not easily accessible within the constraints of the test setting and test items. For example, clinicians are often surprised at the relative paucity of information which is provided when a young child is asked, "Tell me all about this ____" (pointing to a block of wood, an envelope, a toy car, a picture of a hummingbird, etc.) or "Describe how you jump rope . . . no, don't show me, tell me." The resulting attempts to codify past experience with such objects may not fully reflect the child's understanding. Indeed, the task and the child's cognitive abilities may not be able to be separated. Trabasso and others (1978) have found that even a minor task variation can lead to significant changes in performance. However, for an encouraging view of how children may be reliably assessed, in certain developmental sequences and in language, the reader is referred to Bertenthal (1981) and Fischer and Corrigan (in press).

Attention

As noted in the discussion of memory in the memory-schema or inside-outside processing mode, attention is an important component of any model which attempts to deal with how children process information. Selective attention is required when information is encoded or placed in memory. As Norman (1979, p. 28) stated, conscious attending requires the use of attentional resources, which are limited. Selective attention has been described as attending to some mental activities in preference to others (Kahneman, 1973). Such a description of attention is only one way of viewing it (Torgeson, 1981).

As Torgeson points out, there are two ways of viewing the concept of attention in the current literature. However, those who refer children for a "short attention span" to a language specialist or a psychologist are frequently unaware of the fact that the short attention span to which they refer may be viewed in anything but a very global sense. The examiner would be wise to ask for specific information, i.e., when and where was the attention span noted to be "short," so that assessment can be more relevant to the child's abilities and disabilities.

Frequently, those who refer children for inability to attend appear to be making the basic assumption that attention is, indeed, a mental activity or capacity which is independent of specific tasks or settings (Torgeson, 1981). Unfortunately, a corollary to this assumption, then, is that the child may be inattentive under all circumstances. (Anyone who has watched a "hyperactive" child sit entranced for hours by Pac-Man would suspect that such assumptions may not be valid.) Gibson and Rader (1979), and many others, view attention as an information-processing activity directly related to specific goals and tasks. In this sense, attention is dependent rather than independent of the internal and external factors existent at the time of learning new information or processing old information. Attentional deficits noted in language- and learning-disordered children may more accurately reflect "deficiencies in information-processing behaviors that may result from a mismatch between individual and classroom goals, a failure to apply efficient strategies for processing information, or a lack of organized cognitive schemes that can direct appropriate information processing for a given task" (Torgenson, 1981, pp. 52–53). The reader may find excellent examples of the mismatch between individual and classroom goals in Chapters 8 and 14.

There is a considerable body of research literature on attention (Estes, 1976; Norman, 1979; Anderson, 1980, among others.) The application to attentional disorders has begun (Kinsbourne and Caplan, 1971; Sexton and Geffen, 1979; Smith, 1981; Butler, in press). Whether one subscribes to a multi-store, levels-of-processing, or memory-schema analysis of how children process, store, and retrieve information, it is obvious that attentional factors must be taken into account. This brief discussion does no more than alert the reader to its importance.

THE ASSESSMENT OF LANGUAGE PROCESSING

For those who must translate theory into practice well before the theory lends itself to such extrapolation and who must assess language- and learning-disordered children with an eye (or an ear) to appropriate remediation strategies, the road is clearly strewn with boulders and potholes. It is slight comfort that the "experts" are not very expert when it comes to "telling us what to do." Norman (1979) makes the point that we know little about cognitive functions and the mechanisms which may underlie them. We spoke earlier about conscious control processes and automatic processing without conscious awareness, yet we have little information about what it means for a system to be conscious. While we await further understanding of mental representation, processing, and control structures, practitioners must use what is available, knowing full well that no single test or battery is sufficient.

Coles (1978) has extensively reviewed the validation studies of the 10 most frequently recommended procedures for diagnosing learning disabilities, and he finds much to criticize. He cites the Illinois Test of Psycholinguistic Abilities, the Gender Visual-Motor Gestalt Test, the Frostig Developmental Test of Visual Perception, the Wepman Auditory Discrimination Test, the Lincoln-Oseretsky Motor Development Scale, the Graham-Kendall Memory for Designs Test, the Purdue Perceptual-Motor Survey, the Wechsler Intelligence Scale for Children (WISC), a neurological evaluation by a neurologist, and an electroencephalogram (EEG). He concludes that within the "perceptual tests" only Auditory Association, Grammatic Closure, and Sound Blending are minimally predictive of reading success. Within the "intelligence tests" framework, Coles concludes that the significance of WISC scores is obscure, noting that "it is not clear whether WISC results reflect language, perceptual-motor, or academic problems; whether reading achievement is a consequence of abilities comprising intelligence; or whether both reading achievement and WISC scores reflect a third factor" (p. 322). Neurological evaluations and EEG testing are also reviewed and found to be unproductive in Cole's view. However, it should be noted that Cole's statements reflect studies completed in the 1960's and early 1970's, and it is doubtful if sophisticated examiners today would rely solely, or substantially, on the instruments cited. It may be that some of the instruments are used, but for different purposes and using newer forms of analysis (see Chapter 7).

A more positive view, albeit cautionary, is presented by Farnham-Diggory (1980). She touches upon modern cognitive theories and points out that the results of recent experiments open the way toward an understanding of learning disabilities. She, too, points out that traditional tests, like the Illinois Test of Psycholinguistic Abilities, may not be appropriate for "detecting 'now you see it, now you don't' defects that depend critically upon task characteristics" (p. 571). She stresses that new procedures for testing short-term memory, word recognition, and other cognitive functions provide compelling evidence that task characteristics are crucial and that the brain functions differentially. Cited is Ojemann's work (1979a, 1979b; Ojemann and Whitaker, 1978) that brain sites for different tasks are readily distinguishable. For example, when word meanings are tested in bilingual subjects in one language, they appear to be located in one site whereas word meanings in the other language are found in another site. Farnham-Diggory concludes that research into learning disabilities must include a thorough analysis of the experimental tasks which attempt to identify that disability. However, she points out that complex mental processes cannot be measured as yet under ordinary testing conditions since they require laboratory equipment not yet routinely available. She concludes that traditional tests (such as those identified by Coles) are not sufficiently pure measures of the basic cognitive processes and urges that modern diagnostic batteries by closely linked to modern research on cognitive development.

If we are not to assess using the so-called traditional tests, or, at the very least, if we are to use and interpret such tests in the light of recent findings in cognitive psychology, where shall we turn? Emerging from the literature are some initial attempts to develop multidirectional models which address the information-processing aspects of performance (Swanson, 1982) and attempt to look at the knowledge base which influences the development of cognitive strategies, problem solving, and metacognitive skills. It should be remembered, however, that assessment models, evaluation instruments, and the technical aspects of diagnostic batteries are only part of the picture. "Measurement competence" includes the ability to select appropriate procedures and to interpret the data adequately (Bennett, 1981).

In Chapter 1 the reader was introduced to the concept of information processing in reference to Perfetti's 1977 model of reading comprehension. This suggests that research in reading comprehension is of some importance not only to the analysis of reading difficulties, but also to the analysis of language in all its forms. In fact, it is apparent from a review of the literature in speech-language pathology, reading and learning disabilities, and applied linguistics (Brown, 1981; Sajavaara, 1981) that a variety of disciplines have begun to analyze language within an information-processing model. Thus the literature across disciplines can provide assistance in identifying procedures and tasks which will permit the examiner to assess language learning disorders (Perfetti, 1977, Leu, 1981; Calfee et al., 1979; Vetter, 1982). In addition, the chapters which relate specifically tő assessment and intervention strategies for language learning-disabled students may be found in Section III. The reader will find a number of commonalities reflecting the converging interest in assessment of the broad parameters of language comprehension and production (or, as the cognitive scientist would say, in the processing and recall of language.) As later chapters in this volume reveal, evaluation includes not only phonology, syntax, semantics, and pragmatics, but it is suggested that assessment might profitably include metalinguistic and metacognitive skills, narrative abilities, problem solving, and interactional competencies in instructional settings.

Based upon the models of processing discussed earlier in this chapter, it is also recommended that assessment be extended to:

1. *Attention,* focused or divided

2. *Perceptual processing,* by and across modalities

3. *Memory,* short term, long term, and memory schemas

4. *Rehearsal strategies,* maintenance and coding

5. *Search procedures,* automatic and controlled

6. *Retrieval,* recall and recognition

7. *Processing load,* including complexity of message

8. *Temporal aspects of processing,* including response time at the millisecond level, if possible

9. *Facilitation of responses* via *diagnostic teaching*

10. *Metalinguistic and metacognitive* variables.

Not only the quantity and correctness of responses should be noted, but the quality of the responses should be analyzed. Following an analysis of these factors, it is helpful to assess potentially optimal performance by altering the moment of testing, altering the environmental cues, providing pretest cues and pretest training, modifying the level of semantic processing required, using nonlinguistic cues to assist comprehension, and so forth.

Assessment contexts should be varied as well (Butler, 1981a, 1981b). For example, some notion of the child's ability to process information in daily life may be determined by varying:

1. The rate at which input stimuli are provided, noting the differential performance under speeded and nonspeeded conditions;

2. The time between the stimulus and the elicitation of a response, in effect, asking the child to hold an item in short-term memory under maintenance rehearsal conditions;

3. The conditions of testing, providing for auditory or linguistic distractors, noting the effect on attention, perception, and mnemonic strategies;

4. The directions, moving from clear, un-

ambiguous instructions to those requiring metacognitive skills, i.e., deciding whether the instructions can, in fact, be carried out;

5. The context of assessment, moving from an interactive setting with others present and engaged in communication to the decontextualized setting, involving solitary reading performance;

6. The level of semantic networking and memory pool analysis, noting response differences when well known rote information is sought versus the recall of partially known or newly learned information over varying time intervals (adapted from Butler, 1982).

Probe questions have been recommended as a method of eliciting metalinguistic and metacognitive variables (Swanson, 1982), but it should also be recalled that various question *forms* require different degrees of memory processing and place different levels of demands on the child. For example, a Wh-question which requires the retrieval of a specific piece of information (i.e., a recall task) is considered to be more difficult than a yes-no question requiring a recognition response only (Ratner, 1980), to say nothing of the more complex questions attempting to deal with metacognitive variables.

A final note on episodic and semantic memory processing: It has been suggested that episodic memory processing may be less difficult than semantic memory processing since it tends to deal with the "here and now" in large measure. Questions which relate to past and future events will be more likely to elicit memories which are language based and reflect deeper levels of processing. It should be apparent that asking a child to name five pictures present on the table in front of him varies significantly from asking the same child to name five animals he is likely to see at a zoo, and this second task also varies significantly from asking the child to make up a story about Darth Vader.

With this all-too-brief overview of some of the principles of assessment, let us now turn our attention to language processing intervention.

LANGUAGE PROCESSING INTERVENTION: ASSUMPTIONS AND POSSIBLE STRATEGIES

We must return to the research literature on normal processing in order to derive our assumptions about intervention. It is important to recall, however, that in attempting to assist children with language and learning disabilities, application of adult models of processing may not be totally appropriate. There is a growing body of literature on the development of memory in children and how memory strategies may be identified which can assist us in developing both assessment and intervention procedures.

Although there remains a major research emphasis on the operation of children's memory strategies, this is augmented by current interest in the nondeliberate (incidental) memory strategies used by young children. Particularly during the early years, children acquire much of their information in an incidental and nondeliberate manner (Ornstein, 1978). How and why this occurs must be taken into account when designing "memory instruction." As Paris (1978, p. 146) reports, "numerous studies have shown that if children are required to organize, label, elaborate or recall items according to adult strategies, their memory performance improves. However, the enhanced effectiveness is usually short lived ..." Simply instructing children to "listen," to "remember," or to "think" may be insufficient. We must take into account the child's own notion of how *relevant* the chosen memory tasks may be to his or her own memory goals.

Paris (1978, p. 153) points out that even young children "may not need to be taught to be constructive, or inferential, or associative per se, but rather to use these skills appropriately in the context of remembering." This is not to say that *past experience* and *practice* do not also provide children with new relationships and pragmatic inferences among and between words. It does say that word knowledge and the rapid growth of memory between the ages of 6 and 12 among normal children may reflect how children learn to *infer* relationships *to aid memory* as well as the simple acquisition of new information.

How do children, even young children, infer relationships? In a series of experiments (Paris et al., 1977; Paris and Lindauer, 1977), it was found that young children could infer relationships within sentences and use indirect cues to aid recall when the goal was to act out a story or to generate a story rather than to remember the sentences. Intervention, then, should consider the use of tasks which require recall under conditions which call into play nondeliberate processing strategies. Westby (see Chapter 6) identifies three patterns of difficulty in structuring stories, or narratives, for school-aged children with language learning disabilities. These include inefficient processing, organizational difficulties, and insufficient schema knowledge. She also cites some educational implications for such patterns of difficulty. The clinician might consider combining the experimental efforts of Paris et al. (1977) and Paris and Lindauer (1977) which required that children draw inferences through the acting out of stories with Westby's comments in Chapter 6 regarding narrative discourse. Such memory "activities" would also provide the clinician with an opportunity to (1) observe the macrostructure and microstructures of the narrative, or story; (2) observe the relationship between semantic and inferential strategies; and (3) observe the level of language competence as demonstrated by the production of the story. As Westby points out, the only way to have children learn to produce better narratives is to be surrounded by and have opportunities to produce such narratives.

She suggests pretend play as one method of increasing narrative and literate language, since pretend play requires role taking, sequencing and planning of events, increasing degrees of symbolic representations, and decontextualization (see p. 124). She concludes that students need to hear others relate and interpret experiences by and through personal narratives as well as to develop their own. She cautions that children should not be interrupted by questions from adults in this task. While well formed narratives may be modeled by other students or by teachers and clinicians, the child's comprehension and production of a narrative text reflects a holistic schema and should not be interrupted. This is but one example of how research and practice may be wedded to provide an interventional strategy.

The research data also reflect a number of assumptions which can be used as the basis for designing intervention strategies, including:

1. Providing rehearsal training strategies which assist in the organization of information for recall purposes. "Deliberate" memorizing (in contrast to the nondeliberate tasks specified in the earlier example) is of critical importance in the provision of a "data base" or knowledge "storehouse" of memory schemas in long-term memory.

2. Providing tasks which require conscious monitoring strategies and attentional resources for specific lengths of time. Such tasks as "make a mark with your crayon whenever you hear the name of a bird in this word list" require vigilance, attention, and semantic and metacognitive skills.

3. Providing tasks which require different presentation conditions and permitting the child to control the response rate. This permits the child to monitor and to respond to speeded tasks in a self-regulatory fashion.

4. Providing tasks which permit the

child to engage in self-testing procedures. (For example, to ask one's self such questions as, "Do I know this? How much do I know? What are the specifics of what I have just read (or heard)?" The generation of self-monitoring techniques may be provided by the clinician initially, but ideally this becomes part of the child's memorial strategies over time.

5. Providing tasks and materials which permit the child to utilize subskills or component skills of a larger cognitive task prior to performance of that larger task. For example, before asking a child to read a difficult story or passage which contains unknown or partially known words, present the words within the context of a word or phrase from their own experience. Write the word on the board. Have the child write the word. Ask the child to tell you any other words which may be related in some way to the target word(s). Ask the child to group the words into categories which seem relevant. Such activities are referred to as semantic mapping by various authors (Hagen, 1979; Johnson et al., 1982).

6. Providing instruction which assists children in the acquisition of mnemonic devices, such as chunking, clustering, rhyming, acronyms, categorizing, etc. Note that direct teaching of organizational skills is more likely to be effective with children 8 years and older (Bjorklund et al., 1977).

7. Providing instruction in the qualitative aspects of recall. For example, rehearsal type or quality (not just quantity) can be monitored through overt rehearsal, and "active" rehearsal, rather than passive or rote rehearsal patterns, can be encouraged. Teach children to rehearse *all* the stimuli, not just a portion of them; teach them to manipulate the stimuli in the interval between item presentations and request for recall.

These are but a few of the assumptions and suggestions which may prove helpful in the design of intervention strategies and programs. There are a few training programs which utilize the information processing approach. An example is Feuerstein's (1979a, 1979b) instrumental enrichment program. Such programs have been developed to assist children and/or adults who were thought to be mentally retarded, and they can be adapted or utilized, at least in part, for children with language learning difficulties. The reader will find numerous examples of intervention procedures interwoven throughout this volume, either explicitly stated or implicit within the authors' comments about the growth of language skills among normal and language learning-disabled children.

CLOSING REMARKS

This chapter began by suggesting that you conduct a relatively simple processing task, that of saying and "seeing" the alphabet, requiring little in the way of attentional, perceptual, memorial, or cognitive performance. We then discussed how individuals acquire information (much as you early on acquired the alphabet) and suggested that those dealing with language- and learning-disordered children must be interested in not only the child's comprehension and production of language but in how it came to be perceived, attended to, rehearsed, encoded, and stored in memory for later recall. A distinction has been made between process and product, if you will.

There is considerable evidence from cognitive psychology (Sternberg, 1981) that research is having a positive effect on assessment, which will then lead to theory-guided cognitive tasks which can be utilized in training individuals to certain skill and performance levels. A number of models have been proposed into which some cognitive tasks fit more neatly than others. We have identified three possible models, all bearing some similarity to each other: the multi-store model of memory, the levels-of-processing model, and the memory schema model. We have reported that each model brings to us some important information which can be used in assessment and intervention, but we have also noted that each provides some difficulty for researchers and practitioners alike. It has been suggested that there is some important information to be gained from looking at assessment and intervention in the light of these models and in viewing test items and test tasks not only in terms of the child's response to the test or task, but also as to the possible role cognitive processing deficits may play. Finally, we have focused upon memory and memory strategies as likely candidates for assessment and intervention.

Sternberg (1981, p. 1187) points out that "information-processing tests seem to open up diagnostic possibilities that are not available with psychometric testing. Whereas factor or subtest scores ... are useful in pointing out broad areas in which training should take place, they do not specify just what should be trained." He notes that if information-processing tests are used, it is possible to identify whether certain processing components are available, accessible, and efficiently executed, and, if not, to identify the nature of the processing difficulties. However, he notes that such testing is expensive and time consuming and recommends it for exceptional cases only. But then, is not that the type of cases we deal with? Exceptional children require exceptional assessment and intervention.

We conclude the chapter by asking that you attempt to generate from long-term memory an assessment for a language learning-disabled child, jotting down the outline on paper so that you may then evaluate your own ability to process, code, and recall previously learned information in concert with this newly learned information to achieve your own clinical goals.

References

Anderson JR: *Cognitive Psychology and Its Implications.* San Francisco, WH Freeman, 1980.

Atkinson RD, Shiffrin RM: Human memory: a proposed system and its control processes. In Spence KW, Spence JT: *The Psychology of Learning and Motivation.* New York, Academic Press, 1968, vol 2.

Atkinson RD, Shiffrin RM: The control of short-term memory. *Sci Am* 236:82–90, 1971.

Baddeley AD: Short-term memory for word sequences as a function of acoustic, semantic and formal similarity. *Q J Exp Psychol* 18:362–375, 1966.

Bennett RE: Professional competence and the assessment of exceptional children. *J Spec Educ* 15:437–446, 1981.

Bertenthal BI: The significance of developmental sequences for investigating the what and how of development. *Cognitive Dev* 12:43–55, 1981.

Bjorklund DF, Ornstein PA, Haig JR: Developmental differences in organization and recall: training in the use of organizational techniques. *Dev Psychol* 13:175–183, 1977.

Bower GH, Monteiro KP, Gilligan SG: Emotional mood as a context for learning and recall. *J Verbal Learn Verbal Behav* 17:573–587, 1978.

Brown G: Teaching the spoken language. *Stud Linguistica* 35:166–182, 1981.

Butler KG: Language processing disorders: factors in diagnosis and remediation. In Keith R: *Central Auditory and Language Disorders in Children.* Houston, College Hill Press, 1981a, 160–174.

Butler KG: Language disorders: assessment of certain comprehension factors. Presented at the Sixth World Congress of the International Association of Applied Linguistics, University of Lund, Sweden, August, 1981b.

Butler KG: Auditory processing in perspective. In de Montfort-Supple M: *Language Disability: Congenital and Acquired: Proceedings of the Second Seminar in Language Disability.* Dun Laoghaire, Ireland, Boole Press, 1982, 16–38.

Butler KG: Language processing: selective attention and mnemonic strategies. In Katz J, Lasky E: *Central Auditory Processing Disorders: Problems of Speech, Language and Learning.* Baltimore, University Park Press, 1983, 297–318.

Calfee R, Spector J, Piontkowsi: Assessing reading and language skills: an interactive system. *Curr Issues Dyslexia; Bull Orton Soc* 29:129–156, 1979.

Chi MT: Age differences in memory span. *J Exp Child Psychol* 23:266–289, 1977.

Coles GS: The learning-disabilities test battery: empirical and social issues. *Harvard Educ Rev* 48:313–339, 1978.

Collins AM, Loftus EF: A spreading-activation theory of semantic processing. *Psychol Rev* 82:407–428, 1975.

Corsale K, Ornstein PA: Developmental changes in the use of semantic information in recall. Presented at the Psychonomic Society, Washington DC, November, 1977.

Craik FIM: Two components in free recall. *J Verbal Learn Verbal Behav* 7:996–1004, 1968.

Craik FIM: The fate of primary memory items in free recall. *J Verbal Learn Verbal Behav* 9:142–148, 1970.

Craik FIM, Jacoby LL: A process view of short-term retention. In Restle F, Shiffrin RM, Castellan NJ, et al: *Cognitive Theory.* Hillsdale, NJ, Lawrence Erlbaum Associates, 1975, vol 1.

Craik FIM, Lockhart RS: Levels of processing: a

framework for memory research. *J Verbal Learn Verbal Behav* 11:671–684, 1972.

Craik FIM, Tulving E: Depth of processing and the retention of words in episodic memory. *J Exp Psychol* 104:268–294, 1975.

Duchan J: Language processing and geodisic domes. Unpublished data, 1981.

Eich J, Weingartner H, Stillman RC, et al: State-dependent accessibility of retrieval cues in the retention of a categorized list. *J Verbal Learn Verbal Behav* 14:408–417, 1975.

Estes WK: *Handbook of Learning and Cognitive Processes*, vol 4: *Attention and Memory*. Hillsdale, NJ, Lawrence Erlbaum Associates, 1976.

Farnham-Diggory S: Learning disabilities: a view from cognitive science. *J Am Acad Child Psychiatry* 19:570–578, 1980.

Feuerstein R: *Instrumental Enrichment: An Intervention Program for Cognitive Modifiability*. Baltimore, University Park Press, 1979a.

Feuerstein R: *The Dynamic Assessment of Retarded Performers: The Learning Potential Assessment Device, Theory, Instruments, and Techniques*. Baltimore, University Park Press, 1979b.

Finch AJ, Spirito A: Use of cognitive training to change cognitive processes. *Excep Educ Q* 1:31–40, 1980.

Fischer KW: A theory of cognitive development: the control and construction of hierarchies of skills. *Psychol Rev* 87:477–531, 1980.

Fischer KW, Corrigan R: A skill approach to language development. In Stark R: *Language Behavior in Infancy and Early Childhood*. Amsterdam, Elsevier North Holland, in press.

Fischer KW, Roberts RJ: A developmental sequence of classification skills. Unpublished data, Department of Psychology, University of Denver, 1980.

Flavell JH: Developmental studies of mediated memory. In Reese HW, Lipsitt LP: *Advances in Child Development and Behavior*. New York, Academic Press, 1970, vol 5.

Gibson E, Rader N: Attention: The perceiver as performer. In Hale A, Lewis M: *Attention and Cognitive Development*. New York, Plenum Press, 1979.

Glaser R: The future of testing: a research agenda for cognitive psychology and psychometrics. *Am Psychol* 36:923–936, 1981.

Godden DR, Baddeley AD: Context-dependent memory in two natural environments: on land and under water. *Br J Psychol* 66:325–331, 1975.

Hagen JE: The effects of selected pre-reading vocabulary building activities on literal comprehension, vocabulary understanding and attitude of fourth and fifth grade students with reading problems. Unpublished dissertation, University of Wisconsin, 1979.

Hall RJ: Cognitive behavior modification and information-processing skills of exceptional children. *Excep Educ Q* 1:9–16, 1980.

Jacoby LL, Craik FIM: Effects of elaboration of processing at encoding and retrieval: trace distinctiveness and recovery of initial context. In Cermak L, Craik FIM: *Levels of Processing and Human Memory*. Hillsdale, NJ, Lawrence Erlbaum Associates, 1978.

James W: *The Principles of Psychology*. New York, Holt, 1890, vol 1.

Johnson DD, Toms-Bronowski S, Pittelman SD: Vocabulary development, reading and the hearing-impaired individual. *Volta Rev* 84:11–24, 1982.

Kahneman D: *Attention and Effort*. Englewood Cliffs, NJ, Prentice Hall, 1973.

Keogh BK, Glover AT: The generality and durability of cognitive training effects. *Excep Educ Q* 1:75–82, 1980.

Kinsbourne M, Caplan PK: *Children's Learning and Attention Problems*. Boston, Little, Brown, 1971.

Leu DJ, Jr.: Questions from a metatheoretical perspective: the interdependence of solutions to issues involved in the development of reading comprehension models. In Kamil ML, Boswick MM: *Directions in Reading Research and Instruction*. Thirties Yearbook of the National Reading Conference. Washington DC, National Reading Conference, 1981, 96–102.

Lockhart RS, Craik FIM, Jacoby LL: Depth of processing, recognition and recall. In Brown J: *Recognition and Recall*. New York, John Wiley & Sons, 1976.

Mandler G: Organization and repetition: organizational principles with special reference to rote learning. In Nillson L-G: *Perspectives on Memory Research*. Hillsdale, NJ, Lawrence Erlbaum Associates, 1979, 293–327.

Meyers NM, Perlmutter M: Memory in the years from two to five. In Ornstein P: *Memory Development in Children*. Hillsdale, NJ, Lawrence Erlbaum Associates, 1978, 191–218.

Mosenthal P: Children's acquisition of classroom competence. Unpublished data, Syracuse University, 1982.

Naus MJ, Halasz F: Developmental perspectives on cognitive processing and semantic memory structure. In Cermak L, Craik FIM: *Levels of Processing and Human Memory*. Hillsdale, NJ, Lawrence Erlbaum Associates, 1978.

Naus MJ, Ornstein PA, Hoving KL: Developmental implications of multistore and depth of processing models of memory. In Ornstein PA: *Memory Development in Children*. Hillsdale, NJ, Lawrence Erlbaum Associates, 1978, 219–231.

Nelson K, Brown AL: The semantic-episodic distinction in memory development. In Ornstein PA: *Memory Development in Children*. Hillsdale, NJ, Lawrence Erlbaum Associates, 1978, 233–242.

Norman D: Perception, memory and mental processes. In Nillson L-G: *Perspectives on Memory Research*. Hillsdale, NJ, Lawrence Erlbaum Associates, 1979, 121–144.

Ojemann G: Individual variability in cortical localization of language. *J Neurosurg* 50:164–169, 1979a.

Ojemann G: Altering memory with human ventrolateral thalamic stimulation. In Hitchcock E, Ballantine H, Meyerson B: *Modern Concepts in Psychiatric Surgery*. Amsterdam, Elsevier, 1979b, 103–109.

Ojemann G, Whitaker HA: The bilingual brain. *Arch Neurol* 35:409–412, 1978.

O'Leary SG: A response to cognitive training. *Excep Educ Q* 1:89–94, 1980.

Ornstein PA: Introduction: The study of children's memory. In Ornstein PA: *Memory Development in Children.* Hillsdale, NJ, Lawrence Erlbaum Associates, 1978, 1–20.

Paris SG: The development of inference and transformation as memory operations . In Ornstein PA: *Memory Development in Children.* Hillsdale, NJ, Lawrence Erlbaum Associates, 1978, 129–156.

Paris SG, Lindauer BK: Constructive aspects of children's comprehension and memory. In Kail RV, Hagen JW: *Perspectives in the Development of Memory and Cognition.* Hillsdale, NJ, Lawrence Erlbaum Associates, 1977.

Paris SG, Lindauer BK, Cox G: The development of inferential comprehension. *Child Dev* 48:1728–1733, 1977.

Parker ES, Birnbaum IM, Noble EP: Alcohol and memory: storage and state dependency. *J Verbal Learn Verbal Behav* 15:691–702, 1976.

Pearson PD: A primer for schema theory. *Volta Rev* 84:25–34, 1982.

Perfetti C: Language comprehension and fast decoding. In Guthrie J: *Cognition, Curriculum, and Comprehension.* Newark, DE, International Reading Association, 1977, 20–41.

Ratner HH: The role of social context in memory development. In Perlmutter M: *Children's Memory. New Directions for Child Development,* no. 10. San Francisco, Jossey-Bass, 1980, 49–68.

Reid DK: Child reading: readiness or evolution? *Top Language Disord* 1:61–72, 1981.

Roberts RJ: Errors and the assessment of cognitive development. In Fischer KW: *Cognitive Development. New Directions for Child Development,* no. 12. San Francisco, Jossey Bass, 1981, 69–78.

Sexton, M, Geffen G: The development of three strategies of attention and memory. *Dev Psychol* 15:299–310, 1979.

Shiffrin RM, Schneider W: Controlled and automatic human information processing. II. Perceptual learning, automatic attending, and a general theory. *Psychol Rev* 84:127–190, 1977.

Siegler RS: Three aspects of cognitive development. *Cognitive Psychol* 8:481–520, 1976.

Smith DC: Attention disorders: implications for the classroom. *Excep Educ Q* 2:viii–ix, 1981.

Spear NE: Retrieval of memories: A psychobiological approach. In Estes WK: *Handbook of Learning and Cognitive Processes,* vol. 4: *Attention and Memory.* Hillsdale, NJ, Lawrence Erlbaum Associates, 1976, 17–90.

Sternberg RJ: Testing and cognitive psychology. *Am Psychol* 36:1181–1189, 1981.

Swanson HL: A multidirectional model for assessing learning disabled students' intelligence: an information-processing framework. *Learn Disabil Q* 5:312–326, 1982.

Tarver SJ, Hallahan DP, Kauffman JM, et al: Verbal rehearsal and selective attention in children with learning disabilities: a developmental lag. *J Exp Child Psychol* 22:375–385, 1976.

Torgeson JK: The use of efficient task strategies by learning disabled children: conceptual and educational implications. *J Learn Disabil* 13:364–371, 1980.

Torgeson JK: The relationship between memory and attention in learning disabilities. *Excep Educ Q* 2: 1981.

Torgeson JK, Goldman T: Rehearsal and short-term memory in second grade reading disabled children. *Child Dev* 48:56–61, 1977.

Torgeson JK, Houck G: Processing deficiencies in learning disabled children who perform poorly on the digit span task. *J Educ Psychol* 72:141–160, 1982.

Trabasso T, Isen AM, Dolecki P, et al: How do children solve class-inclusion problems? In Siegler RS: *Children's Thinking: What Develops?* Hillsdale, NJ, Lawrence Erlbaum Associates, 1978.

Tulving E: Episodic and semantic memory. In Tulving E, Donaldson: *Organization of Memory.* New York, Academic Press, 1972.

Tulving E: Memory research: what kind of progress? In Nilsson L-G: *Perspectives on Memory Research.* Hillsdale, NJ, Lawrence Erlbaum Associates, 1976, pp 19–34.

Vetter DK: Language disorders and schooling. *Top Language Disord* 2:13–19, 1982.

Waugh NC, Norman DA: Primary memory. *Psychol Rev* 72:89–104, 1965.

Wickelgren WA: Acoustic similarity and intrusion errors in short-term memory. *J Exp Psychol* 70:102–108, 1965.

Normal Processes: Implications for the Source of Language and Learning Problems

CHAPTER FIVE

Later Language Learning: Syntactic Structures and Strategies

GERALDINE P. WALLACH, Ph.D.

"Language is for the child at all ages, and particularly between five and eight, a problem area within its own right. Children have to come to grips with the intricacies of the linguistic structures themselves and may spend a number of years organizing linguistic categories into systems of relevant options" (Karmiloff-Smith, 1979, p. 307).

The study of language acquisition has challenged researchers and practitioners for at least two decades. Through the 1960's and 1970's, a wealth of information has been accumulated. Language researchers and clinicians continue to raise questions that reiterate how difficult it is to study, quantify, and interpret language behavior. The intricate relationship between production and comprehension, particularly as they interface with one another during the various phases of development, provides one avenue of study; the interaction between an individual's comprehension strategies and the acquisition of linguistic structures is another. Subtle changes in language use, shifts in children's ability to deal with semantic and syntactic information, and like topics have come to the forefront of research as professionals consider language acquisition during the school years.

As demonstrated in the previous chapters, information about developmental neurology, information-processing systems, and language disorders has only begun to come together. Understanding of the mechanisms and processes that operate in normally functioning individuals represents a challenge in itself. The challenge is taken further as practitioners attempt to connect the proposed stages of neurological, cognitive, and language functioning to the behaviors manifested by children with problems. An interesting dilemma presents itself in that specialists' training in normal language frequently includes the study of children up to the age of 4 or 5 years (see Chapter 7). This appears to be the case even though the innovative work of C. Chomsky, demonstrating that syntactic growth continues above the age of 5 and through the middle school years, was available in 1969. Since Chomsky's (1969) pivotal work was published, relatively little attention has been given to the language of older children. However, renewed interest in Chomsky's research and other research in the area is now coming about, in part at least, because of the language problems associated with learning disabilities. Recent articles by Bowerman (1979), Karmiloff-Smith (1979), and Goodluck and Tavakolian (1982), among others, have also reminded professionals of the scope of semantic, syntactic, and pragmatic changes that occur over time.

This chapter will explore some of the special characteristics associated with language learning after 4 years of age. It will highlight the strategies available to children as they embark on their school careers and as they prepare for reading, writing, and other academic activities. The question of how older children deal with more sophisticated sentence structures will be discussed with an emphasis on comprehension. Linguistic advances involving the coordination and embedding of clauses in sentences will be included in the discussion. These grammatical devices help children to summarize ideas and events. They also reflect, and interact with, higher level comprehension and problem-solving abilities (see Chapter 10). Coordinate (e.g., Mary swam and Bill hiked), complement (e.g.,

Mary wanted John to leave), and relative clause sentences (e.g., The boy who laughed is my brother) are examples of later acquisitions. The ability to use advanced structures such as these enables children to express themselves in an efficient manner. However, by no means are these abilities isolated ones. As we will see in forthcoming chapters, classroom and textbook language requires proficiency with higher level syntactic-semantic combinations. Likewise, children's ability to process and comprehend complex sentences becomes part of a broader picture—a picture that tells us something about the way they organize information in general (see Chapters 10 and 12).

Children move out of the realm of literal translation during the period of language learning after 4. They begin to use inferential and integrational strategies. They get better at "reading between the lines" and develop a more abstract level of language use, beginning at age 5 and continuing for a number of years (Berlin et al., 1980; see Chapter 8). Children also learn how to handle sentences with violations in word order. Thus, sentences like: "The girl is kissed by the boy," and "Before you do your math, do your reading," become easier to comprehend. A major change in children, i.e., the ability to deal with less explicitly stated relationships, underpins many of these advances.

A number of recurring themes will be discussed in this chapter and in the chapters which follow in this section. The issues listed below remind us that cautious optimism is needed when exploring ages and stages of development:

1. The later stages of language acquisition cannot be separated from the earlier stages. Language growth represents a slow, gradual continuum of change and modification (see Chapter 2). However, there may be "spurts" of activity, followed by major reorganizations, followed by new periods of more obvious growth (Cromer, 1976; Karmiloff-Smith, 1979). While it is recognized that language learning interacts with con-

ceptual development (Piagetian stages), it is also recognized that "language development cannot be explained by cognitive development alone" (Karmiloff-Smith, 1979, p. 307). As put by Karmiloff-Smith (1979) in the opening quote used in this chapter, language development is a special area of concern in its own right.

2. Many of the stages of later language learning remain tentative. The relationship between comprehension and production is still unclear. To date, most of the studies on older child language are studies of comprehension (Bowerman, 1979) as reflected in this chapter. Problems arise because different research methods have been used to test comprehension. This also makes age/stage generalizations difficult. However, patterns have emerged that may provide useful guidelines.

3. Production data are available for some of the later acquisitions, but these remain incomplete. "Because," "so," "if," "until," "after," "since," "although," and "as" are listed as later developing conjunctions (Lee, 1974). Norms are also available for some of the complex sentences that appear in the repertoires of first graders. Sentence structures with "and" conjunctions and infinitive complements are among the earliest ones to be used correctly. "Because" and "if" sentences, among others, develop later (Menyuk, 1969). The listing of syntactic milestones, without consideration of a sentence's content and context, warrants reevaluation (Bloom et al., 1980).

4. More information is needed about the interaction between semantic strategies and the development of syntactic knowledge. Study of the subtle linguistic changes that occur after 8 or 9 years old represents a new dimension of language study. It indicates that numerous and various strategies are available to children. It is important to recognize that children sometimes appear to be "regressing" when, in fact, they are developing new strategies. Likewise, children sometimes appear to be advanced when, in fact, they are at an earlier state of language development.

5. Syntactic, semantic, and pragmatic acquisitions in spoken language are related to acquisitions in written language. Increasing knowledge of these later acquisitions is vital to our understanding of older children with language learning disabilities.

LANGUAGE: A CHANGING CONTINUUM

As early as 1962, Miller wrote that "one of the best ways to study the human mind is by studying the verbal system it uses" (p. 761). He went on to say that "learning what different utterances mean is ... a fundamental skill that any language user must acquire" (Miller, 1962, p. 748). For the most part, adult listeners analyze and comprehend messages quickly and, seemingly, effortlessly. Proficient language users have strategies for chunking incoming sentences that are competency based. That is, their knowledge of linguistic rules enables them to use both grammar and strategies to understand sentences. For young children acquiring language and for learning-disabled children, who may not have complete knowledge of the grammar, comprehension may be much more difficult.

Proficient language users make many decisions as they are listening to language. They make decisions about the underlying relationships between word sequences. They make decisions about the relationships that hold between clauses. Listeners also figure out the relationships between sentences as sentences rarely appear in isolation. They attempt to comprehend what the speaker really means. Various strategies are available to listeners (and, by the way, to readers) as they accomplish these tasks with relative ease.

Most of us take comprehension for granted, only becoming aware of its many facets when faced with communication breakdowns. Foreign language experiences may demonstrate how difficult it is to piece together information when we are not completely familiar with the language. We might rely more heavily on extralinguistic cues, knowledge of the context, the speaker's facial expression, etc., to ease the burden of comprehension. Indeed, numerous variables—e.g., the sentence structure itself, the strategies employed, the content of the message, the message's context—come into play. With these basic ideas in mind, we will begin to explore the strategies available to children as they embark on the task of becoming proficient language users.

We mentioned earlier that two related changes occur as children get older. They develop the ability to comprehend sentences that violate canonical order, i.e., the surface structure word order and the underlying meaning are not matched. They also develop the ability to comprehend clausal relationships in sentences. We will begin by discussing some early interactions between comprehension strategies and syntactic development. We might regard these early foundations as examples of the slow, gradual process of language acquisition. Some of the questions relating to the language learning-disabled child, raised in Chapter 1, might be readdressed here. For example, do learning-disabled and normally achieving students use the same strategies? For spoken language? When reading? Do standardized tests and programs allow for the analysis of strategies? What is it about the structure or the content of a particular sentence that is making comprehension difficult? Is classroom instruction appropriate for the child's language comprehension level (see Chapters 8 and 14)? Two strategies, the canonical order strategy and the order-of-mention strategy will be discussed first. Discussion of more complicated syntactic-semantic combinations will follow.

The Canonical Order Strategy

The canonical order strategy refers to the primary, perhaps the most basic method of syntactic analysis used by listeners. With this strategy, the first noun-verb-noun sequence of a sentence is assumed to be the actor-action-recipient of that sequence if there is no clause boundary and if the first verb agrees with the first noun.

EARLY FOUNDATIONS

Canonical order strategies, although not as developed as those in adults, are believed to begin as "first noun/actor" strategies. That is, children as young as 2 interpret any noun preceding the main verb of a sentence as the logical subject/doer of the action in the sentence. However, by 3 years old, children's performances improve on simple active reversibles such as example 1 below by applying the canonical order strategy to the sentence (Bever, 1970).

	Sentence:	Strategy:
(1)	The cow chases the horse.	= "Pick out the N-V-N sequence and assume it is the actor-action-recipient."

RESULT:

COW-CHASE-HORSE (right interpretation)

Three-year-olds have difficulty with reversible passives because they violate canonical order. In example 2, application of the canonical order strategy results in an incorrect interpretation:

	Sentence:	Strategy:
(2)	The cow is chased by the horse.	= "Pick out the N-V-N sequence and assume it is the actor-action-recipient."

RESULT:

COW-CHASE-HORSE (wrong interpretation)

There is controversy regarding the precise nature of children's strategies between 2 and 3 years old. Clearly, children are working toward developing bona fide canonical order strategies, but the role of extralinguistic cues, context, and "first noun/actor" strategies remains open for further discussion (Chapman, 1978).

MODIFICATIONS IN CANONICAL ORDER

According to Bever (1970), children become more aware of semantic constraints by about 4-years old. They become more sensitive to the logical-functional relationships that hold between the constituents of a sentence. For example, sentence 3, below, a nonreversible passive, is not a problem for 4-year-olds to process, even though its syntactic form is difficult. Children may apply the canonical order strategy to this sentence, resulting in a "FLOWERS-WATER-GIRL" interpretation.

(3) The flowers are watered by the girl.

However, at this point in development, they use their knowledge of the world and "second guess" the word order. Four-year-olds know that "flowers do not water girls" so they are able to comprehend certain syntactic forms that might otherwise be difficult for them. A related strategy, "the probable event strategy," is also evidenced during this time. With the probable event strategy children sometimes disregard word order in simple actives such as "The baby feeds the mother." By applying this strategy, they assign the "agent-actor" role to mother (it is the mother who is feeding the baby), even though the word order suggests otherwise (Strohner and Nelson, 1974). Both semantic constraint and probable event strategies tend to be more predominant before 5.

Sometime after 4 and closer to 5, the segmental strategies used by children become more similiar to those used by adults. That is, they segment the first noun-verb-noun (N-V-N) sequence in the sentence and assume that it corresponds to the actor-action-recipient of the sentence. While semantic constraints protect the child from misinterpreting nonreversible passives such as "The flowers are watered by the girl," application of the "N-V-N = actor-action-recipient" strategy results in poorer performances on reversible passives, such as "The boy is kissed by the girl." Many variables, e.g., age, vocabulary, etc., are involved in the process. Nevertheless, research strongly suggests that all children pass through periods where they overapply certain strategies. Over-application of the canonical order strategy leads to misinterpretation of sentences in which the first noun is the object rather than the actor (Bever, 1970, p. 311). The reader is directed

to Bever's (1970) classic chapter for an in-depth discussion.

A number of questions have been raised that relate to children's use of canonical order strategies. Are there different variations of N-V-N sequencing? Do young children always assume that the first noun of a sentence is the actor-subject of the sentence? It has been suggested that some children pass through a stage of development where they use an agent-action strategy. That is, they find a noun-verb sequence (even if it appears at the end of a sentence) and assume it is the agent and action of the sentence (Lempert and Kinsbourne, 1980). In a sense, this pattern represents an incomplete canonical order strategy. Interestingly, the use of agent-action strategies decreases as age increases (Lempert and Kinsbourne, 1980). Lempert and Kinsbourne (1980) point out that " . . . systematic changes in sentence processing take place around age five, particularly since event probability also loses importance at this time" (p. 378) (see also, Lembert and Kinsbourne, 1978). Chapman (1978) reiterates this notion by stating: "It is not until five years old that most children are able to use syntactic cues of word order to understand agent and object in simple sentences" (p. 318). (See Bridges, 1980, and Huttenlocker and Strauss, 1968, for additional information about how extralinguistic variables influence children's use of canonical order strategies.) We might ask whether language learning-disabled children manifest modified, complete, or incomplete canonical order strategies.

Clausal Strategies

At about 4 or 5 years old, children are also learning about clauses and the relationships that hold between them. The order-of-mention strategy, i.e., the assumption that the order you hear represents the order of events, is one of the strategies operating to facilitate comprehension and memory during this time (Clark and Clark, 1968; Amidon and Carey, 1972; Amidon, 1976; French and Brown, 1977; Kavanagh,

1979). Sentence 4 provides an example of how the order-of-mention strategy could be used on main/subordinate clause sentences. In sentence 4, the spoken order matches the order of events so that the strategy is successfully applied.

Sentence:
(4) Move the blue plane before you move the red plane.
    Strategy:
    "Move items in the order you hear them"/ "Follow order-of-mention"
                    RESULT:
    BLUE PLANE—and then—RED PLANE
            (right interpretation)

Information is available about variations in the order-of-mention strategy. It has also been suggested that 4-year-olds perform differently from 5-year-olds, although this remains very speculative (Amidon and Carey, 1972).

Amidon and Carey (1972) note that 5-year-olds tend to "act out" the main clause regardless of the clause order within sentences. The kindergarteners in their study appeared to have more difficulty processing sentences with subordinate clauses (Move the blue plane *before you move the red plane*), even though they had no problems with coordinate commands containing two clauses (Move the blue plane first; Move the red plane last). This supports the notion that errors in subordinate/main and main/subordinate sentences *are not a function of short-term memory difficulties*. More likely, errors made by children involve a lack of understanding of subordinating syntax and the emergence of new strategies (Amidon and Carey, 1972). Clearly, the interaction between short-term memory rehearsal strategies and comprehension warrants careful scrutiny (see Chapter 4).

Amidon and Carey (1972) hypothesize that, while order-of-mention strategy may be an all-encompassing strategy for interpretation of temporal clauses at age 4, it apparently undergoes certain modifications at age 5. For example, 4-year-olds tend to follow the order regardless of linguistic-lexical variations. Thus, they would move

the blue plane and then move the red plane in sentences 5 and 6, below.

(5) Move the blue plane $\left\{ \begin{array}{l} \text{after} \\ \text{before} \end{array} \right\}$

                    you move the red plane.

(6) $\left\{ \begin{array}{l} \text{After} \\ \text{Before} \end{array} \right\}$ you move the blue plane,

                    move the red plane.

Five-year-olds, however, tend to act out the main clause only, which involves "moving the blue plane" in sentence 5 and "moving the red plane" in sentence 6—omitting the subordinate clause in both cases.

Sentences containing events and sequences that are familiar, i.e., logically constrained sentences, are easier for children regardless of clause order (e.g., French and Brown, 1977; Emerson, 1979, 1980). Sentences such as "The girl feeds the baby before putting it to bed" have been reported as being easier for 3-, 4-, and 5-year-olds than sentences with less familiar or unpredictable sequences. For example, a sentence like, "The girl feeds the baby before picking up a pencil," is more difficult (Kavanagh, 1979). This is reminiscent of semantic constraint and probable event strategies. Kavanagh (1979), among others, has found support for this contention. He points out, however, that children need to learn before/after differences as well as learn how to deal with these words within sentences. Kavanagh's (1979) studies reveal that, when logical constraints are *not* available, "before" sentences are somewhat easier for children than "after" sentences, lending support to Clark's (1971) earlier research on the acquisition of "before" and "after." However, further investigation is warranted, because 6-year-olds, who comprehend the individual vocabulary words, are still known to have difficulty processing before/after structures.

We have seen how, among 4- and 5-year-olds, various strategies emerge and dominate at different points in time. Old strategies are not replaced but they are modified, or they are complemented by others, as children learn language (Amidon and

Carey, 1972). As practitioners dealing with language learning-disabled students, this literature lends itself to practical applications. Numerous items containing clausal sentences appear on standardized tests (see Chapters 12 and 16). We may need to apply qualitative analyses to test results to obtain information about the strategies being employed by a child. Likewise, we might consider reviewing the structures used in reading tests and programs—comparing this material to a child's listening comprehension abilities (see also, Wallach, 1982). In formulating our own informal battery, we can see how the variables mentioned here provide us with tentative guidelines for evaluation and programming. We might include logically constrained sentences, sentences that follow order-of-mention, sentences that have subordinate/main and main/subordinate sequences, etc., in listening and reading comprehension tasks. Let us now turn our attention to the strategies children utilize above the age of 5.

POSSIBLE PATTERNS OF AGE/STAGE CHANGE IN COMPREHENSION: TOWARD 5 AND ABOVE

C. Chomsky (1969) completed one of the first detailed studies of language acquisition above the age of 5. Her research demonstrated that there is a long period of language development that goes beyond the preschool years. Chomsky (1969) investigated children's processing of sentences whose relationships are not explicitly stated in the surface structure. She showed how processing demands increase as grammatical relations become more difficult to figure out.

The Chomsky research provides examples of a number of structures and principles related to later language learning. Although children begin to learn about clausal relationships at a young age, there are many syntactic relationships still undergoing change and development. For example, important knowledge about pronominalization as part of syntactic and pragmatic development is still being acquired after 5.

Sentences 7 and 8, below, were sentences used by Chomsky (1969) to show how certain semantic restrictions accompany grammatical operations. In sentence 7, the pronoun "he" appears before the noun in the main clause. It is restricted to nonidentity because we do not know who "he" refers to when the sentence appears in isolation. Sentence 8, on the other hand, shows how the pronoun can refer to John *or* to someone else.

(7) *He* knew that *John* was going to win the race.
   ("He" and "John" refer to different people)
(8) *John* knew that *he* would win the race.
   ("He" can refer to "John" or "he" can refer to "Bill," "Mario Andretti," etc.)

Its function is not restricted.

Chomsky (1969) found that 5-year-olds demonstrated a specific strategy regarding pronominalization. That is, they assume that "he" and the noun always refer to the same individual regardless of where the pronoun appears in the sentence. It is not until after 5½ that children start to realize that "he" can refer to someone else. This advancement may relate to a statement made at the beginning of this chapter, i.e., children above 5 move out of the realm of literal translation and get better at making inferences. The pronominalization strategy may be an important one to consider when studying both listening and reading comprehension. It has been suggested that some poor readers use a strategy similar to that of Chomsky's 5-year-olds. Dalgleish and Enkelmann (1979) report that the poor readers in their study tended to assume that "he" and a given noun always referred to the same person even when clauses were switched to allow for a broader translation (that "he" can refer to someone else). (See Dalgleish and Enkelmann (1979) for a reading comprehension study that uses Chomsky's (1969) pronominalization strategy as a starting point.)

Chomsky (1969) also identified a number of phases that children go through as they learn to deal with "tell," "promise," and "ask" sentences. She studied the now classic "minimal distance principle" (MDP). By MDP, Chomsky (1969) meant that, when faced with confusion, children will interpret the noun "closest" to the infinitive as being the subject/actor of the infinitive. Sentences 9 to 12 show how the principle works. Sentence 9, a "tell" sentence, adheres to the MDP. "Bill," the closest noun, is the doer/actor in the sentence.

(9)   John told *Bill* to leave. (Bill does the leaving.)

Sentence (10), a "promise" sentence, violates the MDP. John is now the doer/actor.

(10)   *John* promised Bill to leave. (John leaves.)

Finally, sentences 11 and 12, both "ask" sentences, present a dilemma. Sentence 11 follows the MDP. It functions like "tell." Sentence 12, on the other hand, violates the MDP. The verb ask, unlike both tell and promise, is inconsistent in terms of the minimal distance principle.

(11)   John asked *Bill* to leave. (Bill gets going.)
(12)   *John* asked Bill what to do. (John does the "doing.")

Chomsky (1969) found a widespread use of the minimal distance principle. She reports that children start out using the minimal distance principle exclusively. They assume that the noun closest to the infinitive verb is the subject of the verb. Children assume that "promise" follows MDP even though they knew the meaning of the word "promise." The MDP strategy was predominant in the younger groups (5- and 6-year-olds), although there were children as old as 8 who still misinterpreted some "promise" and "ask" sentences (such as example 12, above). In the second phase of acquisition of tell/promise/ask sentences, children learn that the MDP does not always apply. This represents a transition period because children are not sure about the precise nature of MDP violations. After a while, however, the uncertainty is reduced. "Promise" constructions stabilize before "ask" constructions. As Chomsky (1969) points out, "promise" always violates MDP, whereas "ask" constructions remain inconsistent.

Young children generally start our interpreting "ask" as "tell." Thus, when told to "Ask Bozo what time it is.", they say: "I don't know." From this research alone, we can certainly see that 5-year-olds have newly modified strategies, but 6- to 9-year-olds continue to refine and change these strategies as their linguistic knowledge advances. (The reader is directed to the original work of C. Chomsky, 1969, for additional information.)

MDP in the Age of Semantics and Pragmatics

Researchers have recently questioned the minimal distance principle on the grounds that it overemphasizes the structural aspects of children's interpretation strategies (Maratsos, 1974; Lederberg and Maratsos, 1981). It is proposed that children make errors on tell/promise sentences for semantic reasons (Maratsos, 1974). The semantic role principle, sounding very much like a pragmatic strategy, suggests that children look for the goal-recipient of the spoken message. This goes beyond the notion that children choose the *closest noun* to carry out the action of the infinitival complement. Lederberg and Maratsos (1981) point out that a message has three components: *the message* being transmitted, the person who sends the message, *its source*, and the person who receives the message, its *goal-recipient* (Maratsos, 1974; Lederberg and Maratsos, 1981, p. 92). In a sentence such as: "John told Mary to leave," "John" is the source and "Mary" is the goal-recipient of the message.

Lederberg and Maratsos (1981) found that a noun's proximity to the verb was not the predominant influence on 4- to 6-year-olds' processing of sentences. Their subjects chose the goal-recipient of the message as the actor/subject of the complement verb 85% of the time. The Lederberg and Maratsos (1981) research provides some support for the application of semantic/pragmatic strategies on ask/tell/promise sentences *at the 4- to 6-year-old age level.* It may be that syntactic-based strategies, such as those defined by Chomsky (1969), predominate or interact with other strategies, such as those defined by Lederberg and Maratsos (1981), at later points in development. Lederberg and Maratsos (1981) also report that the verbal responses of children in their study support the notion that children are beginning to use infinitive constructions in their speech between 4 and 6. Use of goal-recipient strategies was also manifested in the production data.

Lederberg and Maratsos (1981) relate the semantic strategy to children's knowledge about imperative sentences. When giving commands to people (e.g., "Be quiet"), it is the person who gets the message who must "do it." They also point out that responses for "action" verbs may be different from responses for other verbs like "want" (John wanted Mary to leave). The interaction of semantic, syntactic, and pragmatic variables is demonstrated again. Children as young as 4 and 5 years old are sorting these out as they learn grammar and as they experiment with old and new strategies. It is interesting to note that the MDP strategy and the semantic goal-recipient strategy can lead to the same result for a different reason (Lederberg and Maratsos, 1981). In some cases, the noun closest to the infinitive is also the goal-recipient. Thus, a wide variety of sampling across sentence types and situations is required when attempting to deduce strategy preferences. As practitioners, we recognize that numerous possibilities may account for children's misinterpretation of sentences. As we have seen in this section, sentences may be short but difficult. Likewise, a subtle shift in the placement of a pronoun may cause processing difficulties for younger children (and children with language learning disabilities). MDP and semantic role strategies can account for a correct or incorrect performance.

The Parallel Function Strategy and Relative Clause Sentences

It is generally agreed that relative clause sentences are difficult for children. The parallel function strategy, as defined by Sheldon (1974), is one of the strategies employed by children when they attempt to process and comprehend relative clause sentences. Parallel function refers to the underlying role the modified noun has within a sentence; i.e., is it the actor or recipient of the various actions? A noun has a parallel function if it is the actor/subject or recipient/object in both clauses. Sentence 13 provides an example of how a noun, in this case the noun, "giraffe," has a parallel function. "Giraffe" is the actor/subject of both main and relative clauses.

(13) The giraffe (that bites the wolf) kicks the hippo.
        GIRAFFE does everything.

Sentence 14 provides another example of parallel function. Now the giraffe is the recipient/object of all the actions.

(14) The hippo bumps into the giraffe (that the zebra kicks).
        The GIRAFFE is "done in" (bumped into and kicked) by the other animals.

Sentences 13 and 14 are examples of subject and object relatives, respectively. In a subject relative, such as sentence 13, the relative clause modifies the subject of the main clause. In an object relative, such as sentence 14, the relative clause modifies the object of the main clause. Sentence 13 is an example of an embedded sentence, i.e., the relative clause interrupts the action of the main clause, whereas sentence 14 represents a nonembedded sentence.

Sheldon (1974) reported that parallel function sentences were significantly easier for children to process than sentences that did not follow parallel function. She also found that clause embeddedness was not a significant variable, i.e., children did not make more errors on sentences where the relative clause interrupted the action. However, Sheldon's data revealed that the parallel function-subject relatives, such as sentence 13, showed the greatest improvement with age. Five-year-olds performed better than younger children on these sentences. It may be that "first noun/actor" strategies, i.e., the assumption that the first noun is the doer/actor of all the actions, may be interacting with parallel function strategies. According to Sheldon (1974), performance on object relatives, such as sentence 14, even if they followed parallel function, remained about the same between 3 and 5 years old. These findings suggest that subject relatives with parallel function are the earliest acquisitions—with significant improvement in comprehension occurring around age 5.

Wallach (1977) used the same sentence types and the same procedures as Sheldon (1974) to test comprehension of older children between 8:6 and 13:9. The Wallach study, mentioned in Chapter 2, also included a group of learning-disabled (LD) students of the same age. While information is not available for the in-between ages, Wallach (1977) reports that of the 20 normal children tested, 65% obtained perfect or near-perfect scores. The only normal children who did make errors were below the age of 9. The normal children, by about 9½, obtained perfect scores on a variety of relative clause sentences. As opposed to Sheldon's (1974) findings, however, all the normal children showed perfect performances on the object relatives—even if they did not follow parallel function. Sentence 15 is an example of an object relative that does not follow parallel function.

(15) The hippo bumps the giraffe (that kicks the zebra).
GIRAFFE gets bumped (object)/
GIRAFFE kicks zebra (subject).

In this example, the "giraffe" does not have a semantic consistency (a parallel function). He is the object/recipient of the action in the main clause and the subject/doer of the action in the relative clause. The performance of the normal children in the Wallach (1977) study suggests that the position of the clause made a difference. That is, the nonembedded sentences were easier. Interestingly, the LD children *followed* Sheldon's proposed pattern of order of difficulty—with parallel function-subject relatives being the easiest to comprehend. The parallel function strategy was a more

important strategy for most of the LD subjects *at this age range*. Reflecting back on the discrepancies noted regarding the minimal distance principle, it may be that children alternate between semantic-pragmatic strategies and syntactic strategies. Perhaps younger children prefer (or start out with) semantically oriented strategies. They may advance to syntactically oriented strategies, e.g., becoming more sensitive to embeddedness or nonembeddedness of clauses, as they get older According to Wallach (1977), the learning-disabled subjects were indeed favoring a semantic-based strategy even at the older age ranges (11 to 13). Further investigation of these kinds of discrepancies is certainly warranted. As seen in the clinical section and elsewhere in this text, numerous differences are reported about the language strategy differences between normally achieving and learning-disabled students (e.g., Chapters 2, 6, 9, 11, and 12). Before any generalizations can be made, however, the significance of parallel function and other strategies needs to be investigated with constructions other than relative clause sentences and with children across a variety of age levels and abilities.

LATER SYNTACTIC STRUCTURES: COMPREHENSION, PRODUCTION, AND METALINGUISTICS

In the preceding sections, a number of strategies were outlined that interact with children's advancing syntactic knowledge. While this chapter highlights various aspects of later language learning, we have seen how foundations at the earlier periods of development set the stage for those acquisitions that follow. Van Kleeck also makes this point about the development of metalinguistics in Chapter 7. Canonical order, order-of-mention, pay attention to the main clause, and parallel function strategies operate at various times on various sentences. The 5-year-old has access to all of these strategies. Let us now turn to a discussion of some additional structures, including "and," "because," and "if" sentences. "And" was chosen for exploration because it is listed as one of the "earlier" conjunctions used by children in their speech (Lee, 1974; Bloom et al., 1980). However, the acquisition of "and" sentences, as we shall soon see, represents a slow, gradual process. The various concepts underlying its use, e.g., cause/effect concepts, must be accounted for in addition to describing its syntactic functions. "Because" and "if" sentences, on the other hand, are usually listed as much later acquisitions. "Because" and "if" structures are not fully developed until 8 or 9 years old and above. The issue of how children deal with main/subordinate and subordinate/main constructions, raised earlier when the order-of-mention and pay attention to the main clause strategies were discussed, will be revived in light of the application of these strategies on "because" and "if" sentences. Implications regarding the relationship between comprehension and production will also be addressed in this section.

Coordinates ("and" Sentences)

Ardery (1979) took an in-depth look at the acquisition of coordinate sentences in children. She studied 10 different coordinate types. As with many other studies, Ardery had children manipulate objects to demonstrate comprehension. In a departure from other studies, however, she had children watch objects being moved and then asked them to *tell* what they saw.

The comprehension data revealed that, by far, intransitive verb coordinates such as "The dog *ran and fell*," were the easiest. All of Ardery's subjects (children between the ages of 3:11 and 5:9) demonstrated 100% accuracy when processing the intransitive verb coordinates. Other "and" sentences that were comprehended by most of the children below 5 included object noun phrase coordinates (The giraffe bumped into *the tiger and the cat*), sentence intransitives (The dog ran *and* the cat fell), and verb phrase coordinates (The dog bumped into the horse *and* jumped over the tiger). It is interesting to note that "first noun/

actor" strategies may facilitate comprehension of object noun phrase coordinates and verb phrase coordinates (The "giraffe" and the "dog" do everything).

Five-year-olds, in addition to getting better with variations of the above sentences, begin to work through a more difficult set of coordinate sentences. For example, sentences such as 16, below, involve two subject-verb-object strings with four animals involved in the various actions.

(16) The turtle bumped into the dog and the cat jumped over the rabbit.

It may be that the use of jungle animals in one clause and pets in the other when teaching structures such as that in example 16 might prove facilitative should we be thinking about practical application of these data. Ardery (1979) discusses a number of possibilities and presents a developmental hierarchy, showing that, in terms of comprehension, coordinate sentences are still being acquired as children approach 6 years old and as they get ready to enter the first grade.

The production data revealed that the four easiest sentences to comprehend (those mentioned as acquisitions below 5 at the beginning of this section) were the sentences expressed more frequently by the children when they described what the examiner had done with the animals. However, sentences such as 16, which were understood by 5-year-olds with a 67% accuracy level, were *produced correctly* 80% of the time. A number of other discrepancies between comprehension and production are reported by Ardery (1979). She also discusses some of the issues surrounding the testing, quantifying, and interpretation of language data.

Athey (1977) showed how, in addition to the syntactic advances noted by Ardery (1979), we must also consider semantic-conceptual aspects of the development of "and" sentences. She provides examples of ways in which children's comprehension and use of the conjunction "and" becomes more sophisticated. For example, a coordinate sentence like: "It was growing darker and the rain was coming down heavily," expresses *similarity of elements*. According to Athey (1977), the two thoughts (growing darker and rain coming down) constitute a theme—perhaps that of a "gloomy evening." Sentences like: "John is tall and Bill is short," and "The dog bared its teeth and Bill ran in terror" express *comparative* and *causal relations*, respectively. A developmental trend is suggested by Athey (1977) suggesting a largely random use of the conjunction at grade 1 (6- and 7-year-olds), to adherence to similar elements at grade 4 (9- and 10-year-olds), evolving to more complex rules at grade 10 (Hutson and Shub, 1974; Athey, 1977, p. 74). Through Athey's examples, we can see how the listing of syntactic milestones alone is not sufficient. We must also consider the underlying ideas being expressed by the coordinate sentences (see Athey, 1977, for a fascinating discussion; see also Chapter 10).

"Because" and "if" Sentences

Children's developing ability to deal with "because" and "if" constructions is affected by such variables as imagery, context, prior experience, understanding of various cause-effect relationships, syntactic complexity, and like variables (Corrigan, 1975; Kuhn and Phelps, 1976; Hood, 1977; Emerson, 1979, 1980).

In a series of experiments, Emerson (1979, 1980) dealt with syntactic and semantic relations that underlie "because" and "if" sentences. She used picture identification, sentence verification, and sentence correction tasks to test children's knowledge of these constructions. Emerson (1979) constructed sentences that involved concrete-physical cause-effect relations. A sentence like "He fell off his bicycle because the road was icy," represents a concrete-physical cause-effect relation. It expresses a situation, according to Emerson (1979), that would be familiar to most children. Other cause-effect relations, e.g., motivational ("She ran out of the room because she was angry"), were not considered in the study (see Corrigan, 1975, and Johnson and Chapman, 1980, for additional information on different types of causal relations).

Emerson (1979) studied middle-class children between the ages of 5:8 and 10:1. She used a number of clever picture sequence tasks to obtain information about "because" sentences. We might think about these procedures for assessing older children with language learning disabilities—recognizing that they overlap with metalinguistic abilities.

In the picture-sequence task (PST), two different story sequences were placed in front of the child. A cartoon strip format was used. The children were told stories by the examiner. Emerson (1979) provides this example (p. 284):

For cartoon sequence (1): This is a story about a boy. The boy was feeling very happy. He went out to play with his friends. He is playing with his friends.

For cartoon sequence (2): This story is a bit different. The boy is feeling lonely. He went to play with his friends. Then he was very happy.

Children were asked to decide which story went with a particular sentence. A target sentence for the above stories might be:

"Because he went to play with his friends, he was feeling happy."

This sentence is logical for cartoon sequence 2. While the sentence is a subordinate/main construction, we might note that the order of events spoken follows the actual sequence of events in the story.

Emerson (1979) also used what she called the first-last task (FLT). In the FLT, children were asked to sequence pictures to match sentences. Thus, unlike the PST described above, where picture sequences were always in the child's view, children had to create the sequences in the FLT. In warm-up sessions, children practiced with the first-last idea. That is, they were taught (with sentences other than "because") to move pictures around to show what happened first and what happened last as indicated from spoken sentences. Emerson

(1979) points out that the children had no difficulty understanding the task.

A number of interesting developmental differences were found. The finding that performances were affected by the tasks, which we will return to in a moment, should be of interest to those of us who are working with children. The overall findings indicate that sentences where semantic probability and order-of-mention strategies can be applied are relatively easy for all subjects, including those below 7:6. Nonreversible sentences were easier for the children to process on both PST and FLT. A sentence like "The snowman started to melt because the sun started to shine," has semantic constraints attached to it as well as being nonreversible. One cannot say "The sun started to shine because the snowman started to melt." Emerson's findings revealed that, whenever possible, children try to make use of semantic-logical probability to process "because" sentences.

Improvement on more complex reversible sentences, those not helped by semantic probability, occurred *after 7:6*. A sentence like "He could hear loud noises and the laughing because he went outside," can be reversed. One can also say: "He went outside because he could hear the loud noises and the laughing." The improvement with age was related to the tasks. Children performed better when the picture sequences (the cartoon bubbles) were in front of them (the PST). The first-last task was more difficult for all subjects. Even the 9- and 10-year-olds performed with only 60% accuracy on reversible sentences ("He could hear loud noises, etc.") on the FLT. Having the picture sequences in view on the PST appears to have facilitated comprehension. As put by Emerson (1979):

"Only gradually does 'because' become independent of content and context, so that the child can define event order in the sentences solely on the bases of the meaning of 'because' and its position in the sentence" (p. 287).

Emerson (1979) also asked children in her study to make judgments about "because" sentences. She introduced the younger children to teacher and clown puppets to ensure that they understood the task. The children were told that the teacher says sentences that are "sensible" and the clown says sentences that are "silly." Children were then asked to judge whether they were hearing "silly" or "sensible" sentences. They were also asked to "fix" sentences such as, "The river was frozen over because we wanted to go skating tonight."

It was found that consistent judgments about sentences were not made until 8 years old. Thus, even though children could comprehend many of the sentences, they could not judge them as "sensible" or "silly" until 8 (see Chapter 7). A number of interesting strategies emerged when the children were asked to fix sentences, i.e., to make silly ones sensible. The younger children (the 5- and 6-year-olds) used *reduction* and *content change* strategies. A reduction strategy was demonstrated when a sentence such as "The river was frozen over because we wanted to go skating tonight," was made "The river was all right to go skating." A content change strategy was demonstrated when "The glass of water fell over because the chair got very wet" became "The glass of water spilled because the chair hit it." *Clause reversal strategies* were reserved for the oldest groups (the 9- and 10-year-olds). This strategy was used when "The knife was very sharp because the little boy cut his finger," became "The little boy cut his finger because the knife was very sharp." Finally, *connective changes*, i.e., a change made in the conjunction, were mixed and showed no specific improvement with age. A connective change occurred when, "The boy fell off his bicycle because he scraped his knee" became "The boy fell off his bicycle *and* he scraped his knee."

"If" sentences present as many problems as "because" sentences because they are more difficult syntactic forms and because they represent difficult conceptual-semantic relations. In a follow-up study, Emerson (1980) had children make judgments about "sensible" and "silly" sentences. Sentences

17 and 18 provide examples of logical and illogical "if" constructions:

(17) LOGICAL: I take the bus to school if it starts to rain.
(18) ILLOGICAL: The sun comes out if the snowman melts.

If children are using order-of-mention strategies, misinterpreting or ignoring "if," they should be making more inappropriate judgments about illogical sentences. In other words, if sentence 18 is interpreted as "The sun comes out and then the snowman melts," it would be judged as a sensible sentence. As with "because" sentences, numerous content and clause order variations were used by Emerson (1980) in the "if" sentence study.

The findings for "if" sentences were similar to those reported by Emerson (1979) for "because" sentences. Interestingly, judgments were better when the "if" component came first. This was also the case for "because" sentences, particularly when semantic constraints were present as in nonreversible sentences. Children's ability to deal with "if" in the second clause improved with age. Thus, the position of clauses, i.e., subordinate first/main second versus main first/subordinate second, warrants further investigation.

Strategies for making sense out of "silly" sentences were similar to those mentioned earlier for "because" sentences. Reduction and content changes were predominant in the 4- and 5-year-olds. "If flowers grow very tall, it rains," was changed to "If flowers and trees grow very tall, *I cut them down*," by the 4- and 5-year-olds. The 8-year-olds would be more likely to say: "If it rains, flowers and trees grow very tall." Certainly, younger children make changes that show awareness of the clausal structure of the language, but they need time to become proficient with specific syntactic alterations. Children also made more correct judgments on logical-correct order sentences than on illogical-reverse order sentences. Thus, they may possess some basic discrimination mechanism for differentiat-

ing logical-illogical sentences, although they are not sure of the changes that are needed.

Closing Remarks about Structures and Strategies

Additional information is certainly needed about the subtleties and nuances attached to children's language learning as they approach the early school years and as they move through the grades. All the studies presented thus far have provided examples of the depth and scope of language learning. The studies bring to mind some of the difficulties related to testing complex structures in normally achieving children and should provide us with directions relating to the testing and teaching of these structures and strategies in language learning-disabled children. "Because" and "if" sentences, among other complex forms, are difficult for many reasons, some of which have been pointed out. The role that presupposition plays in the comprehension and use of sentences such as these should also be considered. The sentence, "I'm going to walk if Jane is driving," suggests that the listener knows something about Jane's driving competence (Emerson, 1979, 1980). Likewise, the labeling of sentences as "logical" or "illogical" is not always clear-cut. "Because" sentences remain difficult to test in isolation because people tend to construct relationships in their heads to make sense out of what they are hearing. One cannot help being reminded of Bransford and Johnson's (1973) classic example. They asked people if they comprehended the sentence, "Bill is able to come to the party tonight because his car broke down." People indicated that they could understand the sentence by making up a situation that makes sense, e.g., "Bill lives out of town and was planning on going home, but his car broke down so ... he went to the party." In some cases, then, the "because" structure acts as a cue to create a situation that brings the two phrases into a meaningful relation (Bransford and Johnson, 1973). One of the "if" sentences used by Emerson (1980) and listed as an "illogical" relation (and, without constructing a context, it certainly is) was: "She became ill if she missed school." If one follows a Bransford and Johnson (1973) model, one might make sense out of this sentence by constructing a context: "Because Sally is such a conscientious (if not compulsive) student who wants to graduate at the top of her class, she became upset, to the point of being ill, if she had to miss even one class."

Regardless of the difficulties we might have studying or testing these sentences, we can safely say that children, even until 8 or 9 years old, have more to learn about language. Full comprehension of "because" and "if" and some aspects of "and" are later acquisitions. The role that "constructive" strategies play in these acquisitions warrants further consideration. Let us turn to some fascinating developmental issues regarding children's abilities to "go beyond" sentences themselves, using knowledge in their heads, prior experience, and inferential strategies to comprehend and remember language.

CONSTRUCTIVE ASPECTS OF CHILDREN'S COMPREHENSION AND MEMORY

The research in children's sentence memory and their ability to integrate information that they hear provides an additional avenue one might take to understand later language learning. It is interesting to consider how these strategies interface with syntactic, semantic, and pragmatic knowledge above 5. Clearly, children are becoming better organizers as they are becoming proficient language users. This section will provide some examples of the development of inferential and integrational strategies. It will highlight a number of acquisitions that are reported in children between the ages of 7 and 10 years old (grades 2 to 5). The research presented here and elsewhere in this text (see Chapter 12) provides implications for reconsidering the kinds of

"processing" problems manifested by learning-disabled students.

The question of when children begin to "read between the lines" and make guesses about sentences based upon what they know about the world provides a stimulating base for discussion. As seen earlier, children at 4 do second guess the sentence so to speak, when they interpret "The flowers are watered by the girl" correctly. They also ignore word order in sentences like "The baby feeds the mother," with semantic probability strategies, showing that they are certainly *actively* organizing information during the comprehension process. It seems clear that from 6 to 11 years old, children increase the amount of both explicit and implicit information they can handle (Paris and Upton, 1974). These strategies may be all important during the school years, perhaps setting the stage for problem-solving and other abilities (see Chapter 10).

Inference

In an early study, Paris and Carter (1973) observed children's ability to make inferences as they listened to short stories. They presented seven short paragraphs to children from grades 2 to 5. Each story consisted of three simple, active declarative sentences such as examples 19 to 21:

(19) The bird is in the cage.
(20) The cage was under the table.
(21) The bird is yellow.

After hearing the little stories, the children were presented with four sentences. These sentences were related to the story in some way. They were asked to decide which sentences they had heard before. The recognition sentences, sentences 22 to 25, represent different variations of parts of the story:

(22) The bird is in the cage. (OLD TRUE PREMISE)
(23) The cage is over the table (OLD FALSE PREMISE)
(24) The bird is under the table. (NEW TRUE INFERENCE)

(25) The bird is on top of the table. (NEW FALSE INFERENCE)

Sentence 22 is a verbatim representation of one of the story's sentences. It is called an old true premise. Sentence 23, on the other hand, is a false premise. Vocabulary items are similar to what children were given in the story, but the information is incorrect. Sentence 24, while never given in the story, is a true inference. If children "fused" information in memory, making inferences during processing, they might think they had heard sentence 24 before.

It was found that children could not discriminate old true premises from new true inferences. In other words, they thought they had heard sentences such as 24 even though they had not appeared in the stories. This finding suggests that the children made inferences during processing, e.g., if the bird is in the cage and the cage is under the table then the bird must be under the table, too. All the children in this study made these "errors." This does not imply that syntactic and vocabulary factors are not important or that they are not remembered. It suggests, however, that between 7 and 10 years old, children are actively constructing relations and making inferences as they attempt to organize and remember information (Paris and Upton, 1974; Klein-Konigsberg, 1977; see Chapter 12).

Paris and Lindauer (1976) looked further into developmental changes in inferential processing. They studied children between 6 and 12 years old. Paris and Lindauer (1976) constructed sentences with both explicitly stated instruments as example 26 and sentences with omitted instruments such as example 27:

(26) The workman dug a hole in the ground *with a shovel.*
          (Instrument explicitly stated)
(27) Her friend swept the kitchen floor.
          (Instrument omitted)

Paris and Lindauer (1976) hypothesized that if children spontaneously generated the implied and appropriate instruments, then using "broom" as a prompt for sentence 27 would prove as effective as using "shovel" as a prompt for sentence 26.

They presented children with lists containing four explicit and four implicit sentences. Explicit sentences actually contained the correct instrument (as in 26). Implicit sentences did not contain mention of the correct instrument (as in 27). Children were told to listen carefully and try to remember as many of the sentences as they could. Four minutes after presentation, the experimenters prompted the children with the instrument of each sentence. They asked each child to tell them which sentences from the list came to mind.

Both cue type (explicit versus implicit) and grade level (first, third, fifth) had an effect. First and third graders (6- to 8-year-olds) recalled more sentences with explicit instrument prompts. There was a shift at the fifth grade. Ten- and 11-year-olds recalled the implicit and explicit sentences equally well. Thus, the older subjects (the 10- and 11-year-olds) apparently generated the implicit information during processing. These subjects also incorporated this information into memory representations for use in assessing the entire sentences' meaning (Paris and Lindauer, 1976, p. 221).

Paris and Lindauer (1976) added another part to their experiment. They instructed the first graders (6- and 7-year-olds) to act out the sentences with gestures. Children were told that using gestures would make the sentences easier to remember. They believed that acting out sentences might "force" the child to process the implied instrument. Gesture also provides a readily observable response. The results were simple and dramatic: the young children now recalled implicitly and explicitly cued sentences equally well (with a proficiency on the average of about 71%). This finding certainly has implications for remediation, as discussed later by Klein-Konigsberg in Chapter 12.

Integration

Additional questions have been raised about children's ability to integrate information in memory. Brown (1976) studied children between the ages of 4 and 10 years old. She reports that children as young as 4 have an awareness of coherent story sequences, using semantic strategies early on. Even her youngest subjects were able to distinguish semantically inconsistent pictures when they were asked to resequence pictures to form a story they had been given previously. Too, young children integrated semantically consistent pictures into the story even though they had not seen them before. Westby deals with the development of narratives in greater detail in Chapter 6. Much of this new information mirrors current views of the dynamic nature of memory and comprehension systems. Indeed, "memory for logical narrative sequences involves the retention of the gist or theme into an integrated unified representation of meaning rather than a series of discrete events" (Brown, 1976, p. 247).

SYNTAX, SEMANTICS, AND PRAGMATICS: FROM SPEAKING TO READING

We mentioned earlier in this chapter that, in addition to learning about language development between 4 and 7 years old, we needed to learn more about the subtle changes that occur after 8 years of age. We discussed some of these acquisitions in the previous section. The studies on inference and integration have complemented the discussion by highlighting additional changes that occur in children's processing between grades 2 and 5. The Paris and Lindauer (1976) studies on sentence memory prompts showed how 10- and 11-year-olds' abilities to make inferences improve. We might ask a number of questions with regard to later language learning as we complete our discussion: What constitutes a subtle change in language acquisition? Are the strategies used for listening comprehension similar to those used for reading comprehension?

Syntactic Forms and Pragmatics above 8: An Example

Karmiloff-Smith (1979) discusses developmental changes that occur in children's use of certain determiners (e.g., "a", "the"). In examples from French children, she presents many insights about older children. Karmiloff-Smith (1979) reiterates two very important points about later language learning: (1) On the surface, children appear to use certain linguistic forms correctly. However, on deeper analysis, developmental changes are noted as they get older. (2) The phases of language learning represent gradual shifts with subtle changes that warrant careful observation.

Karmiloff-Smith (1979) explains how children start out being very explicit when using morphological markers. They overmark sentences, using syntactic devices redundantly, to be sure the listener gets the message. Sentences 28 and 29 highlight Karmiloff-Smith's (1979) clever observation. Sentence 28 represents a response that might occur between 5 and 8 years of age. Note the use of multiple marking.

(28) The girl pushed *a* dog and then the boy he *repushed once more the same* dog.

(29) The girl pushed *a* dog and then the boy pushed *the* dog.

Sentence 29 represents a response that would be more typical of a child above 8 years of age. Thus, at 8 years plus, children are making linguistic changes that are not present in the repertoire of younger children (Karmiloff-Smith, 1979).

Other examples are provided by Karmiloff-Smith (1979) that demonstrate aspects of language learning between 8 and 12 years of age. For example, children at this age level are more capable of using linguistic cues to understand subtle changes in stories. When children were asked how they knew a story was about only *one* apple, 9-year-olds referred to linguistic cues. The 9-year-old might say: "I knew you were talking about only one apple because you said, 'the apple,' and if there were more, you could have said 'a' apple, or 'one of the apples'" (Karmiloff-Smith, 1979, p. 321).

Language Strategies and Reading: Directions for Future Research

Blachowicz (1977/78) questioned whether elementary school children would exhibit constructive comprehension strategies when confronted with a silent reading task. She studied second graders (ages 7:1 to 7:8), fifth graders (ages 10:1 to 10:11), seventh graders (12:2 to 12:10), and adults. Subjects were asked to read 10 short paragraphs silently. The paragraphs consisted of three short sentences such as examples 30 to 32. The sentences are reminiscent of the ones used by Paris and Carter (1973).

(30) The birds sat on the branch.

(31) A hawk flew over it.

(32) The birds were robins.

(Taken from Blachowicz, 1977/78, p. 192)

The subjects were given the following instructions: "Please read the following paragraphs carefully so that you will understand and remember them. Later you will be asked questions about them." After reading the paragraphs, subjects participated in a 3-minute transition task. They were then given additional instructions: "You will now read some sentences. If you saw a sentence in the stories you read, mark YES in front of it. Mark YES only for those sentences that are *exactly* the same as the ones you read in the stories."

Sample recognition items are presented in sentences 31 to 34. As with the Paris and Carter (1973) study on inferences, sentence 33 represents a true inference.

(31) The birds sat on the branch.
(TRUE PREMISE)

(32) A hawk flew under it.
(FALSE PREMISE)

(33) A hawk flew over the birds.
(TRUE INFERENCE)

(34) A hawk flew under the birds.
(FALSE INFERENCE)

Blachowicz (1977/78) reported that there was a strong tendency for all subjects to "recognize" (mark YES on their answer sheets) more semantically consistent true inferences than either true statements, false statements, or false inferences. According to Blachowicz, these inferential "errors" are not attributable to poor memory because true inferences and false infer-

ences had the same first and third term and were of similar length and syntactic construction. This research, and the research on listening comprehension, supports the notion that people use inferential strategies when trying to comprehend and remember information.

Wallach and Goldsmith (1975) studied the interaction between listening comprehension and reading comprehension by observing older children's processing of relative clause sentences. They hypothesized that children's strategies for processing written sentences would be similar to those used for processing spoken sentences. Twenty normally achieving and 20 learning-disabled children between the ages of 9 and 12 years were the subjects for this investigation. None of the children manifested any overt expressive language problems as determined by the examiners' screenings and teachers' judgments. Subject relative clause sentences were the stimuli used. Half of the subject relatives followed parallel function, i.e., the relativized noun was the subject/actor of all the actions, as in the sentence: "The giraffe that bites the wolf kicks the hippo." The other half did not follow parallel function, i.e., the relativized noun was the subject/actor of the action in the main clause and the object/recipient of the action in the relative clause, as in the sentence: "The giraffe that the wolf bites kicks the hippo." All the children took part in a listen-manipulate objects and read-manipulate objects task. For the listening task, subjects were told to listen carefully to the sentence and then make the animals (objects) do what the examiner said. For the reading task, subjects were instructed to read the card and then make the animals do what it said. As part of a pretest procedure, subjects were taught (if necessary) to read the individual vocabulary words. Linguistic complexity (parallel versus nonparallel sentences), mode of presentation (spoken versus written sentences), order of presentation (spoken sentences given first versus written sentences given first), and group differences (normal versus learning disabled) were the variables studied.

Wallach and Goldsmith (1975) found that the most significant variable affecting the performance of both groups was linguistic complexity. The subject relatives that did not follow parallel function were very difficult to process—regardless of whether they were presented auditorily or visually. They also found that, when children made errors on sentences (when they used strategies that did not work), they were consistent. Lending evidence to Wallach and Goldsmith's (1977) original hypothesis, both normal and LD subjects used the same strategies on spoken and written sentences.

As a group, the normal children performed better than the learning-disabled group. That is, they made fewer errors overall and the errors tended to be made by the younger normals (those below 10 years old), supporting Wallach's (1977) findings on the listening comprehension study which was discussed earlier in this chapter. What is interesting, however, is that the learning-disabled subjects in the Wallach and Goldsmith (1975) study were not uniformly poorer on visually presented items. That is, they were not just having problems reading but they were having problems comprehending complex structures. It is important to note that "the problems of the learning disabled child which are commonly recognized when reading skill becomes critical for academic success, may be present on an auditory level (comprehension processing level) as well" (Wallach and Goldsmith, 1975, p. 14).

One final difference between normal and learning-disabled subjects is worth mentioning as it has implications for intervention. Order of presentation was significant for the normals but it was not significant for the learning-disabled group. That is, the normal children who received the spoken sentences first performed better on the written sentences. Order of presentation had no effect on the performances of the LD children. It may be that, whereas the normal children took advantage of the auditory first, "practicing" with spoken language, the LD children did not. This issue, and the other issues raised by Wallach and Goldsmith (1975), provides a base for future investigations of the relationship between spoken and written language in normal and language learning-disabled students.

CLOSING REMARKS

This chapter has attempted to outline some of the developmental changes in language and language strategies that occur after age 4. It is by no means complete. Westby and Van Kleeck will consider narrative development and metalinguistic development in the next two chapters. Nelson will show how many of the latter language acquisitions interact with the language of instruction and the school curricula in Chapter 8. Other strategies related to vocabulary and word association will be discussed later in the text (see Chapter 11). The area of phonological development between 7 and 12 years of age, including morphophonemic and intonational changes in spoken language ability that occur during this period, needs to be considered when discussing language learning. The interaction of phonology with syntactic and pragmatic development was beyond the scope of this chapter (for further information see Ingram, 1976; Cruttenden, 1974; see also Chapters 7 and 13).

It is hoped that professionals continue to study language development that occurs during the school years. It is clear that children learn both analytic and integrative strategies. The research presented should contribute toward our understanding of how strategies available to children become dominant or repressed at different points in time. Children may appear to "regress" in language when, in truth, they are working on new strategies. For example, younger children (3- and 4-year-olds) may appear to be at a higher stage of development when "first noun/actor" strategies predominate. There are periods, early in development, where "ask" and "promise" sentences are interpreted correctly and "tell" sentences, the supposedly "easier" ones, are interpreted incorrectly (Chomsky, 1969; Tavakolian, 1977; Bowerman, 1979). We must recognize these changes, understanding that stages and phases are not neatly ordered, if we are to better understand children with language learning disabilities (see Chapter 2). Likewise, we need to recognize that conclusions about children's abilities should be interpreted within the context in which they were observed as well as the tasks through which behavior was measured (Bransford and Johnson, 1973; Emerson, 1979, 1980; Johnson and Chapman, 1980; see also Chapters 1 and 9).

Goodluck and Tavakolian (1982, p. 20) remind us that there are three levels where children's errors on interpretation might occur: at the level of grammatical competence, at the level of process, and at the level of pragmatics. They indicate that processing difficulties can obscure issues related to the grammar. Pragmatic factors can also obscure underlying competence. Some strategies work well for certain sentences and not others. Those that work well for relative clause sentences may not work for infinitive complements (Goodluck and Tavakolian, 1982). In this age of pragmatics, it is essential not to obscure the importance of syntactic knowledge (H. S. Cairns, personal communication, 1982). In another arena, we are reminded by Hood (1977) that children's abilities to deal with cause-effect relations may change in that physical-logical relations are different from the early life experiences that involve motivational-psychological ones.

We have much to learn about later language learning. Nevertheless, we have learned much over the past decade. It is certainly clear that 5 years of age represents the beginning of a new phase of language development. Perhaps another phase begins at 8 (Karmiloff-Smith, 1979). As practitioners, we can apply many of the ideas presented in this chapter, *if we exercise caution*. Developmental differences are frequently difficult to sort out. Much more information is needed about the interaction of syntactic, semantic, and pragmatic variables—and the intersection of these aspects of spoken language and reading (Myers and Paris, 1978). We may have a long way to go but, clearly, we have come a long way from asking: "After 'is . . . ing,' what next?"

References

Amidon A: Children's understanding of sentences with contingent relationships. *J Exp Child Psychol* 22:423–437, 1976.

Amidon A, Carey P: Why five-year-olds cannot understand "before" and "after." *J Verbal Learn Verbal Behav* 11:417–33, 1972.

Ardery G: The development of coordination in child language. *J Verbal Learn Verbal Behav* 18:745–756, 1979.

Athey I: Syntax, semantics, and reading. In Guthrie J: *Cognition, Curriculum, and Comprehension.* Newark, DE, International Reading Association, 1977, pp 71–98.

Berlin L, Blank M, Rose S: The language of instruction: the hidden complexities. *Top Language Disord* 1:47–58, 1980.

Bever TJ: The cognitive basis of linguistic structures. In Hayes JR: *Cognition and the Development of Language.* New York, John Wiley & Sons, 1970, pp 279–362.

Blachowicz, CLZ: Semantic constuctivity in children's comprehension. *Read Res Q* 13:188–199, 1977/78.

Bloom L, Lahey M, Hood L, et al: Complex sentences: acquisition of syntactic connectives and the semantic relations they encode. *J Child Language* 7:235–261, 1980.

Bowerman M: The acquisition of complex sentences. In Fletcher P, Garman M: *Language Acquisition.* New York, Cambridge University Press, 1979, pp 285–305.

Bransford J, Johnson M: Considerations of some problems of comprehension. In Chase W: *Visual Information Processing.* New York, Academic Press, 1973, pp 383–438.

Bridges A: SVO comprehension strategies reconsidered: the evidence of individual patterns of response. *J Child Language* 7:84–104, 1980.

Brown AL: Semantic integration in children's reconstruction of narrative sequences. *Cognitive Psychol* 8:247–262, 1976.

Chapman R: Comprehension strategies in children. In Kavanagh JF, Strange W: *Speech and Language in the Laboratory Schools, and Clinic.* Cambridge, MA, MIT Press, 1978, pp 308–327.

Chomsky C: *The Acquisition of Syntax in Children from Five to Ten.* Cambridge, MA, MIT Press, 1969.

Clark EV: On the acquisition of the meaning of "before" and "after." *J Verbal Learn Verbal Behav* 10:266–275, 1971.

Clark HH, Clark EV: Semantic distinctions and memory for complex sentences. *Q J Exp Psychol* 20:129–139, 1968.

Corrigan R: A scalogram analysis of the development

of the use and comprehension of "because" in children. *Child Dev* 46:195–201, 1975.

Cromer R: Developmental strategies for language. In Hamilton V, and Vernon MD: *The Development of Cognitive Processes*. New York, Academic Press, 1976.

Cruttenden A: An experiment involving the comprehension of intonation in children from seven to ten. *J Child Language* 1:221–231, 1974.

Dalgleish B, Enkelmann S: The interpretation of pronominal reference by retarded and normal readers. *Br J Psychol* 49:290–296, 1979.

Emerson H: Children's comprehension of "because" in reversible and nonreversible sentences. *J Child Language* 6:279–300, 1979.

Emerson H: Children's judgments of correct and reversed sentences with "if." *J Child Language* 7:127–155, 1980.

French L, Brown A: Comprehension of "before" and "after" in logical and arbitrary sequences. *J Child Language* 7:247–256, 1977.

Goodluck H, Tavakolian S: Competence and processing in children's grammar and relative clauses. *Cognition* 11:1–23, 1982.

Hakuta K: Grammatical description versus configuration arrangement in language acquisition: the case of relative clauses in Japanese. *Cognition* 9:197–236, 1981.

Hood L: A longitudinal study of the development of the expression of casual relations in complex sentences. Doctoral dissertation, Columbia University, 1977.

Hutson BA, Shub J: Developmental study factors involved in choice of conjunctions. Presented at the American Educational Research Association Conference, Chicago, 1974.

Huttenlocker J, Strauss S: Comprehension and a statement's relation to the situation it describes. *J Verbal Learn Verbal Behav* 7:300–304, 1968.

Ingram D: *Phonological Disability in Children*. New York, Elsevier, 1976.

Johnson HL, Chapman RS: Children's judgment and recall of causal connectives: a developmental study of "because," "so" and "and." *J Psycholinguistic Res* 9:243–260, 1980.

Karmiloff-Smith A: Language development after five. In Fletcher P, Garman M: *Language Acquisition*. New York, Cambridge University Press, 1979, pp 307–323.

Kavanagh RD: Observations on the role of logically constrained sentences in the comprehension of "before" and "after." *J Child Language* 16:353–357, 1979.

Klein-Konigsberg E: Semantic integration in normal and learning disabled children. Unpublished doctoral dissertation, The Graduate School and University Center of the City University of New York, May, 1977.

Kuhn D, Phelps H: The development of children's comprehension of causal direction. *Child Dev* 47:248–251, 1976.

Lederberg AR, Maratsos M: Children's use of semantic analysis in the interpretation of missing subjects: further evidence against the MDP. *J Psycholinguistic Res* 1:89–110, 1981.

Lee LL: *Developmental Sentence Analysis*. Evanston, IL, Northwestern University Press, 1974.

Lempert H, Kinsbourne M: Children's comprehension of word order: a developmental investigation. *Child Dev* 49:1235–1238, 1978.

Lempert H, Kinsbourne M: Preschool children's sentence comprehension: strategies with respect to word order. *J Child Language* 7:371–379, 1980.

Maratsos M: How preschool children understand missing complement subjects. *Child Dev* 45:700–706, 1974.

Menyuk P: *Sentences Children Use*. Cambridge, MA, MIT Press, 1969.

Miller G: Some psycholinguistic studies of grammer. *Am Psychol* 17:748–762, 1962.

Myers M, Paris S: Children's metacognitive knowledge about reading. *J Educ Psychol* 70:680–690, 1978.

Paris S, Carter A: Semantic and constructive aspects of sentence memory in children. *Dev Psychol* 9:109–113, 1973.

Paris S, Lindauer B: The role of inferences in children's comprehension and memory for sentences. *Cognitive Psychol* 8:217–227, 1976.

Paris S, Upton L: The construction and retention of linguistic inferences by children. Presented at the Western Psychological Association meeting, San Francisco, April, 1974.

Sheldon A: The role of parallel function in the acquisition of relative clauses in English. *J Verbal Learn Verbal Behav* 13:272–281, 1974.

Strohner H, Nelson K: The young child's development of sentence comprehension: influence of event probability, nonverbal context, syntactic form, and strategies. *Child Dev* 45:567–576, 1974.

Tavakolian S: Structural principles in children's acquisition of complex sentences. Unpublished doctoral dissertation, University of Massachusetts, Amherst, 1977.

Wallach GP: The implications of different language comprehension strategies in learning disabled children: effects of thematization. Unpublished doctoral dissertation, The Graduate School and University Center of the City University of New York, 1977.

Wallach GP: Language processing and reading deficiencies: assessment and intervention for children with special learning problems. In Lass NJ, McReynolds LV, Northern JL, et al: *Speech, Language, and Hearing*. Philadelphia, WB Saunders, 1982, vol 2, pp 819–838.

Wallach GP, Goldsmith SC: Sentence processing in normal and learning disabled children: a look at auditory-verbal and visual-verbal channels. Presented at the American Speech-Language-Hearing Association Convention, Washington DC, November, 1975.

CHAPTER SIX

Development of Narrative Language Abilities

CAROL E. WESTBY, Ph.D.

> Mary was on her way to school.
> She came to the corner.
> She saw a red light.
> Then she saw the green light.
> Then she went on to school.
> 1. What was the girl's name? (Mary)
> 2. Where was the girl going? (to school)
> 3. What did she see at the corner? (red or green light)
> 4. What did she do when she got to the corner? (she stopped or waited for the green light)
> 5. Why did she stop at the corner? (red light was on or to wait for green light)
> 6. Where did she cross the street? (at corner or at light)
> 7. Where did she go then? (to school) (Spache, 1981, p. 6)

The passage and questions above are from the Spache Diagnostic Reading Scales. Although the answers to questions three through six are not explicitly given in the text, first-grade students have no difficulty giving the appropriate responses. The children's comprehension of the text is not, therefore, determined by their comprehension of the individual words and sentences alone. Meaning exists in the text that is not present in the component parts. As discussed in the previous chapter, children are active participants in the comprehension process. The constructive aspects of comprehension cannot be minimized.

In the past decade, there has been a growing dissatisfaction with the adequacy of transformational grammar to describe and explain language comprehension and production. Transformational grammar approaches have dissected sentences removed from context and communicative intent and have ignored the fact that the meaning of a total discourse is more than can be explained from the sum of the meanings in the individual words and sentences. The necessity for textlinguistics systems to explain discourse comprehension has been recognized by anthropologists, sociologists, cognitive psychologists, literary scholars, and computer scientists. The turn from the study of syntax to the study of pragmatics or communicative functions of language in the mid-1970's led to the analysis of utterances in both their linguistic and nonlinguistic contexts. This necessitated the study of more than single utterances. It required the study of entire texts. Many of these pragmatic approaches (Searle, 1969; Dore, 1975; Bates, 1976) explored the perlocutionary (effect) and illocutionary (intent) forces of the texts, rather than the structure of meaning within texts.

In order to study the structure of texts, it is necessary to define what constitutes a text. Halliday and Hasan (1976, p. 1) used the term "text" to refer to "any passage, spoken or written, of whatever length, that does form a unified whole." A text can be anything from a single sentence to a novel or all-day committee meeting. According to Halliday and Hasan (1976, p. 2):

"A text is a unit of language in use. A text is not something like a sentence, only bigger; it is something that differs from a sentence in kind. A text is best regarded as a semantic unit; a unit not of form but of meaning.   ... a text does not consist of sentences; it is REALIZED BY, or encoded in, sentences. If we understand it in this way, we shall not expect to find the same kind of structural integration among the parts of a text as we find among the parts of a sentence or clause. The unity of a text is a unity of a different kind."

Methods of defining, analyzing, and interpreting texts are developing rapidly, yet few of the advances in textlinguistics have been applied to the textual language development of children, particularly learning-disabled children. This chapter is divided into three sections. In the first section, current trends in textlinguistics are reviewed. In the second section, the development of a specific type of text, the narrative, is discussed. The third section presents implications of research in textlinguistics and in narrative development for the learning-disabled school-age child.

TRENDS IN TEXTLINGUISTICS

Text Genres

The structuring of meaning within texts is dependent upon the functions and genre of the texts. Halliday (1975) used the term "texture" to refer to this text-forming component of meaning. The texture of a discourse depends not only on structuring the text parts in an appropriate way and in joining them together, but also in doing so in a way that relates both the nonlinguistic situations and the linguistic context.

PRAGMATIC AND MATHETIC TEXTS

Halliday (1975) proposed two general types or genres of texts, pragmatic and mathetic. Pragmatic texts are used as a means of satisfying needs: to request objects, actions, and information; to seek interactions; or to share feelings and information. Mathetic texts are used to construct reality and problem solve: to narrate, explain, hypothesize, or predict. Numerous other dialectical approaches to types of texts have been suggested.

PARTICIPANT AND SPECTATOR TEXTS

Pragmatic and mathetic texts can be viewed in terms of the roles taken by the producers (speakers or writers) or recipients (listeners or readers) of the text. Britton (1970) used the terms participant and spectator for these two roles. In pragmatic discourse, the producers and recipients are participants. They use language to work on a joint task, to exchange information, to instruct, to persuade, to complain, or to argue. In mathetic discourse, text producers and recipients are spectators. They use language to re-create experiences in order to reflect on, contemplate, and evaluate the experiences. Discourse participants try to make sense of the current situation by acting on bits and pieces of information as they receive them. Discourse spectators focus on maintaining the unity and coherence of the total representation of experiences presented in a text. In this way they work upon the experiences they have participated in, or may participate in, but are not *now* participating in. Evaluation and organization of feelings and attitudes are important in the spectator role. Britton (1979, p. 192) stated that, "as participants, we use language to shape experience in order to handle it; as spectators, we use language to digest experience." This digesting or evaluation of experience is considered particularly important in relating personal experience. Personal narratives or stories are considered pointless if they do not include an evaluation of the experience, whether this evaluation is explicitly or implicitly stated (Labov, 1972; Tannen, 1980). The texts of pragmatic, participant language need not have a point or theme beyond the immediate contextual need.

OBSTRUSIVE AND NONOBSTRUSIVE TEXTS

In obstrusive and nonobstrusive texts (Harweg, 1980) the emphasis is on the texts rather than on the roles of producers and recipients. Texts are classified according to the way they approach the listener/reader recipients. Obstrusive texts occur in every-day conversation or personal written notes and letters. Obstrusive texts move toward the recipients; they confront the recipient. Nonobstrusive texts include lectures, es-says, novels, encyclopedia entries; they wait for the recipients to come and meet them. The recipients of obstrusive texts can do little to avoid receiving a letter or being asked to close a door. Their only option is to choose either to respond or to ignore the message. In contrast, it is the recipient's choice to become involved in nonobstrusive texts. Such texts do not confront or seize the recipients. The recipient of nonobstru-sive texts can choose to attend a lecture or read a book.

According to Harweg (1980) information cannot be presented in the same way in obstrusive and nonobstrusive texts. Be-cause nonobstrusive texts do not confront the recipient, it is allowable to begin with information as far removed from the im-mediate communicative situation as de-sired. For example, the children's book *Harriet the Spy* begins, "Harriet was trying to explain to Sport how to play Town." There is no explanation of who the people are or when and why their actions are oc-curring. Obstrusive texts lack such an al-lowance and, consequently, must begin with sentences designating states of affairs in the present situation, often assisted by deictics, such as I, you, here, there, today, yesterday. Information removed from the communicative situation may be presented later in the obstrusive discourse, if appro-priate transitions are made. A story or a personal narrative can be introduced into a conversation, but only if it is in some way tied to the present situation. Although non-obstrusive texts are not required to set the scene as are obstrusive texts, titles can function like deictics to aid the recipients. If nonobstrusive texts lack titles, recipients have to expend greater effort and concen-tration on building hypotheses about the context. This is easily recognized when one reads the following paragraph from Brans-ford and Johnson (1972, p. 400):

"The procedure is actually quite simple. First you arrange items into different groups. Of course, one pile may be sufficient depending on how much there is to do. If you have to go somewhere else due to lack of facilities, that is the next step; otherwise, you are pretty well set. It is important not to overdo things. That is, it is better to do a few things at once than too many. In the short run this may not seem important but complications can easily arise. A mistake can be expensive as well. . . ."

Without this title, "Washing Clothes," this passage is nearly incomprehensible. Com-prehension of a text is significantly im-proved when the text is given a title (Brans-ford and Johnson, 1972; Dooling and Mul-let, 1973; Bock, 1980), yet frequently chil-dren are given tasks of reading a passage and then deciding what the title should be.

Nonobstrusive texts are restricted in where they can occur. Nonobstrusive texts must normally be presented at appropriate places; for example, in libraries, churches, a specific sign in a certain location, or in the story corner of the classroom. Obstru-sive texts are restricted in regard to audi-ence rather than location. Producers of an obstrusive text must judge their degree of familiarity with the audience and the inter-ests the audience may have in the topic when structuring the discourse. This ob-strusive/nonobstrusive text distinction provides a basis for understanding the structural differences of text beginnings in terms of communicative situation and the interactions of producers and recipients. The producers of texts must understand who the recipients of their texts are and where the recipients are in order to struc-ture the meaning within the texts so that it is viewed as comprehensible and socially appropriate by the recipients.

Text Modality: The Oral Literate Continuum

Many of the differences in the structure of meaning among texts can be understood when considered in terms of the modality of text presentation, that is, whether the text is presented in an oral or written mode. There are differences in strategies used in remembering oral and written texts. Oral and written texts also differ in their functions and in the relationship between text and thought. These differences result in structural variations in the organization of meaning between the two types of texts. Orality and literacy should be considered on a continuum rather than as a dichotomy (Tannen, 1980). At the extreme oral end of the continuum would be the pragmatic, obstrusive, participant texts; at the extreme literate or written end would be mathetic, nonobstrusive, spectator texts. Within the mid-range of the continuum some oral forms are more like writing and some written forms are more like oral language. For example, a speech or a lecture is more like written language, while a personal letter is more like oral language.

BASES OF STRUCTURAL DIFFERENCES

The differences between oral and literate modes can be considered in two subcategories: those dealing with the message and those dealing with the medium (Rubin, 1980). The message varies along the dimensions of function (pragmatic or mathetic), topic (everyday objects and situations and shared knowledge versus abstract or unfamiliar objects and situations and unshared knowledge), and structure (familiar words, imprecise, redundant, syntax versus unfamiliar words and formal complex syntax).

Spoken and written language have different functions, and, as a consequence of their different functions, they frequently have different topics. In addition, literate language, according to Olson (1977), allows one to engage in a type of logical thought that is not possible in oral language. Written text permits people to contemplate sentence meaning per se, rather than merely to use the sentence as a cue to the meaning intended by the speaker. Oral language is a universal means of sharing our understanding of concrete situations and practical actions. Written language, by providing definitions and making all assumptions and premises explicit as well as observing the rules of formal logic, is an instrument of considerable power in building an abstract theory of reality.

The modality of the message, that is, whether the message is presented in an oral or a written mode, markedly affects the structure of the message. The differing modes of presentation result in differing levels of interactions and involvement among the producers and recipients, differences in spatial and temporal commonality, and differences in concreteness of referents and separability of characters within the text or discourse. In oral language the participants share the same spatial and temporal context and frequently the objects and events referred to are visually present; hence, the language used can be and is situationally dependent. The speaker and listener are usually jointly involved in the message. If misunderstanding arises, the speaker and the listener can interact to correct the misunderstanding (even though they may not do so). Literate language is decontextualized. The producer and recipient do not share the same spatial and temporal commonality or concreteness of referents, and the producer and recipient are not mutually involved in the message and do not have the opportunity to interact to correct any misunderstandings. Meaning is in the situation in the oral language and in the text in the literate language (Olson, 1977). The oral mode allows considerable information to be conveyed via stress, gestures, and other prosodic cues. The spatial and temporal commonality permits the use of deictic markers, such as this, that, here, there, now, today, last night. Spatial and deictic markers are not interpretable in written text, and temporal deictic markers require that the listener/reader switch from his present context to the temporal context of the narrator or characters within the story.

Because literate language does not involve sharing of spatial and temporal commonality, the ability to interact, and the difference of stress and intonation variables, literate text must be structured differently than oral text. These structural variations, however, are not simply to make explicit in written language what was implicit in the situational context of oral language. The noetics, that is, the process of shaping, storing, retrieving, and communicating, in oral and literate mediums are different. Structural variations reflect noetic differences. In the oral tradition, ideas are elaborated by stitching together formulaic language, that is, familiar cliches and proverbs, in a manner which Ong (1978) called rhapsodic. The language is dependent upon prosodic features, repetitions, proverbial phrases, and shared situational knowledge. In the literate tradition, ideas are expressed in an analytic, sequential, linear manner with specific lexical items and minimal redundancy of ideas. These structural differences result in differences of mnemonics between orality and literacy. The parallel constructions, repetitions, formulaic phrases, and almost poetic-like structures of oral language facilitate memorization. Some of these characteristics are seen in this Navajo holy way chant (Reichard, 1944, p. 59):

"At Rumbling Mountain,
Holy Man who with the eagle tail-feathered arrow
    glides out,
  This day I have come to be trustful
  This day I look to you . . .
  With your strong feet rise up to protect me,
  With your sturdy legs rise up to protect me,
  With your strong body rise up to protect me,
  With your healthy mind rise up to protect me,
  Carrying the dark bow and the eagle tail-feathered
    arrow with which you transformed evil,
  By these means will you protect me."

These repetitive, rhythmical phrases facilitate ease of memorization. Ease of memorization is essential for the continuation of information in an oral culture. If we are literate, we do not need to memorize. In an oral culture, knowing means having memorized. In a literate culture, knowing means knowing where to find the information in a book. It has been suggested that, in the graduate student culture, knowing means, "I've made a Xerox copy and have it in my files."

The mainstream American culture values literacy highly and is quick to assume that literacy is always better than orality. Literacy may not, however, always be better than orality. Bright (1981) suggested that "literacy is like a wooden leg—useful only when one is maimed." In embracing the literature style, we have given up types of memory skills. The Navajos have experienced a strong push toward literacy in the last 30 years and recently are reporting that their children are having great difficulty learning the traditional chants that have been passed down through the generations in the oral tradition. At the 1981 Georgetown Linguistics Roundtable, a participant in the audience made the following comment after hearing the values of literacy extolled:

"I'm from Gambia in West Africa which is a quite oral tradition, and I'm also a griot. . . . Griots are the orators who pass on stories and the history of the people from generation to generation. I am where the line stops because my parents are griots. They can tell the histories of my people, but I'm not able to do that because I'm supposedly educated."

The structural variations of oral and literate language result in differential encoding of the message and, as a result, in different memories of the material presented in an oral or written mode. Even with structure held constant, however, the modality of the message alone also affects the manner of encoding. Hilyard and Olson (1978) demonstrated that children remembered different components of texts depending upon whether they listened to or read the printed texts. Listeners were more accurate in verifying statements referring to the gist and details important for overall story comprehension. The readers, on the other hand, were more accurate in verifying the incidental statements which were not essential to the story as a whole. Although many strategies for listening and reading do overlap, the brain apparently organizes information differently depending upon the modality of presentation. It should be realized that many children entering school come from a primarily oral tradition and, consequently, may not have at their disposal the encoding strategies necessary for literate language.

STRUCTURAL DIFFERENCES

The medium-related differences between oral and literate texts necessitate syntactic and vocabulary differences that are just beginning to be explored. Spoken language has as one of its most salient aspects the use of stress, intonation, and other prosodic features. We rely on stress in oral language as an indicator of such discourse-organizing topics as given information versus new information. Information which is coded prosodically in oral communication must be coded syntactically and semantically in written language. Chafe (1982) noted that spoken discourse presents propositions without overtly marking the relationships to each other, or with the minimal cohesive conjunction "and," whereas written discourse makes use of subordinating conjunctions, subject deletion, and other complex syntactic constructions to achieve cohesion. In many oral communications the listener is involved in the text and already knows the relationships among the people, objects, and events being discussed and, hence, does not need to have these relationships explicitly stated.

Many complex syntactic forms, for example, complements and relative clauses, were discussed in Chapter 5. The use of these forms in oral compared to literate conversational strategies shows interesting differences. These structural differences were observed by Collins and Michaels (1980) in a study of the relationship of oral/literate conversational strategies to the acquisition of literacy in first- and fourth-grade children. Ability to use a literate conversational style was associated with higher reading skills. In the more oral style narratives of children, complements tended to be verbal complements, that is, added information about a given verbal process. For example:

(1) and then he dro--ve off *with 'em*
(2) and he had a wreck *on his bike*

The prepositional phrases added informa-

tion about the verbal activity. In contrast, in the literate style narratives, complements were frequently embedded against key nominals denoting major characters in the overall narrated events. For example:

(1) a man . . . *that was pickin' some* . . . pears
(2) this boy *on this bike* came along

In these examples, the "that" complement and the prepositional phrases added information about the nominals and the pronouns. The embedded information was then used to maintain explicit reference identity throughout the narrative. The oral style narrators were less inclined to use embedded nominals to signal identity of characters and instead employed prosodic conventions. Thus the distinction between or the separability of the characters was handled differently in the oral versus the literate style. Contrast the literate style example in which the character is introduced

There was a man . . . that was . . . picking some . . . pears and

then later referred to again

and then . . . they . . . walked by the man/who gave/ . . . wh-who was picking the pears

with the oral style narrative in which vowel elongation and a high rise-fall contour on "man" serves as a cue that old information is being talked about:

it was/ . . . about this mān
he was um/ . . . . . . take some um . . .
pēach--/some . . . pēa-rs off the tree
. . . and when that . . . when he pa--ssed/
by that ma--n/ . . . the man . . .
the ma--n came out the tree/

This high rise-fall contour functions almost as if to say, "You know what I mean, that man I already told you about."

Children who were classified as literate style narrators also made greater use of intraclausal complements such as infinitives and "that" complements and greater use of clausal connectives such as but, so, on the other hand, conversely. In written language clausal connectives serve to integrate meaning in the absence of prosodic and situational cues (Hirsch, 1977). In spoken language they serve a similar function of semantic integration, either by replacing an intonation or contextual cue or by reduplicating this function. They make the semantic relationships between clauses fully explicit.

Collins and Michaels (1980) reported that those students using the oral style in narration had more difficulty expressing themselves in writing than the children who used a more literate style in their oral discourse. The oral discourse strategies work only if one shares either in the in-group or has an awareness of this oral signaling convention. The oral strategy does not transfer to writing where the accompanying prosodic cues are lost. The literate style which relies on explicit lexical elaboration and clausal embeddings works well in both oral and written discourse.

Approaches to Text Analysis

So far the structural characteristics of different text genres and modalities of presentations and the reasons for structural differences have been discussed. An explanation for how meaning coheres within texts has not been provided. For this, a theory of text structure is needed. Van Dijk and Kintsch (1978) proposed a grammatical theory of discourse consisting of three components:

1. A theory of semantic representations for propositions, sentences, and sequences of sentences which comprise the microstructures of the discourse.

2. A theory of semantic representations for global discourse structures, the text macrostructures that are organized into an overall superstructure which is the theme of the text. Each text genre has a particular macrostructure organization.

3. A theory of cohesion that relates the microstructures to each other and to the macrostructure.

An analysis of a text should consider these three components. Whereas transfor-mational grammar has generally provided an adequate understanding of text microstructures, that is, propositions and sentences, the majority of the most recent research in text analysis has focused on macrostructure systems and cohesion principles. Hence, these two areas of text structure will be discussed.

COHESION

The most familiar work in the area of cohesion is that of Halliday and Hasan (1976). They defined cohesion as the set of possibilities that exists in language for making a text hang together. Cohesion is expressed partly through grammar and partly through vocabulary. Halliday and Hasan's listing of cohesive techniques includes:

1. Reference—pronominals, demonstratives, and comparatives that "instead of being interpreted semantically in their own right . . . make reference to something else for their interpretation" (p. 31). There are two types of reference:

a. Anaphoric reference which presupposes for its interpretation an element that has come earlier in the text, for example:

> Champaign is a duck. He sleeps standing on one leg.

In the second sentence, *he* is an anaphoric reference to Champaign.

> I jogged three miles in 22 minutes yesterday. That's a record for me.

In the second sentence, *that* is an anaphoric reference to jogging 3 miles in 22 minutes.

b. Cataphoric reference which presupposes for its interpretation an element that will follow in the text, for example:

> She could continue no longer. Ann had been swimming in the cold water for two hours.

In the first sentence, *she* refers to Ann in the second sentence.

> I can't believe it. We won a trip to Hawaii.

In the first sentence, *it* refers to the entire second sentence.

2. Ellipsis—the omission of one or more surface expressions within one format, under the provision that a structurally complete version of the format is recoverable in the vicinity, for example:

> Michael enjoys swimming, and Susan does too.

in which *does too* implies enjoys swimming.

> The marble cheesecake was delicious. Bill asked for more.

More in the second sentence presupposes marble cheesecake.

3. Substitution or paraphrase—the reuse of the same content in a different surface pattern, for example:

> Bill failed the first math exam. His roommate said the next one would be easier.

in which *one* substitutes for math exam.

> Everyone was leaving. They were all going out the door.

in which the second sentence is a paraphrase of the first.

4. Lexical—the selection of related vocabulary which may include reiteration of the same word, a synonym or near synonym, or a word representing a superordinate category, for example:

> There's a boy climbing that old oak. The child could fall.

in which *child* is a superordinate of boy.

> The Sierra Club's tour included a hike to the top of the volcanic crater. The trek was arduous.

in which hike and trek are near synonyms.

5. Conjunction—the connecting of surface structures (phrases, clauses, and sentences) with conjunctions.

SCHEMA THEORIES

A variety of theories to explain global discourse structures, that is, macrostructures, have been proposed. A macrostructure approach to text organization is not new. Bartlett (1932), one of the first psychologists to study narrative discourse, proposed a macrostructure theory. He suggested the term schema to refer to the organization of narratives in memory. Schema theory has been further developed by Anderson (1977), Rumelhart, (1975), Schank and Abelson (1977), and Spiro (1977). Overall, the term schema has been used to refer to a hypothetical construction of knowledge. Other terms, such as frame, script, and plans, have been used both synonymously with schema and with a slight variation.

Beaugrande (1979) suggested that the organization of knowledge can be approached from four perspectives. First, knowledge can be viewed as a frame which is an array of elements (Charniak, 1975; Minsky, 1975; Winograd, 1975). For example, a zoo frame would be a network of entries such as animals, foods, cage types, etc., that zoos have. A frame has a conceptual center (in this case, a zoo) with no commitment to a sequence of actualization. Second, knowledge can also be viewed as a progression in which elements occur during actualization. This perspective is called a schema (Bartlett, 1932; Rumelhart, 1975, 1977; Kintsch, 1977; Mandler and Johnson, 1977; Rumelhart and Ortony, 1977; Thorndyke, 1977; Freedle and Hale, 1979). For example, a zoo schema could describe the order in which people can walk through the zoo or the order of experiences in watching the monkeys. Third, knowledge can be viewed in relation to a person's plans or desires in which elements advance the planner toward a goal (Abelson, 1975; Schank and Abelson, 1977; Beaugrande, 1979). For example, someone could summon up plans for visiting a zoo. Fourth, knowledge can be viewed as a script in which elements are instructions to participants about what they should say or do in their perspective roles (Schank and Abelson, 1977; Culling-ford, 1978). For example, a restaurant script has instructions for the customer, waiter, and cashier to be enacted in an established manner. Frames and schemas are more oriented toward the internal arrangement of knowledge, whereas plans and scripts reflect human needs to get things done in everyday interaction. Frames, schemas, scripts, and plans are all necessary to have a total representation of a personal experience.

NARRATIVE SCHEMAS

Schema approaches to macrostructure analysis have been applied primarily to the narrative genre texts in order to understand how they are comprehended and remembered. A variety of narrative schemas have been proposed (Rumelhart, 1975, 1977; Thorndyke, 1977; Stein and Glenn, 1979; Johnson and Mandler, 1980). These narrative schemas are frequently called story grammars because, like other grammars, they make explicit the syntactic structures of narratives. Although there is some variation among the different grammars, they basically all include similar components.

All story grammars include a setting and a goal which is met in an episode system. The setting introduces the main character and/or describes the social, physical, or temporal context of the story. All components other than the setting are subsumed under the category of episode. Most stories have two or more episodes. Episodes have a beginning which is an initiating event, a reaction of the characters to the initiating event, an action or attempt by the characters to deal with the initiating event, an outcome or consequence of the attempt, and an ending. The beginning or initiating event of an episode can be a natural occurrence, such as a flood; an action, such as the three pigs leaving home; an internal physiological state, such as hunger, pain, or sickness; or the perception of an external event, such as seeing a lion. A reaction is the characters' internal response to the initiating event. The reaction has two components: an internal response which is the

characters' emotional response to the initiating event and an internal plan which is the characters' thinking about their reaction and planning what to do about the initiating event. The internal response can be an affective response, such as happiness or despair; or it can be a desire or intention, like the wolf wanting the pig. An internal plan involves ideas about how to deal with the response. The attempt includes statements referring to the characters' overt actions. The outcome or consequence of the attempt is a natural occurrence, such as the rain stopping for Noah; an action, such as the pig cooking the wolf; or an end state, such as marriage. The ending is frequently an affective response, such as they lived happily ever after; but it can be a thought or idea, such as Lamont knowing he had found a friend; or an action, such as riding off into the sunset.

These submacrostructure categories must be related to each other, and the component propositions or microstructures must be related to each other. Three relations are used in story grammars: and, then, and cause. The relationships may or may not be explicitly stated in the text. The following is a story produced by a 12-year-old boy. The sentences have been numbered for purposes of analysis. Figure 6.1 presents a macrostructure analysis of the story using a modified Stein and Glenn (1979) grammar.

1. Once upon a time there was a terrible beast in the mountains.
2. He'd eat people at nighttime. And he'd come down in the town at night, and he'd eat people.
3. And the people, they were getting pretty tired of finding bones—people bones, and stuff everywhere.
4. So they decided to do something about it.
5. So one night they come out of their houses with torches and they went up in the mountains to get him. And they come up in these mountains.
6. And they see this monster. And so they throw their torches at him.
7. And he just . . . fire doesn't hurt him.
8. And so they get their guns and they're shooting at him.
9. And none of them can hit him.

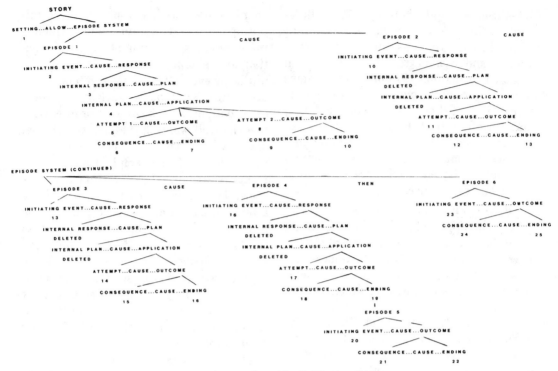

Figure 6.1. Analysis of an oral narrative produced by a 12-year-old boy.

10. And they find out he's not the one doing it 'cause he can talk and he tells them that. He says that he wasn't the one doing it. It was his brother.

11. And so they went into these mountains again another night to find his brother. And this time they brought elephant guns.

12. And they see his brother.

13. And his brother says he's not the one doing it, but it's his sister.

14. So the next night they go out again with elephant guns and stuff and fire.

15. And they find his sister.

16. And she says that she's not the one doing it either. And it's their dad.

17. And so they go out another night.

18. And they find their dad.

19. And he's the one doing it he says. And so they take him into town ... took him captive and take him into town.

20. And bring him to the lie detector thing, and said, and they asked him questions. They said, "Are you the one that's killing all the people?"

21. And he said, "Yeh." And it was a lie.

22. And a and so they let him go.

23. And they they found this lion and it was the one doing it all.

24. And they shot him.

25. And that's the end.

The first episode is a complete episode in that all components of the narrative macrostructure are explicitly stated. Episodes 2, 3, and 4 are, on the surface, less complete, but they are implicitly complete because the responses and plans have been stated in the first episode; they are inferable in later episodes and, therefore, can be deleted (Johnson and Mandler, 1980). Episodes 5 and 6 include only an initiating event, consequence, and ending. There is no response or plan to cope with the initiating events, only a consequence of the events.

One of the first attempts to define components of narrative episodes was suggested by the Russian folklorist Propp (1928). Propp worked with a collection of Russian fairy tales. He noted that the tales have a variety of episodes and characters, but that their plots are quite similar. He contended that the plot of a story was made up of a series of functions. Propp defined function as "an act of a character, which is defined from the point of view of its significance for the course of action of a tale as a whole" (p. 20). Propp argued that all stories are composed of a limited set of functions and that these functions occur in a set order, although no story includes all functions. Botvin (1976) modified Propp's analysis to make it suitable for any story. His analysis yielded 91 elements subcategorized into beginning (introduction, preparation, complication), middle (development), and ending (resolution and ending) functions. The introduction and endings are fomulaic expressions, such as "once upon a time" and "the end." The preparation includes elements that precede disequilibrating events and can involve elements such as threats, warnings, or deceptions. The complication involves a disequilibrating situation either of lack or of villainy. The development section can involve a wide variety of functions including counteractions, translocations, transformations, reconnaissance, alliance, or defense. The resolution involves functions such as rescue and release, lack liquidated or not liquidated, villainy overcome or not overcome. The following story by a seventh-grade student is analyzed according to the functions present:

Once in a small peaceful town a long time ago before cars or electricity some people went on a hike (INTRODUCTION—background information). Little did they know that there was a big monster in the mountains. They kept going (PREPARATION—threatening situation). The monster made an avalanche (COMPLICATION: VILLAINY—physical attack). The people ran from the avalanche (DEVELOPMENT: ESCAPE—escape from a threatening situation). They kept marching because they knew there was something up there and they wanted to know what it was (DEVELOPMENT: RECONNAISSANCE—search). And they got to the top and they see the monster running (DEVELOPMENT: RECONNAISSANCE—find object of search). And they pull out their guns and start shooting at him (DEVELOPMENT: RECONNAISSANCE—prepare for physical counterattack and physical counterattack). They miss every time (DEVELOPMENT: ESCAPE—escape from attack). The monster goes into his cave and sees his two children. His children are throwing food and he scolds them. The people find out where

his cave is and they close it off (RESOLUTION: VILLAINY OVERCOME—threat nullified).

These story elements or functions can be grouped into five metafunctions—two that have to do with states of equilibrium, two with states of transition, and one with states of disequilibrium (Todoruv, 1971). In narratives, an initial state of affairs (equilibrium 1) is changed in some way (transition 1) into a state of affairs that is opposite to it (disequilibrium). This state is then changed in some way (transition 2) so that we get back to a state that is analogous to the initial one (equilibrium 2). This pattern is reflected in the above story. The people who live in a peaceful town go for a hike (state of equilibrium). Their hike is disrupted (transition) by the monster's avalanche (state of disequilibrium). The people cope with this event by first running and then searching for the monster (transition). They find the monster and barricade him in his cave (thus restoring a state of equilibrium). Not all stories include the full cycle; but any narrative must deal with a sequence of at least three metafunctions. Sad stories deal with the first three metafunctions while happier stories deal with the last three.

Propp's functions and the various story grammars are abstract metalinguistic representations of people's worldviews. These worldviews are reflections of six basic knowledge domains (Graesser, 1981):

1. Linguistic knowledge which includes phonemic, lexical, syntactic, semantic, and pragmatic knowledge.

2. Rhetorical knowledge which involves awareness of the superstructures and macrostructures of different genres. This knowledge does not have to be at a meta or conscious level, but rather only at functional level so that a person can carry out the tasks of telling a narrative or arguing.

3. Causal conceptualizations which refer to sequences of events and states that unfold in a mechanistic or nonintentional manner.

4. Intentional conceptualizations which

refer to actions that are planned and goal directed.

5. Spatial knowledge which refers to providing spatial contexts for the actions, events, and states that are expressed in the text.

6. Knowledge about roles, personalities, and objects. This includes knowledge of attributes of people and objects that determine states and events.

All knowledge domains must be integrated in texts. Certain texts require more of some knowledge domains than others. Thus, expository texts are more dependent upon causal conceptualizations, whereas narratives are more dependent upon intentional conceptualizations (Graesser, 1981). Intentional knowledge is, in fact, critical for comprehending and producing narratives because actions in narratives represent steps in a plan. Perception of the plans plays a role in structuring social reality and, consequently, in producing and comprehending narrative texts (Bruce, 1980). The person who has difficulty in planning his own behavior and in recognizing plans and social actions in the behavior of others will also have difficulty in understanding narrative episodes because many of the motivations, reasons, and causes of states and events must be inferred.

The basic assumption of these various schema theories of macrostructure organizations is that what is experienced or learned is organized or stored in the brain not in a static unchanging form but in a way that permits modification through further development. Development occurs when what is known about an object or event interacts with what is new but related. Schema theories have been extremely popular in attempting to explain how written material is comprehended. In this context, it is assumed that the various grammars represent an individual's schema knowledge and that comprehension is as dependent on the schema in the reader's head as it is on what is on the printed page. As the individual reads, the schema is in-

stantiated, that is, the components are filled in (Durkin, 1981).

The text analysis systems have been applied almost exclusively to narrative texts produced by adults. The primary application to children has been in using this analysis procedure on material read by children, and then asking the children to retell the information that they have read and reporting on the story components that the children omit or distort in their retellings. It has been assumed that the retellings reflect the children's comprehension of the texts they have read. Omanson et al. (1978), however, showed that story retelling was independent of story comprehension as measured by inference questions that required the children to integrate the propositions in the text in order to answer the questions. This approach to text understanding has focused on schema processing (Spiro, 1980). When reading, a reader must select (retrieve) the schemas appropriate for the text, and, as the discourse proceeds, the schema must be instantiated. The reader must also be able to maintain and/or change schemas as the discourse proceeds because different schemas will have to be brought to bear at different times depending on signals from the text. In addition, it may be necessary to combine schemas in order to understand a given part of a discourse. The combination may result in an interpretation that was not inferable from additive combinations of the schema parts.

Children may exhibit difficulty in comprehending and/or producing narratives either because of having few and incomplete schemas or because of inefficiency in processing the schemas they do have. Efficient schema processing is certainly imperative for comprehension of text, but even more basic is whether the individual possesses the schema knowledge that must be retrieved and instantiated. The next section will discuss children's acquisition of narrative schemas.

DEVELOPMENT OF NARRATIVE ABILITIES

How do children develop text abilities? Children must first have knowledge in each of the knowledge domains suggested by Graesser (1981). They must be able to represent knowledge linguistically in the appropriate rhetorical mode, and they must possess a knowledge of causal, intentional, spatial, and role relationships. Although this is a book about language disabilities in school-age children, narrative development in preschool children will first be reviewed because even many learning-disabled midschool students do not possess the narrative skills of 4- and 5-year-olds (Westby and Martinez, 1981).

Pitcher and Prelinger (1963) had, until quite recently, contributed the major work on text or story development in children. Their orientation was not, however, on the organization of meaning within the stories but rather on the psychosocial story themes of preschool boys and girls. Applebee (1978), using the Pitcher and Prelinger stories and Vygotsky's (1962) model of concept development, proposed a system for studying the development of story organization. With age, children's stories grow longer and more complex on virtually any dimension of complexity. Narrative structures become more tightly controlled, evolving from a collection of events related to each other only by their proximity in time or space, to stories that have a physical or psychological center, that is, a central character or theme; to stories that have a chaining of events in temporal or cause-effect sequences; to highly structured narratives in which the events are linked structually both to a common center or theme and to other events which immediately precede and follow it in cause-effect and true temporal relationships.

Figure 6.2 presents the stages of story development as suggested by Applebee (1978). These stages of text development are best viewed as steps toward the narrative genre. The earliest prenarrative structure is termed "heaps." In heap stories, children talk about whatever attracts their attention. As a consequence, there is no relationship or organization among the elements or individual microstructures, and there is no story macrostructure. Such stories consist of labeling items or describing activities as exemplified by the following story:

> The gorilla is climbing up the mountain. Snow's comin' up. And the people are down there and all the houses and all the trees. It's all black and it's all brown.

The sentences in such stories are generally simple declarative sentences, almost always in the present or present progressive tense. True cohesive techniques are not used. Children who tell heap stories often do not appear to recognize that the characters on each page of picture books are the same characters. Without this realization, there is no basis for a sequence of related sentences because the child is not aware of the relationships between the pictures.

Applebee termed the second stage of prenarrative development "sequences." The term sequence for this story structure is misleading because, although there may be an apparent time sequence in the story, it is not intentionally planned by the storyteller. Sequence stories, unlike heaps, have a macrostructure. The macrostructure involves a central character or a setting or a topic. The microstructure elements of the story may involve activities of the central character; activities occurring in a particular setting, such as on a snowy day; or similar activities (the topic) carried out by different characters, such as a bird flying, a bee flying, and a ghost flying. The story elements are related to the central macrostructure through concrete associative or perceptual bonds; for example, Superman is perceptually associated with flying or a snowy day is perceptually associated with making a snowman. The following is a typical sequence story with central characters forming the macrostructure:

> A gorilla and robbers were in the house. They were stealing things. They turned off the lights. They stoled

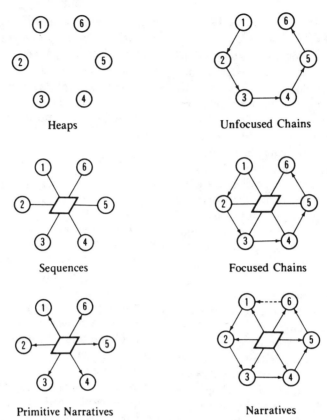

Figure 6.2. The structure of children's stories. *Arrows* indicate complementary attributes; *straight lines*, shared attributes; *parallelograms*, centers; *circles*, incidents or elements. (Reprinted from Applebee AN: *The Child's Concept of Story*. Chicago, © 1978, with permission of The University of Chicago Press.)

all the food in the church and they stoled the money and they stoled a bunch of things. And they were walking in the snow at night. They didn't see the gorilla.

The next conceptual level of stories is termed "primitive narratives." Like sequences, primitive narratives have a macrostructure that consists of a person, object, or event that forms a concrete center. Primitive narrative stories are, however, differentiated from sequence stories by the relationship that exists between the story center and the individual elements. In sequence stories, the characters, objects, or events are put together because they are perceptually associated with or resemble each other is some way; in primitive narratives, the characters, objects, or events are put together because they complement each other in some way. In a primitive narrative, the elements of the story follow logically from the attributes of the center. These attributes are seldom perceptually obvious as they were in sequence stories. They are, instead, internal to the characters, objects, or events, and it is these attributes that determine the types of elements that can occur. For example, a good character will do good deeds and be rewarded for them.

The primitive narrative schema represents the child's first use of inference in stories. Drawing inferences requires that children go beyond explicit and perceptually obvious information and that they be aware of the reciprocal causality between thoughts and external events (Tyler, 1978). Thoughts can be both the consequences of and the causes of external events. Children producing primitive narratives recognize and label facial expressions and body postures, and in their stories they make frequent reference to the associated feelings of the characters. Although they are beginning to expect characters' feelings to be related to the events of a story, this understanding is incomplete. It often goes in only one direction, from thought to event or from event to thought. The children do not always perceive the reciprocal causality between thoughts and events. Hence, children might recognize that Millicent the Monster (in the book by the same name) is sad or lonely because no one will play with her, but they cannot predict what Millicent might do about the situation. Or they might recognize that the hermit in *Once a Mouse* is angry with the lion and will change the lion back into a mouse, but they do not understand that the hermit is angry because of the lion's boasting and lack of gratitude for what the hermit has done for him. The following story produced by a learning-disabled mid-school student shows the developing awareness of the effects of feelings on events:

There was this gorilla and this town people. And the town people went to go see if they could catch the gorilla. And the gorilla says, "Oh, I'm lonely. Look at these people down there. I wish I could go meet them, so I won't be all alone any more." So the townspeople go, "Let's go get him. Let's put him up. Let's catch him as a hostage." Then the gorilla goes, "Oh I wish those people would be nice to me. I wish they'd quit chasing me, trying to beat me up." So the townspeople and the gorilla get together and they live happily ever after. The end.

The next developmental stage toward the true narrative structure is the "unfocused chain." In unfocused chain stories the individual elements or events are linked together in logical or cause-effect relationships, often through the use of conjunctive cohesive techniques. (Recall from the previous chapter that 4- or 5-year-old children are using semantic probability strategies and are learning to deal with sentences having logical conceptual relationships such as before or because). The awareness

of these temporal and cause-effect relationships represents a significant change in children's understanding of relationships among events in their world. Although the elements or microstructures of the unfocused chain are related to each other, they are not related to any macrostructure. Unlike the sequence and primitive narrative stories, unfocused chain stories have no central character or topic. Without this macrostructure there is no story theme or plot, and, consequently, there is no basis for including some events and excluding others. The child produces chains of associated events as one thought leads to another. Any two consecutive microstructures or propositions may have some attributes in common, but later elements frequently share no attributes or relationships with earlier elements in the story. The focus of the child's attention is constantly shifting. This shifting change of focus is apparent in the following story by a 4-year-old girl:

Once upon a time there was a bee that said, "Buzz, buzz, buzz, buzz." The duck went, "Quack, quack, quack." The sun went up down, up down until it came back up. There was a house which was the duck's house and they all went to his house to have supper. They ate hamburgers and drank their favorite punch. And then they all went out to take a little ride with a dog. Then they went to the church to look around. They saw a married girl getting married. She was marrying a boy. The boy and girl went home. They ate dinner. After dinner the baby came out.

Pure unfocused chains are rarely produced by most children. Almost as soon as children begin to deal with cause-effect and true sequential relationships, they begin to tie the story microstructure elements not only to each other but also, simultaneously, to a story macrostructure. As a consequence, we see the development of focused chain and true narrative schema stories. Children's focused chain narratives resemble adult stories in surface appearance because they consist of a central character with a true sequence of events. The understanding of attributes of characters which began to appear in primitive narratives is still weak, however. Because the child lacks complete awareness of, or understanding of, reciprocal relationships between characters' attributes and events and the relationships between events, the stories do not have strong plots. In a plot, the events must build on the attributes of the characters and should result in growth of the characters' personalities by modification of their attributes. In stories without strong plots, the characters' actions seldom lead to attainment of a goal; consequently, if no goal is perceived, then, in the child's thinking, there is no need for an end to the story, or, at least, the ending does not have to follow logically from the beginning. In the focused chain stories, the endings may follow from the preceding event, but one may not be able to tell from the ending how the story began (Westby, 1982). The following story is typical of the focused chain schema:

King Kong was on top of the mountain at night. There was lots of snow all over. He was gonna throw rocks down on the town, and kill all the people. The people knew he was up there. They got fire to burn him up with, and they climbed up the mountain. King Kong threw rocks at them and ran down the other side of the mountain. The end.

As indicated in the previous chapter on later language learning, age 5 represents a new frontier in language acquisition. Beginning at age 5 to 6, children reach the stage of conceptual thought that enables them to formulate a true narrative that has all the components of a story grammar (Botvin and Sutton-Smith, 1977; Applebee, 1978). True narratives integrate chaining of events with the complementary centering of the primitive narrative, and, as a consequence, they have well developed plots. The microstructure elements are sequenced to each other through temporal and cause-effect relationships and are linked to the macrostructures because they are generally motivated by the intentions or the goal directedness of the main character/protagonist, and perhaps also by other characters, particularly antagonists. The intentions or goals of the characters are dependent upon their attributes and feelings. Thus, the ending of a story must be related in some way to issues presented in the beginning of the story. The following story written by a 6½-year-old boy is an excellent example of a story with a true narrative structure. The child's spelling has not been corrected. Sentences have been numbered for purposes of analysis. Figure 6.3 presents an analysis of this story using a modified Stein and Glenn (1979) grammar:

1. Both mother and father dipladacus were afraid to leav the vally.
2. Mother dipladacus was afraid of the great tyranosoras rex.
3. So one day little dipladacus wint to the rocks.
4. He didn't have anething to do.
5. Then he began to thro rocks at the mowntons!
6. The the big tyranasoras rex heard him!
7. He lomberd forward fild with rege!
8. Little dip was frighten but he was brave!
9. He knew what to do!
10. He began to throw rocks at tyranosores rex!
11. He hadd no more rocks!
12. So he began to hit tyranasoras rex with trees!
13. Tyranosores rex fell into the water!
14. And dip was saved. (Westby, 1982, p. 7)

Story grammar analysis can be done on stories with the focused chain or narrative structure. Focused chain stories omit the internal response and internal plans and sometimes the attempt macrostructure components. These components are dependent upon internal motivation and social planning, rather than more perceptually obvious physical causality. Bruce (1980) suggested that the development of planning and awareness of planning is a slow to develop ability and a lifelong learning. The characters' internal plans to deal with problems set up in the initiating events are not frequent in stories told by children under 9 years of age. The internal response and plan are dependent upon the attributes of characters, such as the slyness of the fox or the cleverness of the third son, third pig, or third goat. These attributes and responses are also heavily dependent upon cultural expectations that are not generally elaborated in the story. The characters' feelings and planning cannot be conveyed in picture form as well as the initiating events and consequences of the story. Characters' attempts to cope with the prob-

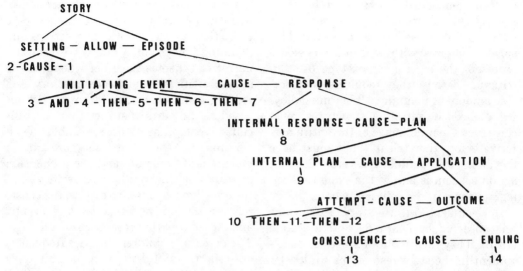

Figure 6.3. Analysis of a narrative written by a 6½-year-old boy. (Reprinted from Westby CE: *Cognitive and linguistic aspects of children's narrative development.* In Bradford L: *Communicative Disorders.* New York, Grune & Stratton, 1982, vol 7, no 1, with permission.)

lems of the initiating events can only be understood in the light of cultural expectations and the characters' attributes.

Botvin and Sutton-Smith (1977) proposed a structural analysis of stories that can be used to extend story grammar analysis. Their early stages of narrative development are similar to those suggested by Applebee. When the true narrative structure emerges around age 5, Botvin and Sutton-Smith analyzed children's narratives as composed of two types of plot units: primary and secondary. Primary units are elements which represent both the motivation or impetus for action or potential action, on one hand, and the resolution, on the other hand. The primary plot units are like the initiating events and consequences in story grammars. A narrative having only a primary plot proceeds from state A (the initiating event) to state B (the consequence). Secondary plot units are elements which represent action or potential actions, preparations, and intermediate actions. Secondary plots include the response, plans, and attempts of story grammars.

These secondary units function as transition elements between states A and B.

Four- to 5-year-old children become aware that actions in stories are organized around disequilibrating events. Their stories have themes that involve the story functions of lack and lack liquidated or villainy and villainy nullified. Six-year-old children begin to elaborate and expand narratives of this elementary type by including mediating thoughts, actions, and events (the responses and attempts of story grammars) as exemplified in the diplodocus narrative.

The next stage of narrative development suggested by Botvin and Sutton-Smith is the ability to conjoin multiple action sequences into a series of episodes. These initially may be repetitions of the first episode such as repeating lack plus lack liquidated, or they may involve use of a different type of episode in subsequent episodes, for example, lack plus lack liquidated and villainy plus villainy nullified. The use of complex narratives, that is those with embedded episodes, does not appear to emerge until around 11 years of age and around 12 years of age for narratives with multiple embedded structures. The story analyzed in Figure 6.1 represents a story with multiple episodes and one embedded episode. Stories with embedded episodes represent the most complex type of story structure because they require a considerable amount of planning. Children employing embedded narrative structures must construct a mental image of the entire narrative before they tell it. They must have the ability to coordinate several different action sequences and at the same time integrate them into a coherent whole.

Development within story resolutions was observed by Maranda and Maranda (1970). They reported four stages of development in the story resolutions. In level 1 were tales in which one power overwhelms another and there is no attempt at response. In level 2 were tales in which the minor power attempts a response but fails. In level 3 tales, the minor power nullifies the original threat. In level 4 tales, not only is the threat nullified, but the original circumstances are substantially transformed. Tales of the last sort are the hero tales in which, having destroyed the monster, the prince returns, marries the princess, and takes over the kingdom. The resolutions are age related, with older children telling stories with higher level endings. In cultures where there was no belief in one's ability to overcome fate, Maranda and Maranda reported that stories did not rise above levels 1 and 2 endings.

One sees with children's narrative development, the developing use of the metafunctions of states of equilibrium, transitions, and disequilibrium. This pattern of equilibrium, transition to disequilibrium, and transition back to equilibrium is characteristic of all cognitive development. Piaget's approach to cognitive development focused on equilibrating and disequilibrating experiences with physical objects. Stories represent equilibrating and disequilibrating experiences in the social world.

The early stories of children consist only of beginnings and endings. As children develop narrative schemas, more and more of the macrostructure components are added, with the last components to emerge being those that refer to emotional reactions and planning. The majority of investigations on narrative schemas have been done in the area of artificial intelligence, memory, and reading comprehension. Attention has focused on the parts of stories that are difficult to comprehend or remember. With children, however, the issues are not so much ones of memory and comprehension of stories as they are lack of awareness of the effective responses to events, the causal relationship among attitudes and events, and the concept that responses are planned. The deficits in children's stories frequently are reflections of deficits in the children's awareness of relationships in the world. The deficits manifest themselves not only in the children's oral narratives and reading comprehension, but also in their social interactions with peers and adults (Kronick, 1981; Westby and Martinez, 1981).

IMPLICATIONS FOR THE LEARNING DISABLED

The recent work in texlinguistics has significant implications for how we analyze children's skills, our understanding of how these skills develop and how they can be facilitated, and what the requirements of the educational system are in light of various developing linguistic skills.

Obtaining a Narrative Language Sample

Although a rose is a rose is a rose, language is not language is not language. Clearly, language has a wide variety of functions, both pragmatic and mathetic, and the way meaning is structured can vary markedly, depending upon the function of language. A child's language cannot and should not be assessed by a single language sample. The language must be analyzed in the light of both its content and context, and both pragmatic participant and mathetic spectator texts should be considered. Even within narrative language tasks, which tap one type of spectator language, there can be considerable variation depending upon the instructions used in presenting the tasks and the specific materials used to elicit the narratives. Relating a personal narrative, something scary or funny that has happened, generally yields a more orally structured narrative with intonation and gestures included to convey the meaning and keep track of the characters. The request to tell a story is likely to result in a more literate style narrative, whereas the request to "make it a story like I find in a book; one that I can write down," is likely to yield an even more literate type of narrative in some children. When the examiner or another individual is present and can see the same stimulus picture as the child, there is a tendency for some children to resort to a more oral style, because so much information is jointly shared in the situation and pictures that there is no need to make the narrative language explicit. Poster pictures that display an action may trigger the child to describe the action and little more; whereas pictures that display primarily a setting often yield a more complex story, if the child has the ability to organize a story. Wordless picture books, such as Mercer Mayer's frog stories, can facilitate discussion about feelings and motivations which are the response categories of story grammars. Telling a story from a wordless picture book is a conceptually easier task than formulating a story about a single poster picture. Wordless picture books require only that the child recognize the schemas depicted. Formulating a story from a poster picture requires that the child evoke the necessary schemas rather than simply recognize them. The instruction to make up a story when no stimulus material is provided is the most demanding for the child, because all schemas must be evoked and organized rather than simply recognized. It has, however, the potential for yielding the most literate language from children, because they must be as explicit as possible if adult listeners are to understand the story.

Narrative Disabilities

Some children show minimal, if any, differences in style or structure of the narratives they produce under the different instructions or in response to different stimuli; other children seem almost to switch channels from an oral to a literate mode, depending upon the task and instructions. Such children have a metalinguistic awareness that different types of tasks require different types of language. Thus, different types of mathetic language, including narratives, require code switching just as different types of pragmatic language require code switching, depending upon the persons, roles, and speaker/listener relationships.

Ong (1978) suggested that cultures evolve from using loosely structured oral styled texts to using highly focused literate styled texts. Children's language also develops from an oral style to a more literate style. With this oral/literate continuum in mind, several questions can be asked about the child who exhibits language difficulty in school:

1. Does the child have an adequate oral language system?

2. Is the apparent language difficulty only within the school context and due to limited knowledge of literate language structure?

3. Is the child able to switch between the oral and literate codes as required by the tasks?

Children from predominantly oral cultures or backgrounds frequently experience school difficulty, but it would be inappropriate to call these children language learning disabled if they are capable of telling a well structured oral narrative.

For school-age children with true language learning disabilities, three patterns of difficulties in structuring narratives have been observed:

1. Inefficient processing. Some students may produce narratives with appropriate macrostructures but appear to have inefficient processing systems. Porch (1974) has provided a model for viewing processing

efficiency of the system, considering behaviors such as response delays, difficulty changing tasks, and the need for repetitions and cues. If these patterns appear on the Porch Index of Communicative Abilities in Children (PICAC), they almost always also appear when the child is attempting to produce a narrative. Some children, however, who have processing problems and difficulty with narratives, may not exhibit such difficulties on the PICAC because the PICAC does not require more than single sentence responses. Such students are slow to retrieve schemas and have difficulty maintaining or changing schemas as needed (Spiro, 1980). In addition, they rely on vague, nonspecific vocabulary. If the student's narrative difficulties are limited to inefficient processing, they are usually able to cope in regular classroom placements if allowed sufficient time to produce their work, although their academic skills will be below that expected for children of their overall intellectual ability.

2. Difficulty in organizing a personal narrative or producing a narrative from limited stimulus material such as a picture. These students are able to tell adequate narratives from wordless picture books and are able to give appropriate responses to questions about the characters' motivations and cause-effect relationships within the stories such as, "How did the big frog feel when the boy got a new baby frog for a birthday present?" or "Why did the big frog bite the baby frog?" These same students, however, may produce little better than a sequence type narrative when asked to relate a personal experience or formulate a story about a poster picture. The individual sentences they produce may be quite adequate, but they are not organized in a systematic, coherent manner so that the listener can understand the story, and their stories lack a theme or plot. This pattern is characteristic of a great many students classified as learning disabled. They lack what Anderson (1977) termed the executive system, that is, the ability to plan and monitor behavior. Some of these students

even have difficulty producing a story from wordless picture books unless they are given focusing questions. They will attend to irrelevant parts of pictures that do not contribute to the forward movement of the story theme or plot. These students are able to recognize schemas, but they cannot evoke them without assistance.

3. Insufficient schema knowledge. This category of disability includes those students who not only cannot relate a personal experience or narrative based on a poster picture, but who also exhibit marked misinterpretations of stories in wordless picture books. In its most marked form, the student does not recognize that the pictures in the book present a story. They describe each picture separately and do not link the events in one picture with the preceding and following pictures. In less marked forms, the student recognizes that the book does present a story, but either does not perceive or else misinterprets the cause-effect and motivational relationships within the book. These students lack not only the executive functioning of the second group, but, in addition, they lack representations for world knowledge. They can neither evoke appropriate schemas nor adequately recognize schemas presented to them.

Both the second and third groups exhibit difficulty with planning. The second group exhibits little planning of their own behavior, but, if given a plan, they understand it and will follow through with it, and they will recognize that story characters plan their actions. What they cannot do is organize their own plans. The third group not only has difficulty planning their own behavior, but also in following through on a plan that is given to them and in recognizing that people do or must plan. Without this awareness that social actions are planned, students will have significant difficulty comprehending narratives as well as in producing them.

The patterns of language learning difficulties that appear on narrative tasks will seldom be detected on more traditional testing methods. Mid-school learning-disabled students in an Albuquerque, New Mexico public school were asked to tell stories from a wordless picture book and poster pictures and to relate a personal narrative. All students had intelligence scores within at least the low-average range. The school was located in a middle-class area of town where a large percentage of parents were professionals. On the Clinical Evaluation of Language Functions Battery (CELF) (Semel and Wiig, 1980), all students scored at or above grade level, yet these students all exhibited varying degrees of difficulty with the narrative tasks. Why was performance on the narrative tasks apparently so discrepant from other test results? Standardized tests such as the Wechsler Intelligence Scale for Children-Revised (1974) and the CELF tend to be discrete point tests. That is, they test specific factual, static information rather than dynamic integrative information. These discrepancies between the students' performance on the narrative tasks and traditional standardized tests reiterates the problems of discrete point versus integrative testing (Oller, 1979; see Chapters 1 and 2). The majority of present tests do not require that the child integrate information as is required by narration; or if the test has required such integration, the analysis procedures have not considered the integrated product—only the components of vocabulary, morphology, or syntax.

Implications for Educational Approaches

Whatever the nature of learning-disabled students' difficulty on narrative tasks, all learning-disabled students exhibit greater difficulty with literate than oral language skills. Although their oral language abilities may not be commensurate with other students their age, their literate language skills are even more delayed and frequently become proportionately more delayed as they continue through the educational system. These learning-disabled children have difficulty learning to read and consequently have less exposure to the school's literate language than non-learning-disabled students. This could be somewhat ameliorated by reading to the students, but time for such activities is often restricted because it is believed that the students must acquire a variety of specific subskills before they will be ready to read. The problem is circular. Learning-disabled students cannot read so they are not exposed to literate language, and they are not exposed to literate language so they cannot read.

The learning-disabled student relies on an oral language system in a school culture that is predominantly literate. The lack of literate language puts the learning-disabled child at a considerable disadvantage in our society. Being literate enables us to amass more information more quickly than is possible in an oral language system alone. We can write down what someone tells us to do or we can check back to our notes or books if we cannot quite remember what an instructor said. Our auditory systems are not equipped to encode something on the first presentation. In cultures that rely on an oral tradition, important information is said more than once and/or in a marked prosody that will facilitate recall. Language learning-disabled children, particularly in the early school years, are heavily dependent on oral language, yet they are treated as though they are literate. How often are such children told, "Now I'm only going to say this once, so you had better listen"? As literate adults, we have the option of resorting to written codes to facilitate our memory. The child has no such option, yet we seldom change our style of presentation to a more oral style with its repetitions, rephrasing, parallel sentence constructions, and poetic-like phrases and intonation that facilitate memory, if memory is what is wanted.

Research on the development of narrative abilities in children has yielded several concepts that could have far-reaching educational consequences. First is the concept that narrative and literate language requires progressive distancing from the here and now. Narrative and literate language requires increasing levels of symbolic representational abilities. Sachs (1980), Scarlett and Wolf (1979), and Vygotsky (1978) all suggested that narrative and written language have their origins in pretend play. Pretend play requires distancing from reality, increasing degrees of symbolic representation, role taking, sequencing, and planning of events, all the skills that are required for narration and written language. Studies show that children who engage in pretend play exhibit longer and more complex utterances, more explicit use of language, and are more sensitive in responding to the cues of others (Freyberg, 1973; Marshall and Hahn, 1967; Smilansky, 1968). Whereas in the 1960's, the emphasis in early childhood education was on cognitive product training, that is, rote memory and drill of linguistic structures, children are now being allowed to play in order to learn in preschool programs. It is difficult, however, to convince teachers, principals, and school administrators of the values of pretend play in elementary school, let alone at junior high levels or above.

Second, the work of Rubin and Wolf (1979), Sachs (1980), Snow (1981), and Vygotsky (1978) showed the need for social interaction for the development of narrative abilities. Narrative language is not immediately reinforcing as is pragmatic need-meeting language. A narrative does not result in receiving an object or in an event changing. Narrative language does not involve the same degree of one-to-one mapping of language onto context as does pragmatic language. Because of these factors, the development of narrative language requires more specific and sustained social interaction than the development of pragmatic language. A child must be shown how to talk about the there and then, that is, how to tell a story. Culturally, the narrative first develops in nonfocused participant stories in which the audience contributes as much or more to the story as the storyteller. Similarly, with 2-year-olds, the development of narration first occurs in a sharing give and take interaction with adults (Snow and Goldfield, 1981). Gradu-

ally, cultures and children become more focused in their narratives until they can maintain a total spectator narrative without any participation or guidance from another. To develop narrative language, children must hear many well formed narratives and have the opportunity to produce narratives.

Narratives are structurally mid-way between the language of the oral tradition and the language of the essayist literary tradition. Research has shown that not all texts are comprehended in the same way or at the same time developmentally. Freedle and Hale (1979), for example, found that children better remember information when it is put in story form than when it is written in an expository form. Narratives, the earliest literate structure that is acquired, arise out of the oral tradition yet have a mathetic function and can, thus, be used to ease the transition from the oral to literate language mode. Folktales are particularly useful for this purpose, because they arise from the oral tradition. Written oral narratives frequently contain the repetitions of the oral tradition (repetitions of episodes and formulaic phrases by the characters), while at the same time using the syntactic cohesion (anaphoric pronoun reference, relative clauses, and conjunctive ties) of the literate form. The majority of basal reading texts make minimal use of folktales and well structured narratives. Basal texts remove the identifiable, stylistic components of texts and reduce the syntax and sentence length according to readability formulas, although Greene (1981) reported that even kindergarten children are highly responsive to and aware of stylistic differences in stories, and Pearson (1974) showed that reducing syntactic complexity does not increase understanding and may, in fact, reduce it. Stories and literary books are relegated to free time or sustained silent reading (SSR) but are seldom read during the regular school day.

Smith (1973) stressed that the only way that children learn to read is by reading. The only way that the learning-disabled student will learn to produce and comprehend texts, particularly literate styled texts, is to be surrounded by such texts and to have opportunities to produce such texts. Texts are whole units, and they must be learned as whole units because they represent holistic schemas of the world. We can analyze the components of a text, but we cannot train these components in isolation and then expect students to be able to comprehend and produce texts. Underlying narrative comprehension is an understanding of complex relationships within the world which include: (1) the effects of environment on people/animals and the effects of people/animals on the environment; (2) the effects of environment on events and the effects of types of people and animals on events; and (3) the effects of feelings on events and the effects of events on feelings. In addition, students must be able to plan their own actions and from this develop an awareness that the actions of characters in narratives are planned (Westby and Martinez, 1981).

In order to develop mathetic spectator comprehension and production, students must hear others relate and interpret experiences either by sharing personal narratives or by hearing a variety of well formed story narratives, and they must have the frequent opportunity to produce such narratives themselves without interrupting questions from adults.

References

Abelson R: Concepts for representing mundane reality. In Bobrow D, Collins A: *Representation and Understanding: Studies in Cognitive Science.* New York, Academic Press, 1975.

Anderson R: The notion of schema and the educational enterprise. In Anderson R, Spiro R, Montague W: *Schooling and the Acquisition of Knowledge.* Hillsdale, NJ, Lawrence Erlbaum Associates, 1977.

Applebee AN: *The Child's Concept of Story.* Chicago, University of Chicago Press, 1978.

Bartlett FC: *Remembering: A Study in Experimental Social Psychology.* Cambridge, Cambridge University Press, 1932.

Bates, E. *Language in Context.* New York, Academic Press, 1976.

Beaugrande R de: The pragmatics of discourse planning. *J Pragmatics* 3:15–42, 1979.

Bock M: Some effects of titles on building and recalling text structures. *Discourse Processes* 3:301–312, 1980.

Botvin GJ: The development of narrative competence: a syntagmatic analysis of children's narrative. Unpublished doctoral dissertation, Columbia University, 1976.

Botvin GJ, Sutton-Smith B: The development of structural complexity in children's fantasy narratives. *Dev Psychol* 13:377–388, 1977.

Bransford JD, Johnson MD: Contextual prerequisites for understanding: some investigations of comprehension and recall. *J Verbal Learn Verbal Behav* 11:717–726, 1972.

Bright W: Recent research. Georgetown University Rountable on Language and Linguistics: Pre-Conference Session—Spoken Written Language, Washington DC, 1981.

Britton JN: *Language and Learning.* London, Penguin Press, 1970.

Britton JN: Learning to use language in two modes. In Smith NR, Franklin MB: *Symbolic Functioning in Childhood.* Hillsdale, NJ, Lawrence Erlbaum Associates, 1979.

Bruce BC. Plans and social actions. In Spiro RJ, Bruce BC, Brewer WF: *Theoretical Issues in Reading Comprehension.* Hillsdale, NJ, Lawrence Erlbaum Associates, 1980.

Chafe W: Features distinguishing spoken and written language. In Tannen D: *Spoken and Written Language.* Norwood NJ: Ablex, 1982.

Charniak E: Organization and inference in a frame-like system of common-sense knowledge. Castagnola, Institute for Cognitive Studies, 1975.

Collins J, Michaels S: The importance of conversational discourse strategies in the acquisition of literacy. In: *Proceedings of the Sixth Annual Meeting of the Berkeley Linguistics Society.* Berkeley, CA, 1980.

Cullingford R: Script application: computer understanding of newspaper stories. Doctoral disseration, Yale University, 1978.

Dooling DJ, Mullet RL: Locus of thematic effects in retention of prose. *J Exp Psychol* 97:404–406, 1973.

Dore J: Holophrases, speech acts, and language universals. *J Child Language* 2:21–40, 1975.

Durkin D: What is the value of the new interest in reading comprehension. *Language Arts* 58:23–43, 1981.

Freedle R, Hale G: Acquisition of new comprehension schemata for expository prose by transfer of a narrative schema. In Freedle RO: *New Directions in Discourse Processing.* Norwood, NJ, Ablex, 1979, vol 2.

Freyberg JT: Increasing the imaginative play of urban disadvantaged kindergarten children through systematic training. In Singer JL: *The Child's World of Make-Believe.* New York, Academic Press, 1973.

Graesser AC: *Prose Comprehension beyond the Word.* New York, Springer-Verlag, 1981.

Greene G: Competence for implicit text analysis: literary style discrimination in 5 year olds. In Tannen D: *Analyzing Discourse: Text and Talk.* Washington DC, Georgetown University Press, 1981.

Halliday MAK: *Learning How to Mean: Explorations in the Development of Language.* London, Edward Arnold, 1975.

Halliday MAK, Hasan R: *Cohesion in English.* London, Longman, 1976.

Harweg R: Beginning a text. *Discourse Processes* 3:313–326, 1980.

Hilyard A: Children's production of inference from oral texts. *Discourse Processes* 2:33–56, 1979.

Hilyard A, Olson DR: Memory and inference in the comprehension of oral and written discourse. *Discourse Processes* 1:91–117, 1978.

Hirsch E: *The Philosophy of Composition.* Chicago, University of Chicago Press, 1977.

Johnson NS, Mandler JM: A tale of two structures: underlying and surface forms in stories. *Poetics* 9:51–86, 1980.

Kintsch W: On comprehending stories. In Just MA, Carpenter PA: *Cognitive Processes in Comprehension.* Hillsdale, NJ, Lawrence Erlbaum Associates, 1977.

Kroňick D: *Social Development of Learning Disabled Persons.* San Francisco, Jossey-Bass, 1981.

Labov W. *Language in the Inner City.* Philadelphia, University of Pennsylvania Press, 1972.

Mandler JM, Johnson NS: Remembrance of things passed: story structure and recall. *Cognitive Psychol* 9:111–151, 1977.

Maranda EK, Maranda P: *Structural Models in Folklore and Transformational Essays.* The Hague, Mouton, 1970.

Marshall H, Hahn SC: Experimental modification of dramatic play. *J Pers Soc Psychol* 5:47–57, 1967.

Minsky M: A framework for representing knowledge. In Winston P: *The Psychology of Computer Vision.* New York, McGraw-Hill, 1975.

Oller JW: *Language Tests at School.* London, Longman, 1979.

Olson D: Oral and written language and the cognitive processes of children. *J Commun* 27:10–26, 1977.

Omanson RC, Warren WH, Trabasso T: Goals, inferential comprehension, and recall of stories by children. *Discourse Processes* 1:323–336, 1978.

Ong, W: Literacy and orality in our times. *Assoc Dept English Bull* 58:1–7, 1978.

Pearson DR: The effects of grammatical complexity on children's comprehension, recall, and conception of certain semantic relations. *Read Res Q* 10:155–192, 1974.

Pitcher EG, Prelinger E: *Children Tell Stories: An Analysis of Fantasy.* New York, International Universities Press, 1963.

Porch BE: *Porch Index of Communicative Ability in Children.* Palo Alto, CA, Consulting Psychologists Press, 1974.

Propp V: The morphology of the folktale. *Int J Am Linguistics* 4:1–134, 1958. (Originally published in Russian in 1928.)

Reichard G: *Prayer: The Compulsive Word.* American Ethnological Society Monograph 7. Seattle, University of Washington Press, 1944.

Rubin A. A theoretical taxonomy of the differences between oral and written language. In Spiro RJ, Bruce BC, Brewer WF: *Theoretical Issues in Reading Comprehension.* Hillsdale, NJ, Lawrence Erlbaum Associates, 1980.

Rubin S, Wolf D: The development of maybe: the evolution of social roles into narrative roles. *New Direct Child Dev* 6:15–28, 1979.

Rumelhart DE: Notes on a schema for stories. In

Brown DG, Collins A: *Representation and Understanding: Studied in Cognitive Sciences.* New York, Academic Press, 1975.

Rumelhart DE: Understanding and summarizing brief stories. In LaBerge D, Jay S: *Basic Processes in Reading: Perception and Comprehension.* Hillsdale, NJ, Lawrence Erlbaum Associates, 1977.

Rumelhart D, Ortony A: The representation of knowledge in memory. In Anderson HC, Spiro RJ, Montague WE: *Schooling and the Acquisition of Knowledge.* Hillsdale, NJ, Lawrence Erlbaum Associates, 1977.

Sachs J: The role of adult-child play in language development. *New Direct Child Dev* 9:33–48, 1980.

Scarlett WG, Wolf D: When it's only make-believe: the construction of a boundary between fantasy and reality in storytelling. *New Direct Child Dev* 6:29–40, 1979.

Schank R, Abelson R: *Scripts, Plans, Goals and Understanding.* Hillsdale NJ, Lawrence Erlbaum Associates, 1977.

Searle JR: *Speech Acts.* Cambridge, Cambridge University Press, 1969.

Semel EM, Wiig EH: *Clinical Evaluation of Language Functions—Diagnostic Battery.* Columbus, OH, Charles E Merrill, 1980.

Smilansky S: *The Effects of Sociodramatic Play on Disadvantaged Preschool Children.* New York, John Wiley & Sons, 1968.

Smith F: *Psycholinguistics and Reading.* New York, Holt, Rinehart and Winston, 1973.

Snow C, Goldfield BA: Building stories: the emergence of information structures from conversation. In Tannen D: *Analyzing Discourse: Text and Talk.* Washington DC, Georgetown University Press, 1981.

Spache GD: *Diagnostic Reading Scales.* Monterey, CA, CTB/McGraw-Hill, 1981.

Spiro RJ: Remembering information from text: the state of schema approach. In Anderson RC, Spiro RJ, Montague WE: *Schooling and the Acquisition of Knowledge.* Hillsdale, NJ, Lawrence Erlbaum Associates, 1977.

Spiro RJ: Constructive processes in prose comprehension and recall. In Spiro RJ, Bruce BC, Brewer WF: *Theoretical Issues in Reading Comprehension.* Hillsdale, NJ, Lawrence Erlbaum Associates, 1980.

Stein NL, Glenn CG: An analysis of story comprehension in elementary school children. In Freedle RO: *New Directions in Discourse Processing.* Norwood, NJ, Ablex, 1979, vol 2.

Sutton-Smith B: *The Folkstories of Children.* Philadelphia, University of Pennsylvania Press, 1981.

Tannen D. Implications of the oral/literate continuum for cross-cultural communication. In Alatic JE: *Current Issues in Bilingual Education.* Washington DC, Georgetown University Press, 1980.

Thorndyke PW: Cognitive structures in comprehension and memory of narrative discourse. *Cognitive Psychol* 9:77–110, 1977.

Todorov T: The two principles or narrative. *Diacritics* 1:37–44, 1971.

Tyler SR: *The Said and the Unsaid.* New York, Academic Press, 1978.

van Dijk T, Kintsch W: Cognitive psychology and discourse: recalling and summarizing stories. In

Dressler WU: *Current Trends in Textlinguistics.* New York, Walter de Druyter, 1978.

Vygotsky LS: *Thought and Language,* Cambridge, MA, MIT Press, 1962.

Vygotsky LS: *Mind in Society: The Development of Higher Psychological Processes.* Cambridge, MA, Harvard University Press, 1978.

Wechsler D: *Wechsler Intelligence Scale for Children—Revised.* New York, Psychological Corporation, 1974.

Westby CE: Cognitive and linguistic aspects of children's narrative development. In Bradford L: *Communicative Disorders.* New York, Grune & Stratton, 1982, vol 7, no 1.

Westby CE, Martinez B: Facilitating narrative abilities in mid-school students. Presented at the American Speech-Language and Hearing Association Convention, 1981.

Winograd T: Frame representations and the declarative-procedural controversy. In Bobrow A, Collins A: *Representation and Understanding: Studies in Cognitive Science.* New York, Academic Press, 1975.

CHAPTER SEVEN

Metalinguistic Skills: Cutting across Spoken and Written Language and Problem-solving Abilities

ANNE VAN KLEECK, Ph.D.

In all realms of human activity, a distinction is often made between practical skill (or know-how) and conscious knowledge of that skill. Language is no exception. As a practical skill, language is a means of communication. We use it automatically, rarely thinking about what we do. We concentrate on what we want to say, with little attention being paid to the actual language used to convey our meaning. As the Duchess heeds to Alice in *Alice in Wonderland*, "Take care of the sense and the sounds will take care of themselves." Were Carroll a

linguist, he might as well have said, "Concentrate on the meaning and the forms will be automatically regulated." While our focus is normally on meaning, we can, if we choose to, consciously reflect upon the things we say. In the previous chapters, Wallach and Westby outlined a number of important acquisitions that relate to higher levels of language learning. As indicated by both authors, development is an ongoing process, with later acquisitions having roots in earlier points of time. In this chapter, we will consider those cases in which the language user stops to think about language itself. Specifically, we will be concerned here with the developmental unfolding in the child of this ability to focus upon and think about the language is (i.e., what its parts are and how those parts relate to each other). On a more complex level, one might focus on both how and why language works as it does. Thinking about language from any of these perspectives is referred to as language awareness or metalinguistics.

LANGUAGE AWARENESS DEFINED

One helpful approach to defining metalinguistics is to consider how it relates to several other similar and indeed often overlapping areas of study. In this section, the terms pragmatics, metacommunication, metapragmatics, and metacognition will be defined. A more careful consideration of the boundaries of each domain helps define the domain of metalinguistics.

Pragmatics

To understand more fully the notion of language awareness, it is helpful to distinguish it, albeit somewhat artificially, from the practical skill of using language in a social context (i.e., pragmatics). In most social conversation, language serves to transmit thought. In these instances, both the speaker and the listener are attuned to the meaning of the message. The specific language being used (i.e., the actual sounds, how they are arranged, and most often even the process of choosing specific words) remains below the level of conscious awareness. That is, neither the listener nor the speaker particularly notices or attends to how the message is being conveyed until something unexpected occurs during the conversation. For example, we may notice a particular word because it was incorrectly produced or produced with an unfamiliar accent, because its meaning was not known to us, or because the speaker played with its meaning (e.g., a pun) or used its meaning metaphorically in an unusual context. In all of these cases, language takes on a metalinguistic character. There is a temporary shift in our attention from what is being said to the language used to say it. The mere activity of our reflecting upon the word entails thought, and language itself temporarily becomes the object of our thoughts. We may, for example, get "caught up" in a foreign speaker's accent, in the stutterer's block, or in the lisper's lisp at the cost of missing some or most of the messages conveyed to us. Although unexpected events within a conversation often serve as catalysts for shifting focus from meaning to form, in other situations children spontaneously ask questions or make comments about the linguistic code in the absence of any apparent event triggering such a shift. Some examples include their questions or comments about pronunciation, grammar, social rules for language use, or the meanings of words.

In addition to these metalinguistic shifts that sometimes occur in spontaneous conversation, children occasionally delight in playfully manipulating language for no apparent utilitarian purpose. They simply derive joy from the activity itself, verbal play being its own reward. We witness them playing with sounds and words. They create strings of highly inflected jargon, nonsense words, rhymes, and alliteration, all often framed with giggles of pleasure and mischief. In a somewhat related vein, the older child will gleefully join in playground chants and jump rope rhymes. In all of these cases, the children are focusing on language as an object having its own existence. Like all other objects, language is a potential item of play. Indeed, unlike concrete objects, it has the added attraction of being creatively "called up" by the resourceful child.

While all of the above examples of language awareness occur more or less spontaneously, there are also numerous tasks presented to the child (by educators or researchers) that are designed to intentionally elicit "metalinguistic reflections" (or thought about language) from the child. For example, one metalinguistic task is the prereading exercise which requires the child to circle all the pictures on a page that depict words beginning with a certain sound. These tasks require the child to focus primarily on the *form* of language rather than on its implied meaning. Psycholinguistic researchers have devised numerous experimental tasks which likewise require a shift from the child's habitual focus on meaning to some aspect of the language used to encode (or produce) that meaning.

Such examples point out situations in which the distinction between practical linguistic skills and metalinguistic skills becomes apparent. Cazden (1974) captures this general distinction metaphorically. She discusses how we normally "hear through" language to its intended meaning and thus treat language forms transparently. In attending to the language itself, it becomes, in a sense, temporarily opaque.

Several catalysts that might potentially promote language awareness can be isolated. *Communication failure* (real or potential) serves as one such catalyst, resulting in awareness reflected by efforts to avert or rectify the failure or breakdown. For example, I might correct a mispronunciation quite automatically to this end. On a far more conscious level, in the face of potential communication failure, I might dramatically alter my vocabulary in attempting to explain my research to my mother as opposed to explaining it to another language development researcher. *Having fun* seems to be another catalyst revealed in early language play. Later, having fun in combination with the pressure of peer socialization is displayed in ritualized forms of language play. The need for creative, verbal *self-expression* might serve as a catalyst to the creation of figurative language. Yet another catalyst, *curiosity*, invokes various types of questions about the linguistic code and language use. Finally, awareness can be provoked by adults questioning the child about language.

We might think of any automatically regulated activity as moving into our awareness due to these same catalysts. Consider, as an example, the sensorimotor activity of walking. We rarely consciously think about walking until one of these same catalysts provokes our awareness. When there is a breakdown—as a temporary tripping or more permanent leg break—the act of walking might become very conscious indeed. In a related vein, we might become aware of walking when we need to adapt this habitual activity to markedly different terrain, such as a steep hill or loose sand. From yet another perspective, the dancer becomes aware of walking in order to enhance that movement. In this case, walking becomes a means of creative self-expression. We might simply be curious about the ordinary act of walking or have awareness provoked by someone else's thoughtful questions about the act. Finally, awareness of the act of walking may constitute a professional, lifelong concern, as it does for the orthopedic surgeon or the physical therapist.

This discussion is not intended as a request to abandon or even deemphasize our current efforts to acknowledge, describe, and explain the nature and development of the ability to use language as a pragmatic tool. Rather, the purpose is to consider another aspect of the language development process—namely, how children learn to treat language as a focus of cognitive reflection. The importance of pragmatic skill is evident; language is the fundamental means of participating in and managing human relationships. The importance of language awareness, although perhaps less apparent, is no less real. Language awareness appears to be the crux of initial learning of the basic literary skills of reading, writing, and spelling. These foundations are crucial to success in our academic institutions and in our highly literate society in general. Indeed, although not always labeled as "meta-" skills, the relationship of language skills, such as auditory analysis and synthesis, to academic skills, such as reading, is clearly not a new concept. But the notion of language awareness does not merely reiterate this obvious connection; it also unites many other skills previously unrelated by any underlying construct (see also Chapter 1). These skills, like reading, are often deficient in the older language-disordered child. They involve dealing with nonliteral and ambiguous language manifested in dual meaning words, puns, idioms, metaphor, etc. Furthermore, language awareness does not always stand in contrast to practical language skill, as it can serve to enhance it.

Metacommunication

We have so far discussed the prefix "meta-" in relation to reflecting specifically on language itself. This prefix has also been used in a different sense with communication (Jakobson, 1960; Watzlawick et al., 1967; Bateson, 1972; Goffman, 1974; Hymes, 1974). The term metacommunication defines a domain (although it is not synonymous for all who use it) that is quite distinct from metalinguistics.

Metacommunication refers to communication that "goes along with" language. This is quite different from metalinguistic reflections on language itself. Metacommunicative messages serve to negotiate both the flow of conversation and the context in which a particular utterance is to be interpreted. As a speaker talks, much more than words are exchanged—messages accompanying language communicate such things as how the speaker feels about what he or she is saying, how he or she feels about the listener (along power and affect dimensions), how the message is to be interpreted (e.g., as a joke, seriously, ironically), whether the speaker would like to continue talking some more before the listener takes a turn, etc. All of these messages can be said in the actual words, but none of them has to be communicated in the actual talk. They are often conveyed simultaneously with (hence, "meta-" in the sense of "along with") a linguistic message by nonlinguistic means. These nonlinguistic devices include kinesics (eye contact, facial and body gesture, touching), proxemics (use of distance and space), paralanguage (suprasegmentals of intonation, pitch, loudness, etc.), and artifactual devices (e.g., clothing, badges, hair style).

In contrast to metalanguage which decontextualizes language in order to make it an object of thought, metacommunicative messages are intrinsic parts of using language in context. As such, metacommunication is actually in the realm of pragmatics, since it addresses what gets communicated in actual social interactions and how this occurs. While understanding that the development of a child's ability to both interpret and produce metacommunicative cues—such as gaining access to a conversation, taking turns, etc.—is of utmost importance, it is beyond the scope of the present chapter to address these pragmatic issues. However, metacommunicative skills will be discussed in Chapter 14.

Metapragmatics

Yet another "meta-" term that is used in the literature is metapragmatics (Bates, 1976). Pragmatic skills allow the effective use of language in context. The use of pragmatic rules for carrying out an interaction generally remains below the level of con-

sciousness. Furthermore, the general flow of a conversation is generally maintained implicitly and through nonverbal channels. However, at times a child's conscious awareness of the social rules for language use is reflected in explicit comments the child makes. With this conscious reflection on the use of language, pragmatics enters the realm of metapragmatics. Such comments might focus on what is socially acceptable behavior or may simply point out what is going on in terms of the content of the talk (specific words or perhaps entire topics); the manner of talking (e.g., how loudly one can talk); the manner of conducting the conversation (e.g., regarding opening and closing conversations and turn taking), etc. For example, the child may make statements such as: "You're not supposed to interrupt" (turn taking), "Let her finish talking" (turn taking), "Don't use your loud voice in the classroom" (manner), or "You're not supposed to talk about other people" (topic). These types of comments focus on the social use of language and stand in contrast to spontaneous metalinguistic comments which focus on the language itself (i.e., elements, grammars, and meaning).

Relationship between Metalanguage and Metacognition

Metacognitive skills involve insights one can have regarding cognitive processes, i.e., the internal mental actions carried out in achieving various goals. The goals of such processing are numerous and include such things as memory, comprehension, learning, attention, and using language. For this reason, metalinguistic skills are sometimes thought of as a subset of the broader domain of metacognitive skills (Brown and DeLoache, 1978; Flavell, 1981). However, there is one clear distinction between the other metacognitive skills mentioned above and language. Most of these skills have mental goals (e.g., to remember, to learn, to attend, to comprehend) but not observable products. For example, people can be conscious of what types of things they tend to remember best and thus be engaging in metacognition. However, there is no observable, quantifiable entity called "remember" that can be recorded and analyzed. In contrast, language requires cognitive processing in order to be understood and produced, but it is also an external product (the actual acoustic energy) that can be observed, recorded, and analyzed. So, to the extent that the focus of one's awareness is on internal cognitive processing, metalinguistic and metacognitive skills do indeed overlap. Those metalinguistic skills that are different from metacognitive skills are those in which one focuses on and reflects upon language as a decontextualized object.

In summary, metalinguistics is defined in this chapter as having some differences as well as some overlap with both pragmatic and metacognitive skills. In contrast it rarely overlaps with the domains of metacommunication or metapragmatics.

FOCUSES OF LANGUAGE AWARENESS

The question of what behaviors constitute evidence of awareness is not an easy one. The range of language awareness is tremendous. It extends from the playful manipulations of sound by the infant to the sophisticated and subtle manipulations of language meanings by the poet or novelist, the intentional and skillful switching between languages of the professional translator, and the esoteric ruminations of the linguist attempting to explain the nature of language itself. The common thread uniting such diverse skills seems elusive at best. The literature has failed thus far to bring coherence to this area of study. One helpful approach, however, is to consider the variety of specific focuses language awareness can take.

Since any property of language can potentially be consciously thought about, the categorizing of metalinguistic skills should be based upon a clear and consistent definition of language. As used in Chapter 1, Bloom and Lahey (1978, p. 4) define language as "a code whereby ideas about the world are represented through a conventional system of arbitrary signals for communication." Using this definition, we can conceive of metalinguistic skills as those which reflect an awareness that language is (1) an arbitrary, conventional code; (2) a system of elements and rules for their combination; and (3) used for communication.

Language as an Arbitrary Conventional Code

Language represents other things. In becoming aware of this aspect of language, the child eventually learns that the word is separate from the thing it represents.* Such an awareness is rarely, if ever, manifested spontaneously in everyday life. Experimental tasks designed to tap a child's emerging awareness of this particular aspect of language are called "word-referent differentiation tasks." These tasks typically require a child to do such things as define words, give examples of words with certain properties (e.g., long, short, or difficult words), and make judgments of whether sound sequences presented by the examiner qualify as words. As will be seen in Chapter 11, we often infer children's abilities from their performances rather than ask them things directly.

In addition to language, the symbol-referent relationship also exists between a picture and the object it depicts as well as between a map and the territory it represents. These representations reproduce fairly directly the proportions and relations of what is being denoted. Language, however, is unique in that the correspondence between sound (or manual sign) and meaning is an arbitrary one. These arbitrary symbols are effective for communicating because they are conventional, i.e., they are agreed upon by members of the linguistic community. We could, for example, just as

* Bateson (1979, p. 30) suggests that "the distinction between the name and the thing named or the map and the territory is perhaps really only made by the dominant hemisphere of the brain. The symbolic and affective hemisphere, normally on the right-hand side, is probably unable to distinguish name from thing named." This may be an important consideration when dealing with brain-damaged individuals.

well call a "chair" a "bink" if everyone agreed to do so, since the particular sound sequence does not in any way correspond to the object chair. Awareness of the arbitrary nature of language form is evidenced in numerous ways. Among these are included (1) foreign language awareness, (2) synonymy, (3) comprehension of linguistic ambiguity, and (4) appreciation of figurative language (i.e., metaphors).

FOREIGN LANGUAGE AWARENESS

Different arbitrary sound sequences are used in different languages to refer to the same things. One researcher has demonstrated that bilingual children develop an awareness that words are arbitrary at a younger age than monolingual children (Ianco-Worrall, 1972). Indeed, given that a child lives in an otherwise growth-stimulating environment, it is logical that exposure to two languages in childhood would provide an advantage in revealing that different sound sequences can be used to refer to the same thing (Cazden, 1974). Children might demonstrate such an awareness by asking for the foreign language equivalents of English words.

From a different perspective, Tervoort (1979) discusses how, between the ages of 5 and 9, his Dutch-speaking daughter spontaneously learned some French by noting in particular the arbitrary nature of language, i.e., that similar sound sequences had totally different meanings in French than they did in Dutch. For example, at the age of 5 she stated that one could get ice cream in a French cafe by saying the Dutch word for "glass" (these two words are pronounced the same in the two different languages). This child eventually built up an entire vocabulary through this strategy of establishing the alternate meanings of Dutch-French homonyms.

Children learning one language also gradually become aware of the arbitrary relationship between a word and its referent. Experimental tasks designed to tap this ability have asked children if the name of an object can be changed (Vygotsky, 1962; Osherson and Markman, 1975). An-

ecdotal evidence of children spontaneously and playfully changing the names of objects has also been reported (Horgan, 1979).

SYNONYMY

The fact that one idea can be coded in a variety of ways also reflects the arbitrary nature of language. In other words, neither the exact words nor their ordering necessarily has any direct influence on meaning. The choice of word in cases where varying word orders are possible is essentially an arbitrary decision. For example, the following sentences result in the same semantic representation. (Although there are admitted subtle pragmatic distinctions implicit in the various choices):

> John kissed Mary.
> Mary was kissed by John.
> It was Mary who John kissed.

In synonymy tasks, one must determine first that the forms are different. Furthermore, the meanings must be essentially identical. Hakes (1980) summarized his general findings regarding children's developmental changes in synonymy judgments performance. Younger than 6 years, children make judgments on the basis of form alone. This formal bias was concluded by considering what the results on this kind of task would look like if children were using the response strategy that, if forms are different, then the sentences are judged as nonsynonymous. This would result in correct responses when the sentences were in fact nonsynonymous and incorrect responses when they were synonymous. This is precisely the pattern they found with younger children. "Their judgments of nonsynonymous pairs were correct significantly more often than chance, but their judgments of synonymous pairs were *incorrect* significantly more often than chance" (p. 86). Children older than 6 judged on the basis of both form and meaning, yielding many more successful responses in this type of task.

LINGUISTIC AMBIGUITY

Within the same language, identical words or sentences can have very different meanings. In French, for example, the word "avocat" refers to both an avocado and an attorney. Likewise, the sentence, "The mayor ordered the police to stop drinking" (Kessel, 1970) also has two different interpretations. In one case, the police themselves—and in the other case the public they protect—have developed an excessive habit which concerns the mayor. This fact of language can potentially lead to ambiguity but rarely does in ongoing discourse due to information supplied by the linguistic or nonlinguistic context. For example, if a group of people were discussing the mayor's tendency to impinge on the private lives of the police force, the interpretation of the above sentence would be clarified by the context.

Once children become aware of the arbitrariness of language, it becomes possible for them to "play" with language. For example, potentially ambiguous linguistic forms are sometimes exploited to create a type of humor. Through contextual cues, the humor based on linguistic ambiguity first biases the listener toward one interpretation of a particular word or sentence and then uses an alternate interpretation in the punch line. The expectancy violation created by shifting to the alternate meaning is the basis for the humor. The following riddle provides an example:

Question: Why can't your nose be 12 inches long?
Answer: Because then it would be a foot.

Here the alternate meanings of the word foot as a unit of measurement or as a body part are responsible for the humor.

FIGURATIVE LANGUAGE

Ambiguity results when similar or identical forms can have various interpretations. Another property of language stemming from its arbitrary nature is that new meaning can be "added to" to the conventional meaning of an existing form. That is, language can be used figuratively, where a clear step beyond the literal conventional meaning is achieved. As long as a recognizable fiber of the original meaning is retained, conventional meaning can thereby be "stretched," thus allowing the language user to become the language creator. This process of using conventional forms in new contexts to convey subtle variations or extensions of meaning underlies the creation of literary devices such as metaphor, simile, proverbs, and personification. (Besides resting upon ambiguity, humor also occasionally rests upon figurative uses of language.)

A representational system with a direct rather than an arbitrary correspondence between symbol and referent would lack this flexibility to create subtle modification of meaning, since nonarbitrary terms could not be so easily transferred to different but somehow related contexts. As such, the richness of nuances in meaning that can potentially be achieved in language derives from its arbitrary nature. To some extent, conventional meanings must be adhered to in order to make communication possible. And yet, as the phrase "poetic license" suggests, the linguistic community united by the conventions understands at the same time the aesthetic need to allow deviation from these conventions. As such, an almost legal right is granted (as indicated by the word license) to the artist to capitalize upon the arbitrary nature of language to create anew. The artist becomes the arbiter, making judgments regarding new extensions of meaning.

Numerous experimental studies addressing the unfolding of figurative language have been conducted. These have focused mainly on the comprehension of metaphor and its production (Billow, 1975; Gardner et al., 1975; Winner et al., 1976). There has been some interest in simile (Malgady, 1977) and proverbs (Honeck et al., 1978) as well. Spontaneous productions of figurative language have also been reported (Winner, 1979).

Language Is a System

Another property of language is that it contains elements and rules for the combination of those elements. The elements of language include the sounds, words, and grammatical morphemes. These features are combined in predictable ways by phonological, syntactic, and morphological rules, respectively. A child's growing awareness that language consists of elements which are combined in systematic ways is the crux of many metalinguistic skills. Recent work has tended to focus on reading as a metalinguistic skill (Mattingly, 1972; Lundberg, 1978; Read, 1978; Ehri, 1979; Ryan, 1980).

Segmentation and synthesis skills, in addition to being important to reading, also underlie such skills as rhyming, forming alliteration, resolving some linguistic forms of humor, and learning secret play languages (such as Pig Latin).

In a different vein, children's emerging awareness of the structural nature of language has been experimentally tapped by having them make judgments regarding the grammatical acceptability of sentences presented to them. Children must at some level realize that there is a system to how such elements can be combined. This "system" allows them to make these judgments.

Language Is Used for Communication

While communication is one of the most obvious properties of language, there are fewer systematic investigations of children's developing awareness of how language is used for communicating. Numerous studies have revealed the pragmatic functions children employ in their own speech (Bates, 1976; Dore, 1977, 1978), but those considering the unfolding awareness of this capacity in children are just emerging.

An initial step in this direction is found in two studies which elicited judgments from young children regarding the appropriateness of utterances in different contexts (Bates, 1976; Leonard and Reid, 1979). Bates explored children's sensitivity to the politeness of various syntactic forms of imperatives (explicit versus implicit). Leonard and Reid explored children's judgments of the appropriateness of seven types of illocutionary acts and found developmental changes in the strategies employed by their 3- through 6-year-old subjects.

More recent studies in this area have been conducted by Flavell et al. (1981); see also Lloyd and Dunn, in press.

FUNCTIONS OF LANGUAGE AWARENESS

Some metalinguistic skills serve very utilitarian purposes for the child, but others do little more than assuage the linguist's curiosity regarding the child's knowledge of language. Although the linguist's needs constitute a noble enough cause, our interest here is in the utility of language awareness *for the child*. Several broad functions can be delineated, including facilitating (1) the use of language in context, (2) the development of further knowledge of the linguistic code, (3) the acquisition of literacy skills, (4) social development, and (5) aesthetic use and appreciation of language.

Facilitating the Use of Language in Context

Two major categories of metalinguistic skills serve to enhance communication—correcting errors in one's speech and adapting to the needs of one's listener. Researchers suggest that such corrections are metalinguistic since they require at least some awareness of the linguistic form itself. Without this focus, errors in the form would go unnoticed. The truly metalinguistic nature of the very early occurring (by 2 years) self-corrections might be questioned, since children of this age are unsuccessful when asked to judge consciously the correctness of linguistic forms.

The second group of skills that serve to enhance communication involves adapting to the needs of one's listener. This is reflected in the various general speech styles (or "registers") a speaker can adopt to assure effective, appropriate communication in a particular social setting. These are considered metalinguistic skills since the speaker presumably chooses (and, therefore, to an extent focuses on) the specific language forms—the syntactic structures and vocabulary—that are most appropriate to the situation. And the child may in certain situations be quite aware (or at least quite explicitly reminded) that certain language forms or manners of speaking are or are not appropriate to a given social situation. Admonitions to say "thank you" to the adult proferring a compliment and to keep the playground-volume voice out of the classroom are examples of such context-sensitive reminders. Children undoubtedly internalize some of these rules without explicit teaching, such as in monitoring (and softening) playground expletives in the presence of authority-wielding adults.

Indeed, while much explicit socialization is of this nature, there is also undoubtedly much listener adaptation that is not determined by sociocultural norms and that takes place quite automatically and unconsciously. Examples include evidence that young children adjust numerous aspects of language form when speaking to a 2-year-old versus an adult (Shatz and Gelman, 1973), to a sighted person versus one they are told is blind (Maratsos, 1973), or to a hearing-impaired versus a normal-hearing adult (Shiff and Ventry, 1976). That these types of adjustments are not the result of explicit socialization or even modeling is suggested by the Shatz and Gelman study where 4-year-olds with and without 2-year-old siblings made similar kinds of adjustments in their language addressed to 2-year-olds. Quite possibly, even these more automatic kinds of listener adaptations might eventually come under more conscious control. In this sense, metalinguistic skill might enhance the speaker's facility in using language as a social-interactive tool.

Piaget (1976) discusses how, without awareness, success in practical skills is achieved by trial and error. In the process of becoming aware of the action, the child comes to understand all the possibilities in the situation. This allows deliberate choice of the most effective means to replace the less efficient trial and error solution. Extending this notion into the language domain specifically, we can see how awareness might potentially enhance the instrumental use of language in context. In conversation, the child could deliberately choose the topics and attendant vocabulary and syntax that were most suitable to the specific situation.

Using language in play and game situations is one mechanism for enhancing such awareness. In play, children can try out new variations of old behaviors without attendant consequences. In this way, they build up their repertoire of potential future responses.

Furthering Knowledge of the Linguistic Code

Synder-McLean and McLean (1978) discuss how metalinguistic skills provide one strategy through which children might further their own practical linguistic skills of comprehension and production. Very early in the language acquisition process, children will frequently point and ask, "What's that?" for countless items they encounter, thereby indicating an awareness that objects and events in the world can be talked about. At a later age, a child who is aware that all words mean something might spontaneously demonstrate this awareness by asking a question about the meaning of a particular word.

In addition to asking for labels and asking questions about meaning, children sometimes further their knowledge about the linguistic code by asking specific questions about word pronunciation or word boundaries. One delightful example of this capacity was provided by a 4-year-old child studied by Gleitman and her colleagues, who asked, "Mommy, is it AN A-dult or A Nuh-dult?" (Gleitman et al., 1972, p. 139).

Besides using adults as a resource, children sometimes further their knowledge quite on their own. They have been observed engaging in intentional practicing of sounds and syntactic frames, most often without an addressee even present. The famous presleep monologues of Ruth Weir's son Anthony at age 2 years and 10 months provide numerous examples (Weir, 1962). The following short excerpt illustrates Anthony focusing on phonology:

berries/*not* barries/barries, barries/not barries/
berries/ba ba (p. 108)

Several investigators suggest that detecting and repairing errors made in
conversation is metalinguistic in nature.
This is believed to be so since "conscious
intervention is then required and the
language user is—momentarily at least—in
some fashion aware of the linguistic entity
that causes the problem" (Levelt et al.,
1978, p. 9). While children's repairs are
often viewed as motivated by attempts to
help the listener understand, Clark and
Andersen (1979) argue that they are often
not really needed to help understanding.
Instead they seem often to function as
repairs to the child's own growing system
of knowledge regarding language. Indeed,
such repairs often reflect monitoring of
"just those parts of the system the child is
in the process of acquiring" (p. 7). Clark
and Andersen plot the growth of such
repairs as moving from being primarily
focused on phonology, to morphology, to
lexicon, and finally to syntax.

Karmiloff-Smith (1979) discusses the
impact of language awareness on language
growth from yet another perspective.

Facilitating the Acquisition of Literacy

Several aspects of language awareness
that have been posited as related to learning to read include word, sound, and grammatical correctness. It is often suggested
that these metalinguistic skills facilitate
the acquisition of reading, but the exact
nature of the relationship between reading
and metalinguistic skill is far from clear.

It has been argued on the one hand that
word consciousness is prerequisite to learning to read (Ryan, 1980; Bereiter and En-
gleman, 1966) and on the other hand that
it is a consequence of learning to read
(Francis, 1973; Ehri, 1979). Similar polar
positions have been taken regarding phonological awareness—that it is prerequisite
to reading (Elkonin, 1973; Fox and Routh,
1976; Liberman and Shankweiler, 1977)
and that we cannot rule out the possibility
that it is a consequence of learning to read

(Read, 1978). Two other positions hover a
middle ground regarding the relationship
of reading and metalinguistic knowledge.
One suggests that metalinguistic skills and
reading *interact*, i.e., that metalinguistic
knowlege is both a contribution to and a
consequence of learning to read (e.g., Ehri,
1979; Vygotsky, 1962). The other middle
position considers the possibility that these
skills correlate not because one causes the
other but because both rely on a common
underlying cognitive ability (Hakes, 1980).
In Chapter 13, Blachman explores the reciprocal relationship between phonological
awareness and reading.

Facilitating Social Development

Certain metalinguistic skills may be
helpful to a child's social acceptance and,
consequently, to his or her social development. The culture of the child perpetuates
its own lore (Opie and Opie, 1959) through
numerous, essentially metalinguistic, tasks.
Included here are playground chants, jump
rope rhymes, hand-clap songs, punning,
ritualized insults (e.g., "I'm the king of the
castle and you're the dirty rascal" (Sanches
and Kirshenblatt-Gimblett, 1976, p. 72)),
and secret languages. These various forms
of linguistic play are distinctive in that they
do not represent creative linguistic acts by
individual children but are instead traditions transmitted within the child's culture.
Children essentially socialize each other in
these traditions of language play. Bernstein
(1960) discusses the interrelated social
functions served by these "public" forms of
language—public in that they "continu-
ously signal the normative arrangements of
the group rather than the individual experiences of its members" (p. 179). Because it
is public language in the child culture,
speech play serves to (1) insulate the child
from full responsibility for what he says,
(2) reinforce group solidarity, and (3) make
the child "sensitive to role and status and
also to the customary relationships connecting and legitimizing the social positions
within his peer groups" (p. 179). Regarding
secret language specifically, "a common

function of (these) play languages is concealment and a corresponding delineation of social groups and subgroups" (Sherzer, 1976, p. 34). Facility with these various forms of language play allows the child access to and membership in the childhood culture.

Facilitating the Aesthetic Use and Appreciation of Language

Perhaps the richest, if also most rare, contribution of language awareness lies in its potential to foster aesthetic awareness. In contriving figures of speech, words become clay. Their literal forms are shaped into novel, unique creations. Here language enters the realm of art. Like other art forms, figurative language use serves to communicate on an intensely personal plane. It does so by allowing expression of the subtle nuances of meaning of an individual's experience in ways that conventional language fails to capture.

Whether created by ourselves or another, "we gain pleasure, inspiration, and often deep insight from instances of figures of speech" (Gardner et al., 1978, p. 30). Their use is an often overlooked means of creative expression for the child.

The numerous functions language awareness serves for the young child are often the same skills that appear to be lacking in older, language-disordered children. One hears many clinical anecdotes of the subtle problems of these older children: "They cannot appreciate humor. They are too literal. The idioms of language often elude them. They often fail to learn to read or they read with great difficulty. Their social language skills are often deficient." These problems are all metalinguistic in nature. To date, however, our approach to helping such children has been intuitive. Indeed, language specialists' training in normal language reflects the state of the art in research—they are experts in language development of normal children up to 4 or 5 years of age (see Chapter 5). Their caseload, on the other hand, may include elementary school children with subtle linguistic deficits. In Chapter 16 Lee and Fine point out some of the dilemmas relative to high school caseloads and the needs of older language-disordered children. A knowledge of normal metalinguistic development, then, may begin to provide the empirical basis that has previously been lacking in our approach to dealing with these older children.

The Development of Metalinguistic Skills

Regardless of which aspect of language is being focused upon or which functions these skills serve, there are some general similarities in how children approach a wide variety of metalinguistic tasks at a given point in their development. The following discussion uses the child's cognitive skills as a parsimonious framework for not only integrating but also for explaining the order of emergence of the various manifestations of language awareness.

Since Chomsky's publication of *Language and Mind* in 1968 in which he suggested that linguists should also be cognitive psychologists, language development research has evidenced a concerted effort to determine cognitive correlates and determinants of language acquisition, pioneered by the work of Bloom (1970, 1973). From these efforts has arisen a general notion that certain aspects of cognitive development appear to be necessary, although not sufficient, prerequisites for certain aspects of linguistic development. Maxwell and Wallach also discuss some of these issues in Chapter 2. To date, the research on cognitive prerequisites has focused mainly on the earliest stages of language development. Attempts have been made to tie early linguistic accomplishments to the cognitive achievements accrued during the sensorimotor period of development in infancy. With a few notable exceptions (Sinclair and Ferreiro, 1970; Ingram, 1975, 1976; Tremaine, 1975), there has been little effort to determine correspondence between cognitive and linguistic advances in later stages of development. Indeed, Furth (1969) suggested that to attempt to do so would be to misconstrue the nature of language, with its primary purpose as a tool for communication. As children learn more about the shared linguistic form of their particular linguistic community, their language becomes better suited to the purpose of communication and simultaneously decreases in its capacity to directly reflect underlying cognitive structure.

Caution is only necessary if one continues to search for a direct correspondence between increasing cognitive knowledge and learning to map that knowledge linguistically, i.e., being able to represent semantically what is cognitively known. There are undoubtedly other ways that cognitive growth can influence linguistic advances besides being reflected in the semantic content of language. Indeed, recent work relating to the pragmatic aspect of language development has sought to establish some of these less direct correspondences. For example, Bates and her colleagues (1975) found that a child's attainment of the ability to invent new means to familiar ends, which occurs in sensorimotor stage 5, was a cognitive prerequisite for gestural performatives. Words were used in the same performative sequences in stage 6. It is not that the children talked *about* means/end relationships, but rather that they began to use language, as they would any other "object," as a means to an end. It is likely that the influence of cognitive advances on later stages of language development are likewise of this less direct nature, i.e., that it does not always consist of a direct translation of cognitive knowlege into semantic representations of that knowledge. Because the linguistic medium itself is an "object" in the child's environment, cognitive advances in which the child learns new ways of reasoning about or acting upon other objects in the environment would also be reflected in the ways that the child learns to act upon language. It is precisely this *less direct* type of influence of cognition on language development that has been postulated as responsible for the flowering of metalinguistic abilities in the middle childhood years.

In two of his most recent works, Piaget (1976, 1978) provides a model which captures the essence of the process of moving inward, i.e., the ability to reflect. While this model was developed to look at the growth in awareness of sensorimotor actions (such as crawling on all fours), it provides a helpful framework for considering growth of awareness in language as well. The model considers the child, the objects in his or her environment, and the practical actions resulting from the interactions between them. Awareness can occur at any of these three points and begins with the child's awareness of the goals and results of her or his practical actions. In a sense, this awareness is peripheral to both the child and the object used in carrying out the action. Later, the child becomes aware of the object, notes its special properties, etc. Finally, the child's own part in the action can potentially become a focus of awareness. That is, the child might consciously consider what kind of mental manipulations he or she did in order to carry out the action.

In extending Piaget's model to consider language awareness specifically, this notion of "types of awareness" clarifies the diverse skills considered by researchers to be metalinguistic in nature. The failure to distinguish between these levels creates much confusion regarding both what one is willing to call metalinguistic and when metalinguistic skills develop. There have been some attempts to deal with levels of awareness by explaining variation in the degree of accessibility of various aspects of language, but none offered to date has the clarifying power of the present extension of Piaget's model. In Figure 7.1, the practical sensorimotor action in Piaget's model is replaced by another practical skill—language. At this level, we are referring to the instrumental use of language in context. As a practical skill, language is a utilitarian, pragmatic tool. Its goal is to convey meaning. Awareness at this point focuses on the success or failure of language in achieving that goal. One asks if the message was

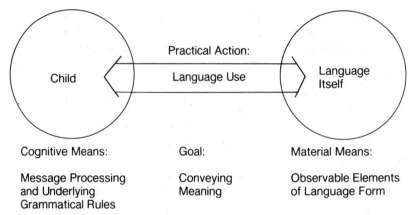

Cognitive Means:	Goal:	Material Means:
Message Processing and Underlying Grammatical Rules	Conveying Meaning	Observable Elements of Language Form

Figure 7.1. Three focuses of language awareness.

successful, in other words, was the meaning conveyed? Only the end product needs to be considered to make this judgment. For example, if the child gives a command which is subsequently carried out, the message is judged successful according to such criteria.

Moving from a focus on the practical action where the child considers *what* is said, the child can focus on the language itself and consider *how* the message was phrased. Here, the focus is on the observable elements of language—the sounds, the words, the syntactic structures.

Finally, the child can consider the cognitive processes he or she utilizes producing and interpreting messages. Even more abstract than these processes are the general rules systems underlying language processing. It is frequently suggested that the grammars of language remain inaccessible to conscious awareness (Read, 1978; Seuren, 1978; Sinclair, 1978). Indeed, explaining the internal processing mechanisms and the rules of grammar is the type of awareness which the linguist or psycholinguist seeks.

Stage One of Language Awareness: The Preoperational Child

The first stage of metalinguistic development occurs between the onset of language and approximately 6 years of age. This corresponds with Piaget's preoperational stage of cognitive development. In-

deed, the metalinguistic skills demonstrated by children in this age range can be explained by looking at the general cognitive skills they typically possess. According to Piagetian theory, two interrelated characteristics of children's thought in this stage are centration and irreversibility. Centration refers to the children's tendency to concentrate on one aspect of a situation at a time and their inability to shift back and forth easily between aspects of a situation.

These limitations in the reasoning capacity of preoperational children directly influence their metalinguistic skills. Metalinguistic performance in the preoperational stage directly reflects the child's tendency to focus on only one aspect of a situation at a time. Children seem capable of focusing on language either as a communicative tool designed to convey meaning or as an object of play divorced from use in a meaningful communicative context. Thus, we see two separate threads of development in this first stage. This is depicted in Figure 7.2 by the separation of language use from language itself.

When using language as a practical utilitarian tool, one does not consciously think about the correct ordering of phonemes or words when conveying or interpreting a message. Unlike the older child or adult, the child at stage one is *limited* to focusing on meaning when using language commu-

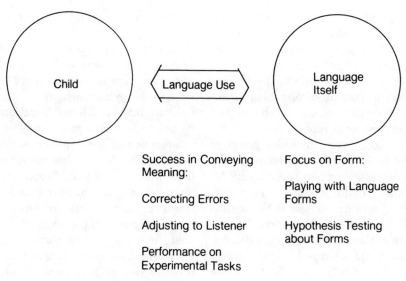

Figure 7.2.   Stage one of language awareness.

nicatively. Here, awareness focuses on the success or failure of language in performing its utilitarian function, i.e., conveying meaning. This awareness is triggered by failure or by accommodation to different situations. The awareness triggered by failure is manifested in the corrections made by the child when an error occurs. The awareness triggered by accommodation to the situation is manifested by how the child varies his or her remarks according to the listener and the setting. In both of these cases, the primary emphasis is placed upon using language in context more effectively. Communication becomes the primary focus; alterations in language form serve this primary end.

CORRECTING ERRORS

Researchers suggest that corrections are metalinguistic in nature since they require at least a marginal level of focus as the linguistic form itself (whether phonology, morphology, lexicon, or syntax). In natural conversations, repairs can involve correcting oneself or correcting others. Self-corrections can be either spontaneous or elicited by others (as in a request for a clarification). To the extent that such repairs are carried out in order to help facilitate the listener's understanding, they serve the

goal facilitating the success of communication. (Recall the earlier discussion of repairs also potentially facilitating language learning.) There is ample evidence that this metalinguistic skill occurs from the very earliest stages of language development.

Regarding elicited repairs, Gallagher (1977) provided evidence that in the earliest stages of language development (Brown's stage 1, mean length of utterance = 1.5) children either repeat or, more frequently, attempt to make revisions or corrections in their own speech when there has been an indication of communication failure (e.g., in response to an adult asking, "What?"). Reflecting back on Maxwell and Wallach's discussion of the language-learning disabilities connection (Chapter 2), it was noted that language-disordered children do not make revisions in the same manner as normal children of the same language level (Gallagher and Darnton, 1978).

A second type of repair occurs in response to children's self-monitoring of their own speech. Scollon (1976) reports examples of a 1½-year-old repeating words several times, often changing a subsequent production to more closely match the adult pronunciation. Clark and Andersen's

(1979) longitudinal study of the spontaneous repairs in three children (ages ranged from 2:2 to 3:7) extends beyond Scollon's findings. Like Scollon, they note that children's earliest repairs tend to be phonological. The proportion of phonological repairs subsequently decreases with age, and lexical and syntactic repairs increase. Finally, they noted that an older group of children (4 to 7 years) made repairs to the speech style register when role playing father, mother, child, doctor, and nurse. Here, the repairs are aimed at the appropriate use of language in context. Within the domain of these pragmatic type repairs, the developmental change in which aspect of form was focused upon reflected those found in the spontaneous non-role play repairs of the younger children studied. The earliest repairs were related to the sound properties of language and generally involved altering pitch. Later repairs began focusing on lexical and syntactic choices.

Children will also monitor others. A common manifestation of this begins around the age of 4 when children will sometimes comment on or correct the mistakes of younger siblings. Weir (1966) provides an example:

Michael (2:4):   Record 'top. Mine.
Anthony (5:4):   Mike says only *top* instead of *stop*.

This monitoring may take the form of teasing as in the example provided by Maccoby and Bee (1965) where a child mimicked his younger brother's pronunciation of merry-go-round as "mewwy-go-wound."

ADJUSTING TO ONE'S LISTENER

Many form variations in children's language use occur in response to varying characteristics of their listener. These are often considered metalinguistic because they involve form manipulations. However, we might question that their mere spontaneous occurrence truly reflects awareness, since early occurring adjustments may not be conscious and deliberate. Indeed a large body of research on adults' communicative behavior indicates that participants in conversations often become similar to each other, i.e., converge on rate, intensity, pitch, accent, linguistic structure, etc. Furthermore, these adjustments may be enacted automatically with little or no conscious awareness (Berger, 1980).

As children eventually become able not only to make such modifications but to consciously judge appropriateness, more awareness can be assumed. At this point, these skills would be considered both metalinguistic (because form is consciously manipulated) and metapragmatic (because the form adjustments are sensitive to the use of language in context). Children demonstrate an ability to make linguistic adjustments as a function of listener characteristics very early in their careers as communicators. Not surprisingly, judgments emerge at a developmentally later time.

The ability to make listener adjustments occurs as young as 2 years of age. In a study of 2-year-old children of deaf parents, Shiff and Ventry (1976) noted that these children adjusted their communicative style depending on whether their listener was a hearing or deaf adult. In talking to deaf adults, they used more gesture, shorter utterances, and more deaf-like distortions. Similar skills at adjusting to listener's needs have been well documented for 3- and 4-year-olds. Shatz and Gelman (1973) found 4-year olds able to differentially adjust the form of their language (length, complexity, etc.) to the age of their listener (2-year-olds, age peers, and adults). Maratsos (1973) found that when told their listener was blind, children in this age range gave more explicit messages. Guralnick and Paul-Brown (1977) found that 4-year-olds used shorter, simpler sentences when addressing developmentally delayed peers than they did when addressing their normal peers. Children also demonstrate their awareness that speech and language behaviors differ according to characteristics such as age, status, role, etc., by their role-taking abilities. Andersen (1977) had children 4 to 7 years of age do the voices of puppets for a father, mother, and baby and for a doctor, nurse, and child patient. She found that even her youngest subjects adjusted their speech to differentiate among the three family roles. For example, in assuming the father's role, the propositional content of the children's talk centered on business-oriented issues. The style was straightforward, unqualified, and forceful. In assuming the mother's role, the propositional content revolved around issues of family care. The style was more talkative, polite, qualified, and softer. The pronunciation contained more baby-talk forms.

While the previous studies noted adjustments in children's spontaneous speech as a function of their listener, several others have elicited judgments regarding similar role-dependent language variations. In adjusting one's language to the status of one's listener, varying degrees of politeness can be achieved by altering the surface structure of language to make it more or less direct. Bates (1976) tested the awareness of this type of stylistic variation in Italian children by having them judge which request would be more likely to get sweets from an old lady puppet, "I want a sweet" or "I would like a sweet." As young as 4½ years, children were able fairly consistently to choose the least direct request as the nicer one. Edelsky (1977) studied changes in judgments of sex attributes of linguistic features by first, third, and sixth graders (e.g., the linguistic counterparts of males as strong, having conviction, angry, mean and the converse for women as powerless, lacking in convictions, and polite). The first graders were very much attuned to the meaning rather than the form of the sentences presented, although they did attribute swearing to males. Thus, for example, "Damn it, get me that perfume" was attributed to women because perfume is associated with women. By the sixth grade, form rather than meaning was consistently used in making sex role judgments. The ability to make these judgments clearly lags behind children's ability to differentiate effectively between the sexes in role play, which is evidenced even in preschoolers (Andersen, 1977). Once again, we see the stage one child's tendency to focus on meaning rather than on language form in making these judgments.

EXPERIMENTAL TASKS

The tendency of the stage one child to focus on the goal of conveying meaning rather than focusing on the forms used to convey meaning is evidenced in his or her performance on a number of experimental tasks designed to tap language awareness (in addition to the status and sex role type judgments discussed above). Such meaning judgments are often made against real-world knowledge rather than knowledge about language. That is, these children focus on "the real world situation that the words or sentences describe" (Berthoud-Papandropoulou, 1978, p. 62).

One category of tasks reflecting this bias is designed to tap what is referred to as word consciousness. This consciousness (or lack thereof) is demonstrated by having children (1) define what a word is, (2) judge which of the sound sequences presented to them are words, (3) judge which segments of a sentence are words by breaking the sentence down into its component words, and (4) demonstrate a conceptual differentiation between words and their referents.

In responding to all of these tasks designed to reflect word consciousness, stage one children often display word realism. That is, they perceive the word as "cosubstantial with the thing" or as "an invisible quality of the object" (Piaget, 1929). Vygotsky (1962, p. 128) likewise noted that "the word, to the child, is an integral part of the object it denotes." The following examples of children's reponses to a variety of word consciousness tasks demonstrate how language has not yet emerged as an object in its own right, separate from the physical reality it represents.

When asked to define the term "word," stage one children suggest that words are words because they refer to concrete things. They define words as the act of speaking itself, often giving as examples an entire sentence (Berthoud-Papandropoulou,

1978). In judging which words are words, the criterion of needing to have a physical referent in order to be a word is again demonstrated. For example, one child responded, "Strawberry is a word because it is grown in the garden" (Berthoud-Papandropoulou, 1978). For the same reason, when presented with words to judge or when segmenting a sentence into words, children will more readily identify concrete nouns and adjectives as words than they will prepositions, conjunctions, possessive pronouns, and other type of function words (Huttenlocher, 1964; Karpova, 1966; Holden and McGinitie, 1972; Berthoud-Papandropoulou and Sinclair, 1974; Ehri, 1975, 1976; Fox and Routh, 1976a). Function words are likely more difficult to identify than concrete nouns because they are context-dependent, i.e., they have no independent semantic status. Indeed, children do not consistently count articles and other functors as words until age 11 (Berthoud-Papandropoulou, 1978).

Word realism is once again demonstrated when children are asked to provide examples of words having certain characteristics such as being long, short, or difficult. Stage one children would typically focus on the real-world referent and supply a word such as "train" when asked for a long word (Berthoud-Papandropoulou, 1978). They focus on properties of referents rather than on linguistic elements per se.

Yet another task asks children if the name of an object could be arbitrarily changed. For example, they might be asked "Could you call a cat a dog?" Stage one children will play this game and agree that you can indeed change names. However, the attributes of the animal cling to the word. In the above example, these children might insist that a cat called a dog could now also bark (Vygotsky, 1962; Osherson and Markman, 1975).

Also possibly related to a tendency toward word realism is the stage one child's inability to consider that one word could have two different meanings. It seems logical that if the word were part of the thing it denotes, it would be difficult to simultaneously conceive of the same word as being part of another different object. For this reason, stage one children are unable to resolve lexical ambiguity humor which turns on the same word having two different meanings (Fowles and Glanz, 1977; Hirsh-Pasek et al., 1978). As such they would not appreciate our earlier riddle (Why can't your nose be 12 inches long?) that required switching the meaning of the word "foot" from a unit of measurement to a body part.

In a similar vein, stage one children cannot comprehend the two meanings of dual function adjectives. For example, words such as bitter, sweet, or hard have both a physical and a psychological meaning. One might refer to both a candy and a person as being sweet. A study by Asch and Nerlove (1960) found that children in the preoperational age range were only aware of the physical meanings of such adjectives.

ACCEPTABILITY JUDGMENTS

Another type of metalinguistic task referred to as acceptability judgments again reflects the young child's "real-world" meaning focus. Here, a child is presented with either grammatically acceptable or unacceptable sentences and asked to judge them. For example, the child might be asked to respond to a given sentence as either "good" or "silly." Sometimes they are simply given a sentence and asked, "Is that right?" Wallach (Chapter 5) discussed a number of these procedures when describing "because" and "if" sentences. Emerson (1980) used the clown and teacher puppets to help children make "sensible" and "silly" judgments (see Chapter 5). In such studies, there are three ways in which sentences can be made unacceptable. One type involves violating what are called lexical selectional rules. It is unacceptable, for example, to talk about a "married bachelor" or a "hungry rock," except perhaps metaphorically. These types of sentences, then, require judgments of meaningfulness. Another type of agrammatical sentence changes acceptable word order. "Tree the climb" is an example. Yet another type of unacceptable sentence violates synactic agreement, although meaning is preserved. "They is boys" is an example of this type of unacceptable utterance. Whereas selection restriction rules require a focus on meaning, these latter two types of agrammaticality require a focus on the syntactic form of the sentence.

By 4 years of age, children can accurately judge sentences that present selection restriction rule violations (Howe and Hillman, 1973; James and Miller, 1973; Carr, 1979). Success on this type of task is in line with the meaning focus of the preoperational child. These same children, however, are unsuccessful on syntactic acceptability judgments for the same reason. They appear to judge the truth value or assertion of these utterances rather than focusing on whether the linguistic form is acceptable (Gleitman et al., 1972; James and Miller, 1973; deVilliers and deVilliers, 1974; Bohannon, 1975; Leonard et al., 1977; Hakes, 1980). Gleitman and her colleagues (1972) provided an excellent example of this deficiency. The suburbanite children in their study negated the grammatical accuracy of "The men wait for the bus" on the grounds that only children wait for buses.

There are, then, several metalinguistic tasks on which preoperational children demonstrate their focus on the message. As shown in Figure 7.2, occasionally the preoperational child focuses exclusively on the linguistic form of language.

One well documented example of a spontaneous focus on linguistic form is the sound play in which even very young children engage. Such play focuses on the sounds of language without regard for meaning. In this sense, this play represents a primitive level of language awareness. Children will also sometimes play with meaningful words by altering the pronunciation or adding endings. One 3½-year-old observed by the author pronounced the word *yes* in several ways in one conversation. She said, "yeah," "yes," "yup," "yuppie," and "yippie," all within the span of 13 utterances of one conversation. The tendency to engage in this type of play with language may foreshadow later skill in manipulating language for verbal humor and using metaphors.

One experimental task in which preoperational children have demonstrated some success in focusing on linguistic form involves segmenting language into its component parts. Segmentation can involve different elements, either words, syllables, or phonemes. Liberman and his colleagues (1974) have found that children as young as 4 years of age can segment words into syllables. The ability to segment into words and phonemes emerges later. It has been suggested that this occurs because it is simply easier to determine syllable boundaries in the acoustic signal. There are no equally discrete boundaries for word and phonemes. Although we separate them in our minds, they are not actually separated in the sound sequences we hear.

In general, the metalinguistic performance of stage one children is marked by their strong focus on language's ability to convey meaning and judgments are focused primarily on how well real-world tangible reality is met with language. Other budding metalinguistic tendencies can be noted in various forms of language play

Stage Two of Language Awareness: The Concrete Operational Child

The limitations of the preoperational child's thought, both centration and the lack of reversibility, are overcome in the transition to concrete operations, a stage which spans from approximately 7 to 11 years of age. Corresponding to the terms centration and irreversibility, the thought of the concrete child is characterized by decentration and reversibility. Decentration refers to the ability to hold in mind and relate more than one aspect of a situation at a time. Related to this, reversibility allows thought to shift back and forth between aspects of the situation. Stage two of language awareness reflects these changes in children's reasoning ability.

Because of their ability to decentrate,

concrete operational children can simultaneously think of language in two ways. They can consider language as a medium for conveying meaning and as an object in its own right. In other words, language communicates, but it is also simultaneously an entity that can be acted upon. This integration of awareness of the goal of language use with language itself is depicted in Figure 7.3.

The metalinguistic skills that emerge during stage two of language awareness can be divided into two broad categories. First, children in this stage are able to focus upon and compare two meanings of one particular linguistic form at a time. Second, they are able to manipulate the linguistic form while retaining the semantic content of the message.

EXPERIMENTAL TASKS

Tasks on which concrete operational children demonstrate their ability to hold in mind two meanings simultaneously are the same as those on which preoperational children are unsuccessful. First, as children make the transition to this stage, they begin being able to understand humor which involves linguistic ambiguity. As such, a 6- or 7-year old who knew both meanings of the word "foot" (as a body part and as a unit of measurement) could find the riddle which asked "Why can't your nose be 12 inches long?" to be quite humorous. It is important to note that, although children begin experiencing success in comprehending humor at this age, it is a number of years before they can comprehend all the various types of humorous ambiguity. The

developmental unfolding of language humor is discussed next.

AMBIGUITY

Ambiguity can occur at several levels of linguistic form. The various types include (1) lexical, (2) phonological, (3) deep structure, (4) surface structure, and (5) morpheme boundary. Children's ability to resolve the various types of ambiguity emerges over a number of years. The ability to resolve lexical ambiguity emerges earliest, at around 6 or 7 years. This form of ambiguity results when a single phonological sequence (spelling may or may not be identical) identifies two separate words that have different meanings. In the following example, the resolution rests on the dual meaning of the word "club" as either a social organization or a large stick:

Q. Do you believe in clubs for young people?
A. Only when kindness fails (Shultz, 1974, from W.C. Fields).

At around 8 or 9 years children begin to comprehend ambiguity humor relying on alternate interpretations of deep or underlying structure. Here the ambiguity results when a single sequence of words has two transformational sources identifying different sentence meanings. In other words, two deep structures can be projected into a single surface structure. An example follows:

Q. Will you join me in a bowl of soup?
A. Do you think there is enough room for both of us? (Hirsh-Pasek et al., 1978)

The remaining three types of ambiguity—phonological, surface structure, and morpheme boundary—all require the child

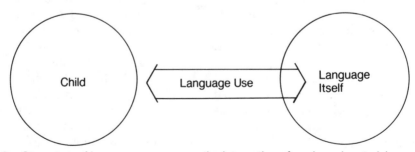

Figure 7.3.   Stage two of language awareness: the integration of goals and material means.

to combine awareness of *two* aspects of language. First, as with the other forms of ambiguity, the child must have some awareness of the arbitrariness of language. In addition, the child needs to become aware of the fact that language consists of elements and rules for their combination. Knowledge of this latter aspect underlies the ability to "manipulate" the elements of language. In phonological ambiguity, for example, two similar phonetic sequences (which differ only in a single sound segment) identify two separate words, which have different meanings. The child must be able to focus upon the single sound segment, as in the following example where the joke "turns" on the initial sound segment of "crackers" as opposed to "quackers."

Q. If you put three ducks in a box, what do you have?
A. A box of quackers (Hirsh-Pasek et al., 1978).

It is interesting that the ability to resolve all three of these types of ambiguity humor emerges latest, when children are approximately 12 years of age.

The second task on which concrete operational children demonstrate an ability to appreciate two meanings is in comprehending both meanings of dual function adjectives. They are now aware of both the physical and psychological meanings of words like soft, hard, warm, and so forth.

Their ability to understand lexical ambiguity humor and dual function adjectives indicates that concrete operational children can shift from one conventional meaning to another. That is, both meanings are shared by speakers of the language. Comprehending and producing figurative language such as metaphor poses a somewhat different problem. Although this task also involves a shift from one meaning to another, the second meaning is not conventional. Instead, when language is used figuratively, a clear step beyond the literal conventional meaning is achieved. Concrete operational children seem to have little flair for figurative language. On the con-

trary, they are often even resistant to figurative language. For example, in a study done by Gardner and his colleagues in 1975, one child of this age protested strongly that "A tie can't be loud." During this stage, children are consolidating literal meanings and are reluctant to allow violations of these recent acquisitions. Their literalness is exemplified in responses obtained by Winner and her colleagues (1976). The children were asked to paraphrase metaphoric sentences such as, "After many years of working in a jail, the prison guard had become a hard rock that could not be moved." Six- and 7-year-olds used a magical approach. One child responded, "A witch turned the guard to rock." Eight- and 9-year-olds focused on a concrete physical feature. One responded, "The guard was like a rock because he had hard muscles." Only by 10 to 11 years were children able to appreciate the metaphors. The onset of metaphoric competence can again be explained by cognitive advances.

Some researchers, such as Elkind (1969) and Inhelder and Piaget (1958), have suggested that a flowering of metaphoric skill requires the onset of Piaget's formal operational stage, which begins somewhere between 10 and 12 years of age. One characteristic of children's reasoning as they advance to formal operations is an ability to deal with possibilities. Correspondingly, comprehending and producing figurative language involves stretching meaning into hypothetical realms. The concrete operational child is beginning to enjoy success in dealing with two meanings. Success, however, is limited at this point to dealing with literal, conventional meanings.

Unlike the stage one child, the stage two child can often perform tasks requiring form manipulations. Recall that stage one children were often unsuccessful due to their semantic or meaning focus. For example, one word-referent task required the children to name a long word. The stage one children named something which was long, focusing on the meaning of the word. Stage two children, on the other hand, focus on the number of letters in the word.

In making grammaticality judgments, once again stage two children can focus on the syntax. They are able to shift their focus on the form used to convey meaning and to judge whether it is accurate.

Segmentation skills, where language is in some way broken into its elements, sometimes also require retaining meaning at the same time. Secret languages such as Pig Latin provide an example. To produce Pig Latin, children must resequence phonemes and add in an extra meaningless syllable. At the same time, they are either comprehending or producing meaningful messages. This rather complex task becomes possible in stage two, although it remains difficult or impossible for many children to master.

Other segmentation skills, such as segmenting words into their component parts, do not require simultaneous retention of meaning. Preoperational children are able to segment words into syllables. The ability to separate words into phonemes emerges at the onset of stage two. Since some segmenting skills do emerge prior to stage two, it seems implausible to suggest that successful performance on segmentation skills requires concrete operational reasoning ability. Perhaps the ability to segment words into sounds is better explained by factors such as instruction in prereading rather than by a general change in the child's reasoning.

Summarizing the metalinguistic accomplishments of the concrete operational child, we have noted that success is witnessed on two types of tasks. First, these children are now able to hold in mind and to compare two conventional meanings. With this achievement, proficiency with linguistic ambiguity begins. Second, the concrete operational child can simultaneously manipulate linguistic form while retaining semantic content. Words now achieve independence from their referents,

grammaticality judgments are performed successfully, and the manipulations of language form become possible. Furthermore, during the early part of the concrete operational stage, most children are taught to read, another impressive metalinguistic accomplishment where language form must be focused upon and deciphered in order to obtain the meaning encoded. Some metalinguistic skills, such as dealing effectively with figurative language, remain beyond the capacity of even the concrete operational child.

CLOSING REMARKS

I have suggested that children's metalinguistic strategies reflect their general cognitive reasoning abilities at the various points in their development. I have argued that the child's awareness of language as being simultaneously both an object in its own right and a medium for communication awaits the onset of concrete operations. If one makes the assumption that concrete operational thought emerges at around 6 or 7 years of age, numerous studies demonstrating differences in children's approaches to metalinguistic tasks in the 5- to 7-year age range offer indirect support for this position.

To date, only the study by Hakes (1980) has directly addressed the issue of a relationship between concrete operations and metalinguistic skills. This study measured both concrete operational skills (using six conservation tasks) and a set of metalinguistic tasks (synonymy and grammatical acceptability judgments and a phoneme segmentation task). The correlations Hakes found between these two domains of skill provide promising direct support for the relationship postulated here. Clearly, further evidence is needed to corroborate these initial findings and to further substantiate the claims made in this chapter.

Although our discussion has focused on the cognitive growth that underlies metalinguistic abilities, there are undoubtedly many other variables that influence one's language awareness. One recurrent finding in this research is that there are large individual differences in metalinguistic performance (Kessel, 1970; Brodzinsky, 1975; Fowles and Glanz, 1977; Hirsch-Pasek et al., 1978). These differences indicate that there is more variability both within and among individuals on metalinguistic task performance than can be explained by cognitive level alone. Indeed, it appears that the cognitive advances of concrete operations are a *facilatory condition* for the flowering of metalinguistic abilities. Numerous other variables may also influence metalinguistic performance, including both child variables and environmental variables. Candidate child variables might include a child's (1) practical language competence, (2) general intelligence, (3) creativity, or (4) cognitive style (see Van Kleeck, 1982, for an in-depth discussion of these variables).

A controversy exists regarding the influence of practical language skill on metalinguistic skill. Gleitman and Gleitman (1979) argue that practical language skills and metalinguistic skills are basically independent. They base their position on findings of extensive individual differences in metalinguistic judgments among people who have equivalent practical language skills. Other researchers have likewise considered skills within these two domains as essentially autonomous (Foss and Hakes, 1978; Hakes, 1980). Some empirical evidence, however, does support the existence of a relationship between the two domains (Smith and Tager-Flushberg, 1980). Piaget supports the latter view. Furthermore, he suggests that without success in action the conceptualization awareness would remain inoperative (Piaget, 1976).

Indeed, it seems that in certain cases metalinguistic skill would quite directly require basic linguistic skills. In resolving lexical ambiguity, for example, vocabulary skills might come into play in that the child needs to be familiar with both meanings of the particular ambiguous word. It seems that, in general, attempts to discern the relationship between practical linguistic skill and metalinguistic skill have been approached too broadly. It is also possible that instruments which find children's knowledge of language to be equivalent tap only the child's knowledge of language structure. Possible differences in the children's practical use of language would not be tapped by such measures, although these skills may correlate more highly with metalinguistic skills. Research is needed to clarify this issue.

It is also possible that a child's general intelligence might correlate highly with metalinguistic facility. Indeed, numerous subtests on verbal intelligence tests do in fact require metalinguistic skills. Examples include rhyming, solving anagrams, cracking secret codes, generating lists of words beginning with a certain letter, and completing verbal analogies.

A third child variable possibly contributing to metalinguistic performance is creativity. Wallach (1970) discusses the operational aspects of creativity as occurring in persons who have (1) more diffuse deployment of attention, (2) greater readiness to use incidental cues, (3) broader category widths, leading to a willingness to entertain deviant instances as possibly relevant to a given class, and (4) the ability to temporarily suspend evaluation or judgment. Certainly such attributes would enhance one's ability to create figures of speech.

A final child variable possibly related to metalinguistic performance is cognitive style. For example, Brodzinsky (1975) found that reflective children develop a sense of humor earlier than impulsive children. In a similar vein, Horgan (1979) noted that her metalinguistically precocious daughter Kelly would accept almost any object to stand for another in her symbolic play, whereas most children prefer some perceptual similarity. Horgan postulated that "Kelly's tolerance for degraded stimuli may be related to her willingness to 'degrade' or alter established patterns" (p. 11). This may relate to her metalinguistic precocity. Undoubtedly, there are many other child variables which contribute to metalinguistic performance that remain to be determined.

Environmental variables related to metalinguistic skill are perhaps of even greater interest since they are manipulable to a degree, and as such offer suggestions for facilitating metalinguistic growth. The literature to date has merely been suggestive of what these variables might be. Two recurring possibilities include (1) exposure to language games, both within families (Gleitman et al., 1972; Slobin, 1978; Horgan, 1979) and within the culture (Kirschenblatt-Gimblett, 1976) and (2) exposure to foreign languages (Ianco-Worral, 1972; Cummins, 1978; Slobin, 1978; Tervoort, 1979).

As a final note, Piaget suggests that the process of becoming aware is a never ending one. "Neither the reflection on one's own thought processes nor the understanding of physical causality can ever be complete; the biological sources of thought remain forever closed to consciousness, and the ultimate understanding of physical reality is equally unattainable, if only because the observing and thinking subject is himself a part of the universe" (Sinclair, 1978, p. 196). Figure 7.4 displays a hypothetical stage three of language awareness, where all three focuses of language awareness are integrated. Here we place ourselves, as students of the enigmatic world of child language.

References

Andersen E: Young children's knowledge of role-related speech differences: a mommy is not a daddy is not a baby. *Papers Reports Child Language Dev* 13:83–90, 1977.

Asch S, Nerlove H: The development of double-function terms in children: an exploratory investigation. In Kaplan B, Wapner S: *Perspectives in Psychological Theory: Essays in Honor of Heinz Werner.* New York, International Universities Press, 1960.

Bates E: *Language and Context: The Acquisition of Pragmatics.* New York, Academic Press, 1976.

Bates E, Camaioni L, Volterra V: The acquisition of performatives prior to speech. *Merrill-Palmer Q* 21:205–226, 1975.

Bateson G: *Steps to an Ecology of Mind.* San Francisco, Chander, 1972.

Bateson, G. *Mind and Nature.* New York, Dutton, 1979.

Bereiter C, Engelmann S: *Teaching Disadvantaged Children in Preschool.* Englewood Cliffs, NJ, Prentice-Hall, 1966.

Berger C: Self-consciousness and the study of interpersonal attraction. In Giles H, Robinson P, Smith P: *Language: Social Psychological Perspectives.* Oxford, Pergamon Press, 1980.

Bernstein B: Review of "The lore and language of school children" by I. and P. Opie. *Br J Sociol* 11:178–181, 1960.

Berthoud-Papandropoulou I: An experimental study of children's ideas about language. In Sinclair A, Jarvella R, Levelt W: *The Child's Conception of Language.* New York, Springer-Verlag, 1978.

Berthoud-Papandropoulou I, Sinclair H: What is a word? Experimental study of children's ideas on grammar. *Hum Dev* 17:241–258, 1974.

Billow R: A cognitive developmental study of metaphor comprehension. *Dev Psychol* 14:415–423, 1975.

Bloom L: *Language Development: Form and Function in Emerging Grammars.* Cambridge, MA, MIT Press, 1970.

Bloom L: *One Word at a Time: The Use of Single-word Utterances before Syntax.* The Hague, Mouton, 1973.

Bloom L, Lahey M: *Language Development and Language Disorders.* New York, John Wiley & Sons, 1978.

Bohannon J: The relationship between syntax discrimination and sentence imitation in children. *Child Dev* 46:444–451, 1975.

Brodzinsky D: Children's comprehension and appre-

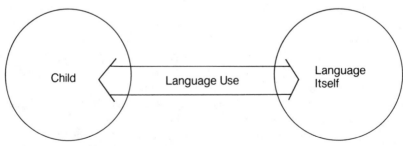

Figure 7.4.   Stage three of language awareness.

ciation of verbal jokes in relation to conceptual tempo. *Child Dev* 48:960–967, 1975.

Brown A, DeLoache J: Skills, plans, and self-regulation. In Siegler R: *Children's Thinking: What Develops*. Hillsdale, NJ, Lawrence Erlbaum Associates, 1978.

Carr D: The development of young children's capacity to judge anomalous sentences. *J Child Language* 6:227–241, 1979.

Cazden C: Play with language and metalinguistic awareness: one dimension of language experience. *Urban Rev* 7:28–39, 1974.

Chamsky N: *Language and Mind*. New York, Harcourt Brace Jovanovich, 1968.

Clark E, Andersen E: Spontaneous repairs: awareness in the process of acquiring language. *Papers Rep Child Language Dev* 16:1–12, 1979.

Cummins J: Orientation to language in Ukranian-English bilingual children. *Child Dev* 49:1239–1242, 1978.

deVilliers J, deVilliers P: Competence and performance in child language: are children really competent to judge? *J Child Language* 1:11–22, 1974.

Dore J: Children's illocutionary acts. In Freedle R: *Discourse Production and Comprehension*. Hillsdale, NJ, Lawrence Erlbaum Associates, 1977.

Dore J: Variation in preschool children's conversational performances. In Nelson KE: *Children's Language*. New York, Gardener Press, 1978, vol 1.

Edelsky C: Acquisition of an area of communicative competence: learning what it means to talk like a lady. In Ervin-Tripp E, Mitchell-Kernan C: *Child Discourse*. New York, Academic Press, 1977.

Ehri L: Word consciousness in readers and prereaders. *J Educ Psychol* 67:204–212, 1975.

Ehri L: Word learning in beginning readers and prereaders: effects of form class and defining contexts. *J Educ Psychol* 68:832–842, 1976.

Ehri L: Linguistic insight: threshold of reading acquisition. In Waller T, MacKinnon G: *Reading Research*. New York, Academic Press, 1979, vol 1.

Elkind D: Piagetian and psychometeric conceptions of intelligence. *Harvard Educ Rev* 39:319–337, 1969.

Elkonin D: USSR. In Downing J: *Comparative Reading: Cross-national Studies of Behavior and Processes in Reading and Writing*. New York, Macmillan, 1973.

Emerson H: Children's judgments of correct and reversed sentences with if. *J Child Language* 7:137–155, 1980.

Flavell J: Cognitive monitoring. In Dickson W: *Children's Oral Communication Skills*. New York, Academic Press, 1981.

Flavell J, Speer J, Green F, et al: The development of comprehension monitoring and knowledge about communication. *Monogr Soc Res Child Dev* 46:1–65, 1981.

Foss D, Hakes D: *Psycholinguistics: An Introduction to the Psychology of Language*. Englewood Cliffs, NJ, Prentice-Hall, 1978.

Fowles B, Glanz M: Competence and talent in verbal riddle comprehension. *J Child Language* 4:433–452, 1977.

Fox B, Routh D: Analyzing spoken language into words, syllables, and phonemes. A developmental study. *J Psycholinguistic Res* 4:331–342, 1976a.

Fox B, Routh DK: Phonemic analysis and synthesis as word-attack skills. *J Educ Psychol* 68:70–74, 1976b.

Francis H: Children's experience of reading and notions of units in language. *Br J Educ Psychol* 43:17–23, 1973.

Furth H: *Piaget and Knowledge*. Englewood Cliffs, NJ, Prentice-Hall, 1969.

Gallagher T: Revision behaviors in the speech of normal children developing language. *J Speech Hear Res* 20:303–318, 1977.

Gallagher T, Darnton B: Conversational aspects of the speech of language-disordered children: revision behaviors. *J Speech Hear Res* 21:118–135, 1978.

Gardner H, Kircher M, Winner E, et al: Children's metaphoric productions and preferences. *J Child Language* 2:125–141, 1975.

Gardner H, Winner E, Bechhofer R, et al: The development of figurative language. In Nelson KE: *Children's Language*. New York, Gardner Press, 1978, vol 1.

Gleitman H, Gleitman L: Language use and language judgment. In Fillmore C, Kempler D, Wang W: *Individual Differences in Language Ability and Language Behavior*. New York, Academic Press, 1979.

Gleitman L, Gleitman H, Shipley E: The emergence of the child as grammarian. *Cognition* 1:137–164, 1972.

Goffman E: *Frame Analysis*. New York, Harper, 1974.

Guralnick M, Paul-Brown D: The nature of verbal interactions among handicapped and nonhandicapped preschool children. *Child Dev* 48:254–260, 1977.

Hakes D: *The Development of Metalinguistic Abilities in Children*. New York, Springer-Verlag, 1980.

Hirsh-Pasek, K, Gleitman L, Gleitman H: What did the brain say to the mind? A study of the detection and report of ambiguity by young children. In Sinclair A, Jarvella R, Levelt W: *The Child's Conception of Language*. New York, Springer-Verlag, 1978.

Holden M, McGinitie W: Children's conceptions of word boundaries in speech and print. *J Educ Psychol* 63:551–557, 1972.

Honeck R, Sowry B, Voegtle K: Proverbial understanding in a pictorial context. *Child Dev* 48:327–331, 1978.

Horgan D: The emergence of Kelly as comedienne: a case study of metalinguistic abilities. Presented at the Second International Conference on Humor, August, 1979.

Howe H, Hillman D: The acquisition of semantic restrictions in children. *J Verbal Learn Verbal Behav* 12:132–139, 1973.

Huttenlocher J: Children's language: word-phrase relationship. *Science* 143:264–265, 1964.

Hymes D: *Foundations in Sociolinguistics: An Ethnographic Approach*. Philadelphia, University of Pennsylvania Press, 1974.

Ianco-Worral A: Bilingualism and cognitive development. *Child Dev* 43:1390, 1972.

Ingram D: If and when transformations are acquired by children. In Dato D: *Developmental Psycholinguistics: Theory and Applications.* Washington DC, Georgetown University Press, 1975.

Ingram D: *Phonological Disability in Children.* New York, Elsevier, 1976.

Inhelder B, Piaget J: *The Growth of Logical Thinking from Childhood to Adolescence.* New York, Basic Books, 1958.

Jakobson R: Linguistics and poetics. In Seboek J: *Style in Language.* Cambridge, MA, MIT Press, 1960.

James S, Miller J: Children's awareness of semantic constraints in sentences. *Child Dev* 44:69–76, 1973.

Karmiloff-Smith A: *A Functional Approach to Child Language.* Cambridge, Cambridge University Press, 1979.

Karpova S: Abstracted by D. Slobin in Smith F, Miller GA: *The Genesis of Language.* Cambridge, MA, MIT Press, 1966.

Kessell F: The role of syntax in children's comprehension from ages six to twelve. *Mongr Soc Res Child Dev* 35:1–59, 1970.

Kirshenblatt-Gimblett B: *Speech Play.* Philadelphia, University of Pennsylvania Press, 1976.

Leonard L, Bolders J, Curtis R: On the nature of children's judgments of linguistic features: semantic relations and grammatical morphemes. *J Psycholinguistic Res* 6:233–244, 1977.

Leonard L, Reid L: Children's judgments of utterance appropriateness. *J Speech Hear Res* 22:500–515, 1979.

Levelt W, Sinclair A, Jarvella R: Causes and functions of linguistic awareness in language acquisition: some introductory remarks. In Sinclair A, Jarvella R, Levelt W: *The Child's Conception of Language.* New York, Springer-Verlag 1978.

Liberman I, Shankweiler D: Speech, the alphabet and teaching to read. In Resnick L, Weaver P: *Theory and Practice of Early Reading.* Hillsdale, NJ, Lawrence Erlbaum Associates, 1977.

Liberman I, Shankweiler D, Fischer F, et al: Explicit syllable and phoneme segmentation in the young child. *J Exp Child Psychol* 18:201–212, 1974.

Lloyd P, Dunn J: Children's awareness of communication. In Feagans L, Garvey K, Golinkoff R: *The Origins and Growth of Communication.* Norwood, NJ, Ablex, in press.

Lundberg I: Aspects of linguistic awareness related to reading. In Sinclair A, Jarvella R, Levelt W: *The Child's Conception of Language.* New York, Springer-Verlag, 1978.

Maccoby E, Bee H: Some speculations concerning the lag between perceiving and performing. *Child Dev* 36:367–377, 1965.

Malgady R: Children's interpretation and appreciation of similies. *Child Dev* 48:1734–1738, 1977.

Maratsos M: Nonegocentric communication abilities in preschool children. *Child Dev* 44:697–700, 1973.

Mattingly I: Reading, the linguistic process, and linguistic awareness. In Kavanagh J, Mattingly I: *Language by Ear and by Eye.* Cambridge, MA, MIT Press, 1972.

Osherson D, Markman E: Language and the ability to evaluate contradictions and tautologies. *Cognition* 3:213–226, 1975.

Opie I, Opie P: *The Lore and Language of Schoolchildren.* Oxford, Clarendon Press, 1959.

Piaget J. *The Child's Conception of the World.* New York, Harcourt, Brace and World, 1929.

Piaget J: *The Grasp of Consciousness.* Cambridge, MA, Harvard University Press, 1976.

Piaget J: *Success and Understanding.* Cambridge, MA, Harvard University Press, 1978.

Read C: Children's awareness of language, with emphasis on sound systems. In Sinclair A, Jarvella R, Levelt W: *The Child's Conception of Language.* New York, Springer-Verlag, 1978.

Ryan E: Metalinguistic development and reading. In Murray FB: *Language Awareness and Reading.* Newark, DE, International Reading Association, 1980.

Sanches M, Kirshenblatt-Gimblett B: Children's traditional speech play and child language. In Kirshenblatt-Gimblett B: *Speech Play.* Philadelphia, University of Pennsylvania Press, 1976.

Scollon R: *Conversations with a One Year Old: A Case Study of the Developmental Foundations of Syntax.* Honolulu, University of Hawaii Press, 1976.

Seuren P: Grammar as an undergound process. In Sinclair A, Jarvella R, Levelt W: *The Child's Conception of Language.* New York, Springer-Verlag, 1978.

Shatz M, Gelman R: The development of communication skills: modifications in the speech of young children as a function of the listener. *Monogr Soc Res Child Dev* 38:1–37, 1973.

Sherzer J: Play languages: implications for (socio) linguistics. In Kirshenblatt-Gimblett B: *Speech Play.* Philadelphia, University of Pennsylvania Press, 1976.

Shiff N, Ventry I: Communication problems in hearing children of deaf parents. *J Speech Hear Disord* 41:348–358, 1976.

Shultz T: Development of the appreciation of riddles. *Child Dev* 45:100–105, 1974.

Sinclair H: Conceptualization and awareness in Piaget's theory and its relevance to the child's conception of language. In Sinclair A, Jarvella R, Levelt W: *The Child's Conception of Language.* New York, Springer-Verlag, 1978.

Sinclair H, Ferreiro E: Etude genetique de la comprehension, production et repetition des phrases au mode passif. *Arch Psychol* 40:1–42, 1970.

Slobin D: A case study of early language awareness. In Sinclair A, Jarvella R, Levelt W: *The Child's Conception of Language.* New York, Springer-Verlag, 1978.

Smith C, Tager-Flushberg H: The relationship between language comprehension and the development of metalinguistic awareness. Presented at the Fifth Annual Boston University Conference on Language Development, Boston, October, 1980.

Snyder-McLean L, McLean J: Verbal information gathering strategies: The child's use of language to acquire language. *J Speech Hear Disord* 43:306–325, 1978.

Tervoort B: Foreign language awareness in a five-to-nine year-old lexicographer. *J Child Language* 6:159–166, 1979.

Tremaine R: *Syntax and Piagetian Operational Thought.* Washington DC, Georgetown University Press, 1975.

Van Kleeck A: The emergence of linguistic awareness: a cognitive framework. *Merrill-Palmer Q* 28: 237–265, 1982.

Vygotsky L: *Language and Thought.* Cambridge, MA, MIT Press, 1962.

Wallach M: Creativity. In Mussen P: *Carmichael's Manual of Child Psychology,* ed 3. New York, John Wiley & Sons, 1970, vol 1.

Watzlawick P, Beavin J, Jackson D: *Pragmatics of Human Communication.* New York, WW Norton, 1967.

Weir R: *Language in the Crib.* The Hague, Mouton, 1962.

Weir R: Some questions on the child's learning of phonology. In Smith F, Miller G: *The Genesis of Language.* Cambridge, MA, MIT Press, 1966.

Winner E: New names for old things: the emergence of metaphorical language. *J Child Language* 6:469–492, 1979.

Winner E: Rosentiel A, and Gardner H: The development of metaphoric understanding. *Dev Psychol* 12:289–297, 1976.

CHAPTER EIGHT

Beyond Information Processing: The Language of Teachers and Textbooks

NICKOLA WOLF NELSON, Ph.D.

The search for the source of language learning disabilities is often aimed at identifying differences in the ways children who exhibit such problems develop and use language (Bloom, 1980; Leonard, 1980). In previous chapters this issue was addressed. It was also recognized that language learning does not occur in a vacuum. Rather, it is largely dependent on opportunities for meaningful discourse (Blank, 1973; Berlin et al., 1980; Bloom, 1980. However, information about the mutual effects of language competence and the context in which it is acquired is rather meager as yet, particularly for the school-age child.

If there are systematic ways in which language facility interacts with the language of teachers and textbooks, then controlling the learning environment may yield beneficial effects for children whose language skills are not well developed. Conversely, children who exhibit language learning problems may be penalized by certain types of instructional methods more than others (Zigmond et al., 1980). As White (1980, p. 43) points out, even normal children have "wobbly competencies," so that many factors affect them:

> A child is not a computer that either "knows" or "does not know." A child is a bumpy, blippy, excitable fatiguable, distractible, active, friendly, mulish, semi-cooperative bundle of biology. Some factors help a moving child pull together coherent address to a problem; others hinder that pulling together and make a child "not know."

It is the responsibility of educators to present information in such a way as to make it maximally comprehensible to learners, to facilitate the "pulling together" of processes for learning (Smith, 1979). Teaching does this largely through processes of communication, with which it has even been considered synonymous (Thompson, 1969).

COMPONENTS OF COMMUNICATION

In presenting his views on teaching as communication, Thompson (1969) emphasizes that every communication or teaching/learning exchange involves four basic components: *sender, receiver, message,* and *medium.*

1. The *sender* is the initiator of the communication cycle and the source of the message. In school settings, teachers are most frequently the "senders." They dominate conversation by speaking most of the time and initiating most of the exchanges (Bellack et al., 1966). Teachers are able to use the shared context of the classroom to augment oral messages they send. The authors of books act as remote senders. They are responsible for encoding more of the information into the text, making it explicit. Some of the ways this is achieved are iden-

tified in Chapter 6 on narrative development.

2. The *receiver* is the interpreter of messages. Communication hinges on meanings being extracted from messages by receivers in such a way that a close match occurs with the meaning intended by the speaker. For the receiver, message reception involves the organization of incoming data in ways that are classifiable in terms of his or her existing store of knowledge.

3. The *message* is the encoded meaning, not the meaning itself. Because the meanings of messages reside in receivers rather than in messages, a single message actually contains as many precise meanings as there are receivers. The messages teachers think they are sending may not match the meanings actually received, particularly when receivers have disordered or different language. Furthermore, the difficulty of message reception has no simple relationship to inherent message complexity. In fact, the "complexity" of messages is almost impossible to define apart from the difficulty receivers have decoding them. This is because the cognitive complexities of deep structure meanings are so completely intertwined with the psycholinguistic complexities of surface structure messages. Both are a function of the available context. In reviewing the literature on the influence of syntax on language processing, Slobin (1971, p. 33) acknowledges this fact in the statement that "the search for a reliable metric of syntactic complexity ... has not been strikingly successful, and the reason for this failure is an important one. We soon discovered that understanding a sentence can depend as much upon the context in which it is used as upon its syntactic form."

4. The *medium* via which the message is transmitted is the fourth component of a communication exchange. Media choices for communicating messages include not only spoken, written, or nonverbal communication. They also include live versus televised, computerized, or film presentation, reading versus being read to, reading

aloud versus reading silently, reading books with pictures versus those without, conversing in groups versus conversing with individuals, and many, many more. Once meaning is encoded in a form which can be transmitted, the medium becomes the message, and the message differs depending upon its medium. In particular, there are important differences among the types of linguistic demands associated with the language of teachers and textbooks. Oral and written language are certainly related, but written language is not just spoken language written down (Kolers, 1970). Listening and reading require a number of distinct abilities (to be considered later in this chapter) which lead to differences in the relative difficulty of language processing in different modalities (Mattingly, 1972).

Attempts to separate the discussion of the four communication components—sender, receiver, message, and medium—are also somewhat artificial in that communication is both cyclical and interactive. In school settings, where teachers are most frequently the "senders" and students the "receivers," this is an important, although not frequently recognized, concept. Although elementary school students are said to spend over one-half of their day listening, and estimates for high school students range as high as 90% (Griffin and Hannah, 1960), communication in the classroom may not be as one-sided as it appears. The completion of a communication cycle requires feedback to be returned from the receiver to the sender. As they speak, senders of oral messages also "receive" input in the form of verbal and nonverbal feedback as to how well their messages have been comprehended. Effective senders "tune in" to the signs of comprehension on the part of their receiving conversational partners.

In one-to-one settings, parents have been shown to adjust their speaking styles for young children (Broen, 1972; Snow, 1972; Moerk, 1975; Snow and Ferguson, 1977). Conversely, as Van Kleeck notes (Chapter 7), children also adjust their styles in a one-to-one context. However, less is known about language addressed to school-age children by teachers and through teaching materials. It would be expected that communicative fine tuning would be more difficult to accomplish in language addressed to children in groups than as individuals. It might be tempting, in such a situation, to judge the success of the communicative event according to the positive responses of just a few students—usually the most successful ones—rather than making certain that all students have understood, before proceeding. There is also evidence to suggest that even parents talking to their individual children do not modify their speech solely in response to attentional and comprehension abilities (Snow, 1977; Wilkinson et al., 1981). Is there any evidence that teachers do the same?

Critical Questions

Information relating features of learning to features of *learning contexts* is still somewhat limited. This chapter examines available information and presents new information on the language of teachers. What is known about the linguistic demands of the school is interpreted in the light of what is known about the nature of language learning disabilities. Facilitating and hindering factors are identified in those areas in which information is available.

As the study of language learning in school contexts proceeds, a number of critical questions are being addressed. For example, what evidence is available for describing the language of teachers and textbooks? What is the nature of teacher-pupil interaction as it usually occurs in regular classrooms? What adjustments are made as students advance in age or have difficulty? What aspects of the learning context can be tied to performance variation by students learning language normally? What is the nature of reading, and how should early instruction proceed? What are the linguistic demands of other textual material? Finally, what implications are there in the answers to these questions for understand-

ing and intervening in language learning disabilities in school-age children?

THE LANGUAGE OF TEACHERS

The importance of language skills to the success of children in school cannot be overemphasized. According to Berlin et al. (1980, p. 48), "verbally based teaching is the medium of instruction through which all other learning is to be fostered." However, Silliman and Leslie (1980) point out that, although all teaching involves talk, not all talk is effective teaching. It would be helpful if the state of knowledge in the area of teacher discourse were sufficiently developed to permit generalizations about what kinds of talk do contribute to effective teaching. However, an experimental era involving careful description of discourse in general, let alone school discourse, has just begun (Dore, 1977).

A major part of teaching is the largely subconscious process of deciding which discourse styles and content will best facilitate learning (Moore, 1977). Teachers also hold the responsibility for determining the pace and style of the larger interactions in the classroom (Mishler, 1972). White (1980, p. 42) characterizes this selection process, often known as "classroom management," as a large part of the art of teaching, "not as a system of discipline, but as a system of dramaturgy." Smith (1975) has suggested that learning might be categorized into three modes: (1) that which occurs through performance or by experience, (2) that which accompanies observation or demonstration, and (3) that which results from being told, from language. Teaching involves a constant selection among these strategies.

To a degree, decisions made depend on the curricular theories of the moment (e.g., the "open clssroom" versus "back-to-basics" movements). They also appear to vary with the developing abilities of children, particularly the ability to shift from strategies which can be used successfully to comprehend the context-bound language of the home to those which are required for understanding the increasingly context-free language of school.

Differences between Home and School Language

In the communication environment of the home, children develop the ability to communicate and interpret meaning within a system of shared communicative assumptions and understandings which arise naturally out of the regularities and rituals of early child-rearing (Cook-Gumperz, 1977). In the communication environment of the school, children must be able to shift away from the expectation of shared assumptions (implicit meaning) to interpreting overtly lexicalized intentions (explicit meaning). These verbally transmitted messages become more and more free of what Cook-Gumperz (1977) calls "situated meaning." In other words, as children advance in school, more of the meaning is encoded linguistically and less of the meaning is available in the nonverbal surrounding context. Consider, for example, the ability of children in the later grades to learn about far away people and places they have never seen, largely through language.

Bernstein (1972) calls the type of communication in which principles and operations are *implicit*, i.e., in which meaning is context bound, "particularistic." He provides an example of a story told by a 5-year-old boy about a picture using particularistic orders of meaning:

They're playing football / and he kicks it and it goes through there / it breaks the window and they're looking at it / and he shouts at them because they've broken it so they run away and then she looks out / and she tells them off (p. 141).

Schools, in serving the role of transferring information from teachers to learners, are necessarily concerned with the transmission and development of "universalistic" orders of meaning. That is, the school makes explicit, by elaborating through language, the principles and operations that apply to objects (science subjects) and to persons (arts subjects) (Moore, 1977).

In a second example, the story told by another 5-year-old child is free enough of the context of the pictures to be understood apart from them:

Three boys are playing football and one boy kicks the ball and it goes through the window / the ball breaks the window and the boys are looking at it and a man comes out and shouts at them / because they've broken the window so they run away / and then that lady looks out of her window / and she tells the boys off (p. 141).

The differences exemplified in these two stories are attributed by Bernstein (1972) to differences in the types of communicative environments children have experienced before coming to school. He concludes that children whose homes include practice listening to language in which elaborated, context-free, universalistic meanings have been encoded are better prepared to understand and produce such sentences.

The elaboration of meaning through language generally demands more complex sentence structures. Noun phrases and other embedded clauses provide greater reference than the pronoun "it," but also require more words and more complex phrase relationships. Berlin et al. (1980) hypothesize that, given the developmental limitations of many normal children, the language-handicapped child can be expected to experience even greater problems when faced with the more complex verbal formulations required for understanding or producing the fully encoded meanings of schools. In such cases, children "might either retain only fragments of the total utterance or, more likely, simply 'tune out' the auditory stream. When this occurs, the language hinders rather than enhances development" (p. 50).

Normal children develop competencies which enable them to shift from strategies which rely on situated meaning to strategies which entail the lexical encoding of intent (Cook-Gumperz, 1977; See also Chapters 5 and 7). An increasing ability to manage the mapping of communicative intent onto surface syntactic structure is acquired. Children also learn to recognize the speech activities that make the context explicit and to "chunk" speech into sequences of recognizable and interpretable social activity (Bruner, 1975). The ability to make meaning explicit conversationally requires an ability to judge what is shared or "old information" held in common with a conversational partner and what is "new information." It is only new, or unshared, information that needs to be made explicit (Bates, 1976). Similarly, listeners must be prepared to pay selective attention to information which has been signaled to be "new" with either semantic or syntactic phrase cues. These are often aided by the use of such supralinguistic devices as contrastive stress. An example is when a teacher emphasizes, "Not the *book*, find the *magazine* that I showed you this morning." Pragmatic judgments of this type require a speaker or a listener to be able to take another person's point of view. These are some of the interrelated cognitive and pragmatic skills that many language learning-disabled children lack (Gerber, 1981). Problems in understanding the use of pragmatic conventions also demonstrate ways in which symptoms of early language disabilities change over time (see Chapter 2).

Change in School Language as Age/ Grade Level Increases

The shift from situated meaning, bound to nonlinguistic contexts, to more completely lexically encoded meaning, is particularly apparent at the point of school entry. An increasing reliance on lexically encoded meaning continues into the upper grades. O'Connor and Eldredge (1980, p. 2) describe the language demands placed upon adolescents as requiring them "to understand and follow the teacher's directions, to focus and derive the main ideas from the teacher's lecture, to organize and store these ideas or facts for retrieval on exams. . . ."

How are children led from the stage of home language to adult language competence? How abrupt are the changes? Bernstein (1972) places much of the responsibility for preparing children to deal with

school language in the communicative styles of their homes. Chomsky (1972) identifies further evidence that parents who read to their children before they enter school provide a major source of practice in dealing with the more completely lexically encoded meanings of school language.

One does not start reading to toddlers by reading the words on the page. One starts by talking about the pictures. Talking about the pictures must also have been preceded by a variety of early conversational and experiential interaction with busy toddlers. Toddlers who squirm when language demands are too high provide powerful feedback, but research suggests that it is more than feedback that allows most adults to have the knack of fitting linguistic tasks to the presumed abilities of young children (Snow, 1977). In a variety of studies, language addressed to toddlers by mothers, fathers, and other adults has been found consistently to be syntactically simple, highly redundant, fluent, and well formed grammatically in contrast to language addressed to adults and older children (Phillips, 1973; Snow, 1977; Wilkinson et al., 1981). Even when addressing language to 2-year-olds while speaking into a tape recorder, adults simplify its presentation. Additional simplifications and repetitions are made when the 2-year-olds are actually present (Snow, 1972). This is viewed as evidence that such simplification is partly a component of adult communicative competence and partly a response to cues provided by the child, such as cues of inattention when speech becomes too complex.

What evidence is there that adults continue fitting communicative tasks to the presumed capabilities of children into the school-age years? This was a question addressed in a study conducted by this author with Cuda (Cuda, 1976; Cuda and Nelson, 1976). In that study, 27 samples of teacher discourse were gathered by placing a high-quality tape recorder with a remote microphone in randomly selected first-, third-, and sixth-grade classrooms (nine each) in

Wichita, Kansas. An electronic switching device was used to turn the tape recorder on and off several times during the school day in an attempt to reduce the effect of reactivity by the teachers to the knowledge that they were being tape recorded. This was also done to increase the likelihood of obtaining a broadly representative sample of school tasks throughout the day.

Each of the tapes yielded a corpus of teacher talk that was selected to meet a number of criteria. Sentences included in the analysis were those addressed to the whole class, to a group within the class, or to an individual, but judged to be for the benefit of all. Any comments or instructions given strictly on an individual basis were not analyzed as part of the corpus. Sentences did not have to be grammatically correct to be included in the study, but were used if they were judged to convey a complete message. Where conjunctions appeared to be used as starters, boundaries between sentences were determined by temporal and contextual cues imposed by the speaker. No attempt was made to control the content of sentences used, and the samples included a wide variety of academic subject matter as well as variation in the intended use of the sentences by the teacher (e.g., to reprimand, explain, instruct, or question). In order to avoid experimenter bias in corpus selection, the 50 sentences included in the analysis were chosen as they occurred consecutively, with the exception that comments which did not meet the criteria were excluded.

The corpus of 50 sentences for each of the 27 teachers was quantitatively evaluated with three measures. *Speaking rate* was measured in syllables per second. *Syntactic complexity* was measured using a syntactic complexity formula (Botel et al., 1973; Miller and Hintzman, 1975) that was designed to incorporate data on children's processing and the theory of transformational grammar (Chomsky, 1965). The formula involves an averaging of the sum of six separate word counts between: (1) beginning and ending sentence boundaries,

(2) the beginning boundary and subject noun, (3) the beginning boundary and main verb, (4) the subject noun and main verb, (5) the subject noun and end boundary, and (6) the main verb and end boundary (Miller and Hintzman, 1975). The third variable measured quantitatively was communicative *style* or *fluency*. This was done by taking counts of four types of "hesitation phenomena" described by Maclay and Osgood (1959): pauses, filled pauses, revisions, and repetitions. Silent pauses were those judged to be of unusual duration for the speaker's rhythm of speech. Filled pauses included not only vocalizations such as "uh, ah, um, er, eh," but also habitual fillers, such as "OK, you know, all right," inserted into a sentence without adding to the linguistic structure of the sentence. Revisions were counted whenever a sentence was begun and reformulated or restarted at any point. This included situations in which either a complete change of thought was made or a word choice was corrected for accuracy of content. Repetitions of sounds, words, or phrases were counted if they occurred without lending emphasis to the sentence. Intentional repetitions for emphasis of a point were not considered nonfluencies and were not counted as repetitions.

The results of the study suggested a positive answer to the question as to whether teachers, like parents, use different speaking styles with children of different ages. Analysis of variance, and post hoc analyses where significant differences were found, showed a steady progression of complexity/difficulty increases in the variables selected for study. Speaking rate was found to be significantly slower for the first-grade teachers than for either third-grade or sixth-grade teachers. Complexity of syntactic relationships was found to be significantly greater for sixth-grade teachers than for either first- or third-grade teachers. Pauses were not significantly different for any of the groups, but significantly more filled pauses, revisions, and repetitions were found for sixth-grade teachers than for either first- or third-grade teachers.

Data for individual teachers are summarized in Table 8.1.

The results were particularly interesting in that they showed syntactic complexity, rate, and fluency indicators to increase in stages rather than all at once. The communicative competence which allows adults to be able to tailor communicative tasks for preschoolers appears to extend to teachers' communicative expectations in the school-age years.

The implications of these findings for language learning-disabled students include a number of considerations. The mean syllable per second (sps) speaking rate for both third- (5.4 sps) and sixth- (5.3 sps) grade teachers was quite fast. In another study, Nelson (1976) found that a rate of 5.0 sps increased comprehension difficulties among normal children up to 9½ years of age. Research with listeners who experience language processing problems of various types suggests that they are even more sensitive than most listeners to increased difficulty related to adjustments in syntactic complexity and speaking rate (McCroskey and Thompson-Nelson, 1973a, 1973b).

The mean rate used by first-grade teachers in this study was 4.5 sps. It was slower than the 5.0 sps rate found to be disruptive to comprehension in the study of normal listeners (Nelson, 1976). Table 8.1 provides individual data to show that the first-grade teachers were also more uniform as a group in their rate of speaking. Third- and sixth-

Table 8.1.
Summary Data and Scores for Individual Teachers (Cuda, 1976)[a]

T	GR	Sch	Yrs	Sex	D	Mean Scores						
						MLU	sps	comp	P	FP	Rev	Rep
1	1	1	7	F	SA	13.10	4.80	34.58	.48	.16	.14	.02
2	1	2	10	F	SA	14.90	4.97	39.94	1.22	.36	.12	.12
3	1	3	1	F	SA	8.86	4.76	23.50	.64	.24	.10	.02
4	1	4	7	F	SA	11.18	4.44	30.64	.66	.14	.04	.04
5	1	5	1	M	SA	15.86	4.00	39.34	1.70	.48	.30	.24
6	1	6	14	F	SA	10.12	4.43	31.00	.52	.24	.20	.02
7	1	8	2	F	SA	11.74	4.86	30.12	.42	.12	.06	.04
8	1	9	27	F	SA	9.50	4.35	23.42	.50	.20	.10	.02
9	1	10	5	F	SA	12.86	3.73	34.78	1.22	.22	.04	.02
1	3	1	15	F	SA	11.90	5.83	32.02	.58	.08	.00	.00
2	3	2	2	F	SA	10.78	5.01	32.42	.80	.24	.14	.04
3	3	3	0	M	SA	15.56	5.68	40.64	.80	.16	.26	.08
4	3	4	4	F	BE	10.92	5.81	28.86	.36	.36	.24	.04
5	3	5	2	F	SA	8.38	6.47	24.66	.52	.12	.14	.02
6	3	6	5	F	SA	10.24	4.23	25.82	.74	.18	.12	.10
7	3	7	16	F	SA	12.26	3.99	35.14	1.20	.16	.18	.14
8	3	8	4	F	SA	13.88	4.65	33.14	1.12	.32	.22	.06
9	3	10	6	F	SA	12.18	5.82	32.42	.54	.34	.14	.02
1	6	1	2	F	SA	10.16	4.83	28.00	.56	.16	.32	.02
2	6	2	8	F	SA	8.82	5.51	28.38	.30	.32	.24	.12
3	6	4	12	M	BE	17.98	4.30	48.04	1.64	1.10	.32	.06
4	6	5	5	M	EA	12.90	6.08	37.10	.64	.54	.28	.20
5	6	6	3	F	SA	15.90	4.64	44.00	1.26	.38	.22	.16
6	6	7	8	M	SA	13.12	4.21	36.34	1.28	.48	.26	.06
7	6	8	11	M	SA	13.52	6.60	38.64	.62	.24	.08	.02
8	6	9	2	M	BE	9.98	6.18	31.74	1.00	1.02	.16	.18
9	6	10	2	F	SA	16.74	5.79	41.44	1.12	.64	.52	.12

[a] Gr, grade; T, teacher; Sch, school; Yrs, Years taught at that grade; D, dialect—SA, standard American; BE, black English; EA, eastern American; MLU, mean length of utterance; sps, syllables per second; comp, complexity scores; P, pause; FP, filled pause; Rev, revisions; Rep, repetitions.

grade teachers demonstrated wider individual differences. Perhaps beyond first grade, some teachers (either consciously or subconsciously) decide that they can talk faster. The increased efficiency of transmitting more information in less time may justify a few errors in comprehension. Older children are also more adept at signaling incomprehension. When problems occur, messages can be repeated or revised as necessary. Third-grade teachers represent a middle ground in this apparent shift. They showed a speaking rate which was similar to sixth-grade teachers but maintained a syntactic complexity which was similar to first-grade teachers. The listening demands of third grade seem to provide an intermediate step toward the dual increased listening demands of speeded rate and greater syntactic complexity in the upper grades.

The individual differences among teachers are also important. Careful selection of teachers for mainstreaming language learning-disabled children should involve consideration of teachers' speaking rates and styles. Teachers who effectively *vary* their speaking rates to call attention to important points may provide the most useful cues for many students.

Discourse Variables in Teachers' Speech to Children

Recalling the discussion of increasingly context-free lexical meanings, it is clear that the increases in complexity of teacher speech as grade level increases are not just structural. In the early grades, instructional emphasis is upon the training of learning *processes* including such language skills as reading and writing. In the later grades, emphasis shifts to the employment of earlier trained skills for the purpose of introducing language *content*.

Mishler (1972, 1975) was one of the first to attempt to analyze the content of teachers' language to their students in units larger than words and sentences. He proposes classification of discourse units according to their purposes to initiate, sustain, and/or control conversation and uses verbatim transcriptions to illustrate his points. In particular, Mishler (1972) argues that the structure of teachers' statements and the type of interchanges developed between them and their children require different cognitive strategies and convey different values and norms.

Mishler (1972) also emphasizes the importance of studying individual differences in teacher style. Indeed, it would be most useful to have a more complete description of the similarities among teachers of different grade levels in the topics and pragmatic functions they use. It would also be useful to have information about the shifts of conversational variables over the school years. To provide data in these areas, further analysis has been made of the 27 teacher discourse samples gathered in the Cuda and Nelson (1976) study using multilevel discourse analysis.

Multilevel discourse analysis is a complex process. Dore (1979) proposes, for example, that, at the very least, a model of conversation must deal with propositional *content*, grammatical *form*, illocutionary *function*, cognitive *process*, conversational *procedure*, and social *frame*. The number of categories needed to classify conversational acts alone (coding for illocutionary function and conversational procedure) is quite extensive. Table 8.2 summarizes Dore's (1979) taxonomy, which eventually splits into 35 categories of conversational acts.*

As an initial step in looking at these variables in teacher language at different grade levels, some segments have been se-

---

* A problem in using Dore's categories to apply to teacher discourse is that the power differential between teachers and students leads to teachers using regulatives to control much more than conversation. Many requestives, particularly action requests, actually serve what are termed in this chapter "regulative functions." These may be either direct ("Would everyone stand up?") or indirect ("Somebody's talking"). Assertives of internal or social phenomena ("I believe we need a wiggle minute") also function in this way at times. These types of acts are usually easily distinguished from the questions, action requests, suggestions, and assertives used to convey lesson content. For the purposes of this discussion, regulative functions performed in the process of organizing students for some activity or another are grouped separately from those used primarily to convey content.

Table 8.2.
A Representation of Dore's (1979) Categories of Primary Conversational Functions, General Conversational Classes, and Particular Conversational Acts, with Examples from the Teacher Discourse Samples Reported in this Chapter

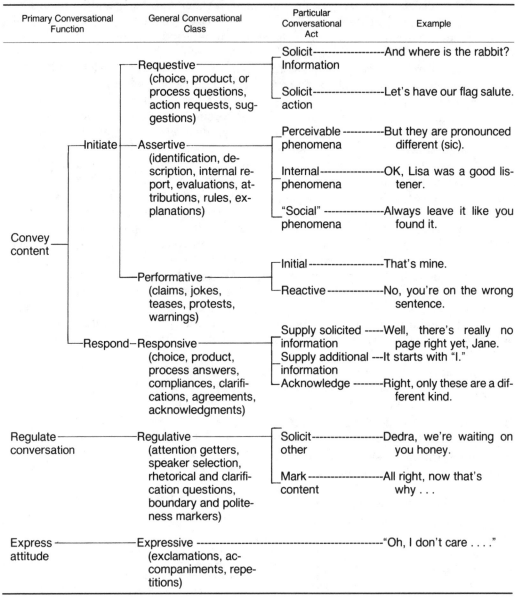

Primary Conversational Function	General Conversational Class	Particular Conversational Act	Example
Convey content	Requestive (choice, product, or process questions, action requests, suggestions)	Solicit Information	And where is the rabbit?
		Solicit action	Let's have our flag salute.
	Assertive (identification, description, internal report, evaluations, attributions, rules, explanations)	Perceivable phenomena	But they are pronounced different (sic).
		Internal phenomena	OK, Lisa was a good listener.
		"Social" phenomena	Always leave it like you found it.
	Performative (claims, jokes, teases, protests, warnings)	Initial	That's mine.
		Reactive	No, you're on the wrong sentence.
	Responsive (choice, product, process answers, compliances, clarifications, agreements, acknowledgments)	Supply solicited information	Well, there's really no page right yet, Jane.
		Supply additional information	It starts with "I."
		Acknowledge	Right, only these are a different kind.
Regulate conversation	Regulative (attention getters, speaker selection, rhetorical and clarification questions, boundary and politeness markers)	Solicit other	Dedra, we're waiting on you honey.
		Mark content	All right, now that's why . . .
Express attitude	Expressive (exclamations, accompaniments, repetitions)		"Oh, I don't care . . . ."

lected from the first-, third-, and sixth-grade teacher discourse samples gathered in the Cuda and Nelson (1976) study. These are naturalistic samples taken from regular education classrooms. In Chapter 14, Silliman provides information on teaching discourse that augments aspects of the process for language learning-disabled students.

FIRST-GRADE TEACHERS PERFORMING REGULATIVE FUNCTIONS

First-grade teachers use a high number of regulative statements to direct the attention of the class and individuals and to control their behavior. For example:

Teacher 1:1†
All right, let's get back to your seats.
Let's have our flag salute.
Dedra, we're waiting on you honey.
Drew, forgot how it starts?
It starts with "I."
Remember you're standing up / tall and straight /
and you look like a letter.

Many of the regulatives and requestives
of first-grade teachers (especially action requests) have to do with classroom organization, working at centers, preparing to
change activities, and so forth. Such types
of communication tend to rely on requestives that may be framed as assertives but
have an implied action request or suggestion. For example:

Teacher 8:1
The chairman of the Arts Center needs to get out
the scrap box and pour a little bit of glue on your
tray.
So whatever chairman I choose has two jobs to do.
I sure do hope you all work this hard at your centers
this afternoon.

Some directly acknowledge the behavioral
needs of first graders:

Teacher 7:1
Push your chairs in please.
I believe we need a wiggle minute.
Would everyone stand up?
We have exactly 1 minute to wiggle—go!
Thank you, now, you should / all be ready to sit
very still.

Others focus directly on the value of attention. In the following sequence a series of
assertives is used to control the listening
behavior of students. The focus is on individuals:

Teacher 2:1
Now, before you start I want to check to see about
my listeners.
OK, Lisa was a good listener.
Randy was fairly good.
aaa, and, and this Randy was fairly good.

_____
† In this section, teachers are identified by subject
number followed by grade level. Numbers correspond
with those of Table 8.1. For example, Teacher 1:1 is
the first subject in the first grade.

Eric / you were not good, you got almost all your
work filled in / you weren't listening.
Vicki, / good listener.
Now boys and girls / listening / is important / for
one reason / you'll need it later on.
Now / some of you know your number words just as
well as you / you know / your name / and you
know your color words.
If you get in the habit of listening / then / no matter
what job you have to do / then we'll have, we'll
have that to do it with.
You know if, if we were going to build, if we were
going to build a dog house, what you need?
What kind of tools would you need?
A hammer, nails, saw, wood / Lisa?
I guess you'd have to see / or make plans to saw the
boards in the right place wouldn't you?
OK, now then, sometimes we need other tools, don't
we?
Remember we talked about / 10 hours of sleep / so
we feel good / at night and a good breakfast / so
you feel good in the morning.
Russel, we're not grouchy / we don't feel bad.
We think "Oh, I don't care if it's orange and purple
I don't feel good."
You've felt like that / I know.
Most of the time / you'll just pull the cover back
over / and you'll stay home that day.
All right / now / that's why I want you to get in a
habit of listening / so you'll know what your're
supposed to be doing.

Notice that Teacher 2:1 uses some abstract
reasoning techniques. Decoding of complex
sentence structures is required. Also notice
the shifting pronominal reference from
"we" to "you." Additionally, the conceptual
demands of the discourse include handling
linguistic analogies and maintaining dual
focus on various meanings of the word
"tool." Children are expected to make a
cognitive shift from the use of the word
"tool" to represent such things as a "hammer" and "saw" to its more abstract use to
mean getting plenty of rest in preparation
for school. Finally, "listening" is identified
as a tool. The language learning-disabled
child would probably sit out this discussion,
not listening. One does not listen to what
one cannot understand.

FIRST-GRADE TEACHERS TEACHING SOME READING AND WRITING FUNDAMENTALS

The content of instructional sequences
of first-grade teachers tends to be aimed

primarily at teaching *how to* do various school-like activities, primarily involving the fundamentals of reading, writing, and math.

Teacher 3:1

What does escalator start with? /ɛ/, /ɛ/, /ɛ/
Apple / or elephant /ɛ/ escalator or Indian octopus, umpire, which one?
No, let's see the "a" sounds like in apple ant, in apron
We're saying /ɛ/, /ɛ/ like in elephant.
So what does it start with?
OK "e" OK
What does Indian start with?
"i" Indian
Let's see/that, that animal is called an ox
Ox / Ox
Very good, Clarence, "o" / "o"
And let's see what else
Oh, let's say umbrella
"u" very good / umbrella

In order to comprehend this activity, a child would have to have the metalinguistic skills to segment words phonemically (see Chapters 7 and 13). This includes phonemic segmentation of vocabulary words that may be totally new. The child also has to grasp the concept that the names and the sounds of letters are different, and that the same letter may represent several different sounds. In addition, it is necessary to recognize that when the teacher asks what a word "starts with," she expects the name of an alphabetic letter (usually) and, in addition to all of this, she expects the students to be able to solve all of these metalinguistic problems quickly. The child who is worrying about keeping up is soon lost.

Another teacher sends a different message. She then needs to use a clarification response when the children have not received the meaning she intended:

Teacher 7:1

What sound does / cat / begin with?
   (Here the language learning-disabled child who does not have a concept of a word might be thinking "meow.")
No / that's not what I asked.
I asked what sound.
Good / We have two letters that make a /k/ sound.
"k" and "c" make the same / sound

How do you know / that cat / does not begin with a "k"?
Because I didn't put a "k" on the paper / so you know it has to begin with a / "c"
Use your sounds and figure out the other words.

In this segment, it is necessary to understand that the same sound may be written by two different letters. The teacher in this segment also uses a process requestive ("How do you know . . .?") to help children solve the problem. However, the answer is not inherent in the linguistic task. Rather, it is available to those who have figured out the strategies of the classroom.

Teacher 7:1

If your first name begins with "s" you may go the gym.
If / your first / name / begins / with "b", "b" like boy, you may go to the door.

These action requestives necessitate multilevel processing. This includes as a minimum: decoding conditional (if-then) sentences both cognitively and syntactically, recognition of the letter the teacher has named, knowing the difference between one's "first" and "last" name, and knowing which letter starts one's first name. In addition, the child must pick all of the important cues out of the surrounding acoustic environment and ignore all of the unimportant ones. Children who have a strong language base can manage these skills, but a child with a language learning disability may have trouble with any one or the combination of these requirements.

The majority of first-grade reading instruction focuses on surface level decoding, but beginning attempts to tie decoding to comprehension are also evident. In the following segment, a teacher begins to lead her children to switch focus back and forth in the context of a phonics and handwriting lesson between sound and letter form and the truthfulness of their textual material. She does this by using a series of choice requestives to lead her students to relate what they see to their broader experiences:

Teacher 4:1

Put your pencils all the way to the top.
What kind of animal do you see at the very top?

(Here one must understand the relational terms "very" and "top.")
And where is the rabbit?
He's sitting on a radio.
Did you ever see a real rabbit sit on a radio?
What does the word rabbit begin with?
"r" / all right / and what about the thing he's sitting on?
Say the word.
Radio, right, very good.
Radio and rabbit both begin with the letter "r."
OK, can you see how that letter is made?
The capital "R" is how many spaces?
Two spaces tall / and the small "r"?
After your name is made / at the space at the top will you make the capital "R" and the small "r" on the lines that are shown / right beside the rabbit?

The preceding sample also provides an example of the highly context-bound activities of the early elementary grades. Many concrete materials are provided to supplement the language of instruction, although children are expected to be able to process information on abstract and concrete levels simultaneously.

Another teacher attempts to lead her students beyond the meaning of individual words to begin to build an appreciation of the macrostructure of reading (larger meaningful units). She even acknowledges that it is acceptable if one cannot decode all of the details:

Teacher 7:1
All right / from now on I would like for you to read a / library book / or a / book from home.
This does not include *Tip, Tip and Mitten, Big Show* and / uh / what you are reading.
You will not know / all of the words.
It's fun to listen to someone if they read with expression.
When is it more fun to listen to someone talk?
Isn't it much / more fun to listen to someone talk with expression?

The children being addressed in the segment below are primarily normal language learners. Imagine the difficulty a language learning-disabled child would have approaching this task, having neither the underlying linguistic competence to draw on, nor the comprehension strategies to apply to the teacher's instructions.

Teacher 5:1
All right / OK / pencils down / pencils down.
OK / now the main / the main reason I was trying to do this today / I wanted to see how / well we're understanding what we're reading / when we're reading in our books, / and / I can understand that we're not understanding what we're reading a single bit.
Because what's happening is / what I'm saying everyday we read a book / and we have this word and / and / and when I'm asking you to find it in a book you don't even know what to do.
Well let me show you / Lorie, what we're supposed to do / using these words / and I'll show you how easy it works.

As in reading instruction, writing instruction is also concentrated at the surface level in the first grade. The verbal instructions of the teacher are closely tied to the actions of the students. The need for context in determining meaning is particularly evident in the next example.

Teacher 5:1
Next one / capital "T" and lower case "t"
Next one / make a capital "E" / and a lower case "e" OK?
You have just completed the first / two rows.
OK / now by the star / put a capital "D" / then a lower case "d"
If I hear anybody else say that "easy peasy" they're gonna stand up / after school and you're gonna say it 150 times.
(This segment provides an example of the context of social frame (Dore, 1979). It also demonstrates Mishler's (1972) comments on the use of teacher/pupil interchanges to convey values and norms. Recall that the same teacher explained how "easy" his word identification exercise was in the previous example.)

In addition to teaching handwriting form, some first-grade teachers also venture into teaching writing content. This type of activity increases in second and third grade (see Chapter 6).

FIRST-GRADE TEACHERS TEACHING SOME MATHEMATIC FUNDAMENTALS

Language activities are also an integral part of mathematics instruction at the first-grade level. In an article entitled. "Everyday math is a story problem: The language of the curriculum," Carlson et al. (1980, p. 61) comment that, "The language used by the classroom teacher can often influence the mathematical success of students." They also propose that teachers may be able to assist students with math problems if they focus on the language of instruction as well as the math concepts themselves (Pollak and Gruenewald, 1976).

Only one example of math instruction occurred in the time-based samples of the nine first-grade teachers in the Cuda and Nelson (1976) study. The following segment includes some comments used by a teacher to accompany an activity where children are writing on the chalkboard. A high number of "product requestives" (Dore, 1979) (e.g., "What did you write, Brian?") and "evaluative assertives" (e.g., "Oh, such smart children you are, really smart!") appear. A high frequency of positive reinforcement in the form of verbal praise, physical contact, and facial expression has been shown to be associated with significant increases in mathematical performance, particularly for young children (Masek, 1970). The teacher in the sample reported here uses a variety of strategies to boost the attitudes and self-confidence of her students before expecting them to work independently in their math books:

Teacher 9:1
　Can you write me down / two things / that will make this number?
　　(Here children must shift from a surface level meaning of numeral formation to focus on underlying additive properties.)
　Oh such smart children you are / really smart.
　What did you write Julie?
　What did you write / uh / Donnie?
　You wrote a different one.
　What do you have Angie? You've got a good one that no one else has.
　All right / now will you erase the chalkboard now?

FIRST-GRADE TEACHERS AND SCIENCE INSTRUCTION

First-grade teachers do not use a great deal of language in lecture-style presentations. Instruction related to content subjects, such as science and social studies, is usually incidental to instruction in the basics of reading, writing, and math. For example:

Teacher 6:1
　That's for the inside temperature not the outside.
　The higher it gets / the warmer it is / the lower it is the colder it is.
　　(This material sounds a little like Bernstein's (1972) "particularistic meanings" example.)
　Which one is the coldest desk?
　Which one is the warmest desk?

THIRD-GRADE TEACHERS PERFORMING REGULATIVE FUNCTIONS

Third-grade teachers continue to use language to control the behaviors of their students, but they tend to rely on written instructions more and the abilities of their students to work independently. For example:

Teacher 2:3
　I'll put your assignment up here on the board.
　When you finish / when you finish your math, why do your Health.
　Some of you haven't read the Health yet.
　Some of you need to read it again.
　All right, look here on the board.

Beyond regulative functions, instruction increasingly focuses on underlying meaning at the third-grade level. Not only is the teaching of reading and writing skills of considerable importance, but content subjects become an integral part of the curriculum as well. A number of new descriptive terms are also introduced in using language to talk about language (necessitating an increasing reliance on metalinguistic skills).

THIRD-GRADE TEACHERS ADDING TO THE FUNDAMENTALS OF READING AND WRITING

The following two sequences provide examples of direct instruction in the use of special case morpho-grapho-phonemic rules for reading, writing, and pronouncing certain words (homographs and homonyms):

Teacher 1:3
　Oh, would you get out your English books please?
　Yesterday we had words that sound alike.
　Today we have words that / look alike
　But they are pronounced different
　There are two ways to pronounce this word. ("tear")
　Do you know what they are?
　That would be /tiɚ/here.

How are you going to know how to pronounce it if
you see it in a sentence?
How would you know whether to say /tiɚ/ or
/tɛɚ/?
Well, there's really no page right yet Jane.
I'm wanting you to pay attention to see if you could
tell me why.
Can anybody get an idea if they would see this in a
sentence if they would know how to say /tiɚ/ or
/tɛɚ/?
But when you see it in a sentence are you going to
say /tiɚ/ or /tɛɚ/?
They mean two different things don't they?
You have a tear in your eye and you tear / the
material.

In the following segment, children are expected to already have learned the special
cases of the homonyms "mail" and "male"
for a spelling test:

Teacher 9:3
OK number two is mail
This is like / talking about a letter that you received
through the mail
We use this word to talk about a man or a boy but
it's not spelled like this.

By the time they reach third grade, children are expected to be able to use syntactic
and semantic cues to complete workbook
activities, such as the one explained by the
teacher in the next segment:

Teacher 2:3
One word in each paragraph does not make sense.
This is your paragraph right here / and there's
one word in there that does not make sense / and
that's where you put your X / on the word that
doesn't make sense.
Well, she has these X'd and circled and everything
else.
That wouldn't be right would it?
Then you should circle the word here / that should
go in there.
(These instructions went on with responsive repetitions and clarifications for five more comments. If children learning language normally
have such difficulty, imagine the perplexity faced
by the child with a language learning disability.)

Reading for meaning as opposed to simply decoding words becomes a more predominant goal by third grade. Research in
educational psychology shows that questions called "cognitive organizers" (Ausubel, 1960) may be used to guide cognitive
processes. Teachers use more memory

questions, i.e., those requiring recall of specific information, than any other category.
The use of higher level questions, such as
more abstract, process-oriented questions,
has been shown to be unrelated to pupil
achievement for most students (Rosenshine, 1971; Dunkin and Biddle, 1974).
Only higher ability students appear to
benefit from the use of higher level organizers to facilitate long-term associative
learning. Less able students appear to use
only the more concrete, specific, and less
generalizable organizers. An explanation of
this phenomenon is that organizers can
only be usable if they relate directly to
existing cognitive structure. Less able students may "file" information by product
questions rather than processing, making
the information more forgettable for low-
ability students (Allen, 1970). These differences may also be related to poorer integrative abilities of some students, as discussed
in Chapter 12.

Mishler (1972) suggests that rules might
be identified in the language of teachers to
represent such teaching strategies as focusing of attention, search and evaluation procedures, and the structure of alternatives.
The teacher in the following segment uses
a variety of conversational acts (product,
process, and action requestives, in Dore's
(1979) taxonomy) to evaluate and to lead
students into strategies of cognitive processing:

Teacher 7:3
Does she get these pajamas?
(This is a product memory requestive)
All right, but what / uh does she get with the
pajamas?
(Another product memory requestive)
What did Kevin say / his Aunt / Gladys had given
him for his birthday?
Who said / "I don't believe it?"
(This is an example of focusing attention. It is
followed by a request for evaluation.)
Why did Homer's mother say that?
Why was Homer's dad so careful / about picking up
the snakes, Todd?
On page 18 / find the paragraph that tells what
Homer said / when his father wanted to know /
if he was telling the truth.
(Search procedures are encouraged.)

All right count down, Pam count down for the
number / of the paragraph.

The fifth paragraph / all right read it for us Pam.

THIRD-GRADE TEACHERS ADDING TO MATHEMATICS FUNDAMENTALS

Mathematics instruction in the third grade continues to rely rather heavily on action requestives. Children are lead to perform overt operations following teacher's verbal instructions. Children who are able to retain and reverbalize instructions for themselves carry an important tool into Piaget's stage of operational thought. In this period the ability to perform mental operations without accompanying overt action appears. The ability to verbalize to oneself both accompanies the child's action and serves mental orientation (Vygotsky, 1962; Pellegrini, 1982).

As children develop, they acquire skill with the internalized manipulation of quantitative symbols rather than the physical manipulation of materials which have previously been used as props. The following segment illustrates a teacher's discourse whereby children perform actions as the teacher gives directions:

Teacher 2:3
The blue line's on top.
Put your finger on 7 / on the blue line / on top.
All right / now find 12 / under 7.
Find 12 under 7 / down there on the yellow line.
Move left / to 5 on pink.
Well move backwards / to 10.
Make left / and what do you have there? / Five
All right that's the way you finally subtract.
You find 12 / find 7 on the blue / find 12 under the 7 / move left to 5 on the pink / line.
Then that's your answer / 12 minus 7 is 5
All right on this page we'll do all of the exercises at the bottom / of the page.

THIRD-GRADE TEACHERS INTRODUCING SCIENCE AS A CONTENT SUBJECT

By third grade, children are spending more time engaged in learning associated with the content subjects, science, health, and social studies. Although direct experience is still often provided, verbal instructions become increasingly important. They are also given in increasingly larger chunks. The teacher in the following segment uses a series of requestives and assertives. These devices are used to direct activity. Successive questions are asked in which previous answers are taken into account (Mishler, 1972). They also provide continuity within the context of classroom experience and beyond. In this way, discourse is used to tie current experience into a larger cognitive framework:

Teacher 3:3
OK, everybody sit down now.
What your're gonna be doing today / is / you're gonna grow / your're gonna grown your own crystals.
If you remember last week / we grew some crystals back there but I kinda put it together didn't I?
Well this week you're gonna grow your own.
How many people in here / know what a tea bag is?
Right / only these tea bags are a different kind of tea tea bag.
These things / they look about the same on both ends but if you're really careful you can open the top part up.

THIRD-GRADE TEACHERS TEACHING LANGUAGE AS A CONTENT SUBJECT

Language has become an official content subject by third grade. The metalinguistic tasks of first grade involve primarily the ability to reflect on the sound patterns of words in order to be able to segment them phonemically. Third graders are expected to be able to categorize language into parts of speech:

Teacher 6:3
Sometimes it's easier if we pick / one noun / and we put an adjective with it.
Because we can think of lots of nouns that we can describe one noun / where it might be very difficult to think of an adjective to describe another noun.
Can you think of another one that might describe decorations and ornaments?
Would wreath be an adjective?
Could I close my eyes and see wreath?
What would wreath be?
It would be a / a noun wouldn't it?
A describing word will only tell me about it.
It won't tell me what the object is.

The type of language used and the cognitive tasks required to reflect upon it are demanding for children learning language normally. Children must also have enough constructive language abilities to be able to handle the teacher's false starts and revisions without losing focus on the task at hand. Recall that second or third grade is the time at which many children with subtle, but significant, language learning problems are referred for the first time for special education services. This is the dilemma of late identification of language learning disabilities discussed by Maxwell and Wallach in Chapter 2.

SIXTH-GRADE TEACHERS PERFORMING REGULATIVE FUNCTIONS

The problem of getting organized operates at all levels of school activity (McDermott, 1977). About 50% of class time is spent getting organized in the average elementary class (Gump, 1975). Success at getting organized depends on how well the participants communicate to each other the importance of the learning tasks (McDermott, 1977). The following two segments illustrate the language for regulating classroom organization at the sixth-grade level:

Teacher 1:6
  You'd better get your / uh / preparatory off the board cause it will be erased.
  If you're not finished / better get it off the board.
Teacher 2:6
  I asked you to quit talking.
  OK when you leave a station always leave it like you found it / then everybody'll be ready to go.

SIXTH-GRADE TEACHERS TEACHING READING AND WRITING AS TOOL SUBJECTS

In the sixth grade, reading has become primarily a tool subject, a mechanism for learning about new people, places, and things, rather than the object of study itself. In the early stages of learning to read, reading is parasitic on language (Mattingly, 1972). In the later stages, additional language learning becomes parasitic on reading.

The teacher in the following segment uses requestives to help her students relate what they have read to what they have heard or studied previously. A variety of pragmatic rules from spoken and written discourse must have been internalized for this process to occur, including the ability to understand the use of noun phrases for referring (Rochester and Martin, 1977). This is one of the techniques used by competent users of discourse to relate "given" to "new" information (Halliday, 1967; Clark and Haviland, 1977; see also Chapter 6). The following sample illustrates that teachers do not always use these conversational strategies with great facility. Normal sixth graders have difficulty in such instances. Language learning-disabled children could be expected to encounter even greater difficulty.

Teacher 9:6
  OK right I just want you to / uh / read at the top.
  Hold it right there.
  Do you remember anything about that when we / uh listened about that in lecture?
  That wasn't in lecture that we / about Mecca was it?
  That was in uh uh the uh special / oh that was in that brochure we had wasn't it?
  It talked about Mecca.
  What's / what was Mecca?
  Does anyone remember?
  OK it was one of the holy cities.

Sixth graders are also expected to be able to write language for others. Most of the instructions in the segment below are directed at teaching students the mechanics of writing. However, the ability to write coherently is dependent on the use of a high level of language abstraction and elaboration (Vygotsky, 1962). Students need to be able to learn that the audience for writing most likely does not share the writer's physical or emotional context (Elsasser and John-Steiner, 1977). They will have to use elaborated "universalistic" meanings (Bernstein, 1972).

Teacher 4:6
  Uh / we've talked about education and what part education can play / as far as the role of / the future's concerned
  And so you know something about education.
  You've heard a lot about it.
  You know what education really should do for chil-

dren and / uh / what education might be able to do for adults.

And also what it can do for a nation.

Uh / since this is what they call a bicentennial year. So the title of this writing / is / education's role in our society.

(Notice here, that a child who knows what a title is will be able to use a type of mental punctuation to bracket the words of the title to assist in comprehending the sentence.)

The introduction to the writing exercise continues for 13 more utterances and includes such comments as:

Now in the first / uh / you know you have marginal lines that you must give attention to.

You may need to use two sheets of paper, you may use / need one.

However, / uh / amount you write depends upon the / what you are capable of doing, and some of you are capable of long paragraphs and / uh / because you have more thoughts uh / on a particular matter.

ending with the statement:

Give it some deep thought / and / uh / and concentrate on it and make sure your handwriting is the best possible that you can put out.

The preceding passage also illustrates the use of language to convey teacher attitudes indirectly as they relate to particular capable students (Mishler, 1972; McDermott, 1977). Language learning-disabled children are quite able to understand that they are not included in that select group who can write "long paragraphs."

Brophy and Good (1970) have studied the ways in which teachers communicate differential expectations for classroom performance. They found evidence that differential teacher behavior occurred which was not attributable to objective differences among children. They interpret these findings as support for the "Pygmalion effect" described by Rosenthal and Jacobson (1968). That is, teacher expectations are seen to function as self-fulfilling prophecies. The combined effects of internal and external contextual factors on the emotionality and educational performance of language learning-disabled children are described by Gerber (1981). A spiraling inter-

action occurs among factors that interfere with adequate language processing in the educational setting. Unrealistic demands result in failure. The child experiences a sense of anxiety and inadequacy. This results in impulsive response behavior which interferes with reflection upon and processing of information. Further failure results.

"In this manner, it is speculated, the child fails to invest himself or herself in the active processing of the information to be mastered. The child, therefore, masters neither the information nor the strategies that the performance of language-related academic tasks requires" (Gerber, 1981, p. 106).

By the time a child reaches sixth grade, reliance on abstract concepts to understand academic tasks has increased dramatically. The following segment illustrates the continuing interaction of verbal and nonverbal concepts. The teacher's direction to focus on "key words" makes this relationship particularly salient:

Teacher 1:6

We look at the properties of addition / on page 28.

Now we glance through these / and you have the commutative property and the / associative property of / of addition.

What's the key word I asked you to underline in / the commutative property / or what is the key word?

What's the key word / in the associative properties that I asked you to underline / or suggested you underline?

Now, does this have anything to do with the order of the numbers when you compare the two sides / or does it have something to do with grouping? (Here, the teacher has embedded process questions as a choice requestive.)

In other words / six is first on this side / on the left side and on the right side six is second.

The importance of language to understanding key concepts in other content areas, such as the current events discussion below, is also brought to the foreground in the use of requestives related to word meaning and broader contextual meanings. In this segment, contingent queries are used successively to frame the topic area:

Teacher 6:6

How many people have the slightest idea or would like to guess what the word detente means?

Talk about / American / Chinese detente, American Soviet detente.

Uh / you're on the right subject matter, but not quite on the right side of it.

Uh / it has more to do with / cooperation / uh a relationship between friends in which they're willing to discuss their disagreements.

Language used to talk about language (metalinguistic functions) also has become increasingly abstract by the sixth grade.

Teacher 7:6

Ok / uh / now we're working with the / base form and the /s/ form of verbs.

The first part / you're supposed to / uh complete the sentence with / uh / with what / either one, either the "s" form or the base form.

Will you please read the sentence?

No you're on the wrong sentence.

THE LANGUAGE OF TEXTBOOKS

Earlier in this chapter, home language was differentiated from school language. Written language, although intimately related to spoken language, also involves special skills and strategies. Understanding the language of textbooks may present particular problems for language learning-disabled students. One has only to review the spoken language samples from teachers in the previous section to appreciate the comment that "written language is not the same as anyone's spoken language" (Smith, 1979, p. 159). In this case, it might be more precise to say that spoken language is not the same as anyone's written language.

If written language included as many incomplete sentences, false starts, revisions, and references bound to nonverbal context as the preceding samples of teacher talk, it is doubtful that many of us would read very much or understand much of what we read. One could argue that relative permanence of the message in written text makes reading less demanding than auditory language—in its mature form at least. Language which has been written down has the opportunity of being reviewed and polished to make sure that its meaning is as clear as possible. Errors and revisions made in spontaneous speaking become an integral part of the message. In listening tasks,

meaning must be gleaned from an acoustic assortment of incidental and transient signals. On the other hand, incomprehensible statements can be restated in conversational interaction. This, and the greater redundancy of oral language, both linguistically and in relation to nonverbal context, gives listening advantages over reading for efficiency of transmission.

Cazden (1972) provides an example of the difference between spoken language and text language. She describes a teacher reading a book about worms to a group of children who had just found a worm in the playground. One passage of the book read, "The worm's mouth is at the fat end. The worm's tail is at the thin end." Cazden points out that if the teacher had been talking instead of reading, the children would have heard something like, "His mouth is here," (as she points) "and his tail is here" (pointing again).

There are differences between reading and oral language that cannot be explained by differences in modality alone. Reading is a language-based skill, dependent upon primary linguistic awareness. Written text "initiates the synthetic process common to both reading and speech, enabling the reader to get the writer's message and so to recognize what has been written" (Mattingly, 1972, p. 145). Two important aspects of reading for the current discussion are that it must be deliberately acquired and that it hinges on linguistic awareness.

Mature Reading

Reading by mature adults has been described by Goodman (1973) as a psycholinguistic process, whereby the reader reconstructs, as closely as possible, a message which has been encoded by a writer as a graphic display. The receptive language processes of listening and reading are not just mirror images of talking and writing. Efficient language users take the most direct route and touch the fewest bases necessary to reach the goal of message comprehension. This is accomplished by cycles of *sampling, predicting, testing,* and *confirming. Sampling* involves a reliance on the redundancy of language and a knowledge of linguistic restraints on phonological, morphological, and syntactic usage. Structures are *predicted* using one's own internalized model of language and *tested* against the semantic context, which is built up from the situation and the ongoing discourse. They are then either *confirmed* or disconfirmed as further language is processed. In the Goodman (1969; 1973) model, three types of cuing systems are used to help make such predictions. These are semantic, syntactic, and morphographemic (sound-symbol associations). Efficient listening and reading depend as much on knowing which ambient details can be safely ignored as knowing which are salient to the comprehension of meaning.

The evidence is fairly strong that units of comprehension to which readers attend occur at several levels, including some that are much larger than single words, or even sentences, although complex or unfamiliar sentence structures have been shown to interfere with comprehension by normal readers (Ruddell, 1965; Bormuth et al., 1970). As discussed by Westby in Chapter 6, understanding text involves analyzing it into highly structured semantic units. A discourse is processed as a multilevel structure. This multilevel structure contains units as "small" as individual concepts and relations and as "large" as macrostructures consisting of networks of connected propositions (Frederiksen, 1977).

Roth and Perfetti (1980) expand on the concept of multilevel textual processing. They point out that a reader must make ongoing decisions about which information to keep "active," in order to comprehend a passage. Failure to keep pertinent information active may interfere with the comprehension of specific sentences because the reader may not notice important relations between nonadjacent concepts in the text. In addition, less attention is available for the constructive elaboration of character motivation, consequences or events, and evaluation or arguments if the reader must devote time and attention to thinking back

to information necessary to comprehend a sentence (Roth and Perfetti, 1980).

Approaches to Early Reading Instruction

Children manifest different strategies when learning to read or having difficulty reading. Most children appear to benefit from being given questions before they hear or read a story (Ausubel, 1960; Bransford and Johnson, 1972). They also tend to recall stories using integrated themes (Bransford and Franks, 1971). Language learning-disabled children, however, rely more heavily on the decoding of individual sentences than upon larger organizational principles to understand and recall stories (Allen, 1970; Klein-Konigsberg, 1977). Klein-Konigsberg also discusses this concept in greater detail in Chapter 12. On the other hand, children with weak decoding skills may need to rely more on discourse-related contextual cues to identify words with which they have difficulty. They may ignore morphographemic cues which might help them test their predictions (Roth and Perfetti, 1980). However, this strategy may not be useful if the context (e.g., pictures and/or introductory sentences to a story) is empty, misleading, or if the meaning is almost entirely lexically encoded. In fact, pictures have been found to hinder, rather than to facilitate, reading (Gibson as reported in Bettelheim and Zelan, 1981).

Mature readers use multilevel cuing systems and units of processing to understand what they read, with *comprehension* the primary goal. The focus of beginning readers is not always the same. Maxwell and Wallach (Chapter 2) describe some of these differences in their discussion of symptoms of reading failure. In attempts to define "reading," comprehension is generally associated with accomplished reading, but *identification* behavior (often termed "decoding skill") is more often associated with reading acquisition (Wiener and Cromer, 1967). In previous chapters we have seen, however, that the relationship between decoding and comprehension is more complex than "either-or" notions might suggest.

The selection of textual materials for

early reading instruction varies according to the approach considered to best represent the various reading processes. For example, the initial teaching units might be letters of the alphabet. During the 1940's and 1950's, a movement arose to analyze reading, and prereading, behavior into even smaller components (Reid, 1980). At that time, "readiness testing" of prerequisite developmental visual and auditory skills was initiated (Havinghurst, 1953). Now it appears that readiness is actually a product of the interaction of the learner and the environment (especially being read to (Chomsky, 1972)), rather than some set of invariant, maturational, prerequisite skills (Durkin, 1968).

The view that component perceptual skills must be identified and remediated prior to initiating practice in such higher level skills as reading for meaning influenced the early literature on learning disabilities and special education (Zigmond et al., 1980). As seen throughout this text, little empirical validity has been shown either for the process training approach (Ysseldyke and Salvia, 1974) or the corresponding perceptual deficit theory approaches to explain learning problems (Vellutino, 1977; see also Chapter 1). However, Bateman (1979) reports that programs based on the notion of training prerequisite skills continue to dominate special education practices. Maxwell and Wallach also address the issue in Chapter 2 in the discussion of visual and verbal strategies in reading.

The child who is just learning to read may need to be instructed in a number of the components of reading (Guthrie, 1978). Goodman (1969) suggests a tool for determining which components may be giving a particular child difficulty. He suggests an analysis of reading "miscues" or errors. For example, a child who reads, "the train was," for "the toy was," is making a word level substitution. One who reads, "Now Skippy was gone," for "Now Skippy was gone?" is making a sentence level error (Goodman, 1969, p. 23). Because all of the information

must be available for the sampling and predicting strategy to operate in the beginning reader, Goodman (1973) argues that the reading process should not be fragmented in its presentation to children.

Most approaches to early reading instruction do emphasize one type of skill or another, depending on their focus. However, one of the greatest controversies in reading instruction has centered around whether the primary units of early instruction should be phonemes (as in phonics approaches, or phonetic approaches using modified alphabets), whole words (as in the sight-word, controlled vocabulary approaches of basal reading series), or larger comprehension units (as in experience story approaches).

Programs that *start* children on individual phonemes have been criticized by many in light of new information. In Chapter 7, Van Kleeck reminded us that this level of analysis is difficult. The examples presented in the teacher dialogues in the first section of this chapter also demonstrate some of the difficulties related to sound-letter activities. As Blachman points out in Chapter 13, individuals learn to segment words into phonemes *after* they acquire the metalinguistic skill to reflect on the relatively invariant clusters of distinctive features that make up sound categories we call phonemes. Some have suggested teaching syllables as the basic unit of reading (Savin, 1972; Liberman et al., 1977), but further investigation is warranted in this area. The progressions suggested by Blachman offer some interesting and new directions regarding the decoding aspects of reading.

Smith (1973, 1975) argues for the use of larger comprehension units as the focus of reading at any level. He points out that we must get the child beyond sound, syllable, or whole word units. Smith uses a whole task, or constructivist, view of information processing to justify his approach to early reading instruction. This approach relies very little on phonics exercises and other decoding practice, but encourages the pursuit of *meaning* as the major focus of learning to read.

Bettelheim and Zelan (1981) question whether traditional textual materials written for children can support the motivation necessary to encourage children to read. Although reading instruction in the first three grades is crucial, they point out that reading materials provided in these grades:

"convey no sense that there are rewards in store. And since poor readers continue to be subjected to these primers well past the third grade, their reading can only get worse as their interests and experience diverge further from the content of the books" (p. 26).

It is largely the attempts to "control" the difficulty of the material presented in early readers that leads to books with "endlessly repeated words passed off as stories" (Bettelheim and Zelan, 1981, p. 27). Wallach and Liebergott also point out that some reading materials require children to make inferential jumps across sentences (Chapter 1).

Linguistic readers comprise one subgroup of materials that particularly illustrate the element of control in design. Children using such series are introduced to monosyllabic word families in an attempt to get them to induce phoneme-grapheme correspondences from such minimal pairs as "cat" and "bat" (Fries, 1963). The problem with these readers is that they produce such semantically sterile sequences as:

> The fat cat played with a bat.
> Dan ran to Fran and Stan.

By eliminating an important set of contextual cues in the unrelatedness of one sentence to another, or to the world, children are presented with one of the most complex decoding tasks possible from the standpoint of paucity of salient cues.

Is There Support for a "Better Way"?

What research is there supporting the use of one instructional method or another? One of the most extensive studies of available methods was conducted by Chall (1967). It was her conclusion that:

"a code emphasis method—i.e., one that views beginning reading as essentially different from mature reading and emphasizes learning of the printed code for the spoken language—produces better results, at least up to a point where sufficient evidence seems to be available, the end of the third grade" (p. 307).

Chall (1967) further mentions that she does not recommend ignoring reading for meaning and that additional work on decoding in the upper grades is probably a waste of time. The methods described by Blachman in Chapter 13 also warrant further study.

In attempting to integrate a variety of conflicting viewpoints, it appears that children need a set of textual materials that will provide them with as many decoding cues as possible (distinctive graphic, phonomorphological, semantic, syntactic, and discourse level features). For example, books using some key words that exceed the usual consonant-vowel-consonant pattern may make early reading easier. "Dinosaur" is more easily discriminated from "the," "and," and "cat," than "dog" is. Emotionally toned topics lead to greater interest in figuring out what is written than empty ones (Ashton-Warner, 1963). Linguistic patterns that are comprehensible encourage children to keep trying. However, in addition to providing multi-level distinctive cues, individual cues must remain detectable so that children are not overloaded. The question of overload is even more important for language learning-disabled children since they are often less able to handle multiple level processing simultaneously.

It is possible to design an approach that can combine alternate focus on the form and function of language for language learning-disabled children. The goal is to facilitate the learning of bidirectional processing skills (both bottom-up decoding to reach meaning and top-down use of meaning to aid decoding). An "eclectic" model of language intervention (Nelson, 1981) using these principles has been shown to be successful with a number of language learning-disabled children in Berrien County, Michigan. The model employs a variety of structured, or form-oriented, techniques with more content, or function-oriented, techniques. Stuctured (or decoding activities) such as those described by Monsees (1972), are presented first separately and then in combination with a variety of more natural, meaning- and function-oriented techniques (such as those described by Smith (1975), Lee and Allen (1963), and Ashton-Warner (1963)). Their purpose is to stretch the developing edge of language competence for language learning-disabled children. Structured and natural techniques are both provided in each day's lessons, and neither approach is considered primary to the other. Rather, the two are viewed as complimentary.

OTHER PERFORMANCE VARIABLES AND IMPLICATIONS

Teachers control the learning environments of their classrooms largely by the things they say and do. Some evidence has been presented here to suggest that teachers at different grade levels control not only the difficulty of the information content they present to students (Berlin et al., 1980), but also vary its form and function (Cuda and Nelson, 1976). Although the mechanism for this process is still unclear, it is likely that teachers use a combination of prior knowledge about the expected linguistic and cognitive abilities of their students along with immediate verbal and nonverbal feedback. In this way they adjust their speaking styles to fit the presumed capabilities of the children they teach. Classroom activities become increasingly reliant on the teacher lecturing to the class as a whole and on individual reading of textual material as grade level increases. The student who falls outside the limits of the teacher's internalized group norm for the language facility of his or her class, or the more formalized vocabulary and word count norms of textbook producers, and who has particular difficulty coping with fully lexicalized meanings or with teacher revisions and dysfluencies will have in-

creasingly greater difficulty staying with the group.

Some of the problems experienced by language learning-disabled children can be directly tied to deficits of language *competence*, i.e., those associated with an incomplete internalized knowledge of the rules of language and communication. For example, a child who does not "know" the vocabulary or sentence structure associated with a particular decoding activity will be unable to perform that task no matter how optimal the conditions. The competencies involved in understanding school tasks and the language used as a part of them also go beyond language processing. They include cognitive strategies related to the internal manipulation of concepts with increasingly less support from nonlinguistic context (Vygotsky, 1962; Gerber, 1981).

Beyond the competence problems language learning-disabled children have in processing the information of school activities, there is also the possibility that *performance* problems, related to specific contextual factors, may exert an added influence. White (1980, p. 43) raises this issue in his description of a child as a "bumpy, blippy, excitable, fatiguable, distractible, active, friendly, mulish, semi-cooperative bundle of biology."

A number of external situational factors in the language of teachers and textbooks interact with internal psychophysiological, cognitive, and social factors inherent in both children and teachers. Some factors have been identified that increase the load and the "noisiness" (degree of nonsensical stimuli) in a language learning-disabled child's working environment. Other features of the external physical environment, such as signal-to-noise ratios and acoustic reverberation in high-ceilinged, hard-floored classrooms, are not discussed here. However, they should be considered in planning optimal learning contexts for language learning-disabled children.

It has been suggested that the best model for a learning environment for language learning-disabled children is one that focuses on various processing levels, followed by deliberate attempts to integrate new forms to serve new communicative and cognitive functions. It is hoped that the information presented here will be of use to teachers and clinicians as they attempt to match the linguistic demands of school tasks more closely to students' capabilities. The key to this process is a continual refocusing of teacher attention to the capabilities of *individual* students. Successful teachers accomplish this, even in group contexts, by addressing leveled tasks and questions differentially to individual students so skillfully that all feel appropriately successful and challenged without anyone feeling singled out. These teachers seem to be guided by an implicit understanding of the monumental tasks facing children in school. They juggle the many variables affecting communicative interactions to achieve a balanced linguistic and nonlinguistic context in which children learn.

References

Allen DI: Some effects of advance organizers and level of question on the learning and retention of written social studies material. *J Educ Psychol* 61:333–339, 1970.

Ashton-Warner S: *Teacher*. New York, Bantam Books, 1963.

Ausubel DP: The use of advance organizers in the learning and retention of meaningful verbal material. *J Educ Psychol* 51:267–272, 1960.

Bateman B: Teaching reading to learning disabled children. In Resnick LB, Weaver PA: *Theory and Practice of Early Reading*. Hillsdale, NJ, Lawrence Erlbaum Associates, 1979, 4 vol.

Bates E: *Language and Context: The Acquisition of Pragmatics*. New York, Academic Press, 1976.

Bellack AA, Kliebard HM, Hyman RT, et al: *The Language of the Classroom*. New York, Columbia University Teacher's College Press, 1966.

Berlin LJ, Blank M, Rose SA: The language of instruction: the hidden complexities. *Top Language Disord* 1:47–58, 1980.

Bernstein BB: A critique of the concept of compensatory education. In Cazden CB, John VP, Hymes D: *Functions of Language in the Classroom*. New York, Columbia University Teachers College Press, 1972.

Bettelheim B, Zelan K: Why children don't like to read. *The Atlantic Monthly*, 25–31, 1981.

Blank M: *Teaching Learning in the Preschool: A Dialogue Approach*. Columbus, OH, Charles Merrill, 1973.

Bloom L: Language development, language disorders and learning disabilities: LD3. *Bull Orton Soc* 30:115–133, 1980.

Bormuth JR, Manning J, Carr J. et al: Children's comprehension of between- and within-sentence syntactic structures. *J Educ Psychol* 61:349–357, 1970.

Botel M, Dawkins J, Granowsky A: A syntactic complexity formula. *Assessment Problems in Reading*. Newark, NJ, International Reading Association, 1973.

Bransford JD, Franks JJ: The abstraction of linguistic ideas. *Cognitive Psychol* 2:331–350, 1971.

Bransford JD, Johnson MK: Contextual prerequisites for understanding: some investigations of comprehension and recall. *J Verbal Learn Verbal Behav* 11:717–726, 1972.

Broen P: *The Verbal Environment of the Language Learning Child*, Monograph 17. Washington DC, American Speech and Hearing Association, 1972.

Brophy JE, Good TL: Teacher's communication of differential expectations for children's classroom performance. *J Educ Psychol* 61:365–374, 1970.

Bruner JS: The ontogenesis of speech acts. *J Child Language* 2:1–19, 1975.

Carlson J, Gruenewald LJ, Nyberg B: Everyday math is a story problem: the language of the curriculum. *Top Language Disord* 1:59–70, 1980.

Cazden CB: *Child Language and Education*. New York, Holt, Rinehart and Winston, 1972.

Chall JS: *Learning to Read: The Great Debate*. New York, McGraw-Hill, 1967.

Chomsky C: Stages in language development and reading exposure. *Harvard Educ Rev* 42:1–33, 1972.

Chomsky N. *Aspects of a Theory of Syntax*. Cambridge, MA, MIT Press, 1965.

Clark HH, Haviland SE: Comprehension and the given—new contract. In Freedle RO: *Discourse Production and Comprehension*, vol 1 in the series *Discourse Processes: Advances in Research and Theory*. Norwood, NJ, Ablex Publishing Corporation, 1977.

Cook-Gumperz J: Situated instructions: language socialization of school age children. In Ervin-Tripp S, Mitchell-Kernan C: *Child Discourse*. New York, Academic Press, 1977.

Cuda RA: Analysis of speaking rate, syntactic complexity and speaking style of public school teachers. Unpublished masters thesis, Wichita State University, 1976.

Cuda RA, Nelson NW: Analysis of teacher speaking rate, syntactic complexity, and hesitation phenomena as a function of grade level. Presented at the Annual Meeting of the American Speech-Language-Hearing Association, Houston, 1976.

Dore J: Children's illocutionary acts. In Freedle RO: *Discourse Production and Comprehension*, vol 1 in the series *Discourse Processes: Advances in Research and Theory*. Norwood, NJ, Ablex Publishing Corporation, 1977.

Dore J: Conversation and preschool language development. In Fletcher P, Garman M: *Language Acquisition*. Cambridge, Cambridge University Press, 1979.

Dunkin MJ, Biddle BJ: *The Study of Teaching*. New York, Holt, Rinehart and Winston, 1974.

Durkin D: When should children begin to read? In *Innovation and Change in Reading Instruction: Sixty-seventh Yearbook of the National Society for the Study of Education*. Chicago, University of Chicago Press, 1968.

Elsasser N, John-Steiner VP: An interactionist approach to advancing literacy. *Harvard Educ Rev* 47:355–369, 1977.

Frederiksen CH: Semantic processing units in understanding text. In Freedle RO: *Discourse Production and Comprehension*, vol 1 in the series *Discourse Processes: Advances in Research and Theory*. Norwood, NJ, Ablex Publishing Corporation, 1977.

Fries CC: *Linguistics and Reading*. New York, Holt, Rinehart and Winston, 1963.

Gerber A: Problems in the processing and use of language in education. In Gerber A, Bryer DN: *Language and Learning Disabilities*. Baltimore, University Park Press, 1981.

Goodman KS: Analysis of oral reading miscues: applied psycholinguistics. *Read Res Q* 5:9–30, 1969.

Goodman KS: Psycholinguistic universals in the reading process. In Smith F: *Psycholinguistics and Reading*. New York, Holt, Rinehart and Winston, 1973.

Griffin K, Hannah L: A study of the results of an extremely short instructional unit in listening. *J Commun* 10:135–139, 1960.

Gump P: Education as an environmental enterprise. In Weinberg R, Wood F: *Observations of Pupils and Teachers in Mainstream and Special Education*. Reston, VA, Council for Exceptional Children, 1975.

Guthrie JT: Principles of instruction: a critique of Johnson's "Remedial approaches to dyslexia." In Benton AL, Pearl D: *Dyslexia: An Appraisal of Current Knowledge*. New York, Oxford University Press, 1978, pp 425–433.

Halliday MAK: Notes on transitivity and theme in English. II. *J Linguistics* 3:199–244, 1967.

Havinghurst R: *Human Development and Education*. New York, Longmans, Green, 1953.

Klein-Konigsberg E: Semantic integration in normal and learning disabled children. Unpublished doctoral dissertation, City University of New York, 1977.

Kolers PA: Three stages of reading. In Levin H, Williams JP: *Basic Studies in Reading*. New York, Basic Books, 1970, pp 90–118.

Lee DM, Allen RV: *Learning to Read through Experience*, ed 2. Englewood Cliffs, NJ, Prentice-Hall, 1963

Leonard LB: The speech of language-disabled children. *Bull Orton Soc* 30:141–152, 1980.

Liberman I, Shankweiler D, Camp L, et al: Steps toward literacy: a report on reading prepared for the working group on learning failure and unused learning potential for the President's Commission on Mental Health. Washington DC, 1977.

Maclay H, Osgood C: Hesitation phenomena in spontaneous English speech. *Word* 15:19–44, 1959.

Masek RM: The effects of teacher applied social reinforcement on arithmetic performance and task-orientation. Unpublished doctoral dissertation, Utah State University, 1970.

Mattingly IG: Reading, the linguistic process and linguistic awareness. In Kavanagh JF, Mattingly IG: *Language by Ear and by Eye*. Cambridge, MA, MIT Press, 1972.

McCroskey RL, Thompson-Nelson NW: A preliminary investigation of comprehension of rate-controlled speech by children with specific learning disabilities. *J Learn Disabil* 6:621–627, 1973a.

McCroskey RL, Thomspon-Nelson NW: Comprehension of rate-controlled speech of varying linguistic complexity by children with reading disorders. Presented at the Annual Meeting of the American Speech and Hearing Association, Detroit, 1973b.

McDermott RP: Social relations as contexts for learning in school. *Harvard Educ Rev* 47:198–213, 1977.

Miller JW, Hintzman CA: Syntactic complexity of Newberry Award winning books. *Reading Teacher*, 750–756, 1975.

Mishler EG: Implications of teacher strategies for language and cognition: observations in first-grade classrooms. In Cazden CB, John VP, Hymes D: *Functions of Language in the Classroom*. New York, Columbia University Teachers College Press, 1972, pp 267–298.

Mishler EG: Studies in dialogue and discourse. II. Types of discourse initiated by and sustained through questionning. *J Psycholinguistic Res* 4:99–121, 1975.

Moerk EL: Verbal interactions between children and their mothers during the preschool years. *Dev Psychol* 11:788–794, 1975.

Monsees EK: *Structured Language for Children with Special Language Learning Problems*. Washington DC, Alexander Graham Bell Association, 1972.

Moore CA: Verbal teaching patterns under simulated teaching conditions. In Freedle RO: *Discourse Production and Comprehension*, vol 1 in the series *Discourse Processes: Advances in Research and Theory*. Norwood, NJ, Ablex Publishing Corporation, 1977, pp 271–306.

Nelson NW: Comprehension of spoken language by normal children as a function of speaking rate, sentence difficulty, and listener age and sex. *Child Dev* 47:299–303, 1976.

Nelson NW: An eclectic model of language intervention for disorders of listening, speaking, reading and writing. *Top Language Disord* 1:1–2, 1981.

O'Connor L, Eldredge P: Language disorders in the adolescent population: A practical approach. Presented at the annual meeting of the American Speech-Language-Hearing Association, Detroit, 1980.

Pellegrini AD: Applying a self-regulating private speech model to classroom settings. *Language Speech Hear Serv Schools* 13:129–133, 1982.

Phillips J: Syntax and vocabulary of mothers' speech to young children: Age and sex comparisons. *Child Dev* 44:182–185, 1973.

Pollak S, Gruenewald L: *Assessment of Language Interaction in Academic Tasks: A Process*. Madison, WI, Madison Public Schools, 1976.

Reid DK: Child reading: readiness or evolution? *Top Language Disord* 1:61–72, 1980.

Rochester SR, Martin JR: The art of referring: the speakers use of noun phrases to instruct the listener. In Freedle RO: *Discourse Production and Comprehension*, vol 1 in the series *Discourse Processes: Advances in Research and Theory*. Norwood, NJ, Ablex Publishing Corporation, 1977.

Rosenshine B: Objectively measured behavioral predictors of effectiveness in explaining. In Westbury DI, Bellack AA: *Research into Classroom Practices*. New York, Teachers College Press, 1971, pp 51–98.

Rosenthal R, Jacobson L: *Pygmalion in the Classroom: Teacher Expectation and Pupils' Intellectual Devel-*

opment. New York, Holt, Rinehart and Winston, 1968.

Roth SF, Perfetti CA: A framework for reading, language comprehension, and language disability. *Top Language Disord* 1:15–28, 1980.

Ruddell RB: The effect of oral and written patterns of language structure on reading comprehension. *Read Teacher* 18:270–275, 1965.

Savin HB: What the child knows about speech when he starts to learn to read. In Kavanagh JF, Mattingly IG: *Language by Ear and by Eye.* Cambridge, MA, MIT Press, 1972, pp 319–326.

Silliman E, Leslie S: Instructional language: a comparison of a regular and special education classroom. Presented at the annual meeting of the American Speech-Language Hearing Association, Detroit, 1980.

Slobin DI: *Psycholinguistics.* Danville, IL, Scott, Foresman, 1971.

Smith F: *Psycholinguistics and Reading.* New York, Holt, Rinehart and Winston, 1973.

Smith F: *Comprehension and Learning.* New York, Holt, Rinehart and Winston, 1975.

Smith F: *Reading without Nonsense.* New York, Teachers College Press, 1979.

Snow C: Mothers' speech to children learning language. *Child Dev* 43:549–565, 1972.

Snow C: The development of conversation between mothers and babies. *J Child Language* 4:1–22, 1977.

Snow C, Ferguson C: *Talking to Children: Language Input and Acquisition.* New York, Cambridge University Press, 1977.

Thompson JJ: *Instructional Communication.* New York, Van Nostrand Reinhold, 1969.

Vellutino FR: Alternative conceptualizations of dyslexia: evidence in support of a verbal-deficit hypothesis. *Harvard Educ Rev* 47:334–354, 1977.

Vygotsky LS: *Language and Thought.* Cambridge, MA, MIT Press, 1962. (Originally published in 1934.)

White SH: Cognitive competence and performance in everyday environments. *Bull Orton Soc* 3:29–45, 1980.

Wiener M, Cromer W: Reading and reading difficulty: a conceptual analysis. *Harvard Educ Rev* 37:618–643, 1967.

Wilkinson LC, Hiebert E, Rembold K: Parents' and peers' communication to toddlers. *J Speech Hear Res* 24:383–388, 1981.

Ysseldyke JE, Salvia J: Diagnostic-prescriptive teaching: two models. *Excep Child* 41:181–195, 1974.

Zigmond N, Vallecorsa A, Leinhardt G: Reading instruction for students with learning disabilities. *Top Language Disord* 1:89–98, 1980.

Assessment and Intervention Strategies for Language Learning-disabled Students: Linguistic and Communicative Competence and Language Contexts

CHAPTER NINE

Assessment and Intervention: Does "Meta" Matter?

ANNE VAN KLEECK, Ph.D.

A number of contributors have discussed the importance of metalinguistic skills in language acquisition and in school success (see Chapters 7 and 8). As a logical sequel to some of the earlier chapters in the text, one might expect (or at least hope) that this chapter would contain some valid and reliable assessment techniques and ingenious intervention suggestions for facilitating the development of language awareness in language learning-disabled children. In recent years speech and language patholo-

gists and other specialists have tended to *assume* that normal developmental data have directly useful applications for children with language and academic problems. Maxwell and Wallach (Chapter 2) reminded us to exercise caution prior to jumping to applications. Indeed, it is crucial to first ask this one very basic question: "How, if at all, does the notion of language awareness change our current thinking about language disabilities in children?" Only a considered answer to this question can ultimately guide us in making, or choosing not to make, applications to the population of children with both early and later language learning problems. For this reason, we will begin this chapter by attempting to address this basic question before considering how the notion of language awareness might influence assessment and intervention issues.

In order to address whether or not the notion of language awareness results in a conceptual change in our thinking about language problems in children and adolescents, we need first to consider the alternative orientations that have been offered in the literature. Only then are we in a position to judge whether such thinking is altered by the notion of language awareness and, if so, *how* it is changed. Are previous orientations being replaced, recombined, expanded upon, complemented, or merely relabeled? Or is it a combination of these various possible types of changes?

EXISTING MODELS OF LANGUAGE DISORDERS IN CHILDREN: THE EFFECTS OF METALINGUISTICS

A normal procedure in scientific investigation involves attempts to impose organization on the particular phenomenon under inquiry, resulting in an organizational framework often called a model. Various implicit frameworks or models underlie the numerous orientations to language disorders in children offered in the literature. The major types of models can be roughly divided into the following three major categories: (1) medical models, (2) processing models, and (3) behavioral product models. In the following section, we will attempt to briefly discuss each genre of model by considering what it contributes to our thinking, what its major shortcomings are, and how it relates to a metalinguistic framework.

Medical Models

As this label suggests, these models arise from traditions set forth in the field of medicine. This involves a search for the etiology of a pathology, in the belief that an accurate diagnosis of the cause provides a direct avenue to the treatment or cure of the pathology. The influence of this medical model is seen in the pioneering work of Myklebust (1954), who discussed language disorders in children by differentiating among the global categories of peripheral deafness, aphasia, psychic deafness (emotional disturbance), and mental deficiency.

In our own definition of the medical model we will include all attempts at understanding language problems in children which attempt to classify children by identifying causal and maintaining factors of the pathology based on anatomical structure and neurological function. Within this paradigm, we can first designate areas of neurological or structural damage or deficit and consider the categories of language disorders that have been associated with each. Neurologically, damage may occur centrally or peripherally. Central damage may be diffuse and global (as in certain types of mental retardation), subtle and undefined (as is often suggested for both developmental aphasia and emotional disturbance), or predominantly affecting the neuromotor system (as in dysarthria and dyspraxia). Peripheral damage is associated with the categories of hearing impairment and visual impairment. Structural deficits that are sometimes considered as causal factors in language disorders include damage to the oral mechanism (cleft palate and/or lip) or the auditory mechanism (some conductive hearing losses) (Table 9.1).

Since social policy often lags considerably behind social science research and theory, the labels generated by a medical model orientation are often necessary for legal and educational placement purposes, as indicated by Wallach and Liebergott in Chapter 1. Furthermore, these labels are all use-

Table 9.1.
Medical Models of Language Disorders in Children

	Associated Categories
Type of neurological deficit	
Diffuse, global central nervous system damage	Mental retardation
Subtle, undefined central nervous system damage	Developmental dysphasia; emotional disturbance
Neuromotor damage	Dysarthria; dyspraxia
Peripheral nervous system damage	Hearing impairment; visual impairment
Location of structural deficit	
Oral mechanism damage	Cleft lip and/or palate
Auditory mechanism damage	Conductive hearing losses due to structural deficits

ful to the extent that they guide certain global types of intervention, such as surgery for clefts or amplification for hearing impairment. However, knowing which category a language-disordered child fits into does not delineate specific language treatment goals, and here the medical model philosophy as an approach to language and learning disabilities breaks down (see Chapters 1 and 2). It is simply not enough to know *only* the category (and indeed, children rarely fit neatly into just one category). One must also look at the actual language and communication behaviors of the child in order to determine language goals (see Bloom and Lahey, 1978, pp. 503–527 for discussion). This is the orientation of the behavioral models we will discuss later.

The medical models focus on observing both language and nonlanguage behaviors in order to determine patterns of behavior indicative of a particular syndrome, which in turn is considered *to identify the cause* of the disorder. The metalinguistic framework we are proposing looks at one specific type of language behavior, i.e., the ability to reflect upon and manipulate language, in order *to describe* a particular child's skill level. As such, there is really no overlap between the end goals of the medical models and a metalinguistic framework (although to the extent that both observe language behavior there is overlap in the procedures used to achieve these goals). Both are valid; they are simply different. Although admittedly limited, the medical model has validity to the extent that it promotes a search for medical causes which in turn may guide very important medical (e.g., surgical repair of cleft) or prosthetic (e.g., fitting of hearing aid) intervention. The metalinguistic framework has validity in that it provides a structure for observing and subsequently describing a category of language behaviors that as a group have previously been either treated unsystematically or have been largely ignored. If one agrees (and not all do) that determining causality and describing language behavior

are both valid goals of the assessment process, these orientations *complement* each other as conceptual frameworks for considering language disorders in children.

Processing Models

The overall objective of processing models is to identify mental processes that may be causing or contributing to language disorders in children. Two general categories within this broader framework are (1) models relating to auditory processing deficits and (2) models relating to general cognitive processing deficits (Table 9.2). Each appears to have different historical roots, and a different relationship to the metalinguistic framework being presented here.

AUDITORY/LINGUISTIC PROCESSING MODELS

In many ways, the auditory/linguistic processing deficit models have arisen from an effort to once again explain causality, primarily within just one of the categories offered by the medical model—developmental dysphasia. As such, they represent a mere *extension* of the medical model just discussed. Dysphasia is traditionally defined by what it is not. That is, by the process of elimination, other potential categories, such as hearing impairment, mental retardation, or emotional disturbance, are ruled out. The specific "language disabilities" (dysphasia) and "learning disabil-

Table 9.2.
Processing Models of Language Disorders in Children

General cognitive processing deficits
  Deficits in information gathering and processing
  Deficits in general symbolic functioning
  Deficits in hierarchical structuring
  Deficits in processing of semantic units, classes, relations, transformations, and implications

Specific auditory/linguistic processing deficits
  Deficits in auditory memory
  Deficits in auditory sequencing
  Deficits in auditory discrimination

ities" connection is reiterated (see Section I). Although some subtle neurological damage is often cited as a potential cause underlying developmental dysphasia, the exact nature of such damage remains elusive since, if such damage does exist, it is beyond the identification capacity of current neurological evaluation techniques. In Chapter 3, Maxwell identifies some of the advances that have been made in the study of developmental neurology. As it stands, however, current efforts have turned from attempting to specify anatomical or physiological deficits characteristic of medical model interpretations of language learning disabilities.

The notion of a central auditory perceptual dysfunction as the basis of developmental dysphasia has a long history in the study of language pathology in children. In 1929, for example, Worster-Drought and Allen discussed auditory imperception of a child with congenital word deafness. Since then, the same general ideas have been expressed by terms such as auding (Hardy, 1965), auditory perceptual dysfunction (Myklebust, 1971), central auditory dysfunction (Keith, 1977), defects of auditory perception (Tallal & Piercy, 1978), etc.

In general, as pointed out in Chapter 1, these models suggest that language disorders result from deficits specific to auditory/linguistic processing, including sequencing, memory, and discrimination processes. Deficiencies in these skills are considered by most proponents of auditory/linguistic processing models to be the cause of the language disorder. As Wallach and Liebergott point out in Chapter 1, it was assumed that the skills should be worked on directly in order to facilitate general language development. We differ from the auditory/linguistic processing models in that we again view the skills they are calling processing skills as one particular use of language.

COGNITIVE PROCESSING MODELS

A more recent orientation to the search for mental processes in language-disordered children has been influenced by a number of fields of study such as information-processing theory, cognitive psychology, and linguistics. Several different models fall under the rubric of general cognitive processing deficits (Table 9.2). Snyder and McLean (1977) suggest that basic information-processing skills, such as the ability to listen selectively and to establish joint reference, may be amiss. Numerous others, influenced generally by cognitive psychology and more specifically by the Piagetian notion of symbolic function, have suggested that the ability to symbolize in general may be impaired in these children. Thus, language, and also other manifestations of the ability to symbolize (symbolic play, deferred imitation, gesture, and drawing), will be impaired (Morehead & Ingram, 1973; de Ajuriaguerra et al., 1976; Inhelder, 1976; Kamhi, 1981).

Cromer's (1978) notion of a hierarchical structuring deficit suggests that language imposes problems on the language-disordered child because of its hierarchical organization. His argument stems primarily from a linguistic orientation. Cromer argues that language structure does not consist of mere associative links between adjacent elements but rather that individual parts derive their meaning from the whole structure. This becomes most obvious when there are interruptions of the surface features by, for example, a relative clause. The written language samples of the children Cromer studied in fact did not contain relative clause structures. He believed this to be evidence that these children were not able to hierarchically organize language structure. This notion is supported in Wallach's (1977) study involving relative clause processing in older children with language learning disabilities (see Chapters 2 and 5). A logical extension of Cromer's position vis-à-vis language is that children with language problems will demonstrate problems in any learning involving the ability to hierarchically organize stimuli. Miller will explore this hypothesis in the following chapter. Here again, the deficit is not restricted to language learning alone, but extends to more general cognitive processing used in the development of language and also used outside of the purely linguistic domain.

Wiig and Semel (1976) present yet another orientation to the notion of cognitive processing. Under this general category they place "the cognitive processing of auditory-symbolic (phoneme sequences) and semantic units (words and concepts), semantic classes (verbal associations), semantic relations (verbal analogies and linguistic concepts), semantic systems (verbal problems), semantic transformations (redefinition of concepts), and semantic implications (cause-effect, predictions, etc.)" (p. 24). Rather than discussing actual processing (as the other cognitive models have), it appears that the components of cognitive processing offered by Wiig and Semel merely describe various uses of linguistic behavior and as such have no particular explanatory value regarding how disruption of cognitive processing would account for language disorders in children. We know only that such uses of language are frequently impaired in this population, but we are offered no insights as to why.

The approach offered by Wiig and Semel deserves further scrutiny, since it has been far more influential in the treatment of language learning disabilities in older children than have the other cognitive processing models discussed. Also, some of the cognitive processes they have delineated overlap with what we are calling metalinguistic skill (e.g., phoneme sequencing, performing verbal analogies and problems). We differ from Wiig and Semel in one very important respect, however. They consider these skills as *processes underlying the use of language,* and we consider that they are *one type of language use.* This distinction is crucial to the eventual applications one might make.

In considering these skills as cognitive processes underlying language, one might believe that remedial work on the processes would affect the social-interactive use of language in context. Indeed, Wiig and Semel appear to make such an implicit as-sumption. Such an assumption is not made when metalinguistic skills are considered as one possible use of language. In this case, it would be expected that work on metalinguistic skills would enhance only the metalinguistic uses of language. There is no reason to believe that other language uses would be affected.

While metalinguistic skills can be considered as one possible use of language, it was earlier (see the chapter on normal metalinguistic development) postulated that certain cognitive processes may *underlie* such skills. It was suggested that the ability to decenter one's focus of attention might be of central importance in learning to treat language as an object in its own right. In this sense, then, this view of treatment of language awareness aligns well with the other cognitive processing models offered in that a potential explanation of metalinguistic deficits (i.e., the inability to decenter) is offered.

The cognitive models (that actually discuss processing) have contributed to our understanding of the connection between early language disorders and learning disabilities. They offer possible alternative explanations for the occurrence of language delays. These explanations in turn point out possible sources of heterogeneity within the language-disordered population. For example, some children may indeed have problems with symbolizing, whereas others may have no difficulty with symbols but with hierarchically organizing information. As such, these models alert us to possible concomitant deficits in children with problems (see Chapter 2). Indeed, it may be helpful to some of these children to work on other areas of symbolic function and for others to also work on hierarchic organization skills in addition to focusing directly on language and communication skills. The chapters which follow in this section will provide direction for such analyses.

Behavioral Product Models

The behavioral product models differ from other models in that they are concerned with describing actual communicative behavior and not with determining causality. They tell us what the child can do communicatively and, by comparing this description with our knowledge of normal developmental sequences, they provide information regarding what the child needs to learn next. It is only from this orientation that we can determine the actual language goals for intervention.

Behavioral product models have as their goal the description of actual observable language and communication behaviors. Within this broad category, two types of overlapping models are evidenced. One group are child centered in that they focus on describing the child's actual behavior. Another, newer group are more interaction oriented in that they attempt to consider the nature of the broader patterns of communication in the environment in which the child participates, i.e., they describe the actual behavior of both the child and significant others in the child's world (e.g., parent-child and teacher-child interactions). Silliman expands on these two frameworks in Chapter 14. She also discusses how conceptual (Piagetian) models and social-interactional models complement each other.

Regarding primarily child-centered models, the form, content, and use model of Bloom and Lahey (1978) provides an overriding framework into which more explicit systems of description can be placed. Practitioners have numerous tools at their disposal which have been developed over the past decade. It is for them to decide and understand the appropriateness of such tools (see Chapter 1). Clinically, the systems of Lee (1974) and Tyack and Gottsleben (1974) are widely used to describe the syntactic development of the language-disabled child. More recently, systems for phonological analysis have become available (Hodson, 1980; Shriberg and Kwiatowski, 1980; Ingram, 1981). Regarding the semantic component of language, Brown (1973) described a number of semantic relations that have frequently been applied to the analysis of spontaneous language of lan-

guage-disordered children. More recently, Bloom and Lahey (1978) have presented a far more comprehensive coding scheme which integrates both semantics and syntax simultaneously. We recognize now that we must move toward understanding the language of older children and developing better coding schemes, etc., at higher age ranges (see Chapter 5). We also recognize that the study of components of language must move toward consideration of the context and purpose for which language is used. In the next chapter, Miller will look at the language components as they relate to problem-solving abilities.

The study of language use in context, or pragmatics, involves addressing the major sociolinguistic questions formulated by Fishman (1965) as who speaks what to whom, when, and to what end. Research attempts to describe children's use of language in context have been a more recent focus than form descriptions. Since there is generally a substantial time lag between such descriptive research and subsequent development of clinical tools incorporating this new information, clinically useful measures of children's use of language are just beginning to emerge, and none as yet are widely agreed upon. Chapman (1981) discusses the nature of and problems with some of the major coding schemes available for considering the communicative intent of children's utterances, i.e., the actual functions that their utterances serve. Miller (Chapter 10) and Silliman (Chapter 14) also follow up with some interesting suggestions.

Besides communicative intent (often referred to as the illocutionary force of the utterance), the use of language in context involves discourse participation. Several interrelated questions dealt with by Silliman in Chapter 14 include: (1) How are successive utterances related to each other? (2) Who controls the conversation, and how is this control negotiated? (3) How is the "floor" passed from one speaker to another? (4) How are new topics introduced and old topics reintroduced? (5) What role does presupposition play in comprehending conversation. Blank and Franklin (1980) offer one clinically useful system of coding the discourse (as well as semantic) aspect of language use that begins to address some of these questions. Silliman (Chapter 14) provides checklists for studying communication breakdowns and for coding language interactions in the classroom.

Interaction-oriented models take an even broader focus in describing actual communication behavior. Proponents of this type of model would advocate coding the semantic, syntactic, and pragmatic aspects of not only the child's language but also that of the child's primary caretaker. The Toledo-McKesson Scale (Quick), for instance, attempts to classify the intents of the adult speaker's utterances into categories that are considered as either facilitatory or non-facilitatory to the child's language development. It allows one to determine on an individual basis which adult behaviors tend to elicit more responses from the child. From an even broader perspective, the general nature of the child's environment (e.g., kinds of stimulation, emotional support) can be tapped by the Home Observation for Measurement of the Environment, a checklist system developed by Caldwell (1978).

In comparing the behavioral product models to the notion of language awareness, we see skills reflecting language awareness as one type of language use, i.e., a reflective use. As such, *metalinguistic skills represent an extension of a thorough approach to language use or pragmatics.* That is, language can be used as a social-interactive tool (the traditional focus of the pragmatic orientation), but it can also be used as an object of reflection. So, in effect, a somewhat artificial dichotomy might be made in the realm of language use between social-interactive uses and metalinguistic uses. We suggest that this dichotomy is somewhat artificial since it is our belief that language awareness can at times enhance the social use of language (see previous chapter on normal metalinguistic development).

In conclusion, we have attempted in this section to relate the notion of language awareness to the various existing orientations to language disorders in children. It is also hoped that the notion of language awareness can be seen as a viable concept for our understanding of older children with language learning disabilities. We have suggested that the medical models are *complemented*, since they focus on causes and the language awareness orientation focuses on actual behaviors. The relationship to processing models is a bit more complicated. The cognitive processing models are *complemented* since they also suggest causality. The models aimed more specifically at auditory/linguistic processing might at first appear to have been merely *relabeled* since many of the tasks used to tap these processing skills are ones we have suggested are metalinguistic in nature. However, from the processing orientation, these tasks are believed to tap skills underlying all language function. We are, in effect, *replacing* this conceptualization in suggesting that children's responses to such tasks do not reflect how they process language but rather reflect their ability to reflect on language. That is, we see this ability to reflect on and manipulate language as but one of the many possible uses of language. As such, we believe this notion *expands upon* the pragmatic component of the behavioral product models. Although we believe the framework to be valid, we need to ask yet another question before turning to applications. Do language-disordered children demonstrate deficits in metalinguistic skills? The next section briefly addresses this issue.

METALINGUISTIC SKILLS IN LANGUAGE LEARNING-DISABLED CHILDREN

We often hear anecdotal evidence, based primarily on clinical observations, that language-disordered children do indeed demonstrate deficient metalinguistic skills. Wiig and Semel's (1976) text on language disabilities in school-age children is replete with examples which draw from their vast wealth of clinical experience. They discuss numerous language deficits of language learning-disabled children which, although not labeled as such, are metalinguistic in nature. Of the kindergartner, they state, "He is not able to sit through listening to a story, learn the alphabet, word rhyming, finger plays or songs, or make one-to-one correspondences between sounds and letter" (p. 5). In the first grade, "they may have problems in same-different discriminations of sounds, in analyzing and synthesizing phoneme sequences, in segmenting words into smaller grammatical units, and in forming stable sound-symbol associations. These deficits may result in limited or slow academic achievement in spelling, reading, and math, among others" (p. 5). Elsewhere, Wiig and Semel note other deficits in skills we would consider metalinguistic, such as interpreting ambiguous sentences, idioms, puns (p. 27), multiple meaning words, metaphors (p. 31), synonyms (p. 33), verbal opposites, and verbal analogies (p. 35). Corroborating Wiig and Semel's clinical observation, Blue (1981) lists five types of utterances to avoid with language-disordered children because they may be difficult for these children to understand. Three of them that require metalinguistic skill are idioms, ambiguous statements, and words with multiple meanings.

Actual empirical studies support the clinical observations cited above that language-disordered children do indeed appear to have difficulty performing metalinguistic tasks. For example, language learning-disabled children lack awareness of the arbitrary, conventional nature of language. This has been demonstrated by their difficulty in comprehending dual meaning words (Myklebust, 1964; Johnson and Myklebust, 1967; Johnson, 1968). Their difficulty in consciously dealing with language as a system (containing parts that are systematically organized) is reflected in the frequent problems they encounter in learning to read. Numerous studies of reading-disabled children show, for example, that they fail to develop the ability to seg-

ment words into their component sounds (Mattingly, 1972; Calfee et al., 1973; Gleitman and Rozin, 1973; Liberman, 1973; Rosner, 1974; Helfgott, 1976; see also Chapter 13). Furthermore, the syntactic judgments which are based on knowledge of the systematic nature of language are also more difficult for language-disordered children than for linguistically normal children of their same age (Liles et al., 1977; Wallach and Brown, 1977).

ASSESSMENT ISSUES

As indicated in Chapter 1, some of the tests used in assessing language are actually testing metalinguistic skills, since they tap skills we have labeled as requiring language awareness. These tests usually tap the child's awareness that language is a system, i.e., they have children focus on and manipulate or judge the component parts of language. Two obvious examples include Wepman's (1973) *Auditory Discrimination Test* and the sound blending subtest of the Illinois Test of Psycholinguistic Ability (ITPA) developed by Kirk et al., (1968).

Wepman's test requires the child to consciously think about the sound properties of English. For example, the child is presented with the words *pat* and *bat* and is asked to judge if they are the same or different. Such judgments emerge later than the ability to simply recognize such distinctions in using language in a meaningful context. Indeed, studies have shown that 2- and 3-year-olds can make sound discriminations which distinguish words with different meanings (Garnica, 1973). On the other hand, Wepman's norms do not even begin until 5 years of age, and many normally developing kindergartners cannot correctly perform this judgment task.

The sound blending subtest of the ITPA requires that the child synthesize phonemes into a whole word. For example, the examiner individually presents the phonemes /b/, /æ/ and /t/, and the expected response from the child is to produce the word *bat*.

Often the initial diagnosis of a language disorder is made by a psychologist on the basis of a child's IQ test score. Typically, a language disorder is suspected when a child is 15 points higher on the performance part of the IQ test (tapping cognitive skills primarily through nonverbal means) than on the verbal part. On closer examination, it appears that verbal intelligence measures require that the child focus on and consciously manipulate language. For example, such tests often contain subtests in which children are asked to give definitions, rhyme, solve anagrams, crack secret codes, complete verbal analogies, etc. Once again, such an assessment tells far more about a child's metalinguistic skill than how he or she functions using language in social interactions.

In addition to the obviously metalinguistic nature of the tests just discussed, it seems quite feasible to make the claim that actually *all* language tests require some metalinguistic skill. Let us consider how we often assess children's language.

A typical evaluation involves administering numerous standardized language tests as well as obtaining and later analyzing a spontaneous language sample. The results obtained from these two data sources are frequently used to support each other, since we are often reluctant to consider alone either standardized tests or one sample of a child's language (usually collected in the unfamiliar clinic setting) as representative of the child's language skills. However, it could be argued that, rather than supporting each other, these two data sources tap *different* aspects of the child's knowledge of language and that they are, therefore, not truly comparable.

Standardized tests measure language skills by taking them out of an interaction context in which they are frequently used and having the child focus on language, often in ways that would be inappropriate in a social context (e.g., repeating *exactly* a sentence that is presented by the examiner). As such, these tests may tell us more about how the child deals with more decontextualized uses of language than how he or she is able to deal with language effectively as a social-interactive tool. In fact, in such a testing situation we are often requiring that the child ignore information about social uses of language and pay attention only to the language itself.

An analogous situation in cognitive testing is discussed by Donaldson (1978). She cites a study by Rose and Blank (1974), using a classic Piagetian conservation task as illustration. In this type of task, for example, the child is first shown two sticks of the same length placed in exact alignment and asked if they are the same length. Once the child agrees, the experimenter asks the child to watch as he or she moves the sticks out of alignment. Next the child is again asked the original question, "Are the sticks the same length?" The conserving child says that they are still the same length; the nonconserving child suggests that one is now longer.

Rose and Blank suggest that the younger children who fail this task may simply be more attuned to a pragmatic parameter of the situation. That is, the children might normally interpret an adult repetition of a question as a cue that they should alter their original judgment. Indeed, the 6-year-olds they tested did perform better on conservation tasks that were altered to require only one judgment after the rearrangement moved the sticks out of alignment. Miller will address additional problem-solving strategies for tasks of this nature in the next chapter.

Even more closely related to language testing are the two studies Donaldson (1978) discusses regarding language imitation. Bloom (1974) conducted a small study in which Peter, a 32-month-old, was asked to imitate utterances he himself had spontaneously produced the day before. His imitations were far shorter than his original productions. For example, "I'm trying to get this cow in there" became "Cow in here." Slobin and Welsh (1973) found a similar drastic reduction in the imitations of a young child whom they called Echo. In both cases, it appears that it was the decontextualized nature of the sentences presented for imitation that caused marked reductions in the length and complexity of the utterances the children produced. The child lacked the contextual support and the true intent to communicate in the imitation task. Language tests which rely on imitation, such as the expressive portion of the widely used *Northwestern Syntax Screening Test,* (Lee, 1969) are likewise assessing the child's ability to deal with decontextualized language.

By arguing that all language tests are metalinguistic in nature, we are in the somewhat unique position of saying that the assessment tools for testing language awareness, a relatively new construct, are already available. We need merely reconceptualize what we are really assessing with language tests currently in use, i.e., that such tests provide information regarding a child's ability to reflect upon the linguistic code.

While many testing devices are available, we believe that the range of metalinguistic function tapped by available procedures is far too narrow. Most deal with focusing on language as a system. There is a need to develop procedures that assess the child's awareness that language is an arbitrary, conventional code as well. This would include tasks designed to reflect the child's ability to differentiate between a word as a linguistic entity and the real-world object it refers to, and to interpret ambiguity and figurative language (puns, idioms, metaphor, simile, personification, proverbs).

An example of an informal procedure for testing word-referent differentiation that we have adopted from research studies with normal children is shown in Table 9.3. Sample items are listed and relevant empirical studies are available as well (e.g., Berthoud-Papandropoulou, 1978; Cummins, 1978a, 1978b). One test which taps an aspect of figurative language comprehension, the *Proverbs Test* (Gorham, 1954, 1956), might be useful for older language-disordered children. Gorham's norms begin

at the fifth-grade level. One might also do an item analysis of a child's responses on a verbal intelligence test in order to make a preliminary determination of deficits in certain metalinguistic skill areas.

With the recent focus on pragmatics in both child language research and clinical intervention, it has often been suggested that formal testing be abandoned altogether in favor of informal procedures that yield far more valid information regarding a child's use of language in context. We would counter this suggestion with our earlier claim that such a view of language is too narrow.

Indeed, language can be used as a social-interactive tool, but it can also be used reflectively. Our plea is to not throw out the baby with the bath water vis-à-vis formal language testing. As we continue to search for valid and clinically useful ways of analyzing children's social-interactive skills, for the school-age child, we should also assess the ability to focus consciously on the linguistic code. Our belief that this latter skill is indeed important to the child's academic success will be argued in the next section.

INTERVENTION ISSUES

The notion of language awareness can potentially influence the treatment of language disorders in two ways. First, it is relevant to the procedures used in intervention, i.e., *how* language development is facilitated. Even when one's goals are to enhance the child's communicative use of language in context, the procedures sometimes involve making the child consciously aware of the elements, rules, and properties of language. This would constitute a metalinguistic approach to facilitating the social-interactive use of language. Secondly, metalinguistic skill development might itself constitute a valid goal for language intervention. Primary linguistic goals consist of the actual form and content expected from a child in using language in interaction, whereas metalinguistic goals involve the child's reflection upon and manipulation of

Table 9.3.
Informal Procedures for Assessing Word-Referent Differentiation Skills

1. Interview questions:
   A. Tell me a long word. Why is it long? _____

   B. Tell me a short word. Why is it short? _____

   C. Tell me a difficult word. Why is it difficult? _____

   D. Tell me an easy word. Why is it easy? _____

   E. I'm going to say some sentences and I want you to tell me how many words are in each.
      (1) The cat climbed the tree. How many words? _____

      What are they? _____

      (2) Six children are playing. How many words? _____

      What are they?_____

2. Word identification: I'm going to say some things and I want you to tell me whether or not they
                         are words. If child says no, ask why.

   house _____   ptib_____
   bink _____   and_____
   a _____
   cat _____
   the _____
   my _____
   mup _____
   boy_____

3. Word length versus referent length: I'm going to say some words and I want you to tell me if they
                                        are long words or short words. Then I want you to tell me
                                        why.

   crocodile (long word; long referent)

   spaghetti (long word; long referent)

   train (short word; long referent)

   fly (short word; small referent)

   banana (long word; long referent)

   hose (short word; long referent)

   toe (short word; small referent)

these items in a conscious way. In this section, we will critically discuss applications of the notion of language awareness to both goals and procedures of language intervention.

Metalinguistic Procedures

Historically, numerous language-training programs have required that the child consciously focus on the linguistic code. We will illustrate by mentioning just a few of these. One program called NON-SLIP (Carrier, 1974) is designed to teach nonverbal children language via an alternate modality (chips with symbols on them). The child begins by labeling, next moves to rote sequencing of items, and then learns subject, verb, preposition, and object selection. For the nonverbal child, this metalinguistic approach requires that the child consciously focus on a language system he or she does not yet know.

Other metalinguistic techniques have been suggested for children who have already developed some syntax. The *Fokes Sentence Builder* (Fokes, 1976), for example, is similar in principle to the NON-SLIP but suggests that the child be combining at least two to three words before beginning the program. From a different (but also metalinguistic) perspective, Shulman and Liles (1979) proposed that language remediation should incorporate judgments of the acceptability of grammatical forms that are being taught. In this case the child is asked to judge the grammatical correctness of a sentence such as, "Tree the climb."

Several investigators (Gleitman et al., 1972; James and Miller, 1973; Bohannon, 1975; Hakes, 1980) have shown that accurate performance on such tasks is beyond the capacity of normally developing children before the age of 6. Certainly these children have been producing sentences with grammatical syntax for quite some time.

For those who espouse a developmental approach to language intervention (MacDonald and Blott, 1974; Miller and Yoder, 1974; Lee et al., 1975; Bloom and Lahey, 1978), the above techniques would likely not be advocated since they defy the normal developmental progression. They would prefer instead providing the child with many examples of a particular language behavior so that the child could *induce* the underlying rule or principle common to them all. Such an approach is often referred to as naturalistic, since it attempts to replicate how the normal child learns language, i.e., through exposure to language in a natural, meaningful context.

From the opposite perspective, others have argued that the language-disordered child has already failed to adequately learn the language, and, therefore, approaches *different* from those of the normal child are warranted. Hence, they might agree that a program such as NON-SLIP could be efficacious with a nonverbal child.

Actual language therapy rarely falls cleanly into either of these camps—the resourceful clinician probably uses both a naturalistic and metalinguistic approach at times. In fact, it would not be unusual for both strategies to occur within the context of one therapy activity. It would be fruitful, however, for the clinician to be consciously aware of which method he or she was using at a particular time and to have a sound rationale for that choice. In order to provide such a rationale, we consider it useful to consider three factors that we tentatively suggest might influence the relative success or failure of a metalinguistic approach to facilitating language learning. These include the cognitive and linguistic level of the child, as well as possible learning style preferences.

COGNITIVE LEVEL

Language learning-disabled children frequently have nonverbal cognitive skills commensurate with their chronological age. That is, if we tap into their knowledge of the world with measures that do not rely on language, such as the *Arthur Adaptation of the Leiter International Performance Scale* (Arthur, 1952), their cognitive skills are often within the normal range for their chronological age. This is certainly true of many aphasic and hearing-impaired children, and even some emotionally disturbed children. As such, since the language learning-disabled children are chronologically older than normal children at a similar language level, they may often be more cognitively advanced than these normal children. This cognitive advantage of the language learning-disabled child may in fact provide avenues for language learning that are not available to the normally developing child. Indeed, we are reminded of this phenomenon in Chapter 2.

In Chapter 7 on normal metalinguistic development, it was suggested that metalinguistic skills which require a simultaneous focus on the form and content of a message emerge in the concrete operational stage of cognitive development when the child acquires the ability to decenter. This is the level of metalinguistic skill required of many of the language intervention techniques we have described. As such, we might expect that a concrete operational child could potentially act on and even learn certain aspects of language in such a manner (if this were not the exclusive method used), whereas a preoperational child might fare better with a more purely naturalistic approach. Admittedly, such suggestions are at this point speculative, and research is clearly needed to support or discredit such a claim.

LINGUISTIC LEVEL

It seems obvious that before a child can reflect upon language, he or she needs to have at least *some* language to reflect upon. *How much* language is necessary, however, is currently little understood. In normal children, we do not expect that they will have the capacity to reflect upon aspects of language they have not yet acquired. So, for example, a young child who has not yet acquired the passive voice would not be expected to be able to reflect upon and judge the acceptability of passive constructions. With language-disordered children, however, the issue is rather different since, if we are using metalinguistic tasks as a means to teach a particular construction, we clearly *do not* expect the construction to already exist in the child's spontaneous language repertoire. The question of what linguistic level is necessary to support metalinguistic skill thus takes on a different character. We might be concerned, for example, about whether the child understands words such as *same* versus *different*, or *silly* versus *correct* that might be used in metalinguistic judgments.

LEARNING STYLE PREFERENCES

For some children, inductive learning may prove extremely difficult. These children might be candidates for an intervention program which emphasizes more metalinguistic techniques. Again, this sugges-

tion is speculative and awaits empirical verification (see Chapter 10).

In summary, we suggest that neither a completely developmental nor a completely metalinguistic approach to language facilitation is generally warranted. The clinician needs to consider the individual child's cognitive and linguistic skills and also determine a learning style preference through trial and error.

Metalinguistic Goals

There is at present certainly no unanimous agreement that metalinguistic skills themselves constitute valid goals for language intervention. On the contrary, in recent years researchers have implored us to conduct language training in a meaningful, relevant context. In light of this prevalent attitude, to propose that we teach children to focus on language devoid of such a context may seem preposterous. We would like to explore this pragmatic approach to intervention in order to explore both its validity and its limitations (see Chapter 15).

In the past decade, volumes of research have been published regarding the linguistic achievements of the preschool child. Work has also progressed on the cognitive developments and their relationships to linguistic developments. The child's accomplishments in the linguistic and cognitive domains share many similarities, and most likely growth in each influences growth in the other.

The infant learns that he or she can influence objects and persons in the environment and soon uses language to those same ends—to regulate activity and interaction. Children are only able to learn language because it is embedded in a meaningful social context. They first learn to make sense of situations and then use this kind of understanding to make sense of what is said to them (Donaldson, 1978, p. 56).

By the time they go to school, children's language and cognitive skills again show parallels. At this stage thinking is oriented to concrete, personally meaningful experiences. In the linguistic realm, "the child has made substantial progress towards mastering the resources of the spoken language and can draw upon those resources appropriately to achieve a wide range of interactional objectives in the familiar contexts of everyday activities" (Wells, 1981, p. 241). The meaning children derive from language is heavily influenced by their common-sense picture of everyday reality. Language is very much embedded in the flow of events which accompany it (Donaldson, 1978, p. 89; see also Chapters 5 and 8).

In applying the above general notions regarding early language development to working with younger language-disordered children, it seems most reasonable to present these children with language in a "real-world" context that is meaningful to their everyday lives. As the recent work in pragmatic development clearly points out, we need to create situations where there is a true need to communicate and wherein the child can learn and practice language in the context of true communication intent. We certainly agree on the efficacy of such an approach to language intervention *as far as the language needs of children functioning at the preschool level are concerned.* We would argue, however, that the boundaries of the "real world," as they are generally conceived of from the pragmatic perspective, are simply too narrow. We are all too painfully aware that children's language problems do not disappear when they enter school. Our definition of the real world, then, must expand to include the very real experiences the child has with language in the course of his or her formal education.

Granted, from the traditional pragmatic orientation, language does continue to be used in the classroom (and throughout one's life) as a social-interactive tool embedded in the context of immediate experience. As such, the socially oriented uses of language remain very important to the language-disordered child's overall development. These uses of language continue to constitute valid goals for intervention. However, language is also used in the classroom in quite a different way and, here again, we see relationships between language and thought. As pointed out by Nelson in Chapter 8, children's thinking becomes increasingly disembedded from a common-sense, concrete, meaningful event. Such thought is referred to as "formal" or "abstract" (Donaldson, 1978, p. 75). To succeed in our educational system, the child has to learn "to turn language and thought in upon themselves" (Donaldson, 1978, p. 90). Language awareness, then, seems crucial to further cognitive development in the school years.

The naturalistic orientations to language intervention (presenting language in a context meaningful to daily experience) are completely valid as far as they go. That is, this orientation accurately reflects the uses of language through the preschool years. The prevalence of the naturalistic orientation is certainly not surprising given the intense research efforts that have been aimed at understanding language acquisition during the preschool years and the relative dearth of information regarding uses of language during the early school years.

Furthermore, the plea for teaching language in a concrete, meaningful context may have been influenced by broader cultural influences. It occurred in the context of a rather widespread reaction against "intellectualism" (formal, analytic, abstract thought) in general. College students were making pleas for courses that were more relevant to their everyday needs, more practical for their daily lives, and more personally meaningful. Sportsmen were writing books on intuitive approaches to various sports, urging us to "feel" rather than analyze the game of tennis or the art of skiing. Therapy groups were forming to put us back "in touch" with ourselves and others, primarily by reemphasizing the social-interactive functions of language. Educators, too, joined in.

As we have seen in Chapter 5, later phases of language development occur wherein language can be used divorced from concrete contexts, allowing logical abstract thought to develop (Olson, 1977a,

1977b; Donaldson, 1978; Wells, 1981; see also Chapter 8). To the extent that academic success is valued in our culture, it seems that facilitating a child's awareness of language would indeed constitute a valid goal for the older or more linguistically mature language-disordered child, who is frequently called "learning disabled" (see Chapter 2).

Perhaps a word of caution is warranted. We believe both the social-interactive and the reflective, disembedded uses of language to be important. We are certainly not advocating the abandonment of facilitating language growth for the purposes of social and practical interaction. We are suggesting, as Silliman does in Chapter 14, however, that the conceptual uses of formalized language not be deemphasized. Wells (1981) reminds us of Sapir's (1921, p. 24) words of over 60 years ago regarding the potential cognitive power of language: "It is somewhat as though a dynamo capable of generating enough power to operate an elevator were operated almost exclusively to feed an electric doorbell." Donaldson (1978, p. 84) cautions us, however, to attempt to achieve a balance since "disembedded thinking ... yields its greatest riches when it is conjoined with doing."

Having established our rationale that metalinguistic skill development does indeed constitute a valid goal for language intervention, we turn our interest to several other issues. First, we might ask when to begin the facilitation of metalinguistic skill development. Next, we are interested in the developmental ordering of both goals and child response expectancies. Finally, we briefly turn to actual activities that might serve to spur such growth.

In Chapter 7, regarding metalinguistic skill in normal children, two stages of development were postulated. The first stage (see Fig. 7.2) occurs during the preoperational phase of cognitive development and contains skills we believe foreshadow the more deliberate, complex metalinguistic functioning possible in the concrete operational stage. One manifestation of metalin-

guistic skill at this earlier stage is play with language divorced from a truly communicative context. This can take several forms, including (1) play with sounds devoid of meaning, (2) creating sound variations with known words, (3) repeating words playfully several times, (4) making up new words for objects the child knows the true word for, (5) replacing words in well rehearsed sequences, such as nursery rhymes or other routines, and (6) creating rhyming word pairs or sequences.

A child's very early environment can encourage the use of these primitive types of language games. Cazden (1974) suggests that language play may facilitate the eventual acquisition of literacy by directing the child's attention to the language as an entity in and of itself. While this particular hypothesis remains to be tested, it seems that attempts to facilitate a playful attitude toward language would benefit the child in other ways. The task of learning language is a difficult, arduous, failure-prone experience for the language-disordered child. Introducing a playful attitude as part of language intervention of children with even very low levels of linguistic ability might lighten the gravity of the task since, in play, there is no right or wrong, merely the attempt. Such consequence-free play might make the child more willing in general to experiment with the linguistic code and might as such help him or her determine its boundaries. In this sense, nonsense might help strengthen the real (Rogow, 1981).

In Chapter 10, Miller will make the point that normal children hypothesis-test about language forms. Snyder-McLean and McLean (1978) talk about ways the child uses language to learn more about language, beginning very early by asking for labels by uttering "what?," "that?," or some variation thereof. Eventually, sophisticated questions regarding word pronunciation, morpheme boundaries, meanings, and even how language works will be evidenced. It is always difficult to urge this sort of curiosity in a child. One can only hope to increase the frequency of such behaviors, if they occur at all, by systematically determining what linguistic or contextual variables (either antecedent or consequent) tend to occur along with such instances of language hypothesis testing. In a like manner, Guess et al. (1974) offer an operant procedure for teaching children to ask "What's that?" and "What are you doing?" in order to expand their lexical repertoires.

As discussed in Chapter 7, the use of repairs may be prompted by either an effort to help the listener understand or to help the child's own language development. Since Gallagher (1977) found that repairs occur from the earliest stages of normal language development, we might attempt to facilitate the child's production of repairs from the very earliest stages of language intervention, even with very low-level children, by introducing "what?" into conversation and observing the child's response. This would seem to be an especially valid concern since Gallagher and Darnton (1978) found that language-disordered children have less flexibility in making repairs than normal children of their same language level.

Other data (Clark and Andersen, 1979) suggest a developmental sequence in the nature of repairs moving from phonological to morphological to lexical to syntactic. This sequence suggests a hierarchy for response expectations from the language-disordered child. At the level of lexical revisions (which characteristically involve giving synonyms), it might also be necessary to work on synonymy, since language-disordered children often have difficulty in this realm as well. The clinician might also interject repairs into his or her own speech of the same type the child is working on in order to provide a model.

Adjusting to one's listener was previously discussed as another potentially metalinguistic skill that has rudiments in early language acquisition. Here again, play may provide a format for very early skill development, since children often practice the speech styles of others through their dramatic role playing. This practice in talking like other people might facilitate the eventual ability to adjust one's language to the needs, status, etc., of others. Actual experience with listeners who have various special needs—such as talking to much younger children, a blind person, etc.—might also prove beneficial and enhance such skills.

For more advanced language learning-disabled children with concrete operational cognitive skills and sufficient language ability, metalinguistic goals might advance to skills characteristic of stage two (see Chapter 7). The broad metalinguistic goals include facilitating the child's awareness that language is (1) an arbitrary, conventional code, and (2) a system. (The third part of the definition, that language is used for communication, falls under the rubric of metapragmatics rather than metalinguistics and as such will not be discussed here.) Tasks which have been designed to test or enhance language awareness in both of these domains vary along two dimensions: (1) which component of language they require that the child focus on and (2) which response is required of the child (see Chapter 1).

Regarding the components, the focus may be on any aspect of language form—lexicon, phonology, morphology, and syntax. The task may also require focusing on several words (a phrase), an entire sentence, or a complete story. Expected responses are also numerous and of varying complexity in terms of the demands they place on the child. Table 9.4 lists and defines the various types of responses required in typical metalinguistic testing tasks (adapted from Franklin, 1979) that are important to keep in mind when developing response hierarchies for teaching metalinguistic skills. Certain of these responses would clearly be easier than others. Merely comprehending, for example, appears to be the least demanding, whereas explaining would pose a far more difficult task.

Table 9.5 summarizes both the focus of

Table 9.4.
Various Response Expectancies Used In Metalinguistic Tasks[a]

Comprehension:	Indicating nonverbally that something has been understood. For example, pointing to the picture (out of a choice of pictures) that corresponds to the correct interpretation of an ambiguous word or sentence or a proverb.
Segmentation:	Separating a stimulus (sentence, compound word, regular word, or syllable) into its component parts (words, syllables, or phonemes).
Synthesis:	Combining phonemes into words or, less frequently, words into sentences.
Evaluation:	Judge by comparing one item to another. For example, one word might be compared to another in an auditory discrimination task. In other situations, the stimulus might be compared to one's stored standard of grammatical or semantic acceptability.
Correction:	Involves identifying the specific errors and changing them to their correct form.
Explanation:	Supplying reasons for comprehension, segmentation, evaluation, or correction.
Relating terms:	Searching the semantic field for relating words to other words. Used in providing homonyms, antonyms, synonyms, analogies, paraphrases, definitions, etc.

[a] Adapted from Franklin (1979).

Table 9.5.
The Focuses of Various Metalinguistic Procedures and the Typical Response Expectancies They Require

Semantic Domain	Component of Language Focused on	Response Expectancies
Language is an arbitrary, conventional code		
Ambiguity	Lexicon, phonology, morpheme boundaries, syntax (deep and surface structure)	Comprehend, explain
Synonymy	Lexicon, sentence	Explain, relate
Analogies	Phrases	Relate
Figurative language	Lexicon (dual function words), phrases (idioms, simile), sentences (proverbs), stories (parables)	Comprehend, explain, relate
Language is a system		
	Phonemes	Comprehend, evaluate, correct, synthesize
	Syllables	Segment into phonemes
	Words	Segment into phonemes, synthesize into sentences
	Bound morphemes	Evaluate, correct, explain
	Syntax	Evaluate, correct, explain

awareness and the typical response expectancies for the two broad areas of awareness—that language is an arbitrary, conventional code and that it is a system. Specific ways of attempting to facilitate the development of some of these skills are offered by Wiig and Semel (1976, 1980). For example, regarding awareness of the arbitrary, conventional nature of language, Wiig and Semel suggest ways to work on multiple meaning words, synonyms, and figurative uses of language. In general, they stress working on nonverbal concept development first. It is also important to build on what is familiar to the child. For example, in developing synonyms, one could start with the child's mother, pointing out that although she is the same person, she is referred to in many ways (e.g., "Mommy," "Mrs. Jessup," "Arlene," or "Honey"). In addition to the relevance of the words to the child, one needs to consider their frequency of use in English and their conceptual difficulty. Miller and Israel provide additional insights into these areas in Chapters 10 and 11.

Many of the tasks designed to enhance the awareness that language is a system have been used for a number of years as part of the reading readiness programs, especially when the focus is on words and phonemes. Numerous detailed programs for facilitating these skills are available. Blachman will expand on these in Chapter 13.

CLOSING REMARKS

In this chapter we have explored several issues regarding the utility of the notion of language awareness for working with language-disordered children. First, we discussed how language awareness relates to various existing orientations to language disorders. Here we developed the position that the notion of language awareness is not a mere relabeling of the processing approach to language disorders but instead should be viewed as a special use of language, one particularly prominent in formal educational settings. Following from our conviction that "meta" does indeed matter, we then explored implications of this construct for both assessment and intervention with language-disordered children.

References

Arthur G: *The Arthur Adaptation of the Leiter International Performance Scale*. Washington DC, Psychological Service Center Press, 1952.

Berthoud-Papandropoulou I: An experimental study of children's ideas about language. In Sinclair A, Jarvella R, Levelt W: *The Child's Conception of Language*. New York, Springer-Verlag, 1978, pp 55–64.

Blank M, Franklin E: Dialogue with preschoolers: a cognitively-based system of assessment. *Appl Psycholing* 1:127–150, 1980.

Bloom L: Talking, understanding, and thinking. In Schiefelbusch R, Lloyd L: *Language Perspectives—Acquisition, Retardation and Intervention*. Baltimore, University Park Press, 1974.

Bloom L, Lahey M: *Language Development and Language Disorders*. New York, John Wiley & Sons, 1978.

Blue C: Types of utterances to avoid when speaking to language-delayed children. *Language, Speech Hear Serv Schools* 12:120–124, 1981.

Bohannon J: The relationship between syntax discrimination and sentence imitation in children. *Child Dev* 46:444–451, 1975.

Brown R: *A First Language: The Early Stages*. Cambridge, MA, Harvard University Press, 1973.

Caldwell B: *Home Observation for Measurement of the Environment*. Unpublished mimeograph, University of Arkansas at Little Rock, 1978.

Calfee R, Lindamood P, Lindamood C: Acoustic-phonetic skills and reading—kindergarten through twelfth grade. *J Educ Psychol* 64:293–298, 1973.

Carrier J: Application of functional analysis and non-speech response mode to teaching language. In McReynolds L: *Developing Systematic procedures for training children's language*. ASHA Monograph 18, 1974.

Cazden C: Play with language and metalinguistic awareness: one dimension of language experience. *Urban Rev* 7:28–39, 1974.

Chapman R: Exploring children's communicative intents. In Miller J: *Assessing Language Production in Children*. Baltimore, University Park Press, 1981.

Clark EV, Andersen E: Spontaneous repairs: awareness in the process of language. *Papers Rep Child Language Dev* 16:1–12, 1979.

Cromer R: The basis of childhood dysphasia: a linguistic approach. In Wyke M: *Developmental Dysphasia*. New York, Academic Press, 1978.

Cummins J: Language and children's ability to evaluate contradictions and tautologies: a critique of Osherson and Markman's findings. *Child Dev* 49:895, 1978a.

Cummins J: Orientation to language in Ukranian-English bilingual children. *Child Dev* 49:1239–1242, 1978b.

de Ajuriaguerra J, Jaeggi A, Guignard F, et al: Evolution et prognostic de la dysphasie chez l'enfant. *Psychiatr Enfant* 8:391–452, 1964. (Reprinted and translated in Morehead D, Morehead A: *Normal and Deficient Language Acquisition*. Baltimore, University Park Press, 1976.)

Donaldson M: *Children's Minds*. New York, WW Norton, 1978.

Downing J, Oliver P: The child's conception of "a word." *Read Res Q* 9:568–582, 1973, 1974.

Fishman J: Who speaks what language to whom and when. *La Linguistique* 2:67–88, 1965.

Fokes, J. *Fokes Sentence Builder*. Hingman, MA, Teaching Resources, 1976.

Franklin M: Metalinguistic functioning in development. In Smith N, Franklin M: *Symbolic Functioning in Childhood*. Hillsdale, NJ, Lawrence Erlbaum Associates, 1979.

Gallagher T: Revision behaviors in the speech of normal children developing language. *J Speech Hear Res* 20:303–318, 1977.

Gallagher T, Darnton B: Conversational aspects of the speech of language-disordered children: revision behaviors. *J Speech Hear Res* 21:118–135, 1978.

Garnica O: The development of phonemic speech perception. In Moore T: *Cognitive Development and the Acquisition of Language*. New York, Academic Press, 1973.

Gleitman L, Gleitman H, Shipley E: The emergence of the child as grammarian. *Cognition* 1:137–164, 1972.

Gleitman L, Rozin P: Teaching reading by use of a syllabary. *Read Res Q* 8:447–483, 1973.

Gorham D: *Proverbs Test*. Missoula, MT, Psychological Test Specialists, 1954.

Gorham D: A proverbs test for clinical and experimental use. *Psychol Rep* 2:1–12, 1956.

Guess D, Sailor W, Baer D: To teach language to retarded children. In Schiefelbusch RL, Lloyd LL: *Language Perspectives: Acquisition, Retardation, and Intervention*. Baltimore, University Park Press, 1974.

Hakes D: *The Development of Metalinguistic Abilities in Children*. New York, Springer-Verlag, 1980.

Hardy W: On language disorders in young children: a reorganization of thinking. *J Speech Hear Disord* 30:3–16, 1965.

Helfgott J: Phonemic segmentation and blending skills of kindergarten children: implications for beginning reading acquisition. *Contemp Educ Psychol* 1:157–169, 1976.

Hodson B: *The Assessment of Phonological Processes*. Danville, IL, Interstate Printers and Publishers, 1980.

Ianco-Worral A: Bilingualism and cognitive development. *Child Dev* 43:1390, 1972.

Ingram D: *Procedures for Phonological Analysis of Children's Language*. Baltimore, University Park Press, 1981.

Inhelder B: Observations sur les aspects operatifs et figuratifs de la pensee chex des enfants dysphasiques. *Probl Psycholinguistique* 6:143–153, 1963. (Reprinted and translated in Morehead D, Morehead A: *Normal and Deficient Child Language*. Baltimore, University Park Press, 1976.)

James S, Miller J: Children's awareness of semantic constraints in sentences. *Child Dev* 44:69–76, 1973.

Johnson D: The language continuum. *Bull Orton Soc* 28:1–11, 1968.

Johnson D, Myklebust H: *Learning Disabilities: Educational Principles and Practices*. New York, Grune & Stratton, 1967.

Kamhi A: Nonlinguistic symbolic and conceptual abilities of language impaired and normally developing children. *J Speech Hear Res* 24:446–453, 1981.

Keith R: *Central Auditory Dysfunction*. New York, Grune and Stratton, 1977.

Kirk S, McCarthy J, Kirk W: *The Illinois Test of Psycholinguistic Ability*, revised ed. Urbana, The University of Illinois Press, 1968.

Lee L: *The Northwestern Syntax Screening Test*. Evanston, IL, Northwestern University Press, 1969.

Lee L: *Developmental Sentence Analysis*. Evanston, IL, Northwestern University Press, 1974.

Lee L, Koenigsknecht R, Mulhern S: *Interactive Language Development Teaching: The Clinical Presentation of Grammatical Structure*. Evanston, IL, Northwestern University Press, 1975.

Liberman I: Segmentation of the spoken words and reading acquisition. *Bull Orton Soc* 23:65–77, 1973.

Liles B, Schulman M, Bartlett S: Judgments of grammaticality by normal and language-disordered children. *J Speech Hear Disord* 42:199–209, 1977.

Lundberg I, Torneus M: Nonreaders' awareness of the basic relationship between spoken and written words. Discussed on pp 85–86 in Lundberg I: Aspects of linguistic awareness related to reading. In Sinclair A, Jarvella R, Levelt W: *The Child's Conception of Language*. New York: Springer-Verlag, 1978, pp 83–96.

MacDonald J, Blott J: Environmental language intervention: the rationale for a diagnostic and training strategy through rules, context, and generalization. *J Speech Hear Disord* 39:244–256, 1974.

Markman E: Children's difficulty with word-reference differentiation. *Child Dev* 47:742–749, 1976.

Mattingly I: Reading, the linguistic process, and linguistic awareness. In Kavanagh J, Mattingly I: *Language by Ear and by Eye: The Relationships between Speech and Reading*. Cambridge, MA, MIT Press, 1972.

Miller J, Yoder D: An ontogenetic language teaching strategy for retarded children. In Schiefelbusch R, Lloyd L: *Language Perspectives—Acquisition, Retardation and Intervention*. Baltimore, University Park Press, 1974.

Morehead D, Ingram D: The development of base syntax in normal and linguistically deviant children. *J Speech Hear Res* 16:330–352, 1973.

Myklebust H: *Auditory Disorders in Children*. New York, Grune & Stratton, 1954.

Myklebust H: Learning disorders: psychoneurological disturbances in childhood. *Rehabil Lit* 25:356–360, 1964.

Myklebust H: Childhood aphasia: an evolving concept. In Travis L: *Handbook of Speech Pathology and Audiology*. New York, Appleton-Century-Crofts, 1971.

Olson D: Oral and written language and the cognitive processes of children. *J Commun* 27:10–26, 1977.

Olson D: From utterance to text: the bias of language in speech and writing. *Harvard Educ Rev* 47:257–281, 1977b.

Osherson D, Markman E: Language and the ability to evaluate contradictions and tautologies. *Cognition* 3:213–226, 1975.

Papandropoulou I, Sinclair H: What is a word? Experimental study of children's ideas on grammar. *Hum Dev* 17:241–258, 1974.

Piaget J: *The Child's Conception of the World*. New York, Harcourt, Brace & World, 1929.

Quick C: *Toledo-McKesson Interaction Scale*. Unpublished mimeograph, Central Institute for the Deaf.

Rogow S: Riddles and rhymes: the importance of speech play for blind and visually handicapped children. Presented at the Second International Congress for the Study of Child Language, Vancouver, British Columbia, August, 1981.

Rose S, Blank M: The potency of context in children's cognition: an illustration through conservation. *Child Dev* 45:499–502, 1974.

Rosner J: Auditory analysis training with prereaders. *Read Teacher* 27:379–384, 1974.

Rozin P, Bressman B, Taft M: Do children understand the basic relationships between speech and writing? The mow-motorcycle test. *J Read Behav* 6:327–334, 1974.

Sapir E: *Language*. New York, Harcourt, Brace, 1921.

Shriberg L, Kwiatowski J: *Natural Process Analysis: A Procedure for Phonological Analysis of Continuous Speech Samples*. New York, John Wiley & Sons, 1980.

Shulman M, Liles B: A sense of grammaticality: an

ingredient for language remediation. *Language Speech Hear Serv Schools* 10:59–62, 1979.

Slobin D, Welch C: Elicited imitation as a research tool in developmental psycholinguistics. In Ferguson C, Slobin D: *Studies of Child Language Development*. New York, Holt, Rinehart & Winston, 1973.

Snyder L, McLean J: Deficient acquisition strategies: a proposed conceptual framework for analyzing severe language deficiency. *Am J Ment Defic* 81:338–349, 1977.

Snyder-McLean L, McLean J: Verbal information gathering strategies: the child's use of language to acquire language. *J Speech Hear Disord* 43:306–325, 1978.

Tallal P, Piercy M: Defects of auditory perception in children with developmental dysphasia. In Wyke M: *Developmental Dysphasia*. New York, Academic Press, 1978.

Tervoort B: Foreign language awareness in a five-to-nine year-old lexicographer. *J Child Language* 6:159–166, 1979.

Tyack D, Gottsleben R: *Language Sampling, Analysis and Training*. Palo Alto, CA, Consulting Psychologists Press, 1974.

Vygotsky L: *Language and Thought*. Cambridge, MA, MIT Press, 1962.

Wallach GP: The implications of different language comprehension strategies in normal and learning disabled children: effects of thematization. Doctoral dissertation, The Graduate School and University Center of City University of New York, 1977.

Wallach GP, Brown S: Synonymy judgments in normal and learning disabled students. Presented at the American Speech-Language-Hearing Association Convention, Chicago, November, 1977.

Wells G: *Learning through Interaction: The Study of Language Development*. New York, Cambridge University Press, 1981.

Wepman J: *Auditory Discrimination Test*. Los Angeles, Western Psychological Services, 1973.

Wiig E, Semel E: *Language Disabilities in Children and Adolescents*. Columbus, OH, Charles E Merrill, 1976.

Wiig E, Semel E: *Language Assessment and Intervention for the Learning Disabled*. Columbus, OH, Charles E Merrill, 1980.

Worster-Drought C, Allen I: Congenital auditory imperception: report of a case with congenital word deafness. *J Neurol Psychopathol* 9:193–203, 1929.

CHAPTER TEN

Problem Solving and Language Disorders

LYNDA MILLER, Ph.D.

ABOUT PROBLEMS AND PROBLEM SOLVING

What Is a Problem?

There are problems and then there are problems. Consider how you would go about the following tasks: (1) finding out how airplanes fly; (2) learning something new without being consciously aware of doing it.

The first task is a relatively narrow one which appears to have a specific outcome, namely, finding out how airplanes fly. To discover how the process works, you would most likely look for the solution by relating airplanes to birds and your previously stored knowledge (assuming you have such a store available) about how birds fly. You might also devise a series of more specific questions about airplanes and flying, determine how to gather the answers to those

mine how to gather the answers to those questions, and try to answer the original question by putting together the information gathered for the more specific questions. There may be other approaches that come to your mind, but the point is that it is rather easy to think of one or two procedures you could use to find your answer.

In contrast, the second task is much more general and unspecified. Most people have difficulty describing exactly how they learn new information. They may be able to state that they have recently become aware of having learned something new, but explaining the actual processes involved remains elusive. Too, they may be able to cite situations which exemplify the new concept, or they may be able to describe other situations which seem similar, but, once again, the actual describing can be a frustrating task in itself.

The point illustrated by the two examples above is that what we call a *problem* can be viewed in a very broad sense, on the one hand or, on the other hand, it can be very narrowly defined. In the more general sense, all of learning can be viewed as problem solving; in the more specific sense, a problem can be as narrow as thinking of the name for something. This chapter has two major purposes. One is to discuss problems, both generally and specifically defined, problem solving, and the role of language and language disorders in problem solving. The other major purpose is to address the issues of assessment and instruction of problem solving, which discussion, as you will soon see, itself presents a problem.

Let us describe the components of a problem. A very general definition of a problem is that it involves decision making or choice making without all the necessary information available. More specifically, Wickelgren (1979) has described problems as consisting of three components:

1. The *givens*, or the declarative, propositional knowledge one uses in attempting to solve the problem, or attain the goal.

2. The *operations*, or the procedural knowledge one uses in attempting to solve the problem.

3. The *goal*, or the end point, the knowledge one expects to gain by using allowable operations in the solving of the problem.

Mayer (1977) views the components of a problem slightly differently from Wickelgren by adding *obstacles* to the givens and the goals of a problem. Mayer indicates that thinking is a process involving the manipulation of a set of operations on knowledge in the cognitive system. In this sense, then, thinking is a directed process in that it results in behavior which solves a problem or is directed toward a solution. Thus, "...thinking is what happens when a person solves a problem..." (Mayer, 1977, p. 6).

Although there may be as many problems as there are minds to conjure them up, for present purposes, we will assume two general types of problems: those that require logical, inferential, sequential problem-solving strategies, and those that require holistic, simultaneous, pattern-seeking strategies. That is, some problems appear to be structured in such a way as to invite solution through the use of linguistic or formal symbolic means (such as mathematics or computer programs). Others seem to be structured in a more nonverbal fashion, perhaps one requiring manipulation of visual-spatial patterns or iconic images. We will return to this apparent distinction in types of problems in several of the succeeding sections.

What Is Problem Solving?

The components of problems and even the types of problems have been generally agreed upon by those studying problem solving, but descriptions of problem solving as a process (or processes) have not been as homogeneous. The psychology literature is replete with descriptions of problem solving which emphasized stimuli, responses, and the establishment of associations between them. Associationist theorists argue that those responses previously practiced in a given situation are more likely to be performed when that situation is presented again. Hence, when a particular problem arises, the individual will be most likely to do whatever he has done before in that situation. In addition, those responses in that individual's response hierarchy that do not help solve a given problem lose strength, whereas those that do help solve the problem move up the hierarchy. The major criticism of the associationist theory of problem solving is that it fails to explain the problem-solving process in novel situations. The theory predicts that the individual in a novel situation will engage in a trial and error application of past habits. This process cannot account for the rapid problem solving which humans are capable of performing in novel situations, particularly in situations requiring nonverbal solutions.

Another theoretical model of problem solving in psychology is the Gestalt description, which can be viewed as almost a direct contrast to the associationist model. The Gestaltists described problem solving as resulting in a structural understanding, or the ability to comprehend how all the parts of the problem fit together to satisfy the requirements of the goal. These theorists emphasized a relatively high-level, creative process in which the emphasis is on organization, or how the elements of the problem fit together to form a structure. This organization is characterized by Mayer (1977) as four general phases:

1. Preparation, or the gathering of information and preliminary attempts at the solution.

2. Incubation, which involves a period of putting the problem aside.

3. Illumination, during which the key to the solution appears.

4. Verification, or a checking out of the solution to make sure it works.

The major criticism of the Gestaltist view of problem solving is that the theory is rather vague to be tested experimentally. The model relies on introspective verification rather than empirical verification.

A third, more recent theory of problem solving which has gained attention in the psychology literature is schema theory. Schema theory is a description of how knowledge is packaged, or re-presented in units called schemata (Rumelhart, 1980). Schemata are data structures, according to Rumelhart, used to store concepts. He argues that there are schemata for representing our knowledge about every kind of concept we store. In addition, each schema contains "...the network of interrelations that is believed to normally hold among the constituents of the concept in question" (p. 34). In Rumelhart's formulation, the most important function of schemata is in constructing interpretations of events, objects, or situations, or what he calls comprehension. These interpretations of events, objects, or situations represent our view of the nature of reality. Schemata are also important in that they provide a source for predictions about unobserved events. Because they provide interpretations for our view of reality, they also provide predictions about what is likely, or probable, to happen next. In related fashion, schemata allow us to "fill in the gaps" when we receive only a portion of the information surrounding an object, event, or situation. In other words, schemata allow us to solve problems by moving from a given to an unknown through the processes of interpretation and prediction. Rumelhart suggests that once one understands a problem, that is, attaches the current situation to available schemata, solving it is virtually complete. "Once we can 'understand' the situation by encoding it in terms of a relatively rich set of schemata, the conceptual constraints of the schemata can be brought into play and the problem readily solved" (Rumelhart, 1980, p. 57).

An integral part of schema theory is a description of how schemata are activated and utilized in the process of understanding and problem solving. Basically, there are two types of processing associated with the utilization of schemata, conceptually driven and data driven processing. Conceptually driven (top-down) processing involves the activation of a schema and all its subcomponents (subschemata) in the following fashion: Suppose you are asked to picture a face. You most likely envision the general components of a face, the eyes, nose, mouth, cheeks perhaps, a chin, and so on. In this example, *face* is the schema activated, and the components of the face are the subschemata which come into mind as your process *face*. This is top-down, or conceptually driven, processing. Suppose, on the other hand, that you are given a picture of discrete and separate elements such as those in Figure 10.1, presented one at a time. By the time the last component has been presented, you have probably realized that the components suggest a face. In this instance, you used the individual

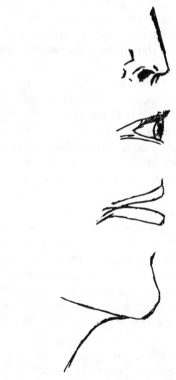

Figure 10.1.   Subschemata for FACE schema.

data, the separate components, to try to work from the bottom up to the more generalized concept, *face*. This latter is an example of bottom-up, or data driven processing. As you can see, when faced with one type of problem, you utilized one problem-solving strategy, top-down processing; a different problem-solving strategy, bottom-up processing, was used to solve the second type of problem. Thus, schema theory provides an explanation for different types of problem solving for different types of problems (see also Chapters 4 and 6).

In 1978 an electrical engineer from Carnegie-Mellon University, David Tuma, and a physicist from the University of California at Berkeley, Frederick Reif, organized a conference called "Problem Solving and Education: Issues in Teaching and Research." One of the contributors, Jill Larkin (1980) argued that one of the most intriguing ideas in the area of problem solving is that there might be strategies underlying problem solving across a wide variety of situations. She suggests that there are three strategies that appear to be both general and powerful in problem solving. The first is means-ends analysis, which is the assessment of the "difference between the current state of knowledge about the problem and the state of knowledge required for the problem's solution" (Larkin, 1980, p. 115). The assessment results in choosing an action that would reduce the difference between these two states of knowledge.

The second type of general strategy described by Larkin is what she calls a kind of planning, which involves "replacing the original problem with an abstracted version in which only certain central features are retained" (Larkin, 1980, p. 115). The abstracted version is then solved, serving as a model solution for the original problem.

The third type of general strategy Larkin discusses is using goals and subgoals as a means of replacing a currently unattainable goal with a simpler subgoal. Once the subgoal is reached, the original goal can be pursued. Larkin goes on to describe instances in which these three strategies have

been used in classroom teaching with good results. However, she cautions that these strategies cannot be utilized without the student already possessing a considerable amount of "domain-specific knowledge" (Larkin, 1980, p. 117), or content-related knowledge. Such specific and considerable domain-specific knowledge is required to know how to go about using the strategies described above. Thus, although there may indeed be general and powerful strategies available to human problem solvers, they appear to require prerequisite knowledge of content before they can be utilized with any success.

The work summarized thus far points to several conclusions. First, although problems may be relatively easy to define generally in terms of component parts, what constitutes problem solving is far from clear. Generally, problem solving can be described as the discovery of relationships, connections between the known and the unknown; the creation of something new; the discovery of something new; or the verification of something thought to be true. The processes one utilizes to achieve these ends have been described in a variety of ways, with the argument that there may be general and powerful problem-solving strategies that are tied to domain-specific knowledge.

Stages of Development of Problem-solving Skills

Especially important in a discussion of problem solving in children is consideration of developmental stages of thinking and problem solving. Because this issue will be particularly pertinent in the final two sections of the chapter on the assessment and instructional considerations of problem solving, considerable detail is presented here.

The developmental model of thinking proposed by Piaget has been the most fully elaborated of all theories of children's development of thinking and problem solving and will serve as the basis for discussion here. Most of the information that follows has been based on work by Copeland (1979).

Before discussing the development of problem solving in children, it is important to distinguish between knowing how to do something versus being conscious of knowing how to do it. Van Kleeck made this same distinction in Chapters 7 and 9. Knowing that one knows how to do something involves a conceptualization or an abstraction of a particular situation. In other words, it involves consciousness of what is going on. Such consciousness requires a representation at an abstract level of what went on at a physical or action level. Knowing how to do something, on the other hand, requires action at a basic sensory and motoric level. It is based on recall of facts or recall of previously successful action patterns. The cognitive structures necessary for many of the logical inferential problems children confront in school curricula remain unconscious until they reach 11 or 12 years of age, according to Piaget (1976). What this means is that the child may be able to solve certain problems as long as several years before that same child is able to know how the problem was solved, or, further, to explain the processes used. An example that illustrates the difference between knowing how to solve a problem and being able to explain how the problem is solved was provided by Copeland (1979). The children were asked to swing a ball in a circle just above a box on the floor in front of them. Then they were asked where the ball would go if they let go of the string. Five-year-olds were able to accomplish getting the ball into the box only through trial and error attempts and were unable to explain where to let go of the string. Eight- and 9-year-olds were successful at releasing the ball at the appropriate spot, but most could not explain where the release had to take place to successfully solve the problem. Eleven- and 12-year-olds were immediately successful at releasing the ball at the appropriate position and were able to describe the concept

of tangential trajectory, even if they did not know the correct words.

The important idea to be gleaned from the above illustration is that knowing how to is not the same thing as being able to explain the processes involved in performing some action or solving a problem. The implication, which will be expanded in the section on instructional considerations, is that our expectations about how children solve problems and transfer their solutions to other problems must be tempered with the knowledge that their consciousness about thinking and problem solving is a late development in relation to their ability to actually solve problems. This consciousness, or thinking about thinking, is called *metacognition* (see also Chapter 7). It develops during what Piaget called the formal operational period of cognitive development (Piaget, 1976). We will return shortly to the concept of metacognition.

To provide a foundation for viewing problem solving in children, it is useful to view the development of problem solving in the child from the Piagetian point of view. Characteristics of the preoperational and concrete operational child were discussed in Chapters 7 and 9. To exemplify the developmental stages and to illustrate how they relate to different aspects of language development, one particular type of problem solving will be described here, that of logical classification.

From the Piagetian perspective, the first experiences in logical classification involve recognizing and naming things in the world, that is, using language to classify. The simplest classification at this level includes sorting based on the idea of a relation between an object and its owner or its habitual place of rest. This basic sorting or classifying forms the basis out of which later come conceptual definitions such as "a family is..." or "a mother is...", etc. Too, these basic and early sorting actions are typically based on the perceptual attributes of the objects. In other words, the child's knowledge of the world is formed around interpretations based on sensory and motor information. This information becomes encoded as a set of perceptual attributes characterizing the child's interactions with objects (and people, events, situations, states, etc.) in the environment. Sorting and classifying at this stage of development, then, relies heavily, if not exclusively, on perceptual attributes rather than on any more abstract, for example, symbolic, attributes. Israel also discusses this notion in Chapter 11, on word knowledge and word retrieval.

Throughout the preoperational stage of development, lasting roughly from 2 to 6 or 7 years of age, the child continues to rely on the perceptual characteristics of the environment in order to "know" it, but the child's thinking and problem solving begin to change somewhat. Children during this stage of development begin to classify and sort on the basis of particular perceptual attributes, most often color or shape and later on the basis of size. Preoperational children are as yet unable to classify hierarchically; they equate fish with animals, for example, because they are not yet capable of distinguishing superordinate classes from subordinate classes. This inability to distinguish superordinate from subordinate class reflects preoperational children's inability to decenter, to separate part from whole. A whole to the preoperational child is equivalent to its parts; all classes are seen as separable and equal parts. Thus, while the preoperational child knows that dogs are animals, when shown a set of six dogs and three chickens, the same child is likely to argue that there are more dogs than animals. To use an illustration more closely exemplifying the process involved in problem solving, consider Figure 10.2. The child is shown an array of circles and squares; all of the circles are blue, one square is blue, and the rest of the squares are red. When asked "Are all the circles blue?" and "Are all circles blue?," the preoperational child will respond as if the same question had been asked. (Recall Wallach's discussion of children's use of "the" after the age of 8 or 9; see Chapter 5, p. 98).

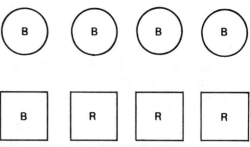

Figure 10.2.   Hierarchical classification.

Perhaps the most described characteristic of preoperational children is that they are unable to track a process through to its conclusion and then mentally reconstruct the process to its original condition; that is, preoperational children are unable to engage in reversible thinking. They are so attracted by the perceptual attributes that they do not mentally let go of the perceptual attraction in order to solve a problem involving reversibility. The most obvious example of lack of reversibility in preoperational thinking is the conservation experiments widely reported in various literatures. Preoperational children are unable to conserve because they are unable to reverse the process they have witnessed to correctly solve the problem. Conservation will be described below as a means for assessing a child's approach to problem solving.

As children enter the next stage of development, the concrete operational stage of thinking, their problem-solving strategies change significantly. They become able to mentally reverse processes in order to conserve, and, at the same time, they develop the concept of *identity*. Identity means that children realize that, although a process they witness, such as pouring equal amounts of water into two differently shaped containers, may appear as if the water changes in amount, the amount remains the same throughout. It is still the same water and cannot have changed amount even though its appearance undergoes modification. During this stage children also become able to sort hierarchically, although they still have some difficulty understanding parts and wholes. They become able to order objects according to relative characteristics, such as size, number of parts, or occurrence in time, and they begin to construct an idea of number. Some examples will illustrate the implications of these developments in problem-solving ability. When concrete operational children are presented with the same problem described above involving the blue circles, blue square, and red squares, 9- and 10-year-olds can differentiate between the two questions, "Are all the circles blue?" and "Are all circles blue?." When asked to pick the one that is different from a set of triangles, all red except one, 8-year-olds can solve the problem. On the other hand, it is not until late in the concrete operational stage of development that children can respond appropriately to the following problem: The children are given three types of cards, one set a picture of trees, one a set of apples, and one a group of blank cards. The children are asked to put the cards into two piles. It is not until the children are 10 or 11 years old that they can do so. Before then, they insist that there are three sets. They are unable to conceptualize one set with pictures and one set without.

By the time children are 11 or 12 years of age, most begin to think in what Piaget has described as a formal operational fashion. At this point of cognitive development children become able to reason or hypothesize with symbols or ideas rather than needing objects physically present as a basis for thinking. What this development implies is that these children can use a hypothetico-deductive procedure in approaching problems. Formal operational children become aware of the implications of certain logical relations, such as the following structures: conditional structures (*if-then*), disjunctive structures (*either-or or both*), exclusive structures (*either-or*), and reciprocal implications. An important development during this stage is that children become able to understand proportions, which then allows them to understand maps reduced to an arbitrary scale,

to solve problems of time and distance, to solve problems of probability, and to solve problems of geometry involving similarity. Also during this stage of development children become able to combine and permute (rearrange) elements in a class and understand hierarchical classification on the basis of part-whole relationships. The formal operational thinker can also classify on the basis of more than one class at once, thus solving problems such as the following: The children are shown a row of leaves of various colors with the last space blank; intersecting this row of leaves at the blank space is a column of green-colored objects such as a house, a human figure, a lamp, a piece of food. The children are asked what would fit into the blank space. Formal operational children can solve the problem easily because they can simultaneously classify two separate sets of members with an intersecting member representing the characteristics of both classes at once.

Perhaps the most interesting development of formal operational thought from the point of view of this chapter is that these children become able to engage in hypothesis formation and hypothesis testing using an orderly (usually deductive) process that is exhaustive. That is, formal operational children can determine all the possibilities involved in a problem and alternative paths to its solution and then develop a procedure for testing the paths most likely to lead to its solution. Again, an example will illustrate the process. Formal operational children are given some materials with which to make a pendulum and asked to determine what makes the pendulum swing faster. The materials include string, weights of various sizes and shapes, and a stick. Formal operational children will proceed in an orderly fashion by formulating several hypotheses, such as "It's the weight of the thing on the bottom of the string," or "It's the length of the string," and then proceed to test them systematically, one at a time until the correct solution is reached.

The stages of development of thinking

and problem solving described above will form the basis for discussion in the following three sections. In the section immediately following, discussion will focus on the role in problem solving of language and language disorders from a developmental point of view. The last two sections will address assessment and instructional considerations for problem solving, again from the developmental viewpoint described here.

LANGUAGE AND LANGUAGE DISORDERS IN PROBLEM SOLVING

As pointed out early in the preceding section of the chapter, problems and problem solving can take two forms, verbal and nonverbal. That is, some problems are presented in nonverbal, perhaps spatial, musical, or mathematical form. Others are presented in verbal, or linguistic, form. In fact, most problems as presented in school curricula take a linguistic form whether the problem to be solved is verbal or nonverbal. Story math problems are a good example of this. However, with the exception of information about the actual unfolding of events, most other information appears to be encoded into one basic storage system, the semantic memory system. Both verbal and nonverbal information is stored in the semantic memory store. Thus, in order to understand problem solving as it relates to children's knowledge and use of language, it is necessary to analyze briefly how they code information in general, both previously encountered information and presently impinging information.

Following the description of information coding in semantic memory, the discussion shifts to a more specific description of how linguistic knowledge appears to be stored in semantic memory and how language disorders can be viewed as specific breakdowns in accessing and/or retrieving linguistic information from the semantic store.

Semantic Memory

The best current model of how all but episodic information is coded is the seman-

tic memory model. Semantic memory has been defined by Wickelgren (1979) as the process by which knowledge is coded in an abstract way, independent of modality of input. Semantic memory is believed to be the device by which virtually all types of information (excluding episodic memory, as pointed out above) is coded, including verbal, visual, spatial imagery, scene and movement analysis (Wickelgren, 1979). However, while it is important in this discussion to include mention of the non-verbal aspects of semantic memory, primary emphasis will be placed on the linguistic components.

Semantic memory is viewed by Wickelgren (1979) as being composed of units which are structured in a hierarchical fashion in order of increasing complexity. He is quick to point out that the units of semantic memory are not arranged or coded in any one-to-one correspondence with the linguistic units of words, phrases, sentences, paragraphs, stories, and so on. However, semantic memory does seem to account for one's coding of linguistic information. In order of increasing complexity, semantic memory is thought to code the following units: concepts, which are signaled by words or phrases; propositions, which are signaled by phrases, clauses, and sentences; and schemata, which are signaled by sentences and larger units of text. A brief description of each follows.

CONCEPTS

Concepts are thought to be the basic level units of semantic memory; that is, they can be envisioned as sitting on the bottom of the representational network in meaningful semantic memory. Concepts can be activated in semantic memory by their constituent attributes, or from above, from the propositions in which each particular concept is incorporated. More specifically, concepts which provoke images, such as TRIANGLE, BOAT, RUNNING, etc., are concrete concepts activated by their lower level constituent attributes. Higher level concepts which cannot provoke concrete images are activated from above, from higher level propositional information. Viewed from this perspective, concept learning is never complete; concepts become increasingly integrated and assimilated into one's semantic memory.

Concepts code two basic types of meaning, referential meanings and relational meanings. Referential meanings represent examples of individual objects, events, states, processes. Relational meanings code all the relationships each concept has to other concepts *and* to specific contexts, including how each relationship emphasizes particular aspects of a concept. Thus it can be seen that concepts are not all-or-nothing, binary creatures. They are, instead, fuzzy in their boundaries. Individual elements exhibit various degrees of membership in a concept because of fuzzy boundaries, for instance, fat dogs, old chickens, green doors. On the other hand, some concepts are prototypical in that they code ideal conceptual members (Rosch, 1975). Rosch has described six prototypes of facial expression for human emotions: happy, sad, angry, afraid, surprised, disgusted. For each prototype, there is an ideal facial expression to convey it; the further away from that expression one moves along a relevant dimension, the less the facial expression is perceived as surprise, for example (Rosch, 1975). Concept development consists of building up prototypes as far as possible in order to be able to perceive variations. One must have seen enough entities in any given class to be able to begin to detect variation; otherwise, all members of a given class are perceived as equal. Until one has seen enough roses, for example, in Gertrude Stein's words, a rose is a rose is a rose is a rose. Rose fanciers, of course, would find such a premise absurd, in part because their experience with roses is so abundant that they can perceive subtle variations undetectable to the novice rose buff.

Wickelgren (1979) argues that concepts are learned through three basic processes: abstraction, propositional learning, and inferential learning. The most basic method of concept learning is thought to be abstrac-

tion, which appears to be largely unconscious in that it is based on observation of instances and noninstances. Abstraction does not involve generating hypotheses, making inferences, or solving problems. It is a gradual and incremental process which seems to underlie all of human learning. Propositional learning of concepts is also thought to be a relatively basic process, although it involves being able to infer on ·the basis of previously available information stored in semantic memory as rules of logical reasoning. Inferential learning of this type involves the selective processing of attributes of examples and nonexamples. Klein-Konigsberg will expand upon aspects of inferential learning in Chapter 12.

PROPOSITIONS

Wickelgren (1979, p. 317) defines a proposition as " ... the semantic memory analogue of a clause, just as a concept is the semantic memory analogue of a word or phrase." Propositions can be viewed as relational terms and one or more arguments; relational terms are most often a verb, an adjective, and a preposition, whereas arguments consist of a noun or a noun phrase, that is, subjects or objects of the relation. An example of a proposition broken into its relational term and its arguments is shown in Figure 10.3.

An important characteristic of human processing is that it involves analysis of information into the same constituent propositions whether the propositions are conveyed by separate sentences, separate clauses, prepositional phrases, or adjective modifiers of nouns. For example, humans

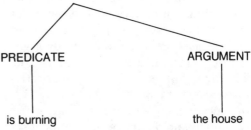

Figure 10.3. Relational terms and arguments of a proposition.

perceive the following as equal propositions: "The book belongs to the boy" versus "That is the boy's book"; similarly, "the table's edge" versus "the edge of the table," and "the blue dress" versus "the dress is blue."

SCHEMATA

Wickelgren (1979) points out that semantic memory must not be thought of as a forest of propositional trees. Rather, semantic memory is a " . . . network of richly interconnected concepts and propositions" (p. 325). This network can be thought of as a matrix of schemata, as described in the first section of this chapter. As the higher order constituents of semantic memory, schemata are important in comprehension of speech and text and in the acquisition and retrieval of information. As was pointed out in Chapter 6, when a proposition is recognized from a word from speech, it activates a schema (or several schemata) in semantic memory. Contextual schemata guide the activation of more specific propositional units and relational or referential units in semantic memory in order to achieve an interpretation appropriate to the context at hand.

Semantic Memory and Language Disorders

One aspect of semantic memory that is of importance in the current discussion is the coding of linguistic information in semantic memory. According to Wickelgren's formulation (1979), different aspects of semantic memory are responsible for the coding of various aspects of linguistic information. For instance, the lower level concept structures most likely encode word and some phrase information (see Chapter 11), whereas higher level proposition structures are the most probable units encoding some phrase, clause, and sentence information. The highest order semantic memory structures, schemata, are thought to account for the encoding of sentences and larger (e.g., paragraph and discourse size) units of spoken and written text (see Chapter 12). This formulation of semantic memory will be

seen to be a useful one in analyzing the level of analysis involved in problem solving, but some translation is required at this point in the discussion in order to integrate the semantic memory model with what is currently known about language disorders. The reader should be alerted that much of what follows is speculative in nature. As pointed out in this chapter and in Chapter 12 on semantic integration, we know very little about how the manipulation of language structures actually occurs during problem solving. However, we are fairly certain that children develop problem-solving strategies at the schema level that depend on rich knowledge of concept and propositional level information, including linguistic information, but the exact nature of that dependence is not yet clear. With these cautions in mind, we now turn to a description of language and language disorders within the framework of the semantic memory model.

Current practice among speech-language clinicians is to divide language disorders into three components, as described in Chapter 1. The three are language disorders based on syntax, semantics, and phonology. In addition, most clinicians analyze the pragmatic aspects of children's communication abilities as an aspect of communication that is supralinguistic, i.e., crossing all linguistic categorizations. Utilizing the semantic memory model outlined above, these linguistic and pragmatic categories can be viewed somewhat differently from current practice. Phonology, syntax, and semantics will be discussed in terms of how each can be viewed using the semantic memory model. In addition, pragmatics will be described from the view of semantic memory. Each component will be integrated into the semantic memory model.

PHONOLOGY

Language at the phonological level is seen as the translation of heard utterances into acoustic constituents according to a specific code, unique to each language, that governs which sets of acoustic features are permitted and in which sequences. Know ing about language at the phonological level can be described as having constructed concepts of phonemes, which are classes of sounds, or families—a basic level of classification for encoding into semantic memory.

A phonological disorder may be viewed as some disruption in the encoding of information into semantic memory at the basic concept level of memory. Children with phonological disorders in spoken language may be experiencing difficulty in extracting from the speech stream those features or attributes that exemplify phonemic categories. The child who says "broiler" for "umbrella" has abstracted some features of the word and not others. Some children may be experiencing difficulty in abstracting the combinatorial features necessary to produce phonemes in the sequences permissible in their own languages. With older children, errors sometimes occur on multisyllabic, complex sound-word combinations (see Chapter 16). The point is that the difficulty may be seen as a breakdown in the encoding of memorial units specifically related to the phonological system of a given language, a breakdown that seems to be occurring at a basic concept level of semantic memory.

SYNTAX

Using the semantic memory model, syntax can be described as the development and access to concepts about grammar. As in the case of phonology, the coding of syntax into semantic memory seems to occur at the basic concept level. It appears to be a process of constructing concepts that are highly specific, having criterial attributes unique to each language, and belonging to sets, or classes of concepts, as the class of nouns, for instance. The boundaries between some of the concepts related to syntax may be somewhat fuzzy, as, for example, the boundary between the preposition *up*, as in "up in the sky," and the particle *up*, as in "He broke up the party." However, there are also prototypical examples of most syntactic categories that exemplify the concept nature of syntactic

categorization. *Table*, for example, could easily be described as a prototype member of the concept NOUN, as *run* could be described as a prototype member of the concept VERB.

A syntactic disorder may be viewed in much the same manner as a phonological disorder, that is, as a breakdown in the abstracting and/or encoding of the criterial attributes corresponding to the grammatical categories (concepts) of a given language. Again, the disorder appears to be related to the process of coding information of a specific linguistic nature, namely syntactic, into the concept level of semantic memory. Perhaps the grammatical features of their language are not salient, or perceptually attractive, to the children who experience problems with this component of language processing.

SEMANTICS

Semantics can also be defined as being coded at the basic concept level of semantic memory. Semantics as vocabulary is nothing more than the attaching of words from one's language to the concepts being constructed in semantic memory. This involves the coding of referential meanings. Semantics may also be thought of as knowledge about the relationships inherent among the conceptual components of one's language, so that it can be seen as an example of the coding of relational meanings, also a concept level process of semantic memory. This representation, shown in Figure 10.4, corresponds quite closely with the propositional level of semantic memory described earlier.

A semantic disorder, then, can be viewed as a breakdown at either of two levels of

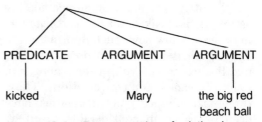

Figure 10.4.   Representation of relational components of a proposition.

semantic memory, depending upon which interpretation is made of semantics. A breakdown in semantics as either vocabulary or knowledge about the relationships among the concepts of one's language can be explained as faulty encoding at the concept level of semantic memory. Children who experience semantic disorders defined in this way seem relatively inefficient at extracting and encoding the criterial attributes of words. They may also have difficulty forming word associations, as shall be seen in Chapter 11.

However, when defined as a description of one's knowledge about the propositions of one's language, or one's knowledge about the relationships between predicates and their arguments, a disruption in semantics is occurring at the higher order propositional level of semantic memory. Thus, children who are thought to have semantic disorders are experiencing problems in figuring out the deep structures of utterances, that is, what utterances mean once syntax is decoded. The interaction between children's semantic (comprehension) strategies and their linguistic knowledge becomes a fascinating area for research (see Wallach's description in Chapter 5).

PRAGMATICS

Although pragmatics is often described as an aspect of language, it is more correctly conceived as a component of communication on a level parallel with language functions. As we have seen elsewhere in the text (see especially Chapters 1, 2, and 7), many aspects of pragmatics have been studied. Included are: how people's intentions underlying communication are mapped into linguistic forms to suit different styles and situations, and the degree of directness with which intentions are communicated; the assumptions speakers make about listeners in order to know how much information to make explicit and how to do it; and the tacitly agreed upon rules people appear to follow in engaging in conversations. These three major aspects of pragmatics have been described in considerable detail by Miller (1981).

Within the semantic memory model, pragmatics can be regarded as a higher level schema level process. That is, pragmatics includes elements that are contextual in the sense that they surround and underlie the actual utterances people use. The pragmatic elements of communication require knowledge that is superordinate to the actual linguistic units within which the message is coded. This superordinate knowledge includes knowledge about who can say what kinds of things to whom and under what circumstances, to paraphrase Hymes's definition (1974; see also Chapter 7). Such knowledge is commonly described as world knowledge, precisely the type of knowledge that appears to be couched in the schemata described in the section on schema theory.

Breakdowns in the pragmatic aspects of communication take many forms, as would be expected when considering schemata about almost everything one knows about how, when, and what to communicate and in what ways. Several characteristics of pragmatic disorders have been described by Miller (1981). One such characteristic is that preoperational and concrete operational children experiencing difficulties with the pragmatic aspects of communication frequently make use of a limited number of linguistic structures in their communicating. That is, they tend to use a restricted language code, preferring general and vague reference and avoiding specific reference to the extent possible within the limits of listener understanding. Examples of what these children often do are the following:

These children (1) use personal and indefinite pronouns when specific nomination is called for; (2) use definite articles when an indefinite is appropriate, which indicates that they have assumed their listeners already know what the antecedent referent is even if it has not been made explicit; (3) make unjustified assumptions about how much their listeners know about the topic at hand and talk about it as if the listener had intimate knowledge; (4) frequently follow the tacit conversational rules of communication without exception, while the exceptions are understood by the majority of speakers as appropriate vehicles for communicating intent. This latter example is evident in the inability of some children to understand that verbal humor is a play on some linguistic form or forms. Van Kleeck pointed this out in Chapter 7, where she also discussed other aspects of pragmatics and metalinguistics. Examples of older children's pragmatic difficulties also appear elsewhere (see Chapter 2).

METALINGUISTICS AND METACOGNITION REVISITED

Problem solving depends on metacognition. In Chapter 7, Van Kleeck pointed out that *metalinguistics* means that one can reflect on language, i.e., the term *metalinguistics* is quite specific to consciousness about language. To be metacognitive, on the other hand, implies a much broader ability. Metacognition is the ability to reflect on thinking in general; it is thinking about thinking. Being metacognitive allows people to devise strategies for thinking, to evaluate strategies, and to modify them— all problem-solving stratagems. To return to the discussion about children with pragmatic difficulties, it should be stressed that, while such children may not be metalinguistic, they are not necessarily also without metacognitive abilities. An illustrative example of a child who is nonmetalinguistic and yet metacognitive is a teenage boy I know who was diagnosed as autistic early in childhood. Kurt developed language abilities adequate for reading at an elementary level, which implies at least the ability to recognize the elements of linguistic structures, but he was unable to use language to discuss linguistic structure. However, Kurt is an accomplished artist who, with limited oral linguistic skill, can explain how he goes about planning and executing his very accomplished paintings. Thus, he is entirely capable of metacognitive strategies, but those strategies do not include any specific to language; hence, he cannot be considered metalinguistic. This distinction is impor-

tant when addressing the assessment and instructional considerations presented in the final sections of this chapter.

Language Disorders and Problem Solving—Some Speculations

In the immediately preceding sections the discussion centered on how the various components of language disorders can be viewed and described according to a semantic memory model of the ways in which children represent and code information. In this portion of the discussion attention will focus on the specific ways in which language disorders may affect children's problem-solving abilities.

Problem solving per se can be described within the perspective of the semantic memory model as well. In its broadest definition, problem solving may be seen as some kind of search for a specific referent at the concept or propositional level of semantic memory. That is, a problem could be said to exist whenever one is faced with the task of interpreting an utterance, which includes a search for referents in one's semantic store corresponding to the heard components of the spoken (or printed) utterance. In this sense, the problem is one of finding the appropriate interpretations for the proposition(s) underlying the utterance, which requires the listener to make use of the propositional level of semantic memory. Listeners employ a variety of comprehension strategies in their attempts to do this (see Chapter 5).

In addition, the listener must make some sort of interpretation of the individual components of the utterance; thus, a search at the concept level is made for concepts corresponding both to individual words and to individual morphemic and phonemic elements. However, in order to make sense of the interpretations at the concept and propositional levels of semantic memory, the listener must fit the estimated interpretation(s) into contextual schemata to see how well the estimate fits with the context within which the utterance is spoken. To make this goodness-of-fit estimate, the highest level of semantic memory, the schema level, is called into play.

To interpret an utterance, then, the listener is required to make use of all three aspects of semantic memory, no easy task, especially for language-disordered children who may be experiencing difficulty in several ways. First, they may not be able to access any appropriate concepts corresponding to the phonemic or morphemic components of the utterance they have heard. Or, they may not have constructed concepts that allow for matching with the individual words they have heard in the utterance, resulting in a misinterpretation of a different type. At a deeper, i.e., higher, level of analysis, if the language disorder involves difficulty at the propositional level of semantic memory, these children are relatively unable to interpret the basic propositional relations between the concepts represented by the utterance. Thus, basic predicate-argument relations either go unrecognized or misunderstood. Finally, if these children are unable to utilize schemata at the schema level of semantic memory in order to make a contextually based interpretation of the utterance, they will be unable to disambiguate potentially ambiguous utterances, or they will not recognize humor, for instance, or devices such as metaphor, simile, analogy, and so on. Not recognizing the contextual cues signaling the use of humor or these other devices, children who show breakdowns with the pragmatic aspects of communication interpret utterances as if they are following explicitly the conversational rules for communicating. These children are unable to interpret violations of these rules, because interpreting violations involves utilizing schemata which represent *both* the rules and their violations. Schemata representing violations of conversational rules most likely are examples of metalinguistic processing in that they are not linguistic rules as such but, rather, rules about particular types of linguistic structures.

In the narrower sense, problem solving can be described as a set of strategies for filling in missing information in order to achieve a desired end state or goal. These strategies are examples of schemata encoded at the schema level of semantic memory and are metacognitive in nature. That is, they are rules about thinking. In addition, however, to the utilization of schemata at the schema level of processing, problem solving in the narrow sense also requires manipulation of information at the lower two levels of semantic memory. In other words, the problem-solving strategies encoded at the schema level include information for how to retrieve information at the lower levels and, more specifically, which particular bits of information would be best to retrieve given the problem at hand. The solving of a problem which is formally presented as a problem requires the use of semantic memory at all three levels, with the schemata operating as guides directing the utilization of the other two levels. To be successful given a problem, children must call into play a set of procedures for how to go about moving from the knowns to the unknown. These procedures involve the use of specific bits of information at the propositional and concept level of semantic memory. As pointed out earlier, there is likely to be a myriad of possible procedures leading to the solution of a given problem. To be efficient, problem solvers must use what have been termed throughout the psychology literature *heuristic methods* for finding the tiny fraction of operations needed to solve a problem.

Wickelgren (1979) has divided problem-solving heuristics into two general sorts: search reduction methods and representation methods. Search reduction methods are ways of pruning the large number of possible solution sequences in clever ways, and they include four approaches. The first is learning to recognize equivalent operations and sequences to avoid going in circles, repeating equivalent steps over and over. This means recognizing that many different sequences may lead to the same point and choosing one out of the many possible sequences for pursuit. The second search reduction method is that of state evaluation, which Wickelgren argues is perhaps the most frequently used problem-solving method. State evaluation involves beginning from the state one is in, the given state of the problem, followed by an evaluation of the alternative states you could reach in one step by performing different operations. What this means is that you are essentially measuring how similar each alternative state is to the goal state. Next you choose to perform an operation that brings you closer to the goal, a choice that is based on the dimensions used to evaluate the similarity of each state to the goal state. The third search reduction method cited by Wickelgren is that of working backward, or beginning at the goal and working back toward the given. Wickelgren emphasizes that for most problems, working *forward* is the best, but in problems for which the goal has more information than the givens, or when allowable operations are reversible, working backward may be the best approach. The fourth search reduction approach is that of defining subgoals that break the problem into more manageable components, a powerful search reduction method according to Wickelgren because each subproblem is much simpler to solve than the original whole problem.

The second major approach to problem solving discussed by Wickelgren is re-presentation, which takes several forms in problem solving. Re-presentation involves reformulating the problem in alternative ways in an attempt to gain a richer understanding of it. Re-presenting may take the form of contradiction, for instance, by which the problem solver constructs a number of possible solutions and contradicts each until arriving at the solution. Contradiction is powerful with problems with a small set of alternatives, such as a multiple-choice problem. Higher order chunking is another way of re-presenting a problem by rearranging the components of the problem in the most general way possible. Using analogy re-presents a problem through dis-covering similarities between the current problem and problems solved before.

Two points about problem solving and children with language disorders need to be made here. The first is that the methods by which children go about solving problems change as the children develop cognitively; their thinking reorganizes several times during childhood, resulting in their approaching the same problems in quite different ways at different times in their lives (see Chapter 2). The problem-solving strategies that have been described most often in the psychology literature are ones that have been gleaned from studying adult problem solvers, people who have achieved formal operational ways of approaching problems. Children are not expected to be able to bring formal operational methods to problem solving until the upper elementary years of their schooling, although this does not mean that children are incapable of solving problems before that time. They most certainly are, but their problem-solving strategies are not characteristic of the formal operational thinker.

The second point to be made is that children with language disorders are not necessarily or by definition limited in their abilities to solve problems. However, because most of the problems they encounter in school are presented verbally, they are relatively inefficient at manipulating linguistic structures and the pragmatic constraints surrounding the use of linguistic forms. Each child, particularly each child exhibiting a language disorder, has spent a lifetime constructing a highly unique set of concepts, propositions, and schemata. Too, each child has developed a particular way of gaining access to these components of semantic memory and of retrieving the information coded there. Because there is so little research available on the relationship between language disorders and problem solving, clinicians must be particularly astute when attempting to assess how language-disordered children approach problems. It is to these assessment considerations that we now shift our attention.

ASSESSMENT CONSIDERATIONS

Assessing children's problem-solving strategies is no easy task. In fact, a measure of the difficulty in such assessment is that there are no standardized instruments designed specifically to assess problem solving in children. Some of the reasons why this is the case are obvious from the preceding discussions. The most apparent is that children's problem-solving strategies change and develop as their thinking changes and reorganizes throughout their development. Another, perhaps not so obvious, reason why assessing problem solving in children is fraught with difficulty is that there is no consensus about exactly (or even not so exactly) what constitutes the structures used for problem solving. We can theorize that a particular model of information-coding structures, e.g., the semantic memory model, provides a reasonable explanation of the structures used in problem solving, but such models provide only the first step in becoming knowledgeable about problem solving in children. As discussed in the previous chapter, it seems quite clear that it is necessary for practitioners to understand the models they use, especially through the study of such models in relation to children as they are confronted with problems.

There are some standardized instruments available that can be viewed as presenting problems that children are asked to solve. However, even the Weschsler scales yield measures of the end result of problem solving, i.e., whether the child achieves some correct goal. None allow for measurement, even indirect, of the actual processes children use in problem solving. A further complication is that the instruments commonly used by speech-language clinicians and teachers to assess language function provide information about children's language functioning only at the first two levels of semantic memory. The bulk of the information is about children's knowledge about the concept level of semantic memory. Only very recently have there been in the literature descriptions of methods for determining how children organize and represent what they know about the pragmatics of communication, but there still exist no standard ways of describing that knowledge. What this means is that clinicians must spend more time and creativity to discover what they need to know about the children with whom they work in order to design instructional and/or remedial techniques emphasizing the pragmatics of communicating.

The discussion in the preceding sections suggests several directions that might be taken in our fledgling attempts to discover more about problem solving in children. The approaches described below represent an attempt to gather in one place some of the "bits and pieces" we can use to discover more about how children go about the tasks involved in understanding problems and solving them. In discussing these approaches an effort has been made to describe how they fit into the information presented thus far.

Developmental Observation

At the present time, the best approach to discovering how any given child approaches problem solving is through observing what that child does when presented with problems of various sorts, constructed carefully so that the child's developmental stage is considered. In other words, in constructing problems for presentation to a particular child, the clinician or teacher first needs to have made some estimate, preferably based on observational evidence, of that child's level of thinking. The Piagetian model described earlier provides a structural framework within which to make such estimates. Once the child's level of thinking has been estimated, problems appropriate to that level can be constructed for presentation and subsequent observation.

Another consideration of major importance in attempting to observe children's problem-solving strategies is their knowledge and use of language structures and their knowledge and facility in using the pragmatic constraints that influence the use of those structures. In other words, the teacher or clinician must also have made a careful study of the child's language and communication functioning in order to choose problems for presentation that are within the child's linguistic and communicative functioning. In either case, the linguistic and communicative load of each problem must be analyzed carefully in order to estimate its impact on the child's problem-solving processes. This point is also made in Chapter 1.

The following examples illustrate representative problems and guidelines for observation appropriate for three different stages of development in thinking: the preoperational, concrete operational, and formal operational stages. Many of the problems are based on descriptions given by Copeland (1979).

PREOPERATIONAL CHILDREN

Problems yielding the richest observational information for preoperational children include classifying, ordering, one-to-one correspondence, conservation, and understanding of connectives. One example will be described for each as a model for others you may devise.

Classifying. Because preoperational children do not yet classify hierarchically, classifying tasks allow the clinician or teacher to discover on what basis or bases the child does classify. Find or construct a set of objects or pictures such as the following: four ducks, one chicken, and one robin. Be sure the child knows the names of each type. Ask the child if there are more ducks or more birds. Be sure the child knows *bird* as a vocabulary item. Preoperational children will respond that there are more ducks.

Ordering. Find or construct a set of six sticks, graduated in length from shortest to longest. Ask the child to arrange them in order from shortest (or smallest, whichever concept the child prefers) to longest. Preoperational children will either arrange the sticks so that one end is graduated with disregard for the other end, as in Figure 10.5, or they will find the shortest stick and compare each of the remaining sticks to the

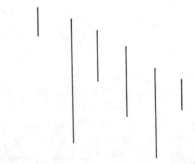

Figure 10.5. Example of preoperational ordering.

shortest, then to the next one discovered to be longer, and so on until all the sticks are arranged in order. Figure 10.5 illustrates how a preoperational child might order the sticks.

One-to-one Correspondence. Find or construct two sets of objects or pictures, one set having one more member than the other. Arrange the sets as in Figure 10.6. Ask the child which set has more members. The preoperational child will insist that the set which is spread out has more members even though it has less.

Conservation. Because preoperational children are so attracted to the perceptual characteristics of things in the world, the conservation problem is a quick index into the type of thinking they are using to solve the problem. Materials include two identical jars, two additional jars of quite different dimensions (e.g., one tall and thin, the other short and squat), and water. (Note: children become able to conserve other types of dimensions at a later stage than when they can conserve water; see p. 217). Have the child fill the identical jars with equal amounts of water until satisfied each contains the same amount. Then have the child pour the water from one jar into the tall, thin jar, and the water from the other jar into the short, squat jar. Ask which has more water. Preoperational children will answer that one or the other has more. They do not yet mentally reverse the process to understand that the water is identical to that poured from the originally equal jars.

Figure 10.6.   One-to-one correspondence.

Understanding of Connectives: Because, Therefore, Then. *Because* implies a relation of cause and effect between two events or phenomena, e.g., "He fell off his bike because he hit a log"; a relation of implication, e.g., "The woman must be going to work because she is carrying her lunch"; or a psychological relation between an action and an intention, e.g., "I slapped Bill because he was laughing at me." Because preoperational children utilize the psychological *because* almost exclusively (Piaget, 1976), it is possible to construct a set of questions to differentiate among the three types. The child's responses can be analyzed according to types. Examples of questions are: "Why does wood float?" (a causal question to which preoperational children frequently give psychological or illogical responses such as "Because it's big."); "Why is it a planet and not a star?" (a logical question to which the preoperational child frequently responds illogically, such as, "Because it's far away."); "Why did you do that?" (a psychological question to which the preoperational child is likely to respond appropriately). Wallach presents additional information on syntactic hierarchies for *because* sentences in Chapter 5.

Therefore is the inverse of *because*; *because* relates cause to effect or reason to logical consequence, whereas *therefore* relates effect to cause or logical consequence

to reason. *Therefore* requires a deduction, which the preoperational child is largely unable to perform. When asked to fill in the blank to the following sentence, the preoperational child responds illogically; "The grass is wet; therefore _____ (it is raining)." The preoperational child may respond with "I will get wet," which shows a cause-effect type of problem solving rather than a logical deduction strategy.

Then is used for a variety of purposes, including to indicate time ("What time will it be then?"), for psychological indication ("What would you like to do then?"), and in the logical *if ... then* constructions ("If the windows are frosty, then it must be cold"). Preoperational children can respond appropriately to the psychological indication question, but they are unable to understand the use of *then* to indicate time. When asked to fill in the missing parts of the following statement, they infrequently use *then*: "If the dog is outside, _____ Dad must be home." The preoperational child's problem-solving strategies can be seen as searches for causes and effects at the perceptual and/or psychological level.

CONCRETE OPERATIONAL CHILDREN

Because concrete operational children have developed thinking constructs about reversibility, transitivity, and identity, they become able to solve problems in quite a different fashion from preoperational children. Too, because concrete operational thinking is characterized by an ability to mentally manipulate information, frequently in a symbolic manner, they are free from reliance on the perceptual characteristics of the materials used in problem-solving tasks. Copeland (1979) summarizes the developments of the concrete operational period of thinking as the putting of objects together to form a class, separating a collection into subclasses, ordering elements in some way, ordering events in time, and so on. One of the easiest ways to gather information about problem solving in children believed to engage in concrete operational thinking is to present them with the same problems described for the preoperational children.

Classifying. Concrete operational children typically classify hierarchically, understanding the class inclusion relation, which means that there exist classes within classes within classes, and so on. Thus, when presented with sets of cards or pictures such as those described in the classification task for preoperational children, concrete operational children understand that there are more birds even though the ducks outnumber the other examples of birds. Too, these children understand reversibility by negation, responding correctly when asked "If all birds died, would there be any ducks left?" and "If all the ducks died, would there be any birds left?"

Ordering. Concrete operational children easily order graduated sticks from shortest to longest, without any trial and error or one-by-one matching to compare the remaining sticks with the previously ordered ones. Children who are concrete operational can also classify more than two sets at once, a feat not accomplished by preoperational children. For instance, find or construct two sets of pictures, e.g., one a set of brown-haired boys and the other of blond-haired boys. Ask the child to classify them into two sets and to tell on what basis they were grouped as they were. Concrete operational children will be able to describe the defining and overlapping features of the two sets.

One-to-one Correspondence. Because concrete operational children are able to decenter, that is, focus attention on features of a process or array of materials other than the most salient perceptual characteristics, they realize that the physical appearance of an array of materials is not the determining factor in deciding whether it contains more members than another set. When presented with the flowers and umbrellas problem described above, concrete operational children understand immediately which one of the two sets has more items, even though one of the sets is spread out to look larger.

Conservation. Concrete operational children are able to understand the reversibility of processes (transitivity); thus, they are able to recognize that the water in the conservation task is equal as long as the two originally equal amounts are kept separate. It should be remembered, however, that there are various types of conservation, and children do not become able to conserve all types at once. They usually occur in order, beginning with number, followed by quantity and weight, and ending with volume at age 10 or 11.

Understanding of Connectives. Because is used and understood by concrete operational children in both its psychological and causal meanings. However, understanding *because* in its logical sense does not typically occur during this stage of development of thinking.

Therefore, because it requires an underlying logical justification, a deduction, is frequently misunderstood by concrete operational children. It is not until children are 11 or 12 years old that they can consider a formal proof of the sort implied by the use of *therefore.*

Then is understood by concrete operational children in its uses to indicate time and to indicate a psychological preference. As in the use of *because* in its logical sense, *then* as a logical term in the *if ... then* deductive sense is not completely understood until the children are in the next stage of development.

The problem-solving strategies used by concrete operational children are characterized by mental, symbolic manipulation of the components of the problem. However, these children still rely heavily on the physical presence of objects and events in their approaches to problem solving.

FORMAL OPERATIONAL CHILDREN

Development into the formal operational stage of thinking marks the emergence of many strategies that underlie much of what is characterized as adult thinking, including strategies for problem solving based on hypothetico-deductive methods. To discover how a formal operational child is thinking and approaching problems is a fascinating process. Formal operational children can reason with symbols or ideas; they no longer need to depend on objects to manipulate as a basis for thinking. The problems described here are designed to illustrate the problem-solving capacities of formal operational children.

Classifying. The formal operational child can classify according to several different relationships between classes, including conjunction, disjunction, and intersection, resulting in problem-solving processes such as logical means-ends analysis and representation in hypothetical form.

Conjunction. Make or find pictures of objects sharing three, four, or even five common attributes. Ask the child to classify according to the appropriate number of classes and to describe the bases upon which the sorting was done. Formal operational children can do this easily.

Disjunction. Make or find pictures of objects which share some common features. Then ask the child to find cards which are neither X nor Y, X and Y being two features not indicated in this set. For instance, if the cards show people, animals, trains, mountains, and cityscapes, ask for cards that show neither mammals nor planets.

Intersection. Make or find cards sharing some attributes in common, but not all. Ask the child to find the pictures indicating two or more common features. For instance, if the pictures are of an airport, a city park, a freighter on the ocean, and a city hall, ask for a picture of commerce and transportation.

The Pendulum Problem. Formal operational children approach the pendulum problem described on page 203 in a logical fashion, forming hypotheses about possible solutions and testing each in systematic fashion until the solution is discovered. Their problem solving does not exhibit any trial and error strategies; rather, they employ logical deductions of the sort: "If I put a weight on the string, then maybe that will cause it to swing faster"; or "When I shortened the string, regardless of the number or total weight of the weights, that caused the pendulum to swing faster; therefore, shortening the string is the solution."

Transitivity. Although concrete operational children understand some types of transitivity problems, it is not until they reach the formal operational stage that children can solve transitivity involving hierarchical classification. The following problem exemplifies this process, which is that if A includes B, and B includes C, then logically A includes C. The child is shown three sets of cards, for example, four yellow roses, four roses of other colors, and eight other flowers. Then the child is asked if there are more yellow flowers than roses *and* if there are more flowers than roses. While few children between 7 and 9 years old respond appropriately to these questions, 73% of 9- and 10-year-olds responded appropriately (Inhelder and Piaget, 1969), indicating that they understood the transitivity within hierarchical classification relations.

Intersection of Sets. Intersection of sets is a special case of conjunction and can involve sets that intersect on the basis of one or more attributes. For instance, given two sets of geometric forms, a red set composed of circles, squares, and triangles, and a blue set composed of triangles, the red triangles can be said to compose a third set intersecting the other two. Figure 10.7 illustrates this principle.

A similar intersection problem (which was described on p. 205) includes two sets, one a set of green-colored objects and the other a set of various-colored leaves, with a blank space where the two sets intersect. In each of these two types of problems, the child can be asked to fill in the members of the "parent" sets to make a third, intersecting set. Formal operational children respond easily, as they understand the concept of intersection.

Disjunction. Similar in principle to conjunction, yet different in underlying logic, disjunction requires the problem solver to discover which members of two sets are either X or Y in order to make a third set. For instance, given a set of geometric forms, the child is asked to construct a set which is composed of all forms that are red or triangles. Again, formal operational thinkers can solve this problem handily.

Negation. Given a proposition of the type "What causes fish to bite?" formal operational children can systematically eliminate probable causes through negation, such as, "It is neither smell nor color that causes them to bite." This problem-

solving strategy will be recognized as an example of re-presentation of the problem by contradicting each of a set of possible solutions until arriving at the correct outcome.

Implication. In similar fashion, given the same proposition, "What causes fish to bite?" children who have developed into formal operational thinkers can use implication to eliminate possibilities, e.g., "If it is not color, then it must be smell."

Understanding of Connectives. By the time a child has developed into a formal operational thinker, understanding the connectives described above is complete. These children comprehend the logical relations implied by all three types of connectives, *because*, *therefore*, and *then*, because their thinking at this stage is characterized by deducing, which underlies the understanding of these forms.

A quite different approach for observing problem solving in children is indirectly suggested by Nickerson et al., who discuss specific identifiable ways in which thinking goes astray. Using their list, it is possible to observe children as they go about solving problems in order to identify what types of confusions or misunderstandings are typical of their attempts to solve problems. It must be kept in mind, however, that the topics presented by these authors are specific to logical thinking; thus, this approach would be useful only for observing children believed to be able to engage in formal operational thinking in their problem solving. What is included here is merely a listing of the "common thinking deficiencies" as the authors call them (p. 117); the authors provide more complete discussion of each. Their list is as follows:

1. Confusion of empirical truth with logical validity.

2. Misusing syllogistic forms in common ways.

3. Assigning different meanings to the same term when it appears in different places throughout the argument.

4. Illogically modifying the argument.

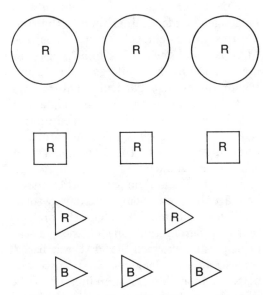

Figure 10.7. Intersection of sets. *R*, red; *B*, blue.

5. Taking alogical strategies or positions in an argument.

6. Persisting with a hypothesis when it is counterproductive.

7. Failing to view one's own opinions objectively.

8. Accepting a hypothesis on the basis of inconclusive evidence.

9. Uncritically accepting social convention as evidence of logical thinking.

10. Gathering information beyond that which is necessary or affordable.

11. Resorting to the ego as logical arguments.

12. Ineffectively applying negative information, i.e., noninstances.

13. Using intuitive statistics.

14. Failing to extract usable information from probability data.

15. Being partial or having a vested interest in the outcome.

16. Rationalizing choices made after the fact.

17. Confusing strength of opinion with its factuality.

18. Allowing one's biases to guide which information to seek in confirming or disconfirming a hypothesis.

19. Overestimating one's own knowledge about a given topic.

Nickerson et al. (p. 117) argue that, "if common thinking deficiencies can be identified, then it makes sense to consider whether training techniques might be developed for the express purpose of correcting those deficiencies." They are arguing, then, that if problem solving suffers from one or more of the "deficiencies" listed above, it is possible to teach people to correct these deficiencies. In the context of the present chapter, it may be more fruitful to view the authors' list as a guide to observing what types of thinking fallacies or deviations from the logical a particular child typically employs in approaching problem solving. In this way, a clinician or teacher will be better able to intervene with instructional materials and plans to aid the child in developing more effective problem-solving strategies.

The Muma Assessment Program

Although directed observation yields rich and valuable information regarding a particular child's problem-solving strategies, determining what one has after having observed is often a difficult and arduous task. Having published materials is a great help to the teacher or clinician in today's school. The Muma Assessment Program (MAP) has been published to fill just such a gap in our present materials. It should be emphasized that the MAP is *not* a test, nor is it a standardized battery. Rather, it is a set of materials and guidelines designed to assist the teacher or clinician in determining how children go about using their cognitive-linguistic-communicative systems and processes (Muma, 1979). Although the MAP was not designed specifically to assess problem-solving strategies, the cognitive component of the program lends itself quite nicely to such an assessment. This is because Muma's intent in publishing the MAP was to focus the clinician's attention on the *processes* children employ rather than on the *status* of their disorders. It also brings attention to the very expectable individual differences found in children with language disorders rather than to the similarities within clinical groups. Thus, the MAP is a tool one can use to help discover how each individual child goes about solving problems of a particular nature. Because it is based on the basic principle that individual children have developed unique strategies for thinking, the MAP provides no normative data for comparison of a child against a standardization group. The teacher or clinician can use the MAP to see how a child goes about thinking to solve problems. Muma points out in the preface to the program that one of the general principles upon which the MAP was based consists of two elements. First, there are patterns in children's thinking, which is what the program attempts to assess; however, second, those patterns are not truly patterns unless they exceed chance. That is, a particular behavior or cluster of behaviors must not be regarded as a pattern until it is used enough times that it can be seen to exceed chance.

The cognitive component of the MAP is comprised of six parts:

1. Perceptual salience, which attempts to ascertain which of several perceptual domains is favored by a child confronted with an assortment, including color, shape, and size.

2. Iconic/symbolic processing modes attempts to determine whether a child refers to group pictures on the basis of iconic processing—visual imagery according to shape and color—or on the basis of symbolic function—the functional properties of things.

3. Rule/nonrule-governed learning is a method for finding out whether a child is adept at extracting rules given a problem of choosing the "right" dimension from a picture on a card. In addition, it is possible to use this subcomponent to discover which of two types of·rules a child prefers to use in solving this particular problem.

4. Technology of reckoning includes a set of cards on which are pictures of objects representing different arrays of attributes, including color, size, shape (static attributes), and agent-action displays, such as running, etc. (dynamic attributes). The purpose is to discover how many attributes a child can deal with at once, up to three-attribute clusters for static attributes and two agent-action attributes for dynamic attributes.

5. Part/whole and alternatives is an attempt to determine an individual child's cognitive style of thinking, e.g., whether a child prefers convergent (synthetic) thinking or divergent (analytic) thinking.

6. Cognitive tempo refers to another aspect of an individual's cognitive style in that it is an attempt to observe the child's rate and accuracy of information processing.

The utility of using the MAP to observe a child's problem-solving strategies is that it provides an opportunity to observe patterns of thinking within a set of six cognitive factors believed to be operating in a child's solving of problems. The MAP allows one to gather descriptive information about a child's cognitive processing in order to structure instructional materials and techniques suitable for each individual child, a process that is frequently the most difficult in the clinical arena.

Protocol Analysis

Perhaps the best known examples of protocol analysis come from the work of Piaget. The techniques used by Piaget and his colleagues involved presenting the child with certain materials and/or questions, probing for the child's understanding of a particular principle or concept. Such observations were recorded and analyzed at a later time in order to discover exactly what the child understood. Examples of the probing question and protocol analysis technique can be found in Piaget (1969) and in Ginsburg and Opper (1979), who describe these techniques in more detail.

An example of protocol analysis specifically geared to children's cognitive structures related to problem solving is provided by Easley (1979), who describes how protocol analysis can be used to yield information regarding the structures underlying children's cognitive structures.

Curriculum Analysis

As children move through the grades in most school curricula, the problem-solving and language demands increase, sometimes rather dramatically. Children are expected to develop academic competence and to acquire skills specific to certain aspects of the curriculum. In addition, children are expected to learn a large volume of content information, especially at the upper elementary grades. One way in which the teacher or clinician can determine how an individual child, for instance, a language-disordered child, is faring in problem solving is to analyze the curriculum carefully to identify those aspects which may be causing breakdowns and to begin to plan for remedial approaches. Nelson (Chapter 8) described a number of factors relating to the language of teachers and the language of curricula.

INSTRUCTIONAL CONSIDERATIONS

Any instructional methods designed to teach problem solving or to enhance the development of thinking skills must be constructed to match each individual child's level of development in thinking. The purpose of this section is to present for discussion topics of importance to those who are attempting to construct instructional programs for teaching effective problem solving. In addition, specific reference will be made throughout the discussion to the special needs of children with language disorders.

Simon (1980) makes a distinction that is relevant to the present discussion about problem solving. He asserts that there is a clear and important difference between the acquisition of knowledge *about* things (declarative knowledge, or knowing a set of facts about something) and the acquisition of the skills necessary to manipulate that knowledge (procedural knowledge, or knowing strategies for understanding one's declarative knowledge). Although the two types of knowledge, declarative and procedural, are different in an important way, they are also interdependent in that one cannot exist without the other. In other words, it is not possible to know how to ride a bicycle (procedural knowledge) without knowledge of what a bicycle is, what it is used for, what it looks like, the major parts, etc. Conversely, without procedural knowledge of bicycling, it is not possible to know how it feels to have the wind streaming past one's face with legs pumping fast, moving along a road lined with sweet-smelling pines, the road ahead and behind filled with cyclists. This latter declarative knowledge is impossible to know without the corresponding procedural knowledge. The

point as it relates to problem solving is that it is impossible to learn how to solve problems without rich knowledge of content to manipulate, nor is it possible to know how to solve math problems, for instance, without some procedural knowledge for solving problems. As mentioned earlier, Larkin (1980) makes this point clear when she argues that general problem-solving strategies probably cannot be implemented without a considerable amount of domain-specific knowledge. What this means for clinicians and teachers is that problem solving will best be thought of as something to teach within the context of a variety of content areas. Providing children with appropriate problems to solve in several different domains is likely to be a more successful method than trying to isolate problem solving from content. The more familiar children are with specific domains of knowledge, the better able they will be to manipulate that declarative knowledge once they have begun to develop procedural skills for solving problems involving that domain. With these introductory cautions as a basis, the next section focuses on some instructional considerations involving general problem-solving skills.

Components of Problem Solving

Descriptions of the basic components of problems and problem solving were given in the first section of this chapter. Generally, problems were seen as comprised of given information, a desired goal state (usually unknown), and operations allowable for use in attempts to achieve that end state. Problem solving was described as a set of schemata that engage in both top-down and bottom-up processing of information in some rather specific ways, including means-ends analysis, re-presenting the problem, and breaking the problem into subgoals for easier solution. Because these latter problem-solving strategies and additional ones seem to apply across a wide variety of problem types and across the developmental stages of thinking, they warrant further discussion.

Means-ends analysis was described earlier as an assessment of the difference between what one currently knows about the problem and the state of knowledge required for its solution (Larkin, 1980). For the preoperational child, such analysis might take the form of trial and error matching in the case of a serial ordering task, or of pouring the water in the conservation task back into the original jars in an attempt to solve the problem. Physical manipulation of objects for the preoperational child is a powerful tool in acquiring the knowledge necessary to solve problems. For the concrete operational child, opportunities to verbally (or symbolically in other than verbal form, perhaps in mathematical notation) state the problem and knowledge necessary to achieve a solution are critical in developing the skills necessary to solve problems. The formal operational child can achieve means-ends analysis through the use of logical inferential statements in verbal or more abstract symbolization (e.g., algebraic notation). Hence, learning of abstract notation is of considerable help to a child who is capable of formal operational thinking.

Re-presentation of the problem is a means for restating the components of the problems in at least one other form in order to discover any similarities to other, previously solved problems. It also allows one to gain insight into the solution because barriers or obstacles present in the original formulation have been removed through the re-presentation. The most obvious way of re-presenting is to paraphrase, using one's own words, a strategy useful for children at all developmental stages of thinking. Another way of re-presenting is to draw pictures to stand for components of the problem. This method is particularly useful when children are given classification problems. Members of sets can be drawn into circles representing each set, so that the relationships between sets are depicted visually. For concrete operational children, math problems can be re-presented using mathematical notation, for instance, reformulating an addition or multiplication problem by actually setting it up on paper. Formal operational children can utilize more advanced notation, such as algebraic symbols, to re-present. This problem-solving method has particular utility for children with language disorders because it allows for a restatement of problems in other than linguistic forms, thus removing one of the barriers these children face in attempting to solve problems.

Breaking the problem into subgoals can be taught as a series of steps toward the overall solution. Once the child has discovered what it is that must be known in order to solve the problem, the teacher or clinician can help the child state (verbally or otherwise) in step fashion exactly what must be done to get to the solution; the child can then solve each step in order, thus arriving at the overall solution through having solved successive subgoals (see Chapter 14). For the preoperational child, problems are typically single step in nature and need no further analysis into subcomponents. Nelson (Chapter 8) showed how the curriculum at the kindergarten and first-grade levels typically requires children to do a series of discrete, one-step problems rather than problems requiring a set of steps for solution. Children are frequently asked to do several related things at once, but each component is usually complete in itself as an individual problem.

For the concrete operational child, setting problems into subgoals may involve providing a piece of paper with the problem stated at the top in original and re-presented forms, followed by a set of numbers down the page corresponding to the number of steps required to achieve an overall solution. The math story problem in Figure 10.8 is used as an example.

Analysis into subgoals is an easy, although not always obvious, task for formal operational thinkers. The trick is usually figuring out what the problem *is* first; once the problem has been formulated, analysis into subgoals becomes a much easier task.

If Jane can paint a room in 2 hours and Sam can paint the same room in 4 hours, how long will it take them to paint the room together?

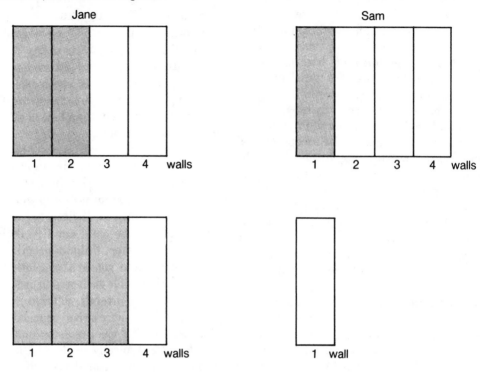

1. Count up how many walls are finished at the end of the hour. (3)
2. How many walls are left? (1)
3. How many walls were painted out of how many total walls? (3/4)
4. Each wall takes how much of an hour to paint? (1/3)
5. The remaining wall will take how long to paint? (1/3)

Figure 10.8. Re-presenting the problem.

Problem-solving Heuristics

In addition to the general problem-solving strategies described above, other authors have postulated a set of heuristics, or methods of inductive reasoning, to assist in solving problems. The heuristics described by Polya (cited in Nickerson et al.) appear to have the most applicability for the purpose of the present discussion and will be presented here in more detail. Generally, Polya distinguishes four stages of problem solving, with associated heuristics for each stage. The four stages and their corresponding heuristics are:

1. Heuristics for understanding or re-presenting the problem
   a. Make sure you understand what is not known, what is given, and how the givens are related.
   b. Draw a graph if possible and represent in suitable notation if possible.
2. Heuristics for designing a plan, or general strategy
   a. Try to think of an analogous problem and solve that.
   b. Try to think of a similar, known problem with the same kind of unknown but which is simpler.
   c. Transform the problem into one whose solution you know.
   d. Look at special cases of the problem to simplify it.
   e. See if you can translate the prob-

lem into a more general one and solve that.

   f. Break the problem into smaller parts until they are manageable.

3. Heuristics for executing a plan (the deductive stage for formal operational thinkers)

   a. Check each step.

4. Heuristics for checking results

   a. Try to solve the problem differently.

   b. Check the implications of the solution.

While the heuristics described here are thought to be useful in approaching the solving of problems, there is not at this time clear-cut evidence that students can always benefit from being taught such methods. For instance, Nickerson et al. point out that it may quite possibly be useless to teach heuristics to people without extensive familiarity with the relevant content area, a point mentioned above. In addition, these same authors argue that students can know both the content area and a set of heuristics without being able to select an appropriate heuristic for any given problem, or they may be unable to apply a given heuristic in detail to a specific problem. Thus, clinicians and teachers cannot expect heuristic approaches to generalize automatically, nor can they expect children to be able to utilize such strategies without adequate knowledge at the declarative level. In addition, it should be kept in mind that language-disordered children will require special modification of the heuristics mentioned above.

Programs for Teaching Problem Solving

Nickerson et al. describe in considerable detail two published programs designed to teach problem-solving skills: deBono's CoRT program (1967, 1968) and the Productive Thinking Program (Covington et al., 1974). In each of the programs, attention is given to providing methods for teaching a considerable range of skills related to thinking and problem solving. Nickerson et al. present an extensive description of each, including the components of thinking and problem solving purported to be taught in each program, an assessment of how well each does what it claims to do, and results of research done regarding the effectiveness of each of the two programs. In general, Nickerson et al. conclude that deBono's CoRT program does seem to lead students "...to take a usefully broader view of problem situations when they are formally posed; whether some of the additional ideas suffer from the problem of quality/quantity tradeoff remains to be determined" (p. 207). What this means is that there is some evidence that the CoRT program leads students to attempt to generate a large number of alternate paths to solution, thus sacrificing quality of solution path for sheer quantity.

Regarding the Productive Thinking Program, Nickerson et al. remark that it is a self-instructional program for fifth and sixth graders and includes some tasks which require divergent tasks with the majority of tasks involving problems with unique answers. The program emphasizes skills involving analysis and inference. The authors conclude that the Productive Thinking Program does seem to "...enhance fluency in the context of problems that resemble its contents, but not particularly otherwise" (p. 232). In other words, there is not much transfer to problems in other contexts.

Games to Teach Problem Solving

Copeland (1979) has described several types of activities in game form for use in assisting children develop both content knowledge and problem-solving strategies. The activities are designed to develop content knowledge about logical classification, logical connectives, and logical relations and are appropriate to late concrete operational and early formal operational children.

Logical classification games are described by Copeland (1979) as providing opportunities for the child to gain operational experience in classifying as a precursor to the development of the logical thought necessary for problem solving. Two of the games are the one- (or two-) property difference game and the intersection game. In the one- (or two-) property difference game, the materials needed are a set of blocks of different shapes, sizes, colors, and thickness, as shown in Figure 10.9.

In the one-property difference game, each child in a group is asked to pick out a block having one property different from the previously chosen block. In the two-property difference game version, the child is asked to pick a block having two properties different from the previously chosen one. Both these games can be done either in a group or with the child and teacher or clinician.

In the intersection game, the teacher constructs a series of cards having three members of a class showing and one space blank. From a set of possible choices, the child is asked to pick out a block to go into the slot, as illustrated in Figure 10.10.

The *logical connective games* are constructed to illustrate conjunction, disjunction, implication, and negation. The games can be constructed either by using real objects, pictures (or drawings of objects), or symbols for objects and relations. The latter is most effective with early formal operational thinkers. When using real objects or pictures, the teacher or clinician needs hula hoops or loops of rope (for real objects) or drawings of circles depicting various relationships and sets of blocks (for real objects) showing a variety of relationships such as color, size, and shape.

The simplest form of conjunction involves asking the child to pick all the blocks that are red *and* square. A more complex form of conjunction asks the child to put all the red blocks in one circle and all the triangles in the other. The child is then asked what to do about red triangles. An

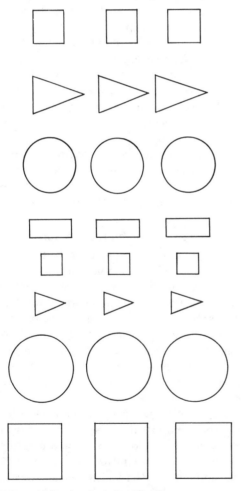

Figure 10.9.   Logical classification.

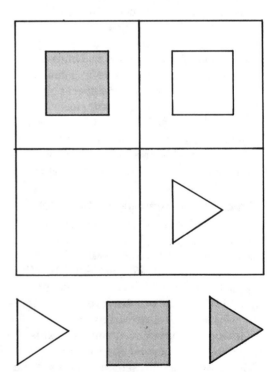

Figure 10.10.   Intersection of sets.

intersecting set is shown in Figure 10.11. An even more complex form of intersection involves three sets, as shown in Figure 10.12.

Disjunction involves the child placing in the circles all the blocks that are red *or* triangles, resulting in a larger set than is the case with conjunction/intersection.

In negation, the child is asked to place in the circles all blocks that are not red, for instance.

Implication requires the child to make a logical deduction to choose between two possibilities when told, for instance, "If it is not red, then it must be _____."

When logical symbols are used, Copeland suggests something along the following lines. Give the sets letter names, for example, the red set = R, square set = Sq, thick = th, thin = tn, conjunction = V, and

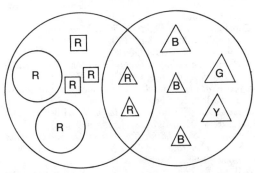

Figure 10.11.   Intersection of two sets. *R*, red; *B*, blue; *Y*, yellow; *G*, green.

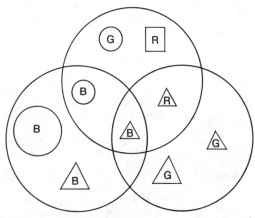

Figure 10.12.   Intersection of three sets. *R*, red; *B*, blue; *G*, green.

disjunction ("or") = ∧. Given that R ∧ Sq, for instance, have the child pick the appropriate block. Alternately, the child can be given block arrangements and asked to provide the appropriate symbolism.

It has been indicated throughout these pages that constant analysis and adjustment must be made for the language-disabled child when considering both content and skills required in problem-solving tasks. Such admonitions are general in that they ask the teacher or clinician to be on continuous alert to eliminate or circumvent possible stumbling blocks for the language-disordered child.

As emphasized throughout this text, adaptation and enhancement of the language components of the curriculum are necessary in order to assist the language-disordered child. Wiig and Semel (1980) have made suggestions regarding the syntactic-semantic components of reading. They state, "The structural complexity of *all* written materials presented for the language and learning disabled student to read should be adapted or reduced" (p. 418). We should be reminded, however, that shorter and simpler sentences are not always easier (see Chapters 1 and 12). Wiig and Semel also argue that "(t)he semantic content of all written sentences should be reduced or edited to reflect the child's current knowledge of word meanings, of linguistic concepts and relationships, and of figurative language" (p. 419). They provide specific ways in which the curriculum can be modified and enhanced for both the syntactic/structural and semantic aspects of language. In addition, Silliman (Chapter 14) presents specific ideas for modifying spoken language input. Although the suggestions made by Wiig and Semel, as well as by contributors in this text, are not necessarily geared to problem solving per se, the techniques can be integrated with the information presented here and translated directly to the problem-solving domains and strategies faced by language-disordered children in the schools.

SOME GUIDING PRINCIPLES

In this chapter we have attempted to bring together a diverse and occasionally complex body of information about problems, problem solving, the development of skills in problem solving, and some of the effects of language disorders on problem solving. As you are well aware at this point in your reading, the picture that has emerged is far from clear. The relationships among the constructs discussed here are not easy to delineate, let alone understand. However, there seem to be some general conclusions that can be drawn from what we know about problem solving (and, I would add, the development of thinking and language in children). These conclusions can be thought of as principles that should guide any teacher or clinician in attempts to train students, language disordered or not, in thinking, especially in problem solving. Nickerson et al. have drawn a similar set of conclusions from their exhaustive discussion of issues surrounding the development and teaching of thinking.

1. Ideas can be absorbed by people who are ready (developmentally and/or experientially) to absorb them.

2. Readiness seems to be genetically determined only to a certain extent; in part it is something that requires nurturing.

3. The more one knows about a domain, the easier it is to learn something new about it or to solve problems within that context.

4. The better children understand why they are being asked to learn something, the more readily they will learn it.

5. By making materials and methods meaningful from the child's point of view, the teacher or clinician can expect more effective learning on the part of the child.

6. All attempts at problem solving, including what are typically seen as "failures," yield valuable information and should be regarded by both the child and the teacher or clinician as important in the child's learning, i.e., learning what something is, or how to do something, often (always?) requires learning what it is not or how not to do it.

7. Any given problem-solving strategy or heuristic should be taught in a variety of problem contexts to assure greater probability of generalization to other domains.

CLOSING REMARKS

Who ever said that learning must be hard work all the time, or boring, or distasteful? And who ever said that humans do not or cannot learn through play, that is, through an enjoyment of the process of toying with alternative avenues toward solution of any kind of problem? Viewed in this general way, as a process of happily exploring various aspects of discovery, then, in an ideal sense, learning may be thought of as the process of playing one's way through life.

References

Anderson JR, Greeno JG, Kline PJ, et al: Acquisition of problem solving skill. In Anderson JR: *Cognitive Skills and Their Acquisition*. Hillsdale, NJ, Lawrence Erlbaum Associates, 1981, pp 19–230.

Copeland R: *How Children Learn Mathematics*, ed 3. New York, Macmillan, 1979.

Covington MV, Crutchfield RS, Davies L, et al: *The Productive Thinking Program: A Course in Learning to Think*. Columbus, OH, Charles E Merrill, 1974.

Cyert RM: Problem solving and educational policy. In Tuma DT, Reif F: *Problem Solving and Education: Issues in Teaching and Research*. Hillsdale, NJ, Lawrence Erlbaum Associates, 1980, pp 3–8.

deBono E: *New Think: The Use of Lateral Thinking in the Generation of New Ideas*. New York, Basic Books, 1968.

deBono E: *The Five-day Course in Thinking*. New York, Basic Books, 1967.

Easley JA Jr: The structural paradigm in protocol analysis. In Lockhead J, Clement J: *Cognitive Process Instruction*. Philadelphia, Franklin Institute Press, 1979.

Ginsburg H, Opper S: *Piaget's Theory of Intellectual Development*, ed 2. Englewood Cliffs, NJ, Prentice-Hall, 1979.

Hayes, JR: Teaching problem-solving mechanics. In Tuma DT, Reif F: *Problem Solving and Education: Issues in Teaching and Research*. Hillsdale, NJ, Lawrence Erlbaum Associates, 1980, pp 141–150.

Hubbell, RD: *Children's Language Disorders: An Integrated Approach*. Englewood Cliffs, NJ, Prentice-Hall, 1981.

Hymes DH: *Foundations in Sociolinguistics: An Ethnographic Approach*. Philadelphia, University of Pennsylvania Press, 1974.

Inhelder B, Piaget J: *The Early Growth of Logic in the Child*. New York, WW Norton, 1969.

Larkin JH: Teaching problem solving in physics: the psychological laboratory and the practical classroom. In Tuma DT, Reif F: *Problem Solving and Education: Issues in Teaching and Research*. Hillsdale, NJ, Lawrence Erlbaum Associates, 1980, pp 111–124.

Mayer, RE: *Thinking and Problem Solving: An Introduction to Human Cognition and Learning.* Glenview, IL, Scott, Foresman, 1977.

Miller L: Remediation of auditory language learning disorders. In Roeser RJ, Downs MP: *Auditory Disorders in Children.* New York, Thieme-Stratton, 1981.

Muma JR: *Muma Assessment Program.* Lubbock, TX, Natural Child Publishing, 1979.

Neves DM, Anderson JR: Knowledge compilation: mechanisms for the automatization of cognitive skills. In Anderson JR: *Cognitive Skills and Their Acquisition.* Hillsdale, NJ, Lawrence Erlbaum Associates, 1981, pp 57–84.

Newell A: One final word. In Tuma DT, Reif F: *Problem Solving and Education: Issues in Teaching and Research.* Hillsdale, NJ, Lawrence Erlbaum Associates, 1980, pp 175–189.

Nickerson RS, Perkins DN, Smith EE: *Teaching Thinking.* Undated manuscript.

Piaget J: *The Child's Conception of Time.* New York, Ballantine Books, 1969.

Piaget J: *The Grasp of Consciousness—Action and Concept in the Young Child.* Cambridge, MA, Harvard University Press, 1976.

Polya, G. *How to Solve It,* ed 2. New York, Doubleday, 1971.

Reitman WR: *Cognition and Thought.* New York, John Wiley & Sons, 1965.

Rosch EH: Cognitive reference points. *Cognitive Psychol* 7:532–547, 1975.

Rumelhart DE: Schemata: the building blocks of cognition. In Spiro RJ, Bruce BC, Brewer WF: *Theoretical Issues in Reading Comprehension.* Hillsdale, NJ, Lawrence Erlbaum Associates, 1980, pp 33–58.

Rumelhart DE, Norman, DA: Analogical processes in learning. In Anderson JR: *Cognitive Skills and Their Acquisition.* Hillsdale, NJ, Lawrence Erlbaum Associates, 1981, pp 335–359.

Scandura JA: *Problem Solving: A Structural/Process Approach with Instructional Applications.* New York, Academic Press, 1977.

Simon, HA: Problem solving and education. In Tuma DT, Reif F: *Problem Solving and Education: Issues in Teaching and Research.* Hillsdale, NJ, Lawrence Erlbaum Associates, 1980, pp 81–96.

Wickelgren WA: *Cognitive Psychology.* Englewood Cliffs, NJ, Prentice-Hall, 1979.

Wiig, E, Semel E: *Language Assessment and Intervention for the Learning Disabled.* Columbus, OH, Charles E Merrill, 1980.

CHAPTER ELEVEN

Word Knowledge and Word Retrieval: Phonological and Semantic Strategies

LEONARD ISRAEL, Ph.D.

"It has been suggested that the same deficit (or deficits) that interfere with the efficient retrieval of verbal labels also interferes with word-sound pattern retrieval during the acquisition of reading" (Bashir, 1973).

The ability to produce age-appropriate word definitions and word associations has received a great deal of attention. The study of an individual's capacity to use words efficiently may provide us with useful information about the selection and sequence of words in spoken and written sentences. One can study the comprehension and production of words as single units, as a series of related elements in sentences, or in the flow of a conversation. The value of studying word knowledge is that it tells us something about the normal use of language. Furthermore, examination of the word processing strategies of children with language learning disabilities may contribute to our knowledge base about the source of some of their reading problems. As suggested by Bashir (1973) and others, the relationship between reading and word retrieval processes warrants careful scrutiny; indeed, naming difficulties may be a good predictor of reading difficulties in some cases (Menyuk, 1980; Wolf, in press). Rapid naming difficulties are also predictive of reading difficulties, as Blachman (Chapter 13) notes. Recent studies have shown a renewed interest in the nature of retrieval problems, i.e., semantic, phonological, accessing, or word generating, in view of their prevalence among children and adolescents with language learning disabilities (Menyuk, 1980; Wiig et al., 1982).

Writing represents the intentional transmission of ideas through a visual symbol system. In planning written messages, one consciously selects appropriate words prior to their organization and placement in sentential contexts. As such, competency in written expression demands facility with oral language. Dysfunctions in the formulation and production of spoken language increase the probability that accompanying difficulties will be generated in written expression. The need exists to scrutinize the effect that word-finding problems, word retrieval deficits, or poor word association skills may have on the acquisition of written language. Such characteristics as word omissions and substitutions, circumlocutions, perseveration, or inappropriate word order may accompany spoken and written language samples (Wiig and Semel, 1980). Written language, as a representational system, demands efficient memorial processing and categorization in much the same way as spoken language.

It is impossible to consider learning independent of language and its meaning, regardless of whether oral or written systems receive the focus of our attention. Dinnan (1971) postulated that learning and communication in any symbolic code are dependent upon paradigmatic knowledge, i.e., a semantic-based organizational system. This includes such categorical relations as superordinate (dog-animal), coordinate (dog-cat), and part-whole (dog-tail). Paradigmatic knowledge is representative of the "expected" mode of response on most standardized tests. Mastery of the academic curricula also requires paradigmatic responding. Dinnan goes on to say that the construction of information in a paradigmatic fashion allows individuals to reason and communicate in similar ways. To some extent, it ensures successful communicative and educational exchanges with other language users. Thus, common references in oral language may facilitate the learning of new linguistic codes such as writing, reading, and spelling. Conversely, coding language to different or idiosyncratic base referents increases the likelihood of unsuccessful communicative and educational in-

terchanges. For example, classification patterns based upon dissimilar referents such as experiential associations (dog-happy; dog-dead) or phonological similarities (dog-log) reflect different levels of organization and lack shared meanings between teacher and student. Consequently, misunderstandings are prevalent.

The delicate interweaving of memorial, word association, and word-finding capabilities dictates that each be a subtopic for discussion in this chapter. The first section will include the identification of learning skills and learning disabilities in each area. Word retrieval and strategic operations that usually enhance accessibility of words in memory will be discussed first. Appraisal of the manner in which normally achieving and learning-disabled children respond on vocabulary tasks will be highlighted throughout the discussion. Differential strategies will be discussed from a variety of perspectives. Assessment and intervention suggestions will follow.

WORD RETRIEVAL: STRATEGIES FOR LEXICAL ACCESS

Complex mental operations mediate between the presentation of a stimulus and the emission of a response. The existence of specific internal processing mechanics responsible for the arrangement and retention of information is now widely accepted. Memory emerges more as a highly structured and interrelated system under the influence of high-level cognitive processes rather than as a random compilation of isolated facts (see Chapter 12). Study of the memorial processes that function to encode and reorganize information provides us with a perspective of how children learn and remember new information.

One strategy that increases the retrievability of information is the recoding of material into a superordinate system. For example, chair, bed, and lamp are individual words subsumed under the superordinate structure "furniture." The ability to organize or cluster related material into its superordinate structure facilitates its retention and retrieval. Thus, randomly presented word lists having membership in several categories, e.g., furniture, clothing, vegetables, may be easier to reproduce if one spontaneously groups the words according to their taxonomic categories. The following words can be grouped into the three superordinate categories mentioned above: chair, socks, lamp, spinach, sweater, bed, coat, lettuce, and carrots. Retrieval of one category member, e.g., coat, can activate the superordinate (clothing) which, in turn, triggers the retrieval of other members belonging to the category (sweater, socks). This clustering strategy acts to reduce memory load. It is illustrative of one type of encoding or reorganizational strategy that can be used with word lists.

This deliberate use of strategic behavior improves as children grow older. With increasing age and maturity, children become more planful in the implementation of systematic categories, as seen elsewhere in this text (e.g., Chapter 5). Their attempts to generate and use more efficient mnemonic strategies develop along with the development of more sophisticated strategies for sentence processing, integration, and other higher level abilities (Hagen and Stanovich, 1977). Concurrent with other aspects of cognitive growth, children's ability to categorize objects shifts from concrete-perceptual organization (grouping by size, color, and shape) to a more conceptual-abstract mode of organization (classification into taxonomic categories) (Rossi and Wittrock, 1971; Naron, 1978). The refinement of efficient coding systems during the preacademic and elementary school years is critical for academic achievement. Developmental research reveals that efficient use of such mnemonic strategies as category clustering and rehearsal result in age-related improvement in memory (Halperin, 1974; Ornstein et al., 1975; Paris, 1978). However, there is less agreement as to how language learning-disabled children process information.

LEXICAL ORGANIZATION, MEMORY, AND LEARNING DISABILITIES

Various researchers have provided information about the processing strategies of learning-disabled children. Poorer performances are found to be highly correlated with a lack of mnemonic sophistication. Torgesen and Goldman (1977) explored the use of verbal rehearsal in late second-grade children with reading problems. The children (mean age of 97 months) were approximately 1 year behind reading grade level. The children were asked to point to drawings of common objects in the sequence presented by the examiner. A 5-second delay period followed the last presentation. All attempts at rehearsal were recorded during the 5-second delay. Upon completion of the recall task, subjects were asked to tell how they remembered the sequential order of the stimuli. Results indicated that poor readers rehearsed less. Deficient rehearsal processes have also been reported in poor readers on free recall tasks (Bryan, 1972; Bauer, 1977a, 1977b). Torgesen and Goldman also reported that the poor readers were less aware of the role of verbal rehearsal. This awareness, or lack of awareness, may also be related to the metacognitive abilities discussed by Van Kleeck in Chapter 7 and Miller in the previous chapter.

There also exists a substantial body of literature demonstrating that recall and clustering strategies are facilitated when stimuli are organized in a "blocked" manner, i.e., when members of the same semantic category appear together rather than when they are randomly ordered (Cole et al., 1971; Ornstein et al., 1975). The generalizability of these results to children with learning disorders is in question, although the notion provides interesting possibilities for intervention.

Freston and Drew (1974) studied the efficiency with which the organization of input facilitates verbal recall. They examined the performance of learning-disabled children (mean age 10:10 years) in recalling auditorily presented stimuli of varying difficulty and degree of organization. Word familiarity ranged from high- to low-frequency usage. Organized lists consisted of blocked conceptual categories (animals, geometric shapes, flowers, and foods). Unorganized stimuli were comprised of randomized instances of the same categories. All lists consisted of five words each. Results showed that recall performance did not differ as a function of the way material was organized. High-frequency words elicited more correct responses than low-frequency words. A subsequent study (Parker et al., 1975) corroborated these findings. Conflicting results were reported by Suiter and Potter (1978). They found that organized pictorial groupings of categorical stimuli were more effectively recalled than unorganized groups when visually presented for recall.

These disparate findings can be attributed to modality differences. Israel (1979) studied the effects of material organization in free recall of learning-disabled and normally achieving children. Subjects received pictorial stimuli as well as the verbal label for each item. Results revealed that the organization of lists exerted a strong facilitative influence on recall and clustering. Although both groups benefited from increased organization, i.e., blocked presentations, recall and clustering were significantly higher for the normal achievers. Several other investigators have studied the interactions among clustering strategies, memory, and learning disabilities (Wong et al., 1977; Bauer, 1979; Ceci et al., 1981). The issue is revealed as being extremely complex, although we now have a greater understanding of why memory "dysfunctions" rarely appear as isolated problems and how they relate to academic success and failure. Much remains to be learned about how children diagnosed as learning disabled make use of memory-coding strategies in learning situations. The limited research to date has only begun to explore the relationship of these strategies to learning problems and underachievement.

The next section considers two interwoven facets of linguistic functioning: word association and word finding. The discussion of word association includes comparisons between normally achieving and learning-disabled students. The section on word finding will focus on learning-disabled individuals. Hypothesis about the interaction between memory and word knowledge will be explored.

WORD ASSOCIATION: SYNTACTIC FOUNDATIONS

The word associations of children are different from those of adults. Information about word association ability is obtained most typically by presenting a word to a person and asking him to say the first word that comes to mind. On such measures, children commonly respond to the stimulus word with a word that could follow in a sentence. For example, if a stimulus word were "dog," a young child would tend to respond with "run." This type of response is known as a *syntagmatic* response. Older children and adults respond differently. When given the word "dog," they tend to respond with "cat." This type of response is called a *paradigmatic* response.

Early investigations of word associations in children held that syntactic learning was responsible for the "shift" from child to adult type associations. Brown and Berko (1960) were among the first contemporary researchers to test empirically the difference between child and adult associations. They classified word associations into two general categories on the basis of the grammatical relations that held between a stimulus word and the response. Association responses were labeled as homogeneous if they shared the same grammatical class (nouns, verbs, adjectives, etc.) as the stimulus word. These were adult-like or paradigmatic. Responses were deemed heterogeneous if they belonged to different grammatical classes. These responses form a linear or sequentially ordered grammatical structure. These are child-like or syntagmatic.

Brown and Berko studied elementary

school-age children and adults. The subjects were presented with two word association tasks. The first task included words representative of six parts of speech (count and mass nouns, transitive and intransitive verbs, adjectives, and adverbs). Subjects were asked to think of a word after hearing the word given by the examiner. A Usage Test, consisting of pronounceable nonsense syllables, was used in the second task. Nonsense words were put into various sentence frames to indicate their part of speech. Subjects were asked to produce a grammatical sentence containing the nonsense word. For example, the examiner said "this is a cat who wants to *niss* something." The subject was then asked "can you make up what that might mean?"

Results indicated that homogeneous responding increased with age on both tasks. Performances were similar across tasks. On both tasks, count nouns and adjectives produced more homogeneous responses across all age levels than other parts of speech. It was concluded that changes in word associations were reflective of the child's developing ability to organize vocabulary into syntactic classes.

Ervin (1961) studied word associations in children from kindergarten through grade 6. In one task, she asked children to select a word from two choices that related best to the stimulus word. As predicted, paradigmatic responding increased proportionately with age with a significant shift to paradigmatic responding by the third grade. Responses included opposites, coordinates, subordinates, and superordinates—all of which share membership in the same taxonomic class. Analyses of responses revealed a number of interesting patterns. Syntagmatic responses consisted frequently of the stimulus word embedded in a phrase. For example, the response *across the street* would be given for the stimulus *across*. Clang associations, or responses governed by sound properties of the stimulus word, included words beginning with the same initial consonants, rhyming words, or words containing similar

syllables. The clang responses were most commonly associated with the younger age groups. Examples of clang responses (in quotes) include: bow—"boat," rat—"cat," and high—"/aɪ/."

Ervin (1961) indicated that responses can be thought of as grammatically equivalent if they share contextual similarity. Responses belonging to the same part of speech as the stimulus word usually occur in the same general slot in a sentence. According to this hypothesis, the association of *a cup of coffee* and *a cup of tea* leads to the word association of *coffee* and *tea*.

The developmental sequence of word associations was investigated further by Entwisle et al. (1964). They studied children between the ages of 5 and 10 years old. Findings were in agreement with earlier reports (Brown and Berko, 1960; Ervin, 1961). The syntagmatic-paradigmatic shift was most marked in ages 6 to 8. Paradigmatic responses for each form class increased with age. These observations were reconfirmed in a second study (Entwisle, 1966) on a larger sample of children.

Syntagmatic and Paradigmatic Responses: Parts of Speech

As discussed in the previous section, maturational changes in word associations have been reflected in changes from syntagmatic to paradigmatic responding. Analyses of these investigations also reveal differential responding according to parts of speech. When the data are analyzed with respect to specific grammatical classes, a common observation is made. The number of paradigmatic responses is highly correlated with specific parts of speech. Entwisle's studies (1964, 1966) show that paradigmatic word associations increase at different rates for different grammatical classes. The qualitative patterns according to grammatical forms are revealed as follows: At 4 and 5 years old, noun responses predominate regardless of the stimuli. Responses tend to involve multi-words or auditorially similar words to the stimulus word. Thus, 4-year-olds would most likely say "run" when presented with *dog* or "fat" when presented with *cat*. Between 5 and 6, the percentage of noun responses decreases. Pradigmatic responses for adjectives increase first. Associations are still primarily syntagmatic. Children at ages 6 to 8 show a decline in noun associates, which peaks at about 8 years old. Between 8 and 10 years old, verb responses increase while paradigmatic responding begins to bear resemblance to adult patterns.

WORD ASSOCIATION: A SEMANTIC ALTERNATIVE

In contrast to explanations that offer a syntactic-grammatical base for word associations are semantically oriented explanations. McNeill (1966) questioned the legitimacy of relating verbal word associates to the development of syntax. He felt that syntactic capacities alone could not account for the syntagmatic-paradigmatic shift. McNeill advocated that nonparadigmatic responding represented an incomplete learning of the semantic properties of words. He went on to say that associations were based on meaning as well as syntactic privileges of occurrence. He contended that until all the featural specifications of words were learned (between 8 and 10 years old), associations would be constrained and fail to match the paradigmatic tendencies characteristic of adult-like responses. For example, syntagmatic responses to the stimulus *man* might illustrate an incomplete knowledge of the featural properties "noun, animate, human, male," etc. As additional features are learned, paradigmatic responses appear. Clark's (1973) "semantic feature hypothesis" represents a similar theory of semantic development.

Rosch (1977) claims that the degree to which items are viewed as "prototypical" referents of a particular semantic category is a function of the number of attributes shared with other referents for the word. The greater the number of common attributes among members, the more prototypical and, hence, the more closely related they are with each other. As such, *apples* and *oranges* are highly prototypical as they

share a large number of properties associated with *fruit*, including sweetness, tree grown, colorful peel, and inedible seeds. In contrast, *apples* and *blueberries* or *avocados* are less prototypical as they share few common features. It is intriguing to draw an analogy to Rosch's description of prototypicality or best exemplars as playing a role in the ability to respond paradigmatically.

Lippman (1971) examined word association responses of kindergarten, second-grade, fourth-grade, and college students in an investigation designed to test semantic feature theory. Subjects were asked to give their reasons for placing the two words together to determine why specific responses to stimuli were given.

Results corroborated earlier reports of age-related improvements in the frequency of paradigmatic responses. Significant grade effects were found for paradigmatic responding. Grade differences were further evident in the ability to justify the pairing of words. Responses typically reflected subjects' knowledge about the featural properties of words. High correlations were noted between paradigmatic behaviors and response justification. For example, subjects responding paradigmatically tended to say that "boy" and "girl" went together because they were children or human beings. Subjects giving syntagmatic associates demonstrated dependency upon perceptual and/or functional attributes of referents. They were likely to respond that a boy and girl go together because a "girl has long hair and a boy has short hair" or "cats and dogs go together because dogs bark and cats meow." The negative relationship between responses patterned on concrete attributes and the level of paradigmatic performance was interpreted as supporting McNeill's theory of feature acquisition. It can be seen that the ability to "talk about language" and improvements in paradigmatic responses also occur around the same time.

In another study, Francis (1972) investigated the basis of 7-year-old children's associations. Children were asked to select two words which they thought were alike from a choice of three. Words such as *sing*, *table*, and *car* were given to the children. One word was from a different grammatical class. In a second task called "directed association," children were provided with word pairs such as *chair* and *carpet* and asked to give a third word like them. On both tasks, semantic class preferences were observed. It was concluded that cognitive-linguistic reorganizations (similar to those discussed by Van Kleeck and Miller in Chapters 7, 9, and 10) were related to children's ability to isolate words and make comparisons about them on the basis of semantic relations.

In a variation of the above-described studies, Emerson and Gekoski (1976) hypothesized that paradigmatic word associates would likely be a function of the subject's knowledge of categorical and interactive relations. Categorical responses were based on shared characteristics as in *bicycle-wagon: you ride them*. Interactive responses were a consequence of placing the stimulus into an action sequence as with *bicycle-boy: boys ride bicycles*. Emerson and Gekoski used word association and picture-grouping activities with preschool and elementary school children. Subjects selected one of four nouns which went better with pictorial stimuli. Thus, subjects were presented with a picture of *train* and asked to decide which word, *bus*, *tracks*, *moon*, or *telephone* went with the picture.

Data analysis showed syntagmatic associates to be positively related to interactive responses. A concomittant age-related progression in the ability to produce categorical responses was noted. The authors concluded that the classification of word association responses by grammatical form class alone was insufficient to explain age-related changes in performance. They felt that classification of responses into interactive and categorical patterns was related to the observed shift in responding.

Despite the accumulation of data that lends evidence to the syntagmatic-paradigmatic shift, the mechanics responsible for the developmental change are still not well understood. The following section presents a semantic-cognitive approach to the study of underlying processes acting to influence and nurture the operation of word association.

Reasons for Word Selection

From the foregoing discussion, it becomes apparent that semantic principles are basic to the process of word selection. Yet the behaviors responsible for selecting an appropriate word for a stimulus word can only be inferred from an individual's performance on a contrived task. Clark and Clark (1977) speculate about the procedures leading to paradigmatic word choice. They postulate a three-stage sequence:

Stage 1. The stimulus word is represented in some semantic form. With young children, it may be represented by the phonological form first.

Stage 2. The representation undergoes semantic transformation.

Stage 3. A word that is meaningfully related to the modified representation, constrained by semantic properties, is produced. The outcome is a word association, i.e., a word with taxonomic similarity.

To illustrate, the stimulus word *man* might elicit the verbal associate *woman*. In accordance with the above hierarchy, *man* should first be conceived as male-adult-human, then altered to *woman* and finally construed as female-adult-human.

Clark and Clark elaborate on the semantic reconstruction of stage 2 by proposing that the changes are rule governed. These rules are of three types: (1) Replace one or more components. This dictates that male can be replaced by female and leads to the response *woman*. (2) Delete one or more components. With the permissible deletion of the features male and adult, *man* can be represented as human and evoke the response *person*. (3) Add one or more components. This would allow, for example, the negative attribute *not* to be added to adult (not adult), giving rise to man-human-equals *boy*.

They acknowledge that, although convenient to explain a large percentage of paradigmatic responses, these rules fail to cover syntagmatic associates. They interpret syntagmatically based responses as emanating from shallow "depths" of processing linked to diverse internal representations. A rule to generate such responding might read: "Find a well-known phrase that begins with the stimulus word and produce the next main word in the phrase" (Clark and Clark, 1977, p. 481). As discussed previously, this syntactic principle strategy describes the preferred mode of response of young children.

Dinnan (1971, 1973) reminds us that the origin of nonconventional responses to word associates may reflect internalized sets of private experiences (perhaps autobiographical). Context-defined relationships are often unknown and meaningless to others. Petry (1977) demonstrated that many of the word-grouping principles behind young children's associations were disciplined and connected to real-world experiences. These situationally formed relationships characterized less mature responses initially. They gave way eventually to context-free, semantically based adult organization. Children's use of situational/ real-world strategies on word association tasks may be similar to the "probable event"/semantic strategies described by Wallach in Chapter 5.

Nelson (1977) argues that neither syntactic nor semantic explanations satisfy the shift to paradigmatics among older children. She ascribes to a two-dimensional viewpoint. On one hand, the shift in response types represents cognitive reorganization. This reorganization increases the availability of information stored in memory. Nelson relates cognitive changes to children's abilities to deal with the numerous conceptual relations such as superordinate, coordinate, and subordinate classifications. A second factor partially responsible for the prevalence of certain responses concerns how children approach word association tasks, i.e., whether the task is viewed as meaningful or contrived.

In conclusion, the ability to perform word associations does not involve study and preparation. However, success may necessitate familiarity with verbal tasks and the inclination to perform meaningfully. Yet, under certain conditions, instruction and direct training in this aspect of linguistic functioning become necessary. Investigations of verbal word associates of learning-disabled children and the reasons why treatment decisions are often necessary follow.

WORD ASSOCIATIONS AND LEARNING-DISABLED CHILDREN

Research on the language development of learning-disabled individuals indicates cognitive and linguistic delays and differences along a number of dimensions. Problems have been reported in the comprehension and production of logical relations (Wiig and Semel, 1976), embedded clause structure (Wallach, 1977), and ungrammatical temporal sentences (Goldsmith et al., 1974). Production difficulties have been noted for complex sentences (Kallail and Edwards, 1980), morphological rules (Vogel, 1975), and pragmatic-communicative skills (Bryan et al., 1981; Soenksen et al., 1981). There is a paucity of literature regarding the nature of syntagmatic and paradigmatic abilities in learning-disabled children. Questions remain, as indicted in the opening remarks, as to the relationship among paradigmatic abilities, learning, and reading.

An early word association investigation using normal achievers and children with school problems was conducted by Dinnan et al. (1971). Subjects were elementary school-age children identified by their teachers as good or poor readers. Each subject was asked to respond orally to 30 stimulus words. Analyses showed a significant difference in the number of paradigmatic responses of good readers ($\bar{x} = 30$) in comparison to poor readers ($\bar{x} = 10$). Although the precise nature of this difference was not explored, the study makes one think about why word association and word-finding difficulties frequently coexist with reading problems.

Bartel et al (1973) employed a free word association task using nouns, verbs, adjectives, and prepositions. Their subjects were normally achieving students and students diagnosed as learning disabled between the ages of 8 and 11 years. Surprisingly, a similar pattern of paradigmatic responding was found for both groups. However, significant differences were found for age, IQ, and part of speech. Paradigmatic associates occurred more frequently for nouns and adjectives. It was concluded that learning-disabled subjects developed categorization skills at comparable ages as academic achievers. It should be noted, however, that young learning-disabled children with lower IQ levels gave significantly fewer paradigmatic responses than older learning-disabled children with comparable IQ's. As the authors point out, the syntagmatic-paradigmatic shift did not occur until after 10 years of age for these children. It is possible that the performance of older children with higher IQ compensated for the reduced performance of the younger group. With the elimination of age and IQ variables, the learning disabled students responded similarly to normally achieving students.

To further assess the verbal behavior of learning-disabled children, Israel (1980) examined verbal associations of learning-disabled children between the ages of 7.5 and 12.3 years with a mean age of 9.8 years. Subjects received 60 high-frequency stimulus words equally distributed among nouns, verbs, adjectives, and prepositions. Subjects were credited with a paradigmatic association if the response to a stimulus word was within the same form class. Thus *chair* for the stimulus word *table* was counted as paradigmatic. On the other hand, *eat* for *table* was counted as nonparadigmatic. Table 11.1 provides an example of the stimuli used in the Israel study. The word lists may be incorporated into an assessment protocol as demonstrated by Shilo (1981).

Table 11.1.
High-frequency Words in Israel's (1980) Study of Verbal Associations of Learning-disabled Children

Nouns	Verbs	Adjectives	Prepositions
coat	cry	both	with
teacher	run	large	in
town	kill	middle	at
street	remember	near	after
friend	catch	three	against
man	travel	nice	under
farm	hang	simple	beside
hill	follow	yellow	among
bottle	come	different	on
bird	eat	big	below
uncle	sit	modern	up
car	talk	soft	from
table	raise	fast	between
hand	look	wise	above
star	carry	tall	beyond

Table 11.2.
Means and Percentages of Paradigmatic Responses for Learning-disabled and Nondisabled Subjects

	Nondisabled		Learning Disabled	
	Per Cent	Mean	Per Cent	Mean
Nouns	87.9	13.2	38.6	5.8
Verbs	68.8	10.3	16.4	2.5
Adjectives	91.9	13.8	36.9	5.5
Prepositions	70.7	10.6	28.8	4.3

Qualitative Response Differences in Learning-disabled Children

Table 11.2 provides the mean scores and percentages of paradigmatic responses achieved by the normal achievers and learning-disabled subjects. Learning-disabled children were found to respond nonparadigmatically to a much greater extent than normal children. Normal children did not utilize rhyming responses, but learning-disabled children utilized such clang expressions 14% of the time.

A curious pattern emerged. There was a greater number of "refusal" or "I don't know" responses (22%) in the normal group. In comparison, the learning-disabled group used "I don't know" responses 14% of the time. This differential may be indicative of greater selectivity on the part of the normal subjects. It may be that the normal children operated with the strategy "if in doubt, don't respond." In contrast, learning-disabled children appeared to work with a "respond with some form" strategy. The "respond with some form" strategy may be attributable to impulsive responding. It may also be equated with a history of prior educational failure. Further investigation of the "whys" behind these responses is warranted.

These findings support those of Dinnan et al. (1971), but they are in stark contrast to those of Bartel et al. (1973). The source of these discrepancies, as with much learning disability research, is attributed to a number of variables. Subject selection and task design can affect the results. The identification and selection of learning-disabled populations represents a tremendous problem, as discussed throughout this text. Age ranges, prior educational experiences, and degree of learning dysfunction are all part of the problem. Differential task designs, e.g., word list composition and scoring criteria, also need to be considered when comparing results across studies. Bearing in mind the heterogeneity within any learning-disabled sample, generalizations should be exercised with care.

The Older Student with Language Learning Disabilities

The studies mentioned thus far concerned children between the ages of 7 and 11. Shilo (1981) studied the word associations of older learning-disabled children. She compared the responses of normal achievers and learning-disabled children between the ages of 10 and 13 years old. Shilo constructed lists with high-frequency mass and count nouns, transitive and intransitive verbs, and prepositions. Items 1 to 5 below provide examples of Shilo's stimuli:

(1) Count nouns: coat, teacher, town, street, friend
(2) Mass nouns: air, water, sugar, money, grass
(3) Transitive verbs: kill, catch, follow, eat, raise
(4) Intransitive verbs: cry, run, travel, come, sit
(5) Prepositions: with, in, at, after, against

Findings showed that learning-disabled subjects did not display the degree of paradigmatic dominance that characterized the performance of the normal achievers. Significant differences between the normals and learning-disabled subjects were word class specific. That is, more paradigmatic responses occurred for the normal children on the verbs and prepositions. Further analysis revealed that count nouns yielded comparable successes, i.e., all children demonstrated a greater number of paradigmatic responses on count nouns. Transitive verbs generated the greatest differences. Intermediate, with respect to degree of differences between normals and learning-disabled students, were prepositions, mass nouns, and intransitive verbs. Overall, a significantly different 67% and 48% characterized normal and learning-disabled children's paradigmatic associations, respectively.

Refusals comprised a sizable segment of nonparadigmatic responses. The ability to respond with refusals was interpreted as representing a sophisticated utilization of the strategy "when in doubt, don't respond." The Shilo conclusion supported Israel's 1980 conclusion. It is the contention, therefore, that learning-disabled children, although following a normal course of paradigmatic development, remain less proficient and lag behind their normal counterparts.

There are a number of issues raised by the word association studies. It may be that learning-disabled children's differential abilities with word association reflect another instance of difficulties or differences with linguistic competency. In Nelson's (1977) terms, learning-disabled children may be using organizational schemes that are more appropriate for early phases of development. Consequently, they are more reliant upon functional and/or perceptual relationships than higher order taxonomical organization. A corrollary (in accordance with Rosch's (1977) doctrine) might be the failure to develop "best exemplars" or prototypicality.

The relationship among semantic features, word knowledge, and memory dysfunction surfaces again. Indeed, what is the source of observed differences between learning-disabled and normally achieving children on word-finding tasks? As Vellutino (1978) asserts, facility with word knowledge and usage, whether on word association or word-finding activities, becomes dependent on the ability to generate and use efficiently mnemonic coding devices for the storage and retrieval of information.

WORD FINDING AND LEARNING DISABILITIES

Children with learning disabilities frequently exhibit vocabulary deficits throughout their school years. The incidence has been estimated to be as high as 80% (Wiig, 1981). Johnson and Myklebust (1967) have suggested that learning-disabled individuals know fewer words, retain restricted word meanings, and are concrete and literal in symbolization and conceptualization skills. They have classified this type of word selection disorder as a problem with reauditorization. By reauditorization, they meant that difficulty with verbal naming and retrieval of words for conversational usage persists in spite of intact comprehension, oro-motor skills, and verbal imitation of spoken words. Among the linguistic parameters cited by Johnson and Myklebust as illustrative of word-finding and retrieval problems are: (1) use of nonverbal vocalizations as in the production of *meow* to name *cat*; (2) pantomime or gesture; (3) circumlocutions, descriptions, and/or definitions inclusive of perceptual and functional attributes—for example, instead of producing the verbal label *ball*, one might say "it's round, it rolls and bounces; you play with it"; (4) word substitutions from within the same taxonomic category, as *car* for *truck* or *spoon* for *fork*; (5) words lacking specificity such as *thing* and *junk*; (6) perseverative repetitions; and (7) excessive or delayed response time prior to labeling pictures or reading words.

Additional characteristics cited by Wiig and Semel (1980) include: (1) phonological relationships such as *telephone* for *telegraph*; (2) antonymy or contrast words such as *wet* for *dry*; (3) semantically empty filler items or placeholders such as *wh, er*, and *well*; (4) overuse of meaningless phrases as exemplified in *you know* and *right*; (5) sentence starter devices such as *well* and *then*; and (6) overuse of indefinites (*this, that, something*) as replacements for substantive words.

Support for these lexical error patterns stems from a number of sources. In a series of studies (Wiig and Semel, 1975; Wiig et al., 1977), accuracy and speed ratings were obtained for learning-disabled adolescents and academically achieving peers. Both groups were asked to: (1) name verbal opposites; (2) retrieve verbal labels in response to pictures of objects, actions, numbers, and colors; (3) name members of the semantic categories of foods, animals, and toys; and (4) define words. In addition, ratings of conversational speech characteristics (among them word finding, word substitutions, and circumlocutions) were recorded.

Learning-disabled subjects exhibited reductions in the speed and accuracy of recalling verbal opposites (within-class substitutions predominated), naming associated members of a semantic category (inefficient retrieval from memory), and defining words (typically described functional attributes). Accompanying these quantitative differences were qualitative differences. Learning-disabled subjects frequently demonstrated idiosyncratic and unpredictable preferences. Rather than utilizing apparent grouping strategies to facilitate recall, they tended to name items by shifting unsystematically from one category to another. Whereas normal learners named members of foods belonging to the subcategories of fruits, vegetables, meat, etc., or by time of day (breakfast, lunch, dinner), learning-disabled subjects shifted erratically among groupings.

Similar findings have been reported by

Denckla and Rudel (1976). They compared poor and normal readers between 7 and 12 years old on a rapid automatic naming task. The groups differed on both accuracy and latency measures. Poor readers made more errors and took longer than normal readers to generate names of common objects, letters, colors, and numerals presented visually. Corroborative evidence of word-finding and retrieval deficiencies is also provided by Perfetti and Hogaboam (1975) and German (1979). German (1982) provides additional information about retrieval strategy preferences in learning-disabled children between 8 and 11 years old.

The issues raised earlier in the text by Maxwell and Wallach (Chapter 2) are reiterated here. Word retrieval and word knowledge deficits persist into adolescence. Many of these problems do not disappear or self-remediate as children get older. We need to learn more about the delicate relationship between memory dysfunction, language deficits, and learning underachievement. An immediate advantage earned from this research should be the construction and implementation of innovative assessment and intervention protocols. The remainder of the chapter concentrates on these two areas.

MEASUREMENT OF VOCABULARY: FORMAL ASSESSMENT

Several commonly used test instruments designed to assess various aspects of vocabulary knowledge are presented here to help practitioners think about the state of the art and possible alternatives. The tests that might be appropriate for school-age children are emphasized. A number of choices are available to the examiner when attempting to assess aspects of vocabulary. The most common and, perhaps, traditional method of vocabulary testing is to have the subject point to picturable words named by the examiner. Another method involves asking the subject to define words that are given by the examiner. Both types are discussed.

Peabody Picture Vocabulary Test

The Peabody Picture Vocabulary Test (PPVT) (Dunn, 1965, 1981) is one of the most widely used and abused vocabulary tests. According to its author, the PPVT provides an estimate of a person's verbal intelligence by assessing his hearing vocabulary. The test is applicable within the age range 2:3 through 18:5 years. Additional data have been made available for older adult subjects. The examiner presents each stimulus word orally, and the subject points to one of four pictures best depicting the meaning of the word. Raw scores convert into percentile rankings, mental age equivalents, and IQ.

Criticisms are many. Among the more prevalent are: outdated lexical items, culture-bound vocabulary, restricted standardization sample, and lack of equivalence between alternate test forms. Modifications have been made in a recently revised edition (1981) that address several of the above-mentioned limitations. A primary modification is the elimination of IQ conversions. However, in view of the scope, complexity, and general nature of word knowledge and word usage, continued use of this test needs to be carefully evaluated. Likewise, the subtle nature of vocabulary changes that occur throughout the school years makes this type of testing (and retesting) questionable (see Chapter 15).

Boehm's Test of Basic Concepts

This test (Boehm, 1971) was designed to measure children's knowledge of frequently used basic concepts including space (location, direction, dimensions, and orientation), quantity, number, and time. It can be used for children between 5 and 8 years old. Fifty pictorial items are arranged in approximate order of increasing difficulty. As the examiner reads aloud statements descriptive of the pictures, the child marks his/her choice that best illustrates the concept being tested from an array of three to four items. The subject receives a point for each correct response. Scores are converted to percentile rankings and grade equivalents. Recommendations for remediation are provided. Examples of the items include *top, farthest, most, second,* and *half.* While attempting to tap a wide range of "basic concepts," we are reminded by Silliman (1979) that the comprehension of spatial terms represents a complex process. This is important since the test contains a disproportionate number of spatial concepts. The complexity is demonstrated further by the difficulty one has in representing certain concepts, e.g., spatial relationships, pictorially. Silliman (1979) should be consulted for an in-depth discussion. Other difficulties include a restricted standardization sample and culture-bound test items.

Test for Auditory Comprehension of Language

This 101-item test (Carrow, 1974) assesses comprehension of selected vocabulary and morphosyntactic structures. Vocabulary items are drawn from the grammatic classes of nouns, verbs, adjectives, and adverbs. Morphological stimuli include the derivational suffixes "er" and "ist," number, prepositions, and interrogatives. Syntactic items include noun-verb agreement, adjectival modifiers, and simple, complex, and compound imperatives. Sets of plates, each with three pictures, are presented. One drawing represents the linguistic form tested; remaining illustrations are decoy items. The child is to point to the designated picture. Norms cover the period 3 to 7 years. Scores translate into age equivalents and percentile rankings. Limitations include poor picturability of target items (e.g., Wh- questions and personal pronouns), confounding of sentence length and grammatical complexity, limited size and geographic distribution of the standardization sample, and the effect of vocabulary knowledge upon performance on syntactic and morphological test structures.

Illinois Test of Psycholinguistic Abilities

The Auditory Reception subtest, perhaps labeled inappropriately, measures knowledge of verbally presented noun-verb vocabulary. This process is tapped by yes/no responses to three-word questions, such as "Do airplanes fly?" or "Do bananas telephone?" Language ages and scaled scores are available (Kirk et al., 1968).

The Detroit Test of Learning Aptitude

This instrument (currently under revision) (Baker and Leland, 1967) contains a number of subtests for vocabulary. The *Likenesses and Differences* subtest requires a child to tell how two words are alike and then how they differ. The child would be asked to judge how a *pen* and *pencil* or *spoon* and *fork* are alike and how they are dissimilar. This subtest may provide information about the superordinate structures children are able to discuss. It may also provide some information about the characteristics, or features of items, that are picked upon by the child.

Bankson Language Screening Test

The design of this test (Bankson, 1977) is to screen expressive language. The subsection assessing semantic knowledge includes body parts, nouns, verbs, categories, functions, prepositions, colors, and opposites. Items are scored as either correct or incorrect. However, items missed expressively can be tested receptively at the discretion of the examiner. Scores convert into age levels for children aged 4 through 7.

Test of Language Development

The Test of Language Development (TOLD) (Newcomer and Hammill, 1977) evaluates a child's ability to process syntactic structures. Five subtests comprise the test: Picture Vocabulary, Oral Vocabulary, Grammatical Understanding, Sentence Imitation, and Grammatical Completion. The Picture Vocabulary subtest (ages 4:0 to 8:11) consists of 25 items and measures comprehension of individual words. The child selects from an array of four drawings the picture which best represents the meaning of the word. Responses are credited with a 1 or 0. Scores convert to language ages and scaled score equivalents. The Oral Vocabulary subtest (ages 4:0 to 8:6) requires the child to define 20 common vocabulary words. One point per test item may be earned. Criteria for successful performance include precise definitions or the provision of two descriptive attributes. The Detroit subtest for Likenesses and Differences mentioned above uses a similar point system scoring. Scores convert to language ages and scaled score equivalents. Examples of test items include *bird, ocean, season, village*, and *north*. Two commonly cited limitations are the narrow age range and small sample size used to obtain measures of test-retest reliability.

Wechsler Intelligence Scale for Children (Revised)

Children ranging in ages 6.0 to 16.10 years are asked to define words presented by the examiner on the word definition subtest (Wechsler, 1974). Thirty words are rated on a 3-point scale with higher scores indicative of greater explicitness. Many items are archaic and not functional for common usage (e.g., hari-kari, belfry, nitroglycerine).

Clinical Evaluation of Language Function (CELF)

The Confrontation Naming subtest evaluates the speed and accuracy of word retrieval involving the names of geometric configurations (circle, square, triangle), colors (red, blue, black, and yellow), and color and form combinations (Wiig and Semel, 1980). Each subsection consists of 36 visual stimuli. Raw scores are found for grades kindergarten through 10. Modifications on the elementary level CELF are now available.

Other measures may be located in the McCarthy Scales of Children's Abilities (McCarthy, 1970). The word knowledge subtests of picture vocabulary and oral definitions are procedurally identical to those instruments just reviewed.

General Limitations of Formal Vocabulary Measures

Professionals interested in learning about a child's vocabulary knowledge must recognize what they are testing when using standardized instruments. For example, picture recognition and word definition tests tap different underlying processes. Whereas recognition requires the subject to be familiar with a given word in order to associate it with a picture, the ability to define words includes the capacity to formulate verbal or written definitions. That is, adequate performance is dependent not only on the ability to use words to describe specific stimulus items, but it also requires that the person retrieve the word and its meaning from memory prior to verbal expression. Verbal expression may present a more complex and demanding activity than recognition, although comprehension and expression are not always representative of a clear-cut either-or phenomenon.

Individual vocabulary tests may differ in the extent and type of language behaviors sampled. For example, the Peabody Picture Vocabulary Test consists primarily of nouns and the Boehm Test of Basic Concepts of relational information. One must exercise utmost caution in equating performance across such a diverse range of test items. Many of these tests also require higher level metalinguistic and metacognitive abilities (see Chapters 1, 7, and 9).

The most important consideration concerns the need to supplement quantitative measurements with qualitative analyses. Quantitative assessments rarely do more than report scores as language-age equivalents (below, at, or above age expectation) after comparison with a normative sample. These product-oriented approaches typically fail to address the nature of poor scores and, perhaps, idiosyncratic problems. In some instances, they even overestimate vocabulary knowledge. Product-oriented approaches do not offer guidance in the formulation of effective intervention procedures. The superficiality of vocabulary recognition tests is further realized in their inability to generate data on how words are used in everyday functional communication. Van Kleeck reminded us in Chapter 9 that most tests, at best, measure children's ability to deal with decontextualized language. Even successful recognition of individual test items does not ensure usage in spontaneous speech exchanges. Muma and Pierce (1981) address the need to look at intentional and referential meaning. Lucas (1980, p. 23) best summarizes the state of the art by writing: "spontaneous and consistent linguistic use of the lexicon is a more accurate indicator than vocabulary tests of children's comprehension of concepts . . . . The child's consistent use of vocabulary demonstrates a more complete understanding of the language." It should be easy to see how formalized vocabulary measures restrict in-depth assessments of verbal capacities and command of vocabulary when reduced to age-graded functions.

Thus, practitioners need to use standardized tests within the context of current theoretical and research frameworks. They also need to initiate informal alternatives and understand the processes and products being evaluated. A complete and well rounded evaluation of a child's lexical knowledge must include procedures designed to explore the use of words for functional purposes. Probes should examine the use of words in context, overextensions (or perhaps overrestrictions), and self-invented entries. Inherent to these procedures would be observation of the use of synonyms, antonyms, and prototypicality of class membership (Muma and Pierce, 1981; Wiig and Semel, 1980).

Among a host of sample techniques, one might ask children to: (1) select from an array of functional objects the item best related to the examiner's request; (2) act or manipulate objects in a manner corresponding to verbal directives, such as "put the boat next to the bridge"; (3) indicate whether two or more utterances are similar or dissimilar in meaning when differing by a single word. For example, "Joe has a *small* boat" versus "Joe has a *tiny* boat" (Wiig and Semel, 1980).

Regardless of the method chosen to informally evaluate vocabulary knowledge, nonstandardized procedures allow freedom of choice and may yield a richer and more meaningful body of information than quantitative measurements. Assessments should consider not only the quantity of material learned but, more importantly, the mode of learning.

MEASUREMENT OF WORD ASSOCIATION: FORMAL ASSESSMENT

Another mechanism for the evaluation of vocabulary proficiency is the administration of word association tasks. Despite a multitude of standardized instruments for the assessment of language deficits in children, only a few relate specifically to word association. Two common methods involve the use of "free" and "controlled" tasks. In "free association tasks," subjects are instructed to produce as many different words as possible within a specified time period. "Controlled associations" consist of naming as many members as possible in select semantic categories within a predetermined time frame. Sidestepping stylistic differences, both tasks may reveal internal organization of material and problem-solving skills.

Free Word Associations

The Free Association subtest of the Detroit Tests of Learning Aptitude (Baker and Leland, 1967) provides a measurement of the ability to say as many words as possible within a prescribed time period. Time limitations are recommended for particular ages, ranging from 1 minute for 3- to 7-year-olds to 5 minutes for 14 years old and above. It is permissible to extend the test beyond these cut-offs into the next time allowance if the subject is "going strong." One point is earned for each word with scores convertible to age level equivalents (range 3:0 to 19:0 years).

Wiig and Semel (1975) report that learning-disabled subjects frequently exhaust their fund of words after the first 1-minute interval. Subsequent responses generally reveal a random, haphazard search pattern for words with few associative groupings among them.

This finding underscores a basic constraint of this approach. The failure to provide a mechanism to score associated or "chunked" items (items belonging to common semantic categories) does not permit the practitioner to readily discern the grouping strategies utilized by the child to guide word retrieval. As such, qualitative analyses remain subjective and at the discretion of the examiner. Confinement to quantitative interpretations alone prohibits the surfacing of information related to organizational processes.

Controlled Word Associations

The Verbal Fluency subtest of the McCarthy Scales of Children's Abilities (McCarthy, 1970) measures the ability to classify and think categorically. Subjects are told to name as many words as possible within 20 seconds from the categories of foods, clothing, vehicles, and animals. One point is earned for each correct response with an allowable maximum score of 36. Score sheets of acceptable responses are provided. Application is restricted to the ages 2:6 to 8:6 years.

Although norms only offer a quantitative product, McCarthy acknowledges that qualitative analyses may yield substantial insight into the originality and flexibility of the response pattern. The perceptive clinician should document the number and type of subcategories with each general category. For example, the names of vegetables, fruits, and meats may comprise "things to eat," whereas zoo, domestic, and farm may represent animals. A tabulation of the number of responses simply does not capture this information.

Similarly, examination of originality or prototypicality of responses should be undertaken. To illustrate, the items *broccoli*, *Swiss cheese*, and *bacon* are more creative than *apples*, *corn*, or *cookies*. Two subjects with an identical number of responses may differ in their originality yet be regarded as performing comparably. Likewise, greater fluency, i.e., the more items named, does not guarantee creativity. Analyses such as these provide valuable data and may further serve to isolate bizarre or perseverative tendencies.

A pilot study by Israel (1981) on preaca-demic children sought to determine the effects of increasing the time allowance from 20 to 60 seconds. Preliminary data indicated that two-thirds of the children profited from additional time. On the average, 2.5 words were added to three categories (the lone exception was vehicles, with one addition). It often reflected a shift to different subclasses. Excessive searching behaviors or strain were not evident. Children frequently responded "I don't know" or began to perseverate when exhausting their mental search for categorical members. Findings suggest that time constraints may serve to underestimate actual ability. This study indicates that the installation of a brief time span, originally thought to prevent strain in the search for additional words by earlier researchers, may not be accurate.

The Verbal Opposite subtest of the Detroit Tests of Learning Aptitude (Baker and Leland, 1967) represents a straightforward word association task. This subtest, whereby the examiner gives a word and the child provides its opposite, might lend itself to a syntagmatic-paradigmatic analysis. Sample items include *boy*, *dirty*, *shut*, and *pretty*.

The word association unit of the Clinical Evaluation of Language Function (Wiig and Semel, 1980) measures the fluency and speed of retrieval (within 1 minute) of semantically associated words from the categories of food and animals. Raw scores are available for grades kindergarten through 10. The authors recommend qualitative investigations to determine the presence or absence of organizational strategies behind performance. This includes looking at the number and type of subclassifications named and the occurrence of shifting from one to another. Adherence to these suggestions should become routine during the course of interpretation.

The Processing Word Classes subtest of the Clinical Evaluation of Language Function might also provide information about the strategies available to children. On this subtest, children are provided three or four words, e.g., *truck*, *pilot*, *bus*, and *horse*. They are asked to tell which two go together. Analyses of error patterns may prove useful. It must be remembered that what appears to be an inappropriate connection to the examiner may be appropriate in the real-life experiences of the child (recall the discussion by Nelson on pp. 237 and 239).

Precautions with Word Association Measures

The relative paucity of information dealing with the paradigmatic shift in children with learning disorders must be kept in mind. The research findings provide suggestions for the development of assessment tools. It may well be worthwhile to devise association tasks to assess paradigmatic responding and word-finding skills. To do so, however, demands that we proceed cautiously in both their design and interpretation.

German (1979, 1982) warns that choice of vocabulary items warrants careful consideration when constructing new assessment tools. She points out that the learning-disabled subjects in her study performed as well as the normal achievers with high-frequency words. Familiarity with stimuli can yield inflated performances and mask underlying or subtle problems. German's findings also suggest that mode of presentation differentially affects performance. She reports a hierarchy of difficulty as a function of stimulus context. The best performances occur on picture-labeling tasks, followed by naming to open-ended sentences (e.g., "You eat ice cream with a ____"), followed by naming to description (e.g., "What is something you use to eat ice cream, is round on one end, etc.?"). The need to devote considerable effort to word list composition was also cited by Shilo (1981) in her recommendation to distinguish between mass and count nouns and transitive and intransitive verbs.

A different position is promulgated by Nelson (1977). She argues that cognitive reorganization and increased availability of conceptual information are the most significant factors responsible for the shift to paradigmatics. She contends that association lists based on form class and frequency of word usage are less than adequate measurements of developmental status. Nelson (1977) proposes that stimuli be classified on the basis of their conceptual relationships such as superordinate, coordinate, contrasts, etc. Such words as animals and clothing, dog and cat, and give and take reflect these relationships. Data obtained may provide information about salient relationships between stored lexical information and conceptual organization at different age levels.

Nelson advocates further that the manner in which children approach word association or word-finding tasks affects their performance on these tests. She speculates that the disposition to respond paradigmatically varies as a function of how children perceive these activities. A playful or egocentric approach, in which the task is viewed as "meaningless," may lead to the appearance of "silly" responses as in clang or multi-word associations. Nelson maintains that paradigmatic dominance depends upon the refinement of appropriate approaches to task demands.

Finally, administration variables can adversely affect performance. It has been demonstrated (Entwisle and Forsyth, 1963) that a greater number of syntagmatic associates appear under written conditions than with oral output. The procedural differences may also affect the frequency of superordinate, subordinate, and contrast responses.

To conclude, the methods deployed to evaluate word skills differ in efficiency and effectiveness. Quantitative scores allow comparison against normative behaviors but fail to offer insight into specific problem areas and strategy usage. Qualitative assessments provide a wealth of information not available from standardized testing. Certainly, the utility of word association and word-finding tasks as viable diagnostic measures of linguistic ability are enhanced when qualitative concerns augment numerical indices. Acknowledgment of the aforementioned precautions should be a priority of all diagnosticians. They can better serve us in the construction and implementation of appropriate programs to ameliorate deficit areas. Practical suggestions for the remediation of vocabulary dysfunctions follow.

INTERVENTION GUIDELINES

A fundamental characteristic reported of many learning-disabled youngsters is that they have difficulty organizing information. Given the diversity of response patterns, remedial programs should be individualized to address the uniqueness of the learning dysfunction. Confirmation of a reduced but qualitatively similar performance suggests that instructional methodology be aimed to increase rate of learning and, where appropriate, progression through normal developmental stages (Tarver et al., 1977). Programs of vocabulary enrichment should include consideration of individual personal experiences as well as levels of cognitive and linguistic functioning. Since semantic deficits persist into adolescence, therapeutic objectives must undergo periodic changes to keep abreast with cognitive advances (see Chapter 2).

The development of paradigmatic organization might include strategies for learning category membership (superordinate-subordinate-coordinate), criterial features of referents, and the relationships of synonymy, antonymy, and contrasts. Inherent in this challenge is the need to foster strategic awareness for remembering and retrieving information and to inspire their prolonged use in obligatory and novel situations. One certainty is that the teaching of categorization and organizational schemes, together with increasing self-monitoring behaviors, represents a slow, laborious process (Brown, 1977). Preliminary evidence of success is reported by Cartelli (1978) in a training paradigm constructed to facilitate cognitive awareness of paradigmatic structures through teaching contrast relations. Findings revealed that paradigmatic structures were "teachable

and testable thought processes" (p. 316) which did not dissipate over time and which generalized (with additional training) to written language.

Gerber and Bryen (1981) speculate that training learning-disabled youngsters in the use of classification and organizational properties of the lexicon might (1) stimulate increased awareness that associations exist among words, (2) enrich the meaningfulness of words, and (3) compensate for word retrieval disorders through activation of potentially facilitative self-cuing strategies.

What follows are sample exercises frequently utilized to promote semantic classification and retrieval skills.

Remediation of Categorization Deficits

The ability to structure several items into one "chunk" provides ease of storage and retrieval. By "chunking," individual but related items are placed into a form of organization characterized by integrated and enriched information units. For example, *cows*, *horses*, and *goats* can be assigned a superordinate label and be recorded as "animals." These consolidated units afford greater cognitive economy and are unlimited in the amount of information which may be packaged into them. This consolidation, in turn, potentially assists in information retrieval.

Among the variety of procedures to assist the establishment of word classification skills are:

1. Association between the names of category members with labels for the categories to which they belong. For example, "A pigeon is a ___" or "Is a pigeon a *bird* or *fish*?" Or, "lions, tigers, and elephants are ___."

2. Association of category names with individual members. For example, "Which of these is a fruit—potato, cheese, or apple?"

3. Identification of an item from a series that is not a member of a particular semantic category. For example, "Which does not belong—arm, leg, hat, or nose?"

4. Selection of an item from a mixed

array that represents an instance of a named category. For example, "Which one is a food? Which is an animal?"

5. Identification of featural properties of referents that serve to differentiate meaning. For example, "How are a newspaper and book alike? different?"

6. Identification of taxonomic subclasses. For example, zoo versus farm animals; breakfast versus lunch versus dinner foods.

7. Association of items composed of shared features. For example, "Find all the objects that need gas to move."

8. Categorization practices to develop visual imagery and self-cuing strategies. For example, "Close your eyes and imagine that you're in a supermarket, classroom, etc. Tell me the names of the things you see." (Group into subclasses)

In addition to working within superordinate networks, similar activities may be utilized to emphasize perceptual or functional attributes, contrast relations, and synonymy. Several can coexist simultaneously to demonstrate grouping traits. For example, "People use scissors to cut paper. Knives also cut paper. Both are pointy and sharp."

Intervention techniques for specific word classes (nouns, verbs, etc.) and word relations (homonyms, antonyms, comparatives, etc.) receive extensive treatment by Wiig and Semel (1980). The reader is encouraged to consult their suggested procedures to gain additional objectivity in exercises whose purposes are to strengthen semantic organization and speed of retrieval as well as associative grouping strategies.

Remediation of Word Retrieval Deficits

Various tasks relate to facilitation of storage, retention, and retrieval. Two probable areas in need of intervention are rehearsal and retrieval operations.

REHEARSAL

Exercises employed to develop rehearsal behaviors initially serve to improve attention. They may ultimately facilitate storage

and retrieval. A common approach is to expose the child to a visual display of X number of items. After a brief study interval, the child closes his/her eyes while a set number of items are removed. Verbal identification of the missing items is required. Related or unrelated referents may be utilized.

A second practice is to request the child to repeat aloud (and eventually covertly) sequential items first as single items, then as binary units, and followed by triplicate sets. For example, *cat, cat-dog, cat-dog-horse*. This manner of instruction has its counterpart in developmental psychology where it has been found (Naus et al., 1977) that, with increased age, children tend to rehearse in pairs or small groups rather than name single items.

RETRIEVAL

A number of cuing techniques are available to facilitate word recall. They may be used in isolation or combination or be externally imposed. Even more desirable is the graduation to self-cued monitoring. Among the most typical cuing strategies are: (1) naming the taxonomic category of the target word; (2) providing highly associative words in the form of paired verbal associates as in "bread and butter" and "in and out"; (3) sentence completion or "fill-in" tasks via the provision of leading utterances such as "we wear shoes on our *feet*"; (4) confrontation naming by labeling a series of referents belonging to specified semantic categories; (5) phonemic cuing with the production of the initial sound, syllable, or syllables of the target word; (6) gestural or pantomime cues; (7) presence of printed or graphic stimuli; (8) use of alternate words such as synonyms or antonyms; and (9) use of subordinate words.

Regardless of the methodology selected to enhance word retrieval, the fundamental objective remains a stable and coherent organizational network of information.

CLOSING REMARKS

An ongoing need exists to understand more thoroughly the word knowledge and word retrieval capacities of children with learning disabilities. Most important is the need to continue research on the interaction of these problems with various facets of academic difficulties. We need to know more about the development of these abilities and their relationship to academic success. Hopefully, our knowledge will continue to expand from incoming information about the extent and type of categorical and paradigmatic thinking, the kinds of associations established, and the nature of memorial strategies and information retrieval. As the data becomes available, we will be in a better position to design more appropriate intervention and educational programs to meet the needs of these children. As the data base undergoes modification, we must be flexible enough to change with it. The challenge is ours to answer.

References

Baker H, Leland B: *Detroit Tests of Learning Aptitude.* Indianapolis, Bobbs-Merrill, 1967.

Bankson NW: *Bankson Language Screening Test.* Baltimore, University Park Press, 1977.

Bartel NR, Grill JJ, Bartel HW: The syntactic-paradigmatic shift in learning disabled and normal children. *J Learn Disabil* 6:59–64, 1973.

Bashir A: *Error Behavior and the Reading Process: Some Germinal Thoughts.* Cambridge, MA, Harvard University School of Education, 1973.

Bauer RH: Short-term memory in learning disabled and nondisabled children. *Bull Psychonomic Soc* 10:128–130, 1977a.

Bauer RH: Memory processes in children with learning disabilities: evidence for deficient rehearsal. *J Exp Child Psychol* 24:415–430, 1977b.

Bauer RH: Memory, acquisition, and category clustering in learning disabled children. *J Exp Child Psychol* 27:365–383, 1979.

Boehm AE: *Boehm Test of Basic Concepts.* New York, Psychological Corporation, 1971.

Brown AL: Development, schooling, and the acquisition of knowledge about knowledge: comments on Nelson. In Anderson RC, Spiro RJ, Montague WE: Hillsdale, NJ, Lawrence Erlbaum Associates, 1977, pp 241–254.

Brown R, Berko J: Word association and the acquisition of grammar. *Child Dev* 31:1–14, 1960.

Bryan T, Donahue M, Pearl R: Studies of learning disabled children's pragmatic competence. *Top Learn Learn Disabil* 1:29–39, 1981.

Bryan TS: The effect of forced mediation upon short-term memory of children with learning disabilities. *J Learn Disabil* 10:605–609, 1972.

Carrow E: *Test for Auditory Comprehension of Language.* Austin, TX, Learning Concepts, 1974.

Cartelli LM: Paradigmatic language training for learning disabled children. *J Learn Disabil* 11:313–318, 1978.

Ceci SJ, Ringstrom M, Lea SEG: Do language-learning disabled children (L/LDS) have impaired memories? In search of underlying processes. *J Learn Disabil* 14:159–162, 1981.

Clark EV: What's in a word? On the child's acquisition of semantics in his first language. In Moore TE: *Cognitive Development and the Acquisition of Language.* New York, Academic Press, 1973, pp 65–110.

Clark HH, Clark EV: *Psychology and Language: An Introduction to Psycholinguistics.* New York, Harcourt, Brace, Jovanovich, 1977.

Cole M, Frankel F, Sharp D: Development of free recall learning in children. *Dev Psychol* 4:109–123, 1971.

Denckla M, Rudel R: Naming of object drawings by dyslexic and other learning disabled children. *Brain Language* 3:1–16, 1976.

Dinnan JA: Key to learning. *J Read Behav* 3:1–13, 1971.

Dinnan J: Categorization of paradigmatic-syntagmatic oral responses. *J Read Behav* 5:207–211, 1973.

Dinnan JA, Bickley AC, Cowart H: An analysis of semantic products of disadvantaged and advantaged 2nd, 3rd, and 4th grade good and poor readers. *J Read Behav* 3:22–26, 1971.

Dunn L: *Peabody Picture Vocabulary Test.* Circle Pines, MN, American Guidance Service, 1965.

Dunn L: *Peabody Picture Vocabulary Test-Revised.* Circle Pines, MN, American Guidance Service, 1981.

Emerson HF, Gekoski WL: Interactive and categorical grouping strategies and the syntagmatic-paradigmatic shift. *Child Dev* 47:1116–1121, 1976.

Entwisle DR: Form class and children's word associations. *J Verbal Learn Verbal Behav* 5:558–565, 1966.

Entwisle DR, Forsyth DF: Word associations of children: effect of method of administration. *Psychol Rep* 13:291–299, 1963.

Entwisle DR, Forsyth DF, Muuss R: The syntactic-paradigmatic shift in children's word associations. *J Verbal Learn Verbal Behav* 3:19–29, 1964.

Ervin SM: Changes with age in the verbal determinants of word associations. *Am J Physiol* 74:361–372, 1961.

Francis H: Toward an explanation of the syntagmatic-paradigmatic shift. *Child Dev* 43:949–958, 1972.

Freston CW, Drew CJ: Verbal performance of learning disabled children as a function of input organization. *J Learn Disabil* 7:34–38, 1974.

Gerber A, Bryen DN: *Language and Learning Disabilities.* Baltimore, University Park Press, 1981.

German DNJ: Word-finding substitutions in children with learning disabilities. *Language Speech Hear Serv Schools* 13:223–230, 1982.

German DNJ: Word-finding skills in children with learning disabilities. *J Learn Disabil* 12:43–48, 1979.

Goldsmith S, Wallach G, Beilin H: Processing ungrammatical time sentences: a normal and learning disabled population. Presented at the New York State Speech and Hearing Convention, 1974.

Hagen JW, Stanovich KG: Strategies of acquisition. In Kail RV, Hagen JW: *Perspectives in the Devel-*

opment of Memory and Cognition. Hillsdale, NJ, Lawrence Erlbaum Associates, 1977, pp 89–111.

Halperin MS: Developmental changes in the recall and recognition of categorized word lists. *Child Dev* 45:144–151, 1974.

Israel L: Memory processing in learning disabled children. Unpublished doctoral dissertation, Graduate School and University Center, City University of New York, 1979.

Israel L: Free word associations of learning disabled and nondisabled children. Presented at the American Speech-Language-Hearing Association Convention, Detroit, 1980.

Israel L: Word associations of young children. Unpublished manuscript, 1981.

Johnson D, Myklebust H: *Learning Disabilities: Educational Principles and Practices.* New York, Grune and Stratton, 1967.

Kallail KJ, Edwards HT: A modified Cloze procedure as a test of comprehension and expression in adolescents. *J Commun Disord* 13:325–333, 1980.

Kirk SA, McCarthy JJ, Kirk WD: *Illinois Test of Psycholinguistic Abilities.* Urbana, University of Illinois Press, 1968.

Lippman MZ: Correlates of contrast word associations: developmental trends. *J Verbal Learn Verbal Behav* 10:392–399, 1971.

Lucas EV: *Semantic and Pragmatic Language Disorders: Assessment and Remediation.* Rockville, MD, Aspen Systems, 1980.

McNeill D: A study of word association. *J Verbal Learn Verbal Behav* 5:548–557, 1966.

Menyuk P: Syntactic competence and reading. Presented at the Symposium on Language, Learning, and Reading Disabilities: A New Decade, City University of New York, May, 1980.

Muma JR, Pierce S: Language intervention: data or evidence? *Top Learn Learn Disabil* 1:1–11, 1981.

Naron NK: Developmental changes in word attribute utilization for organization and retrieval in free recall. *J Exp Child Psychol* 25:279–297, 1978.

Naus MJ, Ornstein PA, Aivano S: Developmental changes in memory: the effects of processing time and rehearsal instruction. *J Exp Child Psychol* 23:237–251, 1977.

Nelson K: The syntagmatic-paradigmatic shift revisited: a review of research and theory. *Psychol Bull* 84:93–116, 1977.

Newcomer PL, Hammill DD: *Test of Language Development.* Austin, TX, Empiric Press, 1977.

Ornstein PA, Naus MJ, Liberty C: Rehearsal and organizational processes in children's memory. *Child Dev* 46:818–830, 1975.

Paris SG: Memory organization during children's repeated recall. *Dev Psychol* 14:99–106, 1978.

Parker TB, Freston CF, Drew CJ: Comparison of verbal performance of normal and learning disabled children as a function of input organization. *J Learn Disabil* 8:386–393, 1975.

Perfetti CA, Hogaboam T: Relationship between single word decoding and reading comprehension skill. *J Educ Psychol* 67:461–469, 1975.

Petry S: Word associations and the development of lexical memory. *Cognition* 5:57–71, 1977.

Rosch E: Human categorization. In Warren N: *Advances in Cross-Cultural Psychology.* London, Academic Press, 1977, vol 1.

Rossi S, Wittrock MC: Developmental shifts in verbal recall between ages two and five. *Child Dev* 42:333–338, 1971.

Semel EM, Wiig EH: *Clinical Evaluation of Language Function.* Columbus, OH, Charles E Merrill, 1980.

Shilo V: Word Associations in learning disabled children. Unpublished master's thesis, Emerson College, Boston, 1981.

Silliman E: Relationship between pictorial interpretation and comprehension of three spatial relations in school-age children. *J Speech Hear Res* 22:366–388, 1979.

Soenksen PA, Flagg CL, Schmits DW: Social communication in learning disabled students: a pragmatic analysis. *J Learn Disabil* 14:283–286, 1981.

Suiter ML, Potter RE: The effects of paradigmatic organization on verbal recall. *J Learn Disabil* 11:63–66, 1978.

Tarver SG, Hallahan DP, Cohen SB, et al: The development of visual selective attention and verbal rehearsal in learning disabled boys. *J Learn Disabil* 10:491–500, 1977.

Torgesen J, Goldman T: Verbal rehearsal and short-term memory in reading-disabled children. *J Learn Disabil* 48:56–60, 1977.

Vellutino FR: Toward an understanding of dyslexia: psychological factors in specific reading disability. In Benton AL, Pearl D: *Dyslexia: An Appraisal of Current Knowledge.* New York, Oxford University Press, 1978, pp 63–111.

Vogel S: *Syntactic Abilities in Normal and Dyslexic Children.* Baltimore, University Park Press, 1975.

Wallach G: The implications of different comprehension strategies in learning disabled children: effects of thematization. Unpublished doctoral dissertation, The Graduate School and University Center, City University of New York, 1977.

Wechsler D: *Wechsler Intelligence Scale for Children.* New York, The Psychological Corporation, 1974.

Wiig EH: Language-learning disabilities in school age children. Presented at the American Speech-Language-Hearing Northeast Regional Conference, Philadelphia, 1981.

Wiig EH, Lapointe C, Semel EM: Relationships among language processing and production abilities of learning disabled adolescents. *J Learn Disabil* 10:38–45, 1977.

Wiig EH, Semel EM: *Language Assessment and Intervention for the Learning Disabled.* Columbus, OH, Charles E Merrill, 1980.

Wiig EH, Semel EM: Productive language abilities in learning disabled adolescents. *J Learn Disabil* 8:578–586, 1975.

Wiig EH, Semel EM: *Language Disabilities in Children and Adolescents.* Columbus, OH, Charles E Merrill, 1976.

Wiig EH, Semel EM, Nystrom L: Comparison of rapid naming abilities in language-learning disabled and academically achieving eight-year-olds. *Lang Speech Hear Serv Schools* 13:11–22, 1982.

Wolf M: The word-retrieval process and reading in children and aphasics. In Nelson K: *Children's Language.* New York, Gardner Press, in press, vol 3.

Wong B, Wong R, Foth D: Recall and clustering of verbal materials among normal and poor readers. *Bull Psychonomic Soc* 19:375–378, 1977.

CHAPTER TWELVE

Semantic Integration and Language Learning Disabilities: From Research to Assessment and Intervention

ESTELLE KLEIN-KONIGSBERG, Ph.D.

"Memory emerges as a highly structured and interrelated system under the influence of higher level cognitive processes rather than the compilation of isolated facts" (Israel, Chapter 11).

AN INTRODUCTION TO LONG-TERM MEMORY AND SEMANTIC INTEGRATION

Memory is quite complex, and almost all studied variables have some effect on memory (Paivio and Begg, 1981). Factors such as an individual's intensity of attention, the meaningfulness of material, the structure of material, one's interest in the subject, and the strategies used for remembering, among others, must be accounted for when discussing memory. Average learners appear to develop all the memory skills necessary to enhance learning, but children with problems often have "poor memories."

This statement signals an immediate dilemma for practitioners who understand that the "poor memory" label may mean different things to different people. Indeed, it would be an understatement to say that, within language learning disabilities circles, characterizations of memory and memory disorders vary significantly. The differences of opinion regarding memory problems and their interaction with learning disabilities are due, in part at least, to the different theoretical and practical orientations of professionals involved in serving these children (Maxwell et al., 1982).

Through the years, our conceptualizations of memory have become more sophisticated. Researchers in the area of human memory have provided us with descriptions of the levels and mechanisms involved in the receiving, processing, interpreting, storing, and retrieving of information (Craik and Lockhart, 1972; Lindsay and Norman, 1972; Massaro, 1975; Crowder, 1976; Baddeley, 1978; Lemme and Daves, 1982; see also Chapter 4). Descriptions of processing, i.e., theoretical models of memory and comprehension, may provide useful information, as long as we understand that all models, no matter how useful or innovative, are abstract summaries of complex behaviors and interrelations (see Chapters 7 and 9). For example, in an earlier model, Lindsay and Norman (1972) and Norman (1969, 1970) outlined three representational levels of the human memory system which included a sensory information storage, a short-term or "primary store," and a long-term or "secondary store." Each of these memory levels was believed to serve a different function, store a different form of information, and have different capacity limitations. The sensory information storage system was described as the one that selectively reduced, or filtered, incoming stimuli so that relevant information would be processed. The short-term store, or "working memory system," enabled a person to "hold onto" the information from sensory store (for a limited amount of time) so that it could be processed further. Finally, the long-term system was responsible for assimilating, storing, and retrieving information when needed (see Chapter 4). The division among the various storage systems was understood as being somewhat hypothetical even in earlier models, but current research has helped us understand some of the aspects of memory to an even greater extent.

Many current theorists have gone as far as to suggest that the division of memory into separate short- and long-term components may be too rigid and that a better approach to take when trying to understand memory is to investigate the different types of coding mechanisms or strategies available to individuals in their attempts to retain information (Kintsch, 1977; Baddeley, 1978; Lemme and Daves, 1982). For example, one might verbalize aloud the sequence of numbers when trying to retain a new phone number. Different strategies would be in order when trying to remember the events and themes of a novel (see Chapter 6). Reflecting on these differences, Lemme and Daves (1982, p. 368) write that "acoustical phonemic encoding occurs as a short-term memory process when semantic coding is not possible." Going back to the phone number example, it may be the case that rehearsal strategies (short-term acoustic-phonemic coding) may be used initially until certain phone numbers (at least the desirable ones) end up in a more permanent, long-term store.

Underpinning many discussions of memory today is the notion that individuals are *actively* involved in the process. Storage processes are intimately related to attention, perception, and comprehension (Lemme and Daves, 1982; see also Chapters 1 and 2). The "transfer" of information from one storage system to another is extremely dynamic. According to some researchers, people's performances on many short-term memory tasks are directly related to what they *already have* in long-term store (Baddeley, 1978). Baddeley (1978) says that "larger memory traces" and "pre-existing associations" have a tremendous effect on short-term memory. As we will see later in this chapter, the memory for sentences is basically an interpretive, integrative process. Likewise, children's performances on certain "sentence memory" tasks may need to be viewed within a broader context.

We have much to learn about both short-term and long-term memory systems. However, regardless of our theoretical biases, we recognize that to function in a successful manner, people must remember things. It may be as seemingly simple as remembering where we parked our car, where we left our books, or the gist of our most recent conversation with a friend (Bellezza, 1982). Throughout our lives, we make judgments about how and how much we will remember (Meyer, 1977). Most importantly, we relate past experiences to current ones, integrating separate bits of information as we go along (Shaw, 1982). If we did not, each experience would be unique with no connection to previous experience and learning. We modify our strategies for remembering based upon the situation. We are just beginning to learn about how young children develop strategies for memory (and comprehension), and we cannot help but ask how language learning-disabled children make decisions about what to remember.

This chapter will explore some of the interactions among memory, language, and learning strategies. Underpinning the discussion is the role that integrative strategies play in helping adults and children remember information. The first section will review some of the classic studies done in the area of semantic memory. The concept of "constructive" processing will be addressed as it relates to adults and children. The second section will present the results of a research study on semantic integration with language learning-disabled children. The final section will provide suggestions for assessment and intervention within the context of this new research.

CONSTRUCTIVE ASPECTS OF MEMORY

We Are Actively Involved

We said before that individuals are actively involved in the memory process. We also said that short-term memory abilities are sometimes influenced by what a person "brings" to the situation. The constructive nature of memory refers to listeners' and readers' active use of past experience and knowledge of the world when processing spoken and written information (Bransford and Johnson, 1973; Bransford and Nitsch, 1978; Lorch, 1982). The notion that active participation in the learning process produces better retention, although not new, should encourage us to review some of the drills and exercises we sometimes give language learning-disabled students.

As early as 1932, Bartlett (pp. 213–214) explained how recall hardly ever involved an exact, or rote recapitulation. He postulated that people assimilate new information into their own "schemata" or organizational framework of past experiences that influences their current perceptions (see Chapters 6 and 10). Readers of this text, for example, whether conscious of it or not, will use their past knowledge of the subject, their experience with children, information from other texts, etc., to facilitate the process of comprehending this material. Butler's discussion of memory pool schemas in Chapter 4 reiterates this point and brings to mind many exciting and new concepts in the area. (See also, Pearson and Spiro, 1980, for an in-depth discussion of "schemata" and reading comprehension.)

What Do We Remember and Where Do We Put It?

People recall certain pieces of information and forget others. Certain pieces of information are also more accessible than others. For example, we might remember that "John Kennedy was President" more easily than we would remember that "John Kennedy was in the Navy" (unless we are old Navy persons) (Lorch, 1982). It is generally believed that material stored in long-term memory rarely maintains its original or actual form (Peleg, 1982). Rather, what is stored is an abstract unit containing an idea, or theme, or, in some cases, a person's interpretation of the information (Bransford and Nitsch, 1978; Peleg, 1982). In the general scheme of things, long-term memory assumes a most important role as an organizational storehouse of an enormous amount of information (Lemme and Daves, 1982). Tulving (1972) helped us understand the facets of this storehouse by making a distinction between *episodic* and *semantic* memory. Episodic memory involves the storage of personal experiences in terms of when they happened and the setting in which they took place. Semantic memory, on the other hand, is a repository of all permanent knowledge relating to things like linguistic rules, mathematical calculation rules, and the like (Tulving, 1972; Bellezza, 1982; Lemme and Daves, 1982). Many tasks require both types of memory, and the levels and strategies involved in the processes are both intriguing and complex.

Descriptions about what actually "remains behind" in long-term store and how it is organized will probably remain vague for quite some time (Bransford and Johnson, 1973). Nevertheless, some innovative researchers are studying various aspects of long-term memory. The classic research of Bransford et al. (1972), Bransford and Franks (1971), and Bransford and Johnson (1973), for example, shows how higher level strategies (inferential and integration strategies) influence the type and amount of information people remember. This research was among the first of its type to provide data about the constructive aspects of semantic memory. The Bransford research provides information about the contributions made by listeners during processing, and it hypothesizes about the structure of sentences in memory. Descriptions of Bransford et al.'s (1972) now classic "turtle" studies and Bransford and Franks's (1971) integration study are among those discussed in the following sections. The research is presented in some detail because it not only contributes to our understanding of information processing but also because it provides a direction for additional research in language learning disabilities. As practitioners, we might look to the research for the construction of contemporary assessment and intervention tools. We might ask ourselves whether standardized tests tap the processes being discussed. We might also consider how these concepts in semantic memory and the strategies involved in remembering relate to the tasks encountered by children every day in school.

Studies of Constructive Aspects of Memory in Adults

USE OF INFERENCES

Bransford et al. (1972) used a sentence recognition task to investigate the nature of sentence representation in memory. They presented subjects with a list of sentences differing only in the italicized prepositions, as in examples 1 and 2. Subjects were told that they would be asked questions about the sentences later.

(1) Three turtles rested *beside* the floating log and a fish swam beneath it.
(2) Three turtles rested *on* the floating log and a fish swam beneath it.

After reading the lists, subjects were given a 3-minute break. They were presented with a new list and were asked to decide whether they had seen any of the sentences before. Sentences such as 3 and 4 appeared on the new list:

(3) Three turtles rested *beside* the floating log and a fish swam beneath *them*.

(4) Three turtles rested *on* the floating log and a fish swam beneath *them*.

The results indicated that subjects tended to confuse sentences 2 and 4. They thought that sentence 4 had appeared on the original list. Sentences 1 and 3, on the other hand, were more likely to be recalled accurately. According to Bransford et al. (1972), the process of inferencing explains this difference. That is, sentence 4 can be inferred from sentence 2 because if the turtles are *on* a log, and a fish swims *under* the log, it logically follows that the fish also swims under the turtles. However, the same inference cannot be made with sentences 1 and 3. If the turtles are *beside* the log, and a fish swims beneath it, it cannot be assumed that the fish also swims under the turtles.

The findings suggest that the representation of sentences 2 and 4 in memory is identical. Bransford et al. (1972) showed that inferences were used in the normal course of language processing. Subjects in their study did not base memory judgments on the information expressed solely by the sentence. Rather, they responded by using their overall knowledge of the spatial relations, which, consequently, resulted in "fusing" the two sentences (2 and 4) into one schema—a schema that includes a visual picture of the turtles, the fish, and the log.

Johnson et al. (1973) also demonstrated that listeners make inferences during processing. They read stories to subjects and then gave them a recognition test. Subjects had to decide whether any of the sentences on the recognition list appeared in the stories. They were instructed to say "no" to sentences which were changed in any way. An experimental group was given stories that were designed to suggest a particular inference: Story 5 represents a sample used for the experimental group. In this story, one could infer that John was using a hammer.

(5) John was trying to fix the bird house. He was *pounding* the nail when his father came out to watch him and help him do the work.

A control group was given a story which was virtually the same as story 5 except for a verb change. With this change, one would be less likely to infer that a hammer was being used. Story 6 represents a sample used for the control group.

(6) John was trying to fix the bird house. He was *looking for* the nail when his father came out to watch him and to help him do the work.

Both groups were given the same sentence, e.g., sentence 7 below, on the recognition task.

(7) John was *using the hammer* to fix the bird house when his father came out to watch him and to help him do the work.

Experimental subjects were much more likely to think that sentence 7 had been part of the story, demonstrating, as in the Bransford et al. (1972) study, the spontaneous use of inferential processing during this memory task.

Although the studies provide some interesting information, we should reiterate that discussions about a sentence's representation in memory include many complex issues. Just how and when sentences merge in memory remains speculative. Jenkins (1974) utilized the same stimuli as Bransford et al. (1972) to obtain information about how people processed individual sentences (sometimes referred to as on-line comprehension) that required inferencing. Specifically, Jenkins (1974) asked subjects to answer questions about individual sentences, such as: "Three turtles rested on a floating log and a fish swam beneath *it*" and "Three turtles rested on a floating log and a fish swam beneath *them*." The question, "Did the fish swim beneath the turtles?" requires a "yes" response in both cases. Jenkins found that people took longer to answer the "it" sentences. He concluded that whereas the information necessary to answer the them-sentences is *explicitly* stated, it is *implicitly* stated in the it-sentences. Thus, according to Jenkins (1974), the two sentences appear to be distinct, at least at the point where they are

presented individually and where a response is required immediately. He goes on to propose that there are actually two representations of meaning available for sentences—the first a basic meaning derived from immediate comprehension processes, and the second an "enriched" meaning resulting from inference and integration as a sentence is stored in memory.

Researchers are continuing to explore interrelations between memory and comprehension (Bransford, 1979; Paivio and Begg, 1981; Lorch, 1982; Peterson and Potts, 1982; see also Chapters 4 and 5). As practitioners involved in testing and teaching children with problems, we should consider applying some of the concepts discussed to our daily work. For example, we might analyze the amount and type of information presented to children. We might also be aware of the kinds of responses being required of them. It is important to recognize that children's performances may vary depending upon whether we give them individual sentences or groups of sentences, use a time delay or not, etc. Diagnostic and educational labels, particularly when talking about "comprehension" and "memory" problems, must be used with caution (see Chapter 1).

INTEGRATION

Integration is a process of combining independently represented, yet functionally related stimuli into a single organized unit. Integration is a generic term for an operation by which information is succinctly stored. The concept of "semantic integration" originated from research on how adults remember sentences (Bransford and Franks, 1971; Franks and Bransford, 1972; Barclay, 1973; Bransford and Johnson, 1973; Bransford and Nitsch, 1978). In one of the first studies of its type, Bransford and Franks (1971) demonstrated that it is the "meaning" of the sentence which is remembered, not necessarily the sentence itself. In addition, they found that the meanings of sets of sentences dealing with the same idea tend to be integrated into a single representation. It is this single representation which is retained in memory, rather than each individual sentence.

Bransford and Franks (1971) constructed a number of complex sentences that could be broken down into four simple sentences. For example, "The ants in the kitchen ate the sweet jelly which was on the table," was a complex (complete idea) sentence used in their experiment. The four basic propositions or simple sentences that form the complex sentence were:

(8) The ants were in the kitchen.
(9) The jelly was on the table.
(10) The jelly was sweet.
(11) The ants ate the jelly.

Sentences 8 to 11 were called ONES. Correspondingly, the complete ideas containing all four interrelated propositions were called FOURS. Other sentences related to a complete idea were also formed. TWOS combined two propositions (e.g., "The ants in the kitchen ate the jelly.") and THREES combined three of the propositions (e.g., "The ants in the kitchen ate the sweet jelly.").

The experimental procedure used by Bransford and Franks (1971) consisted of an acquisition phase followed by a recognition phase. During the acquisition phase, subjects were presented with lists of sentences that included ONES, TWOS, and THREES. All of the sentences on the acquisition lists were derivable from a FOUR. However, subjects were never presented with a FOUR during acquisition. As part of the acquisition task, subjects were asked to answer a question about each sentence after it was presented. After 24 sentences had been presented (various combinations of ONES, TWOS, THREES), they were given a 5-minute break. The recognition test was presented next. The recognition list was made up of FOURS (which the subjects never actually heard), as well as THREES, TWOS, and ONES.

Three types of sentences were included in the recognition test: OLDS (sentences that were actually presented during the acquisition phase); NEWS (sentences which were not presented during acquisition but whose meanings were derivable from one of the complete ideas); and NONCASES (sentences whose meaning was not derivable from one of the ideas being communicated). For example, if one of the complete ideas (FOURS) was "The girl who lives next door broke the large window on the porch," the NONCASE could be "The man who lives next door broke the large window on the porch." The recognition sentences were presented one at a time, and the subjects were asked to judge whether they had actually heard the sentence before. They also gave a confidence rating for each sentence along a 5-point scale.

The results of the Bransford and Franks study showed that the order of recognition and confidence rating was FOURS > THREES > TWOS > ONES. This is interesting in view of the fact that the subjects had never actually heard FOURS. OLDS and NEWS received comparable ratings at the levels of FOURS, THREES, and TWOS, supporting the hypothesis that people retain information about holistic semantic structures and are much less likely to retain information about the particular sentences used to express the structure. In addition, NONCASES received lower ratings than OLD and NEW sentences, suggesting that subjects were not responding to sentence length, or complexity, or key words found in the acquisition sentences.

The Bransford and Franks (1971) research contributed information about semantic integration that was previously unavailable. However, some researchers noticed that the sentences used by Bransford and Franks (1971) expressed concrete ideas (Marschark and Paivio, 1977; Paivio and Begg, 1981; Belmore et al., 1982). That is, the sentences were ones that tended to evoke visual images. A sentence like, "The spirited leader slapped a mournful hostage," could be classified as a concrete sentence whereas a sentence like, "The arbitrary regulation provoked a civil complaint," could be classified as an abstract sentence (Paivio and Begg, 1981). Begg and

Paivio (1969) were among the first to hypothesize that concrete images are stored as visual images, whereas abstract sentences are stored as verbal images, i.e., as words. Studies have produced conflicting results. Some have suggested that the integration effect (as per Bransford and Franks, 1971) may not be as strong for abstract sentences for which visual images are not readily constructed (e.g., Begg and Paivio, 1969). More current research suggests that the storage of abstract and concrete sentences may have common properties because the "semantic analysis . . . (of sentences) . . . requires an abstract level of encoding which is neutral with respect to imagery" (Belmore et al., 1982, p. 348).

We recognize the "common properties" notion regarding the storage of sentences, but there is some evidence suggesting that visual imagery facilitates language processing. Marschark and Paivio (1977) and Belmore et al. (1982), for example, found that concrete sentences were somewhat easier for people to recall and comprehend than abstract sentences. Belmore et al. (1982) reported processing time differences between concrete and abstract sentences (with and without inferences) with subjects answering questions about concrete sentences faster than they answered questions about abstract sentences. However, Belmore et al. (1982, p. 349) caution us by writing: "In the absence of a well-developed model of sentence comprehension which includes the use of imagery, it is difficult to offer a detailed understanding of the role of imagery in on-line sentence processing." The reader is directed to Paivio and Begg (1981), Belmore et al. (1982), and Marshark and Paivio (1977) for additional information regarding the procedures and conclusions drawn from the research. Nevertheless, we are reminded (once again) to consider the type (or level) of material (e.g., concrete versus abstract) we present to language learning-disabled students (see Chapters 1 and 14).

INFERENCE AND INTEGRATION: RESEARCH AND CLINICAL IMPLICATIONS

The studies discussed thus far focused on the inferential and integrative aspects of memory. The act of inferring is an expansion process. It enables the listener and the reader to go beyond given informtion. This is an important process because it enables us to make connections and to "read between the lines." Integration allows us to collapse redundant and extraneous information. Both processes involve active, organizational strategies. Both processes are contingent upon a person's past experiences and knowledge of the environment. The ability to elaborate or make inferences, coupled with the ability to integrate ideas, allows individuals to deal with all kinds of information. As practicing professionals, we are apt to ask: If these abilities develop spontaneously, can they be taught? We need to know more about these processes in children, and we should continue to pose questions that link research and practice. Are the strategies similar in normally achieving and learning-disabled (LD) children? Will modifications in instructional language facilitate the use of these strategies? These issues will be examined further in the next section as we explore the relevance of these concepts for students with language learning disabilities.

Constructive Aspects of Children's Memory: Normal and LD

As outlined in Chapter 5, further research on children's inferential and integrational abilities is warranted. Available data show that between the ages of 6 and 12, children significantly alter their ability to apply inferential processes to the tasks of sentence memory (see Chapter 5). The subtleties and nuances of these aspects of acquisition are still unknown. Collectively, however, the research indicates that children construct inferential relationships and integrate ideas when attempting to comprehend and remember information (Paris and Carter, 1973; Barclay and Reid, 1974; Paris et al., 1974; Glick, 1975; Brown, 1976; Paris and Lindauer, 1976: Wallach and Lee, 1980; see also Chapter 6).

To date, a limited amount of empirical evidence is available about the integration and inferential strategies employed by learning-disabled children. We have seen through the contributions of the authors in this text that continued exploration into the organizational strategies of LD children and adolescents is needed. The relationship between comprehension strategies and exhibited limitations in auditory memory for nonlinguistic (e.g., digits) and linguistic (e.g., sentences) stimuli deserves careful attention (Wiig and Semel, 1976, 1980; Swisher and Aten, 1981). Although we have come a long way, the relationship between sentence comprehension and specific memory functions remains somewhat vague. New concepts and constructs are needed to better understand the developmental aspects of information processing in learning-disabled children. The research presented in the next section will address this need. Assessment and intervention suggestions will also be discussed.

A STUDY OF SEMANTIC INTEGRATION IN LEARNING-DISABLED CHILDREN

This research investigates the ability of learning-disabled children to go beyond given information when trying to understand and remember sentences. Do they spontaneously construct inferential relationships like adults and other children, or do they attend differentially to individual sentences or specific sentence constituents? The experimental design was inspired by Bransford and Franks (1971) and Franks and Bransford (1972). However, rather than being a study of adults, this one involves children between the ages of 7 and 11 years old. Thus, this research also concerns developmental changes in integrative skills. Concrete and abstract sentences were used to obtain additional information about the role of visual imagery in semantic integration. Concrete sentences, e.g., "The old farmer milked the brown cow

in the barn," were believed to be easier to visualize than abstract sentences, e.g., "The proud poor people were disappointed by the high taxes" (Klein-Konigsberg, 1977). The procedures, statistical analysis, and results of the original research are summarized below. Readers are directed to Klein-Konigsberg (1977) for a more detailed discussion.

An Experimental Test

WHO SHALL BE CALLED "LEARNING DISABLED" REVISITED

Sixty normally achieving and 60 learning-disabled children between the ages of 7:0 and 10:11 years were tested. The normal achievers, chosen by their respective classroom teachers, were performing on appropriate grade levels in all academic areas. They were attending grades 2 through 5 in New York City public schools. The learning-disabled children were classified as such by a psychoeducational diagnostic team. Complete histories (educational, medical, speech-language, psychological, etc.) were available for LD subjects. They were attending special education classes in New York City public schools. Both normal and learning-disabled subjects were from middle-class socioeconomic backgrounds.

The problems involved in defining the "learning-disabled" population, as discussed throughout this text, were recognized when this research was undertaken. The factors for subject selection for the learning-disabled group included a number of criteria. All LD children demonstrated auditory acuity within normal limits and obtained Wechsler Intelligence Scale for Children Verbal IQ scores above 85. Additional criteria included:

1. Educational test scores at least 2 years below chronological age levels in two or more academic areas; reading and math scores were obtained by using the Wide Range Achievement Test (Word Recognition, Math, Spelling), the Gray Oral Reading Test, the Key Math Diagnostic Test, the Durrell Test of Reading Analysis, and the Peabody Individual Achievement Test

(Reading, Math, Spelling, General Information).

2. Language test results within 1 SD from the mean for various tests administered, including the Peabody Picture Vocabulary Test and selected subtests of the Illinois Test of Psycholinguistic Abilities (ITPA). Given the problems of both these instruments, it should be noted that the learning-disabled subjects in this study did not exhibit gross linguistic deficiencies as measured by the instruments mentioned above, despite their more subtle learning and language problems. This issue mirrors those raised by Maxwell and Wallach in Chapter 2 about symptoms of language disability "washing away" over time. It also brings to mind the problems raised by many other authors in this text about test-retest myths and population selection (see Chapters 14 and 15).

3. Evidence of organicity as derived from neurologists' and psychiatrists' reports. Regarding this criteria, it was recognized that the *concept* of brain damage may be far different from the *fact* of brain damage (see Stark and Wallach, 1980, p. 2). Indeed, the fact that brain damage exists may be a presumption in some cases, a point which is also made by Maxwell in Chapter 3 and by Wallach and Liebergott in Chapter 1. (Chapter 3 should be consulted for more specific information on the neurological correlates of language learning disabilities.)

PROCEDURES

The children were tested individually. Each child was presented with a list of sentences, on tape, one by one. A question followed each sentence. The child was required to answer the question about the sentence before the next one was presented. This was part 1.

After a 2-minute break, the children were presented with another list of sentences. They were asked to decide whether they had heard any of the sentences before. The examiner explained that some of the sentences were the same as they had just heard and some of the sentences were different. This was part 2.

Children were tested on CONCRETE and ABSTRACT sentences.

STIMULI: CONCRETE SENTENCES (I)

Table 12.1 provides examples of some of the CONCRETE sentences used in the Klein-Konigsberg (1977) Semantic Integration Test. A list of simple sentences, each expressing part of a complete idea, was constructed. Sentences 11 to 14 represent the most basic type of sentence used. These sentences were called ONES because they expressed one of the basic propositions contained in the "complete idea" sentences.

(11) The bear was big.
(12) The bear ate the candy.
(13) The candy was chocolate.
(14) The bear was in the woods.

An example of a complete idea sentence, i.e., a sentence that contains all four interrelated ideas (from sentences 11 to 14), is provided in example 15. Sentences of this type were called FOURS.

(15) The big bear ate the chocolate candy in the woods.

TWO- and THREE-idea sentences were also constructed. Sentences 16 and 17 represent TWOS and THREES, respectively.

(16) The big bear ate the candy. (This sentence combines "The bear was big," and "The bear ate the candy") = TWO IDEAS
(17) The big bear ate the chocolate candy. (This sentence combines "The bear was big," "The bear ate the candy," and "The candy was chocolate.") = THREE IDEAS

The children were presented with various combinations of ONES, TWOS, and THREES in part 1 of the test where they were required to answer questions about the sentences. FOURS were presented in part 2 only. The two complete idea sentences (FOURS) used in the CONCRETE sentence section were: "The big bear ate the chocolate candy in the woods," and "The old farmer milked the brown cow in the barn."

Three types of recognition sentences were used in part 2 where the children had

Table 12.1.

Examples of CONCRETE Sentences Used by Klein-Konigsberg (1977) to Test Semantic Integration

Target FOURS: (1) The big bear ate the chocolate candy in the woods.
            (2) The old farmer milked the brown cow in the barn.

Part 1: (8 sentences in complete test)[a]

1. The cow was brown. (ONE)	What color was the cow?
2. The bear ate the candy in the woods. (TWO)	Where did the bear eat the candy?
3. The old farmer milked the brown cow. (THREE)	What did the farmer milk?
4. The farmer was old. (ONE)	Who was old?

Part 2: (24 sentences in complete test)[b]
1. The farmer was old (OLD ONE) (appeared in part 1)
2. The old farmer ate the chocolate candy in the woods. (TYPE I, NONCASE FOUR) (a false inference)
3. The bear ate the chocolate candy. (NEW TWO) (derived from original)
4. The old farmer milked the brown cow. (OLD THREE) (appeared in part 1)

[a] Children answer questions about sentences.
[b] Children decide whether they have heard sentences before; original test contained eight OLDS, eight NEWS, and eight NONCASES

to decide if they had heard the sentences before:

1. OLD sentences, i.e., sentences that had actually been presented in part 1.

2. NEW sentences, i.e., ONES, TWOS, THREES, and FOURS, derived from the complete idea targets but never presented in part 1.

3. NONCASE sentences, i.e., sentences whose meaning is not derivable from one of the complete ideas being presented.

Two types of NONCASES were formed: (1) TYPE I—a false inference (e.g., "The farmer ate the chocolate candy in the barn."); and (2) TYPE II—a sentence whose idea is not related to either of the complete ideas but which contained a similar lexical item of one of the complete ideas (e.g., "The *cow* ate the grass.")

STIMULI: ABSTRACT SENTENCES (II)

Table 12.2 provides some examples of the ABSTRACT sentences used in the Klein-Konigsberg (1977) Semantic Integration Test. The format, sentence types, and number of sentences used in this section were the same as in the CONCRETE section. The list of ABSTRACT sentences was constructed with the help of a psychoeducational team. Further screening consisted of

matching the CONCRETE (section I) and ABSTRACT (section II) sections for word frequency (Carroll et al., 1971). The two complete ideas sentences (FOURS) used in the ABSTRACT section were: "The smart children did not understand the important new rules" and "The proud poor people were disappointed by the high taxes."

Within the limitations of the present study, semantic integration was defined in the following way: (1) NEW sentences should receive positive or "yes" responses because they are derivable from the complete idea. Subjects should think that they heard NEW sentences even though they did not actually hear them before. This is the case if we follow the model suggested by Bransford and Franks (1971) and Franks and Bransford (1972). (2) Both types of NONCASE sentences should receive negative or "no" responses because they are not derivable from the complete idea. NONCASE data are very important for interpreting results. TYPE I NONCASES would show that subjects were not just responding to sentence length or complexity, inasmuch as they are just as long and complex as the other sentences. TYPE II NONCASE results would also indicate that subjects were not merely responding

Table 12.2.
Examples of ABSTRACT Sentences Used By Klein-Konigsberg (1977) to Test Semantic Integration

Target FOURS: (1) The smart children did not understand the important new rules.
 (2) The proud poor people were disappointed by the high taxes.

Part 1: (8 sentences in complete test)[a]

1. The children did not understand the rules. (ONE)　　What didn't the children understand?
2. The proud people were disappointed by the　　Who were disappointed by the taxes?
 taxes. (TWO)
3. The smart children did not understand the new　　What kind of children did not understand
 rules. (THREE)　　 the new rules?
4. The taxes were high. (ONE)　　What were the taxes?

Part 2: (24 sentences in complete test)[b]

1. The taxes were high. (OLD ONE) (appeared in part 1)
2. The proud poor people were disappointed by the smart children. (TYPE I, NONCASE FOUR)
 (a false inference)
3. The children did not understand the new rules. (NEW TWO) (derived from original)
4. The poor people were disappointed by the high taxes. (OLD THREE) (appeared in part 1)

[a] Children answer questions about sentences.
[b] Children decide whether they heard sentences before; original test contained eight OLDS, eight NEWS, and eight NONCASES.

to the key words from part 1 sentences. This ability to distinguish subtle differences in sentences suggests precise discrimination of semantic information remembered. (3) OLDS and NEWS should receive similar "yes" responses since responses are based on combined information of a sentence set, not just individual sentences actually heard.

RESULTS

Highlights of Significant Findings. Differences emerged between LD and normal groups. Sentence *type* (OLD, NEW, and NONCASE), *image* factors (CONCRETE versus ABSTRACT), and number of *elements* (ONE, TWO, THREE, and FOUR) were the significant variables affecting the children's performances. Interestingly, *age* was not a significant variable. The discussion will concern the differential effect of these variables on the LD and normal children in this study.

Type. LD children responded "yes" a significantly greater number of times for OLD and NONCASE sentences than did normals. In fact, the LD children accounted for all "yes" responses for TYPE I and TYPE II NONCASES.

The mean number of "yes" responses by the normals for OLD and NEW sentences was not significantly different (i.e., OLDS = NEWS). These data show that normal children exhibited a response pattern indicative of semantic integration. The normals thought they had "recognized" the novel sentences (NEWS) consonant with the ideas presented. Unlike the LD children, the normals were also quite sure that they had not heard NONCASE sentences.

Imagery. Data related to the effect of CONCRETE versus ABSTRACT sentences on semantic integration revealed that, on the average, a greater number of "yes" responses occurred for CONCRETE than for ABSTRACT sentence types. This is not surprising in view of the age of the subjects (7 to 11 years old) in this experiment. A more detailed analysis revealed another difference between normal and LD populations. The differences between normals and LD's become greater at the level of ABSTRACT sentences. The normal children, performing significantly better across the board, gave more "yes" responses to NEW ABSTRACT sentences (i.e., sentences that had not been given before). This is a departure from their pattern of responses with the CONCRETE sentences, where "yes" responses equaled each other for OLD and NEW sentences. In comparison, the LD children had much more difficulty than the normals integrating information when it involved NEW ABSTRACT sentences. The poorest performance by the LD children involved NEW ABSTRACTS. As compared with the normals, the LD's scored significantly higher for ABSTRACT OLDS and significantly lower for ABSTRACT NEWS.

Elements. Perhaps the most significant difference between the normal and LD subjects is revealed in the data involving number of ELEMENTS within sentences. Figure 12.1 highlights this extremely important CATEGORY X ELEMENT interaction. Collapsing over OLD/NEW and CONCRETE/ABSTRACT sentences, it was found that the increase in the number of "yes" responses for the normals is a function of the increase in the number of ELEMENTS per sentence. In other words, the normal children tended to be confident that they had heard NEW THREES and FOURS before. This is important because the information contained in the NEW THREES and FOURS could only have

been learned by integrating information from the various sentences actually presented. For the LD children, however, the mean number of "yes" responses significantly increased from ONES to TWOS, remained the same from TWOS to THREES, and started to decline from THREES to FOURS. Thus, the LD children scored significantly higher for ONES than did NORMALS and equaled the performance of normals at TWOS (the point at which the behavior of integration would start to occur). As can be seen in Figure 12.1, the normals then surpassed LD children at THREES and continued the significant rise to FOURS.

DISCUSSION

This research represents one way of studying semantic integration. The mode of storage, or performance of integration, was measured by testing the children's abilities to recognize sentences that were never actually presented but which would be derived through a comprehension of relationships among semantically related sentences.

It appears from the results that normal children spontaneously integrate information expressed by a number of nonconsecutively presented, but semantically related, sentences. The learning-disabled children appeared to attend to smaller units, short sentences, and individual lexical items (as demonstrated by their response to NONCASES). Interestingly, their performance was shown to be similar to normals at the level of TWOS, where integrating begins. Perhaps they can integrate up to a certain point, beyond which additional information is in excess of their integrative capacities.

It appears to be the case that learning-disabled children did not adopt a recoding strategy similar to normal children. Such a strategy might have allowed for more *efficient* processing of information. In one sense, the LD children may have been trying to remember too much, i.e., discrete elements/events or too much of the "wrong thing." The LD children in this study at-

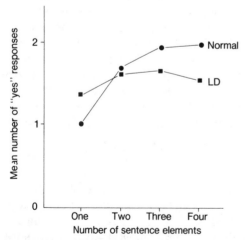

Figure 12.1. Mean number of "yes" responses by learning disabled and normal children as a function of sentence elements (category × element interaction).

tended to individual sentences as well as to specific sentence constituents when attempting to remember information. They did appear to be abstracting the semantic relationships in a manner that was qualitatively similar to the normal children. However, the LD children appeared to be functioning at a level where integration begins.

The role of imagery in facilitating integration warrants further investigation. To some degree, it appears as if imagery facilitated the performance of the LD children. From the CONCRETE test, we can see that the performance of the LD's on OLDS and NEWS is "closer." The NEW ABSTRACTS were really beyond their capabilities. It was almost as if the LD children were trying to memorize each sentence—based upon their performance on the ABSTRACT OLDS (recognizing more of them—even exceeding the normals). The normal children, on the other hand, "improved" in their performances on the NEW ABSTRACTS. The degree and kinds of imagery, context effects, and prior experience all need to be considered.

The present study does not shed any new light on developmental differences, except to say that, above the age of 7, normal children are spontaneously integrating information. This is similar to the findings of Paris and Carter (1973) and Moeser (1976), as discussed in Chapter 5. As suggested by Paris and Upton (1974), children from 6 to 11 years of age increase the amount of both explicit and implicit information they comprehend from paragraphs. The better responses overall on the CONCRETE sentences may also be suggestive of developmental trends we might explore further.

SEMANTIC INTEGRATION: INTRODUCTION TO ASSESSMENT AND INTERVENTION

The principles underlying the experimental tasks presented in the previous section may be similar to the principles which underlie some of the children's everyday experiences in school. They are required to comprehend and remember meaning from stories, films, and teachers' instructions. It may be that certain kinds of training and/or instruction in academic subjects do not always enhance the integrative abilities of learning-disabled students. Shorter verbal directions are not *always* easier (see Chapters 1 and 5). Children may be able to handle more information if it is presented appropriately. Blanchowitz (1977–78) made the same point when discussing reading (quoted in Chapter 1). She pointed out that the overuse of simple declarative sentences in children's early readers may actually "go against" normal integrative processes (see Chapter 1). Current trends such as these, as discussed throughout this text, suggest the need to change remedial teaching procedures in order to maximize learning. As we approach these changes, some of which are presented in the assessment and intervention section that follows, we might remember that individual differences exist within both normal and LD groups, and continued investigation is needed regarding the relationship between these skills and the learning process.

Assessment

Important issues involved in the assessment of language processes of learning-disabled children include: (1) the overall adequacy of currently available assessment instruments (particularly within the areas of memory processes and sentence comprehension); (2) the appropriateness of these instruments for use with a heterogeneous group of youngsters; and (3) interpretation of data from assessment instruments for use within an assessment-intervention paradigm.

Regardless of the specific area to be assessed, concern about the adequacy of assessment procedures is not new (see Chapter 9). In examining the adequacy of measures of memory processes and sentence comprehension, we must consider whether available instruments contradict, complement, or have much or little to do with a current and meaningful theoretical foundation. Many traditional tests used for the identification of specific memory functions in learning-disabled children are ineffective in terms of delineating the relationship between memory processes and sentence comprehension. However, practical application of newer concepts is sometimes difficult because: (1) tests often lead us in other directions; and (2) we are not used to interpreting children's behaviors as parallel functions. More often than not, our mode of operation, clinically and educationally, has been to separate the various functions. Wallach and Liebergott discussed the "discrete skills" dilemma in Chapter 1. Maxwell and Wallach followed up with the example of an assessment team's search for a child's language, *or* perception, *or* memory problem. Can the various functions (processes) be separated when, for example, memory and retrieval processes impinge on all linguistic levels? Is it not the case that this separation becomes even more unrealistic as children get older? Indeed, gaps may be more difficult to evaluate as memory and comprehension skills merge and children learn to compensate.

ASSESSMENT OF AUDITORY MEMORY PATTERNS

Auditory memory and strategies for remembering are involved in comprehension. Because these overlap, it is important to understand that it is difficult (if not meaningless) to continually try to separate "auditory memory" from other processes. As put by Gerber (1981, p. 83), "The relationship between memory and language appears to be reciprocal in that memory is acknowledged to play a critical role in ... language and language has been demonstrated to be a potential facilitator of memory."

A number of clinical instruments are available that measure various aspects of "memory." Many of the tests currently used are limited to various aspects of short-term memory and sentence memory. Tests of semantic integration functions are not available as yet, although in Chapter 16 Lee and Fine will discuss some new trends.

Examples of widely used procedures in the auditory areas include:

1. Recall of number of digit sequences
   —McCarthy Scales (numerical memory)
   —ITPA (auditory sequential memory)
2. Recall of unrelated word sequences
   —McCarthy Scales (recall of unrelated words)
   —Detroit Test of Learning Aptitude (DTLA) (auditory attention for unrelated words)
3. Sentence repetition
   —McCarthy Scales (verbal memory, part I)
   —Detroit Test of Learning Aptitude (auditory attention for related syllables)
   —Clinical Evaluation of Language Function (CELF) (producing model sentences)
4. Recall of oral directions (serial commands)
   —Token Test (parts I to IV)
   —Detroit Test (oral directions)
   —CELF (processing oral directions)
5. Recall of information in spoken passages
   —McCarthy Scales (verbal memory, part II)
   —CELF (processing spoken paragraphs)

As practitioners we need to understand the demands being placed on the child. We should think about the relationships of the skills being tested and the "real world." Wing (1982) reminds us that, although immediate verbatim repetition is not a usual natural response, many tests use repetition tasks to measure short-term auditory memory for phonemes, morphological and syntactic structures, and related and unrelated words. Retrieval, sequencing, and comprehension are all part of the successful completion of such tasks in varying degrees. Semantic strategies become more involved, especially at the word and sentence levels. The DTLA's Auditory Attention for Related Syllables and the CELF's Producing

Model Sentences are both sentence imitation tasks, although their titles can be misleading to the naive examiner, who might suspect that it is auditory attention that is measured in the Detroit subtest and production or expression in the CELF. As the sophisticated examiner is well aware, different titles can mean the same thing, and similar titles may mean different things.

In Chapter 6, Westby showed how memory for sentences is not the same as memory for text or connected discourse. Poor performances on "oral directions tasks" (e.g., before I point to the red line, but after I point to the blue line, you . . ., etc.) do not automatically lead to poor performances on "processing spoken paragraphs" tasks. The concept of success or failure with one- versus two- versus three-level commands also requires reevaluation. Indeed, we do not process sentence sequences in a stilted one-at-a-time manner. Contextual, logical-semantic, and syntactic variables affect the amount of information we recall. Wallach discussed semantic constraints on two-clause sentences in Chapter 5. Sentences 18 and 19 (see p. 87, Chapter 5) represent two commands that are a bit different.

(18) The girl feeds the baby before putting her to bed.
(19) The girl feeds the baby before picking up the pencil.

They both require sequencing and "memory," but the logical connections in sentence 18 could make it somewhat "easier." Certainly, when logical constraints are not available, we may rehearse (i.e., say it aloud to ourselves) or employ specific syntactic strategies (e.g., try to keep words in mind, etc.), and the like. The important point for practical application is to be aware of what the child may be doing (what strategy is being employed). It is also important to recognize what it is about the material that facilitates memory processes. Does Johnny "act out" the main clause and omit the subordinate clause in sentence 20 because he has a "memory" problem and/or because he is using a "pay attention to the main clause" strategy (see Chapter 5, p. 87).

(20) After you point to the red line, point to the green line.

Are memory span and language strategy playing off one another? Does Johnny use a sentence-by-sentence strategy instead of a "get the whole idea" strategy when listening to stories?

To complicate the issue, instruments measuring language comprehension are, at best, generally limited to the measurement of the *literal* meaning of spoken and written passages. As put by Rees and Shulman (1978, p. 210), whether the examiner asks the child to point to a picture, or to move objects around, or repeat a sentence, these techniques "have in common the goal of tapping the child's verbal comprehension in terms of literal sentence meaning."

Van Kleeck (Chapter 9) reminds us that many of the listen-to-sentence/point-to-picture tasks fall into metalinguistic and metacognitive domains. Children have to "hold" the stimulus sentence in memory, compare it to the test's pictures, and then make a judgment about the sentence-picture match. *The Auditory Test of Language Comprehension* (Carrow, 1969), the *CELF* Processing Spoken Sentences (Semel and Wiig, 1980), and other tests using the sentence-picture format present problems from this point of view.

The Token Test for Children (DiSimoni, 1978), requiring manipulation of tokens of different colors, shapes, and sizes, taps the literal level of comprehension. It should also be noted that parts I to IV may prove to be especially difficult for some children. The analyses of specific comprehension strategies may be useful for a more meaningful interpretation of part V (as shown in sentence 20 above). New tests as illustrated by portions of the Holland (1980) *Communicative Abilities in Daily Living* have been constructed in a manner which permits the consideration of certain aspects of comprehension that go beyond literal translations. Rees and Shulman (1978), Bransford (1979), and Swisher and Aten (1981) should be consulted for additional ideas.

GOING BEYOND LITERAL TRANSLATIONS

It is important for us to remember that in daily discourse, listeners distinguish between old and new information. In the case of

(21) Mother is watching baby.

and

(22) Mother is at the park.

we would conclude by integration that

(23) Mother is watching baby at the park.

Another relation exists between old and new information, resulting in information never explicitly expressed. For example, from

(24) Dad was fixing the car.

and

(25) Dad asked for a wrench.

the listener may infer that

(26) Dad needed a wrench to fix the car.

The information in sentences 24 and 25 must be combined, or integrated, before an inference takes place.

These examples show that, to comprehend sentences, listeners must be able to relate old information to new information. The old information may be contained in the sentences themselves, in related situational contexts, or in prior knowledge of the listener.

As mentioned, available clinical instruments measuring language comprehension are designed, for the most part, only to examine the individual's ability to comprehend lexical items and relational or grammatical meanings. The test items do not go beyond the literal meaning of words and sentences. The ability to relate presupposed information to new information and to draw inferences is not assessed by these formal tests. Limiting the clinical measurement of comprehension abilities and deficits to the literal meaning aspect will fail to provide a full picture of the child's abilities and deficits. Obviously, formal tests have serious limitations for assessing the use and comprehension of spoken language.

Until these gaps are filled, the clinician is directed toward reviewing the current research available for descriptive examples of comprehension and memory skills and techniques for observing them. Utilizing the information provided in this chapter, along with an instrument such as the Konigsberg Semantic Integration Test, can provide for a more comprehensive approach to the measurement of inferential and integrative processes. While the Konigsberg Semantic Integration Test is still experimental, it may help us interpret a child's pattern of responses when planning for language intervention. In conclusion, assessment data of a qualitative nature can help answer several questions which quantitative data alone cannot fulfill, e.g., What can/can't the child do? (strengths/deficits); what helps the child respond appropriately?; how does the child try to compensate for deficits?; what strategies are/are not being used by the child?

Intervention

As we have seen, children with language learning disabilities frequently have significant problems retaining and recalling information. Many of these children appear to have less efficient strategies for recoding information. As a result, they may recall irrelevant details in subject matter and miss or misinterpret significant information. These problems may inhibit their ability to comprehend the meaning of monologues, dialogues, conversations, and written materials. On a basic level, we might ask ourselves whether we present subject matter to these children in an integrated way. Are classroom and/or therapy sessions structured in a way that encourages children to make connections between concepts? Does the child learn on one occasion about "rain" and other aspects of climate and on another occasion about "flowers and plants" without being shown on either occasion that one affects the other? Is subject matter in successive grades repeated without showing children how events and concepts are related? It is suggested that associative functions are developed when teachers help students relate subject matter with ideas discussed later in class and, in the older grades, across subject matter (Chapters 8, 14, and 16).

We recognize that it is extremely difficult to discuss, test, or teach memory strategies independent of other learning processes, but we also recognize that it is possible to devise more effective techniques to help children store, retrieve, and organize information (see Chapter 11). Let us explore some possibilities in the next section.

INFERENTIAL AND INTEGRATIONAL STRATEGIES

Wallach and Lee (1980) provide suggestions to enhance inferential and integrational skills. For example, to grasp the concept of "inferences," clinicians could present simple sentences to students as,

(27) The man cut the bread.

and have the child guess (or infer) the implicit tool of the sentence (e.g., with a *knife*). This can be done through either listening or a reading task. Multiple sentences and corresponding answers can be provided for a matching game.

Following an experimental paradigm of Paris and Lindauer (1976), memory games involving inferential relationships can be devised. Sentences can be constructed to include an instrument commonly employed to accomplish the action of the verbs, e.g.,

(28) Mother baked a cake in the *oven*.

The instrument of the sentence (*oven*) could be stated explicitly, as above, or it could be omitted and only implied by the sentence. If the child ordinarily supplies missing, but implied, information to a sentence in order to understand its meaning, then he/she should derive equivalent memory representation for sentences (i.e., recall) with either explicit or implicit instruments. Subsequently, children should be

able to use a retrieval cue such as the instrument to recall sentences with implicit or explicit instruments with equal facility. If children do not spontaneously generate implied relationships such as appropriate instruments, then an instrument cue could be ineffective for retrieval unless it was stated directly in the sentence. Thus, in such a memory task, following sentence presentation, children are told that they are to receive a word which is a clue to one of the sentences they heard. The sentences given could be exclusively "explicit," "implicit," or a combination of both, with regard to instrument used, to determine where the child needs help. For example, task sentences presented could be:

(29) The boy cut the paper plane.
(30) The baker sliced the bread.
(31) The woman swept the floor.

Retrieval cues for this task are (not necessarily in this order)

> scissors
> knife
> broom

And thus the child would try to recall the appropriate sentences for each cue given.

As an additional adaptation to the task, children can be asked to act out the described actions. This might help the child to process the implied instrument. Or perhaps imagery instructions of the type "Make a picture of this sentence in your head" might facilitate recall (Paris et al., 1974).

Another method of testing/training inferential and logical reasoning would involve presenting a paragraph to the child to be completed. Direct the child to listen to or read a paragraph, taking note that it is not finished and to select the word which *best* finishes the paragraph. For example,

(32) The lion tamer protects himself with a whip and gun when working with the ferocious beasts. The job of the lion tamer is
    (a) difficult   **(c) dangerous
    (b) skillful   (d) important

The child should discuss how he/she

solved the problem and arrived at the *best* answer.

The process of semantic integration may be facilitated by helping children understand how information in one sentence is related to information in other sentences. Games would be based upon synthesizing information for simplification of recall of main ideas, prediction of story outcomes, and getting the entire idea of a story (Wallach and Lee, 1980).

Intervention can begin by having children combine related simple, declarative sentences and choose a single more complex form. With sentences such as:

(33) The boy ate too much cake.
(34) The boy ate too much candy.
(35) The boy got sick.

children could choose the sentence form which best tells the whole idea. They might have to choose between:

(36) The boy ate cake and he ate candy and he got sick.

or

(37) The boy ate too much cake and candy and got sick.

Tasks should progress in complexity from sentence pairs to short paragraphs where children have to identify sentences which are inappropriate to the rest of the story. They could be asked to add additional sentences to paragraphs where essential, related information has been omitted.

Learning-disabled children must be directed to "make" learning happen by actively manipulating and organizing the material to be learned. Through various methods and activities, we may help them to become more active, flexible, and organized in the use of certain learning strategies. With a complete understanding of inferential and integrational processes, clinicians' and teachers' only constraints are the limits of their imagination in planning intervention activities.

CLOSING REMARKS

The development of integrative skills involves the composite of many factors. Jenkins (1974) reminds us that we cannot deal with memory without dealing with instructions, perception, comprehension, inference, problem solving, and all other processes that contribute to the construction of events. He goes on to say that "to study memory without studying inference is to be baffled by the transformations that the subject puts on his experience" (Jenkins, 1974, p. 794). Indeed, to study memory without studying language and the experiences a person brings to the task of remembering makes little sense.

It is necessary to view learning as an active, integrative process which does not necessarily rely on repeated exposure to specific stimuli as the basis of acquiring information. In principle, the understanding of a concept continues to be elaborated and embellished even though the concept may never be directly encountered again. This continuous accumulation of the stored information within the memory system has profound effects on the way new information is acquired. We accept the notion that young normal children acquire new concepts through a considerable amount of rote learning. However, understanding is slowly elaborated as properties are accumulated. Initially, therefore, most concepts are only partially defined and are not necessarily well integrated with other learned information. Later, through the accumulation and organization of interconnected data, new information may be learned primarily by association or analogy. As we have seen, language learning-disabled children often experience difficulties in just such organizational strategies.

It is hoped that this chapter has provided readers with an integrated view of theory, research, and practice in the area of semantic integration. It is also hoped that it has contributed information to the understanding of these skills as they relate to language learning-disabled children.

References

Baddeley AD: The trouble with levels: a reexamination of Craik and Lockhart's framework for memory research. *Psychol Rev* 85:139–152, 1978.

Baker H, Leland B: *Detroit Test of Learning Aptitude.* Indianapolis, Bobbs-Merrill, 1967.

Barclay JR: The role of comprehension in remembering sentences. *Cognitive Psychol* 4:229–254, 1973.

Barclay JR, Reid M: Semantic integration in children's recall of discourse. *Dev Psychol* 10:277–281, 1974.

Barlett FC: *Remembering.* Cambridge, Cambridge University Press, 1932.

Begg I, Pavio A: Concreteness and imagery in sentence memory. *J Verbal Learn Verbal Behav* 8:821–827, 1969.

Bellezza F: Updating memory using mnemonic devices. *Cognitive Psychol* 14:301–327, 1982.

Belmore SM, Yates JM, Bellack DR, et al: Drawing inferences from concrete and abstract sentence. *J Verbal Learn Verbal Behav* 21:338–351, 1982.

Blanchowitz C: Semantic constructivity in children's comprehension. *Read Res Q* 13:187–99, 1977–78.

Bransford J: *Human Cognition: Learning, Understanding and Remembering.* Belmont, CA, Wadsworth, 1979.

Bransford JD, Barclay JR, Franks JJ: Sentence memory: a constructive vs interpretive approach. *Cognitive Psychol* 3:193–209, 1972.

Bransford JD, Franks JJ: The abstraction of linguistic ideas. *Cognitive Psychol* 2:331–350, 1971.

Bransford JD, Franks JJ: The abstraction of linguistic ideas: a review. *Cognition* 1:211–249, 1972.

Bransford J, Johnson M: Considerations of some problems of comprehension. In Chase W: *Visual Information Processing,* New York, Academic Press, 1973, pp 383–483.

Bransford J, Nitsch K: Coming to understand things we could not previously understand. In Kavanaugh J, Strange W: *Speech and Language in the Laboratory, School and Clinic.* Cambridge, MA, MIT Press, 1978, pp 267–307.

Brown AL: Semantic integration in children's reconstruction of narrative sequences. *Cognitive Psychol* 8:247–262, 1976.

Carroll J, Davis P, Richmond B: *Word Frequency Book.* New York, American Heritage, 1971.

Carrow E: *Auditory Test of Language Comprehension.* Austin, TX, Southwest Development, 1969.

Craik F, Lockhart R: Levels of processing: a framework for memory research. *J Verbal Learn Verbal Behav* 11:671–684, 1972.

Crowder RG: *Principles of Learning and Memory.* Hillsdale NJ, Lawrence Erlbaum Associates, 1976.

DeRenzi E, Vignolo L: The token test: a sensitive test to detect receptive disturbances in aphasia. *Brain* 86:665–678, 1962.

DiSimoni F: *The Token Test for Children.* Hingham, MA, Teaching Resources Company, 1978.

Franks JJ, Bransford JD: The acquisition of abstract ideas. *J Verbal Learn Verbal Behav* 11:311–315, 1972.

Gerber A: Problems in the processing and use of language in education. In Gerber A, Bryen DN: *Language and Learning Disabilities.* Baltimore, University Park Press, 1981, pp 75–112.

Glick J: Interview at CUNY Graduate School and University Center, December 19, 1975.

Holland AL: *Communicative Abilities in Daily Living.* Baltimore, University Park Press, 1980.

Jenkins JJ: Remember that old theory of memory? Well forget it! *Am Psychol* 64:785–795, 1974.

Johnson M, Bransford J, Solomon S: Memory for tacit implications of sentences. *J Exp Psychol* 98:203–205, 1973.

Kintsch W: *Memory and Cognition.* New York, John Wiley & Sons, 1977.

Kirk S, McCarthy J, Kirk D: *Illinois Test of Psycholinguistic Abilities,* revised ed. Urbana, University of Illinois Press, 1968.

Klein-Konigsberg E: Semantic integration in normal and learning disabled children. Unpublished doctoral dissertation, The Graduate School and University Center of the City University of New York, 1977.

Lemme M, Daves N: Models of auditory linguistic processing. In Lass N, McReynolds L, Northern J, et al: *Speech, Language and Hearing.* Philadelphia, WB Saunders, 1982, pp 348–376.

Lindsay P, Norman D: *Human Information Processing: An Introduction to Psychology.* New York, Academic Press, 1972.

Lorch R: Priming and search processes in semantic memory: a test of three models of spreading activity. *J Verbal Learn Verbal Behav* 21:468–492, 1982.

Marschark M, Paivio A: Integrative processing of concrete and abstract sentences. *J Verbal Learn Verbal Behav* 16:217–231, 1977.

Massaro DW: *Understanding Language.* New York, Academic Press, 1975.

Maxwell DL, Maxwell S, Wallach GP: Brain-related relationships in language learning disabilities: a developmental perspective. Presented at the American Speech-Language-Hearing Association Convention, Toronto, November, 1982.

McCarthy D: *McCarthy Scales of Children's Abilities.* New York, Psychological Corporation, 1970.

Meyer BJF: What is remembered in prose. In Freedle RO: *Discourse Production and Comprehension.* Norwood, NJ, Ablex Publishing Company, 1977, pp 307–336.

Moeser SD: Inferential reasoning in episodic memory. *J Verbal Learn Verbal Behav* 15:193–212, 1976.

Norman D: *Memory and Attention.* New York, John Wiley & Sons, 1969.

Norman D: *Models of Human Memory.* New York, Academic Press, 1970.

Paivio A, Begg I: *The Psychology of Language.* Englewood Cliffs, NJ, Prentice-Hall, 1981.

Paris SG, Carter AY: Semantic and constructive aspects of sentence memory in children. *Dev Psychol* 9:109–113, 1973.

Paris SG, Lindauer BK: The role of inference in children's comprehension and memory for sentences. *Cognitive Psychol* 8:217–227, 1976.

Paris SG, Mahoney GJ: Cognitive integration in children's memory for sentences and pictures. *Child Dev* 45:633–642, 1974.

Paris SG, Mahoney GJ, Buckhalt JA: Facilitation of semantic integration in sentence memory of retarded children. *Am J Ment Defic* 78:714–720, 1974.

Paris SG, Upton LR: The construction and relation of linguistic interferences by children. Presented at the Western Psychological Association meeting, San Francisco, April, 1974.

Pearson PD, Spiro R: Toward a theory of reading comprehension instruction. *Top Language Disord* 1:71–88, 1980.

Peleg ZR: The representation of time and location in memory for sentences. *J Psycholinguistic Res* 2:169–182, 1982.

Peterson SB, Potts GR: Global and specific components of information integration. *J Verbal Learn Verbal Behav* 40:403–420, 1982.

Rees N, Shulman M: I don't understand what you mean by comprehension. *J Speech Hear Disord* 2:208–219, 1978.

Semel EM, Wiig EH: *Clinical Evaluation of Language Functions.* Columbus, OH, Charles E Merrill, 1980.

Shaw ML: Attending to multiple sources of information: the integration of information in decision making. *Cognitive Psychol* 14:353–409, 1982.

Stark J, Wallach GP: The path to a concept of language learning disabilities. *Top Language Disord* 1:1–14, 1980.

Swisher L, Aten J: Assessing comprehension of spoken language: a multifaceted task. *Top Language Disord* 1:75–85, 1981.

Tulving E: Episodic and semantic memory. In Tulving E, Donaldson W: *Organization of Memory.* New York, Academic Press, 1972.

Wallach GP: The implications of different comprehension strategies in normal and learning disabled children: effects of thematization. Unpublished doctoral dissertation, The Graduate School and University Center of the City University of New York, 1977.

Wallach GP, Lee AD: So you want to know what to do with language disabled children above the age of six. *Top Language Disord* 1:99–113, 1980.

Wiig E, Semel E: *Language Disabilities in Children and Adolescents.* Columbus, OH, Charles E Merrill, 1976.

Wiig EH, Semel EM: *Language Assessment and Intervention for the Learning Disabled.* Columbus, OH, Charles E Merrill, 1980.

Wing C: Language processing and linguistic levels: a matrix. *Language Speech Hear Serv Schools* 13:2–11, 1982.

Zangwill OL: Remembering revisited. *Q J Exp Psychol* 24:123–128, 1972.

CHAPTER THIRTEEN

Language Analysis Skills and Early Reading Acquisition

BENITA A. BLACHMAN, Ph.D.

It is likely that readers of a book entitled *Language Learning Disabilities in School-Age Children* will intuitively accept the premise that reading is a language-based skill. It would seem to follow, logically enough, that reading disabilities might indeed be related to language problems. Nonetheless, it is important to preface a chapter on reading with the acknowledgment that, until recently, the most popular explanation of reading disabilities focused not on language problems but on purported deficits in visual perception. It was only in the 1970's that numerous reviews of the literature began to appear that questioned visual perceptual explanations of reading difficulties and provided data that directly contradicted them (Benton, 1975; Larsen and Hammill, 1975; Vellutino, 1977, 1979). One obvious contradiction is the disparity in reading achievement in deaf and hearing populations. It was well known for many years that deaf and hearing-impaired children achieve considerably lower reading levels than would be otherwise expected— despite the fact that they have unimpeded visual access to print (Furth, 1966; Lane and Baker, 1974; Trybus and Karchmer, 1977; Liberman and Shankweiler, 1979).

The emphasis on purported visual deficits in poor readers had a profound effect on the field of learning disabilities during its early history (see Chapters 1 and 2). It has been observed that a "common thread" in the theories of Frostig and Maslow (1973), Getman (1962), Kephart (1960), and other early writers in the field was "the view that developmental reading disability is primarily the result of problems in visual organization and visual memory" (Vellutino, 1978, p. 72). Moreover, despite extensive documentation that remediation programs based on this premise were not effective in improving reading skills (Masland and Cratty, 1971; Hammill, 1972), untold numbers of children continue to receive such training even to this day.

It is easy to understand why this emphasis on visual perceptual problems persists. Reversals of letter orientation and order made by some poor readers are evident and easily describable, even by a lay observer, and might conceivably be accounted for by problems in visual perception. (One often hears it said that "dyslexics see things backwards.") It is of interest to note that Orton, a pioneer in the field, who first saw reversals as central to dyslexia, did not view them as a visual perceptual problem in the usual sense (although he is often misinterpreted on this point). Instead, he saw dyslexia as a language-based problem (Orton, 1925). He attempted to explain the basis for developmental dyslexia in neurological terms as an anomaly in the maturation of cerebral function, specifically related to poorly established dominance of the language hemisphere. Suggesting that reading-disabled children had thus not developed a dominant hemisphere for the recognition of graphic symbols (e.g., printed letters and words), Orton proposed that the mirror images of these symbols represented in the opposite hemisphere were not suppressed. He concluded that this was responsible for the tendency to reverse letters seen in children with reading problems.

Whatever the merits of any explanation of reversals, it is fair to say that reversals themselves are not nearly as frequent a source of error as might be expected from the emphasis they have received. Vowels and consonants, other than the reversible ones, cause the poor reader much more trouble (Liberman et al., 1971). In the Liberman et al. (1971) study, reversals of orientation and order together accounted for fewer than 25% of the mistakes made by second-grade poor readers on a list containing words which lend themselves to such errors (e.g., dig/big; was/saw). A further analysis of the reversals made by the disabled readers also revealed a lack of a significant correlation between the two types of errors (those of orientation and order), a correlation one would expect to find if a perceptual deficit existed in these children. Nonetheless, reversal errors continue to fascinate the researcher and lay public and have surely played an important role in the development of a perceptual-deficit hypothesis as an explanation of reading disability. Perhaps the high visibility of these errors and their early recognition by practitioners diverted attention from the more subtle language-processing problems that are now capturing the attention of investigators of the reading process.

Alternative explanations that implicate "verbal labeling" problems rather than visual perceptual confusion as the basis for these reversal and orientation errors have received empirical support from studies conducted by Vellutino et al. (1972, 1975). In the first study, poor readers between the ages of 9 and 14 were able to graphically reproduce from memory three- and four-item letter and word strings and strings of two and three graphic symbols as accu-

rately as normal readers. These results were replicated in a second study (Vellutino et al., 1975) with good and poor readers between the ages of 7 and 11. Although the second-grade poor readers were here less accurate on the longest strings which taxed the young child's short-term memory, in both studies the poor readers were consistently better at copying than they were at naming. These findings would support the Liberman et al. (1971) contention that linguistic intrusion errors, rather than perceptual confusion, may account for reversals. Vellutino (1978, p. 73) offered this simple summary of the language-based interpretation of reversals:

> "It is our contention that children who called b d or *was saw* do not literally 'see' these configurations differently than normal readers, but, because of one or more deficiencies in verbal processing, cannot remember which verbal label is associated with which printed symbol."

More recent research has also indicated that differences in good and poor readers that were originally interpreted in terms of visual memory deficits in the poor readers more accurately reflect differences between the groups in the ability to process linguistic information. For example, a recent study (Liberman et al., 1982) found that good and poor readers did not differ in recognition memory of photographed faces or nonlabelable abstract designs but did, in contrast, differ markedly in the memory of linguistic material—specifically, nonsense syllables. Evidence continues to mount against both visual organization deficits and visual memory deficits as comprehensive explanations of reading disability. This is not to say that visual problems never account for poor reading, but only that in most cases alternative explanations, relating to linguistic rather than visual-processing deficits, appear to have more salience. Recall Maxwell and Wallach's discussion of visual perceptual issues and developmental changes in Chapter 2.)

There is now a growing body of evidence in the literature that underscores the importance of language-based skills in all aspects of the reading process (Gleitman and Rozin, 1977; Liberman et al., 1977; Liberman and Shankweiler, 1979; Perfetti and Lesgold, 1977, 1979; Vellutino, 1977, 1979; Liberman, 1982). These studies and others offer ample evidence that deficits in the recognition of, and ready access to, linguistic units may be critical in early reading failure. Focusing on beginning aspects of the reading process, this chapter will deal specifically with the ability of the young child to access from the speech stream that unit—the phoneme—that is represented in an alphabetic orthography.

THE RELATIONSHIP BETWEEN SPEECH AND THE ALPHABET

It has been said that "the mere fact that a child understands what is said to him tells us little about what speech segments he perceives" (Savin, 1972, p. 321). It might be even more accurate to say that a child's comprehension of speech tells us little about how well he can *analyze* his speech into its constituent segments. Although of little consequence in becoming an adequate speaker-hearer of one's language, the realization that speech can be segmented and that these segmented units can be represented by printed forms is the fundamental task facing the beginning reader (Liberman, 1971). When reading an alphabetic writing system such as English, in which the graphic symbols more or less represent the sounds of speech, the child must understand not only that the speech stream can be segmented into words and syllables, but ultimately that even smaller sublexical units (phonemes) are accessible.

It is important to understand that the nature of the writing system interacts in very specific ways with the unit the reader must access from the speech stream. As discussed by Liberman et al. (1974) and Gleitman and Rozin (1977), to develop a written representation of a language, one must decide what kind and size of unit will be represented. In the earliest writing systems a meaningful unit—the word—was indicated with a single character or symbol.

The Chinese logographic characters and the Japanese *kanji* characters (borrowed from the Chinese) are examples of this type of writing system. The young child learning to read Chinese need only make the link between the meaningful unit in the speech stream and the printed symbol, a task that we shall see is conceptually less difficult than abstracting smaller, meaningless units. Rozin et al. (1971) were able to demonstrate that American poor readers in second grade were able to learn selected English words more easily when they were represented by Chinese characters. Despite the ease with which poor readers might initially decipher a logographic system (much the way a preschooler initially identifies words on cereal boxes and soup cans by the holistic visual configuration), there are obvious disadvantages to dealing with an alphabetic system in this way. By memorizing an endless series of whole words, the economy of our alphabetic system, which allows us to read words never before encountered in print, is lost.

Historically, writing systems representing meaningless units, specifically syllables and phonemes, were developed after those systems representing whole words (Gelb, 1963). The syllabary, in which the printed symbol stands for a unit of syllable size, is exemplified by the Japanese *kana*. Syllabaries typically represent a simple, open syllable (CV) structure, unlike the more complex syllable structure in English. There is some evidence from the high literacy rates reported among certain cultures using syllabic scripts (i.e., Cherokee, Japanese) that creating a link between syllabic units in the speech stream and the printed notations representing these units is relatively easy for young children (Makita, 1968; Walker, 1969; Sakamoto and Makita, 1973; as reported by Gleitman and Rozin, 1973, and Rozin and Gleitman, 1977). There is also evidence, which will be discussed at some length later, to show that children can segment speech into syllables before they can segment speech into phonemes (Rosner and Simon, 1971; Liberman et al., 1974).

The last (and relatively recent) developmental milestone in the history of writing systems was the abstraction of the phonemic segment from the speech stream and the development of a written notation to represent these small, abstract units. Some alphabetic languages, such as Finnish, are more nearly phonetic transcriptions than English. Nonetheless, like all the other alphabetic orthographies, English writing is, despite its greater abstractness, basically "a cipher on the phonemes of the language" (Liberman and Shankweiler, 1979, p. 110). Once the student unlocks the alphabetic principle (understanding the relationship between speech and an alphabetic orthography), he is eventually able to read words seen in print for the first time by at least approximating their spoken form. *However, there is nothing inherent in becoming an adequate speaker-hearer of English that illuminates for the child the specific linguistic units represented in our alphabetic script. Herein lies a significant problem for many beginning readers.*

THE PROBLEM OF SEGMENTATION

Although it is obvious to literate adults that we have an alphabetic system in which graphic symbols more or less represent the sounds of speech, there is now ample evidence that this level of understanding of the structure of our language develops over time and cannot be taken for granted in the kindergarten and first-grade child (Bruce, 1964; Rosner and Simon, 1971; Liberman et al., 1974). The work of A. Liberman et al. (1967) and A. Liberman (1970) has helped us understand the complex relationship among the phonemes in the speech stream, which makes it difficult for the young child to access these phonemic segments. When we produce the word "bag," for example, information about each segment is actually being transmitted simultaneously. The vowel /æ/ exerts influence over the entire syllable, and the pronunciation of each phoneme is dependent on the

context in which it occurs. Although the three segments of the written word *bag* can be easily identified, the individual phonemes that they represent are coarticulated during speech production (the consonants are folded into the vowels), creating a "merged" (A. Liberman et al., 1967; Liberman, 1971) or "shingled" (Gleitman and Rozin, 1973) effect. The result is that we hear only a single acoustic unit—the syllable. (For a more detailed discussion, see A. Liberman et al. (1967), Liberman (1971, 1973, 1982), and Gleitman and Rozin (1977).)

Given the complex nature of the message the child must analyze in order to construct a link between the sounds of speech and the signs of print, it is not difficult to understand why a 6-year-old beginning reader might have some difficulty. However, there is now evidence that children who are proficient at this level of linguistic analysis (segmenting spoken language into phonemes) at an early age are more likely to become good readers.

SEGMENTATION RESEARCH
Segmenting Speech into Words

It has been suggested that the order of difficulty of segmenting speech into words, syllables, and phonemes might parallel the historical development of writing systems (Liberman and Shankweiler, 1979). Indeed, it has been demonstrated that it is easier for children to segment speech into words and syllables than into phonemic units (Liberman et al., 1974; Fox and Routh, 1975).

Numerous researchers (Karpova, 1955; Huttenlocher, 1964; Holden and MacGinitie, 1972; Francis, 1973; Downing and Oliver, 1973–1974; Ehri, 1975, 1979; Fox and Routh, 1975; Kirk, 1979) have investigated what Ehri (1975, 1979) calls "word consciousness," the awareness that language is composed of separate words. The specifics of several of the studies are presented here to highlight some of the questions raised about the influence of task difficulty on our interpretation of the results. In one of the earliest studies, Karpova (1955) trained Russian children between the ages of 3 and 7 to count pictures and orally presented words. The children were then asked to repeat sentences and answer the question "How many words are there?" Several stages in a slow developmental progression leading to word segmentation were identified. Initially, the children were unable to identify words but would break the sentences into semantic units (e.g., S (age 4): "Galya and Vova went walking." E: "How many words?" S: "Two" ... "Galya went walking and Vova went walking."). More of the older children, athough still unable to completely segment into words, were able to break sentences into subject and predicate. Those at the most advanced stage, about 25% of the 5- to 7-year-olds, were able to segment sentences into individual words, although most continued to have difficulty isolating conjunctions and prepositions. Introducing a motor component into the task, moving a plastic counter for each word in the sentence, did make the task easier for many of the children.

Kindergarten children were taught to play a "talking and tapping game," requiring the child to repeat a taped sentence or phrase and then repeat it again while tapping one poker chip for each word (Holden and MacGinitie, 1972). As in the Karpova study, it was found that function words are more difficult to isolate than more concrete words. Aligning a function word with the subsequent content word was the most common error made by the children. Correct segmentation increased as the proportion of content words in an utterance increased. Nonetheless, with appropriate practice prior to testing, Kirk (1979) found that children between the ages of 4:9 and 5:10 could be taught to segment simple declarative sentences into words, although they continued to have the most difficulty with function words. (See Van Kleeck, Chapter 7, for additional discussion of the difficulty with function words in segmentation tasks.)

Yet another experimental variation on

the task of segmenting speech into words resulted in accurate sentence segmentation for even the 4-year-olds (Fox and Routh, 1975). Children ages 3 to 7 were asked to "say just a little bit" of a sentence (two to seven words in length) spoken by the examiner. If the child responded with a multiword phrase, the examiner repeated the direction of "say just a little bit," and then repeated the phrase rather than the entire sentence. In this way the child was allowed to progress from sentence to multiple-word phrase to single word and, in fact, 50% of the youngest children were successful. (This procedure was also successful in teaching children to segment words into syllables and phonemes at a younger age than was typical in other studies.) Some important questions have been raised about the amount of examiner prompting in this task and whether the successful task performance by these young children actually indicated awareness of words as separate units (Ehri, 1979). Although this concern might be valid in a testing situation, the continued prompting described by Fox and Routh (1975) might be a positive modification during segmentation instruction with beginning readers. This study did illustrate an important point: specific task demands, during both training and testing, do significantly influence performance.

Other attempts to clarify a child's understanding of a word have led investigators to ask about instructional terminology used with beginning readers, specifically use of the word "word." Several investigators attempting to determine the child's ability to segment speech into words have perhaps confounded the results by using this lexical item to describe to the child the task to be performed (Kirk, 1979). Downing and Oliver (1973–1974, p. 581) investigated the conception of the "word" in youngsters 4 to 8 and concluded that "the young beginners in this study do not have the same concept of a spoken word as their teachers would possess." Although the child's understanding improved with age, even the 7- to 8-year-olds confused words with syllables and phonemes when asked to respond "yes" (it is a word) or "no" to eight classes of auditory stimuli. A study with 5:9- to 7:3-year-olds (Francis, 1973) confirmed Downing's findings and reinforced the fact that many children experience confusion when first confronted by the terms "letter," "word," and "sentence." Francis interpreted the findings as a reflection of the child's non-analytic approach to speech. She suggested that the idea that language has identifiable units seems to emerge as children learn to read and are expected to analyze print. This analysis then leads to new insights about spoken language.

Despite a lack of complete agreement in the literature about when children develop an awareness that spoken language can be segmented into words, it seems clear that kindergarten prereaders can be taught this skill, although function words may continue to present a problem. The Fox and Routh (1975) technique (i.e., "tell me a little bit ... ") might be useful if children persist in attaching function words to ·adjacent content words. Certainly teachers should not assume that prereading children are linguistically aware of the word units in speech or the connection between these segments and conventional printed forms. As demonstrated by Rozin et al. (1974, p. 93), a considerable number of inner-city second graders (after 1 year of reading instruction) still did not understand that "words that take longer to say are written with more letters." When asked which of two printed words—MOW or MOTORCYCLE—is MOW, many were still unable to answer correctly. Even a nonreader who understood the basic relationship between the printed word and word segments in speech should have had no difficulty. As noted by Van Kleeck (Chapter 7 and 9), knowledge of such a basic relationship is actually metalinguistic in nature. As teachers and clinicians, we cannot assume that young children have developed the language awareness to make even this most basic connection between speech and print.

Segmenting Speech into Syllables and Phonemes

The ability to segment spoken language into words is only the first level of language analysis required of the child ready to embark on reading. Considerable research has been devoted to investigating the child's ability to analyze the words in his language into their component parts—ultimately into the phonemic segments that are represented in an alphabetic orthography. Much of this research suggests that those children who have greater facility for analyzing the structure of their language are more likely to be among the better readers. Investigators have studied the developmental nature of segmentation skills, their relationship to reading, the ability to train these skills, and the effect of this training on reading ability.

DEVELOPMENTAL STUDIES

During the past 15 years several investigators have found that the ability to analyze the spoken word into syllables or phonemes follows a developmental pattern (Bruce, 1964; Rosner and Simon, 1971; Savin, 1972; Gleitman and Rozin, 1973; Zuhrova, 1973; Liberman et al., 1974; Fox and Routh, 1975). Again, various experimental measures have been used in these studies and, as will be discussed later, several of these can be adapted for both assessment and remediation activities. For example, an elision task was used by Bruce (1964) to test the child's ability to analyze the spoken word. The examiner pronounced a word, such as /fan/, and asked the child to produce the word which would result if one eliminated either the first, last, or middle sound. The subjects, who ranged in age from 5:7 to 7:6, were selected from three English Infant Schools. Children were grouped according to mental ages obtained on the *Stanford Binet Intelligence Test*, and results indicated that the children with a mental age below 7 were unable to perform the task. Between the mental ages of 7 and 8 the variability in scores reflected the different teaching techniques in the three different schools, with those children obtaining the highest scores on the elision task having had the most direct phonics teaching. By age 9, children from all three of the schools were able to perform the task with 80% accuracy.

This elision task was expanded to include words to be produced by the child after eliminating a syllable (e.g., Say /cowboy/ without the /cow/), as well as items which called for the oral manipulation of phonemes (e.g., Say /belt/ without the /t/) (Rosner and Simon, 1971). This expanded task, the *Auditory Analysis Test* (AAT), was administered to children in kindergarten through sixth grade. Mean scores improved progressively from kindergarten upward, with the biggest change occurring between kindergarten and the end of grade 1. Rosner and Simon suggested that, while reading instruction was most likely a significant factor in a child's ability to analyze his language, language analysis skills might in turn affect his early reading ability.

A tapping task was developed by Liberman et al. (1974) to measure the child's ability to segment spoken words into syllables and phonemes. The child was required to indicate, by tapping a wooden dowel on the table, the number of segments (syllables for one group, phonemes for another) in a word spoken by the examiner. The subjects included 4-, 5-, and 6-year-olds in preschool, kindergarten, and first-grade classes. The results clearly indicated that it is easier for words to be segmented into syllables than into phonemes and that there is a developmental hierarchy in the performance of these language analysis tasks. At age 4 nearly half of the children could segment words into syllables, but none could segment into phonemes. Although there was not a marked increase in the ability to segment syllables at age 5, 17% of the children could now segment by phonemes. By the end of the first grade, 90% could successfully perform the syllable segmentation task, while 70% were able to succeed in phoneme segmentation. Liberman et al., like Rosner and Simon (1971)

and Bruce (1964), suggested that it was impossible from existing studies to sort out the effects of maturation and instruction when attempting to explain the steep rise during the first grade in the child's ability to analyze his spoken language. Liberman postulated, however, that regardless of instruction, results indicated a greater level of maturity was necessary to analyze words into phonemes than into syllables (Liberman, 1973).

Others have confirmed the relative ease of syllable segmentation compared to phoneme segmentation using the Liberman Tapping Task (Leong and Haines, 1978; Blachman, 1981, in press; Zifcak, 1981) and other experimental measures of segmentation ability (Fox and Routh, 1975; Goldstein, 1976; Treiman and Baron, 1981). A reasonable question to ask would be why segmentation into syllables is easier than segmentation into phonemes. Liberman et al. (1980b, p. 196) offered the following explanation:

"As we noted earlier, the consonant segments of the phonemic message are typically folded, at the acoustic level, into the vowel. The result is that there is no acoustic criterion by which the phonemic segments are dependably marked. However, every syllable that is formed in this way contains a vocalic nucleus and, therefore, a peak of acoustic energy. These energy peaks provide audible cues that correspond to the syllable centers (Fletcher, 1929). Though such auditory cues could not in themselves help a listener to define exact syllable boundaries, they should make it easy for him to discover how many syllables there are and, in that sense, to do explicit syllabic segmentation."

CORRELATIONAL STUDIES

In addition to the developmental findings, many researchers were also interested in whether a relationship exists between the acquisition of beginning reading skills and the ability to segment words into phonemes. Rosner and Simon (1971) found significant partial correlations (with IQ held constant) between the *Auditory Analysis Test* and the language arts subtests of the *Stanford Achievement Test* for grades 1 through 5. Liberman and her colleagues (1974) were particularly interested in the

30% of the first graders in their study who could not segment words into phonemes at the end of first grade. They administered the word recognition subtest of the *Wide Range Achievement Test* (WRAT) to all children from the original study at the beginning of second grade and found that half of the children in the lowest third of the class for reading had been unable to analyze words into phonemes on the tapping task administered the previous year. However, no children in the upper third of the class in reading had failed the segmentation test in grade 1.

In several more recent studies, significant relationships were also found between the child's ability to analyze language on various segmentation tasks and the acquisition of beginning reading skills. A significant correlation was found between phoneme segmentation and reading on the reading recognition subtest of the *Peabody Individual Achievement Test* (PIAT) (Fox and Routh, 1975). In a later study, Fox and Routh (1976) investigated the ability of bright 4-year-olds to learn to decode pairs of letter-like forms (e.g., ▷| ±) having a one-to-one correspondence to simple English words (e.g., me, see, way). They found that the good segmenters were significantly better than the nonsegmenters at the decoding task. In fact, the nonsegmenters were not able to learn to decode the words in the trials allotted them. In another study of 4-year-olds (Goldstein, 1976), scores on a word analysis/synthesis task accounted for a significant amount of the variance (independent of IQ) on two author-devised reading tests, administered after a 13-week reading training period.

With kindergarten children, ability to segment   consonant - vowel - consonant (CVC) words into three distinct units was significantly related to scores 1 year later on the word recognition subtest of the WRAT (Helfgott, 1976). With first graders, there were significant correlations between phoneme segmentation ability (on the Liberman Tapping Task) and performance on the WRAT word recognition subtest, as

well as the *Gallistel-Ellis Test of Coding Skills* (Blachman, 1981; Zifcak, 1981). In addition, Zifcak compared the ability of the Liberman Tapping Task, the Rosner *Auditory Analysis Test*, and Read's (1971) invented spellings, along with IQ, socioeconomic status, sex, and age, to predict the reading scores of the first-grade sample. The single best predictor was the Liberman Tapping Task, accounting for more than 60% of the variance in reading achievement. The invented spellings also added significantly to the prediction, but none of the other variables made a significant contribution to the prediction of reading achievement. As part of a larger kindergarten and first-grade study investigating the relationship of several reading-related language measures to reading, Blachman (1981) found that phoneme segmentation combined with another reading-related language measure, rapid automatized naming of letters and colors (Denckla and Rudel, 1976), accounted for 68% of the variance in the WRAT reading scores of first-grade inner-city children. Syllable segmentation was not found to be a significant predictor of first-grade reading ability, perhaps because it is a much easier task for first-grade children in general, and thus much less discriminating. According to a recent longitudinal study, however, syllable segmentation measured in kindergarten can significantly predict reading performance in first grade (Liberman and Mann, 1981).

Using the *Lindamood Auditory Conceptualization Test* (LAC) (Lindamood and Lindamood, 1971), an instrument probably more familiar to speech/language pathologists than to others working with learning-disabled children, Calfee et al. (1973) also investigated the relationship between reading and what the authors call "acoustic-phonetic" skills. By manipulating colored blocks, the child indicates his awareness of the phonemic segments in speech. For example, if the examiner said "show me /ip/," the child might present two blocks of different colors. The examiner might then say, "if that says /ip/, show me /pi/," and the student would be expected to reverse the order of the blocks. More complicated items include, "if that says /vips/, show me /ips/" (p. 294). Students in kindergarten through twelfth grade were tested using the LAC and the reading and spelling subtests of the WRAT, and highly significant correlations were found across grade levels between LAC total score and a combined reading and spelling score. Of particular significance in this study was the stability of the relationship between these language analysis skills and reading and spelling scores from kindergarten through high school.

Correlational studies such as we have here, even when the findings are highly consistent, leave many questions unanswered. Of special interest is whether the development of language analysis skills, particularly phoneme segmentation, facilitates learning to read or is developed by learning to read. Of course, there is no reason for one interpretation to preclude the other, when in fact a reciprocal relationship is more likely to be the case (Ehri, 1979; Liberman et al., 1980a). The numerous correlational studies do support the relationship between an awareness of the segmental structure of spoken language and early reading success. In particular, studies with very young children (4-year-olds) suggest that this heightened level of linguistic awareness does facilitate learning to read. At least one study (Morais et al., 1979) suggests, on the other hand, that this awareness is developed as one learns to read an alphabetic system. Comparing literate adults (who only learned to read as adults) and illiterate adults from the same poor peasant background in Portugal on their ability to add or delete a phoneme at the beginning of a nonword, Morais et al. found that only the literate adults were successful. This suggested that the level of linguistic awareness required to segment language into phonemes does not develop as a matter of course, but requires some training that is most often provided by formal reading instruction.

It is possible that for precocious youngsters, mere exposure to print (e.g., being read to, reading signs) triggers this awareness long before formal instruction begins, whereas others who are exposed to formal instruction fail to develop the most rudimentary connections between print and speech (witness the MOW/MOTORCYCLE example (Rozin et al., 1974)). This brings us to several additional questions: Can we train segmentation skills and, as a corollary, how do we do it? Does the training have a positive effect on reading success?

TEACHING SEGMENTATION SKILLS

To some extent, of course, every researcher does some training in segmentation by whatever modeling of the task takes place prior to the presentation of the experimental test items. However, some researchers have made training in segmentation a major focus of their study (Elkonin, 1963, 1973; Zhurova, 1973; Rosner, 1974; Fox and Routh, 1976; Helfgott, 1976; Skjelfjord, 1976; Wallach and Wallach, 1976; Marsh and Mineo, 1977; Kattke, 1978; Lewkowicz and Low, 1979; Williams, 1979, 1980; Lewkowicz, 1980).

After using Rosner's (1973) auditory analysis training program from September to May, 4-year-old preschoolers were successful with two-syllable tasks (e.g., "Say /cowboy/. Now say it again, but don't say /boy/.") and kindergartners were able to perform phoneme elision tasks with initial consonants (e.g., "Say /bat/. Now say it again, but don't say /b/.") (Rosner, 1974, p. 381). Both groups made significant progress from pre- to posttesting. In another type of word analysis task, requiring 4- and 5-year-olds to identify which of two words begins or ends with a given sound, children improved significantly over 4 days of training and appeared to maintain this level of performance during 4 days of transfer tasks (Marsh and Mineo, 1977). In general, continuants (/s/, /m/, /f/, or /n/) were more easily matched than stops (/b/, /d/, /p/, /t/), although there was an interaction between position in the word and phoneme type. In the initial position, subjects were more successful with continuants, whereas the stops were more easily recognized in the final position.

The most detailed description of a successful model for training young children to segment words into phonemes was presented by Elkonin (1963, 1973). Showing children a simple line drawing of the word to be segmented and a row of squares depicting the exact number of phonemes in the pictured word, Elkonin and his colleagues taught the children to pronounce the word slowly and to push a counter into each square as each sound in the word was produced. The success rate of children using the counters, pictures, and diagrams was considerably higher than when the aids were not used in training segmentation skills. Five- and 6-year-old children were able to master segmentation with this procedure. (See additional details in this chapter under "Instructional Procedures.") The segmentation procedure developed by Elkonin is now the first step in reading instruction in Russia (Ungaro, 1974), and it has received considerable attention in the United States, although more from researchers in psychology and reading than from practitioners.

An attempt has also been made to evaluate the effectiveness of each of the visual aids (counters, squares, and pictures) used in the Elkonin procedure (Lewkowicz and Low, 1979). Testing kindergarten children at the beginning of the year, the authors found that squares and counters were the most important in helping the children segment successfully. However, once children had learned to segment two-phoneme words correctly using the aids, the use of the aids did not improve three-phoneme segmentation. Based on their subjects' mastery of two- and three-phoneme word segmentation, the authors suggested that this skill is not too difficult to teach to kindergarten children, a finding confirmed by other researchers (Helfgott, 1976; Kattke, 1978) using the diagram and other elements of the Elkonin procedure in their

training. All of these researchers emphasized initial training with kindergarten children on two-phoneme words (consonant-vowel and vowel-consonant), having found them easier than three-phoneme words to segment.

Several other researchers have looked at analysis (segmentation) and synthesis (blending) skills in 4-, 5-, and 6-year-olds and evaluated attempts to teach both. (See Richardson et al. (1977) for a review of the relationship between sound blending and reading.) Blending was found to be easier than segmentation for kindergarten children (Helfgott, 1976). Similar results were found in 4-year-old subjects (Goldstein, 1976) and in a study of 5- and 6-year-olds in three English schools (Roberts, 1975). Not surprisingly, Roberts found that both analysis and synthesis using sound alone were easier than those tasks combining the use of sound and printed symbols (either decoding or encoding):

"Clearly, in developing the particular skills of analysis and synthesis, an initial approach through sound alone may be most effective. Most commonly, where 'ear-training' does occur in schools, it is confined to the discrimination of different sounds, but a child must learn to do something with the sounds he can discern—to synthesize and analyze them. It is doubtful whether children are given sufficient opportunity to 'manipulate' sounds in this way" (p. 8).

In addition, Roberts emphasized the relationship of analysis skills to writing, suggesting that a child must have some strategy for analyzing the sounds in words, together with the recall of the letter shapes that represent these sounds, in order to write independently.

EFFECTS OF TRAINING ON READING

Despite numerous studies supporting the contribution of segmental ability to beginning reading success, and despite evidence that we can develop phoneme awareness in young children, few researchers have investigated whether training has a direct effect on reading. Elkonin (1973) reported that the kindergarten children in his studies were able to master "sound analysis of words" and this was followed by "improvements in various aspects of literacy" (p. 569). However, we are not given the data to support this success. Rosner (1971) trained a small (n = 8) experimental group of nonreading first graders in segmentation skills, using the auditory component of an earlier version of his 1973 Perceptual Skills Curriculum (e.g., Say /fat/. Now say it again without the /f/.). A control group matched for IQ and auditory analysis scores prior to training did not receive this special instruction, although both groups were being taught to read during this period. At the end of about 3½ months of training, the experimental group had significantly higher scores on the *Auditory Analysis Test*. In addition, the children were also tested on their ability to read words from the instructional material and "transfer" words not included in the training program. The experimental group was able to read significantly more words from both reading lists than the control group. This finding provided some preliminary support for the effect of language analysis skills on the development of reading.

Another first-grade study demonstrated the effectiveness of a tutorial reading program that included training in analysis and synthesis (Wallach and Wallach, 1976). Low-readiness first graders in an inner-city school were tutored by minority mothers, in addition to receiving regular classroom reading instruction. Part I of the program emphasized recognition of sounds at the beginning of words, and sound-symbol relationships; part II emphasized recognition and manipulation of sounds in all positions of the word and direct instruction in blending phonetically regular CVC words; and part III moved into the regular classroom reading materials. At the end of the year, the experimental children performed significantly better than the control children on experimenter-devised and standardized reading measures.

In a more recent study, Williams (1980) evaluated the effectiveness of her program (The ABD's of Reading), designed to teach phonemic analysis, blending, and decoding to learning-disabled children between the ages of 7 and 12. Specific materials were prepared for the teacher to instruct children in analysis of words into syllables, analysis of words into phonemes (first working with syllables of two and then three phonemes), and blending of two-phoneme and then three-phoneme CVC units. A modification of the Elkonin (1973) visual aids was used, with wooden squares representing first the syllables and then the phonemes. After the emphasis on segmental analysis, letter-sound correspondences were taught and letter symbols were placed on the wooden squares. The students were then taught to read (decode) and construct (encode) CVC combinations and later CCVC, CVCC, and CCVCC combinations, followed by two-syllable words with these same patterns.

Classrooms were randomly assigned to either an instructional treatment or nontreatment control group. The program was used for 20 minutes a day, three to four times a week, for about 6 months to supplement whatever reading program was used in the classroom. There were no differences between groups on a pretest measuring sound-symbol associations, phoneme analysis and blending, and decoding of CVC words. However, on posttests based on data from 20 experimental groups (n = 60) and 14 control groups (n = 42), the experimental groups performed significantly better than the control groups on eight of nine subtests. To measure the child's success at decoding novel CVC nonsense and real word combinations (half of the items had been included in the instructional program and the other half were new combinations), two transfer tasks were administered at two different points in the training program. Again, results (based on 28 experimental subjects and 28 control subjects who completed both tests) indicated that correct responses were significantly higher for the experimental than the control subjects. Williams's work demonstrated the effectiveness of teaching these skills to older (ages 7 to 12) learning-disabled students. Williams agreed with others (Elkonin, 1963, 1973; Liberman, 1971; Liberman and Shankweiler, 1979; Liberman et al., 1980b) that these skills should be emphasized in beginning reading instruction.

The Wallach and Wallach (1976) and the Williams (1980) studies evaluated many program components; consequently, the specific effect on reading of training in phoneme analysis skills cannot be isolated. One might also suggest that the effectiveness of the training may have been due to the increased reading time given to experimental subjects, rather than the specific activities used. However, when these studies are reviewed in conjunction with all of the other research (developmental, correlational, and training studies), three overriding conclusions must be reached. First, language analysis skills are consistently related to success in the beginning stages of reading. Second, these skills can be trained. And third, this training appears to positively influence the development of beginning reading skills. In light of this evidence, some suggestions can be made for modifying both assessment and instructional procedures.

ASSESSMENT ISSUES

Linguistic factors known to be critical in the reading process, such as language analysis skills (e.g., phoneme segmentation), are generally overlooked in kindergarten and first-grade screening instruments. Most of the major batteries do, however, include a diversity of perceptual-motor tasks (e.g., blocks, puzzles, drawing, sorting). It would be useful to develop a screening device that more accurately reflects the role of specific linguistic abilities in reading success—or at least to supplement existing tests with such tasks. For example, a recent study (Blachman, 1981, in press) investigated the relationship of several reading-related language measures and the *McCarthy Scales of Children's Abilities* (MSCA) to kindergarten and first-grade reading achievement. Results indicated

that it was possible to significantly increase the predictive power of the MSCA by using selected MSCA scales in conjunction with several language measures known to relate specifically to reading. In this study, the discriminating language tasks at the first-grade level included rapid automatized naming (RAN) of letters and colors (Denckla and Rudel, 1974, 1976) and phoneme segmentation (Liberman et al., 1974). The overall results of this study indicated that children who have greater facility for generating verbal labels (RAN tasks) and analyzing language structure (phoneme segmentation) are more likely to be among the better readers at the end of first grade. Although extensive discussion of these results is beyond the purview of this chapter, the results at both the kindergarten and first-grade levels also indicated that children deficient on rapid naming tasks (i.e., RAN objects, colors, and letters) do not necessarily perform poorly on language analysis tasks (i.e., rhyme production, syllable segmentation, and phoneme segmentation). These two sets of reading-related language measures appeared to be tapping somewhat different components of linguistic processing in these kindergarten and first-grade subjects. It is not known yet if deficiencies in one or the other of these linguistic abilities are reflected in different reading error patterns (a question that we are currently investigating). This study does emphasize the importance of attending to these aspects of linguistic processing when assessing kindergarten or first-grade children, to determine who might be "at risk" for reading failure. There are as yet no data to indicate whether assessment of these skills in preschool children will predict later reading failure. This too needs investigation through longitudinal studies.

Both the *Lindamood Auditory Conceptualization Test* (1971) and Rosner's 13-item *Auditory Analysis Test* (1971) can be used to supplement more traditional assessment procedures when evaluating the prereading or beginning reading child or the older disabled student. In addition, some of the experimental tasks previously described (Elkonin, 1963, 1973; Liberman et al., 1974; Fox and Routh, 1975) could easily be modified and used more informally during assessment to measure a child's competence in language analysis skills. In a reading evaluation with a student who has had exposure to reading instruction, the assessment typically includes an analysis of the child's knowledge of sound/symbol relationships, the ability to decode phonetically regular words (beginning with CVC trigrams), sight word recognition, and oral and silent reading in context. Particularly for those students who are unsuccessful at the most basic level (i.e., identifying letter/sound correspondences and decoding CVC trigrams), the assessment should include an analysis of segmentation ability (segmenting speech into words, syllables, and phonemes). Training in these skills can then be included in programming recommendations.

INSTRUCTIONAL PROCEDURES

To help children understand that speech can be segmented into words, syllables, and phonemes, numerous language analysis activities can be introduced into the kindergarten and first-grade program and also modified for use with older children. Many of these instructional procedures have been presented in detail elsewhere (see, for example, Liberman and Shankweiler, 1979; Liberman et al., 1980b; Camp et al., 1981); therefore, these ideas will only be summarized here.

For the prereading child, word play should help to draw attention to the segmental nature of speech. Recitation of nursery rhymes, rhyming games, listening to songs (Liberman and Shankweiler, 1979) and listening to "stories with frequent sound repetitions" (Camp et al., 1981) are fun for the child and begin to illuminate the sound structure of spoken language (see also Chapters 7 and 9).

In the kindergarten classroom, language analysis activities should begin with word and syllable segmentation. A simple word-

counting game suggested by Engelmann (1969) is very effective. The teacher presents simple statements, pausing between each word; students repeat these sentences and learn to represent each word unit with a chalk mark, raised finger, or counter. Similar activities can be developed for syllable segmentation, beginning with compound words and proceeding to more complex multisyllable words. Rosner's (1975) syllable elision technique (e.g., "Say cucumber. Now say it again, but don't say /cue/" [p. 141].) can also be introduced at this stage.

Once children are aware that speech can be segmented into word and syllable units, phoneme segmentation can be developed. It is important to note, however, that whereas words and syllables can be separated from the speech stream by pausing between each unit, a similar procedure would distort phonemic segments. Due to the encoded nature of the phoneme, segmenting speech into units of this size is more difficult to model and, therefore, more difficult to teach.

The most extensive description of efforts to instruct children in phoneme segmentation is presented by the Russian psychologist, Elkonin (1963, 1973). As discussed earlier in this chapter, Elkonin presents simple line drawings that represent the word to be segmented (e.g., man, lamp). By keeping the picture of the object in view, the child does not need to rely on auditory memory of the word being analyzed. Beneath the drawing is a rectangle divided into squares corresponding to the number of phonemes in the pictured word. The child is taught to say the word slowly, pushing a counter into each square as each successive sound is articulated. The use of the diagram helps the child to visualize the number of phonemic units in the spoken word, and the placement of counters from left to right emphasizes the relationship between the visual-spatial structure of the written word and the auditory-temporal sequence of the spoken word (Liberman et al., 1980b). After the child is successful at this level of analysis of the sound structure of words, the counters are color coded to represent vowels and consonants. For example, red might be used for vowels and black for consonants. Eventually, the graphic symbol corresponding to each sound would be added to the counters. Several researchers have successfully used components of the Elkonin procedure in their studies (Helfgott, 1976; Williams, 1977, 1979, 1980; Kattke, 1978; Lewkowicz and Low, 1979). We have found that kindergarten and first-grade children enjoy the activity, and teachers find that it is easy to integrate into their classroom program.

Several guidelines can be offered for the selection of syllables for segmentation (and blending) activities (Liberman et al., 1980b). In the initial position, a fricative such as /s/ or the nasal murmur of /n/ or /m/ would be easier to segment. These sounds can be produced in isolation without undue distortion, whereas other consonants, specifically the stops (b, d, p, g, t, k), are distorted due to coarticulation when one attempts to isolate them. In addition, segmenting two-phoneme syllables is easier than segmenting three-phoneme syllables, so training might begin with segmentation of real and nonsense syllables of two phonemes.

Other activities to reinforce phoneme segmentation include the elision technique used by Bruce (1964) and Rosner (1973, 1975). Rosner's program includes many activities to develop this skill, and additional suggestions can be found in *Auditory Discrimination in Depth* (Lindamood and Lindamood, 1969).

When children are successful at phoneme analysis, sound-symbol correspondences can be introduced. (For many children, these will have already been taught, although the older remedial student may not yet be able to use this information to decode new words.) The simplest and most direct procedure is to teach these relationships as paired associates. It is helpful, as suggested by Slingerland (1971), to teach the name of the letter, a key word that begins with the

sound of the letter (as an aid to the recall of the sound), and the sound itself. Although consonant sounds are often taught in kindergarten, it is suggested that whenever the child becomes ready for sound/symbol instruction, this should include short vowel sounds as well as consonants.

Once the child has had adequate instruction in segmentation and has mastered the sound/symbol associations for at least one vowel and several consonants, direct reading (decoding) instruction can begin. However, as emphasized by Liberman and her associates (1979, 1980b), the traditional approach to letter-by-letter blending fails to produce an accurate representation of a word in the child's speaking vocabulary (e.g., "buh-ă-tuh" does not become "bat," despite our best efforts at getting the child to blend the sounds together). To avoid this pitfall, some alternative procedures can be suggested. In one procedure adapted from Engelmann (1969), the child learns to pronounce as a single unit a vowel followed by a consonant or a single consonant (continuant) followed by a vowel. The teacher represents this on the board as:

The first sound is held until the teacher points to or writes the second letter, at which time its sounds is produced. The duration between sounds is decreased until the child has produced a single unit. By adding final consonants (initially, stop consonants) and pronouncing the whole word, a pool of real and nonsense words can be built. Words containing new short vowels are also introduced in this fashion.

A technique developed by Slingerland (1971) and described by Liberman and Shankweiler (1979) and Liberman et al. (1980b) can also be used to help children learn to synthesize sounds without resorting to futile letter-by-letter blending. (Slingerland suggests using a wall pocket-chart for group instruction in this activity. However, we have found that it is more effective to make a small pocket-chart for each child in the group to have in front of him for individual responses.) The teacher first slowly says a word, such as "fan," that the child is going to produce, emphasizing the medial vowel. The child repeats the word, listens for the vowel sound, selects its letter card (color-coded for a vowel) from the top pocket, and places it in the lower tier of the chart. The teacher then repeats the whole word and asks the child for the initial sound. The child selects the appropriate letter card, identifies it, and places it in front of the vowel. The teacher then draws her finger along the two letters that the child has placed in the lower tier and says: "Now we have 'fa.' Let's listen to the word again. Our word is 'fan' (drawing out the sounds). What is the last sound we hear in 'fan'?" The child selects the *n* and places it at the end of the word. The child then reads the whole word aloud. The teacher might suggest changing "fan" to "fat" to "rat." When new vowels have been introduced, "fan" easily becomes "fin," etc. Although one child is primarily responsible for constructing a given word, each child in the group also builds the word in his individual pocket-chart.

All of these activities and others suggested by Lewkowicz (1980) and Williams (1979) can be used to help the child analyze the speech stream into words, syllables, and phonemes, and then to construct the link between the sounds of speech and the signs of print—the first step in learning to read an alphabetic writing system. Although the basic connections between speech and print seem to elude many children with learning disabilities, direct instruction using the procedures described here can help these students overcome this hurdle. When introducing these activities to the learning-disabled student, it is important to remember that the rate of presentation (pacing) of various task components and careful selection of instructional terminology are critical to success. Ideally, these instructional procedures should be built into our kindergarten and first-grade programs, before children have had the opportunity to experience reading failure. Incorporating language analysis activities into our prereading programs offers an ideal opportunity for the collaboration of classroom teachers, speech-language pathologists, and reading and learning disability specialists, and the opportunity to make the relationship between speech and beginning reading clearer for teachers and students alike.

References

Benton AL: Developmental dyslexia: neurological aspects. In Friedlander WJ: *Advances in Neurology.* New York, Raven Press, 1975, vol. 7.

Blachman B: The relationship of selected language measures and the McCarthy scales to kindergarten and first-grade reading achievement. (Doctoral dissertation, University of Connecticut, 1981.) *Diss Abstr Int* 42:606A, 1981. (University Microfilms No. 8115312)

Blachman B: Are we assessing the linguistic factors critical in early reading? *Ann Dyslexia,* in press.

Bruce LJ: The analysis of word sounds by young children. *Br J Educ Psychol* 34:158–170, 1964.

Calfee RC, Lindamood P, Lindamood C: Acoustic-phonetic skills and reading—kindergarten through 12th grade. *J Educ Psychol* 64:293–298, 1973.

Camp LW, Winbury NE, Zinna DR: Strategies for initial reading instruction. *Bull Orton Soc* 31:175–188, 1981.

Denckla MB, Rudel RG: Rapid "automatized" naming of pictured objects, colors, letters, and numbers by normal children. *Cortex* 10:186–202, 1974.

Denckla MB, Rudel RG: Rapid "automatized" naming (R.A.N.): dyslexia differentiated from other learning disabilities. *Neuropsychologia* 14:471–479, 1976.

Downing J, Oliver P: The child's conception of "a word." *Read Res Q* 9:568–582, 1973–1974.

Ehri LC: Word consciousness in readers and prereaders. *J Educ Psychol* 67:204–212, 1975.

Ehri LC: Linguistic insight: threshold of reading acquisition. In Waller TG, MacKinnon GE: *Reading Research: Advances in Theory and Practice.* New York, Academic Press, 1979, vol 1.

Elkonin DB: The psychology of mastering the elements of reading. In Simon B, Simon J: *Educational Psychology in the U.S.S.R.* London, Routledge & Kegan Paul, 1963.

Elkonin DB: U.S.S.R. In Downing J: *Comparative Reading.* New York, MacMillan, 1973.

Engelmann S: *Preventing Failure in the Primary Grades.* Chicago, Science Research Associates, 1969.

Fletcher H: *Speech and Hearing.* New York, Van Nostrand, 1929.

Fox B, Routh DK: Analysing spoken language into words, syllables, and phonemes: a developmental study. *J Psycholinguistic Res* 4:331–342, 1975.

Fox B, Routh DK: Phonemic analysis and synthesis

as word-attack skills. *J Educ Psychol* 68:70–74, 1976.

Francis H: Children's experience of reading and notions of units in language. *Br J Educ Psychol* 43:17–23, 1973.

Frostig M, Maslow P: *Learning Problems in the Classroom: Prevention and Remediation.* New York, Grune and Stratton, 1973.

Furth H: *Thinking without Language: Psychological Implications of Deafness.* New York, The Free Press, 1966.

Gallistel E, Ellis K: *Gallistel-Ellis Test of Coding Skills.* Hamden, CT, Montage Press, 1974.

Gelb IJ: *A Study of Writing.* Chicago, The University of Chicago Press, 1963.

Getman GN: *How to Develop Your Child's Intelligence.* Luverne, MN, Announcer Press, 1962.

Gleitman LR, Rozin P: Teaching reading by use of a syllabary. *Read Res Q* 8:447–483, 1973.

Gleitman LR, Rozin P: The structure and acquisition of reading: relations between orthographies and the structure of language. In Reber AS, Scarborough DL: *Toward a Psychology of Reading: The Proceedings of the CUNY Conference.* Hillsdale, NJ, Lawrence Erlbaum Associates, 1977.

Goldstein DM: Cognitive-linguistic functioning and learning to read in preschoolers. *J Educ Psychol* 68:680–688, 1976.

Golinkoff RM: Critique: phonemic awareness skills and reading achievement. In Murray FB, Pikulski JJ: *The Acquisition of Reading: Cognitive, Linguistic and Perceptual Prerequisites.* Baltimore, University Park Press, 1978.

Hammill D: Training visual perceptual processes. *J Learn Disabil* 5:552–559, 1972.

Helfgott J: Phonemic segmentation and blending skills of kindergarten children: implications for beginning reading acquisition. *Contemp Educ Psychol* 1:157–169, 1976.

Holden MH, MacGinitie WH: Children's conceptions of word boundaries in speech and print. *J Educ Psychol* 63:551–557, 1972.

Huttenlocher J: Children's language: word-phrase relationship. *Science* 143:264–265, 1964.

Jastak J, Bijou SW, Jastak SR: *Wide Range Achievement Test.* Wilmington, DL, Jastak Associates, 1978.

Karpova SN: The preschooler's realization of the lexical structure of speech. *Voprosy Psikhol* 4:43–55, 1955. (Abstracted by Slovin DI: In Smith F, Miller G: *Genesis of Language: A Psycholinguistic Approach.* Cambridge, MA, MIT Press, 1966.)

Kattke ML: The ability of kindergarten children to analyze 2-phoneme words. (Doctoral dissertation, Columbia University Teachers College, *Diss Abstr Int* 39:3472A, 1978. (University Microfilms No. 7822058)

Kephart N: *The Slow Learner in the Classroom.* Columbus, OH, Charles E Merrill, 1960.

Kirk C: Patterns of word segmentation in preschool children. *Child Study J* 9:37–49, 1979.

Lane HS, Baker D: Reading achievement of the deaf: another look. *Volta Rev* 76:480–490, 1974.

Larsen SC, Hammill D: The relationship of selected visual perceptual abilities to school learning. *J Spec Educ* 2:281–291, 1975.

Leong CK, Haines CF: Beginning readers' analysis of words and sentences. *J Read Behav* 10:393–407, 1978.

Lewkowicz NK: Phonemic awareness training: what to teach and how to teach it. *J Educ Psychol* 72:686–700, 1980.

Lewkowicz NK, Low LY: Effects of visual aids and word structure on phonemic segmentation. *Contemp Educ Psychol* 4:238–252, 1979.

Liberman AM: The grammars of speech and language. *Cognitive Psychol* 1:301–323, 1970.

Liberman AM, Cooper FS, Shankweiler D, et al: Perception of the speech code. *Psychol Rev* 74:431–461, 1967.

Liberman IY: Basic research in speech and lateralization of language: some implications for reading disability. *Bull Orton Soc* 21:71–87, 1971.

Liberman IY: Segmentation of the spoken word and reading acquisition. *Bull Orton Soc* 23:65–77, 1973.

Liberman IY: A language-oriented view of reading and its disabilities. In Myklebust H: *Progress in Learning Disabilities.* New York, Grune & Stratton, 1982, vol 5.

Liberman IY, Liberman AM, Mattingly IG, et al: Orthography and the beginning reader. In Kavanagh J, Venezky R: *Orthography, Reading and Dyslexia.* Baltimore, University Park Press, 1980a.

Liberman IY, Mann V: Should reading instruction and remediation vary with the sex of the child? In Ansara A, Albert M, Gallaburda A, et al: *The Significance of Sex Differences in Dyslexia.* Towson, MD, Orton Society, 1981.

Liberman IY, Mann VA, Shankweiler D, et al: Children's memory for recurring linguistic and nonlinguistic material in relation to reading ability. *Cortex* 18:367–375, 1982.

Liberman IY, Shankweiler D: Speech, the alphabet, and teaching to read. In Resnick L, Weaver P: *Theory and Practice of Early Reading.* Hillsdale, NJ, Lawrence Erlbaum Associates, 1979, vol 2.

Liberman IY, Shankweiler D, Blachman BA, et al: Steps toward literacy: a linguistic approach. In Levinson P, Sloan C: *Auditory Processing and Language: Clinical and Research Perspectives.* New York, Grune & Stratton, 1980b.

Liberman IY, Shankweiler D, Fischer FW, et al: Explicit syllable and phoneme segmentation in the young child. *J Exp Child Psychol* 18:201–212, 1974.

Liberman IY, Shankweiler D, Liberman AM, et al: Phonetic segmentation and recoding in the beginning reader. In Reber AS, Scarborough DL: *Toward a Psychology of Reading: The Proceedings of the CUNY Conference.* Hillsdale, NJ, Lawrence Ehrlbaum Associates, 1977.

Liberman IY, Shankweiler D, Orlando C, et al: Letter confusions and reversals of sequence in the beginning reader: implications for Orton's theory of developmental dyslexia. *Cortex* 7:127–142, 1971.

Lindamood CH, Lindamood PC: *Auditory Discrimination in Depth.* Boston, Teaching Resources, 1969.

Lindamood CH, Lindamood PC: *L.A.C. Test: Lindamood Auditory Conceptualization Test.* Boston, Teaching Resources, 1971.

Makita K: The rarity of reading disability in Japanese children. *Am J Orthopsychiatry* 38:599–614, 1968.

Marsh G, Mineo RJ: Training preschool children to recognize phonemes in words. *J Educ Psychol* 69:748–753, 1977.

Masland RL, Cratty BJ: The nature of the reading process, the rationale of non-educational remedial methods. In Calkins EO: *Reading Forum.* (NINDS Monograph No. 11, DHEW Publication No. (NIH) 72-44.) Washington DC, United States Government Printing Office, 1971.

McCarthy D: *The McCarthy Scales of Children's Abilities.* New York, The Psychological Corporation, 1972.

Morais J, Cary L, Alegria J, et al: Does awareness of speech as a sequence of phones arise spontaneously? *Cognition* 7:323–331, 1979.

Orton ST: "Word-blindness" in school children. *Arch Neurol Psychiatry* 14:581–615, 1925.

Perfetti CA, Lesgold AM: Discourse comprehension and sources of individual differences. In Just MA, Carpenter PA: *Cognitive Processes in Comprehension.* Hillsdale, NJ, Lawrence Erlbaum Associates, 1977.

Perfetti CA, Lesgold AM: Coding and comprehension in skilled reading and implications for reading instruction. In Resnick LB, Weaver PA: *Theory and Practice of Early Reading.* Hillsdale, NJ, Lawrence Erlbaum Associates, 1979, vol 1.

Read C: Preschool children's knowledge of English phonology. *Harvard Educ Rev* 41:1–34, 1971.

Richardson E, DiBenedetto B, Bradley CM: The relationship of sound blending to reading achievement. *Rev Educ Res* 47:319–334, 1977.

Roberts T: Skills of analysis and synthesis in the early stages of reading. *Br J Educ Psychol* 45:3–9, 1975.

Rosner J: *Phonic Analysis Training and Beginning Reading Skills.* Pittsburgh, University of Pittsburgh Learning Research and Development Center, 1971. (ERIC Document Reproduction Service No. ED 059-029.)

Rosner J: *The Perceptual Skills Curriculum.* New York, Walker Educational Book Company, 1973.

Rosner J: Auditory analysis training with prereaders. *Read Teacher* 27:379–384, 1974.

Rosner J: *Helping Children Overcome Learning Difficulties.* New York, Walker and Co., 1975.

Rosner J, Simon D: The auditory analysis test: an initial report. *J Learn Disabil* 4:40–48, 1971.

Rozin P, Bressman B, Taft M: Do children understand the basic relationship between speech and writing? The mow-motorcycle test. *J Read Behav* 6:327–334, 1974.

Rozin P, Gleitman L: The structure and acquisition of reading. II. The reading process and the acquisition of the alphabetic principle. In Reber AS, Scarborough DL: *Toward a Psychology of Reading: The Proceedings of the CUNY Conference.* Hillsdale, NJ, Lawrence Ehrlbaum Associates, 1977.

Rozin P, Poritsky S, Sotsky R: American children with reading problems can easily learn to read English represented by Chinese characters. *Science* 171:1264–1267, 1971.

Sakamoto T, Makita K: Japan. In Downing J: *Comparative Reading: Cross-national Studies of Behavior and Processes in Reading and Writing.* New York, MacMillan, 1973.

Savin HB: What the child knows about speech when he starts to learn to read. In Kavanagh JF, Mattingly IG: *Language by Ear and by Eye: The Relationships between Speech and Reading.* Cambridge, MA, MIT Press, 1972.

Skjelfjord VJ: Teaching children to segment spoken words as an aid in learning to read. *J Learn Disabil* 9:297–306, 1976.

Slingerland BH: *A Multi-sensory Approach to Language Arts for Specfic Language Disability Children: A Guide for Primary Teachers.* Cambridge, MA, Educators Publishing Service, 1971.

Treiman R, Baron J: Segmental analysis ability: development and relation to reading ability. In MacKinnon GE, Waller TG: *Reading Research: Advances in Theory and Practice.* New York, Academic Press, 1981, vol 3.

Trybus RJ, Karchmer M: School achievement of hearing impaired children: national data on achievement status and growth patterns. *Am Ann Deaf* 122:62–69, 1977.

Ungaro D: Can Ivan help Johnny? *Elementary English* 51:846–852, 1974.

Vellutino FR: Alternative conceptualizations of dyslexia: evidence in support of a verbal-deficit hypothesis. *Harvard Educ Rev* 47:334–354, 1977.

Vellutino FR: Toward an understanding of dyslexia: psychological factors in specific reading disability. In Benton AL, Pearl D: *Dyslexia: An Appraisal of Current Knowledge.* New York, Oxford University Press, 1978.

Vellutino FR: *Dyslexia: Theory and Research.* Cambridge, MA, MIT Press, 1979.

Vellutino FR, Smith H, Steger JA, et al: Reading disability: age differences and the perceptual deficit hypothesis. *Child Dev* 46:487–493, 1975.

Vellutino FR, Steger JA, Kandel G: Reading disability: an investigation of the perceptual deficit hypothesis. *Cortex* 8:106–118, 1972.

Walker W: Notes on native writing systems and the design of native literacy programs. *Anthropol Linguistics* 11:148–166, 1969.

Wallach MA, Wallach L: *Teaching All Children to Read.* Chicago, The University of Chicago Press, 1976.

Williams J: Building perceptual and cognitive strategies into a reading curriculum. In Reber AS, Scarborough DL: *Toward a Psychology of Reading: The Proceedings of the CUNY Conference.* Hillsdale, NJ, Lawrence Erlbaum Associates, 1977.

Williams J: The ABD's of reading: a program for the learning disabled. In Resnick LB, Weaver PA: *Theory and Practice of Early Reading.* Hillsdale, NJ, Lawrence Erlbaum Associates, 1979, vol 3.

Williams JP: Teaching decoding with an emphasis on phoneme analysis and phoneme blending. *J Educ Psychol* 72:1–15, 1980.

Zhurova LY: The development of analysis of words into their sounds by preschool children. In Ferguson CA, Slobin DI: *Studies of Child Language Development.* New York, Holt, Rinehart & Winston, 1973.

Zifcak M: Phonological awareness and reading acquisition. *Contemp Educ Psychol* 6:117–126, 1981.

CHAPTER FOURTEEN

Interactional Competencies in the Instructional Context: The Role of Teaching Discourse in Learning

ELAINE R. SILLIMAN, Ph.D.

That language is the primary means through which the process of schooling is mediated seems an obvious statement. What is less obvious is how language is organized and used effectively by adults to promote productive intellectual activities (Blank et al., 1978a) and to regulate the acquisition and mastery of new linguistic and discourse skills (Nelson and Nelson, 1978; Cazden, 1979). A related, but no less critical, issue is the kind of interactional competencies that children must display in the instructional setting to be evaluated as effective or successful in the judgement of the teacher (Mehan, 1979). In sum, what must children *know* and what must they *do* to be assessed as competent participators in the instructional setting?

Defining the nature of adult and child contributions to the construction of instructional transactions becomes increasingly relevant because of the awareness that many language- and learning-disabled children manifest subtle problems utilizing efficient higher order problem-solving strategies (McKinney and Haskins, 1980; Meichenbaum, 1980; Roth and Perfetti, 1980; see also Chapter 10). Also recognized is the difficulty encountered by children with language and learning disabilities in managing the language demands of the curriculum and the language demands of teacher-directed instruction, or what is called the language of schooling (Blank et al., 1978a; ASHA Committee on Language/Learning Disabilities, 1980; Wiig and Semel, 1980; Gerber and Bryen, 1981). In Chapter 8, Nelson showed how curriculum content and teacher language use became more demanding with increasing grade level. Nelson reminded us that spoken and written language are the principal tools of both the classroom teacher and the speech-language pathologist for achieving the interrelated goals of education and intervention. This chapter will further elaborate on how adults and children in instructional settings mutually organize conversation to "teach" and to "learn" a broad array of conceptual and social skills deemed appropriate by society to be internalized through the educational process.

The first purpose of this review is to define the instructional context in terms of how teaching discourse is designed to accomplish the attainment of general cognitive and social goals. These cognitive and social aspects include what has been previously referred to as the knowing and doing functions of interactional competency. A second purpose is to consider the nature of interactional competencies in regular education, special education, and language intervention (tutorial) settings. A final objective is to suggest how the development of discoursal procedures can lead to intervention strategies more sensitive to the cognitive and social demands of the classroom. On the broadest level, the chief purpose is for team specialists, such as the reading specialist, the special education teacher, and the speech-language pathologist to recognize the need for coordinating instructional objectives.

THE INSTRUCTIONAL CONTEXT: CONCEPTUAL AND SOCIAL EXPECTATIONS FOR EFFECTIVE PARTICIPATION

The Two Modes of Discourse

EVERYDAY VERSUS INSTRUCTIONAL DISCOURSE

On the most general level discourse is the reciprocal means by which at least a dyad, or two persons, organizes verbal exchanges (Garvey, 1977). The components of organization are defined in terms of function, structure, and content. Functional aspects refer to the communicative intent of conversational acts or speech acts in ongoing conversational sequences (Cole et al., 1978a). As the unit of discourse analysis transcending the sentence level, conversational acts reflect what speakers are doing together through their talk (Dore, 1979). Furthermore, conversational acts are always intended to accomplish a communicative goal or task (Dore et al., 1978). Structural aspects pertain to the participant, or turn-taking, feature of conversational organization (Dore et al., 1978; Freedle and Duran, 1979; Nelson and Gruendel, 1979). The content component involves the construction and maintenance of conversational sequences or the sustaining of topic sharing over extended turns or a series of turns (Nelson and Gruendel, 1979).

In Chapter 8 Nelson presented two qualitatively different modes of discourse. One mode is best described as the everyday use of language, and the other is identified as the language of schooling. These two modes of use can be contrasted along four dimensions: general purpose, nature of comprehension activities, coding complexity, and participant assumptions.

General Purpose. Everyday discourse is that type of interaction serving social functions arising from the regulation of interrelationships among settings, participants, role expectations for participants, and the nature of joint activities or tasks (Bronfenbrenner, 1979). In achieving these primarily social or interpersonal goals, dialogic exchanges are marked by generally cooperative turn taking, shared topics, and a shared frame of reference (Garvey and Berninger, 1981), as the following example from Tough (1978, p. 51) illustrates:

(Tom and Peter are playing side by side in a nursery school setting.)

Tom: Pete I'm going to put a big pile here (Peter abandons his efforts with a tire and watches Tom) ... put them on top ... like this ... you bring yours ... you build the wall ... make it high with those bricks ... make a track around it.

Peter: I'm bringing some bricks for it ... there, putting them on top of these (Peter brings some bricks and begins to build).

In contrast to the social saliency of everyday discourse, instructional discourse has a primary cognitive function in the transmission of scientific or logically based knowledge (Bernstein, 1972; Olson, 1977a, 1977b; see also Chapters 6 and 8). In other words, instructional discourse is intended to structure the transformation from thinking *about* knowledge to thinking *in terms of* knowledge as an objective and reflective mental activity (Bransford et al., 1977). In approaching this cognitive goal, social interactional requirements are altered to reflect the different roles of participants and the knowledge-testing structure of exchanges (Cole et al., 1978a). These alterations are reflected in a classroom example from Sinclair and Coulthard (1975, p. 54):

Teacher: What is "comprehend"?
Class: (no response)
Teacher: Nicola?

Nicola:	(no answer)
Teacher:	In fact if you get this word, you'll comprehend.
Nicola:	Find out.
Teacher:	Yes, find out.

Nature of Comprehension Activities. Everyday discourse is presumed to be less mentally complex (Blank et al., 1978a; Cole et al., 1978b). Applying this statement to the Tom and Peter exchange, their expression of communicative intent was dependent on both linguistic and nonlinguistic encoding. However, the source for interpreting what Tom meant resided in language external sources in that the meaning of what he actually intended was situated in (placed in) the shared situation and in the task to be accomplished jointly (Cook-Gumperz, 1977). (For an elaboration of this concept, see Chapter 8.) As Nelson pointed out, everyday discourse is more dependent on situated meaning for its interpretation since social factors are foregrounded and the linguistic (semantic-syntactic) channel is backgrounded.

Interpretation of instructional discourse, in contrast, involves increased mental complexity (Cole et al., 1978b) since comprehension is more dependent on language internal sources. That is, what is meant is foregrounded through linguistic means and must be reconstructed from what is actually said (Halliday and Hasan, 1976).

Coding of Content. Practical or everyday discourse tends to be coded for social regulation. Tough (1978, p. 50) defines this coding process as the use of language "for directing the actions of others or for directing the self in conjunction with others." An example of selecting content for social regulation directed toward the resolution of a practical problem is taken from the research of Cole et al. (1978b, p. 51). Six children, aged 8 to 10 years, have been participating in an after-school cooking club. On this particular day, they need to resolve how they will collaborate in a bread-baking activity.

Ken:	Look, we can only make, we can only make three breads today, alright? ... Rikki seems

	to be out of the shuffle ... Who's gonna work with Rikki?
Helene:	I had to go with Rikki last time.
Reggie:	Us (tapping Rikki on his arm) ... Rikki, you can work with (pointing to Archie and self) me and Archie.
Archie:	Naw.
Dolores:	Rikki you can work with us.
Lucy:	Archie it's only fair.

In both this example and the Tom and Peter dialogue, a practical problem is constituted—how jointly to build a wall with blocks and, on a somewhat more sophisticated level, how to restructure a set of social relations so that an activity can be initiated. The collaborative means selected to resolve each problem reflect a kind of practical action-oriented knowledge for attaining goals (Olson, 1977b; Cole et al., 1978b).

With respect to the language of schooling, instructional discourse is coded for logical definitions and explanations disembedded from specific real-world contexts of use (Olson, 1977a, 1977b). The cognitive consequence of this bias is the priority placed on self-directive or self-regulatory processes involving metacognitive and metalinguistic means for effectively engaging in logical problem solving (Brown, 1977; Nelson and Nelson, 1978; Hakes, 1980; Meichenbaum, 1980; Cavanaugh and Perlmutter, 1982; see also Chapters 7 and 8). A child requested to define the meaning of a word, as in the classroom excerpt from Sinclair and Coulthard (1975), is expected to understand that the intent is to elicit a metalinguistic statement, which focuses on explaining word meaning in terms of other word meanings, that refers to superordinate and subordinate semantic relations (Litowitz, 1977; Nelson, 1978; see also Chapter 11). What "comprehend" means in its conventional or dictionary sense implies some level of conscious awareness of the mental processes of knowing. It also implies being able to talk about aspects of these processes removed from one's practical or experiential knowledge.

Participant Assumptions. Since, in everyday discourse, what is meant can be recovered from the shared situation and activity, the range of potential meaning options are constrained by the specific context (Halliday, 1973). Although the reader may have been uncertain about what Tom and Peter were referring to, both children clearly understood the other's intention because their shared social knowledge limited available alternatives for how the task of building a wall was to be accomplished. When participant assumptions are matched about what each knows, what is literally meant can be taken for granted and need not be actually stated in the surface structure.

Because instructional discourse is coded to elicit self-regulatory systems for the deliberate consideration of knowledge as an objective entity, participant assumptions about what is known or shared cannot be taken for granted. What is meant must be explicitly stated in what is actually said, a property that increases coding complexity as the means to attain shared understanding. An immediate example of this axiom is the writing of this volume. Since contributors, in their role of speaker, assume that members of the audience for whom they are writing do not share in all respects the same frame of reference, much time is devoted to defining terms and explaining what is meant as procedures for establishing a shared topic context. These linguistic procedures are necessary because the range of possible meaning options is not tied to the specific experience of readers and contributors. To achieve a consensus of understanding, then, necessitates selection of elaborated linguistic means for making meaning explicit and, hence, socially shared.

IMPLICATIONS FOR CHILD DIFFERENCES IN MODES OF USE

Gerber and Bryen (1981, p. 47) propose that a mismatch between the linguistic and cognitive demands of instructional discourse "and the reduced cognitive and linguistic abilities of learning disabled youngsters may account for their behavioral reactions of impulsivity and lack of atten-

tion." (Lee and Fine expand upon matches and mismatches in an upcoming chapter.) The Gerber and Bryen statement emphasizes the "knowing" component of interactional competence. A broader issue pertaining to the mismatch thesis has been framed by several other authors, however. The issue concerns distinguishing "disabled" children from those whose cultural experience differs from the conventionalized norms of schooling. Do certain culturally different children bring to school a system of use which is largely practical and, therefore, insufficient to meet cognitive and social expectations for effective participation?

Culturally Different Children. Nelson (1978), Cazden (1979), and Nelson (Chapter 8) address this possibility. Nelson (1978) argues that the more remote a child's social and cultural experience from the conceptual demands of school, or the more limited the opportunities for experience with these demands, the harder it may be to build on the existing conceptual organization brought to the academic setting.

Cazden (1979) suggests that the greater the interference between "scripts" a child has available for ways of talking at home (first discourse development) and the interactional requirements of schooling (second discourse development), the greater will be the mismatch for how successfully a child can participate in the formal instructional setting. By script is generally meant a set of conceptual structures which forms the basis of long-term memory and function as expectation strategies for representing recurrent experience. Because of these scripts, one need not refigure how to behave when new events and information are encountered (Schank and Abelson, 1977; Tannen, 1979; Estes, 1980). Conversational or dialogic scripts are considered as particular scripts that represent the means or process for organizing what to say. These dialogic scripts also enable one to understand concepts activated by verbal information with the nature of processing a function of participants in a dialogue, the topic being discussed, and the setting in which the dialogue occurs (Freedle and Duran, 1979; Nelson and Gruendel, 1979).

These practical conceptual and dialogic scripts for everyday discourse are assumed, therefore, to reflect the "data" for how daily experience comes to be organized and talked about. That the nature and scope of these data vary according to different cultural and social structures and opportunities seems a reasonable hypothesis. Furthermore, variations in experiential knowledge may account for the mismatch between first and second discourse development of some culturally different children (Cazden, 1970, 1979; Philips, 1972; Labov, 1976; Edwards, 1979).

Language Learning-disabled Children. In the realm of language learning disabilities, many current assessment and intervention approaches are designed to evolve a mode of language use more consistent with the properties of instructional discourse (Silliman et al., 1980). Van Kleeck (Chapter 9) notes that a number of norm- and criterion-referenced measures and subsequent intervention goals and procedures are biased toward the display of metalinguistic skill in their emphasis on a child's ability to reflect on aspects of the linguistic code. This emphasis, as a result, may be more indicative of the conceptual demands of the formal instructional context than of a child's level of first discourse development. Examined next are some of the conceptual and social expectations for effective participation in the instructional context.

Conceptual Expectations

THE FORMAL INSTRUCTIONAL CONTEXT

As discussed in Chapter 8, a formal instructional context is one in which the adult's conversational style structures the types of conceptual schemes the child is to evoke for problem solving (Mishler, 1972; Farnham-Diggory, 1978; Meichenbaum and Goodman, 1979; Vellutino, 1979). These adult conversational strategies are

designed principally as the interactional framework for mediating intellectual activity (Blank et al., 1978a), or "getting the child to know." More strictly, teachers' conversational strategies are supposed to function as an externalized cognitive model through which children are provided with implicit principles for learning how to mediate, or self-regulate, problem-solving activity using verbal processes (Meichenbaum and Goodman, 1979; Gearhardt and Newman, 1980). It is unclear, however, whether these conversational strategies actually do result in the acquisition of new cognitive scripts for planful behavior. Meichenbaum and Goodman (1979) suggest, instead, that such mediating activities may serve to enhance efficiency of information storage and management in short- and long-term memory rather than lead to the development of self-instructional procedures. Teacher dialogues provided by Nelson (Chapter 8) present examples of conversational strategies through the elementary grades.

Research on these topics with language learning-disabled children is surprisingly limited. Two types of research approaches can be identified. One focuses on description of the content or conceptual complexity of teacher-child verbal interactions (Blank et al., 1978a, 1978b). The second approach (Wiig and Semel, 1980) concentrates on task analysis of the language demands of curriculum content. Each of these approaches is discussed below.

CONTENT COMPLEXITY OF INSTRUCTIONAL EXCHANGES

Blank and her associates (Blank et al., 1978a, 1978b; Berlin et al., 1980) have developed a model of teaching discourse based on the concept of controlled complexity (Blank and Milewski, 1981). Controlled complexity is defined as the systematic regulation of adult-child conversational sequences in which the adult/teacher simplifies or reformulates content to reduce the magnitude of the mismatch between the child's conceptual resources and the semantic complexity of question content. The goal of this procedure is to guide the child toward successful problem solving. These simplification sequences, activated when the child fails to supply the specific information being requested, are described as a set of instructional principles which "provide a strategy for problem solving that the child can internalize and apply to other relevant situations" (Berlin et al., 1980, p. 54). Furthermore, this approach is characterized as the language of effective instruction since teacher level of demand is matched to the child's level of comprehension (Blank et al., 1978a).

Model of Discourse Skills. At the core of the model are four levels of demand, or levels of abstraction, which appear to be based on the principle of cognitive distancing (Sigel and Cocking, 1977). According to this principle, the degree of distance, or discrepancy, between the social and perceptual (nonlinguistic) information contextually available and the linguistic content that a child must understand and use to operate successfully on a task (problem) regulates comprehension complexity. These four abstraction levels represent, therefore, a continuum of complexity ranging from no inferencing to inferencing (Blank et al., 1978b).

Level I demands (matching perceptions, with perception representing "the material available to the child" (Blank et al., 1978a, p. 17)) include such teacher verbal formulations as *What is this?*, *Please give me the pencil*, and *What things do you see on the table?* Level II demands (requiring selective analysis of perception) are defined by verbalizations such as *What shape is the bowl?*, *Think of other things that we can bake in an oven*, and *What's happening in the picture?* Level III demands (eliciting the reordering of perception) are characterized by such examples as *Tell me what we put in the bowl before we added the egg*, *Show me the part of the egg that we don't eat*, and *Point to all the pictures that are not cups.* Level IV demands (involving reasoning about perception) are formulations as *Why*

don't we eat this part?, *What will happen to the cookies when we put them in the oven?*, and (given an array of possible objects) *Which one of these things could we use to fix the cup so the juice would stay in?*, followed by *Why did you pick that one?*

Simplification sequences function to minimize missing information in relation to this set of hierarchical discourse competencies. In effect, implicit information, serving as the previous topic of talk, is made explicit by what the teacher says in reformulating (Blank et al., 1978a, p. 91). A modified simplification sequence illustrates the interrelated notions of mismatch and verbal remedies for repairing the mismatch, as provided by Blank et al. (1978a, pp. 92–93). A child is presented with two cups, one with a bottom and the other without a bottom. The child is asked initially which one he would pick so that the juice would stay in. He is then asked to explain his selection.

Teacher: Well, why didn't you pick this one? (referring to the cup without a bottom)
Level IV: explaining the obstacles to an action; requires the child to reason about perception.

Child: (shrugs)

Teacher: Well, let's try this cup (referring to the cup without a bottom). Go ahead and pour the juice in here.
Level I (simplification from previous level IV): following a direction; requires that the child match perception with the appropriate action.

Child: (completes the action)

Teacher: Oh, what happened to the juice?
Level I: naming an action.

Child: It dropped here (pointing to the table)

Teacher: That's right. This isn't a good cup to use. Let's try the other one.
Level I: following a direction.

Child: (pours the juice in the cup with a bottom)

Teacher: Did that work?
Level II: identifying characteristics; requires selective analysis of perception.

Child: (nods)

The sequence continues until the child successfully justifies why one cup should not be used and why one should be used, both level IV demands. Blank et al. (1978a) comment that the goal of the sequence is not only to have the question answered appropriately. Rather, it is the anticipation that "the sequence has also provided them with a model whereby they can identify the information needed for this type of problem" (p. 93). In summary, these simplification sequences are assumed to function as a cognitive model in at least three ways. First, the teacher's discourse strategy assists the child to focus on essential information (*Well, let's try this cup. Go ahead and pour the juice in here*). Second, it constrains the nature of the child's information search (*Oh, what happened to the juice?*), and, third, it helps the child to evaluate taks-relevant hypotheses (Meichenbaum and Goodman, 1979) (*So why shouldn't we use this cup?*). It is through this process that the child is guided to internalize progressively a self-instructional strategy for knowing which questions to ask of self (Berlin et al., 1980). This goal is to be accomplished through a process of reducing the complexity of comprehension demands in order "to make the implicit explicit" (Blank et al., 1978a, p. 93).

One problem with the model, as defined by the four levels of abstraction, is its implicit concept of discourse skills. The four demand levels do not describe the range of discourse skills that, for example, normally developing children bring to school. What the model emphasizes is one highly specialized type of interactional competency common to formal instructional contexts—the ability to answer questions correctly and explain "why." In a specific sense, the model is a set of assumptions about what a child needs to know to be evaluated as a successful "contingent responder."

Furthermore, the model is predicated on adult-dominated topic selection and does not attempt to explain the semantic-syntactic links that permit topic sharing to occur across extended speaking turns. A basic premise is that the language of instruction is characterized by minimal variation in structure (interrogatives and imperatives predominate) and function (requests for information and action occur most frequently). What is proposed to vary maximally is the level of conceptual complexity (Blank et al., 1978a). This particular premise, in terms of actual classroom organization, remains to be verified across a broad variety of different kinds of classroom and intervention activities.

What must also be questioned is the definition of dialogue associated with the model. Since the model appears to concentrate solely on contingent responding skill, dialogue is reduced to question-answer sequences only. The adult determines when the child is to take a speaking turn and what the content of talk will be. Moreover, the model is a "management of failure" approach (Berlin et al., 1980, p. 53) that becomes operative as a type of repair strategy when communicative breakdown occurs or when it is assumed that nontopic sharing happens. Whether other kinds of strategies may be equally effective in initially preventing "failure" will be explored in later in this chapter.

Another area of caution concerns critical differences between levels III and IV. Content grouped into these two levels seems to share in common, as distinct from levels I and II, an emphasis on more logically based (as opposed to practically based) causal thinking and subsequent verbal explanation of how one knows. The specific differences remain in need of clarification, particularly in relation to actual use in simplification sequences. As reviewed in Chapters 5 and 12, children's development of inferential skills is an area warranting further investigation.

A final problem with both the model and the controlled complexity procedure is that neither the level of demand concept nor the derived remedial procedure have been studied in actual classroom interaction with either normally developing or disabled children. One exception is the recent work of Griffin et al., (1982). These authors applied the level of demand coding system to describing participation in a small group lesson by two children in the middle primary grades.

Nature of Research. The empirical base for the level of demand construct originates from the development of the *Preschool Language Assessment Instrument* (PLAI) (Blank et al., 1978b). The primary purpose of this appraisal technique was to identify and define the effects of social class differences on the mastery of those kinds of discourse competencies assumed to be related to the instructional goals of schooling at the preschool level. As a measure of the discriminative validity of the PLAI, 14 children, aged 4 to 5 years, "diagnosed as having language disabilities" (Blank et al., 1978b, p. 7), and from middle-class backgrounds, were tested with the instrument. Patterns of performance were found to be more similar to normally developing children from lower socioeconomic backgrounds, specifically for levels III and IV. The authors concluded that the PLAI did differentiate language-disabled from normal (preschool) children. This conclusion must be accepted with reservations on several grounds.

First, insufficient numbers of language learning-disabled children matched for differences in level of severity and intellectual level have been studied (IQ factors appear to influence PLAI performance according to standardization information). Second, no information is available on how, from a qualitative perspective, responses of language learning-disabled children may differ from those of normally developing children matched for language level. Finally, to return to the controlled complexity teaching procedure, minimal data are available on its long-term effectiveness in a variety of instructional settings. What little information there is tends to be based on dyadic participant structures (Blank and Milewski, 1981). If classroom originated, findings are presented in descriptive form only (McBride and Levy, 1981).

LANGUAGE DEMANDS OF CURRICULUM CONTENT

The previous approach clearly emphasizes that "teaching," in a general sense, is a mutually constituted activity structured by the kinds of verbal transactions taking place between teacher and child. Analysis of the content to be acquired through these transactions is offered by Wiig and Semel (1980). In a detailed examination of the language components of curriculum content at the secondary level, Wiig and Semel (1980) identify numerous barriers confronting the language learning-disabled adolescent in effectively participating in classroom lessons. (Lee and Fine will elaborate further on the disabled adolescent in Chapter 16.) Among these barriers, independent of the particular curriculum area, are the mode and manner in which information is presented and how it must be retained. For example, these grade levels are characterized by a verbal lecture format requiring note-taking skill if information is to be retained in an organized manner. The absolute volume of information presented constitutes another formidable barrier to content mastery.

A limitation of the Wiig and Semel (1980) approach is their focus on internal events taking place within the youngster to the exclusion of interactional events. Since conceptual schemes for how information is actively processed or represented are the core of their intervention approach, the unit of intervention is the student to whom "something is being done." How this "something" actually is accomplished, the interactional process itself, is not a major consideration.

Social Expectations

THE FORMAL INSTRUCTIONAL CONTEXT

The function of teaching discourse is not only one of getting the child to know but also one that serves simultaneously to enforce what McDermott (1977) calls an implicit social contract. In getting the child to do (or display what is known), teacher and clinician discourse strategies function to define the social relation between authority and learning to behave (Bernstein, 1972). In Halliday's (1973) description, learning to speak, irrespective of whether this process is considered as first or second discourse development (Cazden, 1979), is inseparable from learning how to behave appropriately. Both involve an exploitation of language and the context in which it is used (Halliday, 1973).

Specifying the communicative components of competent participation in instructional settings is a relatively new area of investigation for both normally developing and language- and learning-disabled children and adolescents. Two different kinds of research strategies are currently being applied to this task. One approach evolves from ethnography, a method for the study of relations between people applied to instructional contexts (McDermott, 1977). The other, applied to language learning-disabled children, involves the development of procedures for more skilled observation of communicative breakdowns in the classroom setting.

THE ETHNOGRAPHIC APPROACH TO THE CLASSROOM

Ethnographic analysis of the classroom setting attempts to describe the means teachers and students use to relate to each other to work out common-sense agreements as "coparticipants in the educational process" (McDermott, 1977, p. 203). The basic premise is that patterned regularities exist in how teachers and students relate to each other. Specifically, these regularities are reflected in how joint activity is organized and in how language is used to transmit this organization. Furthermore, description of any instructional activity, such as a lesson, asserts hypotheses about what children must learn to participate fully in classroom talk and to be evaluated as interactionally and academically competent (Cazden, 1979; Mehan, 1979; see also Chapter 8).

Social Organization of Effective Participation. Knowing how and when to produce academically correct and interactionally appropriate responses requires integrating the social forms for how to *dis-*

play what one knows with the appropriate content, what one *does* know (Mehan, 1979). Within the school community, being effective means knowledge of the implicit rules for getting the floor (taking a turn at speaking), keeping the floor by being relevant (conveying information clearly linked to the previous topic or topics), and making sense (introducing interesting or original information coherently tied back to what has been said). As Mehan's (1979) research shows, violation of one or more of these rules can result in asynchronies that have negative consequences. As illustrations, a child may "know" the correct answer (content) but violate the rule for gaining entrance to the floor by shouting out the answer (form). In this case, there is a lack of integration between content and form for its display in this particular setting with this type of activity. In another instance, a child may know how to appropriately gain access to the floor (taking a speaking turn only when specifically nominated by the teacher) but may not be able to give the "right" answer. The resulting asynchrony is a gap between correct form and correct content. Having one's contributions accepted, then, is contingent upon knowing when to take a turn. If the turn is not taken at the appropriate time, the probability is that some type of implicit or explicit sanction will occur (having one's turn allocated to someone else, receiving a negative comment, or both). Acceptance is also contingent on the sequential relatedness of one's topic selection to the previous discourse. If one's turn is taken appropriately but what is said is irrelevant, the probability is that the particular contribution will be ignored, another type of implicit sanction. Finally, if a child takes a turn appropriately and provides a related topic but does not make interesting what he or she is saying to the specific set of coparticipants, the probability is that a sanction will occur in the form of either implicit or explicit feedback.

The second set of social skills for effective participation pertains to knowing how to behave appropriately across a variety of classroom activities. The constraints imposed by different types of tasks vary as a function of the task at every grade level (Wiig and Semel, 1980). For example, participatory rules vary within different kinds of teacher-directed group activities such as learning a lesson (Mehan, 1979) versus a cleaning-up activity (Dore et al., 1978). Procedural rules also differ for individual activities as learning how to draw (Gearhardt and Newman, 1980). At the high school level, even practical learning requires a different set of participatory rules, for example, learning how to acquire a set of job skills in community placement (Moore, 1981).

When both of these sets of social skills are integrated with the appropriate academic content, the chances are that a child will be evaluated as interactionally competent (Mehan, 1979). The impact of a language and learning disability on this type of evaluation within the classroom setting has not been investigated. However, a modified form of ethnographic analysis has been applied to a case study of one child previously identified as having a learning disability.

Social Organization for Ineffectual Participation.

Hood et al. (1980) provide a descriptive study of Adam. Adam was one of 17, 8- to 10-year-olds participating in an investigation on the real-life validity of experimental cognitive tasks (Cole et al., 1978b). Hood et al. (1980) take the theoretical position that a learning disability is not the product of an internal structural deficit per se. Utilizing a Vygotskian framework, they propose that whether an "ability" or "disability" will be displayed is dependent on how activities are organized by participants.

This social organizational hypothesis was explored with Adam, using as evidence videotaped information obtained from an after-school club that Adam attended with his private school classmates (Cole et al., 1978b). An "IQ bee," in which children were divided into two teams, served as the shared activity. Detailed observations were made

to determine how Adam reorganized the cognitive complexity of the task (the IQ bee) as the means for modifying others' actions toward him. The central issue was how Adam, his peers, and the adult in the role of examiner all collaborated to try to make it "a good day" for Adam so that he could feel successful and competent.

What appeared to be most salient in this collaborative effort was not the complexity of the task demand (e.g., holding in mind a series of digits to repeat in correct order), but the nature of the social support given to Adam's performance. Hood et al. (1980) describe some restructuring activities that permit Adam to obtain "assisted performance" (Cazden, 1981), the external guidance or support of others as a framework for performing successfully on tasks more advanced than what Adam could accomplish alone. For example, as Adam's turn approaches, he squirms, listens attentively to what his peers say, and organizes "an environment in which everyone feels uncomfortable about his plight" (Hood et al., 1980, p. 164).

How did Adam manage to gain assisted performance? It can be assumed that, based on his previous experience in similar situations, Adam's "script" for how to obtain more effective participation is activated by some self-awareness that the task is genuinely difficult (Hood et al., 1980). This metacognitive capacity for self-awareness (Loper, 1980) leads Adam to develop a strategy for reliance on others in order to preserve his self-identity. In the IQ bee, Adam's sequencing of his activities causes a simpler question to be posed to him and for others to applaud his performance. By seeking cooperative assistance and observing others, Adam succeeds in reorganizing the cognitive complexity of the task to display the skill he has available. Thus, two main tasks daily confront Adam in the instructional setting and, by implication, most language learning-disabled children. One task consists of ongoing assessment of the social constraints imposed by different kinds of activities, events, and participants. The second interdependent task involves devising strategies (which may or may not be effective) for preserving self-identity and participatory rights as a group member.

THE OBSERVATIONAL APPROACH TO COMMUNICATIVE BREAKDOWNS IN THE CLASSROOM SETTING

Almost no information exists on the kinds of interactional competencies language learning-disabled children and adolescents display as a function of different social requirements for effective participation in the instructional setting. This lack of information applies equally to potential differences for classroom participation versus participation in "intervention" activities separate from the classroom. Since classroom and intervention settings may be theoretically characterized by dissimilar social organizations, more systematic description would be a necessary prerequisite for coordinating intervention goals with the conceptual and social goals of the classroom.

What limited information is available derives from two types of sources. The largest source of experimental data on children evaluated as learning disabled is that gathered by Bryan and her associates (Pearl et al., 1979; Donahue et al., 1980; Bryan et al., 1981; Donahue, 1981). (See Chapter 2 for a discussion of this research.) It should be pointed out that none of these data were obtained from actual classroom interactions; therefore, caution is warranted in generalizing research findings.

A second source of information is descriptive and is designed for teacher observation of certain kinds of conversational behavior in the classroom. Developed by Damico and Oller (1980) and indirectly related to the structure of discourse, these behaviors are intended to enhance teacher reliability in referring kindergarten through grade 5 children for language evaluations. It is not yet verified that these five discourse categories reliably distinguish normally developing children from those

with possible disability. Given this warning about reliability, what follows next is an attempt to link the categories proposed by Damico and Oller (1980) with their potential for better describing effective participation (Mehan, 1979).

Nonfluent Self-expression. The child's speech is marked by disruptions due to an excessively high number of self-interruptions. By self-interruptions are meant word and phrase repetitions; an unusual number of silent or filled pauses, the latter characterized by such vocal insertions as *um* and *uh*; and the occurrence of numerous nonproductive reformulations (revisions). Included as nonproductive reformulations would be false starts, initiating a verbal sequence and having to reinitiate because of an apparent planning failure (Sabin et al., 1979).

A basic problem in interpreting the diagnostic import of this category concerns the lack of consensus on "how much" of each of these behaviors, or of combinations of these behaviors, results in a judgment of excessive nonfluency (Starkweather, 1980). What is of potential clinical consequence is that investigations on the type and frequency of these normal disfluencies (self-interruptions) with normal children, adolescents, and adults suggest that occurrence is predictable and patterned. Occurrence is inferred to be related to transient failure either in efficiently preplanning verbal formulations as a function of task complexity (Sabin et al., 1979) or in smoothly encoding what has been selected to be said (Butterworth and Goldman-Eisler, 1979). Either type of failure—in preplanning or in execution—when excessive in occurrence, could affect the ability to keep one's speaking turn since topical relatedness might be disrupted, as might acceptable temporal durations for pause length within utterance boundaries.

Unusual Delays before Responding or Excessive Need for Repetition of the Message. This category is described by Damico and Oller (1980) as one in which child-directed utterances are either not immediately responded to or the child manifests a consistent need for repetition of what has just been said. This apparent failure to comprehend may be conveyed through such requests for repetition as *Huh?* or *What?* When repetition is subsequently offered, it may not be successful in repairing misunderstanding.

Failure to provide a swift response is related to knowing how and when to take a turn in the sense of appropriately interpreting the participatory rules operating for a particular activity. Excessive need for repetition of what is said may also be associated with knowing how to assume a turn. Being able to enter conversation at the right time involves active monitoring of another's turn at speaking or what is often called "paying attention" (Ervin-Tripp, 1979). In either case, whether these behaviors occur frequently cannot be readily separated from the nature of the activities, the participant structure, and the topic being talked about.

Nonexplicit and Ambiguous Vocabulary Use. In his or her turn as speaker, the child consistently uses terms for which referents have not been given either in what the child has just said or in the shared setting and activity. Most crucially, when the coparticipant(s) provide feedback that what was said was not understood, the child does not successfully recode to be more explicit. This pattern may be indicative of taking shared assumptions for granted about what is known.

Irrelevant Responses. Damico and Oller (1980, p. 80) define this behavior as one in which "the child (seems to be) operating on an independent discourse agenda." Put another way, the child has difficulty linking or relating what he or she selects to say to what a coparticipant has just said. This kind of behavior would also affect how successfully one can keep a speaking turn. Persistent failure to link what one says to another's content may indicate ineffectual accomodation to the requirements of both the verbal and social context (Blank et al., 1979).

Poor Topic Maintenance. The last category is defined as rapid and inappropriate changes in topic without giving sufficient transitional information to coparticipants (Damico and Oller, 1980). If the child fails to connect ideas logically across his or her stretch of language use, the resulting lack of cohesion may eventuate in interruption of one's turn (losing the floor) or termination of participation for failing to make sense.

The Damico and Oller (1980) categories, as well as other types of discourse-based categories (Dukes, 1981), appear to have some value for screening purposes within the classroom setting. Category reliability is dependent, however, on both adequate training and systematization of observations through criterion referencing frequency of occurrence using appropriate recording procedures. The limitations of a category approach beyond screening purposes seem obvious when the issue of descriptive specificity is considered for defining the nature of the problem and for program planning (Bloom and Lahey, 1978). A more serious conceptual limitation concerns the implicit assumption that the type of communicative breakdown described by each category resides within the child as the source of the breakdown. The unit of analysis, once again, becomes the individual child without regard for how breakdowns may covary with the social organization of different kinds of classroom events.

Closing Remarks

This overview of some conceptual and social expectations for effective classroom participation by language learning-disabled children and adolescents leads to theoretical implications for the relationship between modes of use and the visibility of a disability.

Conceptual expectations for language learning-disabled youngsters appear similar to those for nondisabled children when the cognitive goals of the formal instructional context are examined. The cognitive modeling hypothesis underlying the selection of a teaching discourse strategy, designed to internalize the verbal mediation of planful reasoning in the service of logical problem solving, seems related to a basic assumption about how knowledge is acquired. As Dore (in press) states, this assumption—the core of Piagetian and information models of cognitive psychology— views internal processes as the primary source of behavior. Development is conceptualized as a relatively autonomous, or self-determined, path of acquisition regulated from within. In relation to notions of a language learning disability, the model becomes expressed in the search for descriptions of internal process restrictions through assessment of the child alone as the unit of analysis (see Chapter 9).

When the social organization of the instructional context is considered, it becomes apparent that expectations for effective participation involve not only how accurately a child displays content knowledge but also how appropriately the child selects the form in which to participate. This focus on the contributions of interactional processes to the acquisition and display of knowledge stems from a social constructivist conception of development (Mehan, 1981). This alternate view argues that social and cognitive structures are constructed by and embedded in the collaborative activities among people. As a consequence, competence need not invariably precede performance. Rather, under certain conditions, as with the example of Adam, performance may precede competence when others function as an externalized source of social support to allow the child to accomplish with help what only later can come to be accomplished alone as an internalized and autonomous operation (Cazden, 1981).

Whether the social constructivist or mental constructivist model is a more valid explanation of the acquisition of knowledge remains to be documented. It may be that a social constructivist description is more appropriate for defining the process of first discourse development and certain aspects of second discourse development associated with schooling. The mental constructivist explanation may be more adequate for describing the end-state of formal language use relative to the capacity to reflect intentionally on the process and content of knowing in an autonomous manner removed from specific contexts of use.

INSTRUCTIONAL LANGUAGE USE: ORGANIZATION AND UNITS OF ANALYSIS

Discourse is hierarchically organized into four interrelated components. These components, or units of analysis, are conversational acts, turns, sequences, and episodes. Each is successively explored in classroom and intervention contexts in relation to three aspects of interactional competence (Mehan, 1979). These aspects are knowing what to mean (selecting appropriate conversational acts), knowing how and when to participate (timing and regulation of turn taking), and knowing how to be relevant, clear, and original (constructing sequentially related conversational sequences and repairing communicative breakdowns). In addition, procedures are suggested for increasing clinical skill in systematically observing and analyzing the three aspects in classroom and intervention settings. These procedures are presented as a practical means for developing better coordinated instructional-intervention goals among the various specialists concerned with language and learning disabilities.

Hierarchical Organization of Discourse

MODEL OF DISCOURSE

The model of discourse to be offered is based on Dore (1978, 1979) and was initially introduced in Chapter 8. Dore's model has been operationalized for practical purposes in his coding manual (unpublished data). Further information also appears in studies on the structure of nursery school conversations (Cole et al., 1978a; Dore et al., 1978; Hall and Cole, 1978).

Conversational Acts. A conversational

act (or C-act) is a functional unit of analysis (Dore, 1979) comparable in meaning to a speech act. As discussed in the Chapter 8, C-acts transcend the sentence, or even the utterance, as the object of analysis.

For the purpose of general designation of intent or function, C-acts can be classified into four broad categories (Cole et al., 1978a; Dore, coding manual). These functional categories are listed below:

1. *Requestives*—function to solicit information or action (requests for information or action grammatically realized by the interrogative and imperative forms).

2. *Regulatives*—serve to organize and regulate the flow of conversation. Regulatives include speaker selection (e.g., *It's your turn, John*), attention getters (e.g., *Look*), topic boundary markers (e.g., *O.K. Let's turn the page*), and acknowledgments which evaluate or provide positive, negative, or neutral feedback (e.g., *You're right* or the more neutral *Hmmm*).

3. *Assertives*—provide information. They include facts, descriptions, internal evaluations, and declarations of rights and procedures. Their grammatical form is typically defined as the declarative.

4. *Responsives*—supply solicited information or provide new information related to the preceding requestive or assertive.

An extensive discussion of the types of C-acts which can be classified into these four broad categories is beyond the scope of this discussion. However, a major problem with coding schemas for C-acts concerns the lack of reliability data (Chapman, 1981). Reliability is affected by a number of factors. One factor is that C-act categories and subcategories may be either too detailed or insufficiently detailed to capture specific intent. A second factor is that decisions about intent cannot be separated from their context of occurrence. A third factor derives from the fact that forms do not always correspond with function. For example, the interrogative form *Can you pass the salt?* is a polite means of obtaining compliance with a directive and leaves the listener with the option of not complying.

Finally, reliability is dependent on how conversation is recorded, transcribed, and segmented (Ochs, 1979). It is also dependent on the degree of a clincian's or teacher's training with the coding system.

Turns. A person's turn at speaking is comprised by one or more C-acts. Dore (coding manual) identifies three basic turn types: (1) an initiating turn which usually takes a requestive or assertive as its C-act content; (2) a responding turn which takes responsives as its C-act content; and (3) an extending turn which may take either assertives or responsives as its content. An extending turn is one in which the topic introduced by the initiating C-act is elaborated upon.

Turn taking underlies conversational contingency. By conversational contingency is meant that successive speaking turns are linked or related in terms of function, form, and content. Many of the practical difficulties raised in conjunction with coding C-acts also apply to identifying turn types. Dore (coding manual) suggests a general criterion relating to the position of a turn in a sequence. For example, the C-act *I'm a boy* can be an initiating turn when intended to be an assertion about self-identification. When this same C-act follows a request for information (e.g., *Are you a boy or girl?*, it is coded as a responding turn. If this same C-act occurred immediately after the assertion *You're a girl*, the turn type could be either initiating or extending depending upon whether the initial assertion was intended as a joke or an insult.

Sequences. C-acts serve as the bases for turns. Turns function as the means by which conversational sequences are constructed and maintained. Some debate exists about whether a sequence consisting of two speakers each taking a single turn structured around a particular topic rigorously meets criteria for conversational sequence status. The most questionable candidate for sequence status is the question-answer structure typical of certain kinds of instructional activities.

Consider the following illustration from

a language therapy activity. A clinician and a 9-year-old language-disabled child are baking a cake (Silliman et al., 1980):

Clinician: What do we do with it? (referring to water in a measuring cup)
Child: Pour.
Clinician: Pour it where?
Child: On the (cake) mix.

The organization of C-acts in this example of clinician-child discourse consists of requests for information followed by contingently related responses. According to Nelson and Gruendel (1979), this sample of a question-answer format reflects the maintenance of a topic *over a single turn*. To qualify for true conversational sequence status, a topic (shared reference) would have to be sustained over extended turns, not a single turn. Thus, sequences consisting of initiating and reply turns only (elicitation-replies) may not be dialogic in a strict sense.

How to segment sequences into types remains a coding problem for which uniform agreement also does not exist. One reason for the difficulty in determining sequence type is that topics often shift temporarily or are interrupted by others. As a consequence, the topic may not be completed or may be returned to later in the conversation (Dore, coding manual; Garvey, 1977, 1979; Garvey and BenDebba, 1978).

Episodes. C-acts, turns, and sequences interrelate in order to accomplish social events. These transactions are called episodes or exchanges, the largest unit of discourse analysis (Dore et al., 1978). Episodes may be topically structured events, such as gossip, telling a story, or discussing current political events among friends (Dore, coding manual). They may also be activity structured events (Cazden, 1979) as seen in the clinician-child cake-baking segment (Silliman et al., 1980). Learning lessons (Mehan, 1979), cleaning up in nursery school (Dore et al., 1978), and learning how to draw under teacher guidance (Gearhardt and Newman, 1980) represent other distinct types of episodes.

Teaching discourse is organized similarly to the hierarchical model of discourse just presented (Dore, 1978, 1979). The organization of teaching discourse is therefore, examined next within regular and special education classroom settings with respect to the three aspects of interactional competency. Where appropriate, data from these settings are applied to the organization of intervention activities.

Knowing How to Mean

SELECTION OF TEACHING C-ACTS IN THE REGULAR CLASSROOM

The primary kind of conversational act (C-act) selected by teachers for implementing the instructional phase of a lesson at both the elementary and secondary levels is the request for information or elicitation (Bellack et al., 1966; Garrard, 1966; Mishler, 1975; Sinclair and Coulthard, 1975; Mehan, 1979; see also Chapter 8). Mehan (1979) identifies four subtypes of elicitations in the instructional phase of the lesson: choice, product, process, and metaprocess.

Choice Elicitations. This class of request can function to: (1) elicit either-or evaluations relative to question content; (2) elicit agreement or disagreement (Cole et al., 1978a); or (3) solicit evaluation of specific information a coparticipant needs to fomulate a reply (Mehan, 1979; French and MacLure, 1981). Specific examples include:

Was it nice or was it a lousy weekend for weather? (optional information supplied for an either-or evaluation (Silliman and Leslie, 1980))
Do you know for a fact if I waved a worm in front of a new baby bird—robin—would it eat it? (agreement-disagreement (Silliman and Leslie, 1980))
Well was he a very *sad* (authors' italics) elephant? (specific item of information supplied for evaluation (French and MacLure, 1981, p. 40))

Product Elicitations. This subcategory of requestive solicits factual pieces of information about social or physical objects, events, actions (functions), attributes, location, time, or quantity. Product requestives typically seek information structurally through the *wh*-interrogative form and require single word or short phrase replies. All examples are from Silliman and Leslie (1980).

> What was Friday's date?
> How many minutes in an hour?
> What day is it?
> What is it called?

Process Elicitations. The process requestive queries, through the *wh*-interrogative, opinions or interpretations (Mehan, 1979). These kinds of requestives usually require a reply in which surface structure is expanded as the semantic-syntactic means for supplying an extended description or explanation. Samples are (Silliman and Leslie, 1980):

> Why would you use a book like this?
> Why does a storm make a light go out?
> How does thunder happen?

Metaprocess Elicitations. This subclass of requestives invokes reflection on the rule, procedure, or mental process by which response content was formulated (Mehan, 1979). For example:

> Before you incubate eggs, what must you know?
> (Silliman and Leslie, 1980)
> And, Carolyn, how did you remember where it was?
> (Mehan, 1979, p. 46)

The classification of teacher C-acts into elicitation types can provide a measure of type and frequency of occurrence. The Blank et al. (1978a) level of demand system, discussed earlier, is an alternate means for the description of content complexity. However, neither of these procedures adequately captures how the instructional phase is organized as a series of initiations and replies in which elicitations, as initiations, co-occur with particular replies, e.g., a product elicitation solicits a product reply, etc., resulting in a minimal conversational sequence (Mehan, 1979; Dore, coding manual). Moreover, a co-occurrence relationship presumes that C-acts, as replies, accurately supply the information being queried. When the reply is inaccurate or the child does not respond, the teacher engages in a number of different kinds of repair strategies to reestablish co-

occurrence (Mehan, 1979). The question arises, however, as to whether differences exist in the selection of teaching C-acts in the regular classroom versus the special education classroom.

A STUDY OF TWO CLASSROOMS

Silliman and Leslie (1980) sought to describe similarities and differences in the organization of teaching discourse in a regular and special education second grade. The focus of study was the analysis of comparable topics. Two classes were selected on the basis of teacher interviews to determine initially in which grade levels similar topics were available for comparison. The regular education and special education classes chosen were located in the same elementary school in a middle-income area of suburban New York. Daily discussion of weather and calendar was selected as the major topic area common to both classes.

Four sessions per class were recorded over a 1-week period near the end of the school year for a total of 60 minutes of conversation per class. One of the four sessions was videotaped and the remaining three were audiotaped. The four sessions for each class were transcribed verbatim and coded independently for C-acts using coding systems developed by Cole et al. (1978a), Mehan (1979), and Dore (coding manual).

The special education classroom consisted of 10 children (five males and five females). These children ranged in age from 7 years 6 months to 9 years 3 months (mean chronological age, 8 years 3 months). Available information indicated that the majority of children came from lower middle-class backgrounds. With one exception, they had been placed in a special education setting by the local committee on the handicapped because of learning difficulties. Five of the 10 children were receiving language therapy as a related service from a certified speech-language specialist. All children in the special education class, all but one of whom where white, had normal intellectual potential in nonverbal and verbal domains, as assessed by the *WISC-R* or *WPPSI* (n = 7; mean performance IQ, 100; mean verbal IQ, 95) or *Stanford-Binet* (n = 3; mean IQ, 98).

Global data on language development skills, obtained from standardized measures, were available for four of the five children receiving language therapy services. (For four of the children not receiving language intervention, case records indicated "no history" of language or speech difficulties.) Not all children were administered indentical test batteries or were administered the same measure at comparable ages, making comparisons difficult across children. In general, except for one child, vocabulary familiarity was above chronological age, as measured by the Peabody Picture Vocabulary Test, while language ages varied within children on tests using such a method of measurement.

The regular second-grade class consisted of 25 children who were taught by a teacher with 13 years' teaching experience. The special education teacher had 3 years' teaching experience.

Quantitative Differences in Teachers' Elicitations. All C-acts (requestives, responsives, assertives, and regulatives) for each teacher and children in both classes were coded independently. Interjudge agreement was 92% for the regular education classroom and 88% for the special education classroom. Mean differences between each teacher's C-acts combined over the four recording periods were statistically significant (t (1, 7) = 2.82, p > .05). Significant mean differences were found for the total C-acts of children in both classes (t (1, 7) = 4.01, p > .01). These findings were interpreted as indicating that the quantity of talk was similar for both classrooms.

Findings also showed that the type of teacher C-act selections for accomplishing the lesson on weather and calendar were also similar to the four elicitation categories defined by Mehan (1979). In short, both teachers used elicitations as the primary means, or plan of action, for attaining the lesson's goals. A major difference between teachers concerned the frequency of each category. Frequency distributions for the regular class teacher yielded product elicitations as the most common occurring type (83), followed by choice (78), process (65), and clarification (19) elicitations. The special education teacher, in contrast, displayed a frequency pattern in which product elicitations were used more often than found for the regular class teacher (137), followed by occurrences of choice (48) and clarification elicitations (26). Process elicitations were used least often (16). Few instances of metaprocess requestives were found for either teacher, consistent with Mehan's (1979) results for a comparable grade level. Finally, it should be noted that clarifications were not a category formally discussed by Mehan (1979). Repetition, confirmation, or specification of aspects of the topic on the floor (Garvey, 1977) were one method used by both teachers to repair communicative breakdowns. Examples of each are given in Table 14.1.

Qualitative Differences in Teachers' Elicitations. From a qualitative perspective, differences between teachers were apparent in the *kinds* of elicitation selected. These differences may have reflected each

Table 14.1.
Examples of Teacher Clarifications

Repetition (from regular education class)

Child:	Um-like yesterday when I was-uh-just about to go jump in the pool with my friend…
Teacher:	What ↑
Child:	I said when I was just about to jump into my pool with my friend.

Confirmation (from special education class)

Child:	Me and N (name of friend)-um-might-um and my father might buy a rowboat.
Teacher:	A rowboat ↑
Child:	Yeah.

Specification (from special education class)

Child:	And then you wind the back and then it goes up the stairs, makes the bed, and everything.
Teacher:	WHAT goes up the stairs ↘
Child:	The person that goes.

teacher's respective assumptions about the general comprehension level of the class. This tentative conclusion is one supported also by Bruck and Ruckenstein's (1981) study on how kindergarten teachers conveyed *similiar* information on the rules of a game in *dissimilar* ways to normally developing children versus children with primary language problems. The following exchange, which occurred in the special education class, illustrates how instructional sequences may be symmetrical (there is a match between elicitation and reply) or asymmetrical (the reply is inappropriate or inaccurate relative to teacher intent) (Mehan, 1979).

Teacher:	How many days are in May?
L:	Thirty one.
Teacher:	Ok. N, how many days in a year?
N:	A-a hundred and thirty one? A hundred and thirty six?
Teacher:	Even bigger than that.
X:	Oh! I know! (raising hand)
Teacher:	F (nominating another child and ignoring X).
F:	Three hundred and sixty five.
Teacher:	Good. Say it, N.
N:	Three hundred and sixty five.
Teacher:	Three hundred and sixty five. A very big number. Ok. S, how many days in a week?

Now consider a second exchange from the regular second-grade class. The topic concerned transforming Fahrenheit as a measure of that day's temperature into its Celsius equivalent.

Teacher:	When we're talking about seven Celsius, who can explain to S a little bit about what seven Celsius means?
G:	Cold!
Teacher:	How cold though? Can you compare it to something?
G:	Seven-seven degrees above zero is cold.
Teacher:	Zero is not only cold. It's what?
Many:	Freezing!
Teacher:	Zero Celsius is freezing. So if you're guessing seven-yeah-you're talking about seven above freezing which means quite a cold morning.

The special education teacher's selection of elicitations was linked to a product-oriented or "Tell what you know" strategy. These product elicitations tended to minimize the opportunities for more expansive use of language since the reply necessitated the formulation of only single words or short phrases irrespective of whether the reply was lexically accurate. When replies were lexically accurate, subsequent evaluation in the teacher's next turn closed the three-part initiation-reply-evaluation instructional sequence (Mehan, 1979) either with a neutral acknowledgment (*OK*) or a positive *Good*. When replies were lexically inaccurate, creating asymmetry, for example, child N's initial turn, feedback (evaluation) was often implicitly negative. One type of implicit negative evaluation was the use of hints (*Even bigger than that*). Another type was loss of the floor for child N when the teacher picked another child to provide the expected reply as the procedure for closing the sequence.

In opposition to the "Tell what you know" function of the special education teacher's elicitations was the "Tell how you know," or process-oriented, functions of the regular class teacher's elicitations. Process and choice requestives, e.g., *Can you compare it to something?*, were used to evoke mental steps for developing a planful course of action to arrive at the solution. This emphasis on metacognitive and metalinguistic functions (explaining, comparing) provided the regular second-grade children with the opportunity to utilize, at some level, verbally mediated problem-solving procedures (see also Chapter 10).

The regular class teacher's method of evaluation also differed. For example, when replies contained lexically ambiguous information (G's *Cold!* reply), the teacher often supplied more specific information for children to consider (*How cold though? Can you compare it to something?*). In other instances, the teacher offered a fill-in tied to immediately preceding information (*Zero is not only cold. It's what?*). Evaluation, therefore, conveyed more explicit, although not necessarily less complex, social, cognitive, and linguistic cues for "figuring out" what the teacher intended in the initiation.

Being an effective participator in the classroom, if restricted to knowing what to mean in the role of contingent responder, may involve three integrated skills. One skill refers to how adequately a child can make "on-the-spot assessments" of what sort of information the teacher is seeking (French and MacLure, 1981, p. 33). A second type of skill appears to require knowing how explicit the teacher wants the answer to be (French and MacLure, 1981). These skills are requisite in addition to having the appropriate linguistic means for formulating a verbal reply. The very nature of the social and cognitive constraints imposed by initiation-reply-evaluation sequences would, therefore, predict increased complexity for the language learning-disabled child, for example, making appropriate, accurate, and ongoing inferences about actual teacher intent in both classroom and intervention settings (see Chapters 2 and 8). Mismatches between participant assumptions about what is intended to be accomplished through particular C-acts may be a primary contributor to ineffectual displays of child competence. Certainly, these mismatches need to be recognized and described in order to increase the probability of successful participation in either the classroom or intervention setting (see Chapter 16).

Knowing How and When to Participate

Broadly defined, verbal turn taking, the second aspect of interactional competency, means knowing the implicit participatory rules for entering conversation at a transition relevant point (Ervin-Tripp, 1979). It also means knowing how to keep the floor until completion of one's turn is reached. Taking a speaking turn requires precision timing the point of entry into a conversation without overlapping the turn of the speaker currently holding the floor. As a minimum requirement, timing entry into conversation demands that one can appropriately anticipate a transition relevant point or be responsive to termination cues (Ervin-Tripp, 1979).

PRECISION TIMING A TURN

Precision timing refers to the prediction

of a transition in conversation that is characterized by a switching pause (Garvey and Berninger, 1981). By switching pause is meant "an interval of joint silence that is initiated by the speaker who has the floor but terminated by a vocalization of the speaker who did not have the floor but thereby obtains it" (Feldstein et al., 1979, p. 76).

Overlap, in contrast, pertains to an interruption prior to complete termination of a partner's turn. Strictly defined, overlap is an interruption that is patterned with respect to "plausible stopping places" (Ervin-Tripp, 1979, p. 392). These plausible completion points increase in predictability with covarying reduction in the complexity of monitoring demands as a function of several social variables. One variable is familiarity. The more familiar are participants with one another, e.g., spouses or parents and children, the more likely one can anticipate what will be said next; hence, the greater the chance there will be for overlapping turns through "filling in" what is inferred to be the remaining content. A second variable involves the nature of the speech event. The more routine or ritualistic is the shared event, e.g., ritualized greetings, such as *Hi! How are you?*, the more likely is the chance that content to be said next by a partner will be predictable. A third variable is interest. The less interested are conversational partners in what one or both are saying, e.g., a male who continually overlaps speech addressed to him by a female, the greater will be the probability of transmitting the implicit social cue that "what you have to say is not worthy of my close attention."

CLINICAL IMPLICATIONS OF PRECISION TIMING

Ervin-Tripp (1979) posits that one influential factor regulating the nature of monitoring demands is the participant structure. In a multiparty participant structure, such as the classroom, high value is placed on the fast processing of speech with the frequent outcome that the student who replies most quickly gets the floor. In dyadic or triadic participant structures, organizations more typical of the intervention setting, greater opportunity may be available for redundancy of content (Bruck and Ruckenstein, 1981). Redundancy can reduce, therefore, the complexity of monitoring demands for how adequately a child can precision time a transfer of speaking turn (Garvey and Berninger, 1981). Descriptive data reported by Ervin-Tripp (1979) suggest that, for children under 4 years 6 months, turn taking is easier in dyadic structures because of the less complex monitoring demands of the dyad. This finding needs clinical replication relative to the monitoring requirements of different kinds of classroom events versus the monitoring demands of intervention activities. More detailed study might resolve the often heard complaint of clinicians that a child performs well in the intervention setting (that is, pays attention) but does not show comparable progress in the classroom setting (Gerber and Bryen, 1981).

A second area of interest concerns the extent to which excessive overlapping, or simultaneous speaking, is a patterned property of turn taking with some children described as language learning disabled. The clearest test of this behavior would be peer interaction since the presumption is that adults more strictly regulate timing to prevent overlaps and long gaps in transferring turns (Ervin-Tripp, 1979). Investigations by Ervin-Tripp (1979) and Garvey and Berninger (1981) on preschool peer interaction have found that excessive overlapping is rare and that, when it does occur, duration of simultaneous speaking is short. What remains unresolved is the specific criteria for differentiating among varying kinds of simultaneous speaking. Bennett (1981) proposes that overlap, versus other kinds of simultaneous speech, may serve different functions depending on the nature of the task. The clinical import of overlap and of simultaneous speaking, in general, remains a tantalizing area of exploration along the entire spectrum of developmental disorders.

Another related area for research with language learning-disabled children and adolescents concerns the interaction between age and the ability to be relevant. Even when 4-year-olds precision time entry into conversation or overlap appropriately, their contributions tend to be ignored more often since they have greater difficulty being relevant (Ervin-Tripp, 1979). Even relevance is not a guarantee of being paid attention. Ervin-Tripp (1979) argues that the most important factors regulating whether contributions are ignored or accepted are the age of the speaker and the communicative power of the speaker to be listened to. Moreover, the extent to which gapping occurs (not assuming a turn within conventional temporal limits) will also determine whether one will be listened to. Gapping, as a regularly occurring behavior, can signify difficulty in the swift processing of a conversational partner's content (Ervin-Tripp, 1979) or in successful recovery of implicitly stated information (Ochs, 1979).

CLINICAL IMPLICATIONS OF SELF-INTERRUPTIONS

Timing features related to knowing how and when to enter conversation have been a research focus. A topic receiving less attention is how self-interruptions affect keeping a turn and, ultimately, evaluation by others as an effective communicator (Ochs, 1979). Certainly, the literature on childhood stuttering has been long concerned with the relationship between normal and abnormal disfluencies (self-interruptions) (Bloodstein, 1975; Myers and Wall, 1981; Conture, 1982), but only recently has interest shifted to the physiological and developmental dimensions of normal fluency (Starkweather, 1980; Adams, 1982, Shapiro and DeCicco, 1982; Wexler and Mysak, 1982). A shortcoming of developmental research on self-interruptions is that it has been conducted primarily in laboratory settings (Sabin et al., 1979). If carried out in a more routine setting, for example, a child's home or a separate room in a nursery school, results tend to be analyzed by type and frequency only without consideration of the context of occurrence (Yairi, 1981; Wexler and Mysak, 1982).

Another procedural problem connected with the setting and method of analysis is how information is recorded. Even when transcriptional procedures are used for language sampling, the tendency is to "clean up" the transcript by filtering out self-interruptions. If self-interruptions are included, another practice is to keep some while eliminating others, depending on the purposes of research (Butterworth and Goldman-Eisler, 1979).

A final problem is an explanatory one. Although the structure of self-interruptions has been identified, their specific functions are not universally agreed upon. A general consensus is that filled and silent pauses, repeats (word and phrase repetitions), and reformulations function as an indirect index of verbally planful behavior (Brotherton, 1979; Butterworth and Goldman-Eilser, 1979; Tannen, 1979). In effect, "Speech must be suspended to enable planning to occur" (Brotherton, 1979, p. 181).

The Special Education Classroom Revisited. In an attempt to explore some of these timing issues, narratives were analyzed from the 10 children in the special education class described earlier. Narratives were extracted from the full transcripts (Silliman and Leslie, 1980), and each was retranscribed for clarity and for notation of self-interruptions.* These personal experience narratives, or personal stories, constituted another regular classroom event, that of "sharing time." A total

---

* Co-investigators were Jeannie M. Sorell and Susan Leslie. The initial intent was to gather comparable narrative data from the regular education second-grade class. However, frequent interruptions by teacher and peers during a child's turn in sharing time made the narrative selection criteria inoperable. The notational system adopted for all self-interruptions, except intraword types, was a modification of Bloom and Lahey (1978) and Ochs (1979). Intraword disruptions, or stuttering types of disfluencies, were notated using a coding system developed by Silliman and Seekamp (1980).

of 25 narratives, representing nine children, were found to meet stringent social and verbal criteria for narrative status (Labov and Waletsky, cited in Kernan, 1977; see also Chapter 6). An important social criterion was how the teacher framed this activity as distinct from other classroom events. One procedure was to open the floor for child contributions on topics of their choice. A second procedure consisted of the teacher selecting the topic with the initiating requestive *What did everyone do yesterday?* or *What did everybody do over the weekend?* Children usually bid for a turn through hand raising. The teacher then selected who would be allowed to take the floor. The child chosen was permitted to keep his or her turn until the teacher terminated the narrative, typically by selecting another child.

Proportional frequencies were determined for the five categories of self-interruptions as a function of total syllables produced by each of the nine children. These data were cumulated from two narratives each for two children. For the remaining seven children, data were based on three narratives for each. The self-interruption categories included: (1) reformulations; (2) word and phrase repetitions; (3) intraword disruptions; (4) filled pauses; and (5) silent pauses. Filled pauses, for example, *um* or *uh*, were counted as a syllable since they were part of what was vocalized within the turn.

No relationship was found between frequency of self-interruption and the stage of narrative development (see Chapter 6). (Data pertaining to narrative stage of development are not discussed in this review.) When the pattern of self-interruptions was examined, certain preliminary trends were discernible for individual children. To contrast these individual differences, a portion of child O's narrative is reproduced in Table 14.2. Two complete narratives from children F and N are also shown.

Child O, the only black child in the class, and one of four receiving language therapy along with children F and N, had the great-

Table 14.2.
Patterning of Self-interruptions in Personal Experience Narratives

Child O (male; CA[a] 8:11; total narrative duration, 92 seconds)

The previous speaker's narrative referred to cocoons in his backyard. O bids for the teacher's attention through hand raising and is recognized. (Only a small portion of the narrative is reproduced).

> I went_I went_I went on a trip with my teacher-the *other* teacher/ She-she-she taked me to-to the little red house when it was big/And-an then we saw a lot of cocoons but the-it was empty/And they were big and fat/so-so the-she boiled them-the lady (.) she boiled them in hot water/The-the cocoons they came out to be little treads/
> (Teacher: Oh! *threads.*)

Child F (male; CA 8:6; total narrative duration, 27 seconds)

The teacher had earlier selected the topic, "What did you do over the weekend?" F bids by hand raising, and the teacher gives him the floor.

> Um-(.)-hmm-oh yeah-um(.)over the weekend you know what I did?/ (children are laughing at another child's actions and are not attending to F) I-I got some (.) I got some uh-/u/-um-dirt and I poked the holes in the-uh-in the-uh-in the-uh-the-uh-hill/ (Teacher: In what hill?) *Our* hill / (Teacher: Did you have a shovel and everything?) Oh yeah oh *yeah*/I mixed-I mixed it up with dry and wet/

Child N (male; CA 7:6; narrative duration, 25 seconds)

The floor was open with children permitted to introduce their own topics; however, N had been previously sanctioned by the teacher for interrupting another child who had the floor and now raised his hand to be recognized.

> My father-he had-he had tilings (.) and once (.) he put them up in my mother's room (.) a long time ago_long:long:long:time ago_and my-/mo-/my mother_my mother was_my-my-uh-mother was leaning down_and it just fell right on top of her/(Laughter) An_aan-um-a co-couple of years ago (.)/ma-/-uh-a a(.) couple months ago (.) my father put (.)-um-(.) tilings up on in the ba(thr)oom-the big bathroom/Nothin' happened/

---

[a] CA, Chronological age.

est frequency of self-corrections or reformulations relative to the total number of syllables produced across three narratives. Most of these reformulations were productive. That is, these reformulations served to clarify previously stated information, for example, *the OTHER teacher* and *she boiled them—the lady.* To some extent the meaning of these self-corrections was dependent on a certain amount of shared information among the group members such as knowing that the "other" teacher was the children's physical education teacher. In spite of this qualification, a number of O's reformulations are consistent with Tannen's (1979) description of a backtracking corrective procedure proposed to be evidence for verbal planning efficiency. Tannen also suggests that backtracking is evidence for the more conscious awareness of having violated the discourse constraint to be both relevant and clear. In addition to the general effectiveness of O's reformulations in enhancing narrative presentation, his expressive style was also a factor in effectiveness. Variations in both prosody and facial expressions functioned to get and keep his audience's attention and also served as a redundant means for focusing key information. (O was mainstreamed into a regular education setting the following academic year.)

Child F, in comparison to his peers, had the highest frequency of total self-interruptions, nearly twice as many as child O and six times as many as the child with the lowest frequency of occurrence. F's patterning of filled and silent pauses specifically tended to disrupt the overall timing of syllables, words, and phrases into clausal units. This pattern was indirectly suggestive of some difficulty with either anticipatory planning or with executing what had been selected (Brotherton, 1979). Reformulations, although low in occurrence, were nonproductive in that new information was seldom added to clarify. These disruptions in timing also had social consequences. Child F's contributions were attended to differently than were the contributions of the other group members. Simultaneous speaking was prevalent during F's turn. As a result, the teacher intermittently sanctioned the group for not paying attention to F. It may have been that previous peer assumptions about, and experience with, F's ability to be both interesting and entertaining assisted in structuring the visibility of F's "disability" in a manner similar to that described for Adam (Hood et al., 1980).

Last, six of the nine children had some minimal instances of stuttering type disruptions (Wingate, 1976). Child N had the highest proportion of which three were isolated elemental repetitions, e.g., *and my/mo-/my mother*, and two were single unit repetitions of words subsequently completed, such as *a co-couple of years ago*. These disruptions, while infrequent and not marked by effort or struggle at speaking, affected the continuity of the narrative flow. Disruptions of this kind were also a factor in how adequately child N was able to hold his audience's attention even when he was being entertaining.

Clinical attention to the types of timing features just outlined, using a descriptive methodology, may provide insight into qualitative differences underlying knowing *how* to participate effectively in the instructional setting. Sustained violations of timing features may be sensitive indicators of different sources of difficulty. One source may be preplanning difficulties in the rapid or automatic selection of linguistic elements as a product of the task and participants (Brotherton, 1979; Butterworth and Goldman-Eisler, 1979; Sabin et al., 1979; Tannen, 1979; Wexler and Mysak, 1982). A second source of difficulty may reside in the precision control of neuromotor processes regulating the temporal execution of speech segments into syllabic, word, or phrasal units (Starkweather, 1980; Wexler and Mysak, 1982).

Knowing How to Be Relevant, Clear, and Original

Relevance is the process of making clear what is said (Dore, 1979). Furthermore, knowing how to be relevant is a skill that must be learned (Ervin-Tripp, 1979). Irrelevance, sometimes referred to as communicative egocentricity, is the linking of utterances to one's prior utterances rather than linking or adjusting them to those of the conversational coparticipant (Nelson and Gruendel, 1979). Appropriateness, on the other hand, encompasses not only the selection of content logically tied to what has been said but also the selection of content that is suitable for the particular discourse context. To sustain a dialogue requires, therefore, knowledge of both the conversational rules for turn taking and a broad array of shared content knowledge for the construction and maintenance of conversational sequences (Nelson and Gruendel, 1979).

Because relevance and appropriateness are predicated on topic sharing, various kinds of verbal strategies are typically employed to establish a shared topic context. Other types of verbal strategies are applied to repair miscommunications or communicative breakdowns. These repair procedures for "fixing up" (Dore, 1979) what is not understood can be classified as preformultive and reformulative procedures. The effectiveness of these procedures for soliciting relevant and appropriate content remains unresolved in relation to their efficacy for meeting the goals of either language intervention or the educational process.

A first step in dealing more effectively with language learning-disabled children's "inappropriate" contributions involves more formal awareness of the kinds of verbal procedures selected by adult partners to convey information on what is about to happen or to repair breakdowns so that topic sharing can continue. An interrelated second step concerns more detailed analysis of the child's contributions so that we can better understand how the child attempts to maintain conversation over extended turns.

PREFORMULATING PROCEDURES

Preformulation is an interactive strategy

intended to evoke the appropriate conceptual scheme in order to establish a shared topic context and to minimize the occurrence of communicative breakdowns. Preformulators serve to orient "children to relevant areas of experience which they must draw upon to supply the appropriate answer" (French and MacLure 1981, p. 35) by prefacing the question.

French and MacLure (1981) identify four types of preformulators. One type functions to direct children to attend to specific aspects of a shared event or activity that is to be queried. The following example is taken from clinician discourse with a 6-year, 7-month-old moderately language learning-disabled child. The prefacing information is also structurally similar to Mehan's (1979) description of the opening phase of a lesson.

I have some pictures here. And we're going to divide them into piles (placing a set of object pictures in front of the child), whether you eat something for breakfast, lunch, and dinner or snack, and say what it is. You can see it. Here choose a picture (child selects potato chips from the pile). What are they?

A second type of preformulator directs children to recent past events actually known to have been shared. This kind of setting information was often conveyed by the regular education second-grade teacher from the Silliman and Leslie (1980) study. For example:

Wasn't that some rain yesterday? That was a dangerous storm and lots of lights went out yesterday because of that. Why do you think the lights went out?

A third class of preformulator seeks to focus attention on prior experience assumed to be commonly shared social knowledge. The following example is from the same regular education second-grade teacher:

And-uh-sometimes babies (birds) like that, if they're not ready and they don't have a big wing span, get down on the ground and they can't fly, and kids come along and pick them up—pick the baby up—and bring it home, the baby is going to have a big big problem in your house. Why?

The last kind of preformulator derives from the teacher assumption that children do not always have shared content knowledge readily available. Thus, "teachers must introduce new interpretive recipes and bodies of knowledge to the child" (French and MacLure, 1981, p. 37). It was commented on earlier that the special education teacher's structuring of elicitations appeared related to her assumption that children often did not have common knowledge available. Despite this apparent inference, she seldom employed preformulative procedures but would give the children instructions without prerequisite information for them to consider as orienting material. There were no examples of the interpretive preformulations such as the one cited by French and MacLure (1981, p. 37):

Those are different sizes and *those* (authors' italics) are different sizes. Can you sort them out? Here's the red ones. And here is the green set. So where does this one go?

If the intent of a style of teaching discourse is to verify what children know through contingent responding sequences, then preformulation as a clinical teaching strategy for minimizing opportunities for failure needs more systematic study. Also needing more thorough investigation is how clinicians' and teachers' failure to preformulate a shared topic context adequately may contribute to children's failure to be either relevant, clear, or original. (See also Chapter 8 for the complexity of the interpretive tasks continually confronting children in the classroom.)

REFORMULATING PROCEDURES

Awareness of a communicative breakdown and the ability to effect suitable repair is a discoursal skill that children appear to bring to school entry (McTear, 1981). Repair devices vary broadly in scope. They can include regulation of turn taking (e.g., overlapping a turn and taking the floor when irrelevance is diagnosed) (Dore, 1979), embedding clarification subsequences into the main topic (Garvey, 1977, 1979; Garvey and BenDebba, 1978), and correcting the form of a message such as correction of an articulatory substitution or the use of a nonstandard syntactic element.

Reformulation is another interactive strategy that adults in instructional roles select when the expected reply does not occur. Mehan (1979) notes that a reformulator extends turn taking as a means for restoring symmetry to an initiation-reply sequence. In other words, reformulations are theoretically intended to clue children on how to direct their information search to select the reply being sought. The purpose of this kind of repair procedure is to make the original elicitation more specific (French and MacClure, 1981) or to make the implicit explicit (Blank et al., 1978a). Frequent reformulative strategies are: (1) prompting of inappropriate or inadequate replies or prompting of replies when initiations do not receive uptake and (2) simplification of the form or content of the original elicitation.

Prompting Devices. Prompts can take many forms, including sound, lexical, and manual-gestural forms. Their basic function seems to be that of an external memory cue to assist performance (Cazden, 1981) in order to reestablish symmetry for the topic introduced in an initiating turn. Three examples follow, all of which are taken from transcripts of clinician-child discourse involving language learning-disabled children in the lower primary grades.

The first example illustrates a lexical "fill-in" prompt. The clinician gives an antonym as a clue for narrowing down the lexical choices for the child to evaluate.

Clinician:	(pointing to a picture of an orange) You remember from the time before how oranges tasted?
Child:	Yeah.
Clinician:	How?
Child:	(3.5 sec.) Uh-uh (6 sec.) (looking at picture)
Clinician:	Sour?
Child:	No.
Clinician:	They were ____?
Child:	Sweet.
Clinician:	They were sweet. Right.

The second example combines three successive repairs, a fill-in which is nonspe-

cific, followed by a request for identification, and then a phonemic prompt as the clinician attempts to elicit the word *fence*. The two children in the group have a picture of a fence in front of them as the shared material.

Clinician:	This whole thing (pointing to the picture) is called a ____? (no uptake) Look. What is this?
Child 1:	A gate.
Clinician:	Looks like a gate but not really a gate. Gate is like a door. This is called a ffff ____.
Child 1 & 2:	(unison) Four!
Clinician:	Fence. Ok.

The final example is of a gestural prompt that seeks to evoke two children's functional knowledge of events, specifically sewing, as neither child was previously able to identify the term verbally.

Clinician:	What do we call this action? Called ____? (simultaneously pretending to sew)
Child 1:	Needle. Sew!
Clinician:	Sewing. Right.

Prompts seem to be another class of hints selected on the basis of clinician (and teacher) assumptions about what is conventionally shared word meaning. In two of the three examples, the prompts were effective leading to closure of the initiation-reply-evaluation sequence. In the noneffective "fence" instance, the clinician simply gave up and moved on to another elicitation whose content related to the lexical item (fence) she had just supplied. The actual linguistic effectiveness of the prompt as a teaching strategy is unknown. It may be that prompts have a primary discourse function in providing external guidance for the extension of turn taking in a relevant and appropriate manner.

Simplification Devices. Simplification procedures are designed primarily to reduce the range of possible replies, when the initiating turn fails to elicit the expected reply. The process of repairing through simplification is considered to be a means of reducing the cognitive complexity of information through reformulations which are more specific (Mehan, 1979; Bruck and Ruckenstein, 1981; French and MacLure, 1981). The simplification process is accomplished by giving children clues for figuring out the most appropriate reply according to the teacher's criteria of appropriateness. Controlled simplification was discussed earlier in the review of the approach developed by Blank et al. (1978a). Table 14.3. shows an extended sequence from a language intervention session which illustrates various types of repairs used by the clinician in an attempt to match her assumptions about the task and the goal with the children's mismatched expectations. The excerpt is taken from a 30-minute videotaped transcription of a school-based language therapy session.

The segment shows simplification at work as a collaborative process. It also demonstrates the nonsystematic nature of the process which reciprocally affects the children's efforts to be relevant, clear (explicit), and original. Research findings suggest that clinicians and teachers are often not aware of the specific procedures by which they seek to repair misunderstanding (Silliman, et al., 1980; Bruck and Ruckenstein, 1981; Panagos and Griffith, 1981). The particular excerpt reproduced in Table 14.3 actually took 31 turns to elicit the expected reply, chocolate chip cookie. This predetermined reply was achieved only when the clinician supplied a reformulation reflecting the least cognitive demand. That is, the children needed only to confirm the accuracy of *Do chocolate chip cookies have these kinds of chocolate chips?* Between the initiating requestive (turn #1) and attainment of the goal in turn #31, the clinician employed a variety of corrective procedures. Most of these repair procedures were ineffectual, relative to her expectations, and inefficient given the number of repairs needed to arrive at the appropriate reply. For more detailed information on classroom-obtained simplification data, French and MacLure (1981) should be consulted as a primary source.

From the perspective of the child participants, they were working hard to be effec-

Table 14.3.
Excerpts of an Instructional Sequence from a Language Intervention Session with Three Children, Aged 6 Years 7 Months (Children B and J) and 7 Years 1 Month (Child T), Described as Having Moderate Language Learning Disabilities

(The conversational goal was to elicit the specific subclass (name) of a class of cookie based on its pictorial representation.)

1	Clinician:	(presenting a picture of a chocolate chip cookie) T, what's this? (pointing to the picture)
	T:	(no response)
2	B:	(raising hand and waving it as a bid to reply) Oh, I know! I know!
3	Clinician:	B.
4	B:	Flower.
5	T:	Oh, it's a ball.
6	Clinician:	No. It's round and it's got some chocolate dots on it.
7	T, B, J:	(choral response) Cookie!
8	Clinician:	J knows it's a cookie because I said (.) what? What *word* made you *think* of cookie?
9	J:	Cuz you said [they have
	T:	*Brown* dots] (seizes turn from J) [indicates overlap]
10	Clinician:	The brown dots made you think of cookie or did I *call* them something else?
11	T:	Brown!
12	Clinician:	No. I said the word.
13	B:	Oh, I know! (raising hand to bid)
14	Clinician:	What? (looking at B)
15	B:	DOTS!
16	Clinician:	I said they were *chocolate*! Does a ball have chocolate on it?
17	B: J:	⎡ Yes! ⎤ (simultaneously ⎣ No! ⎦ responding)
18	Clinician:	Does a flower have chocolate on it?
19	T, B, J:	(choral response) No!
20	Clinician:	Does a cookie have chocolate on it?
21	T, B, J:	(choral response) Yes!
22	Clinician:	What kind of cookie do you think this might be? (pointing to picture of chocolate chip cookie)
23	B:	(Waving hand as bid) OOooh! I know!
24	Clinician:	B (allocating turn)
25	B:	Um-Oreos?

tive despite continued asynchrony between appropriate entry into conversation and inappropriate content, as predetermined by the clinician. This type of asynchrony lends some support to the Pickert and Furth (1980) conclusion that children will give topically related but not necessarily explicitly related responses to keep the dialogue going when they are uncertain of the specific reply that is wanted.

In reality, simplification devices, as well as prompts, may be complex instructional hints whose structures are not yet recognized. The general function of this class of repairs seems to be the provision of indirect guidance to children on relating currently unknown information to what is inferred to be information stored as prior experience. Prior experience can be defined broadly as common knowledge of events or phonological, semantic syntactic, or social knowledge expected to be available as the product of conventionalized experience. Furthermore, teachers' and clinicians' unawareness of how language is being used to link topic relatedness across turns makes a strong argument for considering a controlled complexity approach (Blank et al., 1978a; Berlin et al., 1980). This simplification technique, actually a systematic procedure for repairing mismatched assumptions about the topic and goal of talk, is intended to guide the child to obtain the "right," or most appropriate, response. Whether these controlled simplification sequences do serve as an external model by which generalized, rather than task-specific, strategies for planful behavior gradually become internalized is a separate issue not currently answerable.

CLOSING REMARKS

The overriding purpose of this review on the role of teaching discourse in learning is to center attention on how teachers' and clinicians' organization and regulation of conversation reflects the conceptual and social expectations of the instructional context. The specific outcome of increased awareness of how language is used to meet the goals of education and intervention should be a shift of emphasis from the child as the unit of analysis to the interactional

process structuring the ongoing evaluation of effectual or ineffectual participation. Broadening the unit of analysis to include the notion of participants, irrespective of whether that unit is defined in dyadic or multiparty terms, should lead to better integration of classroom and intervention goals along two practical dimensions:

1. One important dimension concerns refining the function of the specialist in communicative development and disorders as a skilled observer of how routine events in the school setting are organized socially through language. Understanding the nature of social organization should permit increased insight into the specific contributions of all participants to a particular child's ability to know what to mean, how and when to participate, and how to be relevant, clear, and informative. Only through critical examination of these three aspects of interactional competency can a communicative impairment be described in programmatically and pragmatically effective terms.

2. The second dimension refers to the specific goals of intervention or what are the aims of assistance beyond initiation-reply-evaluation sequences? While the goals of intervention often seem to be biased toward the cognitive functions of teaching discourse—getting the child to know—other types of discourse skills need to be incorporated into therapy content. As an example, the data reported on the patterning of self-interruptions in the personal experience narratives of children in the special education class suggest that an important aspect of being interactionally competent in the school setting is knowing how to be entertaining in order to hold the interest of one's audience. To achieve that skill, small group intervention structures, rather than tutorial or dyadic structures, may be more effective in assisting children and adolescents to engage in discoursal events involving the use of language as a tool of communication (Hart and Rogers-Warren, 1978; Muma and Pierce, 1981).

Nelson (Chapter 8) stresses that all

teaching, whether studied in the classroom or intervention setting, clearly consists of talk. It is obvious, however, that not all talk is effective teaching. Since the elements of effective verbally based instruction in its broadest sense are undefined, it remains the clinician's task to become intentionally aware of how his or her style of teaching discourse is organized to accommodate to the conceptual and social requirements of the educational process. The end result of ongoing self-reflection should be the development of new methods for the descriptive analysis of the social constraints underlying different routine events. Only by self-reflection can the appropriate changes be made to maximize, rather than minimize, opportunities for children to become more effective communicators.

References

Adams MR: Fluency, nonfluency, and stuttering in children. *J Fluency Disord* 7:171–185, 1982.

American Speech-Language-Hearing Association Committee on Language/Learning Disabilities. Language and learning disabilities ad hoc develops postion. *Asha* 22:628–636, 1980.

Bellack AA, Kliebard HM, Hyman RT, et al: *The Language of the Classroom.* New York, Teachers College Press, 1966.

Bennett A: Interruptions and the interpretation of conversations. *Discourse Processes* 4:171–188, 1981.

Berlin LJ, Blank M, Rose SA: The language of instruction: the hidden complexities. *Top Language Disord* 1 (1):47–58, 1980.

Bernstein B: A critique of the concept of compensatory education. In Cazden CB, John VP, Hymes D: *Functions of Language in the Classroom.* New York, Teachers College Press, 1972, pp 135–151.

Blank M, Gessner M, Esposito A: Language without communication: a case study. *J Child Language* 6:329–352, 1979.

Blank M, Milewski J: Applying psycholinguistic concepts to the treatment of an autistic child. *Appl Psycholinguistics* 2:65–84, 1981.

Blank M, Rose S, Berlin L: *The Language of Learning: The Preschool Years.* New York, Grune and Stratton, 1978a.

Blank M, Rose S, Berlin L: *Preschool Language Assessment Instrument (PLAI): The Language of Learning in Practice.* New York, Grune and Stratton, 1978b.

Bloodstein O: *A Handbook on Stuttering.* Chicago, Eastern Seal Society, 1975.

Bloom L, Lahey M: *Language Development and Language Disorders.* New York, John Wiley & Sons, 1978.

Bransford D, Nitsch KE, Franks JJ: Schooling and the facilitation of knowing. In Anderson RC, Spiro RJ, Montague WE: *Schooling and the Acquisition of Knowledge.* Hillsdale, NJ, Lawrence Erlbaum Associates, 1977, pp 31–55.

Bronfenbrenner U: *The Ecology of Human Development.* Cambridge, MA, Harvard University Press, 1979.

Brotherton P: Speaking and not speaking: processes for translating ideas into speech. In Siegman AW, Feldstein S: *Of Speech and Time.* Hillsdale, NJ, Lawrence Erlbaum Associates, 1979.

Brown AL: Development, schooling, and the acquisition of knowledge about knowledge. In Anderson RC, Spiro RJ, Montague WE: *Schooling and the Acquisition of Knowledge.* Hillsdale, NJ, Lawrence Erlbaum Associates, 1977, pp 241–253.

Bruck M, Ruckenstein S: Teachers talk to language delayed children. *First Language* 2:201–218, 1981.

Bryan T, Donahue M, Pearl R: Studies of learning disabled children's pragmatic competencies. *Top Learn Learn Disabil* 1 (2):29–39, 1981.

Butterworth B, Goldman-Eisler F: Recent studies on cognitive rhythm. In Siegman AW, Feldstein S: *Of Speech and Time.* Hillsdale, NJ, Lawrence Erlbaum Asociates, 1979, pp. 211–224.

Cavanaugh JC, Perlmutter M: Metamemory: a critical examination. *Child Dev* 53:11–28, 1982.

Cazden CB: The situation: a neglected source of social class differences in language use. *J Soc Issues* 26:35–60, 1970.

Cazden CB: Peekaboo as an instructional model: discourse development at home and at school. *Papers Rep Child Language Dev* 17:1–29, 1979.

Cazden CB: Performance before competence: assistance to child discourse in the zone of proximal development. *Q Newslett Lab Compar Hum Cognition* 3:5–8, 1981.

Chapman R: Exploring children's communicative intents. In Miller J: *Assessing Language Production in Children: Experimental Procedures.* Baltimore, University Park Press, 1981, pp 111–136.

Cole M, Dore J, Hall WS, et al: Situation and task in young children's talk. *Discourse Processes* 1:119–176, 1978a.

Cole M, Hood L, McDermott R: *Ecological Niche Picking: Ecological Invalidity as an Axiom of Experimental Cognitive Psychology.* New York, Laboratory of Comparative Human Cognition and Institute for Comparative Human Development, The Rockefeller University, 1978b.

Conture EG: *Stuttering.* Englewood Cliffs, NJ, Prentice-Hall, 1982.

Cook-Gumperz, J. Situated instructions: language socialization of school age children. In Ervin-Tripp Ş, Mitchell-Kernan C: *Child Discourse.* New York, Academic Press, 1977, pp 103–121.

Damico J, Oller JW Jr: Pragmatic versus morphological/syntactic criteria for language referrals. *Language Speech Hear Serv Schools* 11:85–94, 1980.

Donahue M, Pearl R, Bryan T: Learning disabled children's conversational competencies: responses to inadequate messages. *Appl Psycholinguistics* 1:387–403, 1980.

Donahue ML: Requesting strategies of learning disabled children. *Appl Psycholinguistics* 2:213–234, 1981.

Dore J: Variation in preschool children's conversational performances. In Nelson KE: *Children's Language.* New York, Halstead Press, 1978, vol 1, pp 397–444.

Dore J: Conversational acts and the acquisition of language. In Ochs E, Schieffelin BB: *Developmental Pragmatics.* New York, Academic Press, 1979, pp 339–361.

Dore J: Genesis and ontogenesis. In Schiefelbusch RL: *Communicative Competence: Acquisition and Intervention.* Baltimore, University Park Press, in press.

Dore J: Coding manual for identifying conversational acts. Unpublished manuscript, The Rockefeller University.

Dore J, Gearhardt M, Newman D: The structure of nursery school conversation. In Nelson KE: *Children's Language.* New York, Halstead Press, 1978, vol 1, pp 337–395.

Dukes PJ: Developing social prerequisites to oral communication. *Top Learn Learn Disabil* 1 (2):47–58, 1981.

Edwards JR: *Language and Disadvantage.* New York, Elsevier, 1979.

Ervin-Tripp S: Children's verbal turn-taking. In Ochs E, Schieffelin BB: *Developmental Pragmatics.* New York, Academic Press, 1979, pp 391–414.

Estes WK: Is human memory obsolete? *Am Sci* 68:62–69, 1980.

Farnham-Diggory S: *Learning Disabilities: A Psychological Perspective.* Cambridge, MA, Harvard University Press, 1978.

Feldstein S, Alberti L, BenDebba M: Self-attributed personality characteristics and the pacing of conversational interaction. In Siegman AW, Feldstein S: *Of Speech and Time.* Hillsdale, NJ, Lawrence Erlbaum Associates, 1979, pp 73–87.

Freedle R, Duran RP: Sociolinguistic approaches to dialogue with suggested applications to cognitive science. In Freedle RO: *New Directions in Discourse Processing.* Norwood, NJ, Ablex Publishing, 1979, vol 2, pp 197–206.

French P, MacLure M: Teachers' questions, pupils' answers: an investigation of questions and answers in the infant classroom. *First Language* 2:31–45, 1981.

Garrard J. *Review of the Literature: Classroom Interaction.* Austin, TX, University of Texas, 1966. (ERIC Document Reproduction Service No. ED 013 988.)

Garvey C: The contingent query: a dependent act in conversation. In Lewis M, Rosenblum LA: *Interaction, Conversation, and the Development of Language.* New York, Wiley-Interscience, 1977, pp 63–93.

Garvey C: Contingent queries and their relations in discourse. In Ochs E, Schieffelin BB: *Developmental Pragmatics.* New York, Academic Press, 1979, pp 363–372.

Garvey C, Berninger G: Timing and turn taking in children's conversations. *Discourse Processes* 4:27–57, 1981.

Garvey C, Bendebba M: An experimental investigation of contingent query sequences. *Discourse Processes* 1:36–50, 1978.

Gearhardt M, Newman D: Learning to draw a picture: the social context of an individual activity. *Discourse Processes* 3:169–284, 1980.

Gerber A, Bryen DN: *Language and Learning Disabilities.* Baltimore, University Park Press, 1981.

Griffin P, Cole M, Newman D: Locating tasks in psychology and education. *Discourse Processes* 5;111–125, 1982.

Hakes DT: *The Development of Metalinguistic Abilities in Children.* New York, Springer-Verlag, 1980.

Hall WS, Cole M: On participant's shaping of discourse through their understanding of the task. In Nelson KE: *Children's Language.* New York, Halstead Press, 1978, vol 1, pp 445–465.

Halliday MAK: *Explorations in the Functions of Language.* New York, Elsevier-North Holland, 1973.

Halliday MAK, Hasan R: *Cohesion in English.* London, Longman, 1976.

Hart B, Rogers-Warren A: A milieu approach to teaching language. In Schiefelbusch RL: *Language Intervention Strategies.* Baltimore, University Park Press, 1978, pp 193–235.

Hood L, McDermott R, Cole M: "Let's *try* to make it a good day"—some not so simple ways. *Discourse Processes* 1:155–168, 1980.

Kernan KT: Semantic and expressive elaboration in children's narratives. In Ervin-Tripp S, Mitchell-Kernan C: *Child Discourse.* New York, Academic Press, 1977, pp 91–102.

Labov W: *Language in the Inner City.* Philadelphia, University of Pennsylvania Press, 1976.

Litowitz B: Learning to make definitions. *J Child Language* 4:289–304, 1977.

Loper AB: Metacognitive development: implications for cognitive training. *Except Educ Q* 1 (1):1–8, 1980.

McBride JE, Levy K: The early academic classroom for children with communication disorders. In Gerber A, Bryen DN: *Language and Learning Disabilities.* Baltimore, University Park Press, 1981, pp 269–294.

McDermott RP: Social relations as contexts for learning in school. *Harvard Educ Rev* 47:198–213, 1977.

McKinney JD, Haskins R: Cognitive training and the development of problem solving strategies. *Except Educ Q* 1 (1):41–51, 1980.

McTear MF: Investigating children's conversational development. *First Language* 2:117–130, 1981.

Mehan H: *Learning Lessons.* Cambridge, MA, Harvard University Press, 1979.

Mehan H: Social constructivism in psychology and sociology. *Q Newslett Lab Compar Hum Cognition* 3:71–76, 1981.

Meichenbaum D: Cognitive behavior modification with exceptional children. *Except Educ Q* 1 (1):83–88, 1980.

Meichenbaum D, Goodman S: Clinical use of private speech and critical questions about its study in natural settings. In Zivin G: *The Development of Self-regulation through Private Speech.* New York, John Wiley & Sons, 1979, pp 325–360.

Mishler EG: Implications of teacher strategies for language and cognition: observations in first-grade classrooms. In Cazden CB, John VP, Hymes D: *Functions of Language in the Classroom.* New York, Teachers College Press, 1972, pp 267–298.

Mishler EG: Studies in dialogue and discourse: II. types of discourse initiated and sustained through questioning. *J Psycholinguistic Res* 4:99–121, 1975.

Moore DT: Discovering the pedagogy of experience. *Harvard Educ Rev* 51:286–300, 1981.

Muma J, Pierce S: Language intervention: data or evidence? *Top Learn Learn Disabil* 1 (2):1–11, 1981.

Myers FL, Wall MJ: Issues to consider in the differential diagnosis of normal childhood disfluencies and stuttering. *J Fluency Disord* 6:189–195, 1981.

Nelson K: Semantic development and the development of semantic memory. In Nelson KE: *Children's Language*. New York, Halstead Press, 1978, vol 1, pp 39–80.

Nelson K, Gruendel JM: At morning it's lunchtime: a scriptal view of children's dialogues. *Discourse Processes* 2:73–94, 1979.

Nelson KE, Nelson K: Cognitive pendulums and their linguistic relations. In Nelson KE: *Children's Language*. New York, Halstead Press, 1978, vol 1, pp 223–285.

Ochs E: Transcription as theory. In Ochs E, Schieffelin BB: *Developmental Pragmatics*. New York, Academic Press, 1979, pp 43–92.

Olson DR: The languages of instruction: the literate bias of schooling. In Anderson RC, Spiro RJ, Montague WC: *Schooling and the Acquisition of Knowledge*. Hillsdale, NJ, Lawrence Erlbaum Associates, 1977a, pp 65–89.

Olson DR: From utterance to text: the bias of language in speech and writing. *Harvard Educ Rev* 47:257–281, 1977b.

Panagos JM, Griffith PL: Okay, what *do* educators know about language intervention? *Top Learn Learn Disabil* 1 (2):69–82, 1981.

Pearl RA, Donahue ML, Bryan TH: Learning disabled and normal children's responses to requests for clarification which vary in explicitness. Presented at the fourth annual Boston University Conference on Language Development, Boston, September, 1979.

Philips SU: Participant structures and communicative competence: Warm Springs children in community and classroom. In Cazden CB, John VP, Hymes D: *Functions of Language in the Classroom*. New York, Teachers College Press, 1972, pp 370–394.

Pickert SM, Furth HG: How children maintain a conversation with an adult. *Hum Dev* 23:162–176, 1980.

Roth SF, Perfetti CA: A framework for reading, language comprehension, and language disability. *Top Language Disord* 1 (1):15–27, 1980.

Sabin EJ, Clemmer EJ, O'Connell DC, et al: A pausological approach to speech development. In Siegman AW, Feldstein S: *Of Speech and Time*. Hillsdale, NJ, Lawrence Erlbaum Associates, 1979, pp 35–55.

Schank RC, Abelson RP: *Scripts, Plans, Goals, and Understanding: An Inquiry into Human Knowledge Structures*. Hillsdale, NJ, Lawrence Erlbaum Associates, 1977.

Shapiro AI, DeCicco BA: The relation between normal dysfluency and stuttering: an old question revisited. *J Fluency Disord* 7:109–121, 1982.

Sigel IE, Cocking RR: Cognition and communication: a dialectic paradigm for development. In Lewis M, Rosenblum LA: *Interaction, Conversation, and the Development of Language*. New York, Wiley-Interscience, 1977, pp 207–226.

Silliman ER, Gams-Golub SE, Chizzik SG: Clinician-child discourse: how accommodating is the clinician? In Burns MS, Andrews JR: *Current Trends in the Treatment of Language Disorders*. Evanston, IL, Institute for Continuing Professional Education, 1980, pp 22–33.

Silliman ER, Leslie S: Instructional language: comparison of a regular and special education second grade. Presented at the annual convention of the American Speech-Language-Hearing Association, Detroit, November, 1980.

Silliman ER, Seekamp SJ: A transcriptional procedure and notational system for the assessment of frequency of disfluency. Miniseminar presented at the annual convention of the American Speech-Language-Hearing Association, Detroit, November, 1980.

Sinclair JM, Coulthard RM: *Towards an Analysis of Discourse: The English Used by Teachers and Pupils*. Oxford, Oxford University Press, 1975.

Starkweather CW: Speech fluency and its development in normal children. In Lass NJ: *Speech and Language: Advances in Basic Research and Practice*. New York, Academic Press, 1980, vol 4, pp 143–200.

Tannen D: What's in a frame? Surface evidence for underlying expectations. In Freedle RO: *New Directions in Discourse Processing*. Norwood, NJ, Ablex Publishing, 1979, vol 2 pp 137–181.

Tough J: *The Development of Meaning: A Study of Children's Use of Language*. New York, Halstead Press, 1978.

Vellutino FR: *Dyslexia: Theory and Research*. Cambridge, MA, MIT Press, 1979.

Wexler KB, Mysak ED: Disfluency characteristics of 2-, 4-, and 6-yr-old males. *J Fluency Disord* 7:37–46, 1982.

Wiig EH, Semel EM: *Language Assessment and Intervention for the Learning Disabled*. Colombus, OH, Charles E Merrill, 1980.

Wingate ME: *Stuttering: Theory and Treatment*. New York, Irvington Press, 1976.

Yairi E: Disfluencies of normally speaking two-year-old children. *J Speech Hear Res* 24:490–495, 1981.

SECTION IV

Organization and Delivery of Services for Language Learning-disabled Students

CHAPTER FIFTEEN

Outcomes of Language Intervention: A Challenge for the Future

TERIS K. SCHERY, Ph.D.

Throughout this text, we have discussed many facets of the relationship between language and learning disabilities. Various authors have explored recent theoretical and practical advances in this area including the nature of language disorders after age 5 (see Chapter 5), the subtle or higher level skills that relate to learning and school success (see Chapters 6 and 7), and the interplay of inherent language abilities with the environment (see Chapters 8 and 14). Such contemporary thinking has led to the development of new and innovative language assessment and intervention strategies, some of which were outlined in Section III.

As we embark on a new era of clinical and educational planning, we cannot help but be reminded of an issue raised earlier by Maxwell and Wallach (Chapter 2). This issue, i.e., that children with early language disabilities do not necessarily "catch up" in spite of intervention, leaves conscientious professionals with a number of unanswered questions. For example, what intervention strategies *are* of greatest benefit to language-disordered children? How can early language intervention programs be designed to make use of current knowledge about what works best? Can early and appropriate programming help prevent some learning disabilities? Unfortunately, there are no simple answers to such questions. Evidence on the effectiveness of language intervention programs is scanty and often difficult to obtain. Only in the last decade or so, mostly under the pressure of federal and state funding requirements, have we even begun to look at our efforts critically with an eye to improving techniques and documenting the effectiveness of intervention efforts. This chapter will attempt, first, to review program research that has implications for intervention efforts with language learning-disabled children and, second, to suggest some general guidelines for professionals to consider in designing outcome studies.

CURRENT RESEARCH ON PROGRAM EFFECTIVENESS

The research literature on the effects of intervention programs includes at least two related areas that have implications for work with language-disordered children and that reiterate the language disabilities-learning disabilities connection: the studies of early intervention efforts with disadvantaged and "at-risk" children and the studies on mainstreaming efforts with handicapped youngsters. This section will review the literature in these areas and summarize what is currently known about the effectiveness of speech and language programs.

Early Childhood Education Programs

The largest group of studies on the effects of compensatory education are those that have examined the effectiveness of early childhood intervention programs for disadvantaged or high-risk children. Such early intervention programs have received widespread support for over 50 years. Only in the last 20 years or so has an effort been made to document systematically the impact of such programs on children and their families, mostly in response to explicit requirements for federal funding. Both historically and in many current programs, there is an implicit assumption that "of course" intervention programs enhance children's development. Such high expectations about the outcomes of intervention

programs may have had some basis in the classic and impressive study reported by Skeels and Dye (1939). A group of young children were transferred from a non-stimulating orphanage to an institution for retarded women, where they were given individual care and attention by the adult female residents. Over several years, these children showed a dramatic increase in IQ (up to 30 points), whereas the group of children who remained in the orphanage declined in IQ and eventually tested in the retarded range. A follow-up study some 20 years later (Skeels, 1966) found that the original group of "adopted" children were adequate, socially competent people (measured by occupational status, educational level, marital status, etc.), whereas the "control" group were functioning marginally at best.

Two more contemporary projects designed to prevent retardation due primarily to sociocultural factors are the Milwaukee Project (Heber and Garber, 1975) and the Abecedarian Project (Ramey and Campbell, 1979). These projects enrolled children for up to 8 hours a day over a period of years in addition to providing job-related training for parents. It is not too surprising, perhaps, that such programs made a global impact on the children when compared to unserved controls (IQ up some 30 points after 5 years). Both of these projects represent highly "intense" programs. That is, they focus on multiple aspects of children's lives, not just the school experience. However, such comprehensive compensatory interventions are necessarily quite costly and are the exception rather than the rule in early childhood intervention efforts.

More typical, and undoubtedly the most publicized early intervention, is Project Head Start, a 2½-hour daily program for disadvantaged preschool children. Recent data indicate that over half of the children enrolled in Head Start are identified as speech impaired (U.S. Department of HEW, 1979); however, evaluation studies have only considered language growth as a part of a more general cognitive ability.

Zigler and Balla (1982) suggested that inappropriate use of the global measure IQ almost caused the Head Start program to be abandoned during the Nixon era. When the Westinghouse evaluation report (Cicarelli et al., 1969) asserted that early gains in IQ were not maintained after the children left the Head Start program, the fact that other areas of potential impact (such as health care, psychological, and job-related counseling for parents) were not examined made little difference given the political climate of the times (Zigler and Valentine, 1979). Maxwell (Chapter 3) related the apparent limited success of the project to possible neurological-learning plateaus during this age period. However, follow-up studies after several years showed that children who participated in Project Head Start were more likely to be in the correct grade for their age, less likely to be in special education, and more advanced in mathematics and general information than disadvantaged children who did not receive early intervention (Darlington et al., 1980). Two points are worth noting here. First, effects of early intervention programs may not show up until some time after the program ceases. Second, global outcome measures, such as IQ, are probably inappropriate for assessing the effects of all but the most massive or intense programs. Measures of outcome should be tied more closely to program goals and emphases. Such measurement issues will be discussed later in this chapter. (See also Maxwell and Wallach, Chapter 2, for a discussion of measurable changes in children's growth and development.)

A group of follow-up studies conducted by the Developmental Continuity Consortium (Darlington, 1981; Lazar, 1981; Lazar and Darlington, 1982) examined the long-term effects of early intervention carried out in relatively small experimental projects during the late 1950's and early 1960's. The reported success of these programs was the catalyst for Head Start. These follow-up studies also demonstrated a decline of IQ and achievement test scores after early

intervention children became assimilated into the regular school system. However, using aggregated data from the many consortium studies, Weikart (1981) reported that experimental children had less grade retention, fewer placements in special education, and were more likely to graduate from high school than controls. This consortium examined the effects of 27 different curricula (or "treatments") and found no significant differences in long-term outcomes; all showed some effect.

Weikart (1981) has categorized the 27 curricula into three major types representing the predominant approaches to early childhood education during the late 1960's. The first of these included "cognitively oriented" curricula, based on Piagetian concepts and the assumption that mental growth occurs through children's active exploration and manipulation of their environment. The second, "language training curricula," represented programmed approaches adapted primarily from the work of Bereiter and Englemann (1966), including DISTAR (1968). These approaches were predominantly teacher controlled with direct, programmed instruction used to train specific language patterns and preacademic skills in an atmosphere of "friendly competition" and positive reinforcement. The third type of program Weikart called "unit-based curricula," which he described as characteristic of traditional nursery schools, with a focus on the social and emotional growth of the children, including fantasy play and self-expression.

When comparing these three approaches, some differential effects were apparent immediately upon the conclusion of the preschool program. Children enrolled in cognitively oriented (Piagetian) curricula scored the highest on *aptitude* measures (IQ) at the end of preschool, whereas those enrolled in the programmed models achieved higher scores on *academic* achievement measures. Follow-up studies through the fourth grade and again at grade 8 did *not* support any differential effects. Children from all the model preschool programs were more successful in school, on average, than those disadvantaged children who were not enrolled. Such changes in the growth of disadvantaged children remind us of the uneven changes in language development discussed earlier (see Chapters 1 and 2).

The consortium found that the background of the teacher prior to service (paraprofessional or professional) and the site of the program (home based or center based or a combination) made no difference in the outcome. A cluster of five interrelated program characteristics, however, was related to positive outcomes for disadvantaged children: (1) age of intervention—the earlier the better; (2) adult-child ratio—the fewer children the better; (3) number of home visits—the more the better; (4) direct participation of parents—the more the better; (5) services for families, not just children—the more types the better.

At least one of the program directors attributed the effects of these early intervention efforts to changes in parents' values and expectations for their children (Lazar, 1981, p. 305) and suggested that parent training was of primary importance.

How important *is* the role of parent training in early intervention programs? Clarke-Stewart (1981) has thoroughly reviewed the effectiveness of parent education programs on developmental patterns of young children. She concluded that a wide range of model parent programs with disadvantaged, high-risk, and handicapped infants and children has demonstrated significant IQ and language gains (p. 53). She cautioned, however, against an overly positive reaction to this finding, pointing out the poor nature of much of the research which does not allow answers to the question of *why* these programs work.

Implications of Early Childhood Education Research

What then can this literature on outcomes in early intervention programs suggest to those of us who want to plan, implement, and evaluate the most effective remediation program possible? Although the disadvantaged and high-risk populations to which such programs have been targeted are not specifically language impaired, many evidence communication difficulties (U.S. Department of HEW, 1979), and a sizable percentage will be classified as language disordered or learning disabled when they reach elementary school age (Klein and Randolph, 1974; Lassman et al., 1980; Leske, 1981). First, for the language professionals and teachers serving such a preschool and early school-age population, it would seem important to plan systematic follow-up evaluations as the children move through the regular educational program. Early childhood education (ECE) research has shown that positive effects of early intervention may not be discernible immediately, but rather may have a cumulative influence. Many of the consequences of programs cannot be demonstrated by direct and immediate change in children. Change may be long term and slow to emerge, as pointed out by Wallach and Liebergott in their Chapter 1 section entitled, "Too Late, Too Early; Didn't Test the Right Things Anyway."

Under such circumstances we need to think carefully about the long-range goals of our intervention efforts as well as the immediate instructional objectives. Helping a child to complete workbook B of a given language program is perhaps an easily stated and "accountable" learning task. However, we also need to consider the naturalistic communication behaviors that we wish to foster outside the therapy or classroom. These ECE studies highlight the importance of assessing a broad range of outcome variables, including, perhaps, measures of general communicative competence, adjustment to school and, possibly, parent, teacher, and peer rating of communication in natural environments (see also Chapter 14). Important program influences may affect those individuals around the child, not just the child him- or herself.

Another implication of these studies for practitioners is the notion that parent involvement in intervention efforts is extremely important. The ECE program studies consistently suggested that incorporating mothers into intervention programs increased the likelihood of improvement in children's performances, although it was not clear how or why that effect occurred (Lazar, 1981; Weikart, 1981). There is at least some justification for including a strong parent involvement and -training component in programs for young language-handicapped children. By maintaining careful measures of what is included in the parent-training program, perhaps some of the questions on why such a program is effective can be addressed.

Finally, it is thought provoking to consider that language intervention programs based on such varying educational models as a child-centered Piagetian framework versus a teacher-controlled behavioral design might work equally well, at least with normal children. To date, there are no systematic long-term comparisons of these two approaches in the *language-disordered* literature, although some small-group experimental clinical studies have compared short-term outcomes related to these approaches (Leonard, 1981). Language intervention remains a complex and poorly specified process. In the previous chapter, Silliman provided some excellent narrative examples of the interaction between the conceptual (e.g., Piagetian) and social components of learning. Her case example of Adam (see p. 297) illustrated particularly well how the complexity of a task, the particular situation, and a child's perception of himself or herself can interact in language performance. As we develop our capabilities for evaluating language intervention programs thoroughly, perhaps questions about what particular programs or approaches work best can begin to be answered.

Mainstreaming Programs

In our search for what is already known about effective intervention programs, there is a second body of literature that has implications for professionals working with language learning-disabled children of school age. This is the group of studies that

examines the effects of recent efforts at mainstreaming handicapped children.

The push toward mainstreaming has existed for approximately 13 years, and in most areas of special education it is now the rule rather than the exception. Recent litigation and the passage of federal and state legislation has guaranteed each handicapped child the right to be educated by the "least restrictive alternative to the maximum extent possible with their non-handicapped peers" (Public Law 94-142). Although the direction of future legislation is unknown at this time, the current concept of the least restrictive alternative has become synonymous with the educational practice of mainstreaming (Turnbull et al., 1978; Forness, 1979). Mainstreaming has been defined by Kaufman et al. (1975, p. 4) as "the temporal, instructional, and social integration of eligible exceptional children with normal peers, based on an ongoing, individually determined, educational planning and programming process... [that] requires clarification of responsibility among regular and special education administrative, instructional, and supportive personnel." Gottlieb (1981), however, has subsequently pointed out that, in fact, mainstreaming implementation has focused almost exclusively on administrative issues, such as percentage of time spent with regular peers, with little or no attention paid to the appropriateness of the content of the educational program and techniques.

The movement toward mainstreaming began in the late 1960's spurred forward by publication of a critique of special education by Dunn (1968). The climate was right; the civil rights movement as related to education was well under way, and a series of previous efficacy studies had failed to support the academic superiority of segregated special education classes (Goldstein et al., 1965). In the intervening years, all types of special children, ranging from severely/ profoundly handicapped to mildly behaviorally disordered and/or language learning disabled, have been served increasingly in "mainstreamed" environments. The common service delivery options (i.e., the continuum of services) from most to least restrictive are: residential care, self-contained day class, resource room service, and regular class placement.

The last 5 years have witnessed publication of a large number of studies of the effects of mainstream programs, particularly contrasting self-contained classes with the resource room model and regular education (see reviews by Gottlieb, 1981, and Kaufman et al., 1982). Unfortunately, the empirical evidence is inconclusive and difficult to interpret. Many conclusions in the research appear to be based on the subjective opinions of the investigators. Many studies lack control groups, fail to define what is meant by a specific delivery model, and do not accurately account for such independent variables as age of children, teacher competency, teaching methodologies, and criteria for special class placement.

None of these studies looked differentially at language-disordered children in comparison to children with a primary diagnosis (or special education designation) of retardation or learning disability. While we recall the dilemmas associated with labeling and the overlap among groups (see Chapter 1), let us explore the literature that is available on the mainstreaming of two special education subgroups, the educable mentally retarded (EMR) and the learning disabled (LD), in an effort to obtain information about the kinds of programs that may be most useful. Specific criteria for the definition of these groups were not reported in every study; however, all children were enrolled in special classes based on the traditional special education designations (see Chapter 1). These subgroups are generally considered to be the mildly handicapped categories of special education. The studies will be reviewed separately for ef-

fectiveness in the academic and social adjustment domains.

Academic Effects

The studies that claim success for mainstreaming efforts have primarily focused on academic outcomes after a year or at most 2 years in an alternative environment to a special class. Gottlieb (1981) reviewed the efficacy studies of programs for EMR children between 1932 and 1965 and claimed that five showed no significant achievement differences between children in regular and special classes, and five showed significantly better achievement among EMR children in regular classes (p. 117). Not a single investigator reported achievement data favorable to the segregated classes. Such results were the basis of claims that mainstreaming should be preferred as the more cost-effective alternative. If the achievement of EMR students in regular classes is as good as that in special classes, there is little or no justification for the increased costs that special classes incur (Dunn, 1968). Current research data continue to support this claim. Budoff and Gottlieb (1976) randomly assigned EMR children to segregated and mainstreamed classes and found no significant differences in reading or arithmetic after 9 months. The results of Project Prime, a large-scale investigation of EMR mainstreaming, failed to provide evidence of superiority of one type of class placement over another for academic achievement (Kaufman et al., 1982).

Literature on the academic effects of mainstreaming with learning-disabled students presents a similarly bleak picture of the efficacy of segregated classes. Rust et al. (1978) evaluated the effectiveness of a resource room program for elementary school children with learning problems and found that during 1 year the average gains in this experimental group were approximately equal to controls in regular classes. Ritter (1978) examined the effects of mainstreaming children with learning disabilities who had entered a regular classroom after having spent 1 year in a self-contained learning disabilities class. The annual mean grade-equivalent score gains in reading and math were comparable for both settings. Miller and Sabatino (1978), in a large sample study of learning-disabled youngsters, reported minimal to negative academic gains in reading and arithmetic for two forms of special education intervention (resource room and teacher consultant model) versus mainstreaming in regular classes. Earlier, Sabatino (1971) had demonstrated that resource rooms were as effective as self-contained classes in promoting achievement in learning-disabled youngsters. Beck et al. (1981) not only found little academic advantage for learning-disabled students from placement in segregated classes, but found a regression in their intellectual scores (Wechsler Intelligence Score for Children) over 1 to 2 years in such a placement.

The few studies that claim positive short-term effects for academic achievement in segregated classes (or in a residential setting) (Haring and Houck, 1969; Balow et al., 1978; Abidin and Seltzer, 1981) did not employ control groups. On balance, there appears to be very little evidence for the relative effectiveness of any special education service delivery option in promoting academic achievement for mild to moderately handicapped youngsters, at least as measured by standard academic achievement tests and over a relatively short time span. These students appear to make equivalent progress academically when left in regular classes.

Unfortunately, the long-term prognosis for EMR and LD students' academic gains is not very favorable. EMR children especially seem to do very poorly in academic skills (lower than mental ages would suggest) even after years of special education. Semmel et al. (1979) reported that not a single study on mainstreaming for EMR children has ever reported a mean grade-equivalent for reading higher than 3.8.

To date there are no studies that examine the academic effectiveness of various public school programs specifically for language-disordered children, despite accumulating evidence, as we saw in Chapter 2, that these children have pervasive and long-term achievement difficulties (Wiener, 1974; Ajuriaguerra et al., 1976; Hall and Tomblin, 1978; King et al., 1982). Schery (1980) substantiates the research discussed earlier in the text in that she found an increasingly slow rate of achievement in math and reading as language-disordered children approached adolescence, with mean scores never surpassing the high third-grade level. It appears that academic achievement for all groups of mildly handicapped students may only be facilitated up to a point and that there may be some inherent limit in their formally measured academic skills. In the long run, such youngsters seem to fall further behind their normal peers on standardized achievement tests regardless of the educational setting in which they are served (see also Chapter 2).

Social Adjustment Effects

Assumptions made by proponents of mainstreaming often include the notion that placement of handicapped children in regular classrooms will facilitate interaction with normal peers, provide opportunities for "normal" models, and reduce the stigma of labeling associated with special class placement (Christoplos and Renz, 1969; Fisher and Rizzo, 1974; Bricker, 1978). However, recent studies have shown that neither the self-concept of the handicapped child nor acceptance by normal peers is necessarily facilitated by inclusion in regular classes. These studies have encompassed many categories of handicapped children. The following review will consider the social effects of mainstream placement on EMR, learning-disabled, and behaviorally and emotionally handicapped pupils. Preschool handicapped children are considered separately.

EMR, LD, and Behaviorally Handicapped Students

Gottlieb (1981) reviewed the literature on the effects of mainstreaming on the social adjustment of EMR students. He reports that studies on the acceptance of EMR students by normal peers consistently indicate no advantage to mainstream placement. In fact, there is some evidence to support the notion that nonintegrated EMR children gain more acceptance from peers than mainstreamed EMR children (Gottlieb and Budoff, 1973; Iano et al., 1974). It appears that being in daily classroom contact with handicapped peers may lead to greater rejection by normal classmates.

Greater rejection is not always seen as a disadvantage. Morrison (1981) has suggested that it might serve the useful function of helping handicapped youngsters improve the accuracy of their social perceptions. Lack of such socio-empathy may hinder social relations for many mildly handicapped children (Bruininks, 1978). Bruininks found that learning-disabled children were less accurate in assessing their own social status than nonhandicapped children. Overall, learning-disabled children tended to overestimate their social status with results that often led to increased social rejection. Much of the observational research with learning-disabled children in mainstream classrooms has indicated that they are generally not well accepted, are less accurate in assessing nonverbal cues from normal peers, and may experience increasing peer rejection over time (Bryan, 1976, 1977; Bryan et al., 1976; see also Chapter 2).

A 3-year longitudinal study of thirty 8- to 12-year-old learning-disabled students—half were educated in self-contained classes and the other half attended mainstream classes—indicated both academic and social adjustment advantages to the self-contained class for the first 2 years (Scholom et al., 1981). By the third year children in these classes were only marginally superior in academic achievement, but social and personal adjustment reported by parents and the students themselves had declined sharply relative to ratings from previous years. Teachers' ratings of the pupils' ad-

justment, interestingly, continued to show gains. The authors suggested that at early school ages, a self-contained classroom might be the intervention of choice but as children move into adolescence, when identity issues and peer group influences take on greater importance, mainstreaming might be the more desirable alternative. Of course, we have already reviewed literature which suggests that the peer contact and peer acceptance that is of great value to the adolescent may not be facilitated simply by virtue of mainstream placement.

Gresham (1982) has recently done a comprehensive review of the literature on the social effects of the mainstream experience not only for learning-disabled and mentally retarded children, but also for the emotionally and behaviorally disordered populations as well. He supports the above contentions, finding virtually no evidence to support assertions that mainstream placements for school-age handicapped children result in increased social interaction, social acceptance or incidental learning through observing normal peers.

There may also be detrimental effects of mainstreaming on normal class peers. Chow (1980) showed that the introduction of learning-disabled students into regular classes resulted in decreased instructional time for both mainstreamed and regular students. Examination of the effects (and unintended side effects) of mainstream placement on normal class children is an area that has received little attention and suggests a need for closer scrutiny.

Handicapped Preschoolers

Studies on preschool handicapped children have shown some mixed effects of integration. Some investigators suggest negative results. Cavallero and Porter (1980), looking at gaze orientation and social play in a classroom of 20 young children (10 mentally retarded, 10 normal), found that the children mainly interacted within their own group. Guralnick (1980) investigated the communicative and parallel play interactions of mildly, moderately, and severely handicapped (physically and cognitively) preschoolers with normal peers during a free play situation. Results indicated that only the nonhandicapped children interacted with each other greater than would be expected based on availability, whereas the more severely handicapped children were least likely to be sought out by normal peers.

However, other studies with preschool handicapped children suggest some potential benefits to integration. Guralnick and Paul-Brown (1977) demonstrated that normal preschool children adjusted their verbal language output to match the degree of developmental delay of integrated handicapped peers; their speech was more complex, more frequent, and more diverse when addressed to the more advanced peers. This suggested the possibility that integrated normal peers provided facilitating verbal models for language-handicapped preschoolers, since adults and normal children tend to simplify their speech to younger children (Broen, 1972; Snow, 1972; Shatz and Gelman, 1973) and mothers of handicapped children provide a generally less complex linguistic environment when addressing their handicapped children (Howlin et al. 1973; Marshall et al., 1973). Forbes (1980) described the effects of mainstream integration using six normal preschool children carefully matched on age, sex, and background to six mild to moderately cerebral palsied/developmentally delayed peers. He reported positive benefits for both the handicapped children (increased sociability, decreased dependence, reduction in inappropriate behaviors) and the normals (increased nurturance).

There is a specific need for more longitudinal studies of the social effects of mainstreaming. It is quite possible that handicapped children's viewpoints and sensitivities change over time and that the effect of potential or real rejection by peers can have a motivating influence during certain stages in their development whereas at other times it may prove devastating.

Implications of Mainstreaming Research

What does this mainstreaming literature imply for clinicians, teachers, and other practicing professionals working with language learning-disabled students? Rapid academic gains that "close the gap" with normal peers should probably not be anticipated; a slow (and, we hope, steady) growth curve is more realistic in academic subjects such as reading and math. In view of the complex and pervasive nature of early language disabilities, we should also be cautious about promises to "remediate" an underlying language disability so that academic skills can progress consistent with normal peers. Judging language outcomes with formal reading and math inventories may result in disappointment and frustration for the clinician *and* the student. This is not to say that we should avoid an emphasis on training language skills for academics. On the contrary, it is important to do so, but to do so with an appreciation of the complexity of the task and an awareness of what appear to be natural developmental bounds for many handicapped children. As we learn more about the continuum of language development and language difficulties, we will surely learn more about how and when certain skills can be facilitated (see also Chapter 5).

If rapid academic progress is not a likely outcome of special intervention efforts, the social and emotional implications of communication training become increasingly important. Helping children learn social communication skills may increase their chances for successful peer acceptance in mainstreaming contexts. The ability to express himself verbally can facilitate a handicapped child's acceptance of his limitations by allowing expression of such feelings as disappointment and anger in appropriate ways. Such functional language and communication goals are certainly part of the current emphasis on pragmatic language skills. As we develop better methods for analyzing classroom discourse (see Chapter 14), the social as well as communicative effect of language intervention may be enhanced.

LANGUAGE INTERVENTION PROGRAMS

Studies specifically investigating the effects of language intervention programs with language-disordered populations are very limited indeed. To begin with, there are very few data-based studies, despite assertions proclaiming the efficacy of various intervention approaches. Furthermore, some studies that claim relevant data refer to descriptive data which are not capable of demonstrating intervention *effects* in any rigorous way (Wehman and Garrett, 1978). Those studies that do attempt to assess treatment effects are often limited in scope; they are primarily clinical research studies assessing a specific therapeutic technique or intervention in terms of its effects on one or more clients selected for research purposes.

Clinical Training Studies

Leonard (1981) published a very comprehensive review of these clinical "training studies" with specific language-disordered children. Subjects in these studies had normal nonverbal IQ's with significant delay in expressive and/or receptive language areas documented by formal testing; most were of preschool age. He found that few of the studies utilized appropriate control groups; most designs included a group receiving a presumably unrelated therapy (such as articulation training) or the studies utilized single-subject designs. Very little research compared two training approaches. Leonard found that most language intervention approaches could be categorized in one of six classifications: (1) imitation based, (2) modeling, (3) expansion, (4) focused stimulation (concentrated exposure to particular forms), (5) general stimulation, and (6) comprehension based. He discussed several of the problems with this intervention research, including heterogeneity of subjects, difficulty in judging the status of a language form if the child did not initially produce it, variations in what was considered reinforcement, gener-

alization of forms, and the narrow scope of outcomes for individual studies, e.g., no consideration of language use in functional contexts like interpersonal communication or academic applications. The studies he reviewed showed fairly consistent benefits from language therapy overall, with some mixed results for the modeling, expansion, and comprehension-based approaches. Requiring an active response on the child's part appeared to be important for growth. Comparisons between approaches were inconclusive, partly because of the methodological differences in the studies. As important as these studies are, in many cases it is difficult to generalize the results to actual operating clinical programs.

So far, at least, there is encouraging evidence that intervention does help, at least when a specific intervention or training technique is utilized with an appropriate client or clients. To date there are no specific conclusions that can be drawn on the type of intervention approach that works best. There is positive evidence for the success of highly structured imitation techniques (Gottsleben et al., 1974; Mulac and Tomlinson, 1977) as well as for general language stimulation (Whitehurst et al., 1972; Evesham, 1977). Further, more carefully defined research is necessary before we can choose an approach based on efficacy studies with confidence.

The ITPA Model

An area of controversy in the language intervention literature has centered around use of the Illinois Test of Psycholinguistic Abilities (ITPA) (Kirk et al., 1971) as an organizing framework for language intervention efforts (Karnes, 1972; Minskoff et al., 1972; Bush and Giles, 1977). As we saw in Chapters 1 and 9, such intervention programs are based on the premise that language behavior is made up of discrete components that are prerequisite to language learning and are amenable to remedial activities. Hammill and Larsen (1974) reviewed 39 studies that attempted to train various psycholinguistic processes, predominantly in populations of retarded and disadvantaged children. They concluded that the effectiveness of such training had not been proven. This led to a heated rebuttal (Minskoff, 1975; Lund et al., 1978), with counter-response from Hammill and Larsen (1978). The nature of the subjects, actual treatment, and experimental design were contested. Most recently Kavale (1981) applied Glass's meta-analysis approach (Glass, 1976) to the 34 studies of psycholinguistic training which met basic methodological requirements for the technique. Results of this meta-analysis demonstrated the efficacy of psycholinguistic training across all studies. In fact, Kavale suggested that previous reviews tended to underestimate the positive effects of such training. However, it must be stressed that the effect of such a broad statistical approach to analyzing psycholinguistic training does not suggest *what* aspects of the training were effective nor *why*. It may be that some of the ITPA tasks enhance metalinguistic awareness (see Chapter 7); others may develop vocabulary knowledge and word association abilities (see Chapter 11). Nevertheless, as a group, these studies do suggest that language intervention efforts can make a difference. However, like the clinical training studies with language-disordered children which Leonard reviewed, the ITPA studies are generally short term (25 to 50 hours of treatment) and utilize a small sample (4 to 50 subjects). Unfortunately, there is still little direct information to be gleaned from this literature that suggests the differential effectiveness of any particular approach.

Program Level Research

Outcome studies that deal with language intervention not by examining a discrete clinical technique in a research environment, but rather by looking at a full treatment regimen in a programmatic or educational setting, are few. For one thing, program evaluation (for this is what is meant) has only recently developed appropriate methodology for this kind of undertaking (Guttentag and Struening, 1975; Cook and Reichart, 1979; Berk, 1981). Furthermore, speech and language programs have been slow to adapt this "action research" to school, hospital, and clinic settings. Later in this chapter, guidelines for program level research are presented that may help provide a framework for future studies. Although no really comprehensive program evaluation research in speech and language intervention could be found, there are two recent studies that compare entire treatment alternatives rather than specific clinical techniques.

Cooper et al. (1979) compared groups of similar language-disordered preschool children (N ranged from 58 to 119 for each group) receiving the Reynell Developmental Language Programme (1978) in a language class setting and through a home-based parent program with two groups of control children, one in regular school classes receiving weekly speech therapy and the other in classrooms with no special help (on waiting lists for treatment). The authors used a rating technique to quantify annual assessments. Group comparisons indicated that program children made accelerated development in 12 specified language-related areas of development, including attention, verbal comprehension, and expressive language. A follow-up study was conducted from 6 to 30 months after discharge from the special program. The authors reported that 80 to 90% of the children maintained the accelerated language growth. Seventy per cent of the children were rated by their teachers as making very good progress in regular school 1 year after dismissal.

Weiss (1980) compared the overall effect of her INREAL (INclass REActive Language) method for language-handicapped and bilingual preschoolers and kindergarten children (N = 518) in various education settings throughout Colorado between 1974 and 1977. The INREAL method requires the language specialist to work entirely within the classroom, adopting noncontrolling techniques that allow the child to maintain the communicative focus. Control subjects attended regular preschool and kindergarten programs receiving traditional speech therapy services where the clinician worked with individuals and small groups of children outside the classroom. Children in experimental classrooms showed significantly greater language growth in the areas of vocabulary, phonology, receptive syntax, and expressive syntax after 1 year. A follow-up study over 3 years showed that fewer INREAL children required supplemental special education including resource room assignment and speech therapy. A cost-effectiveness analysis verified that early intervention using the INREAL model resulted in a cost savings when compared to the special education resources necessary for children who had not received this early help.

Weiss's research is a particularly well done example of a group of program level studies that are not readily available through published literature but appear as final technical reports from funded research projects. Other such reports suggest the importance of functional communication as a language intervention goal in working with severely handicapped children (Schiefelbusch and Rogers-Warren, 1980), the relationship between language intervention and reading goals for language-disordered children (Miller, 1977), and the usefulness of relatively highly structured intervention approaches with more severely disabled students in contrast to moderately impaired students who do equally well with less structure (Project Child, 1975).

In summary, the available literature evaluating the effects of speech and language intervention is limited to a relatively small group of small-subject research studies that focus on the efficacy of specific techniques, and to an even smaller number of outcome studies comparing entire treatment alternatives. Clinical professionals operating in field settings find little here to guide clinical or educational program decisions. On the positive side, there is some evidence that language intervention helps children gain communication skills above what

would be expected if no treatment were given. This is not a trivial issue in these days of declining fiscal resources. The claim that language intervention procedures *do* make a difference needs to be documented as clearly and conclusively as possible: this is the justification of the extra costs incurred for our services in schools and clinics. Unfortunately, the available studies are not really definitive on this issue, nor have we made much progress toward explicating the most effective aspects of our intervention programs. We need to know *what* particular aspects of therapy work best with *which* types of children in *which* intervention settings. What we do know is that many preschoolers do not outgrow their early language disabilities. Thus the challenge is ours to develop and document effective approaches for language-disordered children of all ages.

APPLYING THE RESEARCH ON INTERVENTION

What then can we conclude from this review of the literature on outcomes of early intervention, mainstream, and language intervention efforts that might guide us in structuring services for children with language learning disabilities in the schools? There are at least six general points we can recapitulate.

1. *Intervention efforts are helpful.* Foremost, perhaps, this literature provides us with rationale for our intervention efforts. The early intervention literature and work with preschool and school-age language-disordered children demonstrate that intervention efforts can make a difference. On the other hand, studies with older school-age learning-disabled children suggest that their academic growth in self-contained classrooms is unlikely to show significant improvement compared to gains made by similar children functioning in regular classes. However, there *is* evidence that special class settings may facilitate socio-emotional growth for some handicapped youngsters. The kinds of language interactions that occur in regular and special ed-

ucation classrooms and the methods used to observe and quantify these interactions warrant careful scrutiny and offer promise for the future (see Chapters 8 and 14).

2. *The earlier intervention efforts start, the more progress can be expected.* The results of the early childhood intervention programs suggest the adaptability of the preschool age. The mainstreaming studies with this young population are the ones most likely to show positive outcomes. The younger children are when they enter a language intervention program the more progress they seem to make (Schery, 1980). However, much is still to be learned about the course of language development with older language-handicapped students. We know little about the effects of language intervention programs with adolescents who have had time to achieve a greater degree of cognitive and linguistic awareness. Currently some promising new approaches are being developed (see Chapter 16).

3. *Including parents in training efforts will facilitate the effectiveness of intervention.* There is a strong suggestion in the early childhood literature that the involvement of parents in programs designed to provide support for day-to-day living has a very beneficial effect for young children's academic and language progress. A wide variety of parent-training programs proved successful in helping parents develop more appropriate expectations for their youngsters.

4. *A rapid acceleration of academic growth for language-disordered children when they are enrolled in a remedial program is unlikely.* Unfortunately, there is an indication that the majority of children with language learning problems in the early grades will continue to test below grade level on academic tests throughout their secondary education and into young adulthood. It is important to recognize language-based learning problems during the school years and to work with these students to help them deal with the underlying disorder. At the present time, however,

claims that language therapy can "remediate" reading problems will probably meet with less than complete success, and expectations of unequivocal positive outcome can only lead to disappointment and frustration on the part of pupils, parents, and educational personnel. The same may be said of non-language-based reading difficulties, (Satz et al., 1979). The application of some of the newer techniques and knowledge discussed throughout this text offers additional direction for the future, however, and suggests that we may proceed with cautious optimism (Wallach, Chapter 5).

5. *Sensitivity to the social and emotional implications of the service delivery format of language intervention is very important.* The studies on mainstreaming indicate that not all effects of being educated with non-handicapped peers are positive for handicapped children; they may experience peer rejection and discrimination. The best service delivery options may vary according to the severity of the disorder and the age of the student. Preschool and adolescent children may be accepted into integrated settings more readily than children in their middle elementary years. The more severely handicapped a child is, the less likely he or she is to interact with normal peers even in an integrated setting.

6. *As enlightened professionals, we must be prepared to document the efficacy of one intervention approach over another.* The well informed practitioner is aware of the various models of language learning and understands how intervention strategies may or may not be consistent with a model's assumptions, as pointed out by van Kleeck in Chapter 9. It is possible that recent emphases on communication-based approaches will result in differential benefits when compared to earlier programs stressing the more structural (syntactic and phonological) aspects of language. It is also possible that advanced knowledge about metalinguistics (Chapter 7), higher level language strategies (Chapters 5 and 6), and other problem-solving abilities (Chapter 10) may lead to more successful outcomes.

However, we cannot make that assumption without evidence. So far it appears that a wide range of intervention approaches can be useful with young disadvantaged learners (Weikart, 1981). Leonard's (1981) review indicated that a range of specific intervention techniques can be helpful with language-disordered children as well.

LANGUAGE DISORDERS PROFESSIONALS AS CLINICAL RESEARCHERS

If the six general conclusions above are all that we can glean from clinical outcome studies to guide our design of language intervention programs, what do we do next? Throw up our hands and plead ignorance? Do whatever we want with the assurance that probably no one can prove that another approach could be more effective? Another possible alternative is to roll up our professional sleeves and begin to train ourselves in how to find some answers. Speech-language professionals and other practitioners working with language learning-disabled students in clinic or school programs are in an ideal position to conduct or participate in research on the many outcome issues that still remain unanswered. The need for our professions to document their overall effectiveness and to refine aspects of intervention programs with language-handicapped children has never been more apparent (Killen and Myklebust, 1980; Gallagher, 1981; Snyder, 1981; Laney, 1982). The pressure of dwindling economic resources combined with increasing requests for service make it imperative that we take seriously the responsibilities of our human service-oriented profession. We must be willing to prove that what we do makes a difference. And we should search for ever more effective and cost-effective ways of doing what it is we do best. It is only by assuming this responsibility for ourselves that we can avoid having others with less knowledge of our programs and professions do it for us.

A Model for Program Evaluation

"Fine," the speech-language pathologist, school psychologist, or special education teacher might ask, "but where do I begin? I already keep diagnostic and reevaluation data on my students for accountability reasons. Isn't this enough?" Unfortunately, probably not. Evaluation of the effectiveness of a speech-language program, a remedial reading program, or a special education class should look at intervention efforts in a broader context than simply relying on test-retest measures from a standard battery. Table 15.1 (Schery and Lipsey, 1982) suggests a framework for designing a program evaluation. To fully understand the effects of language interventions in educational and clinical settings requires investigation of two separate issues—clinical treatment and delivery of service. A good intervention or treatment can be poorly delivered, and an excellent service delivery system can provide a weak (or even harmful) treatment. From the point of view of the language learning-disabled child, *both* these aspects are vitally important.

For both the treatment and the service delivery aspects, three broad topics must be addressed in order to fully document the nature and results of the program. These include the content of the program, its process, and its outcome. As suggested in Table 15.1, each of these can be considered separately for treatment versus service delivery issues as follows:

PROGRAM CONTENT

Treatment. What is the conceptual model for the intervention? What problem does it address? How is it supposed to work? What results is it supposed to have?

Service Delivery. What is the organizational plan for providing services? Who are the intended clients? What treatment or service regimen is to be provided?

PROGRAM PROCESS

Treatment. What is the integrity with which the intervention plan is actually followed on a day-to-day basis, i.e., if the

Table 15.1.

Sample Topics for a Comprehensive Program Evaluation

Evaluation Issue	Program Aspect	
	Clinical Treatment	Service Delivery
Implementation	Does a specifiable treatment model exist? Are there operating procedures defined for the treatment regimen? Are clients actually receiving treatment?	Is there an organization in place with adequate staff and budget? Are there procedures for identifying, recruiting, and enrolling clients? Are there clients coming through the program?
Process	What clients are receiving treatment? On what schedule and over what time? Does the treatment as delivered actually fulfill the treatment plan? What are the activities of staff, family, other program components, etc., in support of treatment?	Are appropriate clients coming into the program? From where? Do all eligible clients have access to service? Are there delays, attrition, or waiting lists for service? What do services cost? What are the key staff activities in support of service delivery?
Outcome	What effects or changes do clients experience that result from treatment? Does treatment affect other areas of functioning besides language? Does treatment have any indirect or unintended side effects on clients?	How many clients receive full service? What proportion receive less? What amount and type of service are delivered? How satisfied are clients with service? How many clients return for additional service? How widely is service distributed in the target client group?

therapy plan calls for verbal reinforcement for each communication attempt, does that actually happen consistently?

Service Delivery. What services do clients actually receive? How much, how often, and over what period? How are staff time and program resources allocated?

PROGRAM OUTCOME

Treatment. What actual effects does the client experience? This may include not only improved communication but also such things as better social functioning, increased motivation, increased achievement scores, etc.

Service Delivery. What number of children were seen compared to the potential number needing service? How many dropped out with incomplete service? How satisfied or dissatisfied were they with the way they were treated?

A design for a comprehensive evaluation of program outcomes would fill each cell of the model's matrix with specific questions pertinent to the particular program in question. With those questions as a framework, various indicators and measures that could provide appropriate data would be defined and a research design formulated to specify when, where, from whom, and how often those measures are to be obtained. In a language intervention program of any size or complexity, getting together a full-scale evaluation of outcomes is clearly no trivial undertaking. It may be sensible to begin less ambitiously and initially to gather data on only some aspects of the model. The important thing, however, is to specify carefully the nature of the data to be collected so that effort is not wasted and the resulting information can be useful in the task we *must* begin—that of documenting the outcomes of our intervention programs.

In addition to the framework described above, certain methodological and procedural guidelines should direct research in program settings. The following section delineates a few of the most important of these issues.

Choice of Test Instruments

Standardized psychometric tests, including many routinely used to evaluate speech and language abilities, have the property of being very sensitive to individual differences in children's language performance. Such tests were developed to document a particular child's performance against performances of a wide spectrum of children in a normal distribution. This type of test is very appropriately used for diagnostic purposes, i.e., to isolate and identify the child who is clearly functioning below the normal range. The stability and reliability that make these tests effective measures of individual differences, however, *reduce* their sensitivity to change in the performance of a single student (Carver, 1974; Schery, 1981). Criterion-referenced tests would be more appropriate as a sensitive change measure. The overriding importance of diagnostic issues in speech and language test selection can work against the ability of the same tests to document gain or growth in the children once they enter the program. It may be advisable to include some criterion-referenced measures in intake batteries along with the more common standardized instruments. Lee and Fine will expand upon these dilemmas in Chapter 16 (also see discussions in Chapters 1, 2, and 9).

RECOMMENDATION

In designing test-retest studies, include tests which are sensitive to individual growth. Many well standardized diagnostic instruments are not.

Uniformity of Data and Missing Data

In large speech and language intervention programs with many staff members, there is likely to be some diversity in the tests utilized. Different staff may have particular biases or strong preferences for one type of assessment over another. Even if they have all agreed on a standard diagnostic battery, the consistency with which retesting is carried out may vary. A child may be ill at the scheduled reevaluation time

and never be rescheduled. A client is transferred to a new clinician who chooses to supplement information with additional tests rather than readministering the former ones. As children approach the 8- to 10-year range, many language tests are no longer appropriately normed, and clinicians vary on ideas of what procedures are useful with older language-handicapped children. New tests are appearing on the market at an astounding rate. They entice clinicians with claims of new and more up-to-date diagnostic information. Even the format in which progress reports are made can vary widely within one program. For example, in the classrooms of a program for language-disordered children in Los Angeles (Schery, 1980), some language clinicians submitted long narrative reports covering whatever they felt was most important, whereas others used brief check sheets covering specified areas. From teacher to teacher, from year to year, the format and content of this record changed, making it virtually impossible to reconstruct what had taken place in the classrooms, at least without laborious extraction from a widely diverse set of materials. All of these factors may make little difference to routine program operation, but they are very damaging to the quality and usefulness of the data for program evaluation purposes.

RECOMMENDATION

Have staff throughout a language program agree on the measures to be gathered and develop a consistent format. More limited measures that are uniformly and routinely administered are more helpful for program evaluation purposes than files filled with insightful comments that no one has time to read. If new procedures and/or tests *are* introduced, discuss them as a group and implement changes uniformly across the entire program.

Range of Outcome Measures

Sheehan and Keogh (1981) argue for the utilization of a more diverse and less quantitative approach to documenting program impact with handicapped children—including ethnographic methods, participant observers, anthropological field techniques, and longitudinal case studies. Peer ratings of the overall improvement in learning-disordered children's communicative and academic performance in the classroom environment have recently been quantified using the system of "social validation" (Wolf, 1978; Epstein and Cullinan, 1979; see also Chapter 14). Such alternatives (or additions) to traditional formal language tests for measuring pupil progress are quite clearly supported by research in outcomes of early childhood education programs. As the ECE studies reviewed earlier suggest, a full assessment of the effects of intervention must consider other outcome issues as well as pre-post data from standard instruments. Zigler and Balla (1982) argue that the full range of functioning of handicapped children is at issue in *any* intervention effort—social competence, family relationships, motivation, physical well-being, and personality, as well as language performance. There are measurement techniques available that are sensitive to such areas; the use of observational techniques, self-report questionnaires, and interviews are some examples that have been useful in early special education contexts (see Sheehan and Keogh, 1981). For the most part, speech and language clinicians have not made use of these techniques for measuring intervention effects beyond the immediate therapy setting, and we may have been selling ourselves short by not doing so.

Another way in which we might extend our search for outcomes is to look at longitudinal data even after the program is completed. Certainly the effects of the Head Start program showed up several years after the "intervention" was administered. Tracking language-disordered children into the "next environment" (Vincent et al., 1980) can provide important information on long-range effects of the program and can allow staff to verify conclusions about the behaviors that lead to "success" outside the program context. Ideally, the range of outcome measures used in intervention programs should sample effects that extend into wider ranging and subsequent environments.

RECOMMENDATION

Determine areas of the child's life that can be affected by improved communicative competence and design ways of measuring functions within these domains. Do not restrict such measurements to formal tests, but consider observations, interviews, surveys, etc. Build in a follow-up mechanism for some period after the child (or a sample of children) leaves the program.

Service Delivery Information

Many language intervention programs concentrate on client performance data in contrast to service delivery information. It is sometimes difficult to consider information on the service delivery aspects of a program as part of its effectiveness; such "management information" appears mundane. However, the value of such ongoing service information can be illustrated by referring again to the study of the Los Angeles County program (Schery, 1980). Retrospectively, we learned (by digging into program archives and patching data together from diverse sources) that the referral rate from the 92 school districts that had contracted for service was highly uneven. Some districts had never referred a child. Other districts accounted for substantially more than their proportional number of referrals. There had been no way of monitoring this on an ongoing basis despite the potential implications such a pattern had for the equitable distribution of resources. Had this information been available in a timely way, it might have been possible to determine what was happening to the language-disordered children in the nonreferring districts. Another example involves the proportion of children in the program who came from bilingual Spanish-English homes. The overall percentage was 17%, a figure that closely approximated census figures for the bilingual population in the districts represented. The program administrators were greatly relieved—they had been concerned that some classes were disproportionately bilingual. For program evaluation purposes there should be a mechanism for routinely obtaining such information.

RECOMMENDATION

Do not overlook the importance of ongoing systematic documentation of the service delivery component of language intervention programs. Such management information can, in the most pragmatic sense, affect the outcome of an intervention program to an even greater extent than the type of intervention utilized.

LANGUAGE INTERVENTION: PAST, PRESENT, AND FUTURE

This chapter has reviewed literature pertinent to designing intervention programs for children with early language disabilities and later language learning difficulties. Extremely few studies have examined the effectiveness of educational or clinical programs specifically for language-disordered children. Related studies in early childhood education and those that consider the effects of integration of school-age handicapped youngsters provide some information and suggest some general guidelines. However, there is a pressing need to consider this information as it relates to language-disordered children and to extend and focus research on effective outcomes of language intervention. To this end, a framework for designing a comprehensive evaluation of a program's effectiveness has been suggested, and certain methodological guidelines designed to make future outcome studies more meaningful have been discussed. Careful evaluation of our intervention programs can delineate the procedures, techniques, and strategies that are most effective in helping language-disordered children. This is our challenge for the future.

References

Abidin B, Seltzer J: Special education outcomes: implications for implementation of Public Law 94–142. *J Learn Disabil* 14:28–31, 1981.

Ajuriaguerra J de, Jaeggi A, Guignard F, et al: The development and prognosis of dysphasia in children. In Morehead D, Morehead A: *Normal and Deficient Child Language*. Baltimore, University Park Press, 1976.

Balow B, Fuchs D, Kasbohm D: Teaching nonreaders to read: an evaluation of the basic skill centers in Minneapolis. *J Learn Disabil* 11:351–354, 1978.

Beck F, Lindsey J, Frith G: Effects of self-contained special class placement on intellectual functioning of learning disabled students. *J Learn Disabil* 14:280–282, 1981.

Bereiter C, Engelmann S: *Teaching Disadvantaged Children in Preschool*. Englewood Cliffs, NJ, Prentice-Hall, 1966.

Berk R: *Education Evaluation Methodology: The State of the Art*. Baltimore, The Johns Hopkins University Press, 1981.

Bricker D: A rationale for the integration of handicapped and nonhandicapped preschool children. In Guralnick M: *Early Intervention and the Integration of Handicapped and Nonhandicapped Children*. Baltimore, University Park Press, 1978.

Broen P: The verbal environment of the language learning child. *Am Speech Hear Assoc Monogr* 17, 1972.

Bruininks V: Actual and perceived peer status of learning disabled students in mainstreamed programs. *J Spec Educ* 12:51–58, 1978.

Bryan T: Peer popularity of learning disabled children: a replication. *J Learn Disabil* 9:307–311, 1976.

Bryan T: Learning disabled children's comprehension of nonverbal communication. *J Learn Disabil* 10:501–506, 1977.

Bryan T, Wheeler R, Felcan J, et al: "Come on, dummy." An observational study of children's communication. *J Learn Disabil* 9:661–669, 1976.

Budoff M, Gottlieb J: Special class EMR children mainstreamed: a study of an aptitude (learning potential) X treatment interaction. *Am J Ment Defic* 81:1–11, 1976.

Bush W, Giles M: *Aids to Psycholinguistic Teaching*, ed 2. Columbus, OH, Charles E Merrill, 1977.

Carver R: Two dimensions of tests: psychometric and edumetric. *Am Psychol* 29:512–518, 1974.

Cavallaro S, Porter R: Peer preference of at risk and normally developing children in a preschool mainstream classroom. *Am J Ment Defic* 84:357–66, 1980.

Chow S: A study of academic learning time of mainstreamed handicapped students. Final report. Far West Lab for Educational Research and Development, Berkeley, CA, August, 1980 (ED 199 990).

Christoplos F, Renz P: A critical evaluation of special education programs. *J Spec Educ* 3:371–379, 1969.

Cicarelli VG, Cooper WH, Granger RL: The impact of Head Start: an evaluation of the effects of Head Start on children's cognitive and affective development. Westinghouse Learning Corporation, OEO Contract No. B89-4536, 1969.

Clarke-Stewart K: Parent education in the 1970's. *Educ Eval Policy Anal* 3:47–58, 1981.

Cook T, Reichart C: *Qualitative and Quantitative Methods in Evaluation Research*. Beverly Hills, CA, Sage, 1979.

Cooper J, Moodley M, Reynell J: The developmental language programme. Results from a five year study. *Br J Disord Commun* 14:57–69, 1979.

Darlington R: The consortium for longitudinal studies. *Educ Eval Policy Anal* 3:37–45, 1981.

Darlington R, Royce J, Snipper A, et al: Preschool programs and later school competence of children from low-income families. *Science* 208:202–204, 1980.

DISTAR Language Program. Science-Research Associates, Chicago, 1968.

Dunn L: Special education for the mildly retarded—Is much of it justifiable? *Excep Child* 35:5–22, 1968.

Epstein M, Cullinan D: Social validity: use of normative peer data to evaluate LD interventions. *Learn Disabil Q* 2:93–98, 1979.

Evesham M: Teaching language skills to children. *Br J Disord Commun* 12:23–29, 1977.

Fisher C, Rizzo A: A paradigm for humanizing special education. *J Spec Educ* 8:321–329, 1974.

Forbes D: Mainstreaming and preschool children: effects on social behavior of the handicapped and the non-handicapped. Presented to conference on mainstreaming mildly handicapped and preschool education, Cambridge, MA, October, 1980.

Forness S: Clinical criteria for mainstreaming mildly handicapped children. *Psychol Schools* 16:508–514, 1979.

Gallagher J: Days of reckoning—days of opportunity: the 1981 statesmen's roundtable. Reston, VA, ERIC Clearinghouse, June, 1981.

Glass G: Primary, secondary and meta-analysis of research. *Educ Res* 5:3–8, 1976.

Goldstein H, Moss J, Jordan L: The efficacy of special class training on the development of mentally retarded children (United States Office of Education Cooperative Project #619). Urbana, University of Illinois Press, 1965.

Gottlieb J: Mainstreaming: fulfilling the promise? *Am J Ment Defic* 86:115–126, 1981.

Gottlieb J, Budoff M: Social acceptability of retarded children in nongraded schools differing in architecture. *Am J Ment Defic* 78:15–19, 1973.

Gottsleben R, Tyack D, Buschini G: Three case studies in language training: applied linguistics. *J Speech Hear Disord* 39:211–224, 1974.

Gresham F: Misguided mainstreaming: the case for social skills training with handicapped children. *Excep Child* 48:422–433, 1982.

Guralnick M: Social interactions among preschool children. *Excep Child* 46:248–253, 1980.

Guralnick M, Paul-Brown D: The nature of verbal interactions among handicapped and nonhandicapped preschool children. *Child Dev* 48:254–260, 1977.

Guttentag M, Struening E: *Handbook of Evaluation Research.* Beverly Hills, CA, Sage, 1975.

Hall P, Tomblin J: A follow-up study of children with articulation and language disorders. *J Speech Hear Disord* 43:227–241, 1978.

Hammill D, Larsen S: The effectiveness of psycholinguistic training. *Excep Child* 41:5–14, 1974.

Hammill D, Larsen S: The effectiveness of psycholinguistic training: a reaffirmation of position. *Excep Child* 44:402–414, 1978.

Haring G, Houck M: Improved learning conditions in the establishment of reading skills with disabled readers. *Excep Child* 35:341–351, 1969.

Heber R, Garber R: The Milwaukee project: A study of the use of family intervention to prevent cultural-familial retardation. In Friendlander B, Sterritt F, Kirk G: *Exceptional Infant: Assessment and Intervention.* New York, Bruner/Mazel, 1975, vol 3.

Howlin P, Cantwell D, Marchant R, et al: Analyzing mothers' speech to young autistic children: a methodological study. *J Abnorm Child Psychol* 1:317–339, 1973.

Iano R, Ayers D, Heller H, et al: Sociometric status of retarded children in an integrative program. *Excep Child* 40:267–271, 1974.

Karnes M: *GOAL Program: Language Development.* Springfield, MA, Milton Bradley, 1972.

Kaufman M, Agard J, Semmel M: *Mainstreaming: Learners and Their Environments.* Baltimore, University Park Press, 1982.

Kaufman M, Gottlieb J, Agard J, et al: Mainstreaming: toward an explication of the construct. In Meyen EL, Vergason GA, Whelan RJ: *Alternatives for Teaching Exceptional Children.* Denver, Love Publishing, 1975.

Kavale K: Functions of the Illinois Test of Psycholinguistic Abilities (ITPA): are they trainable? *Excep Child* 47:496–510, 1981.

Killen J, Myklebust J: Evaluation in special education: a computer-based approach. *J Learn Disabil* 13:35–39, 1980.

King R, Jones C, Lasky E: In retrospect: a fifteen-year follow-up report of speech-language disordered children. *Language Speech Hear Serv Schools* 13:24–32, 1982.

Kirk S, McCarthy J, Kirk W: *Illinois Test of Psycholinguistic Abilities,* revised ed. Urbana, University of Illinois Press, 1971.

Klein J, Randolph L: Placing handicapped children in Head Start programs. *Child Today* 6:7–10, 1974.

Laney M: Research and evaluation in the public schools. *Language Speech Hear Serv Schools* 13:53–60, 1982.

Lassman F, Fisch R, Vetter D, et al: *Early Correlates of Speech, Language and Hearing.* Littleton, MA, PSG Publication Company, 1980.

Lazar I: Early intervention is effective. *Educ Leadership* 38:303–305, 1981.

Lazar I, Darlington R: Lasting effects of early education: a report from the Consortium for Longitudinal Studies. *Mongr Soc Res Child Dev* 47: nos. 2–3, (serial no. 195), 1982.

Leonard L: Facilitating linguistic skills in children with specific language impairment. *Appl Psycholinguistics* 2:89–118, 1981.

Leske M: Prevalence estimates of communicative disorders in the U. S. *ASHA* 23:217–237, 1981.

Lund K, Foster C, McCall-Perez F: The effectiveness of psycholinguistic training: a reevaluation. *Excep Child* 44:310–314, 1978.

Marshall N, Hegrenes J, Goldstein SD: Verbal interactions: mothers and their retarded children vs. mothers and their non-retarded children. *Am J Ment Defic* 77:415–419, 1973.

Miller M: *Summer Program of Reading for Handicapped Pupils in Special Education Classes: Speech/Language Impaired Pupils and Mentally Retarded Pupils.* Final Evaluation Report, Washington DC, Department of Health, Education and Welfare/Office of Education 1977, (ERIC ED 136482).

Miller T, Sabatino D: An evaluation of the teacher

consultant model as an approach to mainstreaming. *Excep Child* 45:86–91, 1978.

Minskoff E: Research on psycholinguistic training: critique and guidelines. *Exep Child.* 42:136–144, 1975.

Minskoff E, Wiseman D, Minskoff J: *The MWM Program for Developing Language Abilities.* Ridgefield, NJ, Educational Performance Associates, 1972.

Morrison J: Perspectives of social status of learning handicapped and nonhandicapped students. *Am J Ment Defic* 86:243–251, 1981.

Mulac A, Tomlinson C: Generalization of an operant remediation program for syntax with language-delayed children. *J Commun Disord* 10:231–244, 1977.

Project Child. *Programming for the Language Disabled Child: Specific Programmatic Techniques.* Austin, Texas Education Agency, May, 1975 (ERIC ED 100107).

Public Law 94-142: Education for All Handicapped Children Act, 1975.

Ramey C, Campbell F: Compensatory education for disadvantaged children. *School Rev* 82:171–189, 1979.

Reynell developmental language programme. In Cooper J, Moodley M, Reynell J: *Helping Language Development.* London, Edward Arnold, 1978.

Ritter D: Surviving in the regular classroom: a follow-up of mainstreamed children with learning disabilities. *J School Psychol* 16:253–56, 1978.

Rust J, Miller C, Wilson H: Using a control group to evaluate a resource room program. *Psychol Schools* 15:503–506, 1978.

Sabatino D: An evaluation of resource rooms for children with learning disabilities. *J Learn Disabil* 4:84–93, 1971.

Satz P, Taylor H, Friel J, et al: Some developmental and predictive precursors of reading disability: a six-year follow up. In Benton A, Pearl D: *Dyslexia: An Appraisal of Current Knowledge.* New York, Oxford University Press, 1979, 313–347.

Schery T: Correlates of language development in language disordered children: an archival study. Dissertation, Claremont Graduate School, 1980.

Schery T: Selecting assessment strategies for language disordered children. *Top Language Disord* 1 (3):59–73, 1981.

Schery T, Lipsey M: Program evaluation for speech and hearing services. In Miller J, Yoder D, Schiefelbusch R: *Language Intervention.* Trenton, NJ, BC Decker, 1982.

Schiefelbusch R, Rogers-Warren A: *Teaching Language-Deviant Children to Generalize Newly Taught Language: A Socio-ecological Approach.* Final Report. Lawrence, KS, University of Kansas, Bureau of Child Research, 1980 (ED 195 084 and 195 085).

Scholom D, Schiff G, Swerdlik M, et al: A three-year study of learning disabled children in mainstreamed and self-contained classes. *Education* 101:231–238, 1981.

Semmel M, Gottlieb J, Robinson N: Mainstreaming: perspectives on educating handicapped children in the public schools. In Berliner D: *Review of Research in Education,* Washington DC, American Educational Research Association, 1979, vol 7.

Shatz M, Gelman R: The development of communication skills: modifications in the speech of young children as a function of listener. *Monogr Soc Res Child Dev* 38 (serial no. 152), 1973.

Sheehan R, Keogh B: Strategies for documenting progress of handicapped children in early education programs. *Educ Eval Policy Anal* 3:59–67, 1981.

Skeels H: Adult status of children with contrasting early life experiences. *Mongr Soc Res Child Dev* 31: (serial no. 105), 1966.

Skeels H, Dye H: A study of the effects of differential stimulation on mentally retarded children. *Proc Am Assoc Ment Defic* 44:114–136, 1939.

Snow C: Mothers' speech to children learning language. *Child Dev* 43:549–565, 1972.

Snyder L: Have we prepared the language disordered child for school? *Top Language Disord* 1 (1):29–45, 1981.

Turnbull A, Strickland B, Hammer S: The individualized educational program: part 2, translating law into practice. *J Learn Disabil* 11:67–73, 1978.

United States Department of Health Education and Welfare: Report of Office of Human Development, February, 1979.

Vincent L, Salisbury C, Walter G, et al: Program evaluation and curriculum development in early childhood/special education: criteria of the next environment. In Sailor W, Wilcox B, Brown L: *Methods of Instruction for Severely Handicapped Students.* Baltimore, Paul H. Brookes, 1980.

Wehman P, Garrett S: Language instruction with severely, profoundly and multi-handicapped students: two years of data. *Ment Retard* 16:410–412, 1978.

Weikart D: Effects of different curricula in early childhood intervention. *Educ Eval Policy Anal* 3:25–35, 1981.

Weiss R: Efficacy of INREAL intervention for preschool and kindergarten handicapped and bilingual (Spanish) children. Presented at Handicapped Children's Early Education Program Project Director's Meeting, Washington DC, December, 1980.

Whitehurst G, Novak G, Zorn G: Delayed speech studied in the home. *Dev Psychol* 7:169–177, 1972.

Wiener P: A language-delayed child at adolescence. *J Speech Hear Res* 39:202–212, 1974.

Wolf M: Social validity: the case for subjective measurement, or how applied behavior analysis is finding its heart. *J Appl Behav Anal* 11:203–214, 1978.

Zigler E, Balla D: Selecting outcome variables in evaluations of early childhood special education programs. *Top Early Childhood Spec Educ* 1:11–22, 1982.

Zigler E, Valentine J: *Project Head Start: A Legacy of the War on Poverty.* New York, Free Press, 1979.

CHAPTER SIXTEEN

When a Language Problem Is Primary: Secondary School Strategies

A. DONNA LEE, M.S., and JANICE SHAPERO-FINE, M.A.

(1) A supervisor of special education classes asked a school language clinician to provide some language development suggestions to a teacher of one of the specific learning disabilities classes in the district. He described the students' difficulties in the following way:

"This is a class for students with 'auditory perceptual problems.' That's why they're having so much difficulty with reading and spelling. Their teacher has been doing a lot of work on auditory discrimination, sound blending and auditory memory. But, she's noticed lately that their language skills *also* seem to be pretty weak."

This example touches upon some concepts about the nature of language, reading, and learning difficulties that are undergoing reevaluation by specialists and clinicians in the area of language and learning disabilities. As more information has become available about the complex relationship that exists between language, perception, and memory, assessment and intervention techniques that focus upon remediation of these symptoms in isolation are being seriously challenged.

(2) A public school language clinician proposed to a school administrator that her caseload size be reviewed as she felt it was too high to effectively meet the needs of the students she served. She presented caseload statistics of other special education resource and support services and noted that their caseload size was considerably lower. The administrator responded that he was sensitive to her concerns but he indicated that he saw her situation as somewhat different. He pointed out that the other support service professionals required more time with most students because they usually worked on several subject areas in the curriculum, whereas she *only* worked with language.

An interchange like this certainly provides much food for thought in light of current information about language development, language disorders, and the central role that language plays in learning and success with the curriculum. Professionals are becoming increasingly aware of the misinterpretations that may result from viewing language as a complex separate from other aspects of learning and development. Indeed, specialists in the field of language learning disabilities have begun to place more emphasis upon the many varied aspects of language that may require consideration in assessment and management of academic difficulties; for example, the language of the child, the language of instruction, and language skills needed to master the curriculum.

There are many other examples that would similarly illustrate the need to bring theory and practice closer in line with one another. Advances in the study of language have broadened our understanding about the nature of language, its development, and its importance to school and social success. This information has had very significant implications for professionals in public school settings who provide services to language learning-disabled students.

The current picture of language learning disabilities differs considerably from that of the past. At one time, the language-disabled student was the individual for whom vocabulary size, mean length of utterance, and grammaticality of sentence structure were the major areas of concern. With the shifts that have occurred from a primary focus on syntax to the inclusion of semantic and pragmatic considerations and their interactions, a more comprehensive picture of language proficiency has emerged.

A better understanding also exists regarding how language interacts with learning and academics. Academics were often thought of as a group of skills that could be developed and taught apart from language. As stressed throughout this text, a great deal of information has become available within the past decade regarding the relationship between spoken and written language, language and thinking, and language of the classroom and curriculum. This knowledge has led to a critical look at many existing procedures and practices.

As knowledge in the field has grown, there has been a reciprocal broadening of scope in terms of the areas and activities with which professionals have become concerned as they attempt to meet the needs of the language learning-disabled student. This chapter will explore concepts and issues important to consider in the delivery of services to language learning-disabled students in school systems. A major emphasis will be directed toward some of the special issues related to developing language programs at the high school level.

The first section addresses itself to philosophical and practical issues and includes a brief overview of some current theoretical concepts that have been discussed in greater detail throughout the text. This section also provides a discussion of issues and realities that exist when working in a school system.

Next are described some identification and assessment procedures recently developed for use in Scarborough, Ontario's high schools. Preliminary impressions regarding language learning problems that high school students present are also provided.

The last section elaborates on some of the issues raised in previous sections as they relate to intervention and programming in an educational setting. Factors involved in effecting a match between teacher, student, and curriculum, as well as the give and take needed between professionals in the delivery of services, are highlighted.

THEORETICAL AND PRACTICAL CONSIDERATIONS
Starting Points

The starting point of any aspect of programming is in its theoretical underpinnings. With the enormous growth in the field, it is the responsibility of the professional to grow by critically evaluating the old and incorporating the new. Many areas of study have been instrumental in providing a broader and more powerful base from which to approach language learning disorders.

As discussed in Chapter 1 and elsewhere in this text, it has become apparent that language should not be conceptualized as a set of discrete and separate skills, e.g., auditory memory, auditory discrimination, and the like. Similarly, visual perceptual factors, frequently cited as the cause of some of the difficulties that children encounter with written language, are being reinterpreted in light of current theory. Such "perceptual weaknesses" are now being considered within the context of language. Problems with auditory discrimination, visual sequencing difficulties, and sound blending may in fact be symptoms of an underlying language disorder.

In part, as discussed in Chapter 5, such

changes in philosophy have come about due to the expanded concepts that professionals now have about the nature of language and the development of language skills. Language development is no longer seen as a process that ends at age 5. Throughout the school years, children both consolidate and expand upon their earlier acquired comprehension and production abilities. Moreover, school-age children develop facility with new and different aspects of language.

New strategies needed for the processing of more complex syntax, for drawing inferences, and for organizing and integrating information emerge during the school years. These abilities represent some of the more subtle aspects of language proficiency. Certainly, a simple listing of sentence structures that are correctly or incorrectly interpreted is no longer seen as providing sufficient information about an individual's comprehension abilities. An evaluation of "sentence comprehension" must also address the particular strategies employed in ascertaining the meaning of a sentence. For example: Is word order followed? Are clauses confused? .... However, this type of information represents only part of the picture. Other levels and processes that go beyond the individual sentence come into play (Perfetti, 1977). Grasping the relatedness among sentences in discourse, using prior knowledge, and considering pertinent contextual information are important dimensions that contribute to comprehension. Consequently, literal, inferential and integrative elements must all be addressed in any meaningful examination of listening and reading comprehension.

The study of communicative competence is another area that has helped professionals to better recognize some other manifestations of language disorders. During the school-age years, children become increasingly sophisticated and flexible in their social-communicative interactions. They become increasingly skilled at varying the content and style of their communication

to fit the needs of their listeners, and they become more adept at taking into account social skills relevant to communicative interactions.

In Chapter 14, Silliman discussed some of the pragmatic deficits exhibited by school-age learning-disabled students. Indeed, research in this area suggests that such difficulties may have significant implications regarding social and communicative interactions both in and outside the classroom. For some learning-disabled students, perceptions of listener needs, knowledge of conversational turn-taking rules, and other aspects related to their roles as listeners and speakers appear to be areas of concern (Donahue et al., 1979).

Van Kleeck reminds us, in Chapter 7, that metalinguistic awareness represents an important dimension of language ability that appears to show longitudinal development during the school years. The transition between preoperational and concrete operational abilities may be a significant stage in which these language abilities emerge (Hakes, 1980). Moreover, it has been suggested that the emergence of formal operational abilities may be important in the development of metalinguistic skills (Gardner et al., 1975; Gardner and Lohman, 1975; Winner et al., 1976.).

Recent research indicates that metalinguistic abilities may be important in reading acquisition. These abilities are also required for the comprehension and use of such linguistic nuances as jokes, riddles, puns, and figurative language. Not only do most elementary and high school students demonstrate increased functional proficiency with these linguistic devices, but they encounter these aspects of language academically as well. As some elementary and high school language learning-disabled students have difficulty with both the use and awareness of language, this may well be a fruitful area to investigate (see Menyuk and Flood, 1981).

In Chapter 13, Blachman reviews information from speech science and reading research that has provided further insights into metalinguistic abilities that may be important for the acquisition of reading. Auditory discrimination and sound-blending tasks (commonly thought of as important in the teaching of reading) in essence may involve more than meets the eye, or the ear. These skills, in fact, may be a problem area for children learning to read since an explicit awareness of phonological structure is required, and some children may not yet have developed that awareness. Without this ability, it may be difficult for children to grasp the relationship between written and spoken language. Therefore, this may be an important component to address in the assessment and remediation of reading difficulties.

The classroom is a setting that affords teachers and clinicians the unique opportunity to truly see language in action. Intensive interest in this area now exists, and some of the reasons may be intuitively obvious. The purpose of the educational system is to foster the development of new concepts, problem-solving and thinking skills, and mastery of curricula. As language is the major medium for teaching such skills, the dynamics of teacher-student language, the language of curriculum, and potential for match or mismatch between curriculum demands/teacher language and a student's abilities may all be factors influencing progress. (American Speech and Hearing Association, 1982.)

In Chapter 8, Nelson reviews issues surrounding teacher-child language interactions. For example, she notes that Blank et al. (1978) have illustrated how language of instruction may necessitate varying degrees of abstraction on the part of the child. From their research, they have developed a very useful framework for qualitatively analyzing a child's response in relation to the complexity of the language demands posed by a task. Silliman (Chapter 14) shows how such information can help teachers and clinicians to modify their own language of instruction in order to lessen the disparity between it and the child's level of understanding.

Creating congruity between the learner and a program is indeed complex, due to the many varied factors that come into play. Current information has helped professionals to better recognize some of the variables involved and how they may operate. For example, Westby's (1981) research not only sheds light on the development of narrative language abilities in children but, additionally, illustrates the subtle and far-reaching ramifications that this information may have for creating a complement between the learner and the curriculum. She points out that the comprehension level of a given story cannot be measured by reading formulas alone. The type of story schema represented in a child's long-term memory must also be taken into account, as this may influence narrative comprehension (see also Chapter 6).

The foregoing discussion has attempted to provide an appreciation of some current concepts and issues that are important to consider in the identification and management of language learning-disabled students. Certain concepts that gained wide acceptance in the past are now being seriously challenged. Some have been abandoned; others have been reinterpreted within the framework of new information (see Chapter 9). Likewise, through the investigation of dimensions previously unexplored, a more comprehensive understanding of language learning disabilities is evolving. This has tremendous import for professionals in school systems, as it is they who must ultimately translate theory into practice with large numbers of students. Professionals are confronted with enormous amounts of information as well as the day-to-day realities and difficulties inherent in public school systems. Nonetheless, the challenge is exciting for professionals who attempt to promote their own growth and that of the students whom they serve.

Linking Theory to Practice: Questions and Dilemmas

Utilizing current knowledge within the existing realities of a school system brings to mind numerous questions. On the surface, it might seem that the availability of a fixed and prescribed set of procedures and specified steps that could be drawn upon when working with the language learning-disabled population would be an efficient way of going about the job. Although this might be tempting, the very nature of language learning disabilities and school systems precludes such an approach, and fortunately so, as it would undermine the ultimate objective—meeting the individual needs of each student. There are numerous reasons for this. First, the language learning-disabled population is not homogeneous. The continuum of symptoms manifested by language learning-disabled students may range greatly in type and in degrees of severity. Second, use of the same set of procedures with both younger and older students is not possible, as symptoms change over time and needs may have to be met in quite different ways. As a result of this, the procedures and approaches employed with younger elementary students should differ considerably from those employed with older elementary and high school students. Additionally, regardless of grade level and type of problem, each school will have, to some extent, its own unique characteristics which will necessitate further procedural and programming considerations. It becomes apparent that what emerges is not so much exact answers to questions but, rather, an appreciation for some of the interesting dilemmas that need to be considered.

WHAT KINDS OF STRATEGIES ARE NEEDED IN ORDER TO IDENTIFY LANGUAGE LEARNING-DISABLED STUDENTS?

The need for effective identification procedures is self-evident. Before the process of meeting the needs of the language learning-disabled student can be set in motion, a means of identifying those students who warrant further investigation must first be developed. However, the question still remains as to how, since language learning-disabled students manifest a very wide range of difficulties, some more subtle than others. Thus, it may be difficult to recognize every student requiring further investigation. Indeed, there is no simple recipe for identifying students because there are numerous factors that will influence the strategies chosen and the method of implementation. The issue, however, is not whether a single procedure is the answer. Rather, procedures need to be weighed in light of student, professional, and school needs.

Large-scale Screening. Large-scale screening procedures in public school systems have been commonly employed as a means of first-line identification, although their use has been most prevalent in kindergarten and the early primary grades, often as components of early identification programs. However, as discussed in the earlier portions of the text (Chapters 1 and 2), the continuum of language failure is very complicated. As noted in Chapter 1, symptoms of language disability may be overt or more obvious when children are younger. However, as children move on in their school careers some language problems may temporarily go "underground," resurfacing only later when task and curricular demands increase (see Chapter 2). Additionally, it may be the case that some children first encounter difficulties with language only in adolescent years. To know whether this may indeed be the case for some adolescents, we will need to learn much more about neurological, cognitive, and language reorganizations that may be taking place during this period of development.

The above information has important implications for large-scale screening programs. One question that arises is whether large-scale screening is indicated at intervals from primary level through high school. One of the problems surrounding screening at the upper levels lies in the nature of the screening tool. Many screening tools currently available tap into the more obvious symptoms observed in younger children, although this matter is currently receiving attention, as can be seen by the recent development of screening tools targeted for the adolescent population (Prather et al., 1980, 1981).

There exist other issues that also bear upon the nature of the instrument. Given that the basic objective of a large-scale language screening is to determine whether a problem simply does or does not exist, its sensitivity will be dependent upon its content. Many questions come to mind: How much content can conceivably be included in a screening instrument without the device turning into an in-depth assessment? What areas are most important to include? Indeed, can all these areas be tapped through a screening? Current literature regarding the nature, changes, and subtleties of language learning disabilities indicates the choice of a screening tool encompasses more than its brevity (Nelson, 1981; Wallach and Lee, 1981).

It may be that screenings are most appropriate for those students who display more obvious symptoms of language disability, e.g., phonological disruptions or expressive syntax difficulties. However, the sensitivity of a screening to some other aspects of language impairment is open to question. For instance, can a brief screening be sufficiently sensitive or lend itself well to certain aspects related to comprehension, metalinguistic abilities, pragmatic skills, and language strategies important to the development of reading competence? This has even greater implications when considering whether screening should be implemented at the junior and senior high school levels, since it may be those aspects of language that present the greatest problems for language learning-disabled adolescents. These students may not necessarily "look" as if they are language disabled, yet difficulties in areas mentioned above (e.g., metalinguistic abilities, etc.) may be the source of academic and social difficulties

not always recognized as being related to a language problem. Supplying items that would tap a number of higher level language abilities would represent additional content to be included. In addition, a screening tool might also need to include content related to earlier acquired language skills, as the chronological age of the high school student does not preclude the existence of language difficulties more commonly seen in younger students.

There are still other dilemmas inherent in using a structured screening device as the sole approach for identifying students with communication problems at any grade level. For example, mass screening may represent an inefficient use of time because the majority of students screened will *not* be language impaired. On the other hand, large-scale screening possibly may identify some students who would otherwise have been missed through alternative procedures (Nelson, 1981; Wallach and Lee, 1981). If a decision is made to carry out routine screenings at the upper levels, the issue of "time efficiency" is further compounded as an even greater amount of time would need to be allotted for the purpose of screening. Administrators and clinicians must ask themselves whether this represents effective usage of time when considering the totality of their clinical activities.

Alternatives for Identification. Vis-à-vis large-scale screenings, a pool of alternative approaches for identification may need to be employed. Obtaining referrals from classroom teachers and other school personnel represents one such alternative. At least at the elementary level, school systems are structured in such a way that classroom teachers have at their fingertips a great deal of pertinent information. Clinicians can draw upon this potentially rich source of information by encouraging teachers to play an active role in identification. Effective implementation of such an approach would certainly relieve some of the time constraints imposed by mass screening programs. When a large number of students are referred, as an intermediate step, clinicians can carry out a more comprehensive screening than would be possible with mass screening. It could then be determined whether in-depth assessment in a specific language area is warranted. However, as with screenings, dilemmas are certain to arise, since the key to the success of a teacher-based identification program lies in the appropriateness of the referrals made.

The means by which professionals can better achieve more appropriate referrals are currently quite diverse. Instruments such as prescreening and observational checklists, referral guidelines, team consultations, and review meetings are just some examples of strategies that have been employed to meet this end.

However, the high school setting presents a somewhat different picture. Rotary schedules (i.e., where students move from one teacher/class to another throughout the day for instruction in different subjects), increased school staff, and subject compartmentalization of curriculum subjects among many different teachers become the norm. It is understandable that a high school teacher may have less opportunity for forming as global an impression of a student as would the elementary teacher who is able to spend the greater part of the school day with the same student. Thus, as students move into the upper grades, a direct and unmodified adaptation of elementary school referral procedures may be neither appropriate nor effective (Neal, 1976). At *any* level, whatever manner is chosen to obtain referrals, there will be a need to ensure that school staff have an awareness of what constitutes a language impairment.

In-service Programming. An avenue that may be powerful for transmitting information about language learning disabilities might be through the provision of in-service programs. Most school professionals and clinicians probably agree that in-service can play a useful if not critical role in meeting the educational needs of students (Wurtzel, 1981). Once again, however, many questions arise. How much time for in-service needs to be made available if it is to be effective? Given the breadth of the field, can single-session workshops be expected to have the desired impact, or is a continuum of in-service called for? If so, how can such a continuum realistically be built into the already busy schedules of all professionals concerned? Should in-service be on a mandatory or a voluntary basis? What format will be most effective? Informal discussion in a staff lounge? Formal presentations and workshops? Or a combination of both? How much emphasis should be placed on theory versus practice so that the information will still be relevant, meaningful, and useful? At the high school level, answers to such questions may be even more problematic when considering the structure, scheduling, and curriculum specialization amongst teachers in high schools.

No doubt, at both the elementary and high school levels, if in-service is recommended, it must be readily accessible to school staff. They, in turn, would need to feel that such services are warranted. This entails a mutual awareness of the needs of all concerned and will require innovation on the part of clinicians and administrators.

As indicated in the preceding discussion, any decision regarding strategies to be employed in identification is surely not one that can be arrived at without careful thought and thorough planning. Any one strategy, by itself, will likely yield only partial success. Likewise, some may be more effective in a particular school setting and less effective in another. Perhaps the most useful approach is one whereby a variety of strategies are selected that can work in harmony with others.

WHAT KINDS OF DIAGNOSTIC TECHNIQUES AND PROCEDURES WILL PROVIDE APPROPRIATE INFORMATION ABOUT LANGUAGE LEARNING-DISABLED STUDENTS?

"The most useful and dependable language assessment device is an informed clinician who feels compelled to keep up with developments in psycholinguistics, speech pathology and related fields and who is not slavishly attached to a particular model of language or of assessment" (Siegel and Broen, 1976, p. 75).

The informed clinician about whom Siegel and Broen write is immediately faced with many important issues that need to be addressed if the clinician is to obtain pertinent and truly valuable information about a given student's language functioning.

In contrast with the recent explosion of research in the field of language learning disabilities, the majority of published language tests currently available may not tap many of the aspects and processes of language that are better understood today. This is not meant to imply that formal measures cannot provide appropriate and useful information. However, they can at best provide only a sampling of communicative functioning, in what is an artificial "language" situation. The increasing emphasis upon informal assessment procedures highlights the need to go beyond a "test."

Such procedures may entail modifying the administration of a test and/or reinterpreting its results in light of current research (e.g., symptom versus cause issues, etc.), as well as developing one's informal tasks for assessing aspects of language functioning not considered in currently available tests. Moreover, any comprehensive language assessment must also capture the communication event or the student's use of language (spoken or written) in natural contexts such as the classroom. The use of descriptive procedures that allow for this in an education setting is essential, since determining the extent of match or mismatch between a learner and the curriculum is a critical component of the assessment-intervention process. Evaluating match/mismatch can probably be best accomplished through relating assessment findings to the actual language interactions and curriculum in the student's classroom. In this manner, the clinician will likely be able to better meet the needs of *both* stu-

dent and teacher (see Chapters 8 and 14).

Above and beyond the many merits of informal assessment, its use with high school students becomes almost the sole means available, since there is a paucity of formal language tests geared for the adolescent at present. The few tests that have traditionally been used for evaluating language ability in this population are targeted toward a restricted range of language functioning. For instance, it has not been uncommon to find an evaluation of a 16- or 17-year-old's language ability which has been based primarily upon results obtained from a test such as the *Peabody Picture Vocabulary Test* (Dunn, 1965).

Many clinicians, recognizing the shortcomings posed by this dilemma, have attempted to evaluate language functioning on a broader basis. In the absence of available tests, clinicians often draw upon a battery of language tests normed for younger students. The clinician may be careful to note that the tests were given under "nonstandard" conditions but, nevertheless, may conclude that a language problem does not exist if the student performs well on the battery. Such a conclusion is based upon an erroneous assumption, i.e., that language abilities of the older student are merely an extension of, rather than different from, those developed earlier. Older students are learning about aspects of language not available to the younger child. For example, adolescents are acquiring command of more complex syntax, certain discourse strategies, higher level metalinguistic abilities, and the like. These aspects of language may not yet be available to the elementary student; therefore, it is likely that the content of tests normed for younger students will not incorporate these dimensions.

In an attempt to rectify this state of affairs, some formal assessment tools have been developed recently. For example, the *Test of Adolescent Language* (Hamill et al., 1980) has normative data for students up to 18 years, 5 months and includes subtests intended to evaluate vocabulary and grammar in listening, speaking, reading, and writing. The *Clinical Evaluation of Language Functions* (Semel and Wiig, 1980) is another instrument with norms up to grade 12. For evaluating certain aspects of language processing, Rees and Schulman (1978) and Wallach (1982) have suggested turning to sections included in some of the standardized reading tests.

As new formal diagnostic tools for adolescents continue to become available, clinicians must not permit the model and content of a test to define the nature and scope of language. They should always keep in mind that old and new tests alike represent "attempts" at diagnosing language problems, and, as such, these tools must be critically evaluated as to the aspects of language being tapped. If any advice could be given at this point, it would be that one, two, three (or even more) tests does not necessarily a language assessment make!

WHAT SERVICES NEED TO BE AVAILABLE IN ORDER TO PROVIDE FOLLOW-UP FOR LANGUAGE LEARNING-DISABLED STUDENTS?

The provision of services for students identified as language and/or speech disabled is not new to school systems. In the past, the primary model of service delivery was one where students were withdrawn from the classroom to be seen individually or in a small group. Articulation and the early and more obvious forms of language impairment tended to be the focus of programming during the 1960's and 1970's (Garrard, 1979). These programs tended to be carried out somewhat independently from classroom programming with consultation primarily taking the form of periodically reviewing therapy goals and progress with the student's classroom teacher.

With better understanding of the many and varied manifestations of language impairment and its interaction with learning and school success, the scope of language programming has broadened. Although specific language therapy targets may be delineated, remediation in the confines of a resource room only may not be appropri-

ate and/or sufficient for some students. Managing a student's language difficulties as they interact with the language demands of the classroom can be integral to the success of a language remediation program. Therefore, incorporating specific language objectives and programming procedures into classroom curricula will be important. Moreover, since effecting a match between the learner and the classroom program is paramount, follow-up may also require modifications of curricular materials and instructional language so they more closely approximate what the student knows and how he learns. From this, it becomes apparent that effective intervention necessitates the availability of a continuum of service delivery options.

A minimum of programming alternatives suggested by Garrard (1979) range from: (1) classroom assistance, (2) daily resource room support, (3) regularly scheduled intermittent itinerant support, and (4) placement in a self-contained language class. These alternatives should not be viewed as mutually exclusive, because adopting combinations may prove to be most useful for some students. A continuum such as the above can allow for flexibility in follow-up strategies for students in both regular and special education classes. Naturally, each alternative will need to be weighed in light of a student's abilities, presenting language learning difficulties, and programming needs. In particular, some form of classroom assistance would seem to be indispensable in an attempt to avoid compartmentalizing language programming from the total educational program.

Being aware of the issues that warrant consideration is one thing—putting them into action is another. For instance, designing curricular materials to fit the individual needs of a student may necessitate deviating considerably from regular curricular series in reading, math, and other subjects. For teachers of regular grades, who usually have 20 or more other students in their classroom, concerns may understandably arise as to how and when an individualized program can be integrated into the classroom program and teaching schedule.

Likewise, in school systems where functional achievement tends to be evaluated by the level of student progress in, for example, a reading series, deviating from a curriculum series altogether or making major modifications within an existing program makes evaluation on this basis more difficult. Teachers of regular and special education classes alike will need to evaluate progress in reference to individualized objectives recommended for the student.

It is also understandable that, at times, teachers may be uncomfortable with recommended curricular modifications that involve new concepts and procedures with which they may not yet be fully familiar. This is especially so, given the many advances that have taken place in the field of language learning disabilities. It is evident that a continuum of service delivery such as the above represents a significant departure from the traditional model of follow-up employed in the past—a departure that necessitates concomitant change in the perceptions held by both teachers and clinicians regarding their own and each other's roles in the management of language learning-disabled students. Clinicians are moving beyond the resource room, with teachers and clinicians "teaming up" to put programs into the classroom. In order to effect this transition, close co-operation, mutual support, and flexibility amongst all team members will be required. Initially, issues and concerns that do arise in attempts to link theory to practice may sometimes appear difficult to overcome. However, through cooperative problem solving this need not be the case.

PUTTING THE WHEELS IN MOTION: THE SCARBOROUGH EXPERIENCE

Many of the issues raised in the previous section will be explored in the remainder of this chapter. The discussion will focus primarily on the language and speech program developed for high schools in the Scarborough Board of Education in Scarborough,

Ontario. As it exists today, the language and speech program in Scarborough's high schools is essentially new. In 1979 a major reorganization of services to the high schools was initiated in order to better meet the needs of students with communication disorders. A primary emphasis was placed upon developing services for the language learning-disabled population at this level. A discussion of some of the strategies that have been developed, or are being planned, in our efforts to introduce and incorporate this shifting focus follows.

The Scarborough Board of Education is located 15 miles east of Toronto, Canada. Its total student enrollment is 78,793, with 47,572 in the elementary division and 31,221 in the secondary division. Scarborough's school population is representative of a variety of socioeconomic and cultural groups.

High schools in Scarborough begin at grade 8 or 9 and continue to grade 12 or 13, depending upon the high school program in which a student is enrolled. There are three secondary programs within Scarborough's system: collegiates in which curriculum is designed for students intending to go on to university or community college; secondary schools which provide occupational programming in conjunction with programming to strengthen academic skills; and vocational schools that are suited to students who require continued remedial or special class instruction with an emphasis upon vocational training. There is a total of six specific learning disabilities classes in the collegiates and secondary schools. Additionally, in most schools remedial reading classes and itinerant special education support services are available.

Altering Perceptions: When Is a Learning Problem a Language Problem?

At a placement and review committee, a school psychologist presented a child whose academic progress was of great concern. Sheldon, who was an 11-year-old boy in grade 4, had previously repeated grade 1. He was having severe reading difficulties and was highly anxious about his progress. Despite Sheldon's positive attitude, his motivation, and his having received remedial reading instruction for 3 years, Sheldon was reading only at an early grade 2 level. The psychologist's assessment had indicated that Sheldon's intellectual functioning was within normal limits (verbal IQ = 96, performance IQ = 106, full scale = 101), with no evidence of any "perceptual" problems. She also commented that Sheldon was a highly verbal child who conversed in a very mature manner. An assessment by the reading department had been requested in an attempt to determine other possible contributing factors. Mention was made in the reading report that language problems did not appear to constitute a likely source of Sheldon's reading difficulty. (Just for interest; this conclusion was based upon the results of the *Peabody Picture Vocabulary Test* and informal observation of conversational skills.) In summary, the psychologist stated that assessments to date provided no explanation as to why Sheldon was experiencing difficulty learning to read.

Following the review of the case, a speech-language clinician who was a member of the placement and review committee indicated that more information was required regarding Sheldon's language skills. She, therefore, recommended that any decision regarding programming and/or placement be deferred pending an in-depth language assessment.

The language clinicians's findings showed that Sheldon performed poorly on a test for auditory analytic skills, suggesting that he lacked an explicit awareness of phonological structure, which might explain why Sheldon was having difficulties with decoding. The clinician had also observed that Sheldon read in a laborious word-by-word fashion which, upon assessment, appeared to be related to difficulty in utilizing syntactic-semantic context to predict upcoming words. The clinician concluded that *Sheldon did indeed have a language problem.*

Although this example concerns an 11-year-old, age seems to have little bearing when considering the implications for identification, assessment, and remediation of language learning disabilities in adolescence. When students like Sheldon move on to high school, will their academic problems continue to be approached in a similar manner? This example certainly highlights the need for thorough and appropriate language testing at any level. Closely tied with this are the perceptions that educators and other professionals may hold regarding the scope of language, language disorders, and the interaction between academic success and language competence. If a student in elementary school is having difficulty learning the "basics" yet shows proficiency with spoken language, it may be erro-

neously concluded that language difficulties would not play a role in a student's academic problems. If such is the case in elementary schools, what is the situation like in high school?

In high school, curricula are designed with the assumption that, upon entrance into the system, students will have mastered the "basics." Moreover, not only are students assumed to possess intact language skills, but demands of the curriculum require them to use language in new and even more sophisticated ways. At the high school level, it is conceivable that a narrow perspective of language proficiency may be even more entrenched, with language competency becoming even further removed as a possible source of academic difficulty.

In the initial stages of reorganizing language services in Scarborough, the types of referrals received from high school staff appeared to corroborate this. The vast majority of referrals were for students who had minor misarticulations (e.g., lisps) and dialect differences. When a "language" referral was made, it was more often than not for a student who was learning English as a second language. Follow-up revealed that very few of those referred did, in fact, exhibit language disorders. This situation led to a consideration of the following factors: (1) that few language-disordered high school students existed in Scarborough, or (2) that existing identification procedures were not sufficiently sensitive, and/or (3) that high school teachers held somewhat traditional perceptions regarding the role of the speech-language clinician in the high school setting.

Given that Scarborough has had a need to establish remedial reading and specific learning disabilities classes at the high school level, it seemed conceivable that at least in *these* classes, some of the students' learning problems might be language based. Thus, it was felt that the latter two explanations might better account for the types of referrals submitted. Therefore, development of new strategies was initiated in order to better identify and provide subsequent programming for high school learning-disabled students—not only those in remedial and special education programs, but also students in regular stream who possibly manifest learning difficulties of a less obvious nature.

Identification Procedures

REFERRAL GUIDELINES

Obtaining referrals from teachers is a useful method for surveying school populations to identify students who may be language learning disabled. In a study conducted by Neal (1976) related to practices and trends in secondary school speech pathology programs, he found that speech and language clinicians most frequently used and preferred teacher referrals as a case-finding procedure (53.7%). Teacher interviews and observational questionnaires/inventories were less preferred, with their incidence of use being 22.1% and 4.2%, respectively. In our view, these results are not surprising for several reasons. First, it would be unrealistic to expect teachers to complete a questionnaire/inventory or participate in an interview for every high school student, when they deal with so many in the course of a day. Second, a teacher's contact is usually limited to only one or two periods a day, which may include, to some extent, independent course work on the part of the student. These circumstances, no doubt, restrict a teacher's opportunity to form as comprehensive an impression about a student's language functioning as completion of a questionnaire/inventory for each student would likely require. As such, the high school setting may be less conducive to the use of such tools. Moreover, the clinician would be faced with an enormous amount of data. Theoretically, this may seem to be an objective worth pursuing, but, in actual practice, collecting the data, collating it for each student, and interpreting all the data would be disproportionately time consuming for the clinician.

With these considerations in mind, an identification program utilizing, in part, teacher-initiated referrals was implemented in Scarborough. Because language difficulties vary so widely in their manifestations and degree of severity, referral guidelines were provided as one means of input to teachers as to what may constitute a language disorder. Table 16.1 illustrates the language portion of the referral guidelines developed for Scarborough high school teachers.

The items included in the guidelines were selected to capture various aspects of language proficiency. For instance, symptoms such as those described in d, e, f, g, i, and k might be indicative of students who have difficulty comprehending information at different "levels" (i.e., literal → constructive/integrative). Similarly, such items as a, b, and c might alert the clinician to students with pragmatic deficits interfering with social-communicative interactions. Additonally, because some items naturally focus on more than one area, it was possible to design a compact set of guidelines which still would meet the desired objectives. In attempts to maximize the likelihood of appropriate referrals and minimize the use of jargon, the items also allow for similar aspects of language to be considered through varying teacher perspectives. For example, for some teachers, semantic integration may be best represented through the concept of abstracting themes (item e), whereas for others it may be best presented in terms of integrating ideas (item d).

The guidelines are distributed, and each teacher then submits the name(s) of student(s) who are of concern, along with the referral reason. This procedure is not only expeditious, but allows the clinician to note any student who has been referred by more than one teacher. Since each teacher deals with different curricula, he/she will see a given student under a specific set of curricular demands. This can be useful to the clinician in that it may provide an initial clue as to the kinds of concerns that different teachers have about a given student, and it alerts the clinician to students who may be high priority for assessment.

Table 16.1.
Referral Guidelines for the High School
Language Disordered

The Board of Education for the Borough of Scarborough, Department of Special Education, Language and Speech Services

Referral Guidelines for Speech-Language Therapy (High School)

Language Disorders:

Language has basically three components:
(a) vocabulary and grammar or form,
(b) underlying meaning, ideas, concepts, or content, and
(c) appropriateness to the situation/context;
and it is conveyed through: listening, reading, speaking and writing.

A disruption in one or more of the above areas constitutes a language disorder that may span the continuum from severe to subtle. It is the latter that are often more difficult to identify and may sometimes manifest themselves only once the student is in high school.

To help you identify those students with language difficulties, be on the lookout for the following clues; the student who:
(a) has conversational skills that are weak or inappropriate,
(b) appears to have difficulty "reading the situation,"
(c) has difficulty organizing/conveying thoughts (spoken and/or written),
(d) has difficulty integrating information heard or read,
(e) has difficulty abstracting the main idea or theme,
(f) has difficulty following spoken and/or written directions,
(g) has difficulty answering simple direct questions asked in classroom discussion and/or written assignments,
(h) has difficulty answering questions requiring inferences (how, why, what if questions, consequences, etc.),
(i) doesn't seem to "read between the lines,"
(j) in conversation and/or written assignments, has problems finding the right word, can offer only vague explanations or descriptions, may "talk" around the topic,
(k) has difficulty remembering facts and details,
(l) in conversation and/or written assignments, has deviant grammar (*not* slang), and
(m) has not achieved sufficient skill with oral reading.

NOTE: Please keep in mind that the above may be displayed in oral communication, reading, or writing.

IN-SERVICE

In light of Scarborough's recent reorganization of high school speech and language services, an "on-line" strategy has been used thus far for introducing the changes. In using the referral guidelines, teachers have begun to ask questions concerning the language clinician's role and how language demands might be interacting with some of their students' learning difficulties. Dialogue such as this has indicated a need for developing in-service programs as an important component in the identification process. The implementation of formal in-service programs was considered to be premature until the role of the clinician became more firmly established within the high schools themselves. In addition, the clinician was able to use this time to determine what topics would be most relevant as well as which presentation formats would be most meaningful for future in-service programs.

The need for in-service thus far has been approached on an informal basis. For example, a teacher in one of the specific learning disabilities classes, in meeting with the language clinician, commented that many of her students exhibited the symptoms described on the referral guidelines but explained that the source of their problems was "perceptual" in nature. A discussion of alternative perspectives for viewing these learning problems ensued. Shortly thereafter, the teacher asked the clinician for program suggestions that could be incorporated into her curriculum. No doubt, in-service of a consultative nature can be powerful. However, with the large number of high school staff in Scarborough, we are aware that this represents only a "drop in the bucket." The task that lays ahead, then, is a series of in-service workshops that will reach more high school staff. The referrals and requests received thus far appear to indicate that special education, remedial reading, and English teachers would find in-service programs most valuable in terms of both identification and programming.

SELF-REFERRALS FROM STUDENTS

An avenue that may have exciting possibilities and which is currently being explored as a means of identification is obtaining referrals directly from the students themselves. If it is possible to provide adolescents with the "right type" of information about language learning difficulties, it is conceivable that they could relate this information to themselves in ways that younger children usually are not able to do. The level of maturity that many adolescents demonstrate by the time they reach high school may enable them to more actively contribute information that may aid in identification.

Indeed, our own experiences in working with adolescents have shown us that in many cases students are able to offer feedback and "insights" regarding their language difficulties and language strategies which are often less easily derived from a battery of tests. The following example illustrates the potential that such an approach may hold.

The clinician had been invited to speak to a class about speech-language pathology. In attempting to explain what was meant by a language learning problem, the clinician had the students participate in one of the tasks that she often used in her language assessments. Following this, the clinician reviewed types of answers that might possibly indicate a need for further investigation. A significant outcome was that three of the 30 students present requested an assessment. Indeed, the clinician found that all three students did display language learning difficulties.

The Nature of the Problem: Assessment Procedures and Strategies

In developing strategies for assessing high school students, a combination of such strategies has evolved, including informal tasks inspired by experimental and clinical literature, portions of formal tests, innovative tasks developed by clinicians themselves, and informal observation. All are complemented by careful consideration of the students' functional performance in the classroom. Above and beyond the assessment techniques used, the interpretation of the student's performance is guided first and foremost by a strong foundation rooted in current theoretical information, coupled with a problem-solving approach. The latter is of particular importance clinically, in that arriving at an understanding of the language strategies used by the student may not be immediately evident. However, through probing and hypothesis testing, it may become possible to determine the underlying processes and strategies. Furthermore, it is always kept in mind that much is still to be learned about language strategies used by proficient language users, as well as those used by language learning-disabled individuals. No doubt, the clinical setting affords the problem-solving practitioner an excellent opportunity to learn about and develop further insights about language and learning. This has certainly been the case in our attempts to describe and treat adolescent language disorders.

OPERATION HIGH SCHOOL

In attempting to pursue the issue of screening versus testing, a number of factors were considered. The large size of Scarborough's high school population and the shifts in both service delivery and target population significantly influenced the approach chosen.

Following a referral, the clinician attempts to meet three objectives through what might be best described as an in-depth screening, attempting to: (1) determine whether a language difficulty does or does not exist, (2) gain information about areas of difficulty, and (3) gain some preliminary information about possible language strategies or patterns that will provide direction for further in-depth assessment and diagnostic therapy.

The types of procedures and tasks employed permit a reasonable degree of brevity to be maintained, without appearing to sacrifice sensitivity and/or effectiveness. A structured framework is also provided which does not, however, preclude flexibility. Although a specific set of items is always administered, a student's responses may lead the clinician to deviate from the protocol through an "on the spot" activity or continuing with a specific line of questioning. Such tangents allow immediate probing of areas that appear to be significant and may help to confirm or rule out suspicions as to the source of difficulty.

In the construction of the screening, an attempt was made to avoid, when possible, including tasks that would tap only a very specific aspect of language functioning. Rather, the tasks included involved a variety of interacting processes. For instance, the essential purpose of the listening comprehension task to be described is to screen a student's ability to integrate ideas across sentences. Success with the task, however, also necessitates the interaction of all levels of comprehension. If a student has difficulty with the passage, the first purpose of the screening has been accomplished, i.e., determining whether a language difficulty exists. A partial answer is also obtained as to the area of difficulty, in this case, some aspect(s) of comprehension. Qualitative analysis of the student's responses may also provide clues as to possible strategies or patterns, the third objective. If patterns do not seem apparent at the time, the third objective will still be met, as the clinician will at least be alerted that in-depth assessment in the area is definitely warranted. Additionally, the student's answers in themselves may provide clues related to other areas, such as lexical accessing or other expressive skills. As can be seen, there is potential for gleaning a variety of different types of information in addition to the obvious objective of the task.

Although the screening may be sensitive to a variety of language areas, at the same time it was recognized that some significant aspects would not be covered. The dilemma concerning how much can be feasibly incorporated into a screening is one that even an in-depth screening cannot fully resolve. For example, the student's written expression was not included in the Scarborough screening due to time factors. However, these areas may be explored as the clinician goes beyond the screening.

THE IN-DEPTH SCREENING

An outline of the basic screening format used in Scarborough's high schools follows. A student's performance on portions of the screening is also included as an illustration of its use. Space does not permit a detailed account of each task, but a brief description with examples of some items is provided. Modifications and optional tasks given at the clinician's discretion are included as well. Although not explicitly mentioned in the outline, it should be noted that the screening allows for informal conversation to take place. The time required to administer the screening ranges from 20 to 45 minutes, but in the majority of cases 30 to 35 minutes are required.

The Screening Tasks.

1. The student listens to a short passage/story representative of content and concepts likely encountered at a specific curriculum level. The student is then asked to: (1) answer questions about it (literal, inferential, integrative); (2) make up a title; (3) state the theme.

Modifications: having the student retell/paraphrase the passage; asking the student additional questions based on the student's previous answers; if the student cannot answer most questions, the student is then asked to answer questions about an easier story to determine whether performance improves when content is simplified.

2. The student listens to a verbal absurdity of two to four sentences in length (i.e., material that is linguistically acceptable but empirically false). The student is asked whether an absurdity exists and, if so, is then asked to explain why.

Modification: When the student is unable to detect the absurdity, the student is asked to paraphrase what the clinician said to determine whether the student's rendition does or does not include the critical information that makes the item false.

3. The student listens to pairs of synonymous and nonsynonymous sentences and is asked whether they have the same meaning. Examples:

(a) The picture that is finished
was painted by that artist.   (synonymous)
That artist painted the pic-
ture that is finished.
(b) The bird that flew over the
butterfly landed on the
tree.   (nonsynonymous)
The bird flew over the but-
terfly that landed on the
tree.

4. The student listens to a sentence and
is then asked a question about it. Examples:

(a) Mary was hit by Donna.
Who was hurt?
(b) The leopard was killed by the tiger.
Which animal is dead?
(c) The man fed the dog after he read the newspaper.
What did the man do first?
(d) The man ran up to the woman who missed the
bus.
Who missed the bus—the man or the woman?

Note that examples a and b require a semantic inference in addition to comprehension of the passive structure.

5. The student listens to an incomplete
sentence and is asked to complete it. Examples:

The man is taking a shower although _____.
The man is taking a shower because _____.
The man takes a shower if _____.
The man is taking a shower but _____.

6. Using a task from the Language Assessment Task (LAT) (Kellman et al.,
1977), the student is asked to give two
meanings (physical and psychological) for
a double function word. The student is then
asked to explain the relationship between
the meanings. Examples:

cold (cold day versus cold person)
bright (bright light versus bright student)

Modification: If the student has difficulty
defining the psychological meaning, the clinician provides a "verbal scenario" appropriate to the use of the word and notes
whether this "contextual backup" helps the
student arrive at the psychological meaning. If the student is then able to describe
the psychological meaning, the clinician
then determines whether the student can

now explain the relationship between the
two meanings.

7. The student is asked to explain the
meaning of some idioms and common
expressions that work their way into language. Examples:

"What a drag"
"Space cadet"
"When the cat's away, the mice will play"

8. The student is asked to read aloud a
short passage taken from a popular high
school student magazine. The clinician
makes a notation of general fluency and
specific errors are noted and qualitatively
considered. If decoding difficulties or lack
of fluency are apparent, the student is also
asked questions regarding possible strategies employed (e.g., "How did you figure out
what that word said?" "What do you do
when you come to a word you don't know?,"
etc.). Following this, the student's comprehension of the passage is checked by asking
the student questions along a similar format to those asked in task 1.

Modification: If the student has difficulty
answering the questions, he/she is permitted to silently reread the passage and, following this, is again asked the questions.
Special note is taken regarding parallels
between listening and reading comprehension strategies.

9. Observations and notes are made
throughout the screening regarding the student's general skill at engaging in discourse
with the clinician (syntax, organizing and
expressing ideas, presupposition, indirect
speech acts, listener needs, etc.)

Optional Tasks.

10. Student is asked to explain similarities and differences between two words,
e.g., magazine and journal.

11. Verbal Opposites Subtest from the
Detroit Test of Learning Aptitude (Baker
and Leland, 1967) is given.

12. Object manipulation task for further
assessment of comprehension strategies
employed in analyzing "higher level" syntax (e.g., order of mention, subordinate/

main clause, embedded clauses, parallel function, etc.) is used.

13. Further informal probing of the speech-reading relationship through sound segmentation activities similar to those suggested by Elkonin (1973) and Lindamood and Lindamood (1969) (see Chapter 13) is undertaken. Morphophonological aspects may also be informally looked at through presenting the student with printed multisyllabic words that he/she had difficulty reading in task 8 (e.g., institution). The clinician notes how the student segments the printed word into syllables and also attempts to determine whether the student is aware that the addition of morphemes may result in a change in pronunciation.

Table 16.2 summarizes the areas tapped by the tasks. As the summary illustrates, many of the tasks tap into more than one aspect of language functioning.

GOING BEYOND THE SCREENING

Assessment does not come to a close upon completion of the language screening. When screening results appear to indicate a language difficulty, the student's language strategies are considered in greater detail through diagnostic therapy. When appropriate, formal tests may also be employed. Likewise, the student's functional performance is taken into account to gain further insights. Obtaining samples of classroom work and discussions with the referring teacher, other team members, and the student about academic difficulties are helpful in meeting this end. These procedures may also be valuable when screening results do not suggest the presence of a problem, but

Table 16.2.
Areas of Language Functioning Screened at the High School Level

Summary of Areas Tapped in Screening
(digits in parentheses correspond to digits used to number screening tasks)

A. Sentence Comprehension (literal aspects)
—general impressions from—(1) (2) (8) (12)
—specific strategies (e.g., order of mention, parallel function, etc.)—(4) (11)
—comprehension of connectors/concepts (e.g., and, if, after, although, etc.)—(4) (5) (12)

B. Sentence Integration (relating old-new information)
—general impressions from—(1) (2) (8)

C. Inferential Comprehension
—sentence level—(4)
—within discourse—(1) (8)

D. Recalling Facts/Details—(1) (2) (8)

E. Semantic Integration (overlaps with A, B, C, and D)
—themes, titles, paraphrasing stories—(1) (2) (8)

F. Metalinguistic Skills (synonymy judgments, idioms, proverbs, double function words, etc.)—(3) (6) (7) (9) possibly (2)

G. Language/Speech — Reading Relationship (overlaps with F)
—decoding (speech-print relationship morphophonological aspects)—(8) (13)
—use of semantic-syntactic context cues for prediction—(5) (8)

H. Lexical Organization (semantic features, syntagmatic/paradigmatic, etc.)—(10) (11)

I. Language Use—noted throughout screening
—syntax
—organization of ideas
—pragmatic skills
—word retrieval

Going beyond the screening: classroom observation, diagnostic therapy, team conferences, samples of written work, etc.

language ability is still questioned by team members.

BRAD: A HIGH SCHOOL LANGUAGE-DISABLED STUDENT

Brad, who was a 16-year-old student with average intellectual potential, was referred by his remedial reading teacher because he "dragged out sounds" as he read and had "difficulty remembering information." The screening revealed difficulties in several areas.

Brad encountered a great deal of difficulty with the listening comprehension passage first given in task 1, and his performance did not improve when an easier passage was used. Both literal and inferential questions proved to be difficult for him. Even with the second story, Brad showed no understanding of what it was about (a story about what happened while a teenager was on a babysitting job). In order to determine that the girl was babysitting, an inference had to be made because this was never explicitly mentioned in the story. However, ample details were supplied that should have lead to this conclusion. Brad's answers showed that he never made the inference. Brad's answers also provided clues about possible strategies he may have been employing. It appeared as though Brad was processing details within the story as separate and unrelated pieces of information and then drew upon one of these details in his attempt to figure out what the story was about. For example, Brad said the story was about a "girl making chicken." This may have been the result of his focusing on a detail in one of the events mentioned early in the story, i.e., that the teenager got some *chicken* salad from the refrigerator. His strategy for answering other questions about the story was also interesting in that his answers never related to content actually included in the story but instead revolved around what *he thought* the story was about. Brad's processing difficulties appeared to manifest themselves primarily at the level of discourse. For instance, in task 4 and during diagnostic therapy, he showed good comprehension of individual sentences.

Metalinguistic tasks also posed difficulty for Brad. For example, he was usually able to provide only a concrete (physical) meaning for double function words (task 6) and, when told the psychological meaning, he was unable to explain the relationship between the meanings. Fluency with oral reading was weak as well (task 8). Brad read in a laborious, word-by-word fashion and encountered difficulty decoding some words within the paragraph. His usual strategy for these words was to guess at them solely on the basis of the first sound, rarely using semantic-syntactic context as a clue. Types of errors also suggested decoding difficulties related to morphophonological-orthographic rules. It was evident that Brad needed to learn how to better apply his knowledge of spoken language to the printed page.

Preliminary Observations

The foregoing case illustration certainly highlights that language difficulties may be at the source of some high school students' learning problems. Data indicate that Brad is not an isolated case. The case illustration, as well as the observations that follow, provides a flavor for just some of the problems that high school language learning-disabled students experience. Thus far, students with language learning problems that range considerably in type and degree of severity have been identified.

For some of these students, the abilities to make inferences and to integrate information have been significant problem areas. The academic history for some suggests that these problems probably existed prior to high school. An interesting question, however, is whether some students encounter these types of problems *only* when they reach high school because of the curriculum content becoming much more complex, sophisticated, and abstract.

Inefficient language strategies also appeared to be related to reading difficulties exhibited by some of the language-disabled students identified. To date, we have rarely come across a high school student who has not yet acquired the basic knowledge and skills related to *learning* to read. Rather, the problem for most of these students seems to be with the transition into skilled reading. One pattern which may be a contributing factor is that the syntactic-semantic context is often inefficiently utilized in anticipating and predicting upcoming text. This has sometimes been observed to the extent that reading for some students is a task of decoding words only and not one of reading for meaning. The problem for these students seems to be similar to what Perfetti (1977) has described as reading only at a surface level, or "word barking."

For those who exhibit problems in word decoding, it has been found that a basic awareness of the relationship between speech and print (i.e., sound-symbol decoding aspects) exists in most cases. However, many of the students identified experience difficulty with multisyllabic words—decoding them incorrectly or very slowly, particularly when prior context has not been utilized. In "attacking" such words, students have frequently been observed to use a solely phonetic approach, ignoring the morphemes and syllable boundaries within the words that need to be considered as well. These observations may suggest that the learning of orthographic rules, as well as the orthographic mapping of morphophonological patterns, presents considerable difficulty for some language learning-disabled students.

Referrals requesting assessment of written expression also increased when referral procedures and guidelines were reorganized. In analyzing samples of written work, it was noted that some students did not always provide sufficient information, making it difficult to determine intended meaning. For instance, it was not always apparent why a student had included certain information or how information between sentences and/or paragraphs was related. Closely related to this were difficulties in structural organization of written work. Teacher remarks and comments typically seen on these students' classroom work included, "You've gone off topic," "You've talked around the subject," "Vague," and "You've jumped from one idea to the next too quickly." Difficulties such as the above seem to have resulted in poor topic maintenance in written work.

Part of the problem for some students seemed to be related to not fully understanding the demands of the task. For example, it has been noted that some students referred have had difficulty with examination questions such as "Discuss the . . . ." Although they show a general understanding of what a discussion entails, they do not appear to bring this knowledge to the written task. Their answers, too, may appear to be "incomplete," "disjointed," "off topic," and "not hitting the heart of the matter." These types of difficulties also bring to mind the identification of high school students whose pragmatic skills may be weak. As yet, such students have not been referred. It may be that, for such students, more sensitive identification and assessment procedures still need to be developed.

. . . AND MORE ABOUT HIGH SCHOOL: SERVICE DELIVERY

Does Practice Really Make Perfect?: Match/Mismatch Issues

As more information becomes available, professionals are becoming more cognizant of important variables leading to a match or mismatch among teacher, student, and curriculum. Persistent efforts have been made and continue to be made in the search for teaching strategies that can meet the needs of students with learning difficulties. In doing so, however, it is not unlikely that continued use of some long-standing (and "popular") practices will be questioned. One clinician's experience with a high school student for whom she was recommending language therapy is illustrative. The student made it perfectly clear from the outset that he hoped the clinician would be able to help him with his reading. However, he added that if she intended to teach phonics, she could count him out because he had "had it for years and it hadn't worked." This student's remark addresses itself to the title of this section: "does practice really make perfect?" Few would argue that experiences for the consolidation and generalization of new concepts and information need to be provided. The crux of the matter may not necessarily rest in the provision of experiences for carryover but instead, may be related more to *what* the student is being required to practice and the rationale for teaching it. For example, did dealing directly with *symptoms* of an "auditory blending" difficulty through continued teaching of phonics make the above student a better reader?

The source of a mismatch may not always lie in the appropriateness of what is being taught. For example, delineating a curriculum objective, such as "strengthening inferential language skills" for a student who has difficulty in that area, is most likely an appropriate goal. Many curriculum programs which target these very skills are available. However, upon close examination of the materials, what often turns out to be the case is that the tasks fail to explicitly show the student the logistics entailed in arriving at an inference. The student is required to do that which he/she could not do in the first place, that is, make an inference. It is questionable whether continued practice with these kinds of activities will lead to the desired objective. In fact, such practice may only serve to frustrate the student.

Examples like these highlight the importance of seeking out possible sources of mismatch in attempts to lessen disparity between curricular demands and student needs. A variety of variables may influence success in learning. Instructional language, language of the curriculum, the student's language and learning strategies, as well as motivation and teaching style are just some of the dimensions that are significant. Procedures such as those suggested by Blank et al. (1978), Berlin et al. (1980), and Pollak and Gruenewald (1978) may be helpful in analyzing student-teacher-curriculum language interactions. Keeping abreast of current developments in the field will also enable teachers and clinicians to devise innovative activities and to implement curriculum modifications that may more closely approximate the language abilities and needs of the student.

The Discipline of Working Together

The ultimate objectives of any intervention program are (1) helping the student acquire needed learning strategies and (2) promoting effective carryover. After all, what is the value of stimulating the acquisition of skills if they are not *functionally* used by the student in the classroom, not to mention other communicative settings? However, the move from resource room to classroom is not necessarily a smooth transition for the student, clinician, or teacher. Only through a tightly coordinated team effort can the rough edges be smoothed.

In the high school setting, it is often possible to afford students a degree of responsibility that their elementary counterparts cannot, in most cases, be expected to assume. Therefore, it may be appropriate to conceptualize the high school student as someone who actively contributes to the decisions and conclusions arrived at by the team. With assistance, the student may be able to develop more appropriate language learning strategies. Whether such assistance will represent a productive use of the student's, teacher's, or clinician's time rests to some extent upon how receptive the student is. On the other hand, the student's willingness and cooperation are not just a matter of self-motivation. Clinicians need to be adept at demonstrating to the student how their assistance can be of value. This has particular relevance for those high school students who, because of years of frustration and disappointment, may be anxious about or may have come to view the services being offered to them with some degree of skepticism.

The give and take between all team members is critical to the effectiveness of programming. In a high school system this becomes an even greater challenge. Because of the organization of high schools, the needs of students in the regular stream who possess exceptionalities have not been easy to accommodate. With the reorganization of Scarborough's language services, many teachers have gained a greater awareness of the way language problems may be affecting the academic progress of students whom they have referred. However, in most cases, "support" for the students has been relegated to remedial and itinerant professionals. With the thrust toward placement that provides "the least restrictive environment" and with individualized classroom programming, high school classroom teachers will no doubt be required to assume greater responsibility in implementing recommended curriculum modifications. Teachers likely will seek the input of other team members to meet this end. Without question, in-service will become more important than ever.

For students enrolled in Scarborough's special education classes, an integrated team approach has been effected more readily. Individual sessions with the clinician in or out of the classroom combined with consultative procedures have proven to be a valuable approach. Diagnostic therapy has allowed the clinician to not only establish specific language objectives, but it has also enabled the clinician to experiment with curricular materials and modifications that can be of use to the teacher in the classroom. In turn, consultation has encouraged the clinician to incorporate successful classroom strategies and materials into therapy sessions. The results of this give and take are a well coordinated and comprehensive educational program. In short, through an atmosphere of mutual respect and support, programming becomes a complement of efforts to best meet the needs of a common concern—the student with a language learning difficulty.

In many cases, the team will need to extend beyond the language clinician and the classroom teacher. Professionals from several disciplines may be involved. In ed-

ucational planning and implementation, divergent viewpoints may arise. Decisions will need to be reached jointly; therefore, finding common ground will be crucial to a student's progress. If such is not the case, the student might be "better off with no help at all, should he become a battleground for professional feuds" (Martin, 1974).

...AND STILL MORE ABOUT HIGH SCHOOL: CLOSING REMARKS

Many issues have been addressed throughout this chapter in an attempt to bridge the gap between theory and practice. It is evident that language learning disabilities are not exclusive to the elementary school population. Only some of the concerns central to fully understanding and effectively programming for the high school language learning-disabled student have been addressed. As this population is only beginning to be understood, many more theoretical and practical questions need to be asked. Our own experiences have led us to consider issues such as the following: What additional information needs to be learned about growth and changes in language ability that may occur during adolescence? Will current intervention procedures initiated at an earlier age adequately prepare the student for the language demands of high school? Or will some students continue to show difficulty in later acquired strategies needed for dealing with new aspects of language learning? Reflecting back upon the student who did not know what "discuss" meant in an assignment, how much of this may be related to a "language learning disability" versus a "curriculum disability"? Whatever the case, the importance of including professionals on curriculum-writing teams who are knowledgeable in the area of normal language acquisition cannot be stressed enough. Finally, are alternatives such as self-contained language classes viable for some high school students, as they have been for some elementary students?

This chapter has by no means exhausted the many issues and areas that may be significant to the development of effective school programming for the language learning-disabled student. The procedures presented represent an attempt to deal with some of the issues. Ongoing evaluation of all procedures is needed in our continuing attempts to link theory to practice. With every advance in the field, professionals become better able to meet the needs of the language learning-disabled individual. At the same time, every step along the way leads to new questions and challenges. Needless to say, the complexities involved in language and learning make the notion of a "cookbook approach" inconceivable. What may appear to be a frustrating situation at times is truly an exciting and rewarding one for the problem-solving clinician.

References

American Speech and Hearing Association Committee on Language Learning Disabilities: The role of the speech-language pathologist in learning disabilities. *ASHA*, 24:937–944, 1982.

Baker HJ, Leland B: *Detroit Tests of Learning Aptitude*. Indianapolis, Bobbs-Merrill, 1967.

Berlin LJ, Blank M, Rose SA: The language of instruction: the hidden complexities. *Top Language Disord* 1:47–58, 1980.

Blank M, Rose SA, Berlin LJ: *The Language of Learning: The Preschool Years*. New York, Grune and Stratton, 1978.

Donahue ML, Bryan TH, Pearl RA: Pragmatic competence of learning disabled children. *Paper for the University of Illinois*. Illinois, Chicago Institute for Learning Disabilities, University of Illinois at Chicago Circle, 1979.

Dunn L: *Peabody Picture Vocabulary Test*. Circle Pines, MN, American Guidance Service, 1965.

Elkonin DB: Methods of teaching reading. In Downing J: *Comparative Reading*. New York, Macmillan, 1973.

Gardner H, Kircher M, Winner E, et al: Children's metaphoric productions and preferences. *J Child Language* 2:135–141, 1975.

Gardner H, Lohman W: Children's sensitivity to literary styles. *Merrill-Palmer Q* 21:113–126, 1975.

Garrard KR: The changing role of speech and hearing professionals in public education. *ASHA* 21:91–98, 1979.

Hakes DT: *The Development of Metalinguistic Abilities in Children*. New York, Springer-Verlag, 1980.

Hammill DD, Brown VL, Larsen SC, et al: *Test of Adolescent Language*. Allen TX, Developmental Learning Materials, 1980.

Kellman M, Flood C, Yoder D: *Language Assessment Tasks for Ages 9 to 14 and Graes 4 to 8*, ed 1.

Madison, WI, University of Wisconsin—Madison Department of Communicative Disorders, 1977.

Lindamood CH, Lindamood PC: *The ADD Program, Auditory Discrimination in Depth*. Boston, Teaching Resources, 1969.

Martin VE: Consulting with teachers. *Language Speech Hear Serv Schools* 5:176–179, 1974.

Menyuk P, Flood J: Linguistic competence, reading, writing problems and remediation. *Bull Orton Soc* 31:13–28, 1981.

Neal WR: Speech pathology services in the secondary schools. *Language Speech Hear Serv Schools* 7:6–16, 1976.

Nelson, NW: Tests and materials in speech and language screening. *Semin Speech Language Hear* 2:11–36, 1981.

Ontario Ministry of Education. *Bill 82: An Act to Amend the Education Act, 1974*. Toronto, Ontario, The Ministry, 1980.

Perfetti CA: Language comprehension and fast decoding: some psycholinguistic prerequisites for skilled reading comprehension. In Guthrie JT: *Cognition, Curriculum, and Comprehension*. Newark, DE, International Reading Association, 1977, 20–41.

Pollak S, Gruenewald L: *A Manual for Assessing Language in Academic Tasks*. Madison, WI, Midwest IGE Services, School of Education, University of Wisconsin, 1978.

Prather EM, Breecher SV, Stafford ML, et al: *Screening Test of Adolescent Language*. Seattle, WA, University of Washington Press, 1980.

Prather EM, Brenner AC, Hughes KS: A mini-screening language test for adolescents. *Language Speech Hearing Serv Schools*. 12:67–73, 1981.

Rees N, Shulman M: I don't understand what you mean by comprehension. *J Speech Hear Disord* 43:208–219, 1978.

Semel EM, Wiig EH: *Clinical Evaluation of Language Functions*. Columbus, OH, Charles E Merrill, 1980.

Siegel GM, Broen PA: Language assessment. In Lloyd LL: *Communication Assessment and Intervention Strategies*. Baltimore, University Park Press, 1976, pp 73–122.

Wallach GP: Language processing and reading deficiencies: assessment and remediation of children with special learning problems. In Lass N, Northern J, Yoder D, et al: *Speech, Language and Hearing*. Philadelphia, WB Saunders, 1982, vol 2, 819–838.

Wallach GP, Lee D: Language screening in the schools. *Semin Speech Language Hear* 2:53–68, 1981.

Westby CE: Children's narrative development—cognitive and linguistic aspects. In Stark J, Wurtzel S: *Language Learning and Reading Disabilities: A New Decade, Preliminary Proceedings of an Interdisciplinary Conference*. May, 1981.

Winner E, Rosensteil K, Gardner H: The development of metaphoric understanding. *Dev Psychol* 12: 289–297, 1976.

Wurtzel S: The preparation of personnel: past, present and future. In Stark J, Wurtzel S: *Language Learning and Reading Disabilities: A New Decade, Preliminary Proceedings of an Interdisciplinary Conference*. New York, May, 1981.

CHAPTER SEVENTEEN

The Final Word: From Theory to Therapy

KATHARINE G. BUTLER, Ph.D., and GERALDINE P. WALLACH, Ph.D.

Knowing and Using the Research
The Children We Call Language
Disabled
The Practitioner's Challenge

The "final word," as you might suspect, is not the last word on the subject of language learning disabilities in school-age children. Each new journal, text, seminar, or state-of-the-art paper reminds us that there is much yet to be learned. Moreover, our knowledge base in language learning disabilities appears to be accelerating, providing increased opportunities at every level of research and practice. While this chapter serves to summarize and close our current discussion of this topic for the nonce, it also addresses the meaning of basic research for practitioners who are providing services for children and adolescents with such problems. Coming to the realization that we are without a set of carved-in-stone procedures for clinical and educational management, we are then required to face the challenge of identifying and developing meaningful alternatives to current research and practice. Undoubtedly, as has been amply illustrated throughout this text, there exists no single test, no one informal assessment procedure, no lone program for intervention, or even a series of remedial activities that adequately meets the needs of all language learning-disabled students.

Nation and Aram (1982) see the problem-solving practitioner as one who applies information from a variety of sources, adapts techniques to the idiosyncratic needs of individuals, and learns to be creative about the solutions to be devised. Put another way, we would say, "beware of language specialists bearing cookbooks," and

be wary of simplistic solutions to complex research and clinical problems. As we strive to achieve the Nation and Aram ideal, we recognize the constraints that are a part of the daily realities of our respective school assessment teams, committees on the handicapped, interprofessional "turf" issues, and the like. Language specialists providing services have acknowledged (1) the diversity and complexity of the research data, (2) the challenge of attempting to understand the population of children and adolescents known as "learning disabled," and (3) the educational and theoretical biases of both individual practitioners and their work settings. The resultant three-way interaction is fascinating to observers and frustrating to participants.

KNOWING AND USING THE RESEARCH

This text has been dedicated to the proposition that there is much clinical gold in them thar research hills. Mining that gold is sometimes troublesome, since basic understanding of language learning disabilities may lie within neurological and cognitive substrata. It is likely that appropriate assessment and intervention, derived from yet to be developed postulates, will be neither simple nor direct. The authors of this book have attempted the difficult task of mining and refining the available research ore and delivering it to the reader in a form which permits its application. They have done so without going beyond the limits of the data and without violating the customary caveats.

The very complexity inherent in language acquisition, the development of cognition, and the achievement of academic success mitigates against easy solutions. As noted throughout this book, there is a rapidly expanding pool of knowledge regarding the development of language and learning, both normal and disordered. Despite the hundreds of years we have been engaged in language and thought, we are only beginning to learn about how various events—whether neurological, environmental, or otherwise, and regulated by different maturational timetables—differentially affect individuals (Bashir et al., 1983). The research has lead us to ask some provocative questions in the area. What are some of the special characteristics associated with language learning after the age of 4? How do models of language and our interpretations of language behaviors in school-age children differ from those we apply to younger children? Are there crucial times for catching up, changing, and modifying one's learning strategies? What different learning strategy subgroups exist within the language learning-disabled population? For example, how do poor readers *with* segmentation skills (as described by Blachman in Chapter 13) differ from other children? What are the implications of comprehension strategy subgroups proposed by Wallach (Chapter 5), Blachman (1982), and others?

As we know, many "faces" appear when we take a comprehensive view of language. Those who read the research across a number of language-related disciplines—i.e., psycholinguistics, speech-language pathology, reading, applied linguistics, language acquisition, cognitive psychology, education, and so forth—will encounter remarkably similar findings upon occasion. Certainly, a review of the literature related to the comprehension of language, both spoken and read, provides a multi-dimensional view of language acquisition and its disorders. The language specialist, as clinician or teacher, charged with the task of devising intervention or remedial strategies for students with language learning disabilities, needs to be concerned about more than phonology, more than syntax, more than semantics, and more than pragmatics. As this volume suggests, we must look at chil-

dren's narrative abilities as a way of focusing upon both referential and inferential skills. We need to view metalinguistic and metacognitive skills, as well as problem-solving abilities, within a language context. As Miller suggested in Chapter 10, pragmatics might even be considered supralinguistic in that it cuts across all linguistic categories. She also reminds us that problem solving may best be thought of as something to be taught within the context of a variety of content areas.

That individuals re-present and recode information constantly has been stressed by a number of the chapters' authors. Children and their behaviors are flexible and ever changing. Researchers have begun to look into some of the ways in which strategies for learning can be taught at the conscious level. Some are studying the development of self-regulatory and metacognitive skills involved in increased task performance. As Robinson and Robinson (1982) have noted, children need to know "when they don't know enough." Others have begun to explore the differential effects of various kinds of instruction on different populations of children. For example, Pany et al. (1982) offer some interesting ideas about the effects of vocabulary instruction on reading comprehension with normal achievers and learning-disabled students. Indeed, issues related to word knowledge and word retrieval strategies appear in various places in this text (e.g., Chapter 11). Also discussed is the persistence of word-naming and related problems in the language learning-disabled population (e.g., Chapter 2). Few studies are available that demonstrate how the teaching of vocabulary and related word-processing strategies to students affects their reading comprehension and other aspects of their school achievement. The Pany et al. (1982) studies and those by Becker and Snyder (1982), among others, offer promise for the future.

Calfee and Sutter (1982) provide a number of suggestions for the manner in which oral language may be measured within a classroom's formal discussion period, pragmatic and interactive parameters identified, and remediation provided. A predictable outcome of such activities, in addition to those set by Calfee and Sutter, would be the sharing of intervention goals and activities between language specialists and educators and would include the modification of the interactive language components of instruction. Swanson (1982) offers practitioners some guidelines for assessment from an information-processing framework.

Although a surge of optimism has swept through a number of professional fields regarding the expanding knowledge base and its eventual application to practice, all too frequently discipline boundaries fragment information and interaction between and among researchers. Some of the theoretical and practical aspects of this dilemma were discussed in the opening remarks by Wallach and Liebergott in Chapter 1. Does the "language-disordered" child receive one kind of intervention while the "learning-disabled" child receives another? Does the "language-disordered" child with reading problems (a likely combination) see the speech-language pathologist for "language therapy" and the reading specialist for "reading remediation"? Do "language people" read speech-language journals while "reading people" read reading journals, and so forth? In this volume we have attempted to bring together some of the recent research in language disorders, cognitive science, reading, psycholinguistics, and educational practice. The mass of data available makes it impossible to place it all within the covers of a single text. However, it is evident from the material gathered together here that the traditional boundaries have begun to blur and fade. As we progress, we may see additional links being forged. Central to our quest is emerging information from neuropsychological sources, from reading comprehension research, from the seminal works of Piaget and Chomsky, from discourse and narrative research, from second language learning,

and from cognitive psychology and information processing, to name only a few. Certainly, as Glaser (1981) notes, research in how novice learners are transformed into "experts" will provide us with additional information on learning styles and strategies.

THE CHILDREN WE CALL LANGUAGE LEARNING DISABLED

One noted researcher is presumed to have said, "I don't know what learning disabilities are, but they are two per cent of something," a statement in reference to the federal "cap" placed on children diagnosed as learning disabled. This country has seen a rapid expansion of the demand for services for children labeled as "learning disabled" or at high risk for academic failure. "Learning disabilities" now outranks many other high-incidence handicapping conditions, rivaling or exceeding in sheer numbers children reported to have speech impairments or language disorders (Foster, 1982). In a number of states there has been a decrease in children served who were classified as "educable mentally retarded" or "language disordered" and an increase in children served who are classified as having "specified learning disabilities." It is suspected, at least by a few, that such shifts in terminology may reflect funding priorities and fiscal constraints rather than addressing the question of "who" are the children now identified under any number of handicapping conditions or labels.

In this volume, we have attempted to address the issue of how research and practice may serve to clarify this very confusing picture. Lahey (1981) has said that discussions of learning disabilities make her think about the complicated puzzles one sees in stationery stores. Solving these sophisticated puzzles becomes more difficult if one loses a puzzle's box cover. Lahey (1981) has noted the loss of a "frame of reference" or a "mental theme" as we attempt to consider the problems of language learning-disabled children. She goes on to say that learning disabilities (as a category) is like a box of puzzle pieces, many of which seem to interlock, but not all. Professionals are unable to complete the puzzle because they may have lost the puzzle box (or frame of reference). She asks whether more than one box cover will be needed, and she recommends flexibility as our search continues into the next decade.

Research in developmental neurology, language, and other behavioral concomitants to the acquisition of learning has lead to the suggestion that a neurological base exists for language learning disabilities. It is suggested that the child "comes with" a vulnerability—a difference—a subtle, or not so subtle, neurological difference. This notion that some of the difficulties may be intrinsic to the child has been and will remain controversial. We know little as yet about the relationship between events in early life and the problems encountered later in school life. However, it is important to keep in mind the interaction between *internal* processes and the *environment*, a truism which is too oft forgotten. Zigmond et al. (1980, p. 90) succinctly state the position when they say that "learning is a complex product of what the learner brings to the situation and what the situation brings to the learner." Indeed, early school failure may lead children with problems to develop a set whereby they respond passively to cognitively demanding situations (see Chapter 14).

THE PRACTITIONER'S CHALLENGE

Research and practice come into contact with each other at an uneven rate. As the "old hands" know, the cart of therapy and remediation appears to be frequently unhitched from the horse of theory. At times, theory far outdistances the cart of therapy, with little evidence of its existence to be seen in the clinical realm. At other times, the outcomes of research provide a tremendous number of powerful ideas and applications, and the cart is filled to overflowing. It is somewhat disconcerting to the professional novice to learn that horse and cart are rarely in perfect tandem. Rather, the

clinical applications are placed in the cart in seeming disarray. It is the practitioner who is responsible for the ordering and balancing of the contents, thus contributing to the forward movement of the therapeutic enterprise. Equally disconcerting (and perhaps even discouraging to a few) is the realization that clinical applications change over time and that the cart may never achieve either a perfect balance or even permanently stored contents. Theoretical steeds from a wide array of disciplines arrive at erratic intervals, requiring frequent rearrangement of the cart's contents, alternatively slowing and accelerating assessment and intervention. However, for the practitioner who delights in inquiry and in the ferreting out of the relationship between theory and therapy; one who can tolerate a significant level of ambiguity and uncertainty; and one who is wise enough to retain the gold of the old with the best of the new, *that* is the individual for whom the provision of clinical and educational services remains an exciting enterprise. This volume will be successful if it contributes in some small way to such endeavors.

Finally, lest we think that current research and practice in language and its disorders are relatively recent, an excerpt or two from Lewis Carroll's *Through the Looking Glass* (1872) may be in order. Perhaps you recall Alice's conversation with Humpty-Dumpty in which he engaged in turn taking, by forthrightly stating . . . "It's my turn to choose a subject. . . ." Defining the speaker's intent and the listener's processing skills is found in the next comment:

"So here's a question for you . . How old did you say you were?"

Alice made a short calculation, and said, "Seven years and six months."

"Wrong!" Humpty Dumpty exclaimed triumphantly. "You never said a word like it!"

"I thought you meant 'How old *are* you?'" Alice explained.

"If I'd meant that, I'd have said it" (p. 211, 1976).

Alice encountered even greater difficulty in attempting to deal with the Red and White Queens. They objected strenuously to

Alice using "if-then" clauses, ordering her to "Always speak the truth—think before you speak—and write it down afterwards" (p. 251). Parenthetically, how often do we ask children today to identify information as literal versus inferential? Or to engage in such metacognitive strategies as rehearsing and evaluating incoming information before responding? Or to utilize another modality, such as writing, to assist in the storage and retrieval of information from long-term memory?

To conclude, Alice's presumed difficulties in comprehension and expression as viewed by the Red and White Queens continued. Alice protested, maintaining her communicative competence and noting that she had not meant to be unclear. The Red Queen, as someone who evidently believed in direct intervention within a language context, responded:

"That's just what I complain of! You should have meant! What do you suppose is the use of a child without any meaning? Even a joke should have some meaning and a child's more important than a joke, I hope . . ." (p. 251, 1976).

As Carroll's Red Queen reflected 90 years ago, cognition and language intersect, and comprehension and production emerge as significant concomitants.

A child *with* meaning—surely this is the goal of intervention with language learning-disabled children.

References

Bashir AS, Kuban KC, Kleinman S, et al: Issues in language disorders: considerations of cause, maintenance, and change. In Miller J, Yoder D, Schiefelbusch R: *Contemporary Issues in Language and Intervention.* ASHA Report #12. Rockville, MD, 1983, 92–106.

Becker LB, Snyder LS: "Word retrieval intervention: changing the lexicon vs. changing the strategy. Presented at the American Speech-Language-Hearing Association Convention, Toronto, November, 1982.

Blachman B: "Assessing linguistic factors critical in early reading, Presented at the American Speech-Language-Hearing Convention, Toronto, November, 1982.

Calfee R, Sutter L: Oral language assessment through formal discussion. *Top Language Disord* 2 (4):45–55, 1982.

Carroll L: Through the looking glass and what Alice found there. *The Complete Works of Lewis Carroll.* New York, Vintage Books, 1976.

Foster SG: Special-Ed: report cites shortage of teachers, *Educ Week,* December 22, 1982, p 9.

Glaser R: The future of testing: a research agenda for cognitive psychology and psychometrics. *Am Psychol* 6:923–936, 1981.

Jenkins JJ: Implications of basic research: thoughts behind the conference. In Kavanagh JF, Strange W: *Speech and Language in the Laboratory School and Clinic.* Cambridge, MA, MIT Press, 1978.

Lahey M: Learning disabilities: a puzzle without a cover? *Preliminary Proceedings of an Interdisciplinary Conference on language, Learning, and Reading Disabilities: A New Decade.* New York, Department of Communication Arts and Sciences, City University of New York, May, 1981, pp 78–83.

Nation JE, Aram DM: The diagnostic process. In Lass N, McReynolds L, Northern J, et al: *Speech, Language and Hearing.* Philadelphia, WB Saunders 1982 vol 2, pp 443–460.

Pany D, Jenkins JJ, Schreck J: Vocabulary instruction: effects on word knowledge and reading comprehension. *Learn Disabil Q* 5:202–215, 1982.

Robinson EJ, Robinson WP: Knowing when you don't know enough: children's judgments about ambiguous information. *Cognition* 12:267–280, 1982.

Swanson HL: A multidirectional model for assessing learning disabled students' intelligence: an information processing framework. *Learn Disabil Q* 5:312–326, 1982.

Zigmond N, Vallecorsa A, Leinhardt G: Reading instruction for students with learning disabilities. *Top Language Disord* 1 (1):89–98, 1980.

Author Index

Subject Index